May 15–17, 2012
Cagliari, Italy

I0047551

**Association for
Computing Machinery**

Advancing Computing as a Science & Profession

CF'12

Proceedings of the ACM
Computing Frontiers Conference

Sponsored by:
ACM SIGMICRO

Supported by:
**Pacific Northwest National Laboratories
and University of Cagliari**

**Association for
Computing Machinery**

Advancing Computing as a Science & Profession

The Association for Computing Machinery
2 Penn Plaza, Suite 701
New York, New York 10121-0701

Notice to Past Authors of ACM-Published Articles
ACM intends to create a complete electronic archive of all articles and/or other material previously published by ACM. If you have written a work that has been previously published by ACM in any journal or conference proceedings prior to 1978, or any SIG Newsletter at any time, and you do NOT want this work to appear in the ACM Digital Library, please inform permissions@acm.org, stating the title of the work, the author(s), and where and when published.

ISBN: 978-1-4503-1215-8 (Digital)

ISBN: 978-1-4503-1728-3 (Print)

Additional copies may be ordered prepaid from:

ACM Order Department
PO Box 30777
New York, NY 10087-0777, USA

Phone: 1-800-342-6626 (USA and Canada)
+1-212-626-0500 (Global)
Fax: +1-212-944-1318
E-mail: acmhelp@acm.org
Hours of Operation: 8:30 am – 4:30 pm ET

Printed in the USA

Welcome to Computing Frontiers 2012

It is our great pleasure to welcome you to *Computing Frontiers 2012*. The conference, now in its ninth year, provides a forum where researchers meet to exchange ideas in all areas of computer science. True to its roots, this year's conference comprises a set of diversified and interdisciplinary papers and presentations on novel processors and network technologies, supervised memories, energy efficient computing, streaming applications and systems, and performance modeling. New this year are two special sessions on the use artificial intelligence in games and European Exascale projects. To support graduate student research, we reserved space within the poster session for Ph.D. students. The session provides students an opportunity to publish early results and receive critical commentary. We hope that you enjoy both the special sessions and the Ph.D. forum and that both become permanent fixtures at future conferences.

The call for papers attracted 81 submissions from across the World. The peer review process was rigorous with most papers receiving four reviews. Papers were discussed extensively during the program committee meeting. The committee accepted 23 full papers and 11 poster presentations. The papers in the proceedings have been revised by the authors in consideration of referee comments. The poster presentations appear in the proceedings as short papers with a three-page limit. Our keynote speaker this year is Dr. Moray McLaren who will speak on integration of photonic and electronic computing.

A successful conference requires the efforts of many people. We would like to thank our program committee members for their thorough reviews and insightful comments. Special thanks to Francesca Palumbo, the local arrangements chair, and Antonino Tumeo, the publication chair, for their hard work and attention to detail. We thank the University of Delft and Pacific Northwest National Laboratory for sponsoring best paper awards in the memories of Stamatis Vassiliadis and Jarek Nieplocha, respectively. We would also like to thank ACM SIGMICRO, Pacific Northwest National Laboratory, and the University of Cagliari for their generous contributions to our conference. Finally, a special thank to the Conference's Steering Committee for their guidance and giving us the opportunity to organize this year's conference.

Traditionally, *Computing Frontiers* is held in Ischia. This year we chose a larger, but just as beautiful Italian island. We left Wednesday afternoon open to give you time to visit Cagliari's many historical and cultural sites, and its beautiful beaches. Please enjoy Cagliari, Sardinia, and *Computing Frontiers*. Have a wonderful time!

John Feo
General Chair
PNNL, USA

Paolo Faraboschi
Program Co-Chair
HP, Spain

Oreste Villa
Program Co-Chair
PNNL, USA

Table of Contents

Table of Contents

Session 4: Energy Efficiency

Session 5: Massive Parallelism and Streaming

Session 6: Modeling, Benchmarking and Characterization

Poster Session

Special Session 1: Computer Intelligence in Games

Special Session 2: Exascale in Europe

Author Index

CF 2012 Conference Organization

General Chair: John Feo *(Pacific Northwest National Laboratory, USA)*

Program Chairs: Paolo Faraboschi *(HP Labs, Spain)*
Oreste Villa *(Pacific Northwest National Laboratory, USA)*

Workshop Chairs: Alexander Heinecke *(TU München, Germany)*
Josef Weidenforfer *(TU München, Germany)*

Poster Chairs: Hubertus Franke *(IBM, USA)*
Mikel Lujan *(University of Manchester, UK)*

Finance Chair: Carsten Trinitis *(TU München, Germany & University of Bedfordshire, UK)*

Publication Chair: Antonino Tumeo *(Pacific Northwest National Laboratory, USA)*

Local Arrangements Chairs: Luigi Raffo *(University of Cagliari, Italy)*
Francesca Palumbo *(University of Cagliari, Italy)*

Publicity Chair: Carsten Maple *(University of Bedfordshire, UK)*

Scholarships Chair: Nancy M. Amato *(Texas A&M University, USA)*

Web Chair: Joseph B. Manzano-Franco *(Pacific Northwest National Laboratory, USA)*

Steering Committee: Monica Alderighi *(INAF, Italy)*
Nancy M. Amato *(Texas A&M University, USA)*
Steven Beaty *(Metro State College Denver, USA)*
Calin Cascaval *(Qualcomm, USA)*
Sergio D'Angelo *(INAF, Italy)*
Kemal Ebcioglu *(Global Supercomputing, USA)*
Hubertus Franke *(IBM Research, USA)*
Gearold Johnson *(Colorado State University, USA)*
Paul H J Kelly *(Imperial College London, UK)*
Sally A. McKee *(Chalmers University of Technology, Sweden)*
Cecilia Metra *(University of Bologna, Italy)*
Viktor Prasanna *(University of Southern California, USA)*
Valentina Salapura *(IBM Research, USA)*
Giacomo Sechi *(INAF, Italy)*
Pedro Trancoso *(Unversity of Cyprus, Cyprus)*
Carsten Trinitis *(TU München, Germany & University of Bedfordshire, UK)*

Additional reviewers:

Fakhar Anjam
Anthony Brandon
Darius Buntinas
Fabio Checconi
Fei Chen
Michael Chu
Peter Desnoyers
James Dinan
Yang Ding
Miad Faezipour
Lee Howes
Gokcen Kestor
Dries Kimpe

Dong Li
Guangdeng Liao
Changhui Lin
Faisal M. Nadeem
Davide Pasetto
Kalyan Perumalla
Roel Seedorf
Weidong Shi
Nikos Tziritas
Rafael Ubal
Cliff Young
Hanqiao Zhang

Additional reviewers:

Fakhar Anjam
Anthony Brandon
Darius Buntinas
Fabio Checconi
Fei Chen
Michael Chu
Peter Desnoyers
James Dinan
Yang Ding
Miad Faezipour
Lee Howes
Gokcen Kestor
Dries Kimpe

Dong Li
Guangdeng Liao
Changhui Lin
Faisal M. Nadeem
Davide Pasetto
Kalyan Perumalla
Roel Seedorf
Weidong Shi
Nikos Tziritas
Rafael Ubal
Cliff Young
Hanqiao Zhang

Sponsor:

Supporters:

Keynote Talk

Towards Truly Integrated Photonic and Electronic Computing

Moray McLaren
HP Labs
Stoke Gifford, Bristol, UK
moray.mclaren@hp.com

Abstract

The long heralded transition of photonic technology from a rack to rack interconnect to an integral part of the system architecture is underway. Silicon photonics, where the optical communications devices are fabricated using the same materials and processes as CMOS logic, will allow 3D or monolithically integrated devices to be created, minimizing the overhead for moving between the electronic and photonic domains. System architects will then be free to exploit the unique characteristics of photonic communications such as broadband switching and distance independence. Photonic interconnects are very sensitive to the performance of connectors, and so may favor architectures where redundancy and reconfiguration are used in preference to replacement.

Categories & Subject Descriptors: B.4.3 **[Input/Output and Data Communications]**: Interconnections-fiber optics, physical structures, topology

General Terms: Design

Bio

Moray McLaren is a Distinguished Technologist with HP labs, working in the Intelligent Infrastructure Lab. His recent research activities have focused on the impact of nanophotonics on future computer architectures. The two main areas of study have been high speed networking, and memory architectures. Prior to joining HP Labs in January 2007, he worked on the development of high speed interconnects for parallel processors. These interconnects were successfully deployed in a significant number of supercomputing systems around the world. He holds a number of patents in the area of high speed network interconnect design. His previous experience also includes the development of parallel systems architectures, and CMOS microprocessors. He holds a 1st class honors degree in microelectronics from the University of Edinburgh.

Algorithmic Methodologies for Ultra-efficient *Inexact* Architectures for Sustaining Technology Scaling

Avinash Lingamneni
Dept. of ECE, Rice University
Houston, TX 77005, USA
Wireless & Integrated
Systems Div., CSEM SA
Neuchatel 2002, Switzerland
avinash.l@rice.edu

Kirthi Krishna
Muntimadugu
Dept. of ECE, Rice University
6100 Main St, MS-366
Houston, TX 77005, USA
kirthi.krishna@rice.edu

Christian Enz
EPFL, Lausanne 1015
Wireless & Integrated
Systems Division, CSEM SA
Neuchatel, CH-2002
Switzerland
christian.enz@csem.ch

Richard M Karp
Dept. of EECS
University of California at
Berkeley
California 94720, USA
karp@cs.berkeley.edu

Krishna V Palem
Dept. of CS, Rice University
Houston, TX 77005, USA
NTU-Rice Institute of
Sustainable & Applied
Infodynamics (ISAID)
NTU, Singapore, 637332
palem@rice.edu

Christian Piguet
Wireless & Integrated
Systems Division, CSEM SA
Neuchatel, CH-2002
Switzerland
christian.piguet@csem.ch

ABSTRACT

Owing to a growing desire to reduce energy consumption and widely anticipated hurdles to the continued technology scaling promised by Moore's law, techniques and technologies such as *inexact* circuits and *probabilistic* CMOS (PCMOS) have gained prominence. These radical approaches trade accuracy at the *hardware* level for significant gains in energy consumption, area, and speed. While holding great promise, their ability to influence the broader milieu of computing is limited due to two shortcomings. First, they were mostly based on ad-hoc hand designs and did not consider algorithmically well-characterized *automated* design methodologies. Also, existing design approaches were limited to particular layers of abstraction such as physical, architectural and algorithmic or more broadly software. However, it is well-known that significant gains can be achieved by optimizing across the layers. To respond to this need, in this paper, we present an algorithmically well-founded cross-layer co-design framework (CCF) for automatically designing *inexact* hardware in the form of datapath elements. Specifically adders and multipliers, and show that significant associated gains can be achieved in terms of energy, area, and delay or speed. Our algorithms can achieve these gains with adding any additional hardware overhead. The proposed CCF framework embodies a *symbiotic* relationship between architecture and logic-layer design through the technique of *probabilistic pruning* combined with the novel *confined voltage scaling* technique introduced in this paper, applied at the physical layer. A second drawback of the state of the art with inexact design is the lack of physical evidence established through measuring fabricated ICs that the gains and other benefits that can be achieved are valid. Again, in this paper, we have addressed this shortcoming by using CCF to fabricate a prototype chip implementing inexact data-path elements; a range of 64-bit integer adders whose outputs can be erroneous. Through physical measurements of our prototype chip wherein the inexact adders admit expected relative error magnitudes of 10% or less, we have found that cumulative gains over comparable and fully accurate chips, quantified through the area-delay-energy product, can be a multiplicative factor of 15 or more. As evidence of the utility of these results, we demonstrate that despite admitting error while achieving gains, images processed using the FFT algorithm implemented using our inexact adders are visually discernible.

Categories and Subject Descriptors

B.8.0 [**Hardware**]: Performance and Reliability—*General*

General Terms

VLSI Design, Low Power/Energy

Keywords

Average Case Analysis, Cross-layer Co-design Framework, Confined Voltage Scaling, Energy-Accuracy Tradeoff, Error-resilient Systems, Inexact Circuit Design, Probabilistic Pruning

1. INTRODUCTION

Exact hardware is used universally to realize elemental circuits whose behaviors are precise and deterministic in the design of computing systems. Put another way, building computing systems that are known to be faulty and retaining such faults is rather unusual indeed. However, our ability to design and realize deterministic hardware is facing serious challenges today [5], as transistor sizes, diminishing at a pace dictated by Moore's law, are leading to increasing process variations that stem from limits in lithography, and due to increasing parameter variations owing to perturbations such as (thermal) noise. The resulting non-deterministic device and circuit behaviors are deemed to be an inevitable future event as stated in the bellwether international technology roadmap for semiconductors (ITRS) [12] :

> Relaxing the requirement of 100% correctness for devices and interconnects may dramatically reduce costs of manufacturing, verification, and test. Such a paradigm shift is likely forced in any case by technology scaling, which leads to more transient and permanent failures of signals, logic values, devices, and interconnects.

Several innovative approaches have been proposed to overcome this impending hurdle. One obvious way to counter the antagonistic effects mentioned above is through the introduction of error-correction mechanisms using both spatial [14] and temporal [6] redundancies. However, a radically different approach was proposed [22] that advocated realizing useful computations from hardware components designed to be erroneous! This approach, instantiated in CMOS technology, was broadly referred to as *probabilistic* CMOS or PCMOS, and since has expanded into what is now referred to as *inexact design* [2].[1] Inexact design refers to an approach to realizing computing systems which includes transistors, gates, data-path elements or system-on-chip architectures [18]. Such inexact systems are are deliberately designed to be erroneous and used as such, *without adding any error-correction or compensatory mechanisms*.

The surprising insight that makes inexact design attractive is that significant savings in energy, performance and/or area can be achieved in return for embracing error. This insight and its consequences have been shown to be especially attractive in contexts where the quest for ultra-low energy systems and longer battery life is paramount [13]. For example, inexact design is of particular interest in the domain of embedded and portable signal processing and multimedia applications, and in novel application domains of increasing importance such as image recognition, data mining, search, and machine learning, all of which embody inexactness naturally.

To be able to design systems built out of inexact hardware elements efficiently and expeditiously, we will need computerized tools navigating the novel design space relating the cost attributes of the inexact building blocks such as the energy consumed, the area and the speed, to the associated error. In this paper, we develop and validate such an algorithmically well-founded design methodology, for automatically designing inexact data-path elements. Existing ad-hoc approaches generally don't have a methodological and automated approach to designing inexact hardware. As a result, for the most part, the design of an inexact datapath element

---

[1]The phrase *inexact design* used in this paper is an umbrella term for the variants described earlier including but not limited to the design of *probabilistic circuits* [13], [18], *approximate circuits* [19], *stochastic circuits* [29] and *inexact circuits* [2].

meeting a quality constraint can be very laborious and riddled with the usual pitfalls associated with trial and error approaches.

Our proposed cross-layer co-design framework (CCF) spans the architecture and logic-layers on the one hand, and the physical-layer on the other, while synergistically bridging them. Specifically, given the desired quality of a datapath element quantified as a constraint on the *expected error* as an input, our design methodology (heuristically) optimizes the energy consumed, area and time, while meeting the given quality or error constraint. The result is that we simultaneously achieve cumulative gains across all of the three resource dimensions, namely energy, delay and area, without introducing any hardware overheads. We quantify these cumulative gains through the energy-delay-area product or EDAP metric. CCF embodies the probabilistic pruning technique (from [2]) at the architecture-layer, combined with a novel *confined voltage scaling* technique proposed in this paper, at the physical-layer. As one illustrative example of the benefits, the proposed CCF technique achieved a cumulative EDAP savings of a multiplicative factor of 13 in the context of the Hans-Carlson adder [9] using *iso-error* conditions as constraints. These gains were twice as large as those achieved by the probabilistic pruning approach in isolation.

Demonstrating the gains realized through inexact design by measuring the behavior of fabricated integrated circuits is a second significant contribution of this paper. We considered a range of 12 adder architectures, serial and parallel implementations and of varying sizes or bit-widths, which are ubiquitous to computing system design, As one example of measured result, using measurements of the fabricated chips in the TSMC 180nm (low power CMOS) technology process, we are able to show that an inexact parallel Kogge-Stone adder yields energy gains of a multiplicative factor of 3.5, when compared to the same adder designed using exact or conventional hardware. If the cumulative gains are quantified through EDAP, the gains are a multiplicative factor of 7.5, and in both cases we admit a small *expected relative error magnitude* (henceforth referred to as relative error) of 0.25%. If we admit a larger relative error of 8%, our cumulative gains can be as high as a multiplicative factor of 15. Finally, we applied inexact adders to processing images using the FFT and determined that a relative error of 0.54% would be suitable for most applications, whereas images with relative error of 7.5% would still permit image recognition by human subjects.

1.1 Relationship to previous work

Following the foundational work that led to the area of inexact design [22, 23, 24], a plethora of papers have demonstrated the usefulness of this idea either through localized physical-layer techniques such as voltage overscaling [13, 19], or architectural-layer techniques such as probabilistic pruning [2]. Voltage overscaled circuits were used as the basis for realizing cost-accuracy tradeoffs for a wide variety of applications such as datapath circuits [19, 17] through Biased Voltage Overscaling (BiVOS), Motion Estimation [8], Discrete Cosine Transform [21], and Image Processing [30] achieving energy gains from 30% upto 80%. More recent and promising efforts building on the foundational principles referred to above– popularly referred to as *stochastic*

---

computation– involve managing the cost and error trade-offs at the granularity of processor modules [1, 29]. We observe that inexact design in our sense is different from the concepts used in approximate signal processing [15, 28] and algorithmic noise tolerance [10, 11] in that these latter approaches either used error-free hardware components or compensatory error-correction mechanisms to implement error-free low-cost DSP primitives. In contrast, the central focus of our approach is on gleaning cost benefits by using erroneous or inexact circuits.

Returning to voltage overscaled circuits, the basis for realizing cost-accuracy tradeoffs for a wide variety of applications [17, 19] was through Biased Voltage Overscaling (or BiVOS). From an engineering perspective, overscaling– a technique used at the physical layer– of the supply voltage (V_{dd}) has several associated drawbacks:

- Varying the supply voltage to enable critical path violations might lead to timing failures due to metastable conditions, and require flip-flops or latches that can help tolerate metastability, leading to increased overheads.

- Ensuring an accurate fine-tuning of supply voltage leads to a large overhead necessitated by the inherent variations present in the power supply routing [20] and has the associated risk of massive failures beyond a critical voltage overscaling point [29].

- Circuit implementations requiring multiple supply voltages (such as Biased Voltage Scaling (BiVOS) in [13], [19]) are impeded with the overheads of routing multiple voltage planes, and the need to use level shifters.

Based on these drawbacks, more recent efforts for inexact design have moved away from the physical-layer to explore architecture/logic-layer techniques with probabilistic pruning [2] and probabilistic logic minimization [3] being notable examples. While both these design techniques avoid the hurdles that overscaling posed, they are not as potent in realizing significant gains when compared to CCF typically owing to the sub-linear energy gains through pruning when compared to to quadratic energy gains through voltage overscaling schemes.

Building on the foundational work and the early results described above, impressive progress in methods for realizing inexact circuits using cross-layer methods have been reported in [7, 31]. These methods introduce inexactness at the architectural and physical layers. The CCF methodology can be distinguished from these works in two ways. Firstly, we deliberately limit inexactness to manifest only at the architecture/logic-layer and be fixed at design time. Specifically inexactness is not introduced at the physical-layer, thus avoiding the problems associated with voltage overscaling mentioned above. Secondly, our approach allows us to trade costs (thereby, overcoming overheads) across the layers and thus, adopts a co-design methodology. In contrast, prior work involves trading error for cost locally, at the individual physical or architectural layers and hence, most of the overheads are retained.

1.2 Roadmap of the Paper

The rest of the paper is organized as follows : In section 2, we introduce the cross-layer co-design framework CCF

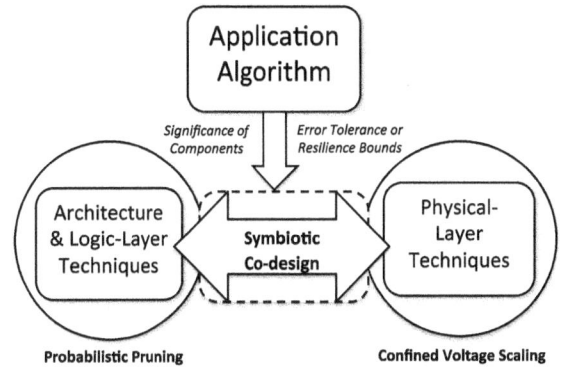

Figure 1: A cross-layer co-design methodology for realizing inexact circuits

(Figure 1) and its use with a focus on refining and improving the probabilistic pruning technique in section 2.1 and proposing the confined voltage scaling technique in section 2.2. The details of the fabricated inexact prototype chip are described in Section 3. In Section 3.1, we describe experimental validation flow that enabled faster design times, manufacturability and testability of inexact CMOS system designs. In Section 3.2, we describe the gains in energy consumption, area and speed achieved by applying CCF to our prototype chip. In Section 3.4, we will also show that our inexact designs produce images that are perceptually acceptable when processed using our inexact adders in the context of the Fast Fourier Transform (FFT). Conclusions and future directions for research on inexact design are the topic of Section 4.

2. A CROSS-LAYER CO-DESIGN FRAME-WORK FOR INEXACT CIRCUITS

As shown in Figure 1, the proposed CCF embodies a combination of optimization techniques applied at the architectural layer, and at the physical-layer. We integrate a version of *probabilistic pruning* [2] to be applied at the architectural layer, complemented by the *confined voltage scaling* (CVS) technique applied at the physical layer. We will now mention the advantages of our approach of adopting both these techniques, with emphasis on exploiting the synergies between them to glean significant savings. First, while the probabilistic pruning does achieve gains simultaneously in terms of energy, delay, and area, the energy gains by themselves are not dramatic owing to the fact that we prune computational elements whose importance in determining the value of the outputs is not too high, which inherently used the notion of having a lower switching activity. On the other hand, it is well known that voltage scaling techniques yield quadratic energy savings in the amount by which the circuit is slowed down, and has concomitant area and other engineering penalties attributed to additional circuitry that is needed. Hence, a judicious mix of exploiting the energy savings from confined voltage scaling, augmented by the area and delay benefits of pruning enables CCF to glean much more in terms of efficiencies than either technique in isolation – when logic- and architecture-layer methods are applied independently of those at the physical-layer. In the sequel, we will demonstrate the effectiveness of CCF by applying it to a wide range of circuits which represent architectures for integer addition.

2.1 Architecture/Logic-Layer Cost-Error Trade-off through Refined Probabilistic Pruning

Probabilistic Pruning is a technique we apply at the architecture and logic layers through which computational blocks and their connecting wires are deleted from a fully functional circuit design. The criterion for deciding that a block can be removed is based on the significance that the node has in contributing to the output value, and also its activity level when the circuit is exercised using a canonical set of inputs. For example, a node whose output has a lot of significance but is pretty dormant across most inputs of interest is a candidate. Application workloads determine the inputs and in our case, we use MATLAB-based pseudorandom number generator which draws inputs from an uniform distribution following the foundations of average case algorithm analysis [26]. Similarly, a very active node can be a candidate for pruning if the values it computes do not have significant contribution to the outputs. The pruning technique we use here is versatile and can be applied at varying node granularities– nodes can be a *micro-block* such as a gate for logic-layer pruning or a *macro-block* such as an adder or multiplier, for architectural-layer pruning. Conceptually, the pruning algorithm is made up of three steps. (*i*). Ranking nodes by their significance which determines their relative priorities as inputs to the next step. (*ii*). Pruning the nodes in the decreasing order of ranks where higher ranked nodes are preserved at the expense of those that have lower ranks and (*iii*). Healing which takes the pruned circuit and *reconnects* the blocks that might have become isolated due to the pruning in the previous step. We will now describe each of these steps in turn.

2.1.1 Ranking Function

We present two heuristics (depending on the evaluation error metric) to assigning significance to nodes in an adder: In the first heuristic, we assign *significance* to a node based on the positional significance of the output nodes directly affected by the current node as shown in Figure 2(a). In the second approach, we assign the same significance to all output nodes irrespective of where they occur in the circuit, as shown in Figure 2(b) . Empirically, we have noticed that the former approach leads to lower relative and average error magnitudes, whereas the latter approach leads to lower error rates.

We compute the probability of a node being active, or the *activity* of a node using a model presented in [25]. From this model, it is easy to see that the probability of any particular path from a pair of input bits A_j or B_j contributing to an output Sum S_i being active is $1/2^{i-j+1}$. The rank of a node is the product of its significance and its activity and we will use SAP to denote this product. In Figure 2, the SAP values of the nodes in a Kogge-Stone adder which are the candidates for pruning are shown inside the boxes for 16 nodes. To reiterate, whenever there is a choice between nodes to be pruned, those with the lowest rank (or lowest SAP value) are chosen first.

2.1.2 Pruning Function

The pruning function works on the nodes of the circuit presented as a graph, sorted in non-decreasing order of rank.

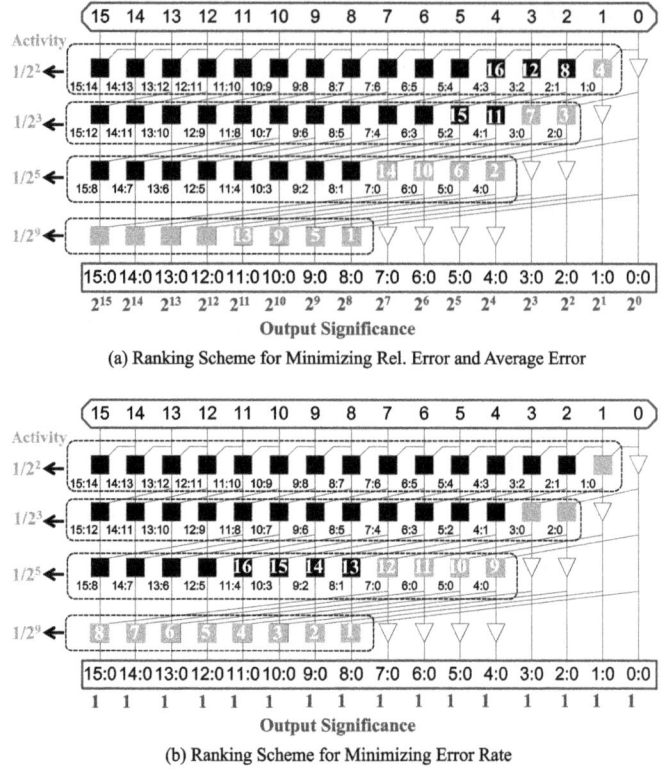

(a) Ranking Scheme for Minimizing Rel. Error and Average Error

(b) Ranking Scheme for Minimizing Error Rate

Figure 2: Ranking functions on a carry path network of a 16-bit Kogge-Stone Adder with Significance and Activity values assigned for each node

Instead of an iterative search for the node to be pruned used in [2], we use *binary search* based node pruning. At each step of binary search, the circuit is exercised using our simulation framework over the set of test inputs. We note in passing that given an adder with N nodes, binary search will be invoked $O(\log N)$ times. Clearly, if we wish to exercise each step of this process with all possible inputs to determine if we are exceeding the specified error bounds, we will need to consider 2^{2n} possible input pairs for an n-bit adder which is a prohibitively large number. Instead, we present an approach to estimating the average error using a *reduced* set of inputs to be used during pruning, where the number of input used grows quadratically in n. Therefore, the total complexity of the pruning step will be $O(n^2 \log N)$ simulations as opposed to $O(2^{2n}N)$ needed before [2]. Our reduced set of test-inputs has proven to be a surprisingly good estimator of the expected error during pruning, compared to using much larger standardized "test benches" which are sets of input pairs. We will now describe our specific approach to constructing the limited sets of inputs for adders, and validating them as being effective in estimating the expected error.

Constructing a set of test inputs for an adder that grows quadratically in n:

Given an n-bit adder and two specific n-bit binary numbers $\mathbf{a} = a_{n-1}a_{n-2}\ldots a_0$ and $\mathbf{b} = b_{n-1}b_{n-2}\ldots b_0$ as inputs to the binary adder, a carry chain is said exist from position

i to position j if and only if

$$a_i = b_i = 1 \; ; \; a_w \neq b_w \; ; \; a_j = b_j$$

where $0 \leq i < w < j \leq n$ (when $j = i + 1$, $0 \leq i < j \leq n$ and $i \neq n - 1$). An indicator function $C_{ij}(\mathbf{a}, \mathbf{b}) = 1$ whenever there is a carry chain from i to j and $C_{ij}(\mathbf{a}, \mathbf{b}) = 0$ otherwise. From our definition, it follows immediately that two carry chains associated with the same pair of inputs cannot overlap, namely there cannot exist $C_{ij}(\mathbf{a}, \mathbf{b}) = 1$ and $C_{xy}(\mathbf{a}, \mathbf{b}) = 1$ such that $i \leq x < j \leq y$.

Therefore, in the *reduced* benchmark, we compute error for each unique carry chain (unique in terms of length and position in the n-bit adder) and then use p_{ij} to find the expected error over the entire sample space (all possible input pairs). In an n-bit adder with inputs $\mathbf{a}$ and $\mathbf{b}$, we will define p_{ij}, for all $0 \leq i < j \leq n$, as the probability that $C_{ij}(\mathbf{a}, \mathbf{b}) = 1$, where $0 \leq \mathbf{a}, \mathbf{b} \leq 2^n - 1$.

Let a' be a number with a binary '1' in the ith position and '0' everywhere else and b' be the number which has the value '1' for any index between i and j and '0' everywhere else, where $0 \leq i < j \leq n$. Clearly, in adding a' and b', we will be generating a carry chain from i to j. The pair of inputs a' and b' ensures that $C_{ij}(\mathbf{a}', \mathbf{b}') = 1$ and $C_{mn}(\mathbf{a}', \mathbf{b}') = 0$ for all $m \neq i$ and $n \neq j$, thus isolating the inputs (and correspondingly the output) to a *unique* carry chain. Therefore, given any carry chain, we can identify such an unique pair that can generate it and denote our test set $\mathbf{T}$ to be set of all such pairs representing all such possible distinct carry chains.

Let $(\mathbf{a}', \mathbf{b}')$ be drawn from the input test set $\mathbf{T}$. The probability p_{ij} can be computed if we are given the distributions of the inputs $\mathbf{a}$ and $\mathbf{b}$. As an example, we will assume a uniform distribution, that is, a_i and b_i, for all $0 \leq i < n$, are each 0 or 1 with probability $\frac{1}{2}$. In this case, $p_{ij} = \left(\frac{1}{2}\right)^{j-i+2}$ [25]. In addition to allowing a lower time complexity, the simplicity of the reduced input set $\mathbf{T}$ allows us to estimate the activity of individual nodes in the adder being pruned through p_{ij}. Consequently, the need to estimate it using expensive simulations, which was the previous approach used in [2], is eliminated.

Let $O(\mathbf{a}', \mathbf{b}')$ denote the output value of the pruned adder $\mathcal{G}^p$ under inputs $\mathbf{a}'$ and $\mathbf{b}'$ from the set $\mathbf{T}$ as defined above. Then the *expected error* $\tilde{E}_{\mathcal{G}^p}$ is given by

$$\tilde{E}_{\mathcal{G}^p} = \sum_{0 \leq i < j \leq n} |\, O(\mathbf{a}', \mathbf{b}') - (\mathbf{a}' + \mathbf{b}')\,| \times p_{ij} \qquad (1)$$

Returning to the question of the time complexity of our approach, we note that $|\mathbf{T}| = \frac{n(n+1)}{2}$ and therefore we have $O(n^2)$ test inputs for each step of the binary search. This is in contrast to a *full* simulation if the entire input space is used requiring of the 2^{2n} inputs per-step. Somewhat surprisingly, we are able to show that estimating error using our set $\mathbf{T}$ of inputs compares very favorably with the expected error determined using a full testbench for varying values of bitwidth n as summarized in Table 1. Therefore, our pruned adders were realized using this reduced input set, and with the associated lower pruning (time) complexity.

2.1.3 Healing Function

After the pruning step, the next and final step involves the healing function. In this step, once the circuit has been pruned, the inputs of the nodes connected to the outputs of

Table 1: Results for the Carry Chain Estimator

Error Estimator	Bit Width	Input cases	Avg. Deviation	Sim. Time
Full Testbench	8	64,536	-	2 min.
	10	1,048,576	-	3 min.
	12	16,777,216	-	5 min.
	16	4,294 967,296	-	??
Proposed	8	36	6%.	1 sec
	10	55	7%	1 sec.
	12	78	6%	2 secs
	16	136	??	2 secs

Table 2: Comparison of Healing functions in Kogge-Stone Carry Network based on Average error and Energy-Delay Product (EDP) Gains over a conventional correct adder

	Connect to Zero		Connect to Input	
Nodes Pruned	Avg. Err	EDP Gain	Avg. Err	EDP Gain
6	38.34	1.62X	17.296	1.07X
8	42.495	1.73X	35.354	1.11X
10	83.516	1.853X	75.978	1.173X

the pruned nodes are undefined. The obvious two choices are to either "hardwire" the undefined values a '0' or a '1', or to bind them to one of the inputs of the pruned nodes. Let us consider the prefix adders as an example. One of the important blocks in such adders is used to compute the boolean function $f = a + b \cdot c$. It is easy to see that if the block implementing this function is pruned and we bind f to a fixed logic '0' (or equivalently implement it as a constant function), the result will be wrong for 5/8 of the input combinations. However, if we connect f to a, its output will be incorrect in only $1/8^{\text{th}}$ of the possible cases! Thus, in this example, connecting dangling connections after pruning to the inputs of the appropriate pruned nodes can result in lower probabilities of error and hence lower expected error at the output of the adders.

We have empirically characterized the error as well as the gains quantified through the energy-delay product using these two approaches to healing, and summarized them for an example Kogge-Stone adder in Table 2. In this paper, we use a simple *greedy* heuristic to select between these two choices using the error induced by each of these choices as a basis. The two choices are applied in turn to the boolean function representing the node, and the choice that introduces lower error is chosen where the inputs are drawn uniformly from the set $\mathbf{T}$.

2.2 Physical-layer Energy-Delay/Area Trade-off through Confined Voltage Scaling

Conventional physical-layer approaches such as voltage overscaling sought to aggressively scale down the supply voltage and strived to limit the resulting (delay) overhead by not reducing the sampling frequency (thereby making errors) [19], [17], [21]. However, imprudent use of such voltage overscaling techniques severely mitigates the gains in a physical realization as a result of unaccounted overheads outlined in Section 1. Hence, it is critical to identify the amount of voltage scaling that would be feasible on a given inexact circuit and in this paper, we propose to identify such a bound on voltage scaling. The proposed *confined voltage scaling* (CVS) technique reduces the supply voltage such that the hardware implementation overheads in terms of delay and area are lower than the gains achieved through architectural-layer approaches. In other words, we intend to trade a small portion of the delay and area savings achieved from architecture and logic-layer techniques for realizing energy gains.

We will use the commonly accepted fact that $V \propto \frac{1}{D}$ and that $E \propto V^2$. Assuming D^P is the critical path delay of the pruned circuit when the supply voltage is V, the minimum supply voltage for the proposed scheme $V_{cvs} = V \times \frac{D^P}{D}$. As a result, the critical path delay is restored to D taking. We reiterate in passing that that the area overhead introduced at this step will not exceed the savings from the pruning done at the logic and architecture-layers. Succinctly, if A_C denotes the area overhead by CVS and A_P denotes the area saved by pruning, $A_P - A_C \geq 0$. Thus, the energy consumption would be $E_{cvs} = E^P \times \left(\frac{V_{cvs}}{V}\right)^2 = E^P \times \left(\frac{D^P}{D}\right)^2$, thereby providing energy reduction that is quadratic in $\frac{D^P}{D} < 1$.

The major difference between the conventional voltage overscaling scheme and the proposed CVS scheme is that while the former induces errors in the circuits by violating the critical path delay that was increased due to lowering the supply voltage, the latter doesn't induce any further errors in the circuits. We provide a succinct description of the CCF algorithm (Algorithm 1 below, while the complete algorithm and framework are described Appendix A).

Algorithm 1: Succinct form of the CCF algorithm

> **function** CCF (Graph $\mathcal{G}$, MaxError, Testbench **T**)
>   //*Step 1 : Architectural-layer – Probabilistic Pruning*
> $(A, D, E) \leftarrow$ Area, Delay, Energy of $\mathcal{G}$
>   RankList = **RankNodes**($\mathcal{G}$, **T**)
> $\mathcal{G}^P$ = **PruneNodes**(RankList)
> $\mathcal{G}^P$ = **HealNodes**($\mathcal{G}^P$)
>   //*Step 2 : Physical-layer – Confined Voltage Scaling*
> $(A^P, D^P, E^P) \leftarrow$ Area, Delay, Energy of $\mathcal{G}^P$
> $V_{cvs} = V \times \frac{D^P}{D}$ when $(A_P - A_C \geq 0)$
>   **return** $\mathcal{G}^P$, V_{cvs}
> end function CCF

3. VALIDATING GAINS THROUGH FABRICATED INEXACT CIRCUITS

Building on the heuristics from the previous section, we validate the effectiveness of the proposed CCF framework by incorporating it into industry-standard design flows. Using this flow, we have designed a test chip which serves as the basis for our post-silicon chip measurements summarized in this section.

3.1 Framework for Designing and Testing our Inexact Circuits

The main objects of interest in the design flow (shown in Figure 3) are the *probabilistic pruner* and the *confined voltage scaler*. The pruner module uses the heuristics from the previous section while the confined voltage scaler determines the permissible amount of voltage scaling from the post-layout netlists based on Algorithm 1. The proposed techniques have been applied to a variety of canonical 64-bit adders designs and the prototype chip has been fabricated

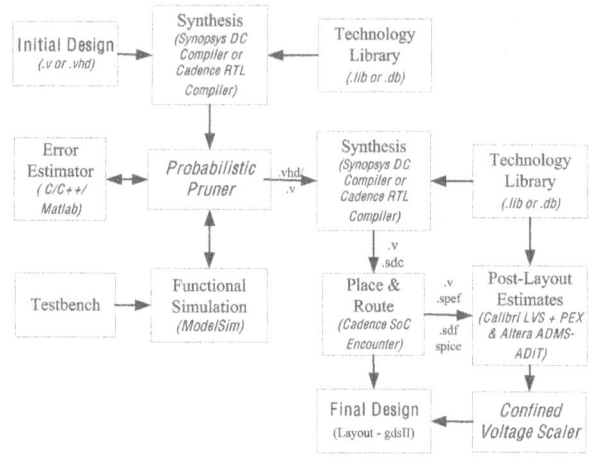

Figure 3: A CAD flow for designing and measuring inexact circuits using the CCF framework

Figure 4: (a) A die photograph of the fabricated prototype chip; (b) The prototype chip integrated into the *icy*board test platform

using TSMC 180nm (low power) technology. A photograph of the 86-pin fabricated chip is shown in Figure 4(a). The various adder circuits which span a combination of both conventional and pruned designs are placed in the PD2 power domain, while the peripheral circuitry including pseudo random number generators, register banks, and other support circuitry to facilitate the functioning and verification of the adder circuits, are placed in the outer PD1 power domain. Finally, the versatile *icy*board [27] platform is used to build the testing framework for the fabricated inexact circuits as shown in Figure 4(b). .

3.2 Results and Analysis

Recall that the resources we are trying to save include the energy consumed, area, and the delay or time it takes to compute. In all of our validations, we have an inexact design, as well as a deterministically correct exact design alongside it. Both versions have been implemented for a total of 12 adder architectures and thus, our measurement based validations are quite exhaustive. The gains in the usage of any particular resource, gleaned through CCF, are simply the ratio of that resource used by the conventional or exact design, to that associated with the pruned and optimized design derived using CCF. In addition to the raw gains for each of the resources, we also show the product of the gains as the energy-delay-area product or EDAP. As shown in Figure 5, we report the gains by varying the rel-

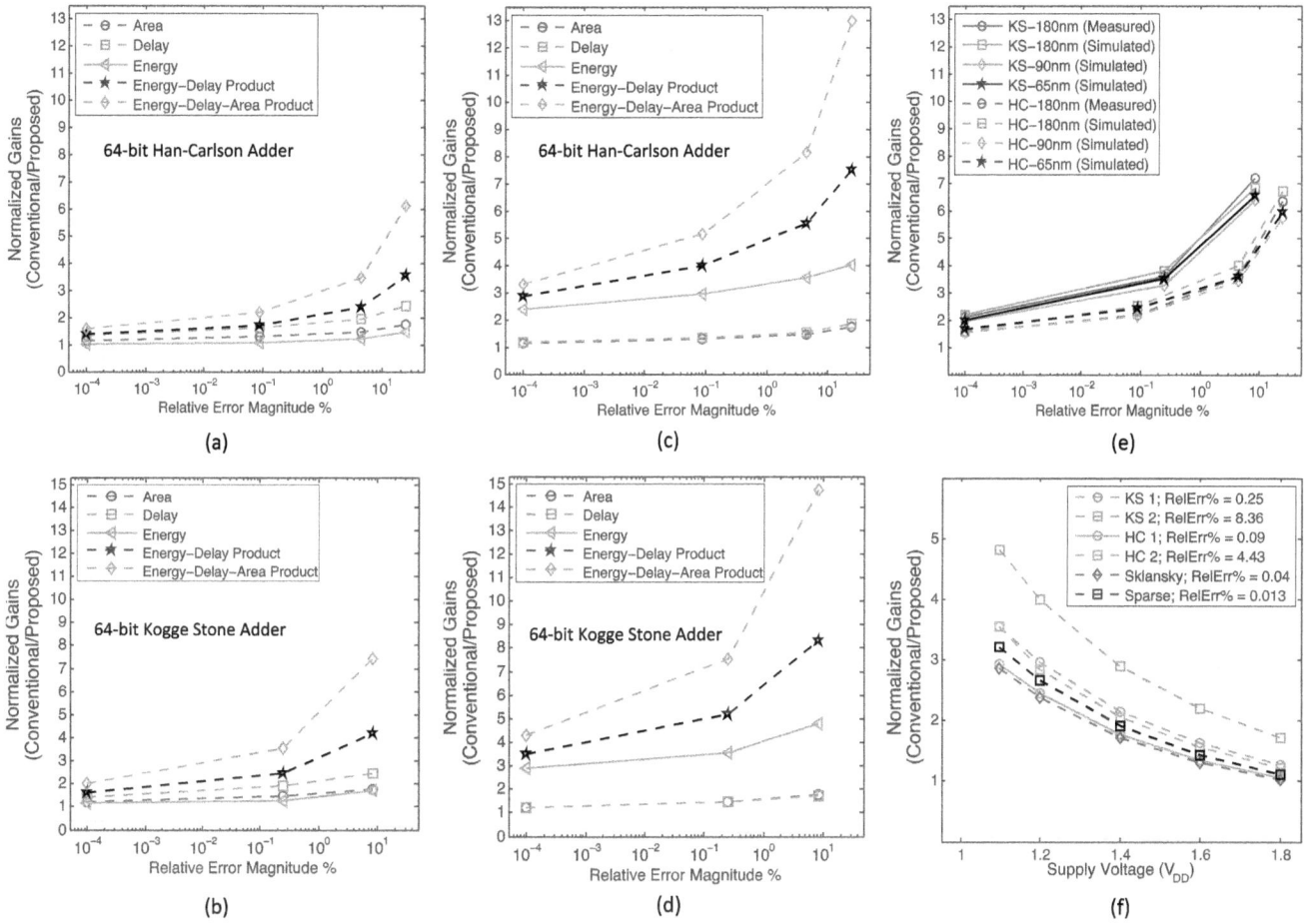

Figure 5: Normalized gains vs relative error percentage of : (a), (b) Adders using only probabilistic pruning technique from chip measurements; (c), (d) Adders through the cross-layer co-design approach from chip measurements, (e) Technology independence of the EDAPgains from probabilistic pruning technique on Kogge-Stone(KS) and Han-Carlson(HC) adders through chip measurements and simulations (f) Normalized energy gains through the cross-layer co-design approach from chip measurements for different adder designs with varying error values

ative error, quantified by averaging over the input test set, and for each pair of inputs, expressing the error as a percentage of the correct magnitude. This relative error is varied from 10^{-4}% to 25 % in all of the measurements; for details of these metrics, please see [4].

We recall that the novelty of CCF is the ability to combine confined voltage scaling with the refined probabilistic pruning technique, described in Section 2. Therefore, it is of interest to quantify the additional gains over those using pruning in isolation. For purposes of reporting in this paper, due to space constraints, we consider measurements from the widely used Han-Carslon and Kogge-Stone adders, both of 64 bit-width, as shown in Figure 5. The results and trends for the other adder architectures follow a similar pattern.

As show in Figure 5 (c) and (d), combining the probabilistic pruning technique with confined voltage scaling through CCF yields energy gains as high as a multiplicative factor of 4.8. This is in contrast to energy gains of no more than a multiplicative factor of 1.6 using probabilistic pruning alone, without invoking confined voltage scaling as shown in Figure 5(a) and (b). However, as shown in these figures, proba-

bilistic pruning combined with confined voltage scaling does incur a penalty in terms of speed. However, through CCF, the amount of area and speed traded away are small when compared to the energy savings achieved. As a result, the cumulative EDAP gains are substantial and can be as high as a multiplicative factor of 15. This is more than twice the EDAP gains of a factor of 7 achieved using probabilistic pruning alone, with a relative error of 10%. For completeness, we also show the energy gains alone for four types of adder architectures in Figure 5(f), which range from a multiplicative factor of around 3 to a value of 4.8.

All of the measured values were determined using the fabricated chip in TSMC 180nm (low power) technology . However, to demonstrate the value of inexact hardware at the architectural layer using probabilistic pruning in the context of technology scaling as the feature sizes decrease to 90nm and below, we also designed adder architectures using IBM 90nm and TSMC 65nm (high V_{th} and low leakage) technologies. In this case, we performed post-layout simulations and the results shown in Figure 5(e) establish the technology independence of the probabilistic pruning technique. The

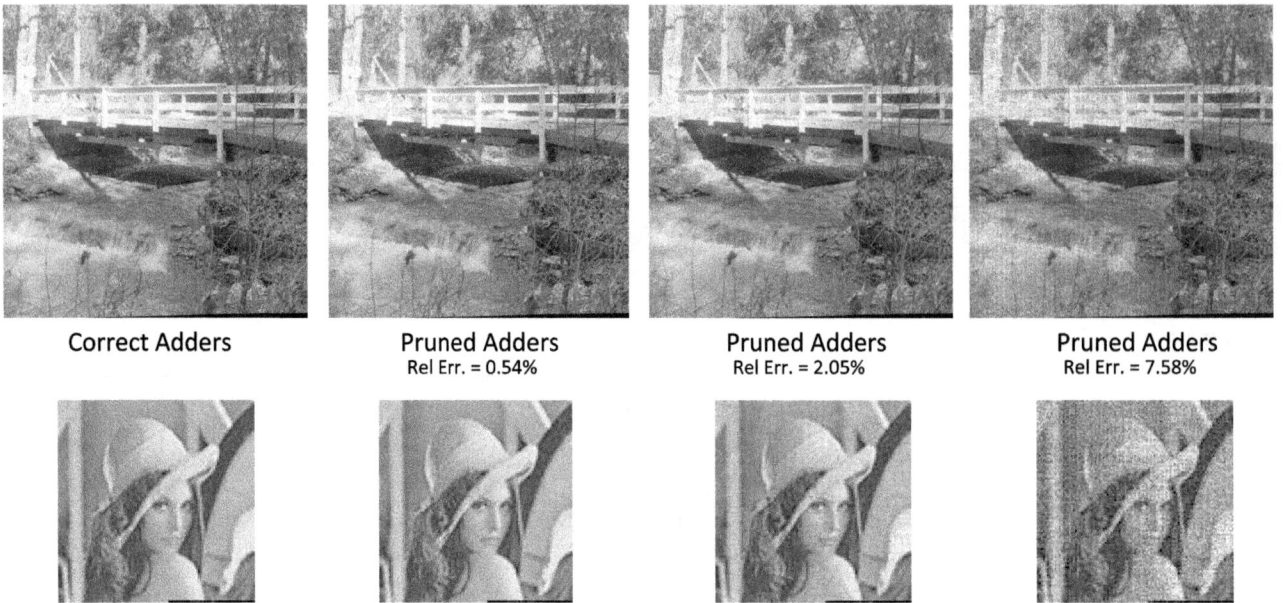

Figure 6: Results for two sets of images after an FFT operation by correct adders and pruned adders with varying relative error

Table 3: Comparison of Probabilistic Pruning and Precision Reduction for a 16-bit Input data over a Kogge Stone Carry Network

Precision reduced to	Rel. Error	Avg. Error	Pruned Adder (extra) EDAP Gains
14-bit	0.007%	3	1.334X
13-bit	0.015%	7	1.239X
12-bit	0.031%	15	1.328X
11-bit	0.065%	31	1.383X
10-bit	0.13%	63	1.231X

main point worth noting is that the EDAP gains for the two types of adder architectures shown are very close in magnitude across technology generations, and establish the fact that they will scale as the transistor feature sizes decrease in the future.

3.3 Comparison to Precision Reduction or Bit-width Reduction

The question as to comparing our CCF approach or probabilistic pruning to standard *precision reduction* by utilizing circuits of lower bit-width comes up often. Precision reduction techniques can be viewed as a special case of the probabilistic pruning algorithm in which the significance of the truncated (output/input) nodes can be assigned as zero or the activity of the truncated nodes is zero, or both. Our results, as shown in Table 3, indicate that the probabilistic pruning technique outperforms the precision reduction technique by achieving 20-40% more cumulative EDAP gains for comparable error.

3.4 Application of Pruned Adders to Images

Since metrics such as relative error do not provide an intuitive idea as to how much an inexact architecture affects an application, we will provide some preliminary evidence demonstrating the effect of inexactness on perceptual quality in the context of media processing applications . For this purpose, we will choose the Fast Fourier Transform, one of the most ubiquitous building blocks in such applications. We have simulated an 8-point FFT architecture designed using pruned adders. The adders used in the FFT were simulations of 16-bit pruned adders implemented using a MATLAB environment. Specifically, we collected the mean and standard deviation of relative error magnitudes from post-layout simulations of 16-bit pruned adders, and injected these statistically determined values into our simulator. The resulting images processed using such inexact FFT architectures with various levels of error are shown in Figure 6. Depending on the perceptual quality needed, the inexact adder with the corresponding error properties could be chosen. From this figure, it can be observed that while images corresponding to a relative error of 0.54% would be suitable for most applications, images with relative error of 7.5% would still allow us to visually recognize the images. Thus, depending on the specific quality needed and after accounting for the compensation provided by our own visual and potentially auditory pathways, inexact architectures can be used at relatively high levels of admissible error indeed!

4. CONCLUSION AND FUTURE DIRECTIONS

We have proposed a cross-layer co-design approach integrating the architecture and logic layers, as well as the physical layer. To the best of our knowledge, this is the first attempt at such a symbiotic co-design methodology, supported by a systematic algorithmic framework for designing inexact circuits. The possible gains by the proposed approach have been conclusively established through measured results of a prototype chip. The CAD framework used to perform these measurements and test this chip, we believe, is a novel contribution in its own right in the context of designing inexact hardware circuits.

We will identify several directions for future research:

- **Algorithmic and optimization questions:** First, the algorithmic techniques used in our co-design framework CCF, are heuristic. Given their simplicity, this framework has yielded surprisingly good results. We believe that a rigorous characterization of the pruning function, analyzing it using methods rooted in the average case analysis of algorithms [26], and most significantly, removing the need for simulation during each of the pruning steps would be interesting. Such methods would also help lower the current dependence on heuristics during the healing phase. We also believe that conventional algorithms for (computer) arithmetic and associated designs for signal processing will have to be reexamined when inexactness is permitted, and will likely result in novel algorithms. Notably, canonical algorithms for addition, multiplication and the FFT are all candidates.

- **Hardware-software co-design for inexact applications:** There is a need for developing a hardware-software co-design framework for efficiently mapping the inexact parts of an application algorithm into corresponding inexact hardware. Here, the problem of characterizing and managing inexact control-flow beyond the datapath component poses very exciting challenges. Efficient software compilers and design automation tools for realizing such a mapping, both statically and at runtime, would be of significant interest. In this context, efficient hardware support would also be crucial. Some preliminary steps have been recently announced [13] that provide interesting frameworks for addressing these significant and interesting challenges.

- **Mixed-signal and inexact SoC design:** While most of the current research in inexact design has focused on digital systems and their memories, analog components which are quite naturally inexact have not been considered in the past. A mixed-signal SoC integrating all these three types of hardware elements, namely digital logic for computing, memories, and analog circuits, would allow for even greater opportunities to explore the value inexactness. Similarly, domain specific co-processors building on the work of [16] are also eminently well-suited candidates for incorporating inexactness.

- **Verification and test of inexact systems:** As inexact systems allow error, the notion of correctness is redefined in a fundamental way. Therefore, conventional verification and test algorithms and their evaluation metrics have to be redesigned and extended to allow for inexactness.

5. ACKNOWLEDGEMENTS

The authors would like to acknowledge and thank Jean-Luc Nagel, Pierre-Alain Beuchat and Marc Morgan of CSEM SA, Switzerland for their valuable help and support in establishing the implementation and validation framework for this paper. The work of Kirthi Krishna Muntimadugu, Richard Karp and Krishna Palem was supported in part by the NTU-Rice Institute of Sustainable and Applied Infodynamics, Nanyang Technological University, Singapore.

6. REFERENCES

[1] A. Kahng et al. Slack redistribution for graceful degradation under voltage overscaling. *in proc. of ASPDAC*, pages 825 – 831, Jan 2010.

[2] A. Lingamneni et al. Energy parsimonious circuit design through probabilistic pruning. *in proc. of DATE*, pages 764–769, Mar 2011.

[3] A. Lingamneni et al. Parsimonious circuit design for error-tolerant applications through probabilistic logic minimization. *in the proc. of the PATMOS*, pages 204–213, 2011.

[4] A Lingamneni et al. Synthesizing parsimonious inexact circuits through probabilistic design techniques. *in the special issue on Probabilistic Embedded Computing, ACM Transactions on Embedded Computing Systems*, 2012.

[5] S. Borkar. Designing reliable systems from unreliable components: The challenges of transistor variability and degradation. *IEEE Micro*, 25(6):10–16, 2005.

[6] D. Ernst et al. Razor: A low-power pipeline based on circuit-level timing speculation. In *in proc. of MICRO*, pages 7–18, Oct. 2003.

[7] G. Karakonstantis et al. Herqules: system level cross-layer design exploration for efficient energy-quality trade-offs. *in the proc. of ISLPED*, (117-122), 2010.

[8] G. V. Varatkar et al. Energy-efficient motion estimation using error-tolerance. In *proc. of ISLPED*, pages 113 – 118, Oct 2006.

[9] D. Harris. A taxonomy of parallel prefix networks. *Asilomar Conference on Signals, Systems and Computers*, 2:2213, Nov 2003.

[10] R. Hegde and N. R. Shanbhag. Energy-efficient signal processing via algorithmic noise-tolerance. *In Proc. Int. Symp. on Low Power Electronics and Design*, pages 30–35, 1999.

[11] R. Hegde and N. R. Shanbhag. Soft digital signal processing. *IEEE Transactions on Very Large Scale Integration (VLSI) Systems*, 9(6):813–823, Dec. 2001.

[12] ITRS. International technology roadmap for semiconductors, 2007.

[13] J. George et al. Probabilistic arithmetic and energy efficient embedded signal processing. In *proc. of IEEE/ACM CASES*, pages 158 – 168, 2006.

[14] J. Ray et al. Dual use of superscalar datapath for transient-fault detection and recovery. In *in proc. of MICRO*, pages 214–224, 2001.

[15] J.T. Ludwig et al. Low-power digital filtering using approximate processing. *IEEE Journal of Solid-State Circuits*, 31(3):395–400, Mar. 1996.

[16] H. Kaul, M. Anders, S. Mathew, S. Hsu, A. Agarwal, R. Krishnamurthy, and S. Borkar. A 320 mv 56 μw 411 gops/watt ultra-low voltage motion estimation accelerator in 65 nm cmos. In *IEEE Journal of Solid-State Circuits*, pages 107–114, 2008.

[17] K.V. Palem et al. Sustaining moore's law in embedded computing through probabilistic and approximate

design: retrospects and prospects. In *in proc. of CASES*, pages 1–10, 2009.

[18] L. N. B. Chakrapani et al. Probabilistic system-on-a-chip architectures. *in ACM Trans. on Design Automation of Electronic Sys*, 12(3):1–28, 2007.

[19] L.N.B. Chakrapani et al. Highly energy and performance efficient embedded computing through approximately correct arithmetic: A mathematical foundation and preliminary experimental validation. In *proc. of IEEE/ACM CASES*, pages 187–196, 2008.

[20] M. Alioto et al. Impact of supply voltage variations on full adder delay: analysis and comparison. *IEEE Transactions on VLSI Systems*, 14(12):1322, Dec 2006.

[21] N Banerjee et al. Process variation tolerant low power DCT architecture. In *Design, Automation and Test in Europe Conference*, Apr 2007.

[22] K. V. Palem. Energy aware algorithm design via probabilistic computing: From algorithms and models to Moore's law and novel (semiconductor) devices. In *proc. of CASES*, pages 113 – 116, 2003.

[23] K. V. Palem. Energy aware computing through probabilistic switching: A study of limits. *IEEE Transactions on Computers*, 54(9):1123–1137, 2005.

[24] K. V. Palem, S. Cheemalavagu, P. Korkmaz, and B. E. Akgul. Probabilistic and introverted switching to conserve energy in a digital system. *US Patent*, (20050240787), 2005.

[25] N. Pippenger. Analysis of carry propagation in addition: An elementary approach. *Journal of Algorithms*, 42:317–313, 2002.

[26] R. M. Karp et al. Average case analysis of a heuristic for the assignment problem. *Mathematics of Operations Research*, 19(3):513–522, Aug 1994.

[27] S. Gyger et al. Hardware development kit for systems based on an icyflex processor. *CSEM Scientific and Technical Report*, 2009.

[28] S. H. Nawab et al. Approximate signal processing. *The Journal of VLSI Signal Processing*, 15:177–200, 1997.

[29] S Narayanan et al. Scalable stochastic processors. In *in proc. of DATE*, pages 335 – 338, Mar 2010.

[30] S.H. Kim et al. Experimental analysis of sequence dependence on energy saving for error tolerant image processing. *in the proc. of ISLPED*, 2009.

[31] V. K. Chippa et al. Scalable effort hardware design: exploiting algorithmic resilience for energy efficiency. *in the proc. of DAC*, (555-560), 2010.

APPENDIX

A. DETAILED PSEUDO- CODE FOR THE CCF ALGORITHM

In this appendix, we provide a more detailed form of the CCF algorithm expanding upon Algorithm 1 described in Section 2 that can be applied to general circuits.

```
// Main Function in the Algorithm
function CO-DESIGN(Graph 𝒢, MaxError, Testbench T)
    //Step 1 : Architecture-layer – Probabilistic Pruning
    (A, D, E) ← Area, Energy, Delay of 𝒢
    RankList = RankNodes(𝒢, T);
    𝒢ᴾ = PruneNodes(RankList);
    HealNodes(𝒢ᴾ);
    //Step 2 : Physical-layer – Confined Voltage Scaling
    (Aᴾ, Dᴾ, Eᴾ) ← Area, Energy, Delay of 𝒢ᴾ
    AreaOverhead ∝ (LevelShifters, VoltageRegulators)
    if A − Aᴾ ≥ AreaOverhead then
```
$$V_{\text{cvs}} = V \times \frac{D^P}{D}$$
```
    end if
    return 𝒢ᴾ, V_cvs
end function
```

```
// Ranking Function : Rank nodes in the increasing order
of their Significance Activity Product (SAP)
function RANKNODES(𝒢, T)
    RunBenchmark(T);
    // Compute the probability of switching of each node
    for all i ← 1 to N do
        node.activity(i)(j) = ComputeNodeSwitchProb;
    end for
    // Compute Significance-Activity Product of each node
    for all i ← 1 to N do
        node.sap(i) = node.significance(i) × node.activity(i);
    end for
end function
```

```
// Pruning Function : Prune maximum number of lowest
rank nodes without exceeding MaxError
function PRUNENODES(RankList)
    high = N, low = 1;
    while low ≠ high do
        mid = ⌊(high + low)/2⌋;
        CurError = ComputeError(𝒢(N − mid));
        if (CurError > MaxError) then
            high = mid;
        else if (CurError ≤ MaxError) then
            low = mid;
        end if
    end while
    for i ← 1 to mid do
        𝒢 = 𝒢(N − i);
    end for
    return 𝒢
end function
```

```
// Healing Function: Finds the input or a fixed logic value
which results in least amount of error upon node pruning
function HEALNODES(𝒢)
    // Iterate over all possible unique nodes in the graph
    and find the minimum error over all possible inputs and
    fixed logic values
    for k ← 1 to K do
        NodeHealChoice_k ←
```
$$\min_{i \in \{i_1, i_2, \dots, i_m, 0, 1\}} \left(\sum_{\forall \text{ inputs}} (f_k \oplus i) \right);$$
```
    end for
    Apply NodeHealChoice_k to all pruned nodes
end function
```

A Reconfigurable Optical/Electrical Interconnect Architecture for Large-scale Clusters and Datacenters

Diego Lugones
The Rince Institute
Dublin City University
Glasnevin
Dublin 9, Ireland.
diego@rince.ie

Kostas Katrinis
Dublin Research Lab
IBM Research
IBM Dublin Technology
Campus, Mulhuddart
Dublin 15, Ireland
katrinisk@ie.ibm.com

Martin Collier
School of Electronic
Engineering
Dublin City University
Glasnevin
Dublin 9, Ireland.
collierm@eeng.dcu.ie

ABSTRACT

Hybrid optical/electrical interconnects, using commercially available optical circuit switches at the core part of the network, have been recently proposed as an attractive alternative to fully-connected electronically-switched networks in terms of port density, bandwidth/port, cabling and energy efficiency. Although the shift from a traditionally packet-switched core to switching between server aggregations (or servers) at circuit granularity requires system redesign, the approach has been shown to fit well to the traffic requirements of certain classes of high-performance computing applications, as well as to the traffic patterns exhibited by typical data center workloads. Recent proposals for such system designs have looked at small/medium scale hybrid interconnects. In this paper, we present a hybrid optical/electrical interconnect architecture intended for large-scale deployments of high-performance computing systems and server co-locations. To reduce complexity, our architecture employs a regular shuffle network topology that allows for simple management and cabling. Thanks to using a single-stage core interconnect and multiple optical planes, our design can be both incrementally scaled up (in capacity) and scaled out (in the number of racks) without requiring major re-cabling and network re-configuration. Also, we are the first to our knowledge to explore the benefit of using multi-hopping in the optical domain as a means to avoid constant reconfiguration of optical circuit switches. We have prototyped our architecture at packet-level detail in a simulation framework to evaluate this concept. Our results demonstrate that our hybrid interconnect, by adapting to the changing nature of application traffic, can significantly exceed the throughput of a static interconnect of equal degree, while at times attaining a throughput comparable to that of a costly fully-connected network. We also show a further benefit brought by multi-hopping, that it reduces the performance drops by reducing the frequency of reconfiguration.

Categories and Subject Descriptors

C.2.1 [**Network Architecture and Design**]: Network topology, circuit-switching networks, packet-switching networks; C.2.2 [**Network Protocols**]: Routing protocols

Keywords

Interconnection Networks, Optical Switching, Multi-Hop topologies

1. INTRODUCTION

High-performance computing (HPC) has already embarked into the Petascale era and yet efforts are already on-going towards further increasing the peak performance of super-computing systems. To sustain this trend, data movement efficiency needs to improve in hand with the tremendous increase in compute density and speed. In turn, this presents a challenge in implementing the fabric interconnecting a massive scale of compute elements at controlled capitalization and operational cost. A similar challenge is presented in large-scale datacenters (DC) due to their constant need for ever increasing capacity computing brought about by emerging applications (e.g. web search, video processing) and new trends in offering computing services (e.g. Cloud Computing). Commodity solutions have typically to date employed full-bisection bandwidth interconnects for this purpose. Although being a safe approach due to covering the worst-case, recent studies [3] in DCs have reported that full bisection can be overkill due to poor utilization. Other researchers [2, 8] have similarly shown that a set of widely used HPC applications exhibits a low communication degree throughout the application lifetime.

As an alternative, various interconnects [2, 6, 16] employing reconfigurable optical circuit switches (OCS) in the core part of the fabric have been proposed. The reconfigurability of an OCS network enables it to dynamically place bandwidth on demand wherever is needed, as opposed to static bandwidth allocation in electronic networks . The attractions of optical circuit switches include a) their high port density allowing the construction of large interconnects with a small number of stages, b) the reduced number of transceivers in the core due to all-optical switching, c) the amenity to protocol and bandwidth upgrades occurring at the electronic edge, d) their power efficiency due to passive switching and e) tremendous link bandwidth using Wavelength-Division Multiplexing (WDM) technologies, whose cost continues to decrease. These advantages come at the cost of switching at circuit (or flow) granularity: unlike high-end electronic switches that can switch a single packet between an arbitrary port pair in the order of micro- or even nano-seconds, commercial MEMS-based optical circuit switches exhibit latencies in the order of tenths of milliseconds to establish an optical cross-connection, which in turn incurs a prohibitive overhead to switch at packet granularity at 10Gbps rates and beyond. This presents one of the main challenges for the deployment of such designs into production systems. Another challenge stems from the point-to-point nature of optical MEMS-based interconnects. Since a fully-connected network in this case is prohibitive cost-wise, it remains questionable whether a low-bisection optical core can sustain the connectivity requirements of all possible workloads.

To address these challenges, this paper proposes a hybrid optical/electrical interconnect architecture. Intended for larger scales, our architecture implements a shuffle-exchange topology to avoid costly multiple stages, while allowing incremental upgrades without the requirement for redesign or recabling, and features communication based on shortest paths and multi-path capability. We also present a novel heuristic for dynamically adapting the optical interconnect to changing traffic patterns that leverages the regularity of the topology to provide for effective adaptation, while striving to minimize the frequency and thus the impact of reconfiguration. To our knowledge, we are the first to evaluate the benefit of having packets traversing the optical domain multiple times (multi-hopping) on their path from source to destination. As our simulation results show, the multi-hop approach can significantly mitigate the effect of lengthy reconfiguration times of MEMS switches, while also yielding good performance for traffic patterns with a core connectivity degree exceeding the physical connectivity of the network edge.

This paper is structured as follows: the next section outlines similar approaches and discusses them in relation to the present work. Section 3 presents the architecture of the hybrid interconnect, while Section 4 enhances the scheme with a dynamic topology optimization algorithm. We present and discuss the simulation results obtained to evaluate the proposed architecture in Section 5 and present our conclusions and outline our on-going work in Section 6.

2. RELATED WORK

The communication patterns of various parallel scientific applications were studied in [4, 12, 15] in order to dimension the architectural requirements of petascale platforms. In [5], authors analyze the impact of the network's non-blocking capability on overall performance and conclude that a significant reduction in the number of inter-stage links can be tolerated causing less than 5% overall loss of performance. Particularly to using circuit-switched optical interconnects as core network elements, [2] layed out the design of a hybrid optical/electrical interconnect, together with a study of the connectivity requirements of various HPC applications, confirming that full bisection bandwidth is an overkill for a class of workloads. A follow-up work [1] has presented a feasibility analysis of a hybrid solution and a related performance analysis. A similar study was presented in [8], based on an exhaustive analysis of application requirements described in [7] and [9]. All the above work has made the case for hybrid optical/electrical interconnects being a cost-competitive and yet effective solution for a specific set of mainly HPC applications and as such it re-inforces the feasibility and potential impact of this work.

Hybrid interconnect architectures have been proposed before in different contexts, such as HPC [2, 9], datacenter networks [6, 14, 16] and stream computing systems [13], addressing various issues towards a production implementation, such as topology design, routing, traffic assignment to the optical resp. electrical network and dynamic reconfiguration algorithms. As such, our work is directly related and shares similar problems with all the above previously proposed designs. Unlike conventional fat-tree like topologies with multiple stages or recent designs using high-radix routers to reduce the network diameter [10], we propose an architecture based on a single-stage regular topology that avoids the complexity and cost of multiple stages, while being able to scale to tenths of thousands of servers. Also, through the inclusion of optical multi-hop functionality, we extend for the first time to our knowledge the scope of hybrid optical/electrical interconnects to applications with higher logical connectivity degree compared to the physical connectivity degree of the network edge, as well as alleviate to a significant extent the impact of high switching latency of commercial optical circuit switches to application performance.

3. INTERCONNECT ARCHITECTURE

For the sake of integrity, we provide here a review of the use of commodity Optical Circuit Switches (OCS) as part of a hybrid optical/electrical HPC and/or DC interconnect, whereby the qualifier "hybrid" refers both to the combination of two distinct switching technologies (optical and electronic switching), as well as to the combination of two distinct switching granularities (circuit vs. packet as switched unit). In this abstracted layout of the OCS/EPS architecture, communication incurred by processing elements is assigned by edge routing to the appropriate part of the hybrid interconnect. Pertaining to point-to-point communication, long-lived, edge-aggregated high-volume flows (source/destination pairs) are switched via the network of OCS switches, whereas low-rate/small-message communication and signalling/control messages are routed via the packet-switched electronic network. The default action for collective communication (broadcast, reduction operations) is to route it via the electronic network, since typically collectives are short-lived and also fit well with the low switching overhead and replication capability of electronic packet switching. As part of our on-going work, we are evaluating the use of optical multi-hop functionality of our architecture for serving collectives all-optically (beyond the edge tier), aiming at further reducing the size/link-capacity of the EPS network.

In what follows, we present the detailed architecture of the interconnect part dealing with the OCS network, since this presents the main challenge in terms of scalability, cost and matching of technology characteristics to workload requirements. We otherwise assume that a low-rate electronic network complements the OCS part and interconnects edge networking elements for the transport of signalling/control messages and collectives.

3.1 Topology and Switching

Prior work on interconnects of this class (cf. section 2) has mostly looked at constrained system scales, primarily because the focus was on "first-principles" issues that had to be addressed to make the case for hybrid reconfigurable interconnects. Instead, our focus is on scalability and this is reflected in the topology selection. Our optical interconnect architecture derives its topology from the *directly connected Single-stage Shuffle eXchange (SSX)* network [11], with specific amendments to leverage the ability of reconfiguration and to enable multi-hop routing in the optical domain.

Figure 1 shows an embodiment of the interconnect topology comprising an edge tier with nine radix-3 electronic packet Switching Elements (SE) and a core tier with a single 27-port optically circuit-switched plane. Each input/output port of the SEs connects via uni-directional fiber to a port of the optical switch, whereby compute nodes/servers connect to packet switching elements directly (not shown in Figure 1). The optical circuit switch plane can be readily implemented using commercially available 3D-MEMS based products (e.g. Calient Fiberconnect 320 or Glimmerglass Intelligent Optical System 600). Aligned with current integration practices, packet switches in our topology correspond to backplanes or top-of-rack switches that implement the switching functionality (exchange) required by the SSX network[1].

More formally, let N be the total number of *radix-k* packet switches attached to the optical switch. Then, port p at packet switch i connects via an optical circuit to packet switch j, where j is given by

$$j = (k \cdot i + p) \bmod N, \quad 0 \le p \le k-1, \quad 0 \le i,j \le N-1 \quad (1)$$

Unlike conventional shuffle-exchange networks that perform first the *shuffling* - routing a packet to the appropriate switch - and then the *exchange*, i.e. picking the right switch output port for a packet towards its destination, in our architecture the exchange is performed first (in the packet switches), followed by the shuffling carried out in an optical circuit switch. Packet switches implement efficient routing of packets sent by compute nodes attached to them, as well as flow control, and the optical cross-connect maintains a shuffle pattern between packet switches. The shuffle topology can be dynamically altered by network control to match physical connectivity to logical communication patterns exhibited by applications (either pro-actively on application request or re-actively as a result of monitoring). A packet needs to traverse at least one hop (i.e. the optical circuit and two fibers) and at most $log_k N$ hops to reach its destination. Compared to multi-stage topologies with a fixed diameter of $log_k N$, the SSX topology allows for shortest path routing, thus minimizing latency, congestion and eliminating cycles (deadlock avoidance). Note also that multiple paths between node pairs are possible over the single-stage shuffle for the purpose of network load distribution and resilience.

As already mentioned in section 1, the typical reconfiguration latency of commercial optical circuit-switching technologies is in the order of milliseconds, a fact that can drastically reduce application performance during logical topology changes. Instead, off-the-shelf core packet switches can switch between distinct port pairs within microseconds. To alleviate this disadvantage of optical circuit switching over

---

[1]In the future, however, we do not preclude the electronic switching functionality being carried out at servers instead of at dedicated networking elements, for it is likely that a more aggressive integration of cores per socket will incur relatively long-lived, low birth/death-rate flows being initiated from or terminated at compute nodes.

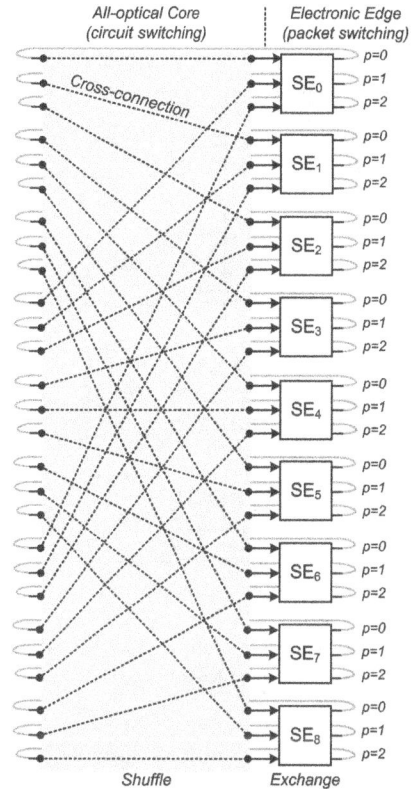

Figure 1: Instance of a reconfigurable optical SSX interconnect comprising N=9 radix-3 packet switching elements at the network edge and a reconfigurable optical fiber cross-connect at the core. Packet switches connect via fiber to input ports of the cross-connect (left side), whereby output ports (right side) of the optical cross-connect are routed via fiber to input ports of the edge switches. Cross-connections within the cross-connect implementing the shuffle are depicted with dotted lines. Nodes connect directly to packet switches (not shown).

established core packet switching solutions, we employ *multi-hopping in the optical domain*: switching elements at the edge are programmed with the ability to switch packets received from the optical domain back to optical switches; thus, packets can cross the optical domain two or more times until they reach their destination terminal. The purpose of this approach is to reduce the number of reconfigurations by prolonging the goodness of an established optical switch configuration to time scales that are significantly larger compared to application flow duration. Of equal importance is the use of multi-hopping in the optical domain to support workloads that exhibit cross-rack logical connectivity degrees that are higher than the maximum number of optical circuits emanating from a rack in the physical topology. If this aspect is seen from a design perspective, multi-hopping opens a design space to trade-off application performance for reduced cost (#ports) of the optical core.

3.2 Scalability

To date, we are aware of commercial MEMS fiber switches with up to 320 bidirectional optical ports. Due to this technology/commercial-drive constraint, the scalability of the architecture presented so far is limited to a few thou-

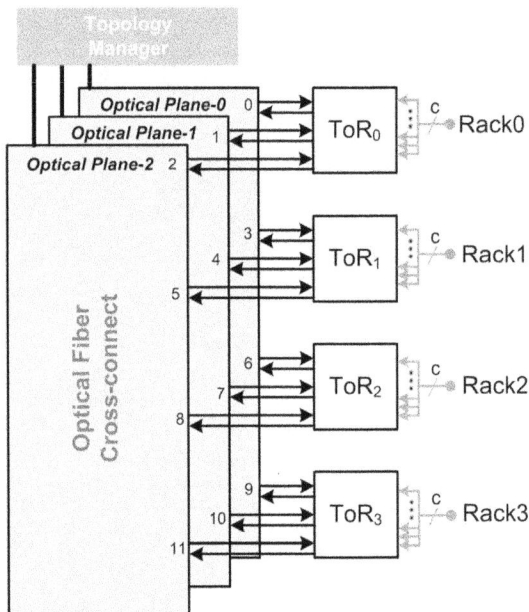

Figure 2: 4-rack instance of the hybrid interconnect with multiple optical planes, employing radix-3 packet switches at the edge.

sands of servers. Beyond departmental and medium-scale enterprise clusters, our work is targetting large-scale high-performance computing systems and data centers in the order of $O(10K)$ of servers. To enable installations of this scale, our architecture employs multiple independent *optical planes* [2], whereby each plane is implemented with an optical circuit switch. Figure 2 depicts an instantiation of the multi-plane extension of the interconnect architecture with three planes and four edge packet switches. Unless otherwise stated and without loss of generality, we assume that each packet Switching Element (SE) connects with a single bi-directional fiber to each plane. We cover the general case of having multiple fibers between an SE and an optical plane in the next section. From an application perspective and taking into consideration that the optical domain is circuit-switched, essentially each optical plane increases the 1-hop connectivity degree of a server rack, allowing each rack to reach at most k other racks within a single hop. For applications exhibiting a logical connectivity degree that exceeds the number of planes, multi-hop is employed, allowing each rack to reach k^h racks in h hops ($2 \leq h \leq log_k N$), thus implementing full connectivity at logarithmic latency.

In our architecture, the output degree (or radix) k of each packet switching element equals the number of optical planes m. Note that the number of optical switches S need not be equal to the number of planes. If r is the number of optical ports per optical switch (uniform to all switches), then we can still have m planes, even if $S \leq m$, as long as $N \cdot k \leq S \cdot r$. We accomplish this by logically clustering port regions of the same optical switch to distinct planes. In the rest of this paper and for the sake of presentation, we assume that $m = S$.

Table 1 presents several configurations using 40 resp. 80 servers per rack integration, assuming 64-port packet switches, 320 optical ports per optical switch and for various core/edge

oversubscription ratios and numbers of planes. In the 80 servers/rack case, we assume two SE's per rack and two distinct ratios for SE-to-SE vs. rack-to-core capacity allocation (1:1 and 1:2). It can be observed that the maximum system size with a single plane is limited to 880 and 1600 servers for 40- and 80-servers per rack respectively. The addition of more planes allows the topology to reach tenths of thousands of servers (25600 servers at maximum with a core:edge oversubscription ratio of 5). Given that 1024-port MEMS-switches are possible [2], a maximum system size of up to 81920 servers can be achieved without having to revert to multi-stage core topologies that complicate network control and cabling. Essentially, the port density of a plane controls the maximum number of racks, while the number of planes controls the core oversubscription ratio. This unveils the value of the independent planes design in terms of incremental deployment: gradual system scaling-out (constrained on MEMS-switch port capacity) and/or capacity scaling-up are both possible without network re-design or re-cabling, as opposed to multi-stage designs that are cumbersome and expensive to scale incrementally. To justify the selection of

Planes	Servers per Rack	SE(s) per Rack	Core Oversub.	Racks (max.)	Servers (max.)
	40	1	1.67	13	520
	40	1	3	22	880
1	80	2	3.33	13	1040
	80	2	5	20	1600
24	40	1	1.67	320	12800
13	40	1	3	320	12800
24	80	2	3.33	320	25600
16	80	2	5	320	25600

Table 1: Scalability of single- and multi-plane SSX hybrid interconnect

the single shuffle-exchange topology in terms of scalability, we compare it against an interconnect topology that is frequently employed in HPC clusters and datacenters, namely a fat-tree. Due to fat-trees exhibiting a full-bisection, this also helps in highlighting the trade-off between full capacity and interconnect cost. We refrain from translating equipment volume to market prices due to price fluctuation and price unavailability for some components. Specifically, interconnecting $H = k^n$ servers in a k-ary n-tree, where k is the input/output switch degree and n is the number stages or levels in the tree, requires $N = (n - \frac{1}{2}) \cdot k^{n-1}$ [$k \times k$] switches and $L = 2 \cdot n \cdot H$ unidirectional links, yielding a $log_k H$ diameter. Compared to the super-linear scaling of the fat-tree, the single shuffle-exchange topology requires $N = H/k$ [$k \times k$] switch elements and $L = 4 \cdot k \cdot N$ unidirectional links to interconnect H servers. This reduction in cost comes at the expense of throughput: while the fat-tree can theoretically achieve throughput equal to H, messages in the single shuffle-exchange may traverse up to $log_k N$ hops, thus incurring throughput equal to $H/log_k N$ messages per communication cycle. In our architecture, we strive to improve this figure by providing for shortest-path routing and a topology optimization heuristic (cf. sections 3.4 and 4), aiming at minimizing average number of hops. We plot in Figure 3 the volume of switches/links of the SSX topology relative to the fat tree against server-number for two distinct switching element degrees. Among others, we observe

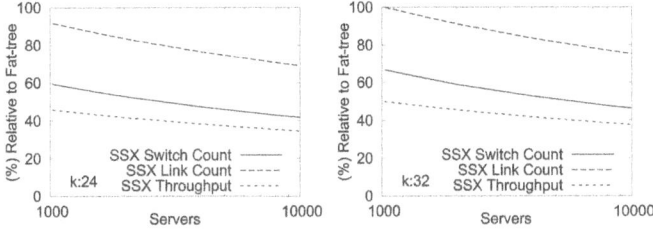

Figure 3: Switch/link volume and theoretical throughput comparison between the SSX and Fat-Tree topologies. Reduction of switch/link count of the SSX relative to a fat-tree is shown for two SE degrees (k: 24 and 32) against a target number of servers.

that $45\% - 70\%$ of fat-Tree resources are needed by the SSX network to connect $O(10K)$ servers executing applications requiring throughput around $\sim 40\%$ of a similar size fat-tree. For specific classes of applications, this is supported by studies arguing that fat-tree resources are under-utilized at all levels (cf. sections 1 and 2), thus justifying the use of a more sparse network with linear cost scaling. For instance, [8] reports that less than 40% of the Fat-Tree resources are utilized near the root, leading to an average potential port reduction of 45% for several scientific applications.

3.3 Optical SSX and Plane Decomposition

Centralized control attached to the control plane ports (typically Ethernet ports) of the optical circuit switches ensures that cross-connections of the various optical planes implement the shuffle topology among attached edge packet switches. Such functionality is provided by a dedicated server termed *Topology Manager (TM)*, as shown in Figure 2. In addition, the TM is responsible for adapting the connectivity of the shuffle to match physical interconnection to dynamic logical topology changes, as it will be presented in the next section.

In our architecture, each packet switch connects with a single bi-directional fiber to each plane[2]. Given that the number of planes m equals the radix k of each packet switch and that the number of planes equals the number of optical switches, we then have each (uni-directional) port p of a packet switch i connecting to optical port i of plane x ($x = 0...m - 1$, $i = 0...N - 1$, $p = 0...k - 1$). In order for the TM to be able to cross-connect the various planes in a manner that it implements the desired shuffle pattern, the assignment of shuffle links to planes and optical input/output ports needs to be unambiguously defined. For this, we employ a decomposition formula to embed the SSX topology to multiple optical planes. Let N stand for the number of packet switching elements directly attached to the optical planes and k be the radix of these switching elements. Then, the plane index x implementing the set of cross-connections that corresponds to the shuffle topology link initiating from

---

[2]Note that as already mentioned in the previous subsection, we can have multiple fiber pairs connecting to the same optical switch. The definition of planes can be logical and not correspond to a single optical switch.

port p of switching element i is obtained as follows:

$$Plane_x = \{ <i, (k \cdot i + p) \bmod N >,$$
$$\forall\, i : 0, 1, ..., N - 1; and\, p\, satisfying$$
$$x = (i \cdot \left\lfloor \frac{h}{N} \right\rfloor + p) \bmod k\} \qquad (2)$$

Where, $x : 0, 1, ..., k - 1$, and h is the greatest common divisor of N and k, i.e. $h = \gcd(N, k)$.

Due to the one-to-one correspondence between electronic (packet switching element) port numbers and optical port numbers in each plane, it suffices then for the TM to cross-connect port i to port j at plane x to implement the shuffle pattern, where j is calculated according to Eq. 1 given i and p. The algorithm running at the TM to cross-connect optical ports at the various planes is given in Algorithm 1.

Algorithm 1 SSX_decomposition (N, k)

1: $h \leftarrow \gcd(N, k)$
2: **for** $i = 0$ to $N - 1$ **do**
3:    **for** $n = 0$ to $k - 1$ **do**
4:       $x \leftarrow (i \cdot h/N + p) \bmod k$
5:       $j \leftarrow (k \cdot i + p) \bmod N$
        {Add element $<i, j>$ to the subset: $plane_x$}
6:       $plane[x] \leftarrow <i, j> \quad \{<i, j> \in plane_x\}$
7:    **end for**
8: **end for**
9: **return** $plane_x$

3.4 Routing

One of the outstanding features of shuffle-exchange networks is its efficiency in data-forwarding: routing is tag-based - at each hop a switching element picks the output port based on the most significant bit of the tag - and thus takes constant time, while eliminating the need for maintaining forwarding state at intermediate nodes. Routing in our architecture borrows from the routing approach presented in [11] that allows for an arbitrary relationship between network size N and switching element radix k. In generalized single-stage radix-k shuffle networks of size N, the routing tag (P_n) of length n is the given by:

$$P_n = C.N + j - k^n.i, \,\forall\, 0 \le P_n < k^n\, and\, C \ge 0 \qquad (3)$$

where i and j are the source and destination switching elements and C is a non-negative integer such that $0 \le P_n < k^n$ [11]. Given that the decomposition in Equation 2 modifies output port connections to properly embed the SSX topology into multiple planes, the routing tag P_n must be also modified accordingly. For this, we initially use the routing tag $P_n : |p_1, p_2, ..., p_n|_k$ (in radix-k representation) for generalized shuffle-exchange networks and then we modify it to obtain the final tag $T_n : |t_1, t_2, ..., t_n|_k$ according to:

$$t_y = (m_y \cdot \left\lfloor \frac{h}{N} \right\rfloor + p_y) \bmod k$$
$$m_y = (k \cdot m_{y-1} + p_y) \bmod N$$
$$m_0 = i$$
$$y = 1...n \qquad (4)$$

The routing algorithm is performed at the network edge where the most significant digit of the tag (in radix-k representation) is used to select the proper output port. Then, the tag is left-shifted to eliminate the most significant digit. This routing function can be performed by modular arithmetic operations, which leads to efficient hardware implementations.

Unlike multistage networks with a fixed number of stages, where the tag has as many digits as stages in the network, the length of the tag can vary in single-stage networks, allowing thus for shortest path routing to minimize latency and congestion. We employ shortest-length tag generation (and thus shortest-path routing) for a given source i and destination j, as outlined in Algorithm 2. Lines *1 through 19* in the algorithm compute the tag P_n with the smallest length n according to Equation 3. Then, the transformation proposed in Equation 4 is performed on lines *20* throughout *25*.

Algorithm 2 SSX_routing (i, j)

1: $A \leftarrow k \cdot i$
2: $B \leftarrow k \cdot (i+1)$
3: $n \leftarrow 0$
4: $J \leftarrow j$
5: **while** 1 **do**
6:    **if** $A \leq J$ **then**
7:       **if** $J < B$ **then**
8:          $P \leftarrow J - A$
9:          *break*
10:       **else**
11:          $A \leftarrow k \cdot A$
12:          $B \leftarrow k \cdot B$
13:          $n \leftarrow n + 1$
14:       **end if**
15:    **else**
16:       $J \leftarrow J + N$
17:    **end if**
18: **end while**
   {Set P to k-radix format (i.e. $P_n : |p_1, p_2, ..., p_n|_k)$}
19: $P_n \leftarrow convBase(P, k)$
20: $m \leftarrow i$
21: **for** $y = 0$ **to** n **do**
22:    $t_y \leftarrow (m \cdot \lfloor \frac{h}{N} \rfloor + p_y) \bmod k$
23:    $m \leftarrow (k \cdot m + p_y) \bmod N$
24: **end for**
25: **return** $T_n \{: |t_1, t_2, ..., t_n|_k\}$

---

4. TOPOLOGY OPTIMIZATION

By allowing to place bandwidth capacity wherever and whenever it is needed, reconfigurability of optical interconnects is the feature that opens up the design space between scalable low-degree and expensive full-bisection bandwidth interconnects. For this, effective algorithms and architectural support to monitor and identify suboptimal configurations of the optical planes with regard to existing/building-up flows, as well as to compute and apply reconfigurations that improve application performance, are required. In this section, we present a greedy heuristic that adapts the shuffle-exchange topology to dynamic traffic requirements.

The proposed heuristic re-aligns the embedding of the SSX regular topology into the physical network topology by directly cross-connecting (i.e. offering an 1-hop optical connection) the most heavily communicating source/destination packet-switching element pairs; the rest of the communicat-

ing pairs are served with multi-hop connections. Specifically, given a non-negative traffic matrix λ with elements corresponding to source/destination packet-switch pairs' communication rates (as measured within a pre-defined historical time window) and the SSX topology as input, our heuristic algorithms implements dynamic topology management in two steps:

Step-1: This step outputs the set $\lambda_{OPT_{i,j}}$ with the N most heavily communicating packet-switching elements. More precisely:

$$\lambda_{OPT_{i,j}} = \{ <i,j> : \sum_{<i,j>} \lambda[i][j] \text{ is maximized}$$
$$and \ |\lambda_{OPT_{i,j}}| = N, \ 0 \leq i, j \leq N\} \quad (5)$$

We compute $\lambda_{OPT_{i,j}}$ as defined in Equation 5 by solving the assignment problem on the packet-switching elements source and destination sets, using the traffic matrix as cost input. For this, we use the *Kuhn-Munkres* algorithm that outputs an assignment that maximizes traffic rate exchange, given the input.

Step-2: For each element in the subset $\lambda_{OPT_{i,j}}$, find an alternative source node s located at 1-hop distance from destination j and swap node i with s, if $\lambda[i][j] > \lambda[s][j]$ and $d_{ij} > 1$, where d_{ij} $(0 \leq i, j < N)$ gives the hop-count between any two packet-switching elements in the current topology. Equation 1 that specifies adjacency in the SSX topology is used for locating alternative sources and thus the shuffle-pattern is preserved after node swapping. Among the k alternative source SE's we can select from, we pick the one that exhibits the lowest traffic rate in the traffic matrix. Essentially, step-2 strives to assign 1-hop cross-connections to src/dst pairs that belong to the most heavily communicating ones and are at least 2-hops away between each other.

The term "node swapping" in step-2 involves having the swapped packet-switching elements swap the i, j indices that identify them in the shuffle-exchange topology, as well as re-configuring cross-connections as necessary to preserve the shuffle pattern in the physical topology. Apart from applying this change at the Topology Manager, the only part of the system that needs to be notified about swapping events is the entity that generates routing tags.

After both steps have executed, the heuristic returns a set R whose elements $<i,s>$ represent the nodes to be swapped and re-connected by reconfiguring optical links as appropriate:

$$R = \{ <i,s> : \lambda[i][j] > \lambda[s][j] \text{ and } d_{ij} > 1,$$
$$0 \leq i, j < N, \ 0 \leq s < N\} \quad (6)$$

To shed more light on the workings of the dynamic topology management heuristic, we present here a topology reconfiguration example. Consider the SSX topology with $N = 6$ and $k = 2$ shown in Figure 4 and an instantaneous traffic matrix with inter-node traffic rates shown in Table 2. In Figure 4, we also depict the source/destination servers - attached to switching elements SE_1/SE_4 and SE_5/SE_0 - that contribute to the rack-level flows λ_{14} and λ_{50} respectively. Note that packets of flow λ_{14} traverse two hops (depicted with dashed lines in Figure 4) to reach their destination, while flow λ_{50} takes three hops from source to destination packet-switching element. Using these instances of topology and traffic matrix as input, *step-1* of the topology optimization heuristic computes among the $(N-1) \cdot (N-1)$ possible alternatives

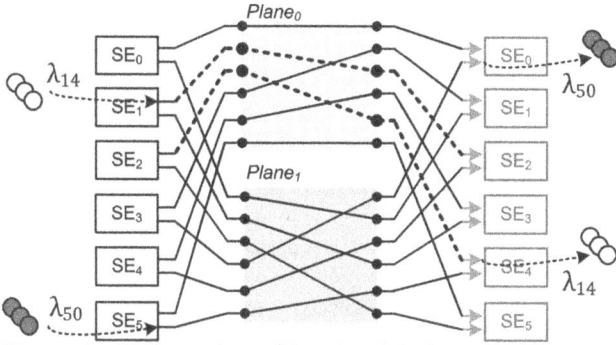

Figure 4: SSX topology (N=6,k=2) before that topology optimization is applied. Servers contributing to flow λ_{14} are depicted with white circles, while black circles correspond to servers sourcing/terminating flow λ_{50}.

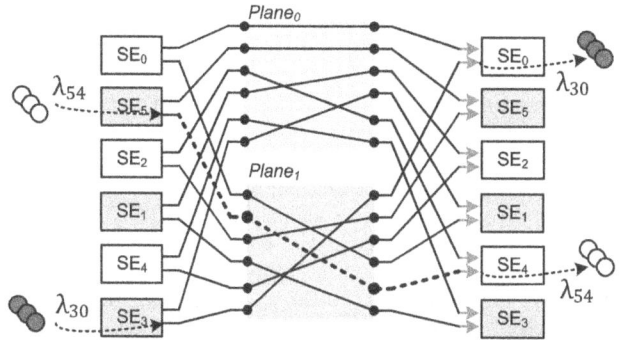

Figure 5: After reconfiguration SE's 1, 3 and 5 are swapped with SE's 5, 1 and 3 respectively, and optical circuits are modified to preserve the SSX topology. From a routing perspective, flows λ_{14} and λ_{50} in Figure 4 are now λ_{54} and λ_{30}, both taking only one hop from source to destination.

Table 2: Traffic Matrix (λ)

S\D	0	1	2	3	4	5
0	0	476	758	876	109	318
1	175	0	436	101	944	181
2	611	107	0	197	446	814
3	38	479	796	0	960	726
4	448	741	825	847	0	410
5	925	29	404	13	54	0

the set $\lambda_{OPT_{i,j}}$ that maximizes aggregate rate. In this particular example, the obtained $\lambda_{OPT_{i,j}}$ is:

$$\lambda_{OPT_{i,j}} = \{<1,4>, <5,0>, <0,3>, <2,5>, \\ <3,2>, <4,1>\}$$

with aggregate rate $\sum_{<i,j>} \lambda[i][j] = 5096$. Subsequently, *step-2* computes the set of packet-switching elements that need to be swapped for minimizing inter-node distance. In this case, the resulting set R as specified by Equation 6 is:

$$R = \{<0,0>, <1,5>, <2,2>, <3,1> \\ <4,4>, <5,3>\}$$

Elements in R indicate that SSX nodes 1, 3 and 5 must be swapped with nodes 5, 1 and 3 respectively. The outcome of swapping is shown in Figure 5, together with the reconfigured cross-connections that preserve the SSX topology. Note that servers are still physically attached to the same SE's and need not be aware of the SE index swapping. It is only the routing tag generation entity that needs to be notified about SE swapping events.

The pseudocode of the topology optimization heuristic is listed in Algorithm 3. *Step-1* is implemented on line 1, where function f_{SA} returns an optimal assignment as output by the *Kuhn-Munkres* algorithm on an input traffic matrix λ. Lines 2-12 implement *step-2*. In the implementation of the heuristic, we add a weighting parameter T_{hres} (line 6 in Algorithm 3) when deciding swapping of packet switching-elements. This allows for selectively trading-off optimality of topology for frequency and extent of reconfiguration (e.g. using a high value for T_{hres} reduces the number of reconfigurations over time, whereas setting $T_{hres} = 1$ yields the best achievable topology over time).

Algorithm 3 SSX_optimization (λ, N, k)

1: calculate $\lambda_{OPT_{i,j}} \leftarrow f_{SA}(\lambda)$
2: **for each** $<i,j> \in \lambda_{OPT_{i,j}}$ **do**
3:    **if** $d_{ij} > 1$ **then**
4:       **for each** $s : d_{sj} = 1$ **do**
5:          select $s : s \notin R$ and $\lambda[s][j]$ is minimum
6:          **if** $\lambda[i][j] > T_{hres} \cdot \lambda[s][j]$ **then**
7:             $R \leftarrow <i,s>$
8:             $R \leftarrow <j,j>$
9:          **end if**
10:       **end for**
11:    **end if**
12: **end for**
13: **return** R

---

5. PERFORMANCE EVALUATION

For the purpose of evaluating the performance of our design, we implemented a packet-level simulator, including server, packet and optical circuit switches models, as well as implementing the full logic of routing, decomposition and dynamic topology reconfiguration. Simulation experiments were conducted for various network sizes and packet switch radices.

5.1 Input Traffic

Instead of using actual application traces that could potentially fit well the low bisection bandwidth of the core part of the interconnect and/or exhibit slow-changing connectivity patterns at the core, we used synthetic traffic (rack-level flows) that was appropriately instrumented to stress the performance of the interconnect against adverse input, similar to the approach followed in [6]. Flow generation in our simulation experiments is controlled by two parameters:

- *Stability period:* defined as the lifetime (in seconds) of a flow between two packet-switching elements (SE's).

- *Topological Degree of Communication (TDC):* defined as the number of simultaneous destinations that a given source SE sources traffic to.

Intuitively, the TDC parameter is appropriately tuned to evaluate performance, both for workloads that exhibit low logical communication degree and thus can trivially benefit from a low-bisection bandwidth interconnect, as well as for workloads that exhibit a much higher logical communication degree and thus are not easy to be effectively handled by a low-degree core. The stability period is used to test the ability of the reconfigurable core to adapt to constantly changing communication patterns. For a given value combination of the stability period and TDC parameters, the servers attached to a packet-switching element source *TDC* simultaneous flows to servers attached to a remote SE (*destination SE*). On expiration of each stability period, a new *destination SE* is picked. This strategy puts maximum strain on the reconfiguration algorithm, since after each stability period, established cross-connections on the optical planes cannot be re-used to serve new flow requests.

5.2 Simulation Scenarios and Parameters

We implemented our reconfigurable architecture in our simulator and experimented with both the Single-Hop (**SH**) and the SSX Multi-Hop (**MH**) approaches. We also implemented two well-known solutions that act as bounds to compare our approaches against, namely: a) a Static SSX network (**ST**) to showcase the impact of reconfigurability and b) a Fully-Connected (**FC**) network that acts as the best-case in terms of performance due to uniform 1-hop distance among all SE pairs.

We first experimented with a small-scale topology (comprising 8 radix-2 SE's with 6 servers attached to each) to observe the temporal evolution of throughput achieved by the Multi-Hop approach and thus evaluate at fine time scales its ability to adapt the interconnect to changing traffic patterns. In the rest of our simulation experiments, we tested larger scale topologies reaching up to 9600 servers. Table 3 summarizes the parameters and parameter values used throughout this set of experiments. Due to space constraints, we don't report results that show the impact of varying the T_{hres} to performance (T_{hres} fixed as shown in Table 3). Across all experiments, the reconfiguration latency of optical circuit switches was set to 50ms and link capacity was set to 10Gbps uniformly for all links in the simulation topology. We also implemented a fully-connected 10Gbps Electronically Packet-Switched (EPS) network that is used to bypass traffic that cannot be carried all-optically during reconfiguration periods.

Table 3: Simulation Parameters

Parameter Description	Parameter Value
Servers/Rack	30
Number of SE/Rack	1
SE Radix (k)	$k \in \{6, 8, 10\}$
Number of SE's (N)	$N \in \{128, 256, 320\}$
TDC (%)	$TDC \in \{1, 10, 15\}$
Stability Period (sec)	1
Threshold (T_{hres})	1.1

5.3 Evaluation Results

We first evaluated the throughput of the Multi-hop approach in the small-scale simulation setup. We configured our simulator with a 2sec warm-up period, after which the throughput is measured up to t=10sec. Multiple runs were executed using the traffic pattern described in section 5.1 with a stability period of 1 sec, and two distinct absolute TDC values, namely 2 and 3. These two TDC values allow

us to create two different scenarios to quantify the potential benefit of the multi-hop over the single-hop approach. Also, we report the throughput obtained in a fully-connected network as a performance upper bound (no circuit reconfiguration is needed), as well as in a static SSX topology.

Figures 6a and 6b depict the results obtained when transmitting at an aggregate average rate of ∼50 Gbps into the core of the interconnect with TDC=2 and 3 respectively. When TDC=2 (see Figure 6a), cross-rack logical connectivity matches exactly the topology radix (k=2). In this case, both MH and SH approaches can adapt optical circuits to satisfy flow requests (incoming at every second), reaching at times the throughput achieved by the costly fully-connected network. We observe though that the throughput of the SH approach reduces to ∼ 10 Gbps (the EPS bandwidth) at the expiration of each stability period (e.g. *time* ≅ 3, 4, 5, ... sec). This occurs because all circuits have to be reconfigured to reach new pairs of racks. Instead, the multi-hop approach, in hand with our topology optimization algorithm, avoided circuit reconfigurations and thus incurred more stable core bandwidth, decoupled from the stability period.

Figure 6b shows the throughput results obtained in the same network, though now using an increased TDC value (TDC=3). Increasing the TDC has a direct impact on the SH approach: since each switching element sources three simultaneous flows to the core and given that k=2, at least one of the flows has to be switched via the EPS network. As a consequence, we observe a degraded throughput of the SH approach that is always far from reaching the ideal throughput of the FC network. On the contrary, the MH approach manages to accommodate all flows in the OCS (in 1, 2 or $log_k N = 3$ hops) and throughput reaches the throughput of the FC network after some reconfigurations. Note that the throughput variations that can be observed between stability periods are not due to network performance, but solely due to the varying (exponentially distributed) traffic generated by servers.

The SH and MH approaches were also compared against a static SSX network (**ST**) in Figure 6 to show the benefit of reconfiguration. In the ST network, only the algorithms 1 and 2 (routing and decomposition, cf. section 3.2) are implemented, whereas topology optimization as implemented by Algorithm 3 is deactivated. Figures 6a and 6b show that reconfigurability together with multi-hop achieved an average improvement in throughput of ∼ 50% over a static SSX network for the input traffic patterns used.

Our second set of experiments targeted the evaluation of the proposed architecture at scale. For this, we simulated all three configurations (SH, MH and ST) for various network sizes and SE radices. We do not report results for the FC case, since these are trivial (maximum throughput). In all setups, the input traffic was set to have a stability period of 1 sec, while we also experimented with three distinct TDC values: 1%, 10% and 15% of the total number of SE's (and thus the number of racks). We plot the results of measured average throughput in Figure 7.

When a TDC value of 1% was used, the number of flows sourced by each packet-switching element is 1, 2 and 3 for N=128, 256 and 320 respectively. Given that in this case the radix is always larger than the number of flows sourced by a rack, the SH approach can always allocate single-hop connections to satisfy cross-rack communication demands. The MH approach has also enough optical connectivity to

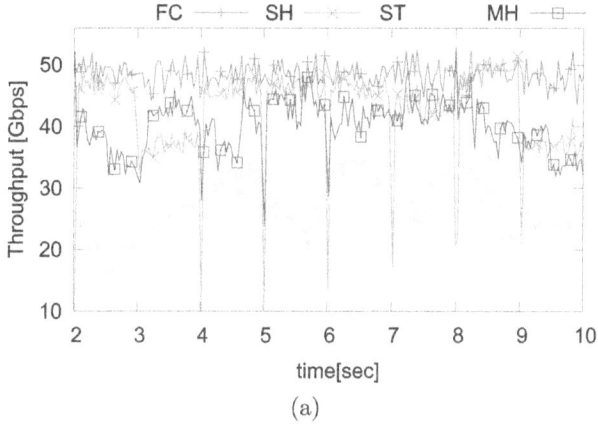

(a)

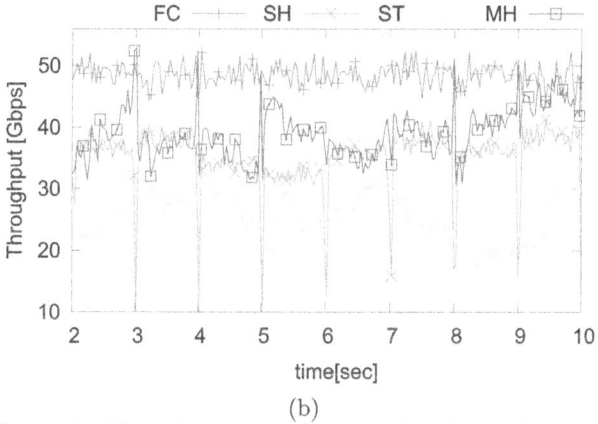

(b)

Figure 6: Throughput over time results obtained in the small-scale scenario comprising 48 servers evenly distributed to 8 radix-2 SE's. The proposed reconfigurable SSX multi-hop architecture is compared against the single-hop approach, a static SSX interconnect and a fully-connected network. (a)TDC=2 and (b)TDC=3.

allocate to incoming flows, though some of the flow requests were served with paths longer than a single hop (up to $log_k N$ hops). For this reason, the SH incurred slightly higher average throughput compared to the MH approach across many setups with TDC=1%. We also observe that this slight superiority of the SH approach diminishes as the radix k increases from k=6 to k=10. As k increases, the diameter of the SSX topology[3] (given by $log_k N$) decreases. Therefore, multi-hop paths employed by the MH approach become shorter with increasing k and thus the throughput improves, outperforming the average throughput of the SH approach at k=10 in two out of three setups tested with TDC=1%.

As we increase the TDC value used to 10% (resp. 15%) of the network size, the number of flows sourced per SE becomes 12(19), 25(38) and 32(48) for the N=128, N=256 and N=320 networks respectively. The more the TDC is increased, the larger are the throughput differences observed, as shown in the bars of Figures 7a, 7b and 7c corresponding to TDC=10% and 15%. Since the TDC in these cases exceeds the physical connectivity of the edge to the core (even for k=10), the SH approach cannot handle the flow demand and thus yields degraded throughput compared to the MH

---

[3]Hop distances vary from 2 to 4 based on the values of N and k used in the various experimental setups

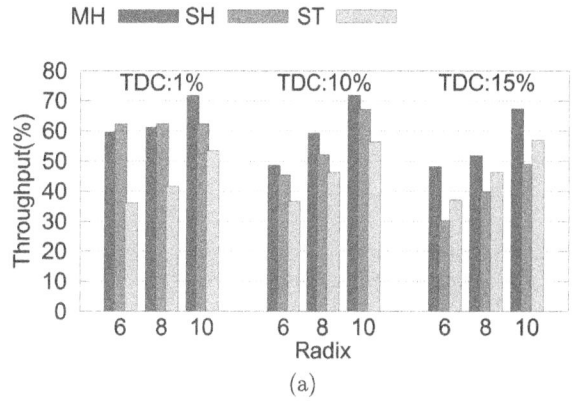

(a)

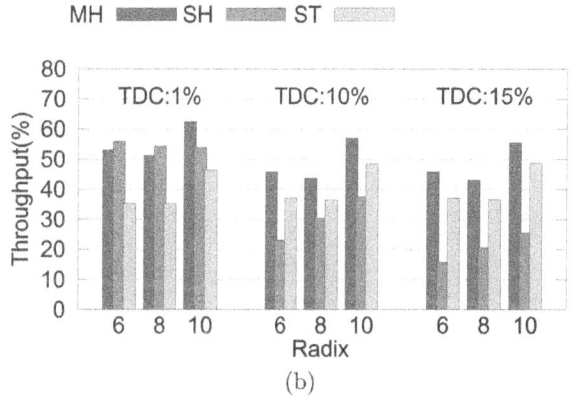

(b)

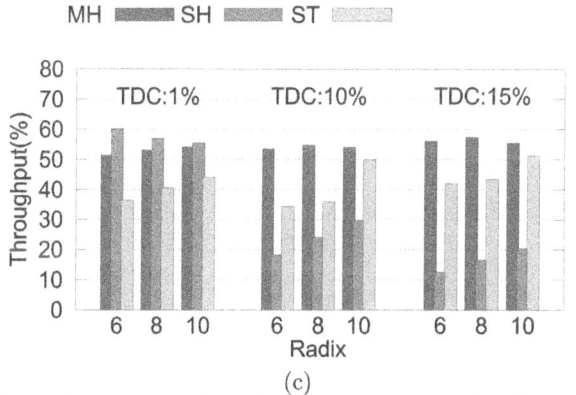

(c)

Figure 7: Average throughput measurements for three different network sizes (a) N=128, (b) N=256 and (c) N=320 SE's and three different radices (k=6, 8 and 10). To evaluate against different communication requirements, TDC parameter was set to 1%, 10% and 15% of the network size. Throughput is plotted as a percentage of aggregate rate injected into the network core.

approach, for the latter can accomodate a higher number of communication pairs between reconfigurations. This has also a direct implication on the capacity that needs to be placed on the EPS network, which is magnified in the case of the SH approach, while the MH economizes to a significant extent in this regard. As the EPS capacity used in our experiments has much lower capacity than the optical core, even the static configuration (ST) achieved higher performance compared to the single-hop approach for TDC values that exceed the SE radix, as it can be observed in Figure 7 (e.g. for TDC 15%).

6. CONCLUSIONS

This paper proposed a new hybrid optical/electrical reconfigurable interconnect architecture for large-scale clusters and datacenters, employing a Single-stage Shuffle eXchange (SSX) topology that allows for scalability, simple cabling and incremental upgrades and multi-hop capability for improved performance. We derived a decomposition formula to embed the proposed topology in the physical fabric and adapted an existing routing algorithm to the decomposition approach, enabling data exchange over shortest paths. We also proposed a heuristic for dynamic topology optimization that takes advantage of the reconfigurability of the all-optical fabric to timely adapt the interconnect to changing communication patterns exhibited by workloads.

In specific configurations and for the input traffic patterns and rates used, the results obtained in our evaluation showed that the proposed architecture yields a performance that approaches that of a fully-connected network in the same experimental setting. One of the novel findings of this work was that the multi-hop approach managed to sustain good performance even when the cross-rack logical connectivity degree exceeded the physical connectivity of the core. We acknowledge that in such a scenario, a build up of back-pressure at edge (packet) switches may thus increase latency or even lead to congestion. Our on-going exploration of the design space will include an investigation of the magnitude of this effect, and its mitigation. Other issues to address include exploring methods for hardware implementation of the proposed architecture and system integration challenges.

7. ACKNOWLEDGEMENTS

This work was supported by the Irish Research Council for Science, Engineering and Technology (IRCSET) through the Enterprise Partnership Scheme and IDA (Industrial Development Agency) Ireland. We are also grateful to Dr. Eugen Schenfeld for sharing his experience and ideas with us during early stages of this work.

8. REFERENCES

[1] K. Barker and D. Kerbyson. Performance analysis of an optical circuit switched network for peta-scale systems. In *Euro-Par 2007 Parallel Processing*, volume 4641 of *Lecture Notes in Computer Science*, pages 858–867. Springer Berlin / Heidelberg, 2007.

[2] K. J. Barker, A. Benner, R. Hoare, A. Hoisie, A. K. Jones, D. K. Kerbyson, D. Li, R. Melhem, R. Rajamony, E. Schenfeld, S. Shao, C. Stunkel, and P. Walker. On the feasibility of optical circuit switching for high performance computing systems. In *Proc. ACM/IEEE SC 2005 Conf. Supercomp.*, 2005.

[3] T. Benson, A. Akella, and D. A. Maltz. Network traffic characteristics of data centers in the wild. In *Proceedings of the 10th annual conference on Internet measurement*, IMC '10, pages 267–280, New York, NY, USA, 2010. ACM.

[4] R. Cypher, A. Ho, S. Konstantinidou, and P. Messina. Architectural requirements of parallel scientific applications with explicit communication. In *Proc. 20th Annual Int Comp. Arch. Symp*, pages 2–13, 1993.

[5] N. Desai, P. Balaji, P. Sadayappan, and M. Islam. Are nonblocking networks really needed for high-end-computing workloads? In *Proc. IEEE Int Cluster Computing Conf*, pages 152–159, 2008.

[6] N. Farrington, G. Porter, S. Radhakrishnan, H. H. Bazzaz, V. Subramanya, Y. Fainman, G. Papen, and A. Vahdat. Helios: a hybrid electrical/optical switch architecture for modular data centers. *SIGCOMM Comput. Commun. Rev.*, 40:339–350, August 2010.

[7] V. Gupta and E. Schenfeld. Performance analysis of a synchronous, circuit-switched interconnection cached network. In *Proceedings of the 8th international conference on Supercomputing*, ICS '94, pages 246–255, New York, NY, USA, 1994. ACM.

[8] S. Kamil, L. Oliker, A. Pinar, and J. Shalf. Communication requirements and interconnect optimization for high-end scientific applications. *IEEE Transactions on Parallel and Distributed Systems*, 21(2):188–202, 2010.

[9] S. Kamil, A. Pinar, D. Gunter, M. Lijewski, L. Oliker, and J. Shalf. Reconfigurable hybrid interconnection for static and dynamic scientific applications. In *Proceedings of the 4th international conference on Computing frontiers*, CF '07, pages 183–194, New York, NY, USA, 2007. ACM.

[10] J. Kim, W. J. Dally, S. Scott, and D. Abts. Technology driven, highly scalable dragonfly topology. *SIGARCH Comput. Archit. News*, 36(3):77–88, June 2008.

[11] S. Kim and A. V. Veidenbaum. On shortest path routing in single stage shuffle-exchange networks. In *Proceedings of the seventh annual ACM symposium on Parallel algorithms and architectures*, SPAA '95, pages 298–307, New York, NY, USA, 1995. ACM.

[12] L. Oliker, A. Canning, J. Carter, C. Iancu, M. Lijewski, S. Kamil, J. Shalf, H. Shan, E. Strohmaier, S. Ethier, and T. Goodale. Scientific application performance on candidate petascale platforms. In *In Proc. of the International Parallel & Distributed Processing Symposium (IPDPS)*, 2007.

[13] L. Schares, X. J. Zhang, R. Wagle, D. Rajan, P. Selo, S. P. Chang, J. Giles, K. Hildrum, D. Kuchta, J. Wolf, and E. Schenfeld. A reconfigurable interconnect fabric with optical circuit switch and software optimizer for stream computing systems. In *Proc. Conf. Optical Fiber Communication - incudes post deadline papers OFC 2009*, pages 1–3, 2009.

[14] A. Singla, A. Singh, K. Ramachandran, L. Xu, and Y. Zhang. Feasibility study on topology malleable data center networks (dcn) using optical switching technologies. In *Proc. and the National Fiber Optic Engineers Conf. Optical Fiber Communication Conf. and Exposition (OFC/NFOEC)*, pages 1–3, 2011.

[15] J. Vetter and A. Yoo. An empirical performance evaluation of scalable scientific applications. In *Supercomputing, ACM/IEEE 2002 Conference*, page 16, nov. 2002.

[16] G. Wang, D. G. Andersen, M. Kaminsky, K. Papagiannaki, T. E. Ng, M. Kozuch, and M. Ryan. c-through: part-time optics in data centers. *SIGCOMM Comput. Commun. Rev.*, 40:327–338, August 2010.

BSArc: Blacksmith Streaming Architecture for HPC Accelerators

Muhammad Shafiq
Barcelona Supercomputing Center
Universitat Politècnica de Catalunya
Barcelona, Spain
muhammad.shafiq@bsc.es

Miquel Pericàs
Tokyo Institute of Technology
JST, CREST
Tokyo, Japan
pericas.m.aa@m.titech.ac.jp

Nacho Navarro
Barcelona Supercomputing Center
Universitat Politècnica de Catalunya
Barcelona, Spain
nacho@ac.upc.edu

Eduard Ayguadé
Barcelona Supercomputing Center
Universitat Politècnica de Catalunya
Barcelona, Spain
eduard.ayguade@bsc.es

ABSTRACT

The current trend in high performance computing (HPC) systems is to deploy parallel computers equipped with general purpose multi-core processors and possibly multi-core streaming accelerators. However, the performance of these multi-cores is often constrained by the limited external bandwidth or by badly matching data access patterns. The latter reduces the size of useful data during memory transactions. A change in the application algorithm can improve the memory accesses but a hardware support mechanism for an application specific data arrangement in the memory hierarchy can significantly boost the performance for many application domains.

In this work, we present a conceptual computing architecture named *BSArc* (Blacksmith Streaming Architecture). *BSArc* introduces a forging front-end to efficiently distribute data to a large set of simple streaming processors in the back-end. We apply this concept to a SIMT execution model and present a design space exploration in the context of a GPU-like streaming architecture with a reconfigurable application specific front-end. These design space explorations are carried out on a streaming architectural simulator that models BSArc. We evaluate the performance advantages for the BSArc design against a standard L2 cache in a GPU-like device. In our evaluations we use three application kernels: 2D-FFT, Matrix-Matrix Multiplication and 3D-Stencil. The results show that employing an application specific arrangement of data on these kernels achieves an average speedup of $2.3\times$ compared to a standard cache for a GPU-like streaming device.

Categories and Subject Descriptors

C.1 [**Processor Architectures**]: Heterogeneous Systems; I.6 [**Simulation and Modeling**]: Simulation Support Systems—*Environments*

Keywords

GPU Simulator, SArcs, GPU, Customized Memory, Reconfigurable Logic, Design Space, Hybrid GPU-FPGA

1. INTRODUCTION

High Performance Computing (HPC) is a term relative to the computing power required for solving a problem in an acceptable time. The complexity of a problem can grow with the passage of time due to the inclusion of new algorithmic ideas and the increasing problem sizes necessary to improve the accuracy of results. This keeps on imposing a need for more and more computational power from HPC systems. This everyday rise in computational demands has given birth to the usage in HPC of throughput oriented processors like GPUs [1]. The key for performance in these streaming architectures is the feeding of continuous data streams to their large number of simple compute units [2]. Normally, processor architectures employ a cache hierarchy to help improve the availability of data for the compute units. However, the efficient flow of data highly depends on the application nature. Therefore, a generic data front-end for a computing device may not generate optimal streams of data for many applications.

GPUs adopt a streaming based compute model in their architectures. These devices expect the user to efficiently arrange parallel sets of data for the computations. A single GPU device contains hundreds of simple processing cores. These use multi-threading to keep a high throughput and hide the memory latencies by switching between thousands of threads. Generally, the architecture of a GPU device consists of dual level hierarchy. The top level is made-up of vector processors, called streaming multiprocessors (SMs) in NVIDIA GPUs and SIMD cores in AMD GPUs. Each of these vector processors contains a set of simple processing cores, called streaming processors (SPs). All processing cores inside one vector processor can communicate through

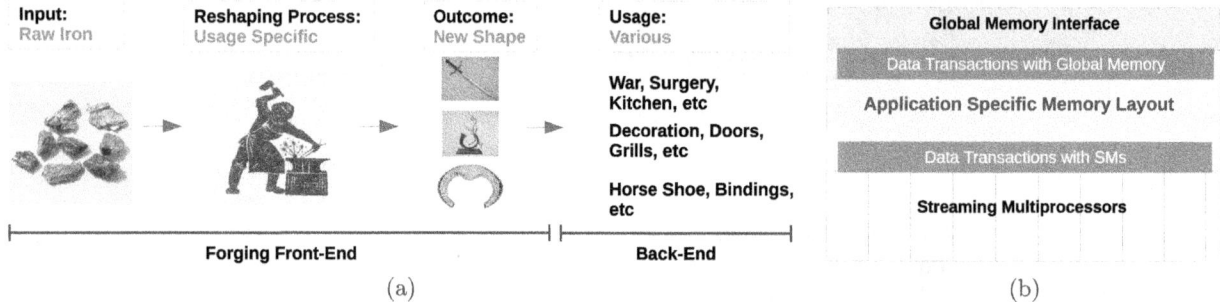

Figure 1: (a) An Analogy for the Blacksmith Computing (b) The simplified target platform model

an on-chip user managed memory, termed local memory in AMD GPUs and shared memory in NVIDIA GPUs. The performance of these streaming multi-core architectures can suffer from the limited external bandwidth and/or from the inefficient data access patterns reducing the size of useful data during memory transactions [3]. The latter issue may be improved significantly for many application domains by including hardware support for the application specific arrangement of data in the processor memory hierarchy.

In this work we present design space explorations for streaming architectures with an application specific configurable frond-end. These explorations are based on the concept of *Blacksmith Computing* performed on a Blacksmith Streaming Architecture (*BSArc*). *Blacksmith Computing* uses a forging front-end to efficiently manage data according to the application nature. A large set of simple streaming processors in the back-end can fetch this arranged data to run computations on it. This computing concept is generic and adoptable for different target platforms. However, in this work we apply this concept to a SIMT execution model and present it as a part of a modified GPU-like device.

For our evaluations of blacksmith computing we use the **Streaming Architectural Simulator** (*SArcs*) [4] which we developed for this purpose. *SArcs* is a trace driven simulation framework. It exploits the fact that an application compiled for any architecture would require to transact the same amount of data with the main memory in the absence of registers or cache hierarchy. Moreover, the computations inside an application can be simulated by the target device latencies. *SArcs* creates an architectural correlation with the target device by passing the source code through a source to source translator followed by a thread aware trace generation. This trace is used by a device mapping process which transforms the trace into a SIMT trace specific for a GPU architecture. The SIMT trace is then passed through a cycle accurate simulator to get performance numbers and related statistics.

SArcs provides an automated framework for simulations of streaming architectures like GPUs. This simulator can be used either as a standalone system – completely independent of a streaming environment – or it can be connected to other existing simulation related tools due to its modular nature. *SArcs* as an independent simulation infrastructure for GPUs does not require to have a physical GPU or any GPU related software tool-chain available. To the best of our knowledge the *SArcs* tool is the first trace based GPU architectural simulator that does not require the presence of

a GPU environment. A detailed design description of the simulator framework is given in section 4.

Our design space explorations for *BSArc* integrate a configurable front-end in a GPU like device. The accuracy of the base line simulator is established against the NVIDIA's Fermi architecture (GPU Tesla C2050). We evaluate the performance difference for the Blacksmith Compute model based design approach against the standard L2 cache in the modified GPU like device. In our evaluations we use three application kernels: 2D-FFT, Matrix-Matrix Multiplication and 3D-Stencil. The results show that employing an application specific arrangement of data can achieve an average speedup of 2.3× compared to the usage of a standard cache in a GPU like streaming architecture.

This paper present the basic concepts behind *Blacksmith Computing* in the next section. The paper propose a modified GPU as a *Blacksmith Streaming Architecture (BSArc)* to achieve the potential benefits from the blacksmith computing. This work also covers the application specific memory designs for three selected application kernels in Section 3. The later section summaries the design of the platform independent simulation tool chain developed for the architectural explorations of *BSArc*. The paper also presents the design space explorations for the example kernels – containing application specific memory layouts – by mapping them at the L2 level of the *SArcs* simulation infrastructure.

2. BLACKSMITH COMPUTING

The basic concept of *blacksmith computing* can be understood more easily from the work of a blacksmith as depicted in Figure 1(a). In this figure, one can see that a blacksmith takes raw iron and uses a hammer to give it a required shape depending upon the final purpose of the produced item. Similarly, in blacksmith computing the raw input data (unprocessed data) is marshaled and laid out inside a specialized front-end memory so that the algorithm running on the streaming multiprocessors in the back-end of the compute device can use this arranged data in an effective way.

2.1 Target Platform Model

Mapping an application design to a GPU device for performance is not a simple task. Each application requires a different set of optimizations and fine tuning to achieve an acceptable level of performance. Furthermore, the stringent hardware restrictions like aligned and fine grained memory accesses do not allow the programmer to fetch data efficiently using different pattern based approaches. This

24

painful exercise of experimentation and restricted ways of fetching data could be completely eliminated by facilitating a configurable front-end while using similar simple configurations of SMs (streaming multiprocessors) in the back-end. This configurable front-end is adjustable to layout data according to the nature of the application running on a target device.

A simplified target platform model for blacksmith computing is shown in Figure 1(b). This model follows the basic concept given in our recent proposal on a template based architecture for reconfigurable accelerators [5]. We embed the idea into a GPU like SIMT architecture which results in a heterogeneous device that could be high level programmable using a CUDA [6] like programing model while at the same time partially reconfigurable. This device essentially results in a modified GPU with a configurable forging front-end. However, the computing cores in the back-end of the target platform model are kept similar to the existing GPU architecture with *WARPs* as the fundamental unit of dispatch within a single SM. The new data front-end can reshape and unfold data-sets specific to application requirements by configuring and incorporating domain specific architectural templates developed by domain experts. The memory layouts for the forging front-end may even be common for various application kernels [7]. This means the programmer does not need to worry about hardware constraints nor the difficult task of software tuning for the modified GPU device.

3. APPLICATION SPECIFIC FRONT-ENDS

In order to explore the potential benefits of Blacksmith computing, we use three example application kernels: 2D-FFT, Matrix-Matrix Multiplication and 3D-Stencil. These kernels use either 2D or 3D data sets. In general, the efficient handling of data in 2D and 3D creates a more complex problem as compared to dealing with single dimensional vectors. Moreover, each of these kernels uses data in an arrangement very different from the other one. We show specialized memory layouts configured for each kernel in the Figures 2, 3 and 4. However, one can choose some other layout according to one's own requirements.

It is very important to mention that many data dependent application kernels may not get any benefit from the specialized memory layouts. In these cases, we consider that the best application specific memory layout will be a standard L2 cache to exploit statistical data locality. Furthermore, there are also some strictly sequential algorithms. We do not consider such algorithms to be suitable for throughput oriented streaming architectures and do not further study them here.

3.1 2D-FFT

The shaded area in the Figure 2 shows the specialized front-end memory design for the 2D-FFT. The complete design consists of two main parts: the data management part (shaded region) and the 1D-FFT computational part using streaming multiprocessors (SMs). Data is processed for the 2D-FFT in two phases shown as phase-1 and phase-2 in Figure 2 . Both phases run the 1D-FFT on orthogonal dimensions of the frame. These phases are executed in the same call to the device. However, their execution occurs in a sequential order. The data management part maintains internally 2D-Frames for transposed accesses by the 1D-FFT executed in the phase-2. The internal 2D-Frames

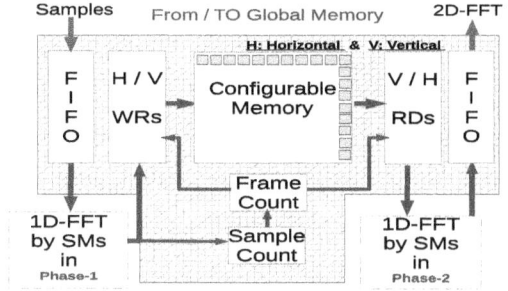

Figure 2: 2D-FFT Memory Layout

are managed by toggling the writing (WR) and reading (RD) sides for the horizontal and vertical order of the configurable memory on the alternative frames. As an example we show the horizontal and vertical memory blocks which are dual ported to help their accesses in two different orders. The size of the individual memory blocks and the number of independent memory blocks is generated according to X (*points*) and Y dimensional parameters for the input frames. It is important that the size of the data frames needing 2D-FFT should fit inside the specialized memory design.

During phase-1, frame data is processed for 1D-FFT and written to the dual ported memory blocks in *H* or *V* order while during the second execution phase for another 1D-FFT, this memory is read in the reverse order. This way the specialized memory design helps a faster 1D-FFT for the orthogonal dimension by providing all data available in a fully ordered way at the level-2 of the memory hierarchy. The hardware support for two dimensional accesses of memory also simplifies the program and the programmer's job.

3.2 Matrix Multiplication

The data accesses in Matrix-Matrix multiplication requires, in general, two basic optimizations: transposed access to one of the matrices and retaining a vector data from a matrix (row vector) for longer period of time to be computed with all the columns of the other matrix. We opt for the same specialized memory design that we already proposed for the template based systems [5]. This memory design is efficient for large sized matrices processed by streaming processors similar as in our case. The specialized memory design for our modified GPU is shown in Figure-3. In this implementation, the matrices are accessed in the same row major order from the external memory. The matrices A and B are fetched in the order of one row and multiple columns. During the run, one row of matrix A is fetched from the external memory into a single circular buffer. It is used element by element while the fetched row from matrix B is scattered around the mul-

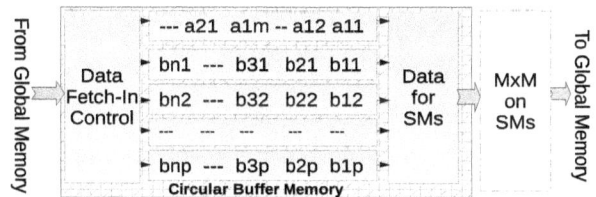

Figure 3: Matrix-Matrix Multiplication (MM) Memory Layout

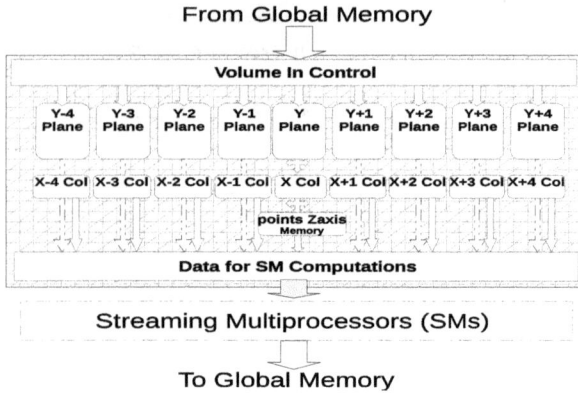

Figure 4: 3D-Stencil Memory Layout

tiple circular buffers proportional to the compute capability in the SMs of the GPU back-end. Therefore, the product of an element from the row of matrix A is done with multiple columns of matrix B. Each SM accumulates the results for the element wise product of allocated rows (matrix A) and the columns (matrix B).

3.3 3D-Stencil

A 3D-Stencil kernel operates on near neighboring points in three dimensions of a volume. We adopt a specialized memory architecture for the $8 \times 9 \times 8$ 3D-stencil from Araya et al. on Reverse Time Migration [8]. However, we modify the design according to the modified GPU needs as shown in Figure 4. The original specialized memory design consists of a specialized 3D memory layout and 3D write and read control corresponding to the three dimensions of the input volume. In our design we use only two dimensions with farthest points (Y-dim and X-dim receptively) while the consecutive data from the Z-dimension is processed inside the registers of the SMs.

The application specific memory layout for the 3D-Stencil (Figure 4) shows the first layer of memory labeled as **Plane** and corresponding to the Y-axis of the volume (therefore named *Y-layer*). This layer in the memory hierarchy consists of 9 dual ported memory blocks. All nine planes in the layer are sequentially writable but can be read in parallel. The second layer of memory is labeled as **Column** and corresponds to the X-axis of the input volume (named *X-Layer*) This layer has exactly the same features as that of the Y-layer except that its size is equal to a column in a plane. The third memory layer corresponds to the Z-axis (Z-layer). As already mentioned, it is being managed inside the SMs. All these memory layers and their controls work in a way that SMs can access data from all three dimensions as parallel streams.

4. THE SARCS DESIGN SPACE EXPLORATION TOOL

The basic goal of the Streaming Architectural Simulator (*SArcs*) is to provide a simulation platform for streaming architectures that could be used for applications performance analysis or to experiment with architectural innovations. These objectives are achieved by working through different stages of the *SArcs* framework. These stages, as shown in Figure 5, consist of *Trace Generation*, *Device Mapping*, *De-*

vice Simulation and *Results Analysis*. Figure 5 also shows that these stages are executed in different steps. Steps 3 to 5 can be repeated for the number of device kernels in an application, and/or as many times a certain device kernel requires to be run with different inputs. A brief introduction about the different stages of the *SArcs* framework is given next.

4.1 Trace Generation

SArcs supports the CUDA programming model. Users of *SArcs* are only required to provide a plain CUDA program (The `main` function and the device *kernel(s)*) for an application. CUDA specific APIs can be used inside the device kernel. However, it is not allowed to call any application specific API's for the standalone version of *SArcs*. The CUDA source files for an application are processed by a source-to-source translator (*S-S Translator*) before compilation with a C compiler in *step-2* as shown in the Figure 5. After compilation, the generated binary of the application is forwarded to a thread aware tracing tool (the *TTrace tool*) to generate the traces. The details on the *S-S Translator* and the *TTrace tool* are given below:

4.1.1 S-S Translator

The *S-S Translator* is a source-to-source translator. It takes a CUDA program and applies appropriate modifications and additions with two main goals: (i) Programs should be compilable by the C compiler, and (ii) The added code inside the source needs to output necessary runtime information to feed the next stages of the simulator. At first, to make the CUDA code compilable with the GNU compiler, we provide the simulator with a modified cuda header file (`mcuda.h`) which satisfies CUDA API calls, internal variables (eg. thread and block IDs) and special identifiers (`__global __shared` etc.).

The *S-S Translator* also inserts additional code at predefined places in the CUDA source file(s) as shown in Figure 6. This code insertion helps the simulator in two ways: (i) To get a detailed trace of the target application kernel that needs to be run on the GPU device, and (ii) To extract certain information from the code at run-time. The code between lines 2 and 19, as shown in the Figure 6, is an example replacement done by the *S-S Translator* for the code in line 1. Line 1 shows a commented CUDA call to a global function (`kernel_name`) that originally has to run on the GPU device. However, the *S-S Translator* commented this call and inserts a code with some assignment statements, `printf` instructions and nested loops. In this example piece of code (Figure 6), lines 2 and 3 copy values of block dimensions to the global variables. Next, lines 4 to 10 show code inserted to extract some runtime information specific to a code and also specific to an execution run. The examples of this runtime information are the pointer addresses assigned to the global variables `dimGrid`, `blockDim`, `blockIdx` and `threadIdx`. This information is used during the later steps of the simulation process. The nested loops in the inserted code from lines 12 to 19 call the target function (`kernel_name`) at the thread granularity (the most inner loop). These nested loops make it possible to generate a complete trace for all the threads (originally CUDA Threads) in a *block* (originally CUDA Block) and for all the *blocks* in a *grid*. It is important to remember that these nested loops work according to the dimensions of a block and the grid dimensions. These

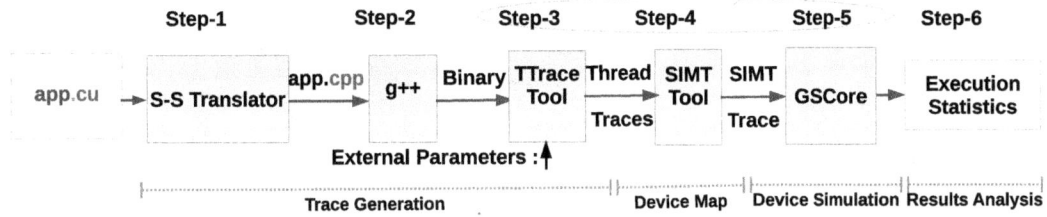

Figure 5: The SArcs Framework

dimensions are defined by the user before calling a GPU target function in a CUDA program.

4.1.2 TTrace Tool

The modified source code generated by the *S-S Translator* is compiled with the C compiler in step 2 of SArcs framework (see Figure 5). The program binary is executed with the thread aware trace (*TTrace*) tool. The *TTrace* tool performs dynamic instrumentation of the programs using the PIN [9] environment. The target kernel function name (originally the GPU device kernel) can either be given as an external argument or is automatically identified by the *S-S Translator* and forwarded to the *TTrace tool*. The name of the kernel function allows the tool to only instrument this function. The *TTrace tool* arranges the instruction level trace information in separate thread groups. The main parameters traced by this binary instrumentation tool include the *Instruction Pointers, Instruction Ops, Memory Addresses, Memory Access Sizes* and any calls to the sub-functions from the kernel function. In a CPU ISA, the instruction set can be very large. Therefore, the current version of the *TTrace Tool* only distinguish the memory Read/Write operations from the all other operations. Separate identifications are given to the heap based memory accesses and the stack based memory accesses. The rest of the operations are accommodated in the trace under a single identification name.

4.2 Device Map

The *Device Mapping* stage provides isolation between the user control over the program and the micro-architectural level program execution by a GPU device. For example, in the trace generation stage, the user has control over the CUDA program to adjust the block and grid dimensions while the number of threads in a WARP is a micro-architectural

feature of a GPU device handled at the *Device Mapping* stage. This stage of the *SArcs* framework uses a *SIMT tool* to map a user program trace (the output of the *TTrace tool*) to a specific GPU device. The output of the *SIMT tool* is a SIMT trace which is fed to a *GPU Core Simulator* in the following stage. The *SIMT tool* passes the user program trace through multiple processing phases. Some important phases are given next.

4.2.1 Removing Built-ins

A real GPU uses some built-in variables represented in CUDA, such as dimGrid, blockDim, blockIdx and threadIdx. These variables act as parts of the GPU micro-architecture. However, in our trace generation methodology, these variables acts as global variables with their accesses from the main memory. *SArcs* removes all accesses to these variables from the trace by identifying their address pointers obtained at the execution of program with *TTrace tool*.

4.2.2 WARP Instructions Formation

The user program trace (the output of *TTrace tool*) only groups the instructions traces at thread level granularity. The *SIMT tool* arranges these trace instructions as WARP Instructions and groups them at the thread block granularity level.

4.2.3 Coalescing Effects

The sets of WARP Instructions created in the previous step are further processed by the *SIMT tool* to add the effects of coalesced data accesses for the memory access instructions. The *SIMT tool* performs an analysis on the data access pointers for the WARP instructions. A WARP Instruction is split into multiple WARP Instructions if the memory accesses are not coalesced inside the original WARP

```
1  /* kernel_name dimGrid , dimBlock >>> ( a_d , b_d , c_d , iter ); */
2        blockDim.x = dimBlock.x;
3        blockDim.y = dimBlock.y;
4  printf("GDim.y , GDim.x , BDim.x , BDim.y , BId.y , BId.x , TId.y , TId.x\n");
5  printf(":>REF:>%p %p %p %p %p %p %p %p<:REF<:\n", &dimGrid.x,&dimGrid.y,&blockDim.x,&blockDim.y,
6        &blockIdx.y,&blockIdx.x,&threadIdx.y, &threadIdx.x);

8  printf("BId.y , DId.x , TId.y , TId.x , GDim.y , GDim.x , BDim.x , BDim.y \n");
9  printf(":>PAR:>%ld %ld %ld %ld %ld %ld %ld %ld <:PAR<:\n",dimGrid.x,  dimGrid.y, blockDim.x, blockDim.y,
10       blockIdx.y, blockIdx.x, threadIdx.y, threadIdx.x );

12  for (blockIdx.y=0; blockIdx.y< dimGrid.y; blockIdx.y++)
13        for(blockIdx.x=0; blockIdx.x< dimGrid.x; blockIdx.x++)
14            for(threadIdx.y=0; threadIdx.y< dimBlock.y; threadIdx.y++)
15                for(threadIdx.x=0; threadIdx.x< dimBlock.x; threadIdx.x++) {

17                kernel_name (a_d , b_d , c_d , iter );

19                }
```

Figure 6: An example code insertion for the replacement of the target gpu kernel call

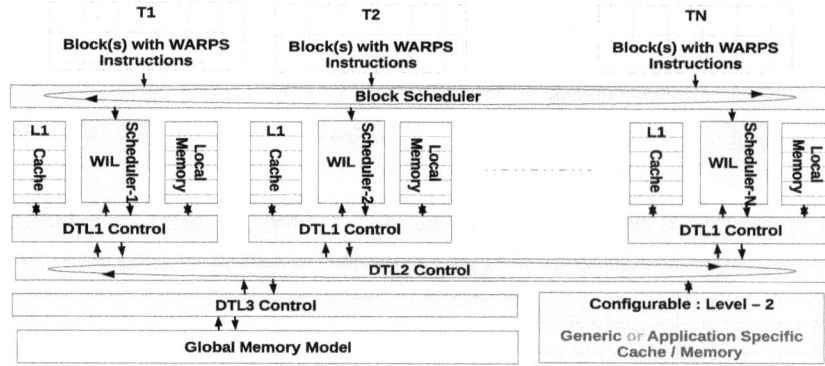

Figure 7: GPU Simulation Core (GSCore)

Instruction. The new WARP instructions contain accesses which are coalesced.

4.2.4 Registers and Shared Memory Handling

In a GPU kernel, local variables are mapped to SM (Streaming Multiprocessor) registers. Therefore, the scope of accesses to these local variables inside a GPU remains inside a block allocated to a SM. *SArcs* categorizes all stack based accesses inside a kernel either as registered accesses or as shared memory accesses. Shared memory accesses are isolated from registered accesses based on the base-pointer of the shared array and its allocation size. Currently *SArcs* does not handle corner cases like dynamic allocation of shared memory. The shared memory accesses are also organized as WARP instructions but with separate identifications.

4.2.5 Grouping Blocks

We call the new formatted trace generated by the *SIMT tool* the *SIMT Trace*. The *SIMT Trace* is arranged into blocks. In order to help the *GPU Simulation Core* (Section 4.3) efficiently access the SIMT Trace, the *SIMT tool* arranges these blocks in multiple files (called SIMT trace files) which are kept equal to the number of SMs in the target GPU device. This means that if there are M number of SMs in a GPU then the first SIMT file will contain 1st, $M+1^{th}$, $2*M+1^{th}$ and so on SIMT trace blocks. However, as it will be seen in the explanations of *GPU Simulation Core*, this arrangement does not create any binding on the choice of SIMT trace block for any specific SM during the simulation process.

4.3 Device Simulation

The *Device Simulation* stage models the dynamic effects for various micro-architectural components of a target GPU device. This stage uses *GSCore* (GPU Simulation Core), a tool specifically developed in-house for simulating the GPU like streaming devices. The functional layout of *GSCore* is shown in Figure 7. This simulator accepts SIMT Trace files generated by the *SIMT tool*. These SIMT trace files contain blocks of WARP instructions as shown at the top of the Figure 7. These blocks corresponds to the thread blocks defined in a grid for the target application kernel. However, these blocks do not contain threads but traces arranged in the form of WARP instructions. The *GSCore* implements a *Block Scheduler* which is responsible for delivering these

blocks to the SMs, initially in a round-robin fashion, and later based on requests from a SM. SMs are represented as *WIL Schedulers* next to the *GSCore's Block Scheduler* in Figure 7. The *WIL Scheduler* is named upon its real function which is to schedule the WARPs Instructions & Latency (WIL).

The *WIL Scheduler* schedules WARPs of instructions from one or more blocks based on the latencies corresponding to the operations these WARPs have to do. The latency values for different operations are loaded by the *GSCore* corresponding to a target device from a *GPU Constants File*. This file of constant parameters is provided within the *SArcs* framework. The GPU constants file keeps architectural and micro-architectural parameters for various GPU devices. The latencies due to instruction level dependencies are normally hidden or unknown in trace driven simulators. In case of *GSCore*, the final performance as compared to a real GPU shows almost no effect for these dependencies. This is because of the inherent nature of the real GPU architecture which switches with almost zero-overhead between the WARPs to avoid performance loss due to these dependencies. However, We consider that this effect depends on an application nature. Therefore, the future development of *SArcs* is being considered to include dependency information inside the trace.

The WARP instructions corresponding to memory transactions are forwarded to the *Data transaction Level-1* (DTL-1) control. The memory WARP instructions are scheduled on a first-come first-serve basis or in a round-robin way if multiple requests are available in the same cycle from different WILs (SMs). These memory WARP instructions go through *GScore's* modeled memory hierarchy corresponding to a real GPU. This includes implementation of a configurable L1 cache and a local scratch pad memory for each of the WIL Scheduler (i.e for each SM in a real GPU), L2 cache or the application specific (AS) memory and the global memory. All levels of *GScore* work in a synchronous way and simulate the latencies when going from one level to another one. In case, a memory WARP instruction is not fulfilled at DTL-1, it is passed to the DTL-2 for L2 cache or AS memory test, and if required it is forwarded to the DTL-3 level which models a global memory access. All WARP instructions which are memory writes are forwarded to the global memory.

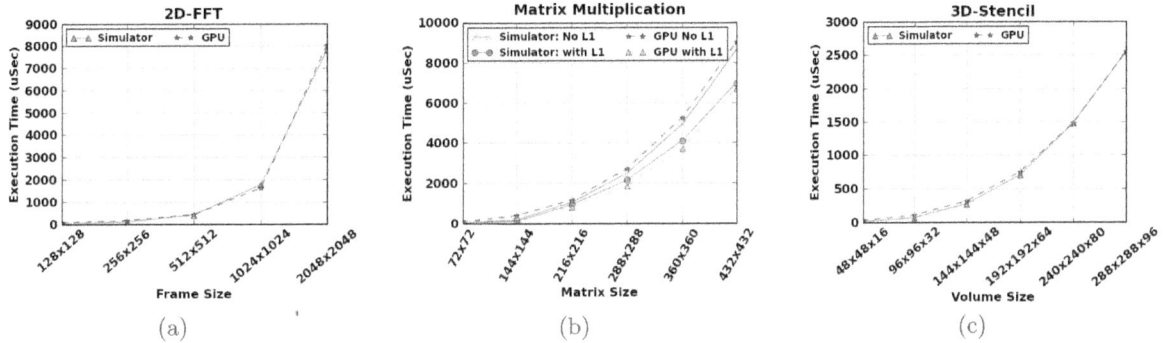

Figure 8: Establishment of the accuracy of the simulator (SArcs) by performance characterization against the real GPU for the base line architecture (NVIDIA's Tesla C2050). (a) 2D-FFT (b) Matrix Multiplication with/without L1 (c) 3D-Stencil Kernel

4.4 The Accuracy of the Design Space Exploration Tool

The simulator accuracy is an important factor to be established before one can proceed for the design space exploration of a target architecture using that simulator. The *SArcs* simulation framework applies a large set of architectural optimizations, including the ones described in Section 4.2, during its simulation process. The original results of the corresponding test cases show that the *SArcs* average error remains around 20% of the real executions on a GPU. It is important to remember that the current version of SArcs is using CPU code projections for the GPU simulation. Therefore, one source of error in the simulated performance for an application comes from compiling the code for a different Instruction Set Architecture (ISA). The difference in compilation platforms appears in the form of different size of the compiled code which ultimately appears as a difference in the execution times. Another source of error includes the choice of instructions for the trace generation from the huge set of CPU instructions at the trace generation phase. Moreover, a lack of the precise information regarding the micro-architectural details of the target GPU device also contributes in the error between the simulated and the real performance.

The results for the design space explorations could be extended for more accuracy and closer to real GPU executions. This is because the *SArcs* simulation results deviate from the real ones with a constant factor for each kernel. In our design space explorations, we adjust the baseline results with a single constant factor for every kernel to make the results matching the real executions. This constant factor adjustment reduces the actual average error of 20% to an error around 5% of the real execution of a kernel. We use the same constant factor for each kernel results during the *BSArc* related design space exploration process. The simulation results of *SArcs* and the reference results of the real GPU (NVIDIA's Tesla C2050) based executions for the performance characterization of different application kernels are shown in Figures 8 (a) to (c). It can be observed that in all cases, the *SArcs* simulated results closely follow the real GPU based executions. The results for matrix-multiplication (MM) kernel also present the real and simulated behavior of the L1 cache. Other kernels use shared memory to exploit data locality thus making only little use of the L1 cache.

4.5 SArcs as BSArc

The GPU simulation core shown in Figure 7 highlights the level-2 of the memory hierarchy as a configurable part like an FPGA fabric. During the application specific (AS) memory configuration for the level-2, the simulator replaces the L2 model with an AS model which simulates the approximate latencies for the real memory layout of an application kernel. In a real system, the AS memory can be configured statically before application execution or dynamically at runtime. The SMs in the back-end of the device communicate with this configurable front-end part through a group of command, control and status registers and a large set of index based circular buffers. These index based buffers exploit the indexed based accesses of data from the existing CUDA programing model. The group of command, control and status registers helps to synchronize the front-end with the back-ends. This requires a CUDA-like programing model with extensions for the modified GPU. However the scope of this paper does not cover the details on these changes for a modified CUDA programing model. Moreover, the fine details on the low-level connectivity and synchronization of the modified GPU architecture are also outside the scope of this paper.

The main job of the front-end memory architecture is to fetch data and arrange it in the specialized memory structures. This makes it possible for the SMs in the modified GPU to process the data in a continuous way or with the least degree of interruption due to the unavailability of data in the specialized memory. We consider the specialized memory layouts to be developed by application domain experts as templates which could be adjusted according to a device and the problem size at the configuration time. These adjustments could use automated template-based generation tools like the one proposed by Shafiq et al. [10].

5. DESIGN SPACE EXPLORATION ENVIRONMENT

In our explorations for the Blacksmith Compute model, we use three application kernels covering 2D and 3D types of data accesses. A brief description of each application kernel and the related application specific memory layout has been given in Section 3. In the following we will introduce the base line GPU configuration and the test platform used in our design space explorations.

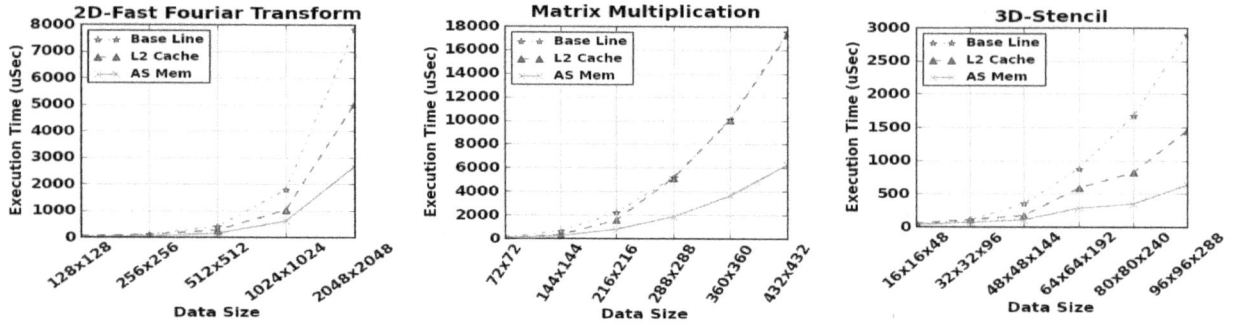

Figure 9: The application kernel's execution times for the three configurations : (i) Base Line (L2 Cache-Disabled and No Application Specific Memory) (ii) L2 Cache: Using only L2 cache (iii) AS Mem: Using only Application Specific (AS) memory.

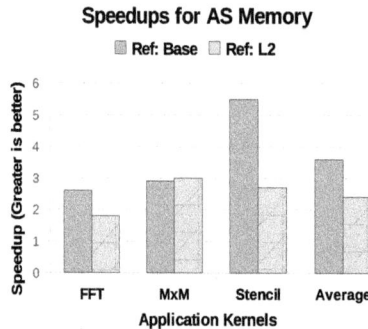

Figure 10: The speedups for the test kernels using Application Specific (AS) memory with reference (Ref) to: (i) The base line (Base) architectural configuration and (ii) L2 Cache Based Executions

5.1 Base Line Architecture

In our design space explorations, the *SArcs* simulation infrastructure uses a base line architecture following NVIDIA's GPU device Tesla C2050. This device belongs to the Fermi generation [11] of GPUs which is the most recent architecture from NVIDIA. This device has 14 Streaming Multiprocessors (SMs) each containing 32 streaming (scalar) processors. The device is capable of performing 32 fp32 or int32 operations per clock cycle. Moreover, it has 4 Special Function Units (SFUs) to execute transcendental instructions such as *sine*, *cosine*, their reciprocals, and square root. On the memory hierarchy side the device is configured to support 48 KB / 16 KB shared memory, 16KB / 48 KB L1 data cache and 768Kbytes of L2 memory. The L2 cache module is replaceable with application specific memory models. The size of the L2 cache is configurable to keep it compatible with the memory sizes used in the application specific memory layouts.

5.2 Simulation Platform

SArcs can be compiled for any host machine. The only constraint is that the PIN environment used in the *TTrace tool* should have support for that used CPU. In our evaluations, we use an Intel Xeon E7450 processor included in an IBM "x3850 M2" machine. The host machine uses x86_64-suse-linux and gcc compiler version 4.3.4. The target application kernels are compiled for optimization level 3 (switch -O3). On the GPU side, we use *nvcc* compiler with cuda compilation tool release 4.0, V0.2.1221. We compiled the

the CUDA codes using optimization level 3. Further, we use compilation switch -Xptxas along with -dlcm=ca or -dlcm=cg to enable and disable L1 cache accesses as required.

6. RESULTS AND DISCUSSION

In our architectural explorations, we used three application kernels: 2D-FFT, Matrix-Matrix (MM) Multiplication and 3D-Stencil. The program configurations and optimizations for all these kernels use only registers inside an SM as the local memory resource. In all cases, we keep the size of the memory used for the L2-cache configurations equal to the size of memory used in application specific memory layouts. As compared to the original GPU configuration, the 3D-stencil uses same size of memory and MM needs only half of that for the largest data set. Due to the nature of the FFT algorithm, we use around 32MB of memory in simulation to retain a complete frame of complex FFT data for the largest execution (2048×2048 points). However, we consider it as a corner case. This is because, in general, contemporary algorithms for signal processing almost never require more than 64×64 point FFTs. This further indicates that the problem domains that could be decomposed into sub-domains are better suited for the proposed architecture. However, this constraint applies generally to all microprocessor architectures because of the upper limit on the size of processor's local storages and the cache memories.

The results for the evaluations of *BSArc* are shown in Figures 9 (a) to (c). All results in the figure include the execution time of an application kernel for the three configuration cases: (i) The base case: L2 cache off and no application specific memory (ii) L2 case: using only L2 cache (iii) Using only application specific (AS) memory. It can be observed that in all cases (in the case of MM only for small matrix sizes) the usage of L2 cache improves the performance for an application kernel as compared to the base line executions but *BSArc* based executions take a significant edge on the cache based performances. The basic reason for this performance impact is the increase in the locality and the parallelism of data according to the requirement of the application. However, this increase in the performance is not free as it comes at the cost of an increased architectural complexity. In this work we consider that the design of these specialized memory layouts is provided by the application domain experts in the form of templates. These templates are adjustable according to a device and the problem size at the device's configuration time.

The Figure 10 shows the speedups achieved by using *BSArc*. These speedups for the test kernels are achieved by using the Application Specific (AS) memory front-end with reference to the the base line execution and the L2 cache based executions. These results show that employing an application specific arrangement of data for these kernels achieves an average speedup of 3.6× with reference to the base case. However, the impact of cache improves the performance of kernels therefore the relative speedup for the BSArc based configuration achieves 2.3× compared to a GPU-like streaming device equipped with a standard cache.

7. RELATED WORK

Most research efforts on computer architecture focus toward enhancing general purpose computing architectures. A large number of design exploration environments like SimpleScalar [12], Simics [13], PTLsim [14], M5 [15], TaskSim & Cyclesim [16], among others, are available for research on general purpose processor architectures. However, streaming architectures like GPUs lack similar level of support from simulation infrastructures. Several teams have developed GPU simulation environments like Barra [17] or GpuOcelot [18], but still most of the efforts are either limited to a specific GPU architecture or require the presence of a physical GPU and its related software environment.

Past researches like the Barrel processor [19] and SMT Architecture [20] worked on the similar lines of the current generations of GPU designs. However, the first graphics processor termed as *GPU* was introduced by NVIDIA in 1999 [11]. The base architecture for the current GPU design was incorporated in the G80 series in 2006 and the first GPU (GT200) with CUDA cores was introduced just in 2008 [11]. The previous contributions related to GPU simulation and performance analysis mostly adopt analytical methods but efforts also have been made to develop GPU simulation tools. In the field of analytical methods, Hong et al. were one of the first to propose a GPU performance model [21]. This model was later extended as an integrated performance and power model for GPUs [22]. *CuMAPz* is a CUDA program analysis tool developed by Kim and Shrivastava [23]. This tool analyzes memory access patterns in CUDA. Their proposal helps in tuning GPGPU applications for better performance by allowing its users to compare the memory performance (both shared and global memory) for an application designed with various versions of memory access patterns. The *CuMAPz* approach is a compile-time analysis tool. Therefore, it can not handle any information that can only be determined during run-time, such as dynamically allocated shared memory, indirect array accesses, etc. In 2009, Bakhoda et al. proposed a detailed GPU simulator [24] for analyzing CUDA workloads. The simulator runs NVIDIA's parallel thread execution (PTX) virtual instruction set for CUDA compiled applications. This simulation tool models the shader cores equivalent to the current SMs in a GPU, the interconnection network between these shader cores, L2 cache and the global memory controller. An adaptive GPU performance modeling tool was presented by Baghsorkhi et al. [25]. This tool uses a compiler-based approach to run a static analysis called *symbolic evaluations* on the program structure. This analysis determines the effects of the structural conditions and complex memory access expressions on the performance of a GPU kernel. Moreover, this tool provides a mechanism to adjust latencies according to the kernel inputs and/or data access patterns.

GROPHECY [26] takes as input a modified CPU code (*termed as Code Skeleton*) and tunes it for a GPU based implementation. In the *code skeletonization* the user abstracts the CPU code's parallelism, computational intensity, and data accesses. The *GROPHECY* tool applies a different set of parameters and optimizations in an automated way to propose one of the best code structure for the GPU based implementation. *GpuOcelot* [18] is another interesting compilation framework for heterogeneous systems. *GpuOcelot* provides various back-end targets for CUDA programs and analysis modules for the PTX instruction set. In addition to the current standalone framework of *SArcs*, we are planning to use *GpuOcelot* as a front-end of *SArcs* to enable a provision to also generate traces directly from the PTX code. MacSim [27] is a *GpuOcelot*-based trace driven simulation tool chain for heterogeneous architectures. The idea behind MacSim is to convert the program trace to RISC style *uops* and then simulate these *uops*. *SArcs*, on the other hand, controls the trace generation process. The generated trace is either from a CPU code or a PTX based GPU code, thus *SArcs* can directly map and simulate the real trace for a GPU generation.

Heterogeneous types of microprocessor architectures containing programmable and configurable parts have also been studied in the past. *Garp* [28], Molen [29], Chimaera [30] and OneChip [31] are all well known examples of such hybrid (programmable and reconfigurable) architectural proposals.

8. CONCLUSIONS

This paper presents the concept of Blacksmith Computing along with an implementation called Balcksmith Streaming Architecture (*BSArc*). This architecture provides an opportunity to improve exploitation of data locality and data level parallelism for an application. The results show the importance of efficient data management strategies for high performance computing. Generic methods like standard cache hierarchies for improving data locality may not achieve the potential performance benefits for an application. Therefore, high performance devices might need to converge for a solution with more specialized memory front-ends.

The physical availability of architectures like *BSArc* may still take time. However, development of precise architectural exploration tools like *SArcs* can be very useful for giving an insight via design space explorations for such architectural proposals. We showed the potential of our developed simulation framework for *BSArc* with example explorations for the design of future GPU devices containing configurable application specific front-end. The results are promising and motivate for further research in this direction.

9. ACKNOWLEDGMENTS

We thankfully acknowledge the support of the European Commission through the HiPEAC-2 Network of Excellence (FP7/ICT 217068), the support of the Spanish Ministry of Education (TIN2007-60625, and CSD2007-00050) and the Generalitat de Catalunya (2009-SGR-980). This project was also partially supported by JST, CREST through its research program: "Highly Productive, High Performance Application Frameworks for Post Petascale Computing." Finally, the authors also would like to thank the reviewers for their useful comments.

10. REFERENCES

[1] "Top 500 Supercomputer Sites," June 2011. [Online]. Available: http://top500.org/lists/2011/11

[2] G. Caragea, F. Keceli, A. Tzannes, and U. Vishkin, "General-Purpose vs. GPU: Comparison of Many-Cores on Irregular Workloads," *HotPar, Berkeley, CA*, June 2010. [Online]. Available: http://www.usenix.org/event/hotpar10/final_posters/Caragea.pdf

[3] S. Asano, T. Maruyama, and Y. Yamaguchi, "Performance Comparison of FPGA, GPU and CPU in Image processing," *IEEE FPL*, September 2009.

[4] M. Shafiq, M. Pericas, N. Navarro, and E. Ayguade, "SArcs: Streaming Architectural Simulator for Performance Characterization," *UPC Internal Research Report: UPC-DAC-RR-2012-14*, March 2012.

[5] M. Shafiq, M. Pericàs, N. Navarro, and E. Ayguade, "TARCAD: A Template Architecture for Reconiñ Agurable Accelerator Designs," *IEEE Symposium On application Specific Processors. San Diego, CA*, June 2011.

[6] "CUDA Programming Model." [Online]. Available: http://developer.nvidia.com/category/zone/cuda-zone

[7] M. Shafiq, M. Pericàs, N. Navarro, and E. Ayguadé, "FEM: A Step Towards a Common Memory Layout for FPGA Based Accelerators," *20th Intl. Conf. on FPL and Apps.*, Aug. 2010.

[8] M. Araya-Polo, J. Cabezas, M. Hanzich, M. Pericàs, F. Rubio, I. Gelado, M. Shafiq, E. Morancho, N. Navarro, E. Ayguadé, J. M. Cela, and M. Valero, "Assessing Accelerator-Based HPC Reverse Time Migration," *IEEE TPDS*, 2011.

[9] "Pin - A Dynamic Binary Instrumentation Tool." [Online]. Available: http://www.pintool.org/

[10] M. Shafiq, M. Pericàs, N. Navarro and E. Ayguadé, "A Template System for the Effcient Compilation of Domain Abstractions onto Reconfigurable Computers," *HiPEAC WRC, Heraklion Crete*, Jan 2011.

[11] NVIDIA, "Whitepaper : NVIDIA's Next Generation CUDA Compute Architecture," 2009.

[12] "SimpleScalar: ." [Online]. Available: http://pages.cs.wisc.edu/ mscalar/simplescalar.html

[13] "simics: ." [Online]. Available: https://www.simics.net/

[14] "PTLsim: ." [Online]. Available: http://www.ptlsim.org/

[15] "M5: ." [Online]. Available: http://www.m5sim.org/Main_Page

[16] "TaskSim and Cyclesim: ." [Online]. Available: http://pcsostres.ac.upc.edu/cyclesim/doku.php/tasksim:start

[17] "Barra - NVIDIA G80 GPU Functional Simulator ." [Online]. Available: http://gpgpu.univ-perp.fr/index.php/Barra

[18] "GpuOcelot: A dynamic compilation framework for PTX." [Online]. Available: http://code.google.com/p/gpuocelot/

[19] "Barrel Processor." [Online]. Available: http://en.wikipedia.org/wiki/Barrel_processor

[20] "SMT Architecture." [Online]. Available: http://www.cs.washington.edu/research/smt/

[21] S. Hong and H. Kim, "An analytical model for a gpu architecture with memory-level and thread-level parallelism awareness," *SIGARCH Comput. Archit. News*, June 2009.

[22] Sunpyo Hong and Hyesoon Kim, "An integrated GPU power and performance model," *ACM ISCA 10*, June 2010.

[23] Y. Kim and A. Shrivastava, "CuMAPz: A tool to analyze memory access patterns in CUDA," *ACM/IEEE DAC 2011*, June 2011.

[24] A. Bakhoda, G. L. Yuan, W. W. L. Fung, H. Wong, and T. M. Aamodt, "Analyzing CUDA workloads using a detailed GPU simulator," *IEEE ISPASS 09*, April 2009.

[25] S. S. Baghsorkhi, M. Delahaye, S. J. Patel, W. D. Gropp, and W. mei W. Hwu, "An Adaptive Performance Modeling Tool for GPU Architectures," *ACM PPoPP10*, January 2010.

[26] J. Meng, V. A. Morozov, K. Kumaran, V. Vishwanath, and T. D. Uram, "GROPHECY: GPU Performance Projection from CPU Code Skeletons," *ACM/IEEE SC11*, November 2011.

[27] H. Kim, "GPU Architecture Research with MacSim ," 2010. [Online]. Available: http://comparch.gatech.edu/hparch/nvidia_kickoff_2010_kim.pdf

[28] J.R. Hauser, J. Wawrzynek, "Garp: a MIPS processor with a reconfigurable coprocessor," *5th IEEE Symposium on FPGA-Based Custom Computing Machines (FCCM '97)*, 1997.

[29] S. Vassiliadis, S. Wong, G. Gaydadjiev, K. Bertels, G. Kuzmanov, and E. M. Panainte, "The MOLEN Polymorphic Processor," *IEEE Transactions on Computers*, vol. 53, pp. 1363–1375, 2004.

[30] S. Hauck, T. W. Fry, M. M. Hosler, and J. P. Kao, "The Chimaera reconfigurable functional unit," *IEEE Trans. on VLSI Systems*, 2004.

[31] Jorge E. Carrillo E. , Paul Chow, "The effect of reconfigurable units in superscalar processors," *Proceedings of the ACM/SIGDA ninth international symposium on Field programmable gate arrays*, February 2001.

A Limits Study of Benefits from Nanostore-Based Future Data-Centric System Architectures

Jichuan Chang[*] Parthasarathy Ranganathan[*] Trevor Mudge[†]
David Roberts[‡] Mehul A. Shah[#] Kevin T. Lim[*]

HP Labs[*], University of Michigan[†], Micron[‡] and Nou Data[#]

ABSTRACT

The adoption of non-volatile memories (NVMs) in system architecture and the growth in data-centric workloads offer exciting opportunities for new designs. In this paper, we examine the potential and limit of designs that move compute in close proximity to NVM-based data stores. To address the challenges in evaluating such system architectures for distributed systems, we develop and validate a new methodology for large-scale data-centric workloads. We then study "nanostores" as an example design that constructs distributed systems from building blocks with 3D-stacked compute and NVM layers on the same chip, replacing both traditional storage and memory with NVM. Our limits study demonstrates significant potential of this approach (3-162X improvement in energy delay product) over 2015 baselines, particularly for IO-intensive workloads. We also discuss and quantify the impact of network bandwidth, software scalability, and power density, and design tradeoffs for future NVM-based data-centric architectures.

Categories and Subject Descriptors

C.4 [**Performance of Systems**];
C.5.5 [**Computer System Implementation**] Servers

General Terms

Design, Measurement, Performance

Keywords

Limits study, system architectures, Nanostores, non-volatile memory, data-centric data centers

1. INTRODUCTION

The amount of data being created in both enterprise and scientific communities is exploding, growing significantly faster than Moore's Law. The size of online data is estimated to have risen nearly 60-fold in the last seven years [1]. Similarly, many scientific disciplines are experiencing a paradigm shift towards data-driven discovery. The annual doubling of gene databases and the petabyte per second produced by the Large Hadron Collider [25] are a few examples representing the unprecedented data challenges for scientists. Richer sensors, digitization of analog content, and new applications like Twitter, web search, etc., will only increase data growth rates. Indeed, it is estimated that only 5% of the world's offline data has been made online so far.

The growth in data is leading to a corresponding growth in data-centric applications that operate on data in diverse ways (capture, classify, analyze, process, archive, etc.). Compared to traditional enterprise workloads (e.g., online transaction processing, web serving), emerging data-centric workloads significantly change assumptions about system design. These workloads typically operate at larger scale (up to hundreds of thousands of servers) and on more diverse data (e.g., structured, unstructured, rich media) with I/O intensive, sometimes random, data access patterns and limited locality. In addition, recent software innovations aimed at improving scalability with commodity hardware (e.g., MapReduce [9]) allow such workloads to be implemented and executed on large-scale distributed systems. This evolution of both workload and software support suggests a re-evaluation of system architectures in the datacenters.

At the same time, non-volatile memories (NVMs) are also challenging many traditional assumptions in system design. Flash memories are already pervasive in popular consumer devices (e.g., smart phones) and are becoming important in the enterprise as well (e.g., Fusion-IO, EMC). New NVMs such as phase-change RAM (PCM) or memristors offer significantly better latencies and energy efficiencies than Flash, enabling a new layer in the storage hierarchy. Looking further ahead, these NVMs are predicted to have comparable performance to DRAM, and with better energy efficiency and device scalability [4, 18].

Both NVMs as new architectural building blocks and the growth in data-centric workloads offer an interesting opportunity for new system architectures. We classify recent proposals that incorporate NVM into the system architecture, and identify a trend towards tighter integration of compute with NVM-based persistent data stores [2][7][33][34][35] (Section 2). Extrapolating this trend points to a future where data-centric systems can be built using compute packaged with persistent NVM data stores that are accessed in memory-based interfaces. However, the design space that realizes this vision has not been fully explored. Similarly, there has been inadequate emphasis on distributed systems in prior proposals.

A key challenge in addressing these questions is the lack of an evaluation methodology for NVM-based designs in large-scale, data-centric system architectures. We address this challenge by developing (and validating) a hybrid analytical and simulation based methodology to evaluate such architectures, using benchmarks representing data-centric applications, and carefully choosing baseline architectures and configurations optimized for each benchmark (Section 3).

We focus on an illustrative design point, "nanostores": an approach to build large-scale distributed systems from a new building block that stacks compute and NVM on the same chip and uses NVM to replace traditional disks as well as main

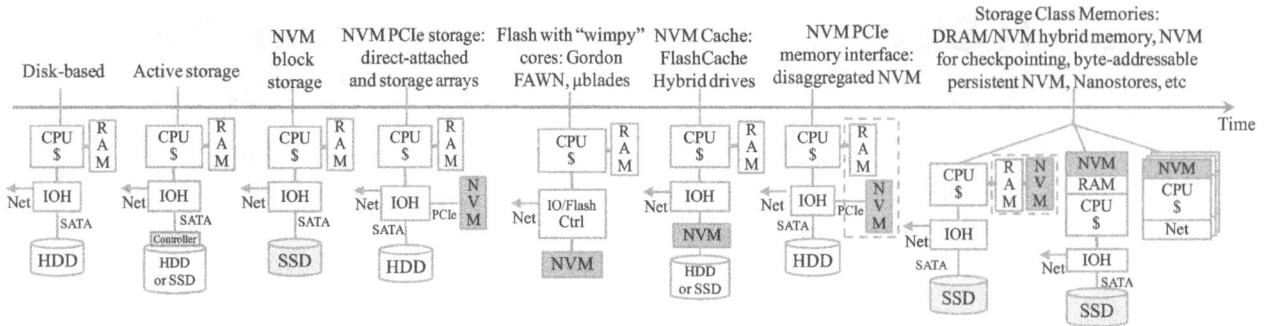

Figure 1: System architectures exploiting NVM

memory. Using carefully chosen architecture parameters for the baseline and proposed designs, our evaluation results (Section 4) indicate significant potential for nanostores, with 3-162X improvements in energy delay product (EDP) for our benchmarks, translating to improved performance as well as better energy efficiency. Concurrently, these results also indicate important future challenges in scaling software, power density, and network bandwidth. Specifically, our design space exploration identifies interesting new tradeoffs and benefits from balanced system designs centered on compute and network provisioning. Using these insights, we discuss other architecture issues and implications for using non-volatile memories (Section 5). Sections 6 and 7 additionally discuss related work and conclusions.

2. BACKGROUND: NVM-BASED DATA-CENTRIC SYSTEM ARCHITECTURES

Figure 1 presents a summary of various current and proposed designs that integrate non-volatile memories into system architectures. Several existing products (e.g., EMC, Fusion-IO, HP, Oracle, Seagate, TMS) expose Flash memories as block devices either through SAS/SATA or PCI Express (PCIe) interfaces, and use them as disk replacements or disk caches, with appropriate software support (e.g., Fusion-IO drivers, Oracle ASM, Facebook Flashcache). Recent research proposals (microblades [18], FAWN [5], Gordon [6]) have additionally noted that coupling such Flash-based storage with "wimpy" lower-power processors can lead to more balanced system designs for cloud workloads, significantly improving energy efficiency. Several research proposals have also discussed DRAM/NVM hybrid memory and NVM as byte-addressable memory devices connected to the memory bus or 3D-stacked on the chip, but using NVM as additional levels in the memory/storage hierarchy and for single-node workloads. These designs do not exploit the non-volatility of NVMs. More recent proposals have begun to examine software support for using NVM as a byte-addressable persistent data store (e.g., BPFS [33], CDDS [34], NV-Heaps [35] and Mnemosyne [7]), and leverage NVM-based data stores in future distributed architectures (Nanostores [2]).

Classifying these designs across two dimensions – (1) the type of NVM interface exposed and (2) the proximity of NVM to the compute resources – and tracing the timeline of design evolution reveals an interesting trend: future designs are ultimately likely to use NVM as the primary data store (merging both memory and storage) and access the NVM through high-bandwidth memory-based interfaces.

The rightmost design in Figure 1 illustrates one such system architecture that we focus on in this paper. In this "nanostore" design [2], the NVM is 3D-stacked on the chip with the processor, but is used as a single-level, memory-addressed persistent data

store replacing the function of traditional main memory as well as disk drives. The two most important aspects of this approach are: (1) the co-location of power-efficient computing with NVM-based data store, and (2) the use of nanostore arrays to build highly-parallel, large-scale distributed systems.

Exploring this architecture invariably identifies open questions representative of the broader design space for future NVM-based data-centric system architectures. How do these new designs compare to aggressive extrapolations of existing architectures? How do the benefits change across the range of data-centric workloads? Do we need to rethink the balance of compute, data, and network for this new architecture for large systems? What are the implications of specific design choices and technology extrapolations, including network bandwidth and packaging assumptions? This paper addresses these questions.

3. EXPLORATION METHODOLOGY

A key challenge in answering these questions is the lack of an evaluation methodology for full-system, distributed architectures with future technology and workloads. Specifically, we need to study large-scale clusters running distributed workloads operating on high volumes of data. We also need to examine tradeoffs at the full system level and model the interactions of compute, memory, storage, and networking subsystems. Conventional architecture simulators cannot model this level of scale and scope. There is also a combinatorial explosion in the design space from various fine-grained and coarse-grained architecture-level options, as well as the choice of technology and workload parameters. To address these challenges, we develop and validate a new evaluation methodology based on hybrid performance models and new data-centric benchmarks.

3.1 Evaluation models and validation

Evaluation methodology

Our evaluation methodology focuses on the application's system-level behavior and allows exploration of broader datacenter issues such as scalability and compute-network-I/O balance. The methodology adopts approaches currently used for database query planning (e.g., [26]) and MapReduce/Hadoop simulation (e.g., [27]). Similar to these approaches, we propose a high-level model using the application's execution template to break down an application's execution into consecutive phases. Each phase consists of compute, network, and I/O subsystem activities, performed sequentially or in parallel. The high-level model takes inputs from low-level performance and power models regarding the performance and usage of compute, memory, I/O and network subsystems to calculate the power and execution time for each activity, phase, and subsequently the whole application.

Figure 2(a) summarizes the model, while additional details and examples are presented later in Section 3.2 and Appendix A1. Specifically, the I/O (data store) and network subsystem performance models calculate the execution time for storage access and communication activities as the ratio between (1) the amount of data need to be transferred to and from the I/O and network subsystems for each activity and (2) the provisioned I/O and network bandwidths. For data stores, we model the combined bandwidth needs of both file and memory accesses in our nanostore designs, and calculate read and write time separately.

To model the performance of the compute/memory subsystem, we first run the workloads (discussed next) on an existing Xeon server configured with minimal storage and network overhead (to isolate the performance impact of network and I/O). We measure the workload's performance with two metrics: (1) the application-level data processing throughput, e.g., in terms of MB/s of data sorted or video transcoded by the compute; and (2) the workload's IPC on this Xeon server. We refer to these two numbers as the workload's base compute throughput and base IPC, respectively. We can then calculate the workload's compute throughput on a simulated processor configuration as the base compute throughput scaled by the ratio of the simulated IPC over the base IPC.

Using COTSon [3] for detailed, micro-architectural simulation, this methodology allows us to model processors with different microarchitectural and architectural configurations. The calculated compute throughput and other simulation outputs such as consumed memory bandwidths are fed into the higher-level model for full-system performance and power estimation.

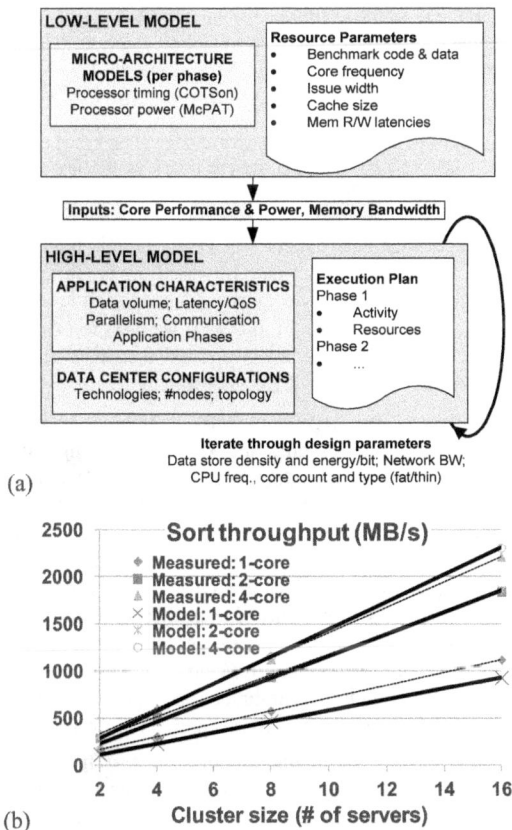

(a)

(b)

Figure 2: Design exploration model and validation. The method in (a) combines application and subsystem level models and simulation results to reason about architecture tradeoffs; (b) presents validation results for an illustrative experiment for *sort*.

For power modeling, we focus mainly on average power consumption (for both active and static power). We also consider peak power, but only to verify compliance with power/thermal density constraints. We use the performance model to compute the utilizations for processor, memory, data store and network. Active power is assumed to scale linearly with utilization. We use the corresponding utilization factors to derate active power based on the component's peak and idle power. We also model static power when appropriate, e.g., for CPU and DRAM leakage power.

During execution phases where the CPU cores are active, we use the read and write memory bandwidth statistics from COTSon to calculate memory utilization. The amortized per-node network power is modeled as its NIC-level power scaled by a network hop multiplier, which corresponds to the average network hops traversed by a packet. Such a multiplier accounts for switch power consumed for packet routing and forwarding. The CPU peak power is determined using McPAT [17], as a function of issue width, frequency and cache size. CPU configurations at each frequency also factor in the power benefits from voltage and frequency scaling supported by McPAT. CPU static power is scaled based on the number of cores and their caches sizes.

Overall, this model provides both sufficient details and a simple way to iterate between various compute, storage I/O, and network options in order to select the optimal designs for a given objective function (e.g., EDP, energy efficiency, or performance).

Model validation

Figure 2(b) presents results validating our model for an MPI-based implementation for one of our benchmark (*sort*), on small cluster sizes ranging from 2 to 16 servers. As discussed later in Section 3.2, *sort* has one of the most complex execution template with multiple phases and concurrent compute, I/O and network activities, which stresses the validation of our approach. Each server in the cluster has 2 dual-core 2.4GHz AMD Opteron processors and a 1Gb/s Ethernet NIC. We use the traffic shaping tool wondershaper (http://lartc.org/wondershaper/) to vary the network bandwidths. Figure 2(b) shows the *measured* and *modeled* system-level sort throughput for different cluster sizes and number of cores per server. The predicted performance from our model tracks the real system fairly well. Note that the discrepancies mainly come from 1-core *sort*, where the real-system throughput is higher because the single core can "unfairly" use the entire shared cache and memory bandwidth.

While the model addresses all the compute, I/O, and network components of the system, and provides a powerful way to systematically explore the large design space at practical simulation times, a few caveats need to be noted. First, we assume that computation and network communication can overlap and are purely bandwidth based (i.e., no queuing models are used). These assumptions are acceptable for the distinct phases and coarse-grained data transfer behavior of our benchmarks (and many important real-world applications), but care needs to be exercised in extrapolating the model to other workloads. Notice we also assume data are distributed uniformly, and load-imbalance or skews are not considered in the model (we study the impact of relaxing these assumptions in Section 4.3).

3.2 Data-centric benchmarks

The space of data-centric workloads is vast, fast-evolving, and characterized by diversity across multiple dimensions. To study a subset of workloads for coverage and representativeness, we systematically classify data-centric workloads to characterize the key dimensions of diversity and pick a subset of workloads that

Response Time	Real-time	Real-time or interactive responses required
	Background	Response time is not critical for user needs
Access Pattern	Random	Unpredictable access to regions of data store
	Sequential	Sequential access of data chunks
	Permutation	Data is re-distributed across the system
Working Set	All	The entire dataset is accessed
	Partial	Only a subset of data is accessed
Data Type	Structured	Metadata/schema/type are used for data records
	Unstructured	No explicit data structure, e.g., text/binary files
	Rich media	Audio/video and image data with inherent structures and specific processing algorithms
Read vs. Write	Read heavy	Data reads are significant for processing
	Write heavy	Data writes are significant for processing
Processing Complexity	High	Complex processing of data is required per data item. Examples: video trans-coding, classification, prediction
	Low	Dominated by data access with low compute ratio. Examples: sort, upload, download, filtering, and aggregation.

Figure 3: Classification of data-centric workloads, used to guide our selection of benchmarks.

exercises all these dimensions. Figure 3 illustrates the taxonomy and attributes of each dimension. Considered dimensions include: response time (real-time vs. background), access pattern (random, sequential or permutation), working set (all vs. partial), data type (structured, unstructured and rich media), read vs. write heavy accesses, and processing complexity (low, medium or high).

Based on this analysis, we choose five representative benchmarks. *Sort*, *cksum* (checksum calculation in data deduplication), and *video* (video transcoding) represent I/O intensive data-centric workloads, an important focus for this study. Additionally, we study *search* and *recommender* (collaborative filtering based recommendation) to represent emerging in-memory data-centric workloads. Within these broad categories, the individual workloads provide coverage of different requirements. Taking processing complexity as an example dimension, *video* requires more computation per unit of data compared to *sort*, which needs more computation relative to *cksum*. Similarly, *recommender* requires more computation than *search*. These workloads also stress different data access patterns: random versus sequential; and different data types: structured, unstructured, and rich media. They also have publicly available implementations that we can use for simulations.

Below we describe these benchmarks and summarize their execution plans (detailed execution plans and performance/power models are presented in Appendix A1).

Sort: This benchmark implements a distributed sort of key-value records. *Sort* is read/write-heavy, and stresses the balance between compute/storage/network subsystems. We model a data-parallel algorithm with two phases: (i) A *shuffle* phase where each server reads records from local storage and, based on the key values, sends them over the network to their destinations. While incoming records fill its buffer, the server sorts the buffer and outputs to storage. (ii) A *local merge* phase after the shuffle, where each server reads previously sorted small files from local storage, performs a merge sort, and outputs the final sort results. We use nsort (http://www.ordinal.com) to model the local merge phase.

Checksum in data de-duplication: The benchmark *cksum* models the checksum calculation task in de-duplication, resulting in mostly read-only sequential accesses and low processing complexity. We model a parallel implementation of *cksum* where each server scans its local files to generate block or file signatures using the SHA-1 hash function. We use the Linux utility sha1sum in our simulations.

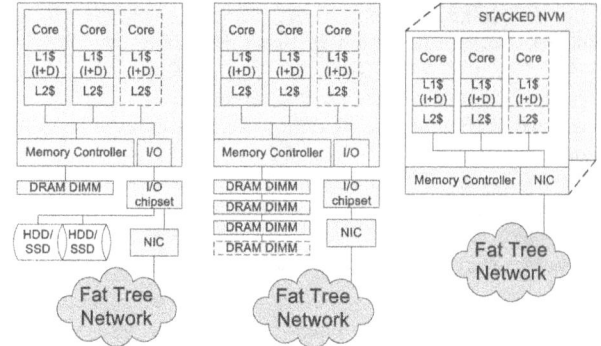

Figure 4: System architectures studied: HDD/SSD-based and memory-based baselines vs. Nanostores (right)

Processor	Baseline	Nanostore
Core count	32	1-128
Frequency (GHz)	2	0.1-2.0
Issue width	4	2, 4
Per-core L1 cache	64K+64K	64K+64K
Per-core L2 cache	1M	512K, 1M
Peak Power/Core (W)	1.83	(model)
Idle Power/Core (W)	0.04	(model)

Network	Baseline	Nanostore
Peak BW/Port (Gbit/s)	40	40
Peak Power/Port (W)	10	10
Idle Power/Port (W)	2	2

Main Memory	Baseline	Nanostore
Peak BW/Unit (GB/s)	25.6	32
Capacity/Unit (GB)	16	25
Peak Power/Unit (W)	10	0.6
Idle Power/Unit (W)	2	0

Hard Disk/SSD	HDD	SSD
Peak BW/Drive (GB/s)	0.5	4.5
Capacity/Drive (TB)	6	1.2
Peak Power/Drive (W)	10	10
Idle Power/Drive (W)	8	1

Figure 5: Evaluation methodology and parameter details.
Notes: (1) Baseline CPU configuration extrapolated from Xeon E7500; (2) per-core cache capacity lowered to model many-core and ultra-low voltage cores; (3) baseline DRAM bandwidth extrapolated from Xeon servers, optimistic power overhead for unused bandwidth (conservative for nanostore benefits); (4) DRAM/NVM capacity based on ITRS extrapolation [4]; (5) HDD baseline extrapolated from 125MB/s 1.5TB as 2011 commodity component, SSD baseline extrapolated from Fusion-IO ioDuo; (6) Network bandwidth and power extrapolation based on [32]. (7) We study a fat-tree network with system nodes as the leaves, but the designs should work equally well or better with other topologies.

Video transcoding: The benchmark *video* models popular video transcoding web services that use the cloud for batch processing. The algorithm reads the video input files, transcodes to a new format, and stores it. For our simulations, we use the ffmpeg code over a large dataset. The video is in FLV format with 320x240 resolution and transcoded to JPEG snapshots.

Recommender: The *recommender* benchmark represents sophisticated machine learning algorithms with high compute complexity and regular communication patterns. We model the Netflix challenge [31] over a 5 Terabyte dataset, using matrix factorization. The algorithm iteratively refines two matrices so their product can best summarize the *movie-ratings* matrix. Large matrices are partitioned across the cluster and stored in main memory. Each iteration has four phases: two of them are matrix operations; the other interleaving phases communicate the new results to each server. It requires large memory to host the matrices and compute/communication balance. For our simulations, we use Matlab based on a parallel algorithm [31].

Search: The *search* benchmark models text search across a 128 terabyte data set, using in-memory indices to achieve sub-second response times. The workload is read-only with random access patterns. Similar to Google's in-memory text search, the entire index is partitioned across a large cluster and stored in main memory. Each server searches its local index first, and sends the top-matching document list to the front-end server. In addition to search query throughput, this benchmark models a quality of service (QoS) requirement of less than 0.5 second average query latency. We use `lucene` in our simulations.

3.3 Specific design choices and parameters

One of the other challenges in modeling nanostores is the existence of a wide range of possible implementations. There are a number of design choices in terms of the provisioning, organization, and balance of the compute, storage, and network resources per nanostore; the sharing model across the individual nodes; as well as the network topology (including potential differences between the on-chip network, interconnect on the PCB board, and cluster-level networks). The design choices are not independent and are often constrained by technology- and circuits-level parameters (e.g., the die size and yield, the number of 3D-stacked or intra-die layers, as well as power/thermal budget per processor socket or server board).

We address this challenge with careful selection of baseline and proposed architecture parameters, and use our methodology to quickly identify key insights through a large parameter space. Figure 4 and 5 summarizes the system architectures and configuration parameters we examine for this study. All the parameters are chosen based on projected data from recent publications and industry sources (e.g., ITRS [4]).

NVM data stores. We assume a nanostore die size of $100mm^2$, based on the cost-efficiency sweet-spot design point for memory chips [4]. For a PCM-based design circa 2015, assuming 8 layers of 3D and intra-die stacking, the on-chip data store capacity is 25 GB per socket. The density/capacity, access latency (150 ns) and access energy (2-20 pJ/bit) are based on published PCM models [15]. We also study other parameters for data store capacity, latency, and energy to understand the sensitivity of our results to alternative future NVMs (e.g., memristors [36]), these results provide similar insights but for brevity are not presented here.

Compute. The processor cores in the compute layer are based on low-voltage power-efficient microarchitectures with simple SRAM cache hierarchies. We study multiple different organizations for the compute layer – varying the number of cores (32 options ranging from 1 to 128; the maximum core count of 128 is based on area estimation from McPAT), the clock frequency (100MHz, 200MHz, 500MHz, 1GHz and 2GHz), the issue width and pipeline depth (2-way or 4-way), and the L2 cache size (512KB or 1MB per core).

Power density. To ensure realistic designs, we limit the power density at the socket level (including all the compute and NVM layers). The power density is limited both by practical thermal density for packaging and cooling, and by the number of available power pins. We use a $32W/cm^2$ "cap" (based on today's 80W Xeon server with die size of $2.5cm^2$) as a design constraint in our performance and energy efficiency evaluation. Later in our sensitivity analysis, we also study the impact of raising this cap to $50W/cm^2$ (corresponding to today's high-power 125W servers) or $100W/cm^2$ (for advanced future packaging/cooling technologies).

Memory bandwidth. For the projected timeframe, we expect 3D stacking to provide significantly improved bandwidth (32GB/s) between the processor and stacked memory using through-silicon vias, similar to PicoServer [11]. A large body of work exists on 3D technology and 3D-based memory organization; we choose this bandwidth as a tradeoff between bandwidth and power.

Distributed system. We model 80Gbps networking bandwidth per server (two 40Gbs NICs as extrapolated for 2015) as in a traditional architecture, and in the sensitivity study we examine the impact of higher network bandwidth. We assume a large-scale, distributed shared-nothing system abstraction, well-matched with current data-centric software. Each nanostore can be viewed as a complete, independent system executing software needed to implement a data parallel execution environment like MapReduce. We also study the effectiveness of software scaling as a variable parameter, and discuss software issues in Section 5.

Baseline architectures

Another evaluation challenge is to provide a fair comparison between the baselines and the proposed architectures. Different workloads have different resource requirements and utilization patterns of compute, memory, storage I/O and network. Therefore, using a single baseline for all the benchmarks will not accommodate workload-specific sweet-spot configurations and may lead to unfair comparisons.

To address this challenge, we choose the best performing baseline specific to individual benchmarks (using the methodology described in Section 3.1). Depending on the evaluation metric (e.g., performance, energy efficiency, or EDP), different baseline configurations are identified and used in our evaluation. For fair comparison, we fix the dataset size across different configurations (i.e., satisfying the same user requirement), and therefore compare designs with the same persistent storage capacity. Based on the node capacity values in Figure 5, this implies the nanostore cluster can have 40-240x more nodes than SSD and HDD based designs.

The *sort, cksum* and *video* benchmarks keep their data on disks and are each allocated a single DRAM DIMM (to save power). For such IO-intensive workloads, we study both traditional hard disks and SSD-based storage. *Search* and *recommender* are in-memory workloads, so the architecture stores large datasets in the main memory and has no hard disks or SSDs. Overall, we examine three classes of designs, corresponding to the HDD-, SSD- and memory-based architectures in Figure 4.

In choosing parameters for the baselines, we ignore any potential end-of-life device scaling limitations when using DRAM or Flash, and instead extrapolate historical scaling trends for capacity and bandwidth. Note that such assumptions produce baselines that make the nanostore benefits estimates more conservative. We assume configurations of 16GB per DRAM module, doubling the capacity of today's GB/$ sweet-spot 8GB DIMMs. The per-channel DRAM bandwidth is optimistically increased from today's 12.8GB/s to 25.6 GB/s bandwidth in 2015, with each DIMM consuming 10W at peak and 2W at idle. For persistent storage, we assume future HDDs each with 6TB capacity and 500 MB/s bandwidth (two generations into the future under Moore's Law scaling), and an active power consumption varying between 8W to 10W from idle to peak. Using Fusion-IO as today's SSD baseline, we model future SSDs at lower capacity per drive (1.2TB), but higher bandwidth (4.5GB/s) and improved energy efficiency (10W peak and 1W idle power).

4. EVALUATION RESULTS

This section presents evaluation results to answer the following questions: (1) Overall, how well do nanostores perform relative to the baselines, and where do the benefits come from? (2) For the evaluated architectures in Figure 4, what are the design tradeoffs with different choices of compute, network, and data store? (3) How sensitive are our results to limiting bottlenecks such as network bandwidth, power density and software scalability?

4.1 Design space analysis

Figure 6 summarizes the results from our design space exploration, focusing on the inverse of energy delay product

(EDP) across our benchmarks. Notice configurations with higher 1/EDP values are better.

Figure 6(a) shows the 1/EDP results of *cksum*, a storage I/O intensive benchmark, for *nanostores* as well as SSD- and HDD-based designs. The entire design space has over 8000 configurations as a result of considering 32 core count options, 5 frequencies, 4 microarchitectural options in cache and pipeline, and a large number of storage and network bandwidths. For illustration, we present only 40 points along the x-axis by fixing the per-socket network bandwidth and number of storage devices, and only examining a smaller subset of processor core-count options – 16, 32, 64, and 128 cores. The x-axis in Figure 6(a) lists the details of these different processor configurations, sorted in ascending order by per-socket theoretical peak compute bandwidth in GIPS (Giga-Instructions-Per-Second). Here *16c_0.1GHz_2w* refers to a 16-core design with 100MHz, 2-way issue cores. For each configuration, we plot the per-socket peak compute bandwidth GIPS, and the relative 1/EDP values for the three system architectures (*HDD, SSD, and nanostores*).

The variation in 1/EDP values across different architectures (between curves) and configurations (within a curve) illustrates several trends. First, *NVM-based data stores remove I/O bandwidth and energy bottlenecks for data-centric workloads, and consequently can exploit a matching increase in compute bandwidth.* This observation is reflected directly in the shape and slope of the different curves. The 1/EDP curve for HDD-based designs is almost *flat,* showing the diminishing returns in EDP improvement after a modest increase in compute bandwidth due

to the storage bottleneck. Higher storage bandwidth and lower energy from SSD and nanostores (the other two 1/EDP curves) can address this limitation, allowing 1/EDP to better scale with increased compute bandwidth.

Second, although higher I/O and compute bandwidth generally improves EDP, none of the best designs (indicated by the three circled data points in the figure) choose the highest GIPS configuration. *Instead, theses designs achieve better EDP by balancing their compute bandwidth to match the storage bandwidth, and by careful performance/power tradeoffs.* Specifically, imbalanced nanostore designs with under-provisioned compute have worse EDP than balanced SSD-based designs, mainly due to lower performance and idle power overhead. Similarly, over-provisioning with peak-performance processors can degrade EDP due to under-utilized high compute power and the mismatch with I/O-intensive workloads.

Third, Figure 6(a) also illustrates *the two key factors contributing to higher compute bandwidth: (1) parallelism from increased socket count and (2) increased per-socket compute provisioning.* Because nanostores have smaller per-socket data stores than SSD- and HDD-based systems, maintaining the same system-wide data store capacity across these designs actually significantly increases the socket-level parallelism for nanostores (shown by the gap between different curves). For data points on the same curve, compute bandwidth varies with per-socket compute configuration.

Figure 6(b) plots the 1/EDP results for the remaining four benchmarks. The figure is dense with data points, but is included to illustrate the *workload diversity.* Comparing the sub-figures

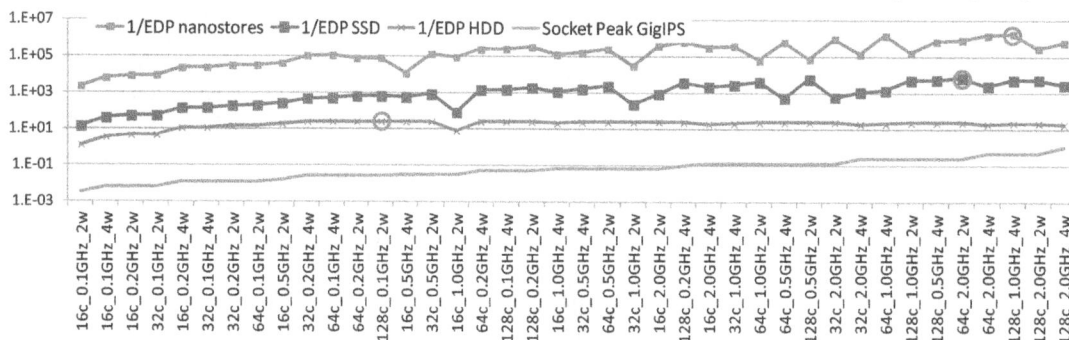

(a) 1/EDP curves for *cksum*. Two trends are highlighted: (1) NVM and in particular nanostores can remove the storage bottleneck of HDD-based designs; (2) optimizing for balance (between compute and I/O, and between performance and power) also has significant impact.

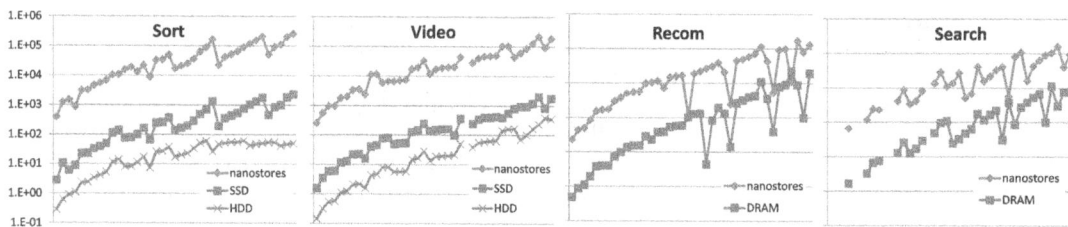

(b) 1/EDP for the remaining benchmarks, showing workload diversity and design implications. The X-axis uses the same 40 points as sub-figure (a).

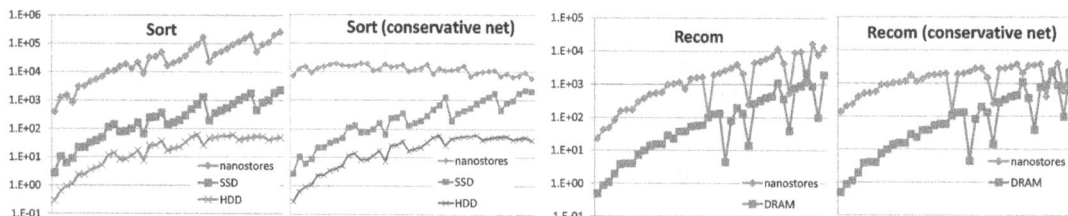

(c) 1/EDP for *sort* and *recommender* with *optimistic vs. conservative* network bandwidths. *Sort* and *recom* figures from (b) are repeated for clarity.

Figure 6: Design space exploration insights.

including Figure 6(a), we observe the gaps and slopes between 1/EDP curves for each workload are different. Focusing only on nanostore curves, the best configurations are also different across workloads. For example, similar to *cksum*, the EDP improvement of *sort* with HDDs is also limited by the storage bottleneck. However the compute bandwidth at the point of diminishing return is much higher than with *cksum*. This indicates *sort* has a different compute to storage ratio requirement and can exploit higher compute bandwidth. For more compute intensive workloads (e.g., *video*), the storage bottleneck is even less visible.

These observations imply the importance of understanding and optimizing for the diversity of workloads for data-centric system architectures. Beside compute, these benchmarks also have diverse communication and quality-of-service (QoS) requirements. For example, the missing points in the *search* subfigure represent invalid configurations with low compute bandwidth that cannot satisfy *search*'s latency QoS requirements. Although not visualized here, workload diversity in these aspects can have significant performance and energy-efficiency impacts, and their combination sometimes can change the balanced design points in non-intuitive ways.

Finally, Figure 6(c) shows the need to further balance compute and IO with another key resource—network bandwidth. When the total network bandwidth of nanostores is conservatively set to be the same as in the SSD design, the EDP improvement for communication-intensive workloads (*sort* and *recommender*) becomes limited, especially for the high-compute configurations.

Overall, from a limits perspective, the nanostore design has the potential to significantly outperform traditional designs. For I/O-intensive data-centric workloads, nanostores can improve EDP by 2-3 orders of magnitude compared to HDD-based baselines, and 1-2 orders of magnitude over SSD-based baselines. The in-memory workloads achieve an order of magnitude better EDP compared to DRAM/DIMM baselines. Note that our aggressively optimized baselines make such benefits estimation more conservative. The next section discusses the benefits in details.

4.2 Performance and energy efficiency

Figure 7 presents the improvements in performance and energy efficiency from the nanostore designs relative to the baselines (for the IO-intensive workloads, HDD-based and SSD-based; and for the in-memory workloads, DIMM-based). For brevity, we plot only the *best EDP-point* from the design space exploration and show the details of the specific configuration in Figure 7(b). The results show that *for all our benchmarks, the EDP benefits from nanostores translate into both better performance and energy efficiency*. For I/O intensive benchmarks – *sort, cksum, and video* – the nanostore designs achieve 1-3 orders of magnitude higher performance improvement with 3X-16X better energy efficiency. For the in-memory benchmarks with DRAM DIMM baselines – *recom, search* – nanostores achieve 2X-6X speedup with 2X-4X better energy efficiency. The relatively smaller performance improvements for the in-memory benchmarks compared to the IO-intensive benchmarks can similarly be traced back to the baseline's high DRAM bandwidth.

Analysis of the results shows that the *greatest improvement correlates with the aggregate data store bandwidth*, resulting from the combination of both the higher per-nanostore bandwidth and lower per-socket capacity. For example, with more than 5000 times higher data bandwidth, the three I/O-intensive benchmarks no longer have any data store access bottleneck. With co-located compute, nanostores also allow significantly higher compute

bandwidths (e.g., *cksum* and *video*) and network bandwidths (e.g., *sort*) to match the increased data store bandwidth, regaining the balance across resource subsystems to improve performance.

Our detailed statistics showed, surprisingly, that *not all potential bandwidth improvements enabled by 3D-stacking were fully exploited*. Further increasing the compute and network bandwidth can potentially realize the full potential of such high bandwidth, but are currently limited by processor power density and network aggregate bandwidth. These newly exposed bottlenecks limit how well the memory and storage bandwidth is used; our additional experiments (data not shown in table for space) show significantly higher performance improvements when these limitations are relaxed. Furthermore, as discussed in Section 3, our performance model and the COTSon-generated per-core memory bandwidth numbers used as input to the model are both conservative about the effect of improved memory bandwidth on performance, likely contributing further to these results. Finally, the nanostore design's *memory-like data store latency has huge performance potential* for workloads that are latency sensitive or dominated by random access patterns. However, the benchmarks we study are throughput-oriented and our performance model is mainly bandwidth based; therefore our results do not demonstrate the potential benefit of better latency.

Focusing on the energy efficiency benefits, our analysis show that *the nanostore benefits stem from three primary sources*: (1) the energy-efficiency improvements of the NVM-based data store, relative to HDDs, SSDs, and DRAM DIMM, due to lower access energy (device technology and 3D stacking) and better power proportionality (almost no idle power), (2) the use of low-power, more energy-efficient, processor cores enabled by compute co-location with lower per-nanostore capacity, and (3) reduced energy for data movement between the logically separate segments of memory and persistent storage in the nanostore's collapsed hierarchy. The last effect is conservatively modeled in the integrated model that we consider, but separate calculations show that it can provide significant benefits (e.g., 10%-30%).

4.3 Impact of the power density and network bandwidth limitations

The significant potential of nanostores motivates us to further understand the limits of such designs. So far our evaluation has focused on exploring the storage and compute subsystems; next, we address the remaining key aspects of system architecture, namely, networking, packaging/cooling (using power density as a proxy metric), and software (in terms of scaling overhead).

Figure 8(a) visualizes the effect of relaxing the socket power density and network bandwidth constraints. The socket-level power density baseline is $32W/cm^2$ (as of today's 80W $2.5cm^2$ Xeon server chips), and is relaxed to 50 and 100 W/cm^2. The aggregate network bandwidth (and apportioned per-socket bandwidth) is relaxed by a factor of 4 and 16 (X4 and X16 in the figure). All results are normalized to the nanostore design with conservatively extrapolated power density and network bandwidth, darker shades illustrate higher benefits.

Allowing higher power density has a positive performance effect for all workloads, matching our analysis in Section 4.2. On the other hand, raising the network bandwidth only affects the two network-heavy benchmarks (*sort* and *recom*), especially *sort* where network is the new bottleneck for performance scaling. Power density is the first bottleneck for *recom*, which has to trade core count with higher network bandwidth within the power envelope to get better performance.

Result	Performance									EE								
Watt/cm2	32			50			100			32			50			100		
Net_BW	x1	x4	x16	x1	x4	x16	x1	x4	x16	x1	x4	x16	x1	x4	x16	x1	x4	x16
Sort	1	4	22	1	4	22	1	4	22	1.0	1.0	0.8	1.0	1.0	0.8	1.0	1.0	0.8
Cksum	1	1	1	2	2	2	2	2	2	1.0	1.0	1.0	0.8	0.8	0.8	0.8	0.8	0.8
Video	1	1	1	2	2	2	3	3	3	1.0	1.0	1.0	0.7	0.7	0.7	0.6	0.6	0.6
Recom	1	2	2	1	3	3	1	3	6	1.0	1.0	1.0	1.0	1.0	1.0	1.0	1.0	0.9
Search	1	1	1	2	2	2	2	2	2	1.0	1.0	1.0	0.6	0.6	0.6	0.6	0.6	0.6

(a)

Result	Performance			EE			1/EDP		
Penalty	x1	x1.25	x1.5	x1	x1.25	x1.5	x1	x1.25	x1.5
Sort	1.0	0.8	0.8	1.0	0.9	0.7	1.0	0.7	0.6
Cksum	1.0	1.2	1.1	1.0	0.7	0.7	1.0	0.9	0.8
Video	1.0	0.8	1.0	1.0	1.0	0.7	1.0	0.8	0.7
Recom	1.0	1.0	0.9	1.0	1.0	1.0	1.0	0.9	0.9
Search	1.0	1.3	1.2	1.0	0.7	0.6	1.0	0.8	0.7

(b)

Figure 8: Impact of (a) power-density and network constraints and (b) software scaling overheads

Another important issue is around scaling of distributed software. The performance improvements from nanostores partly come from the larger scale of the distributed workloads, increasing the node count by factors ranging from 100 to 500. Figure 8(b) summarizes the impact when we consider the penalizing overhead of software execution time due to increased cluster size. The table considers a 25% and 50% additional penalty in overall execution time relative to an ideally scaled system with all nodes instantly starting and finishing execution and perfect load-balance. As expected, software scalability is an important consideration to achieve the benefits from nanostores. EDP degrades with reduced software efficiency in all our experiments. (Since we present a single data point for the EDP-optimal design after the design space exploration, some chosen designs would have higher performance and lower energy efficiency, but the 1/EDP value is lower in all cases.)

In summary, our sensitivity study leads to two key learnings: (1) network bandwidth, power density and software scaling are all potential barriers in further scaling the nanostore designs, motivating holistic optimizations across various design aspects; (2) for different benchmarks, these limitations also manifest themselves in different order and magnitude, demonstrating workload diversity and calling for workload-optimized designs.

5. DISCUSSION

Software scaling. Scaling software for nanostores presents two key challenges. First, current software stacks are developed with decades-old assumptions of traditional rotational disks. They will have to be re-architected to leverage NVM persistent data stores under the memory interface. However, recent work around byte-persistent file systems [33], consistent durable data structures [34], persistent transactions [35], and RAMCloud [10] presage the growing interest in the systems community and progress being made in this space. The second challenge is around horizontal scaling required for large-scale distributed systems. While it is worth noting that over the decade from 1998 to 2009, Google's infrastructure is reported to have scaled performance (queries processed/day) by 1000X while scaling the infrastructure size by 1000X [1], more scalable distributed algorithms are required for future nanostore designs. Recent work on data-centric software stacks (e.g., Google BigTable and MapReduce, Microsoft Dryad, Facebook Memcached) illustrate progress in this area.

Endurance. Write endurance is an important issue to consider for NVM-based architectures. NVMs such as PCM and memristor offer significantly better functionality than Flash (10^7-10^8 or more writes per cell compared to the 10^5 writes per cell, respectively). Optimizations at the technology, circuit, and systems levels [15][20][21][30] have been shown to further address endurance issues, and more improvements are likely as the technologies mature and gain widespread adoption. For the peak memory bandwidth we consider, in theory, storage wear-out can occur in 2 years for PCM based on the nanostore capacity and endurance. However, in practice, not all applications sustain write rates at peak level and the average across the application is much lower, leading to significantly longer lifetimes across the array. Wear-leveling schemes must still be used to spread writes across the memory space to prevent early failure of hot blocks. Assuming a previously proposed approach – start-gap wear leveling – at an efficiency of 90% of optimal wear-leveling [20], and using the memory write bandwidths from our simulations, we estimate per-nanostore lifetimes of 7-18 years for our benchmarks on the PCM-based design. Nevertheless, techniques that carefully manage wear-out warrant further study.

Costs. In this paper, we focus primarily on architectural and technology implications for best future designs, but cost is another issue that also needs to be considered. Current Flash memories have about an order of magnitude higher cost on a $/byte basis compared to disk. The NVMs we consider in this paper have the potential to lower these costs by more aggressive stacking and simpler fabrication processes. The improved energy efficiency of our design can also further reduce the total costs of ownership. Based on these observations, and given the increased performance, we expect the nanostore design to be competitive for performance/$ compared to high-performance storage solutions.

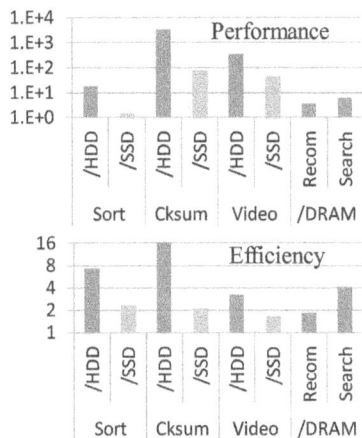

Bench	Scheme	Configuration
Sort	HDD	28-core, 2.0GHz, 2-way issue, 1MB per-core L2$, 2x HDD, 4Gbs network
	SSD	128-core, 2.0GHz, 2-way issue, 1MB per-core L2$, 2x SSD, 10Gbs network
	PCM	22-core, 0.1GHz, 2-way issue, 512KB per-core L2$, nanostores, 0.1Gbs network
Cksum	HDD	40-core, 2.0GHz, 4-way issue, 1MB per-core L2$, 14x HDD, 8Mbs network
	SSD	104-core, 0.5GHz, 4-way issue, 512KB per-core L2$, 2x SSD, 8Mbs network
	PCM	128-core, 0.5GHz, 2-way issue, 512KB per-core L2$, nanostores, 8Mbs network
Video	HDD	40-core, 2.0GHz, 4-way issue, 1MB per-core L2$, 2x HDD, 8Mbs network
	SSD	88-core, 2.0GHz, 2-way issue, 1MB per-core L2$, 2x SSD, 8Mbs network
	PCM	128-core, 0.5GHz, 2-way issue, 1MB per-core L2$, nanostores, 8Mbs network
Recom	DRAM	56-core, 2.0GHz, 4-way issue, 1MB per-core L2$, DRAM, 4Gbs network
	PCM	128-core, 2.0GHz, 2-way issue, 1MB per-core L2$, nanostores, 4Gbs network
Search	DRAM	80-core, 2.0 GHz, 4-way issue, 1MB per-core L2$, DRAM, 8Mbs network
	PCM	128-core, 0.5 GHz, 2-way issue, 512KB per-core L2$, nanostores, 8Mbs network

(a) Factors of improvements   (b) Summary of balanced design points presented in sub-figure (a)

Figure 7: Performance and energy efficiency improvements over 2015 baselines

Workload diversity and implications. The diverse workload requirements shown in our study motivates system architectures that can support a wide range of applications. For workloads that can exploit high memory and storage performance (in bandwidth or latency) from the tight integration of compute and NVM, nanostores can offer significant better performance and EDP. Such compute-to-data integration can be implemented either through 3D-stacking or side-stacking (i.e., 2.5D-stacking via silicon interposer), but the balance between resource types needs to be predetermined at the time of manufacturing/packaging. For workloads that are not memory and I/O bandwidth limited, or instead bottlenecked by network or software parallelism, their preferred architectures are likely to incorporate NVM in different ways. The need to support diversity also stems from distinct phase behaviors within a single application. We believe that such flexibility is likely to be supported by system architectures that integrate and utilize heterogeneous building blocks, either on-chip or distributed across discrete components/systems.

6. RELATED WORK

Section 2 already discussed the large body of prior work on system architectures using non-volatile memory (e.g., [5][6][7][8][13][14][15][16][21][30]). To the best of our knowledge, this work is the first limits study of benefits from such designs in large-scale data-centric system architectures.

The co-location of compute close to the data store in our nanostore designs is thematically similar to Active Storage [23]. However, Active Storage incorporates compute closer to disk, in the form of more powerful disk controllers for offloading and streaming. The main processor is still a deep memory hierarchy away. The IRAM and PIM proposals [12][19] examine integrating a processor with the main memory system, but mainly address challenges with CPU-logic/DRAM integration in the same fabrication process and benefits with vector streaming programming models. In contrast, our work integrates the persistent data store with compute with 3D-stacking and addresses system balance for distributed data-centric workloads.

Recently, the RAMCloud project [19] has proposed distributed systems where all data resides in DRAM. Their research primarily focuses on the software stack, around low-latency RPC, durability, data model, scaling, and consistency, etc. Although several of their motivating arguments are similar to ours, we differ in our assumptions around all data residing in 3D-stacked NVM and in our architectural explorations around balanced designs.

Other recent studies have examined using lower-power "wimpy" cores for energy efficiency [5][6][8][18][24] while also being aware of the impact on quality of service [22]. There has also been prior work on ultra-low-voltage core design [28]. Recent architectural proposals have studied 3D stacking and demonstrated its viability and benefits for improved bandwidth and memory redesign (e.g. [11][29]). We use these techniques as well, but in a different context. Several studies have proposed optimizations to improve endurance [15][21][29][30] and others have identified potential improvements in the future [4].

7. CONCLUSIONS

Data and data-centric computing are steeply on the rise. The recent adoption of non-volatile storage, both in the HPC and business worlds, presents an interesting inflection point and an opportunity for new designs for this market. This paper explores how we should design future NVM-based system architectures targeted at data-centric workloads.

We analyze current proposals for system designs using non-volatile memory and identify an important trend towards using NVM as persistent disk replacement in close proximity to the compute element. We develop and validate a new evaluation methodology, including representative data-centric workloads, and analyze an example proposal in this space, nanostores, that incorporate compute with 3D-stacked NVM on a single chip and use NVM as both memory and storage. Our evaluation shows significant benefits (an order of magnitude or higher improvement in EDP) for such an approach but also highlights the challenges – particularly in software, networking and power density scaling – to achieve this potential. Our analysis also illustrates new insights on the implications of system balance for future architectures. Overall, the findings of our study argue for future NVM-based system designs to incorporate and tradeoff three key principles – co-location of compute closer to data, higher parallelism better supported by modern software stack and networking infrastructure, and emphasis on system balance across compute, network, and storage subsystems to improve energy efficiency along with performance.

We further quantify the impact of potential limitations to this design. Given the smaller capacities of per-node storage, the number of nodes in the system increases dramatically. This can potentially increase the stress on the networking subsystem specifically due to bandwidth contention (particularly for all-to-all communication), topological complexity, port count, and power. Software scalability can also be an issue. While large-scale deployments of data-centric workloads have been demonstrated, latency requirements (e.g., sub-second response time for a search request) will still have to carefully factor in the sizing of the system. Finally, chip-level thermal constraints can limit the amount of compute packaged per nanostore, leading to a potential compute bottleneck (e.g., for machine learning algorithms used in recommendation systems).

Looking ahead, while our results are promising, we believe we have only scratched the surface of what is possible. We are currently examining the rich architectural space enabled by future data-centric designs, including heterogeneous architectures and integrated optics. There are also interesting opportunities for hardware/software co-design including new interfaces and persistent data store resilience. The large scale and low latency of such designs will likely enable new, previously-not-possible applications, allowing for more sophisticated insights from larger diverse data; these will provide even more opportunities for future research.

8. AKNOWLEDGEMENT

This research was partially supported by the US Department of Energy under Award Number DE - SC0005026. The disclaimer can be found at http://www.hpl.hp.com/DoE-Disclaimer.html.

REFERENCES

[1] M. Mayer. The physics of data. *Talk at Xerox PARC*, 2009.

[2] P. Ranganathan, From Microprocessors to Nanostores: Rethinking Data-Centric Systems. IEEE Computer Vol. 44(1), 2011, pp. 39-48.

[3] COTSon: Infrastructure for system-level simulation. *MICRO Tutorial*, 2008.

[4] ITRS roadmap. *http://www.itrs.net/*, 2009.

[5] D. Andersen, et al. FAWN: A fast array of wimpy nodes. *SOSP*, 2009.

[6] A. Caulfield, et a;. Gordon: an improved architecture for data-intensive applications. *IEEE Micro*, 30(1), 2010.

[7] H. Volos, A. Tack, et al. Mnemosyne: Lightweight Persistent Memory. *ASPLOS*, 2011.

[8] A. Cockcroft. Millicomputing: The future in your pocket and your datacenter. *USENIX invited talk*, 2008.

[9] J. Dean and S. Ghemawat. MapReduce: Simplified data processing on large clusters. *OSDI*, 2004.

[10] J. Ousterhout et. al. The case for RAMCloud. *Communications of the ACM*, 54(7):121-130, 2011.

[11] T. Kgil et al. PicoServer: Using 3D Stacking Technology To Enable A Compact Energy Efficient Chip Multiprocessor. *ASPLOS*, 2006.

[12] M. Gokhale, B. Holmes, and K. Iobst. Processing in memory: the terasys massively parallel PIM array. *Computer*, 28(4):23–31, 1995.

[13] T. Kgil and T. Mudge. FlashCache: a NAND Flash memory file cache for low power web servers. *CASES*, 2006.

[14] T. Kgil, D. Roberts, and T. Mudge. Improving nand Flash based disk caches. *ISCA*, 2008.

[15] B. C. Lee, et al. Architecting phase change memory as a scalable dram alternative. *ISCA*, 2009.

[16] D. Lewis and H. Lee. Architectural evaluation of 3D stacked RRAM caches. *IEEE 3D System Integration Conf.*, 2009.

[17] S. Li, et al. McPAT: An integrated power, area and timing modeling framework for multicore and manycore architectures. *MICRO*, 2009.

[18] K. Lim, et al. Understanding and designing new server architectures for emerging warehouse-computing environments. *ISCA*, 2008.

[19] D. Patterson, et al.A case for intelligent RAM. *IEEE Micro*, 1997.

[20] M. K. Qureshi, et al. Enhancing lifetime and security of pcm-based main memory with start-gap wear leveling. *MICRO-42*, 2009.

[21] M. Qureshi, et al. Scalable high performance main memory system using phase-change memory technology. *ISCA*, 2009.

[22] V. Reddi, et al. Web Search Using Small Cores: Quantifying the Price of Efficiency. ISCA, 2010.

[23] E. Riedel, et al. Active disks for large-scale data processing. *IEEE Computer*, vol 34, , 2001.

[24] S. Rivoire, et al. JouleSort: a balanced energy-efficiency benchmark. *SIGMOD*, 2007.

[25] P. Clark, et al. Processing Petabytes per Second with the ATLAS Experiment at the LHC in CERN. *GPU Tech. Conf.*, 2010.

[26] Zichen Xu, et al. Exploring power-performance tradeoffs in database systems. ICDE, 2010.

[27] Fan Yang, et al. Formalizing mapreduce with CSP. ECBS, 2010.

[28] B. Zhai, et al. Energy efficient near-threshold chip multi-processing. *ISLPED*, 2007.

[29] W. Zhang and T. Li. Exploring phase change memory and 3D die-stacking for power/thermal friendly, fast and durable memory architectures. *PACT*, 2009.

[30] P. Zhou, et al. A durable and energy efficient main memory using phase change memory technology. *ISCA*, 2009.

[31] Y. Zhou et al. Large-scale Parallel Collaborative Filtering for the Netflix Prize. *Algo. Aspects in Information and Management*, 2008.

[32] D. Abts et al. Energy proportional datacenter networks. ISCA, 2010.

[33] J. Condit et al, Better I/O through byte-addressable, persistent memory. *SOSP*, 2009.

[34] S. Venkataraman et al. Consistent and Durable Data Structures for Non-Volatile Byte-Addressable Memory. *FAST*, 2011.

[35] J. Coburn et al. NV-Heaps: Making Persistent Objects Fast and Safe with Next-Generation, Non-Volatile Memories. *ASPLOS*, 2011.

[36] D. Stukov, G. Snider, D. Steward, and R. Williams. The missing memristor found. *Nature*, volume 453, pages 80–83, 2008.

Appendix A1: Detailed execution plans and performance/power models

Figure 9 shows the execution plans for our benchmarks: *sort*, *cksum*, *video*, *recom*, and *search*. The horizontal arrows indicate execution time progress, and the dotted vertical lines in each benchmark demarcate the boundary of execution phases. The execution time and power calculation as well as power density and QoS constraints are described in the embedded formulas and equations.

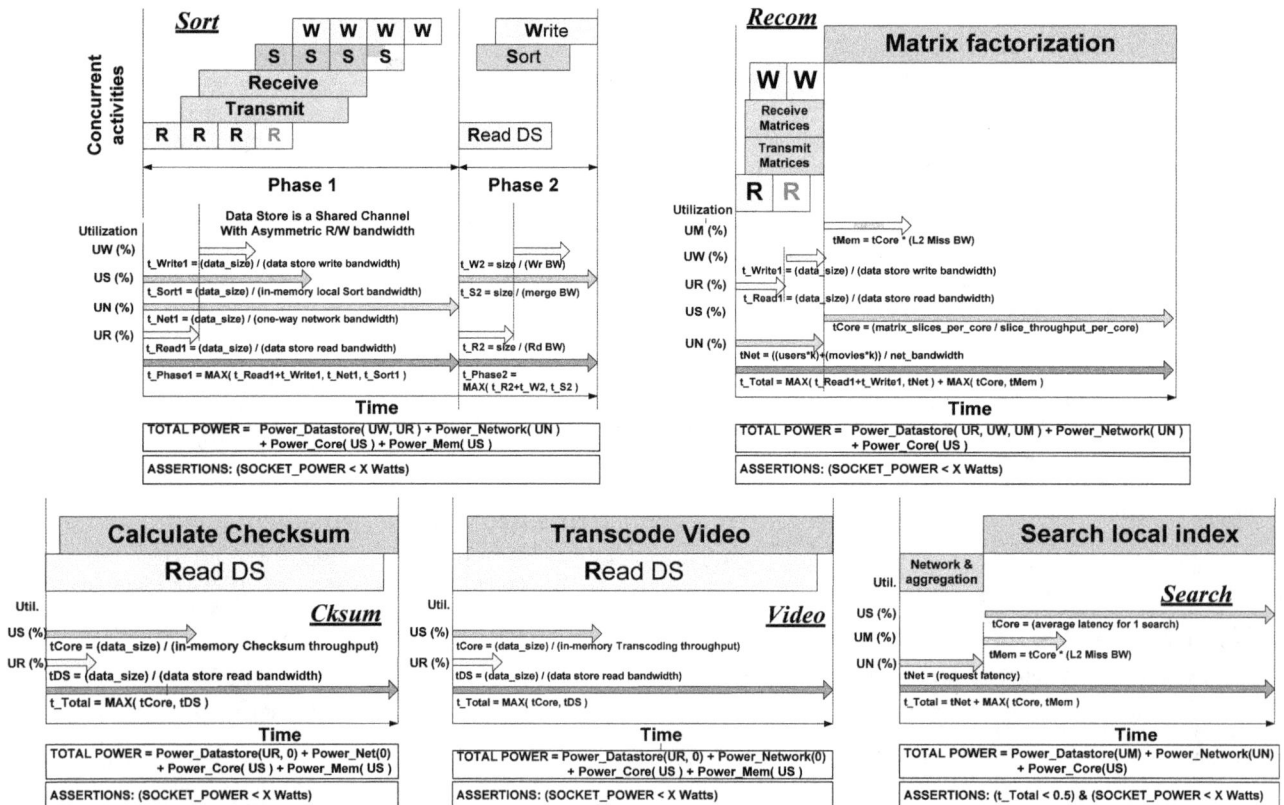

Figure 9: Benchmark execution plans with performance/power models

Mesh Independent Loop Fusion for Unstructured Mesh Applications[*]

Carlo Bertolli
Department of Computing
Imperial College London
c.bertolli@imperial.ac.uk

Adam Betts
Department of Computing
Imperial College London
abetts@imperial.ac.uk

Gihan R. Mudalige
Oxford e-Research Centre
University of Oxford
gihan.mudalige@oerc.ox.ac.uk

Paul H.J. Kelly
Department of Computing
Imperial College London
phjk@imperial.ac.uk

Michael B. Giles
Oxford e-Research Centre
University of Oxford
mike.giles@maths.ox.ac.uk

ABSTRACT

Applications based on unstructured meshes are typically compute intensive, leading to long running times. In principle, state-of-the-art hardware, such as multi-core CPUs and many-core GPUs, could be used for their acceleration but these esoteric architectures require specialised knowledge to achieve optimal performance. OP2 is a parallel programming layer which attempts to ease this programming burden by allowing programmers to express parallel iterations over elements in the unstructured mesh through an API call, a so-called OP2-loop. The OP2 compiler infrastructure then uses source-to-source transformations to realise a parallel implementation of each OP2-loop and discover opportunities for optimisation.

In this paper, we describe how several compiler techniques can be effectively utilised in tandem to increase the performance of unstructured mesh applications. In particular, we show how whole-program analysis — which is often inhibited due to the size of the control flow graph — often becomes feasible as a result of the OP2 programming model, facilitating aggressive optimisation. We subsequently show how whole-program analysis then becomes an enabler to OP2-loop optimisations. Based on this, we show how a classical technique, namely loop fusion, which is typically difficult to apply to unstructured mesh applications, can be defined at compile-time. We examine the limits of its application and show experimental results on a computational fluid dynamic application benchmark, assessing the performance gains due to loop fusion.

[*]This research is partly funded by EPSRC (grant reference numbers EP/I00677X/1, EP/I006079/1), the UK Technology Strategy Board, and Rolls Royce plc through the SILOET programme.

Categories and Subject Descriptors

D.1.3 [**Software**]: Programming Techniques—*Concurrent Programming*

Keywords

Unstructured Mesh Applications, Compilers, Loop fusion, Whole Program Control Flow Analysis

1. INTRODUCTION

An unstructured mesh is an irregular collection of linked vertices, edges, and polygons which provides an effective abstraction within the computational sciences. For example, it can be utilised in the finite volume method that gives approximate solutions to Partial Differential Equations (PDEs). To achieve a reasonable degree of accuracy, however, requires that the unstructured mesh be composed of many millions of elements, leading to a large amount of computation. One such industrial application is HYDRA, which is used by Rolls Royce Plc. in turbomachinery design and is the driving force of our research. In HYDRA the mesh can grow to sizes of over 100 million edges. Furthermore the HYDRA software is extremely complex, with about 1000 separate parallel loops over the mesh. For this reason, HYDRA is currently accelerated with MPI through the OPlus library [6, 5], a predecessor of our research work.

One potential solution to the speedup issue is to utilise multi- and many-core processors, especially because unstructured mesh computations are massively data parallel. However, this assumes that the programmer retains sufficient expertise to program to such a specialised architecture; for example, using the CUDA programming model. A more crucial drawback is that performance portability is greatly inhibited: re-targeting the code base towards different backends requires a fresh implementation, and the idiosyncrasies imposed by particular hardware to achieve optimal performance are unlikely to be satisfied.

A programming layer called OP2 [16, 11, 10] attempts to simultaneously ease the programming burden and performance portability problems. It provides abstractions to declare unstructured meshes in an intuitive manner (i.e., as we show in Section 3, through the sets comprising the mesh) and to express parallel computations on the mesh in terms of iterations over particular sets. A program containing calls to the OP2 API is then compiled using source-to-source transformation tools, before finally being compiled to the target architecture using a vendor-specific compiler. In this way, the source-to-source translator becomes crucial to the optimisation process because it knows which parallel computations are to be performed on the mesh (via calls to the OP2 API) and the architecture of choice.

Using OP2 a single application program (written using the OP2 API) can be transformed to a range of diverse architectures, including multi- and many-core systems. The optimisation challenge is to deliver near optimal performance for each single architecture, and in turn achieve performance portability. For the target applications, loop optimisations are the key to achieve this goal.

This paper investigates the optimisation opportunities applicable to programs written in OP2. With respect to the optimisations, we first show how much of the program can be sliced [18] due to assumptions in the OP2 programming model, thereby making whole-program analysis feasible. Using the whole-program Control Flow Graph (CFG) we then show how to apply loop fusion used to accelerate the parallel loops over the mesh.

The general optimisation problem that we investigate in this paper can be formulated as the compile-time fusion of two loops using non-affine array accesses such as the following ones:

```
! loop over edges
do i = 1, numberOfEdges
 A[n(i,1)] = kernel1 (B[m(i,1), B[m(i,2)], C[i])
enddo

! loop over cells
do j = 1, numberOfCells
 D[j] = kernel2 (B[p(j,1), B[p(j,2)], A[j])
enddo
```

In this example A, B, C, and D are arrays defined for a mesh set, e.g. there is a tuple of elements in the A array for each cell in the mesh. With n, m, and p we denote *mappings* which relate mesh sets between themselves. For instance, n maps an edge identifier to a cell identifier (the second argument of n is used to select one of the cells linked to an edge) and it is used to access A when iterating over edges. Finally, *kernel1* and *kernel2* are user-defined kernel functions, defined for the generic mesh set element (either an edge or a cell).

Obviously, this general loop fusion case cannot be achieved at compile-time. A fundamental piece of information is unknown until run-time, i.e. array accesses derived from the mesh. In this paper we precisely characterise which simpler sub-cases can and cannot be subject to compile time loop fusion. More specifically, the paper concludes that:

- If two loops are iterating over the same iteration space, and one of them is not using indirections (i.e. non-affine array accesses), then compile-time loop fusion is possible. This can be done without the knowledge of the specific details of the meshes on which the program executes, i.e. in a *mesh independent* manner.

- In all other cases, loop fusion can only be performed at run-time, when mesh information (i.e. non-affine accesses) is known. We will address such cases in future work.

The actual application of the first case depends on performance considerations, which are based on: (i) increased data

locality, in case the two loops access same datasets; (ii) to a lower extent, reduced global synchronisations.

The described loop fusion case is a recurring one in large-scale applications. A fundamental trade-off in performance must be studied to understand if loop fusion is actually delivering a performance improvement. In the specific case of OP2 (but equivalent solutions must be applied to any parallel implementation of loops with non-affine array accesses) a loop using indirections is implemented using colouring to control the parallelism. This guarantees that no race conditions can happen during the execution, as two iterations incrementing a common memory location are scheduled serially. Colouring implies that parallelism is reduced from the iteration space size to the average number of iterations of the same colour. In contrast, the implementation of a loop without indirections (henceforth called "direct loop") can use a parallelism degree as high as the size of the iteration set. If two such loops are fused, the resulting fused loop uses indirections, and the implementation is based on colouring. There is hence a decrease in the maximum achievable parallelism degree when comparing the two loops against the single fused one. This must be balanced by the benefits gained in the fusion. In this paper we show that in a two representative examples improvement after loop fusion is obtained.

Another fundamental step to achieve compile-time loop fusion is given by the ability of the compiler to define the relation between two loops, in terms of abstract concepts as iteration spaces, indirections used to access datasets, and type of operations. This is obtained in OP2 through the use of access descriptors, which precisely characterise dependence. Using this abstraction, the compiler is fully capable of deriving if two loops can be fused without further analysis.

We validate our approach by applying loop fusion to a classical computational fluid dynamics application, called *Airfoil*. This is a standard benchmark which we use to characterise the performance of a section of the significantly more complex HYDRA case. Therefore, any performance improvement obtained for the Airfoil application will be directly mapped in specific sections of HYDRA. Our experiments show the performance gains that we obtain on two main-stream architectures including an Nvidia M2050 GPU, and an Intel Xeon X5650 "Nehalem" multicore, with 12 2-way hyperthreaded cores.

The contributions of this paper are:

- We show how program slicing can be defined for OP2 programs, to identify loop optimisation opportunities.

- We show how OP2 access descriptors permit the compiler to analyse if loop fusion can be applied, and what benefits can be obtained.

- We precisely identify in which cases loop fusion can be applied without the knowledge of the mesh, and which other cases require instead that knowledge.

- We characterise experimentally the performance benefits due to loop fusion in two representative examples.

The remainder of the paper is organised as follows: Section 2 places OP2 into context by reviewing related work. Section 3 then presents the OP2 programming layer, outlines the assumptions which are critical to the optimisations proposed, and gives an overview of our compiler infrastructure supporting OP2. Following that, Section 4 formalises the program model utilised by our optimisation framework, and it presents how whole-program analysis and slicing and loop optimisations are applied to the program model. Section 5 focuses on loop fusion, motivating its theoretical performance gain in the OP2 implementation, and describing its feasibility by analysing different loop types. Section 6 evaluates our approach before conclusions are finally drawn in Section 7.

2. RELATED WORK

OP2 is the second iteration of OPlus (Oxford Parallel Library for Unstructured Solvers) [6, 5]. OPlus provided an abstraction framework for performing unstructured mesh based computations across a distributed-memory cluster, using a traditional MPI library approach. It is currently used as the underlying parallelisation library for HYDRA [15, 9] a CFD application used in turbomachinery design at Rolls-Royce plc. OP2 builds upon the features provided by its predecessor but develops an "active" library approach with code generation to exploit parallelism on heterogeneous multicore/many-core architectures.

Although OPlus pre-dates it, both OPlus and OP2 can be viewed as an instantiation of the AEcute (access-execute descriptor) [13] programming model that separates the specification of a computational kernel with its parallel iteration space, from a declarative specification of how each iteration accesses its data. The decoupled Access/Execute specification in turn creates the opportunity to apply powerful optimisations targeting the underlying hardware.

A number of related research projects have implemented similar programming frameworks. The most comparable of these is LISZT [7], which is a domain-specific language based on the SCALA language targeting unstructured mesh applications. Unlike OP2, LISZT attempts to synthesise dependence information from the program, by exposing programmers a stricter programming model. Another notable framework is described in [14], which shares with OP2 the library approach but it is based on a C++ framework.

3. THE OP2 MODEL OF COMPUTATION

From the programmer's point of view, OP2 is an Application Programming Interface (API) enabling the following to be declared:

1. The sets constituting the topology of the mesh. These normally include its vertices, edges, and polygons, but might incorporate various subsets, such as boundary edges.

2. How distinct sets relate to each other via mapping functions. A typical example is the mapping from an edge to the two vertices to which it is incident.

3. The data associated with elements in the sets, e.g. vertex co-ordinates or edge weights.

4. How a specified function can be applied *in parallel* to every element of a particular set.

We demonstrate OP2 through the C++ code shown in Listing 3[1], which will serve as a running example throughout the paper. In this example, we omit the user kernel code, and we focus on the OP2 details useful to show loop fusion feasibility in the next sections. The sample application is Airfoil, a non-linear 2D inviscid airfoil code that uses an unstructured mesh. It is a very simple application, but acts as a forerunner for testing the OP2 library in our compiler framework due to its strong similarities to HYDRA, the CFD application used at Rolls Royce plc. for the simulation of jet engines.

At the top of Listing 3 is one of the user-supplied kernels, `save_soln`, contained in the Airfoil application. It has two formal parameters, namely `p_q` and `p_qold`, which are both arrays of double precision floating-point values. In the function `main`, three sets are defined (`cells`, `edges`, and `bedges`) such that their cardinalities are set to 2, 100, and 10, respectively. Next, data contained in the local variable declarations `q` and `qold` are associated with the set `cells` through `op_decl_dat`, which specifies that there is a vector of four elements associated to each set element. That is, the first element of `cells` has initial values 1.0, 2.0, 3.0, 4.0, while the second element has initial values 5.0, 6.0, 7.0, 8.0. The declaration of an `op_map` is used to define a mapping between two sets. For instance, `pcell` is declared as a mapping between cells and nodes, identifying which nodes (i.e. their identifiers) are at the border of each cell, and thus also how cells are connected between themselves through nodes. This mapping information is obtained from an input array passed to the related declaration call, and it defines the topology of the unstructured mesh. The use of indirect dataset addressing also classifies these applications as *irregular*.

We need to clarify at this point the difference between a loop arising from a programming-language construct, e.g. due to *for* statements, and a loop arising from the OP2 programming layer. We shall refer to the former as a loop and the latter as an OP2-loop.

The remainder of the code contains a doubly-nested loop with OP2-loops (`op_par_loop`) that specify parallel iteration over the declared sets. For example, the first call to `op_par_loop` states that the `save_soln` function is to be applied to each element of the set `cells`. The next six actual arguments in the `op_par_loop` call indicate the OP2 data expected by the kernel function and provide information pertaining to their access. These are the so-called *access descriptors*.

Since `save_soln` has two formal parameters, two OP2 data types, `p_q` and `p_qold`, are supplied. This means that there are three actual arguments in the OP2-loop per kernel formal parameter, which we refer to as an OP2 argument group. The first OP2 argument group (`p_q`, `-1`, `OP_ID`, `OP_READ`) states that the OP2 data type `p_q` is *directly* accessed and is read within the kernel function. Direct access is expressed by `OP_ID` and arises from the fact that the sets over which `save_soln` iterates, and to which `p_q` is associated, are cells; in other words, no mapping is required. In this case, we say that the OP2-loop is *direct*, whereas an OP2-loop containing mappings is *indirect*. The final argument in this grouping, `OP_READ`, signifies read access and arises from the fact that `p_q` in `save_soln` is an r-value. The second OP2 argument group (`p_qold`, `-1`, `OP_ID`, `OP_WRITE`) expresses similar semantics, except `p_qold` is written, i.e. `p_qold` is an l-value in `save_soln`. Note, therefore, how the access patterns of an OP2-loop are explicitly expressed, thereby

---

[1]Unnecessary OP2 declarations are omitted in the code to make reading easier and confined to essential information.

```
int main (void) {
  // Declare sets
  op_set cells  = op_decl_set (2);
  op_set edges  = op_decl_set (100);
  op_set bedges = op_decl_set (10);
  op_set nodes  = op_decl_set (100);

  //Declare maps
  op_map pcell = op_decl_map (cells, nodes, 4,
      map_arr);

  // Declare data
  double * q = {1.0, 2.0, 3.0, 4.0,
                5.0, 6.0, 7.0, 8.0};
  op_dat p_q = op_decl_dat (cells, 4, q);

  double * qold = {10.0, 20.0, 30.0, 40.0,
                   50.0, 60.0, 70.0, 80.0};
  op_dat p_qold = op_decl_dat (cells, 4, qold);

  double *x = {..}
  op_dat p_x = op_decl_dat (nodes, 2, x);

  // ...other declarations...

  for (int i = 0; i < 1000; ++i) {

    op_par_loop(save_soln, cells,
        op_arg_dat(p_q,    -1, OP_ID, OP_READ),
        op_arg_dat(p_qold, -1, OP_ID, OP_WRITE));

    for (int j = 0; j < 2; ++j) {
        op_par_loop(adt_calc, cells,
            op_arg_dat(p_x,   0,pcell, OP_READ),
            op_arg_dat(p_x,   1,pcell, OP_READ),
            op_arg_dat(p_x,   2,pcell, OP_READ),
            op_arg_dat(p_x,   3,pcell, OP_READ),
            op_arg_dat(p_q,  -1,OP_ID, OP_READ),
            op_arg_dat(p_adt,-1,OP_ID,OP_WRITE));

        op_par_loop(res_calc, edges,
            op_arg_dat(p_x,   0,pedge, OP_READ),
            op_arg_dat(p_x,   1,pedge, OP_READ),
            op_arg_dat(p_q,   0,pecell,OP_READ),
            op_arg_dat(p_q,   1,pecell,OP_READ),
            op_arg_dat(p_adt, 0,pecell,OP_READ),
            op_arg_dat(p_adt, 1,pecell,OP_READ),
            op_arg_dat(p_res, 0,pecell, OP_INC),
            op_arg_dat(p_res, 1,pecell, OP_INC));

        op_par_loop(bres_calc, bedges,
            op_arg_dat(p_x,    0,pbedge, OP_READ),
            op_arg_dat(p_x,    1,pbedge, OP_READ),
            op_arg_dat(p_q,    0,pbecell,OP_READ),
            op_arg_dat(p_adt,  0,pbecell,OP_READ),
            op_arg_dat(p_res,  0,pbecell, OP_INC),
            op_arg_dat(p_bound,-1,OP_ID,  OP_READ));

        rms = 0.0;

        op_par_loop(update, cells,
            op_arg_dat(p_qold,-1,OP_ID,  OP_READ),
            op_arg_dat(p_q,   -1,OP_ID,OP_WRITE),
            op_arg_dat(p_res, -1,OP_ID,  OP_RW),
            op_arg_dat(p_adt, -1,OP_ID,  OP_READ),
            op_arg_gbl(&rms, OP_INC));} \\inner loop
  } \\outer loop
  return 0;
}
```

Figure 1: Airfoil application implemented in OP2.

allowing the OP2 compiler to precisely characterise the dependencies between OP2-loops without complex data-flow analyses.

The second OP2-loop iterates over cells and it includes as first parameter an indirectly accessed op_dat. The related argument line indicates that: the op_dat p_x is accessed; as p_x is associated with the node set, the mapping (pcell) is used to translates a cell identifier (i.e. an iteration index) to one of the 4 corresponding node identifiers. The second argument of the op_arg function is used to specify which one of the four nodes connected to the current cell (on which the user kernel is applied at each loop iteration) is to be consider as actual parameter. In this loop we pass all four nodes information related to each cell to the kernel. As this adt_calc loop includes one or more indirectly accessed op_dat arguments, it is then classified as *indirect*.

Finally, consider the res_calc OP2-loop, which iterates over edges, and accesses the p_res dataset through an indirection (from edges to cells) by incrementing it (OP_INC). This means that two iterations of the same loop can in principle increment the same data at the same time (i.e. in parallel, as required by OP2-loop semantics). To solve this parallelism control issue, OP2 takes different strategies, each optimised for a different target architecture. For the sake of loop fusion discussed in this paper, we only consider the case of GPUs and multicores. For these architectures a colouring technique is used, where different colours are assigned to possible conflicting iterations, and then execution parallelises iterations with the same colour, but it sequentialises those with different colours. This — OP_INC over indirect argument — is the only way in which the user can rely on OP2 to avoid potential race conditions. If the user declares a OP_WRITE access to an indirect argument, then it is the user's task to guarantee that no two iterations can modify the same data, through a proper selection of the mapping data.

3.1 OP2 Assumptions

OP2 makes several important assumptions:

- For any indirect OP2-loop, there is only one level of indirection in retrieving the data.

- The order in which elements of a set are processed *in an OP2-loop* does not affect the final result, thereby providing the compiler and run-time support great flexibility in ordering the computations.

- How the data are accessed in OP2-loops is correctly given by the programmer.

- The data associated with sets are not written outside of the parallel iteration space, that is, in the sequential parts of code. In essence, once the data pass into OP2 territory, further modifications to the data can only occur opaquely through the OP2 API. As we observe in Section 5, this property facilitates aggressive program slicing and whole-program analysis.

3.2 OP2 Compiler Infrastructure

Producing a binary for a specific hardware from an OP2 program requires several compilation steps. The first of these utilises source-to-source transformation to transpose the OP2-loops into a parallel implementation compliant with the architecture of choice, e.g. CUDA. The second step then simply compiles the generated code using a vendor-specific compiler.

In order to realise the source-to-source translation, our OP2 compiler, illustrated in Figure 2, performs the following steps:

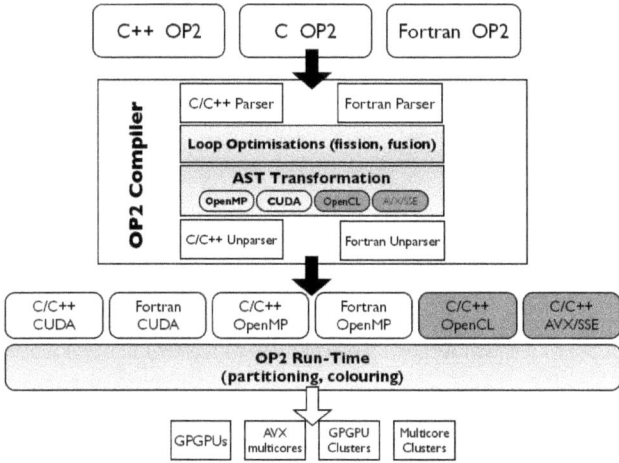

Figure 2: Overview of OP2 Compiler Framework.

- Parses the source code, using the parsers provided by ROSE [1], to obtain the Abstract Syntax Tree (AST) that forms the basis of all subsequent analyses. Currently we support Fortran 77-2003 and C/C++.

- Optimisations of OP2-loops using the AST and the techniques outlined in Section 5.

- Re-writing of the AST to generate functions implementing the parallel computation and replacing calls to OP2-loops with calls to the generated functions. For instance, if CUDA is the target programming model, this step involves generation of the host stub and the CUDA kernel functions. Each OP2-loop call is subsequently replaced by a call to the appropriate host stub.

- Re-writing of the kernel functions supplied by the user. In the case of CUDA, for example, this is needed to label the kernel as a device subroutine.

- Unparsing of the AST to output the generated code using the ROSE unparsers.

Our compiler currently supports generation of CUDA and OpenMP for both Fortran and C/C++, while OpenCL and SSE/AVX backends are in development for C/C++.

Note that the final step in Figure 2 includes linking the generated code against an OP2 library; this provides run-time support to partition the iteration sets (to parallelise) and to colour partitions (to avoid race conditions). Both Fortran and C/C++ generated programs utilise the same implementation of the colouring and partitioning algorithms, which are written in C. As shown in [3], this incurs a small ($\sim$5%)) performance cost for Fortran generated programs due to interoperating with C.

4. PROGRAM MODEL AND SLICING

The previous section gave an overview of OP2 from the programmatic point of view. Here we formalise the model extracted from the analysis stage of our compiler, which serves as the basis of the optimisation process.

An OP2 program consists of several subprograms each of which is characterised by its CFG:

DEFINITION 1. *The CFG $C = \langle V_C, E_C, \mathsf{s}, \mathsf{t} \rangle$ of a subprogram is a directed graph such that:*

- *V_C are vertices representing basic blocks, which are maximal sequences of statements, such that there is only one entry point and a single exit point.*

- *$\mathsf{s}, \mathsf{t} \in V_C$ are distinguished (dummy) vertices, respectively, such that s has no predecessors (the entry vertex) and t has no successors (the exit vertex).*

- *E_C models the branches and fall-throughs between basic blocks. Or, every entry point to the function has s as a predecessor and every exit point of the function has t as a successor.*

This paper assumes that the CFGs are constructed from the AST after parsing of the source code during the compilation process. For this reason, OP2 parallel loop calls merely appear as unique basic blocks in the CFG.

The CFG of the OP2 program appearing in Figure 3 is provided to the left of Figure 3. The outer loop with a bound of 1000 is represented by vertex L_1 and exits to vertex E_1, its outer scope. Similarly, the inner loop with bound 2 is represented by vertex L_2 and exits to vertex E_2.

The optimisations proposed in this paper assume that *natural loops* in a CFG can be identified, which are loops with a single entry point, called the header. Transitions from within a loop to the header are called *loop-back edges*. The nesting relationship between loops can then be represented hierarchically through a Loop-Nesting Tree (LNT):

DEFINITION 2. *For a CFG $C = \langle V_C, E_C \cup \{\mathsf{t} \rightarrow \mathsf{s}\}, \mathsf{s}, \mathsf{t} \rangle$, its LNT $T_L^C = \langle V_{T_L^C} = V_C, \mathcal{H}, E_{T_L^C}, r \rangle$ is a tree with the following properties[2]:*

- *$\mathcal{H} \subseteq V_C$ is the set of internal vertices representing the headers identified in C.*

- *$V_C \setminus \mathcal{H}$ is the set of leaves.*

- *$E_{T_L^C} = \{(header(v), v) | header(v) \in \mathcal{H}, v \in V_C \setminus \mathcal{H}\}$ where $header(v)$ is the representative header of the innermost enclosing loop in which v is contained.*

For example, in the CFG of Figure 3, there are two loop-back edges, `update` $\rightarrow L_2$ and $E_2 \rightarrow L_1$. The LNT is depicted to the right in Figure 3 where internal vertices L_1 and L_2 represent the respective loops. This figure also shows that: L_2 is nested in L_1; the innermost enclosing loop of `save_soln` is L_1; the innermost enclosing loop of `adt_calc`, `res_calc`, `bres_calc`, `update` is L_2.

The final program model that our optimisation framework needs is the call graph, which represents inter-procedural relations between subprograms is needed:

DEFINITION 3. *A call graph $\mathcal{C} = \langle V_C, E_C, \mathcal{B}, \omega \rangle$ of a program is a digraph in which:*

- *V_C is the set of vertices representing subprograms.*

---

[2]We explicitly add the edge $\mathsf{t} \rightarrow \mathsf{s}$ to the CFG C to ensure that it becomes strongly connected. Therefore, all vertices in C are enclosed in a loop and the nesting relationship between loops can be captured in a tree as opposed to a disjoint union of trees, i.e. a forest.

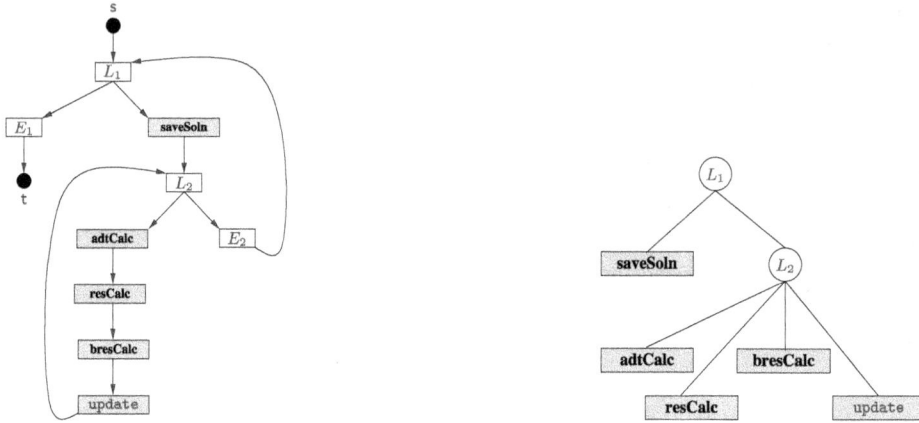

Figure 3: Example CFG and LNT.

- E_C *is the set of edges representing the calling relation between subprograms. In particular, for any $(u, v) \in E_C$, subprogram u calls subprogram v.*

- $\mathcal{B}$ *is the set of basic blocks in the program that transfer control flow to a different subprogram, i.e. the call sites.*

- $\omega : E_C \mapsto (2^{\mathcal{B}} \setminus \emptyset)$ *is a function mapping a call to the call sites leading to that call.*

In this paper, we assume that all indirect function call destinations have been resolved and that there is no recursion so that the call graph is acyclic.

4.1 Slicing to Enable Whole-Program Analysis

Whole-program analysis is a technique that provides visibility to the *entire* CFG of the program. It is particularly desirable because it opens up optimisation opportunities not available to the typical module-wide analyses of modern compilers. However, the size of a whole-program CFG grows exponentially due to the need to duplicate CFG from callees into callers at every call site; that is, for a callee CFG $C = \langle V_C, E_C, \mathsf{s}, \mathsf{t} \rangle$, each inline increases the size of the caller CFG C' by $(|V_C| + |E_C|)^n$, where n is the number of of calls from C' to C.

In practice, the number of vertices and edges inlined can be eased considerably by *slicing* away portions of CFGs which do not apply to the analysis. This is particularly relevant to OP2 as it presumes that the data it effectively owns are not modified in the sequential parts of the code (see Section 3). For this reason, aggressive program slicing can be applied and whole-program analysis enabled. In HYDRA, for instance, there are a mere 700 OP2-loops, vastly reducing the complexity of the whole-program CFG.

The slice of interest in our case is the OP2-loops and the decisions on which their execution is dependent. The latter parts are needed to maintain the basic shape of control flow, such as loops in which OP2-loops are contained or the conditional controlling entry into a specific OP2-loop. This is needed in the subsequent optimisation phase to reason about which loops can safely be fused or split, without changing the semantics of the code.

BUILD-OP2-CFG($\mathcal{C}, C_1, \ldots, C_{|V_C|}$)
1 **foreach** $v \in V_C$ in reverse post-order **do**
2   Compute the control-dependence graph of CFG C_v
3   Slice C_v with respect to the OP2-loops
4   **foreach** $s \in succ(v)$ **do**
5   **foreach** $c \in \omega(v, s)$ **do**
6   Inline C_s into C_v at c

Figure 4: Algorithm to construct the whole-program CFG.

Figure 4 gives the algorithm to produce the whole-program CFG given the call graph $\mathcal{C}$ and the CFGs $C_1, \ldots C_{|V_C|}$) of the program. It moves up the call graph in a bottom-up fashion (Lines 1- 6). For each vertex in the call graph v, we compute the control-dependence relation of its CFG C_v (Line 2), for which there are known algorithms [4]. This allows us to slice the program accordingly with respect to the OP2-loops (Line 3). Every callee s of v is then analysed (Line 4), and at each call site c leading to a call of s (Line 5), we inline the CFG C_s (Line 6).

4.2 Loop unrolling

The biggest hurdle in fusing loops is discovering opportunities in the code, as a user typically writes OP2-loops in an optimised way; that is, a programmer usually spots when two sequentially-composed OP2-loops can be merged as they iterate over the same set. For instance, the code in Listing 3 does not contain any obvious fusion opportunities.

OP2-loop fusion is enabled inside our compiler by unrolling specific loops. In particular, we ignore loops with early exits, as these complicate the unrolling process due to code duplication, and those for which the bound cannot be determined at compile time, since it is impossible to determine the unroll factor. Note that there are known techniques to determine the upper bounds of loops [2, 12, 8]. Armed with this information, the LNT of the whole-program CFG is then traversed in a bottom-up fashion and, as each loop is analysed, we attempt to fully unroll the body of the loop.

We then search in the body of the unrolled loop for maximal sequences of basic blocks that contain OP2-loops over the same set, and fuse depending on the chosen backend ar-

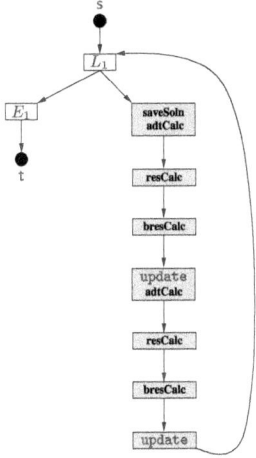

Figure 5: The CFG of Figure 3 after Unrolling and Fusion Transformations.

chitecture. For example, it is not always beneficial to fuse in the case of CUDA, because each thread can only assume the availability of a limited number of registers, otherwise spillage into the L1 cache occurs. Observe that, when complete unrolling becomes too costly due to a large loop bound, we instead limit the unroll factor to a small positive number.

Let us re-consider the (whole-program) CFG and its LNT in Figure 3. Using our technique, loop L_2 is the first encountered during the bottom-up traversal of the LNT; its body is then completely unrolled because its bound is two. This immediately exposes two obvious OP2-loop fusion opportunities which are not feasible without unrolling: `save_soln` and `adt_calc` because they both iterate over the set `cells` (see Listing 3); similarly, `update` and `adt_calc`. The CFG with L_2 unrolled and the OP2-loops fused is presented in Figure 5. Note that completely unrolling loop L_1 is too costly as its upper bound is one thousand; however, unrolling it once would expose another opportunity since, in the CFG of Figure 5, `update` is the last OP2-loop executed, while the fused OP2-loop `save_soln/adt_calc` is the first OP2-loop executed, and both iterate over `cells`.

5. OP2-LOOP FUSION

The program analysis presented in the previous section enables us to spot loop optimisation opportunities, specifically related to OP2-loops fusion. In this section we discuss the benefits deriving from applying loop fusion in the case of the GPU compiler back-end, and the restrictions that we have so far discovered to its application in our programming model. For brevity, we omit a full discussion related to the OpenMP back-end of our compiler. However, the same implementation scheme, based on a so-called *scratchpad* memory (see below), is used also on multicores, to minimise cache misses. Loop fusion is thus valid also in this case.

5.1 Motivation

The CUDA implementation of an OP2-loop proceeds in the following manner. First, data declared by the user to be owned by OP2 (through `op_decl_dat`) is transferred at elaboration time into global device memory through the OP2 run-time support. Second, when control reaches an OP2-loop in the program (generated by our OP2 compiler), a

host stub is called. In the host stub, the grid dimensions, the thread-block dimensions, and the size of dynamically allocated shared memory are set for the CUDA kernel launch. Third, the CUDA kernel is called, which itself consists of three principal steps. In this implementation, the mesh is partitioned and an instance of CUDA kernel is applied to each partition. The kernel steps are:

1. Data needed by the user-supplied kernel is staged in from global device memory into shared memory. In doing so, the compiler coalesces in shared memory the data scattered in device memory, this last being a typical feature of unstructured mesh applications. This means that the shared memory implements a scratchpad memory for the partition execution.

2. The user-supplied kernel is called with the data resident in shared memory.

3. Data is staged out back to global device memory. Evidently, this allows subsequent calls to the OP2-loop to observe changes to the data.

Staging data in and out of the global device memory is a costly activity. In the general case these costs cannot be avoided, since there can be arbitrary control flow between different invocations of an OP2-loop. However, when there are at least two sequentially-composed OP2-loops iterating over the same set which share some data, the overhead can be reduced through loop fusion, potentially leading to significant performance benefits. In addition, the current OP2 CUDA and OpenMP implementation requires a full thread synchronisation between loops (i.e. OP2-loops). Such a synchronisation can be avoided when loop fusion is applied.

Fusing OP2-loops is generally more straightforward than fusing (ordinary) loops since the dependencies between data are explicitly represented in the OP2 programming layer by means of access descriptors. The fusion element, therefore, equates to concatenating several user-supplied kernel function bodies and unioning their formal parameters to create a single, monolithic function. Later we show an example to clarify the fusion process.

5.2 Feasibility of Loop Fusion in OP2

Loop fusion is a well-known technique always applied by optimising compilers to regular applications. However, for irregular applications, using indirect data accesses instantiated at run-time as it is the case of unstructured meshes, this technique is difficult to apply automatically. In this paper we consider *syntactic* loop fusion, where the compiler is able to transform the input program fusing loops. This is possible only in some simple albeit effective cases, as we show in the experiments section, thanks to the use of OP2 access descriptors. In fact, these permit us to analyse straightforwardly dependencies between successive OP2-loops, and to automatically decide if loop fusion is feasible and possibly efficient.

Let's consider that our whole program analysis has spotted that two successive loops can be potentially fused. A first analysis for loop fusion feasibility considers the iteration sets of each loop:

- If the two loops iterate over different sets, we do not apply loop fusion. This is mainly due to the impossibility of easily relating iterations defined over two different spaces.

- If the two loops iterate over the same sets, then loop fusion might be applied, depending on the analysis of the access descriptors.

We further analyse the second case, when the two OP2-loops iterate over the same set. A further loop fusion feasibility classification can be done by considering if two OP2-loops use indirect datasets accesses (i.e. op_maps):

- If the two OP2-loops are direct (no indirect accesses) then loop fusion is feasible. As there are no indirect accesses, an iteration i of the second loop can only depends on the values produced by the same iteration i of the previous loop. The resulting fused loop applies, for each iteration, successively the first and second loops' kernels.

- Consider the case in which the two OP2-loops are indirect. If these have a read-after-write dependency (the first loop using OP_INC) on a dataset indirectly accesses, then it is possible than iteration i from the second loop can depend on two iterations (e.g. j and k) of the first loop. As a consequence, no simple scheduling without the knowledge of the precise iteration set sizes and mapping information can be applied at compile-time, hence no loop fusion can be defined at compile-time. If no data sharing is present, then there is no actual performance gain (see below) derives from loop fusion, even if it is feasible.

- Finally, consider the cases when a direct OP2-loop is followed by an indirect loop, or viceversa. The condition of the previous case cannot hold, as the direct loops cannot access datasets indirectly, and as a consequence a one-to-one dependency between loop iterations is defined. Notice that data sharing can only happen through directly accessed datasets. Loop fusion is hence feasible for these cases, and the resulting single fused loop will have indirect datasets accesses (i.e. it is an indirect loop).

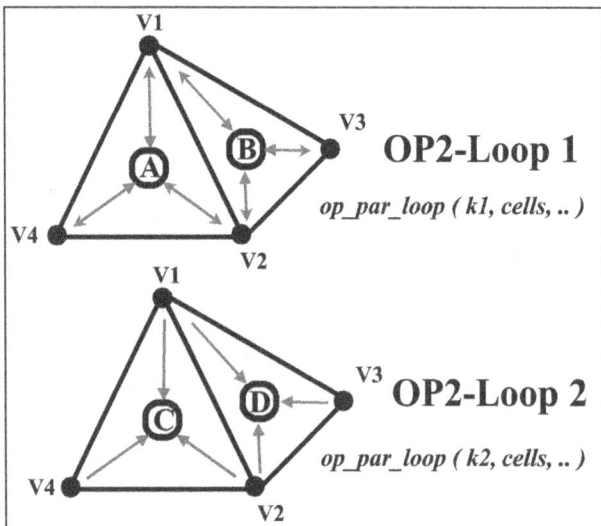

Figure 6: Example of infeasibility of loop fusion, when two indirect loops, iterating over cells, access the same dataset defined over nodes using some mapping.

Figure 6 show a visual representation of the second case. Two successive OP2-loops iterate over cells, the first incrementing data associated to nodes, and the second reading it. In the figure, we show the details of two iterations (i.e. two cells) for each loop. The shared data on nodes is related to nodes **V1** and **V2**. As iteration **A** and **B** modify these nodes, then both iterations **C** and **D** depends on them, i.e. on the results that they produce. Therefore, no loop fusion of iterations can be performed without the knowledge of which nodes connect which cells (i.e. the mesh).

The first case (two direct loops) always delivers a performance improvement if there is data sharing between the loops and the scratchpad memory is efficiently used. The efficiency of the third case depends on the trade-off between the improved data sharing between the loops, and the reduced parallelism degree achievable for the direct loop involved, as the fused loop will be an indirect one, inevitably using parallelism control techniques (e.g. colouring in the considered architectures).

By applying this analysis to the Airfoil application with the inner loop unrolled (see Section 4), we are able to apply loop fusion to the following OP2-loop pairs: save_soln and adt_calc; update and adt_calc. These pairs both iterate over cells, and they include a direct and indirect loop (third case described above).

When loop fusion cannot be defined at compile-time, in a syntactic manner, then run-time loop fusion can be pursued, by properly synthesising fusing code in the compiler. A support for run-time loop fusion can be based on the building of a task graph of the iterations of the two loops, where dependencies between iterations are derived from OP2 maps. This kind of technique can be expressed by using similar frameworks enabling the application of other techniques, like those underlying sparse tiling, as described in [17]. In future work we will introduce this modelling framework in our compiler to achieve run-time loop fusion.

6. EVALUATION

To evaluate the effectiveness of loop fusion we applied it "manually" to the unrolled version of the Airfoil program. We generated three versions of the Airfoil:

- The original version, denoted as *original*, as presented in the previous sections.

- A version with a single loop fusion of the save_soln and adt_calc loops, denoted with *single fusion*. This version is achieved by un-rolling the inner loop, as showed in Section 4.

- A version extending the previous one with a further fusion of the update and adt_calc, again feasible due to the loop unrolling of the inner loop. This version is called *double fusion*.

We then translated the related Airfoil program into CUDA and OpenMP using our OP2 compiler, and executed them respectively on an Nvidia M2050 GPU, and on a multicore node supporting two Intel Xeon X5650 "Nehalem" processors, each including 6 2-way hyperthreaded cores. Configuration parameters for the CUDA architecture are the size of the unstructured mesh partition, which has a direct impact on the size of shared memory/cache needed for the execution of each partition, and the number of threads in a block (called *block size*), executing in parallel the iterations in a same partition (see [3] for implementation details). For the multicore architecture we have again the partition size as a parameter, and the number of threads used in the execution of the OP2-loops, which we instantiate to 4, 8, 12 and 16. Notice that the last value is larger than the actual maximum parallelism degree supported by the multicore. This last cases does not map each thread to a physical core, but the hyperthreading support is used.

The following experiments are related to an Airfoil program using double precision floating point values as datasets, applied to an unstructured mesh including approximately 1.5 million edges, and 700 hundreds thousands nodes and cells. The actual working version of the Airfoil used in these experiments is written in Fortran. It is compiled by our OP2 compiler to the Nvidia GPU, and then compiled again to its executable form using both the PGI CUDA Fortran compiler and the Nvidia CUDA compiler (nvcc). Options passed to this last compilation step are "-fast -O2". For the multicore implementation, we used the Intel Fortran and C compiler, using the following options: "-O3 -parallel"

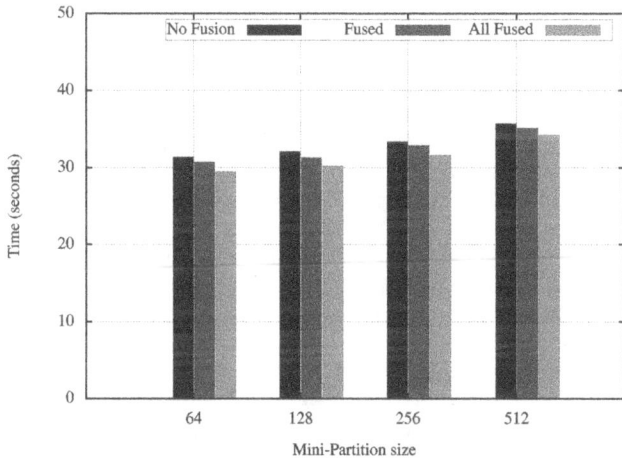

Figure 7: **Results of three Airfoil versions in comparison. For each group, the original version has the leftmost darker line; the single fusion one the medium dark middle line; the double fusion version the rightmost lighter line. On the X-axis the partition size is displayed, and on the Y-axis the total execution time.**

Figure 7 shows the results of the execution of respectively the *original* (darker line), *single fusion* (medium dark line), and *double fusion* (lighter line) versions on the GPU. The figures have on the X-axis the partition size, which in these experiments is equal to the CUDA thread block size. In the Y-axis the execution times in seconds is shown, while different bands for the same X-axis value denote the three different versions of the airfoil. Results indicate that the incremental loop fusion application delivers increasing performance, i.e. smaller execution times, for the three different configurations. In particular, the best configuration (i.e. partition size equal to 64) results in a 6.124% improvement for the double fusion version and 2.19% for the single fusion one.

This performance gain is small compared to the total execution time. This is mainly due to the fact that a loop that is not subject to optimisation, i.e. the `res_calc` loop,

is the most expensive one in this program. Loop optimisations applied to other more lightweight kernels affect only slightly the total performance. However, this result also means that loop fusion delivers a performance improvement even on lightweight OP2-loops.

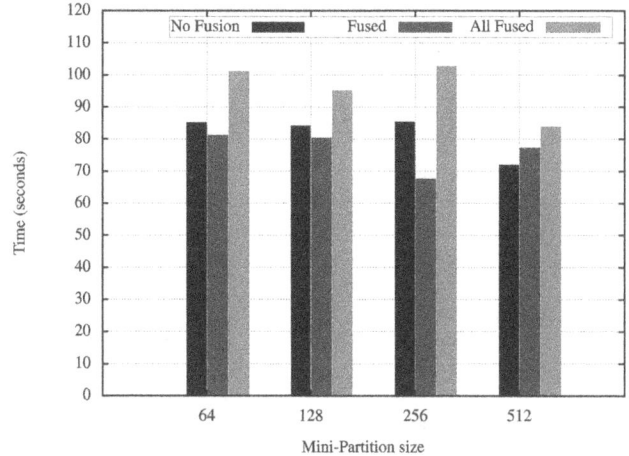

Figure 8: **Results of three Airfoil versions in comparison for 12 OpenMP threads. For each group, the original version has the leftmost darker line; the single fusion one the medium dark middle line; the double fusion version the rightmost lighter line. On the X-axis the partition size is displayed, and on the Y-axis the total execution time**

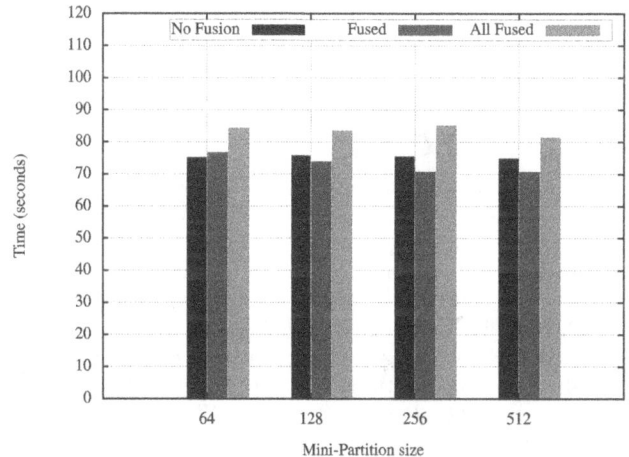

Figure 9: **Results of three Airfoil versions in comparison for 16 OpenMP threads. For each group, the original version has the leftmost darker line; the single fusion one the medium dark middle line; the double fusion version the rightmost lighter line. On the X-axis the partition size is displayed, and on the Y-axis the total execution time**

Figure 8 and 9 show the results of the experiments on the multicore processor for 12 and 16 OpenMP threads. Again, the X-axis models increasing partition sizes and the Y-axis the execution time in seconds. In this paper we only report results for parallelism degrees giving the best performance. The different columns for the same X-axis value are related to one of the three versions of the Airfoil application, as for CUDA experiments.

In general, it can be noticed that a performance improvement is obtained by the single fusion version, with a peak performance improvement of 20.76%. However, the double fusion version is showing generally worse performance. This is mainly given by a cache pollution effect: as in this case the shared op_dat between the two second fused loops is not staged into cache, then fusion benefits are only based on the ability of increasing data locality, against the cache pollution effects.

7. CONCLUSION

OP2 is a programming library which enables parallel iteration over elements of unstructured meshes to be expressed without being tied to a particular implementation. This paper proposes using whole-program analysis to optimise these applications, which is made feasible by aggressively slicing the sequential parts of the code. The whole-program control flow graph then enables loops in the OP2 layer to be fused or split according to the best choice for a particular architecture.

Since a programmer typically writes OP2-loops in an optimal way w.r.t. sequential composition, we showed how loop unrolling can increase the opportunities for fusion. To assess the benefits and practicality of these optimisations, we analysed the Airfoil application, a representative program heavily used in the computational fluid dynamics domain. Our results showed a small performance improvement for GPUs, and a greater one for multicore, due to a better use of respectively shared and cache memory. This suggests us that loop fusion represents generally a performance improvement. Extensive studies of more complex forms of run-time loop fusion to cover the unfeasible cases showed in this paper will deliver additional and higher optimisations to unstructured mesh applications.

8. REFERENCES

[1] The ROSE compiler. http://wwww.rosecompiler.org/.

[2] M. Bartlett, I. Bate, and D. Kazakov. Guaranteed loop bound identification from program traces for wcet. In *Proceedings of the 15th Real-Time Technology and Applications Symposium (RTAS'09)*, April 2009.

[3] C. Bertolli, A. Betts, G. Mudalige, M. B. Giles, and P. H.J. Kelly. Design and performance of the OP2 library for unstructured mesh applications. In *Euro-Par 2001 Parallel Processing Workshops*, LNCS. Springer, 2011.

[4] G. Bilardi and K. Pingali. A framework for generalized control dependence. *SIGPLAN Not.*, 31, May 1996.

[5] D.A. Burgess, P.I. Crumpton, and M.B. Giles. A parallel framework for unstructured grid solvers. In K.M. Decker and R.M. Rehmann, editors, *Programming Environments for Massively Parallel Distributed Systems*, pages 97–106, 1994.

[6] P.I. Crumpton and M.B. Giles. *Parallel Computational Fluid Dynamics: Implementations and Results Using Parallel Computers*, chapter Multigrid aircraft computations using the OPlus parallel library, pages 339–346. 1996.

[7] Z. DeVito, N. Joubert, F. Palacios, S. Oakley, M. Medina, M. Barrientos, E. Elsen, F. Ham, A. Aiken, K. Duraisamy, E. Darve, J. Alonso, and P. Hanrahan. Liszt: a domain specific language for building portable mesh-based pde solvers. In *Proceedings of 2011 International Conference for High Performance Computing, Networking, Storage and Analysis*, SC '11, pages 9:1–9:12, New York, NY, USA, 2011. ACM.

[8] A. Ermedahl, C. Sandberg, J. Gustafsson, S. Bygde, and B. Lisper. Loop bound analysis based on a combination of program slicing, abstract interpretation, and invariant analysis. In *Proceedings of the 7th Int'l. Workshop on Worst Case Execution Time (WCET) Analysis*, July 2007.

[9] M. B. Giles, M. C. Duta, J. D. Muller, and N. A. Pierce. Algorithm developments for discrete adjoint methods. *AIAA Journal*, 42(2):198–205, 2003.

[10] M.B. Giles, G.R. Mudalige, Z. Sharif, G. Markall, and P. H.J. Kelly. Performance analysis and optimisation of the OP2 framework on many-core architectures. *The Computer Journal*, 2011.

[11] M.B. Giles, G.R. Mudalige, Z. Sharif, G. Markall, and P. H.J. Kelly. Performance analysis of the OP2 framework on many-core architectures. *SIGMETRICS Perform. Eval. Rev.*, 38(4):9–15, March 2011.

[12] C. A. Healy, M. Sjödin, V. Rustagi, D. Whalley, and R. van Engelen. Supporting timing analysis by automatic bounding of loops iterations. *Real-Time Systems*, 18(2-3):129–156, May 2000.

[13] Lee W. Howes, Anton Lokhmotov, Alastair F. Donaldson, and Paul H.J. Kelly. Deriving efficient data movement from decoupled access/execute specifications. In *Proceedings of the 4th International. Conference on High Performance Embedded Architectures and Compilers*, HiPEAC '09, 2009.

[14] J. S. Meredith, R. Sisneros, D. Pugmire, and S. Ahern. A distributed data-parallel framework for analysis and visualization algorithm development. In *Proceedings of the 5th Annual Workshop on General Purpose Processing with Graphics Processing Units*, GPGPU-5, pages 11–19, New York, NY, USA, 2012. ACM.

[15] P. Moinier, J. D. Muller, and M. B. Giles. Edge-based multigrid and preconditioning for hybrid grids. *AIAA Journal*, 40(10):1954–1960, 2002.

[16] http://www.oerc.ox.ac.uk/research/op2.

[17] M. Strout, L. Carter, and J. Ferrante. Compile-time composition of run-time data and iteration reorderings. In *Proceedings of the 2003 ACM SIGPLAN Conference on Programming Language Design and Implementation (PLDI)*, June 2003.

[18] Mark Weiser. Program slicing. In *Proceedings of the 5th Int'l. conference on Software engineering*, ICSE '81, 1981.

GA-GPU: Extending a Library-based Global Address Space Programming Model for Scalable Heterogeneous Computing Systems

Vinod Tipparaju[*]
IEEE Member
tipparajuv@ieee.org

Jeffrey S. Vetter
Oak Ridge National Laboratory
vetter@ornl.gov

ABSTRACT

Scalable heterogeneous computing (SHC) architectures are emerging as a response to new requirements for low cost, power efficiency, and high performance. For example, numerous contemporary HPC systems are using commodity Graphical Processing Units (GPU) to supplement traditional multicore processors. Yet scientists continue to face challenges in utilizing SHC systems. First and foremost, they are forced to combine a number of programming models and then delicately optimize the data movement among these multiple programming systems on each architecture. In this paper, we investigate a programming model for SHC systems that attempts to unify data access to the aggregate memory available in GPUs in the system. In particular, we extend the popular and easy to use Global Address Space (GAS) programming model to SHC systems. We explore multiple implementation options, and demonstrate our solution in the context of Global Arrays, a library based GAS model. We evaluated these options in the context of kernels and NWChem, a scalable chemistry application . Our results reveal that GA-GPU can offer considerable benefit to users in terms of programmability, and both our empirical results and performance model provide encouraging performance benefits for future systems that offer a tightly integrated memory system.

Categories and Subject Descriptors

D.1.3 [**Programming Techniques**]: Concurrent Programming—*Parallel Programming*

Keywords

Global Address Space and Global Arrays and ARMCI and GPU and NWChem and PGAS and GAS and GA

---

[*]Currently employed by Advanced Micro Devices Inc. This work was performed while the Author was at Oak Ridge National Laboratory

1. INTRODUCTION

Recent reports from DOE, DARPA [14], and NSF have identified multiple challenges on the road to extreme-scale high performance computing systems. These challenges include the unrelenting issues of performance, scalability, and productivity, yet they also include the relatively new priorities of energy-efficiency and resiliency. Not coincidentally, recently announced HPC architectures, such as Road-Runner, Tianhe, Tsubame2, Keeneland [35], and Nebulae (see [33, 11]), illustrate that scalable heterogeneous computing (SHC) systems using graphical processing units (GPUs) can provide an innovative solution to begin addressing these challenges.

Early experiences on these systems have demonstrated their performance and energy-efficiency benefits [33, 11, 28, 36]; however, SHC systems have other challenges: low programmer productivity, limited portability across systems, lack of integrated tools and libraries, and very sensitive performance stability. Taken together, these issues will slow the adoption of these architectures by application teams.

While multiple groups are addressing the challenge of programming GPUs at the node level, few efforts have tackled the challenge of programming GPUs running one application at massive scale, where the system has hundreds to thousands of GPUs. These node-level approaches use advanced compilers [18, 37], runtime systems [31], and libraries [20, 24] to simplify the data orchestration, scheduling, and synchronization among the host processors and GPUs in a node. By contrast, when computing on large scale SHC systems, such as the architecture illustrated in Fig. 1, current applications are forced to combine multiple programming models, such as MPI [30] for internode communication and synchronization, and CUDA [6] for the intranode communication and synchronization. Even worse, optimizing the performance of these combined models is very fragile and error prone because it requires precise orchestration of data movement and computation across multiple levels of a distributed memory hierarchy, which may change for each SHC architecture.

In fact, future systems, like AMD's HSA [3] (Heterogeneous Systems Architecture) and NVIDIA's Echelon [7], will progressively integrate and unify the underlying memory models at both the node and system scale, bypassing contemporary I/O interfaces like PCI-Express. This integration will reduce data transfer and synchronization latencies between these devices, and undoubtedly force users to reexamine their applications when using these existing low-level, mixed programming models.

Meanwhile, over the past decade, GAS programming mod-

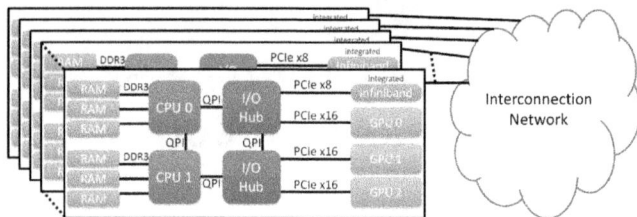

Figure 1: Architecture of a contemporary, scalable GPU system.

els - both the Partitioned (PGAS) [22, 34, 25] and Asynchronous Partitioned Global Address Space (APGAS) - have been developed as alternative models (to the Message Passing Interface [30]) for programming large-scale HPC platforms in order to improve application performance and programmer productivity. For example, Global Arrays [22] implements the GAS model as a runtime library, while UPC [34] extends the C language to implement the PGAS model using both compilers that can generate optimized instructions for GAS hardware support (if any), and specific library calls for bulk data transfers, synchronization, and other operations. In particular, GAS languages and libraries have several user-friendly features that reduce the programming burden by hiding much of the complexity of data movement, addressing, and synchronization. In addition, GAS models typically provide support for multiple memory consistency models, data movement decoupled from synchronization, and, more recently, remote method invocation. With these features, users can typically write more compact applications, and allow the language and runtime system to optimize data orchestration and allow some additional level of performance portability.

1.1 Contributions

To address this programmability challenge of GPU-based SHC systems, we have designed, implemented, and evaluated GA-GPU. GA-GPU is an approach that is based on a Global Address Space (GAS) programming model to programming scalable GPU systems . Specifically, this paper has four main contributions.

- We analyze the characteristics in a GAS programming model that must be implemented in order to extend it to GPUs (§2.2).
- We propose and evaluate several design alternatives for our library-based GAS model (§3), including different consistency models.
- We evaluate our implementation and the alternatives on several pertinent examples that include a major scientific application in computational chemistry - NWChem.
- We describe our experiences and observations, and describe how this infrastructure can be used by other GAS languages or libraries for programming GPU devices in a SHC system.

2. A GAS PROGRAMMING MODEL FOR SHC ARCHITECTURES

GAS models reduce the programming burden on application developers in utilizing the increasingly complex HPC hardware. Applications based on these models have the ability to access any data that resides in the global address space. The Global Arrays GAS Model, for instance, provides intuitive and high-performant interfaces to perform linear algebra operation on dense distributed arrays (the Conjugate Gradient example in §4 shows compact, easy to use Global Arrays example).

Despite all the benefits of a GAS models, extending these models to contemporary SHC systems is not intuitive. This issue is primarily due to the complexities of extending the memory consistency model for GAS to a device like a contemporary GPU, which has distinct memory space apart from the host CPU.

2.1 Design Goals and Options

In the analysis of issues with extending Address Space to GPUs, we first focus on the general goals for extending any GAS/PGAS model to use SHC systems. Then, we focus on specific design choices that are used in extending a popular GAS model - Global Arrays - to use GPUs.

GAS Memory Consistency Model.

The consistency that the GAS model guarantees must be retained despite extension of the model to utilize GPU. A plethora of consistency models have been used in GAS models. The most popular of these are Sequential Consistency [16] , Location Consistency [10] and various hybrid consistency models [1, 29]. When the address space is extended to GPU, the default consistency model of the language must be enforced even for memory that resides on the device.

GAS Coherence and Synchronization.

In GAS models, coherence and synchronization are typically provided with the mechanisms of ordering and fences. Fences synchronize memory in a GAS model. They may be issued implicitly by the system (e.g., triggered by the sequence of operations the application invokes), or issued explicitly by the application. Furthermore, fences must work across multiple levels of the architecture's hierarchy: at a peer-to-peer level or across a group of processes by the user.

As parts of the address space are extended to the device memory of the GPU, the fence operation should continue to provide the expected behavior. For example, GA distinguishes two types of completion of the store operations (i.e., put, scatter) that target global shared memory: local and remote. The blocking version of GA Put operation returns after the operation is completed locally indicating that the user buffer containing the source of the data can be reused. In contrast, the blocking version of GA Put operation is guaranteed to complete remotely only after one of two synchronization operations are invoked: a memory fence or a barrier.

Ordering, on the other hand, applies to the order in which the changes made to an address space appear in memory. Ordering requirements are typically linked with consistency requirements but ordering is used internally within a GAS implementation for various other reasons. For example, ordering is important to define the outcome of multiple memory operations when two different network channels are used to update the same memory. The extension of an address space to the GPU needs to ensure that the coherence guarantees and synchronization primitives retain their behaviors.

Address Space Transparency.

Parts of the address space or an entire address space may reside on the GPU. Having this difference in memory location but still support a uniform way of accessing the memory is preferred but may carry performance penalty.

The alternative to this transparency is to make things explicitly user aware, i.e. completely expose and identify the part of address space that resides on GPU. UPC Shared pointer is an example where something other than a regular C pointer has been used to represent a "shared" address thereby making it explicit to the user that this is different from a local pointer.

Explicit or Implicit Control of GPU.

While both extending the address space and providing a GAS-friendly abstraction to GPU memory are explicit means of extending a GAS model to include a GPU, there are several implicit ways of employing a GPU, which can provide better performance. There have been efforts in the past targeted at implicit utilization of GPU computations, one such effort intercepts linear algebra calls and execute them on GPU [8]. In the GA library example of implicit utilization is the `GA_DDot` operation. Within the implementation of this function, which is transparent to the user, the Global Arrays library may invoke a linear algebra library to perform this operation or launch it on a GPU and await completion. This implicit execution has several benefits including that it does not require any modifications to the programming/execution model or application. Similarly, such implicit control is also possible in language based models such as UPC. For example, consider this simple UPC parallel loop over a shared array:

```
for ( i = 0 ; i < n ; i ++ )
  /*a & b are shared*/
  a[me+i]= a[me+i]*scale+b[me+i];
```

Clearly, this loop can be translated into a linear algebra subroutine call or it can be executed on a GPU when internal aggregation is being performed by the UPC implementation. When such optimizations are performed, they could be accomplished with little or no user intervention. For effectively utilizing GPUs in a PGAS model, we believe that both implicit and explicit usage models should be supported.

Numerical Correctness.

Heterogeneous processors, and GPUs, can have differences in the numerical accuracy of their floating point operations. Recently, GPUs, such as NVIDIA's FERMI [26], have been designed hardware that provides IEEE754-2008 compliant floating point arithmetic, so this is less of a concern that it was several years ago. However, in any case, when a computation that would otherwise be performed on a CPU is ultimately executed on a GPU, the language or library must ensure that all numerical guarantees are enforced.

2.2 Additional Design Challenges

The execution model for a computer system is defined by the properties and behaviors of how it exposes and manages its address space and execution of processes or threads [12]. Contemporary parallel programming systems have, by far, been dominated by control-driven SPMD-based execution models; however, it is unclear if alternative models will prevail in the next decade. Although our actual proposed solution (§3) is implemented on (and consequently limited by) the underlying execution model, the concepts we propose carry no such limitations.

For example, the role of process management will most likely change if and when the GPU can run an entire application process, and not only application kernels. For this to be possible, a regular C, C++ or a Fortran program must be able to compile and execute on the GPU as it would on a CPU and all the associated operating system and communication libraries (such as MPI, etc.) must function natively. This is neither feasible today, nor is it the intended use of today's GPU. However, it may still be possible to run a simple, restricted, task with certain characteristics (that we describe in §3); we refer to these tasks as specialized tasks. For these reasons, we focus on the Address Space and specialized tasks that can be generated both implicitly and explicitly by the GAS model.

3. IMPLEMENTATION AND ALTERNATIVES ANALYSIS

To evaluate these design choices, we have designed, implemented, and evaluated GA-GPU: a model that extends the benefits of Global Address Space (GAS) methods to scalable GPU systems. Our evaluation demonstrates that we can improve the programmability of SHC systems with this model, and that GA-GPU would greatly benefit from changes to the underlying hardware architecture. Namely, today's architectures often relegate GPUs and network interfaces to I/O devices on the PCI-Express interface, which forces many transfers across this interface for every interaction. This limitation is imposed on all programming models. For the GA-GPU concept to be widely successful, the underlying network must have a low latency connection to the GPU, bypassing PCI-Express, and the network interface must support direct, low-latency connections across the system, bypassing host CPU interactions for every transfer.

Indeed, looking to the future, we believe that recent advances in memory and node-level interconnect technology will improve the possibilities for extending GAS/PGAS models to GPUs. Future architectures, like AMDs HSA (Heterogeneous Systems Architecture) and NVIDIA's Echelon, will include GAS support directly on the node to enable a class of applications based on GAS models.

3.1 Global Arrays Library and Runtime System (GA)

Our implementation is based on the open Global Arrays Library and Runtime System (GA)[22]. GA is a library-based GAS model that allows the user to allocate array data-structures of different dimensions and sizes, and access elements of these arrays in a shared memory fashion. GA is a unique model in that it (a) is process-centric, (b) provides a GAS/shared-memory abstraction to a physically distributed array and (c) can provide the performance of a PGAS model by exposing the partitioned nature of the distributed arrays to the user via a special set of interfaces. Specifically, in the GA library, the distribution and locality information is always available through interfaces to query 1) which data portion is held by a given process, 2) which process owns a particular array element, and 3) a list of processes and the blocks of data owned by each process corresponding to a given section of an array. The GA approach attempts to combine the best features of both the shared and distributed memory concepts. For instance, it implements a shared-memory style programming model while still allowing the programmer to exploit data locality. This is achieved by subroutines that provide information on which portion of the distributed data is held locally, and the use of explicit calls to subroutines that transfer data between a global address space (i.e., a distributed array) and local memory. The combination of these functions allows users to optimize their algorithms for locality. Another advantage is that GA, by optimizing and moving only the data requested by the user, avoids issues such as false sharing or redundant data transfers, which have been identified in some DSM solutions. In addition, GA's model exposes the hierarchical memory of contemporary computer architectures to the programmer, and, by recognizing the communication overhead for remote data transfer, it promotes data reuse and locality of reference. For these reasons, GA is well suited as a target for investigating techniques to extend GAS to SHC.

Our approach to extending GA to GPUs has three significant parts: 1) address space extension, 2) encapsulating consistency requirements, and 3) infrastructure to support this solution for GA and potentially other PGAS models. We will describe our solution and discuss how it addresses issues discussed in §2.

3.2 Extending the Address Space to GPUs

Both AMD and NVIDIA are working on software and hardware solutions to support the likes of *Unified Memory* or *Single Address Space*. NVIDIAs solution can be realized by the Unified model Cuda 4.0 provides and AMDs HSA can be utilize by various solutions including HSA runtime, and the consideration of Virtual Memory (SVM) in OpenCL, which has both appeared in literature [17] and is being considered for incorporation into OpenCL standard. These solutions provide complete sharing of virtual memory (potentially allocated with a *special* allocator) and simplify extension of a GAS solution to GPUs. While this is a viable solution and can be directly be adopted with minimal changes to existing GA software stack, past experiences with hierarchical memory systems has demonstrated that such usage might not always be optimal and that techniques such as bulk-prefetching and mirroring may be essential for performance despite *Unified Memory*. The work done by Bell et. al. [2] on Cray X1 (which has hardware support for memory on remote X1 nodes to be directly accessed via. Load/Store operations) discusses the substantial benefit from bulk prefetching on a system that supports direct load/stores to remote memory in hardware.

Our solution for address space extension is to allow for utilizing the GPU and its memory in one of three ways based on usage and algorithm: GPU only, mirroring, and hybrid.

3.2.1 GPU Only

Our first technique for extending address space to GPU is to allocate the data structures directly on the GPU without direct load/store access to it from the host. We label this option *GPU-only*.

For PGAS languages, the translation layer would need to do some bookeeping to identify which data structures actually reside entirely on the GPU and generate necessary communication code to translate accesses. For any computa-

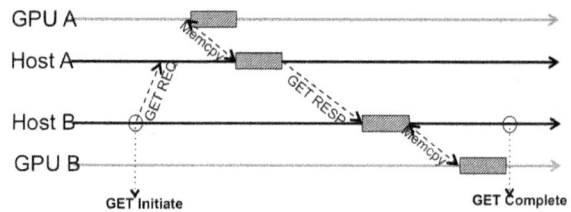

Figure 2: Data Transfer steps for a Get operation on GPU only Array.

tion done on these data structures, either a source-to-source translation to a GPU specific language or copying of the data structures back to the host is possible. Alternatively, these data structures could be explicitly identified (e.g. via a new type specifier).

In GA, the array meta-data, which is accessed usually as often as the array itself (sometimes at very high frequency), resides on the host while the array itself may reside on the GPU. For such arrays, all the GA data parallel operations must have variants written in GPU specific language (an inefficient alternative would be to bring the data back to the host for computation). Any linear algebra operations performed on the arrays will in-turn invoke a GPU specific linear algebra library. While the data parallel operations do pose challenges (coding the non-standard data parallel operations in GPU specific languages), direct access to sections of GPU-only array and consistency semantics add additional complications. Section 3.3 discusses these in detail as they are applicable to other two techniques discussed here. The data transfer steps involved in transfer from one GPU-only array to another are shown in Figure 2. The figure shows a get from GPU A, which is on Host A, into GPU B, that resides on Host B. The transfer is initiated by a user application process on Host B. After a GET operation is initiated on Host B (by an application process on that host), a GET request is generated, sent to Host A which uses a preallocated buffer to copy the contents from GPU memory to Host memory and initiate a GET response. Upon the receipt of the response into a host buffer on Host B, the received data is copied into the GPU memory on GPU B.

If some linear algebra operations such as DOT product or DAXPY are repeatedly performed on a data structure, GPU-only arrays are a viable solution. Another advantage of this approach is that consistency semantics are much simpler given the data structure resides entirely on the GPU and the computation is driven only by the CPU.

3.2.2 Mirroring

Our second option to extend the GA address space to GPUs is *Mirroring*. A copy of the data structure in the host (either the whole data structure or parts of it) can be maintained on the GPU. Any modifications to either the host array or the GPU copy can be lazily synchronized via a *merge* operation.

For PGAS languages, mirroring is particularly useful during communication. For an array that is synchronized, any communication done to/from this data structure can directly use the host copy of it. Round trip latency to the GPU may be avoided. The disadvantage is the cost of the merge

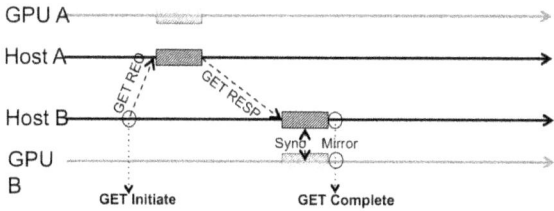

Figure 3: Data Transfer steps for a Get operation on a Array with mirrored address space extension

operation. If there is a need for frequent merge operations, the cost of the merge will typically degrade performance.

The GA library already supports mirroring of arrays in host memory [27] where an SMP-only copy of the entire distributed array can be created to avoid expensive remote memory communication. GA, along with interfaces to create mirrored arrays, also supports interfaces to merge the original array with its mirror. To utilize mirrored address space in GA, instead of creating an SMP-only copy, we allocate memory for the array on the GPU directly. Just as in the GPU-only case, the array meta-data resides on the CPU. The steps involved in a GET operation from Mirrored data are shown in Figure 3. In contrast to the GPU-only version of the GET, the Mirrored version has fewer steps in the best case. When the host and GPU mirror are synchronized, a GET request from Host B can directly be addressed by Host A. Once the data reaches Host B, the copy on the Host must be synchronized with the copy on the GPU. More importantly, this synchronization may also be postponed until the GPU actually has a computation utilizing that data.

The advantage mirroring is that not all the GA data parallel operations need a GPU variant. Some operations may be directly performed on the host and some directly on the GPU; both the arrays can be kept synchronized via merge operations.

While avoiding expensive data transfers and costly synchronization is an advantage, mirroring to the GPU has some disadvantages as well.

First, the amount of memory that can be allocated on the GPU is typically smaller in comparison to that on the host. Mirroring typically keeps a *temporary* copy of an otherwise large distributed array in shared memory on the local node. By mirroring the host array, the size of the array on the host is limited by what can be allocated on the GPU. Second, an advantage of host-mirroring in the original GA implementation is the fact that the mirror is located in shared memory; this feature is not possible in contemporary GPUs (fortunately, this limitation will be addressed by AMDs HSA and NVIDIAs Unified Memory). Any access to any section of the mirror is a relatively fast load/store memory operation (as opposed to a network operation if the section accessed in the distributed array is on a remote node). However, by keeping a copy on the GPU, the transfer to and from GPU memory is more expensive than a typical load/store (though not as expensive as a network operation).

3.2.3 Hybrid

Our final option for extending the address space is *Hybrid*. In our Hybrid model, parts of the address space (even with-in the same data structure) reside either in the host

memory without mirroring, in the host memory with mirroring, or exclusively in the GPU memory. In contrast to mirroring, our hybrid model forces exclusivity for some portions of the address space, and hence, they do not require explicit synchronization.

For PGAS languages, this is the most challenging option to implement. Setting aside the complexities of compiler code generation, if a loop that modifies a section of a data structure is in a critical section, extending this critical section to the part of the data structure that resides on the GPU is extremely challenging. In addition to this, enforcing the required consistency is non-trivial.

On the other hand, for GA, there are some scenarios where this hybrid model is quite useful, and it is relatively straightforward to use. For example, the GA library supports ghost cells (or halo regions)[22]. In GA, the ghost cells can be created during array creation and GA supports several operations on ghost cells. The most significant (in terms of performance implications) operation is the ghost cell update operation, which updates the overlapping ghost regions between processes with local modifications. Utilization of ghost cells is very common in a time-step loop where modifications to local ghost cells are percolated to the neighboring processes via an update operation. This is one example of possible internal usage of hybrid address space extension to a GPU within the GA library (for our preliminary prototype, we have not implemented any implicit utilization of hybrid arrays in ghost cells).

3.3 Consistency Requirements

Enforcing consistency requirements is critical for correct operation of the application, yet it depends on the specific extension technique under consideration. Original GA uses a consistency model that combines access-release consistency with location consistency. For exclusive access to directly modify a section of an array, GA provides access-release semantics. When overlapping accesses update sections of an array, GA follows a model very similar to location consistency for accesses. To compare, several PGAS languages support a spectrum of consistency semantics for accesses, ranging from sequential to relaxed. UPC, for example, has a consistency model that allows marking/identifying address space accesses (or sections of code via pragmas within UPC code) to follow a strict consistency. Then, these consistency models are enforced within the user code.

In our extension to GA, solutions to support different consistencies depend on the design alternative: GPU-only, Mirrored or Hybrid. While we describe how we addressed challenges associated with consistency, it is important to note that the main application processes are still executing on the host, and not on the GPU. Also, strict consistency that requires program order to be enforced across threads is not feasible for execution on GPUs (as this makes extending the model to GPU SIMD challenging).

First, in the case of the **GPU-only** option, since any access to GPU memory and any computation done on the GPU is driven by an application process running on the host, required consistency can be enforced at the host itself. If host-only data structures also exist and sequential consistency is required, then the application process must block until an initiated GPU operation concludes. The limitation is that a GPU kernel can neither access the host memory directly, nor can it copy data to and from the host memory;

this limitation reduces the complexity of the implementation and is a benefit. If the host keeps track of what kernels are currently being executed on the GPU and which data structures the kernels are modifying, it is sufficient to enforce any strict consistency between sections of code that execute on the CPU and sections of code that execute on the GPU. For the GA library, location consistency is enforced through coarse grain address-range data structures internally referred to as *memlock tables*. Despite the array data residing entirely in the GPU for the GPU-only option, the access to it is controlled via the existing memlock tables on the host.

Second, in case of **Mirrored** option, if consistency demands that an operation synchronize the array and its mirror, the synchronization needs to be performed implicitly. If the GAS model requires a strict consistency (with pre-specified order of execution of instructions), the mirroring option will not be a viable solution. For some PGAS languages, it is unclear how a technique such as mirroring can be implemented easily. For example, it may be possible to mirror a data structure that is only accessed with UPC relaxed semantics while it may not be possible to do the same for strict semantics. Every modification in the host might require synchronization between the data structure and its mirror on the GPU, which would lead to disastrous performance. The Mirrored option is unique in that it has its own consistency model that *encapsulates* existing consistency constraints for array element accesses and sequences of instruction execution. While it has several uses in GA[27], the same may not hold true for PGAS languages, which may lack the semantic information on data dependencies.

Finally, in the case of **Hybrid** option, regions of memory that reside on the GPU must be distinguishable from regions of memory that reside on the host. For regions of memory that reside on the GPU, the host has complete control over the kernels that are executed on the GPU, and the modification they might be doing to this memory. For the GA library, the hybrid option does not require any additional steps (other than the support for exclusivity over sections of memory, which is efficiently and asynchronously supported in GA) to enforce consistency. Even when a single host operation (e.g., an atomic update on a section of memory) accesses data that resides partially in host memory and partially in GPU memory, the use of memlock tables ensures access control and satisfies the consistency requirements.

In summary, one problem that is common to all the three options is the need to enforce consistency between remote, local, and GPU accesses. The host memory can only be accessed by the host itself or via the network while the GPU memory could be accessed by any of the following ways: 1) by a remote node, 2) by host CPU, or 3) by user for direct access.

Depending on the consistency model, these accesses may need to be exclusive or consistent by location (such as in Location Consistency). Our solution is to allow each of the access mechanisms that access the memory to be encapsulated within its own access-release control mechanism. Such encapsulation allows for a consistency to be enforced within each type of access and control overlap across accesses. This is an effective way to avoid complications from simultaneous use. With regards to correctness, there are many problem-specific solutions (e.g., for dot-product [38]), that are specialized for kernels running on the GPU.

3.4 Coherence and Synchronization

Two fundamental primitives that subsume fence and ordering are 1) commit a data transfer to memory and 2) to ensure completion of an operation that is being performed on the data structure. In GA-GPU, we have implemented these two primitives for GPU accesses. We have extended the ordering mechanism to include messages that target GPU memory directly and messages that target both host and GPU memory (such as the ones arising from hybrid address space access). For access to and from a hybrid address space, a data transfer is considered complete only after both the host and GPU transfers are complete. For operation such as accumulate that involve computation on the GPU, completion requires GPU threads to be synchronized; this synchronization is implemented from the host as a part of message completion logic.

3.5 GPU Infrastructure for GAS Models

The fundamental primitives required to extend address space and support consistency, synchronization, and other features are applicable to several PGAS models. Our solution can address the above mentioned issues and can go a step further to generalize the usage of GPUs within PGAS models. GA-GPU is an infrastructure that PGAS developers can use to either extend the address space, utilize the additional address space, or just implicitly use GPUs for compute-intensive sections of their applications. Hence, instead of a model-specific solution, we have extracted the required primitives as interfaces that can be available to any PGAS model to leverage GPUs either implicitly (within the model for intensive computations), or explicitly by exposing the usage directly to the user. The primitives that have been identified include

- interfaces to collectively allocate and deallocate GPU memory (this is so that the user can keep pointers to remote GPU address space);
- contiguous and non-contiguous data transfer to and from Remote GPU memory;
- active message style interfaces to launch a remote kernel and await response (the user or PGAS model should be able to specify the kernel that needs to be launched);
- interfaces to order among GPU and CPU and active message style operations;
- interfaces to complete execution of a remote GPU kernel or complete a data transfer operation initiated to a GPU; and,
- interfaces for synchronization across multiple GPUs potentially residing on multiple nodes.

In GA-GPU, we have designed interfaces that implement these primitives. The initial version of these interfaces has been implemented alongside the ARMCI one-sided communication library [23] that GA uses for communication. The collective memory allocation interfaces to allocate GPU memory follow the exact same behavior as ARMCI collective host memory interfaces (`ARMCI_Malloc`). Even if one allocation on one GPU fails, the entire collective allocation is aborted after freeing already allocated chunks. By utilizing ARMCI for the initial implementation of our infrastructure, we get portability across different network.

Interfaces for contiguous data transfers to GPU are built on the ARMCI Communication Helper Thread (CHT) (described in [32]). Our implementation of remote GPU kernel

Table 1: Latency measurements for data transfer and kernel launch functions for Remote GPU.

Platform	xfer init	launch init	xfer init + wait	launch initiation + wait
Opteron system	7.25	12.21	23.2	52.3

launch uses ARMCI Global Procedure Calls (GPC) functionality (described in [15]). Specialized tasks that launch GPU kernels are registered GPC procedures. Note that these tasks are not general purpose as they cannot access all the memory in the host or on the device. We keep track of the fact the GPU operations have been previously initiated on node. If a fence is performed, and the node has prior GPU operations pending, threads on the GPU are synchronized as a part of the fence and merge of any mirrors is also performed.

Since our implementation of the infrastructure is a prototype, few of the individual operations (data transfers or remote kernel launches) have been extensively optimized. Table 1 shows the latency of data transfer operation to a remote GPU, and the latency associated with launching a kernel on a remote GPU for our implementation. We expect the Remote GPU Kernel launch and Kernel launch initiation + completion to drastically reduce with architectures like AMD HSA.

4. EXPERIMENTAL EVALUATION

We have evaluated performance of our three different options with micro-benchmarks, conjugate gradient kernel, and major scientific application (NWChem). Our experimental platform was an AMD Opteron Cluster at Oak Ridge National Laboratory; it has 32 nodes, each node has four 2.3GHz AMD Opteron quad-core sockets (16 cores in total) with 64 GB of memory, and 2 NVIDIA 8800 GTX GPUs. We will refer to this platform as the Opteron system.

4.1 One-Sided communication to GPU Memory

These benchmarks create a global array that spans different host nodes and GPUs, and then measure latency for accessing parts of the global array that reside in the memory of the local node, in the memory of the local GPU, and in the memory of a remote node and remote GPU.

The benchmark executes each of the GET, PUT and Accumulate tests for several iterations for each size. There are two sets of benchmarks: the second set has been designed for PUT and Accumulate tests. The first set pipelines the communication operations – it does not synchronize memory after each communication call. Instead, the synchronization (fence, in this case) is done at the end of all the iterations for each message size. While Pipelined benchmark shows the best case scenario, the Synchronized benchmarks highlight the actual cost of doing the data transfer and realizing consistency.[1]

Figure 4 measures the transfer cost for one dimensional (contiguous) data on Opteron system. Figure 4(a) shows latency numbers for a PUT operation (write) to local (within

[1]Note that the pseudo code does not show the logic that picks a different source and destination address for each step.

the same node) memory of both the host and device for data structures that reside in GPU-Only, Mirrored, and Hybrid address spaces. Figure 4(b) shows the latency of a PUT operation with synchronization to local (within the same node) memory of both the host and device for data structures that reside in GPU-Only, Mirrored, and Hybrid address spaces. It can be seen in the figure that there is a significant overhead ($\tilde{1}6$ μs) for accessing the GPU memory. In this test, the PUT to a mirrored address space is first done to the GPU memory and subsequently synchronized. PUTs to the GPU copy of mirrored address space are the most expensive because they incur a round-trip to GPU memory: the trip to the GPU memory is to do the PUT, and the trip back is during synchronization with the host copy. §3.5 describes how remote GPU operations are implemented. With future optimizations to our infrastructure, we will eliminate the need for this round trip and cache the PUTs to GPU memory until a future synchronization.

Figure 5(a,b) is similar to Figure 4 – both measurements capture latency of a PUT operation (write) to GPU memory. However, in Figure 5, the destination of the PUT operation is a remote node. This is the first step in validating the functionality of our infrastructure by utilizing it in an actual GAS model.

Figure 6 shows the latency of a GET operation for GPU-only, Mirrored, and Hybrid address space. The completion of a GET operation is marked by the arrival of the data. Hence, the GET operations need not be explicitly synchronized, the completion of the GET is itself a synchronization.

Another rather important Global Arrays one-sided operation to consider is the *Accumulate*. This operation involves a DAXPY like computation on remote data. For sections of the array that reside on the GPU, the accumulate operation is performed on the GPU itself via customized accumulate GPU kernels. Figure 7(a,b) illustrates the latency of accumulate for GPU-only, Mirrored, and Hybrid address spaces for both the Pipelined version and Synchronized version of the microbenchmark. Hybrid address space outperforms the native GA accumulate for larger message sizes. With future hardware, and GA-GPU optimizations, we anticipate substantial benefits for large accumulates.

4.2 Conjugate Gradient Benchmark.

The Conjugate Gradient (CG) benchmark solves an unstructured sparse linear system. It uses the inverse power method to find an estimate of the largest eigenvalue of a symmetric positive definite sparse matrix. The CG benchmark is quite memory intensive; it tests irregular, long distance communication and employs unstructured matrix vector multiplications. This benchmark has been parallelized and studied in context of multiple programming models[19, 9].

Several GPU-based solutions to the CG benchmark exist ([5, 4]). Most of this work is limited to a shared memory node, but some of the implementations can work for distributed memory systems using MPI between nodes [13]. The common goal for this prior work was high efficiency and scalability. *In contrast, our goal is to demonstrate a productive, distributed memory implementation of CG written in an existing high-level programming model that seamlessly uses GPUs on a SHC architecture by merely extending the model and its implementation.*

There are three significant parts of the CG benchmark:

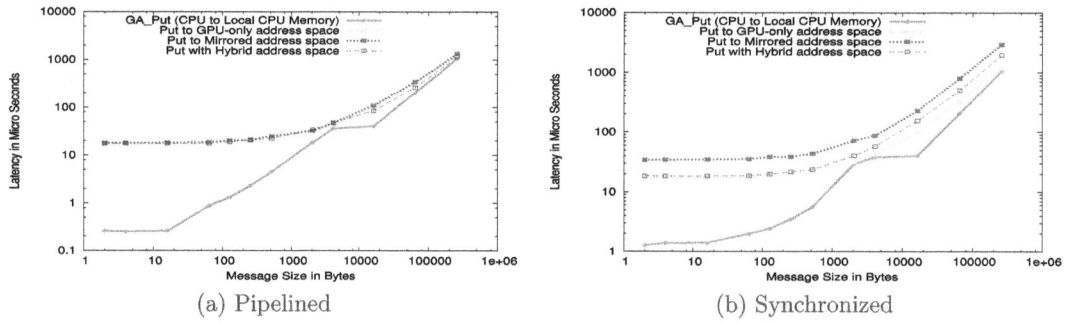

Figure 4: Intra-node (local) Latency of GA_Put to GPU-only, Mirrored and Hybrid address spaces

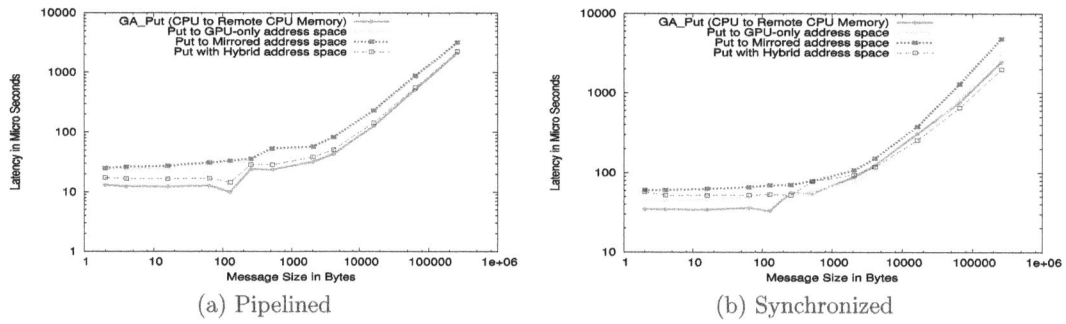

Figure 5: Inter-node (remote) Latency of GA_Put to GPU-only, Mirrored and Hybrid address spaces

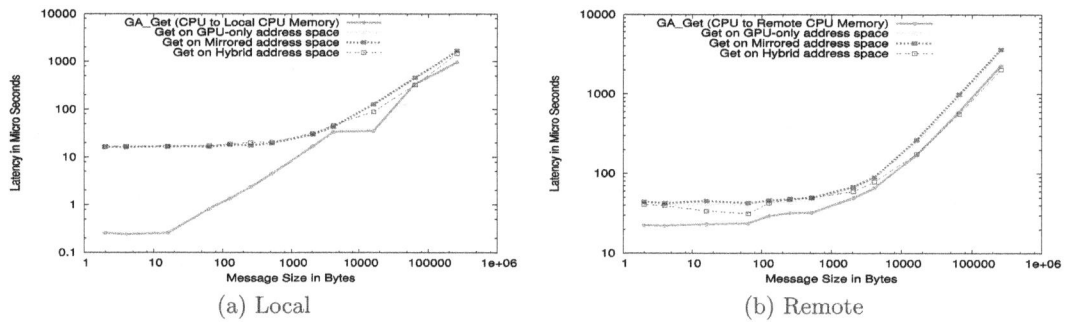

Figure 6: GA_Get latency for intra-node (Local) and inter-node (Remote) GET operation

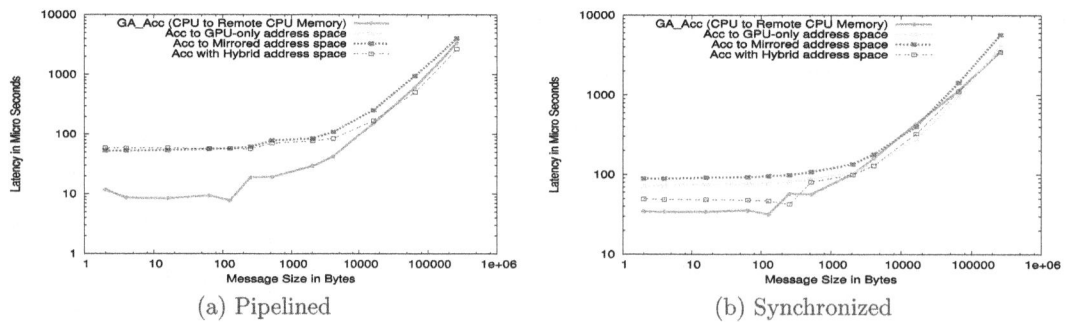

Figure 7: GA_Acc latency for three address space extensions for Pipelined and Synchronized benchmark

Program 1 Steps in a Conjugate Gradient algorithm and its equivalent GA pseudo code

```
/* deltanew = r.r_tranpose */
deltanew = GA_Ddot(dvec,rvec);         δ_new = r.r^T
/* delta0 = deltanew */
delta0 = deltanew;                     δ_0 = δ_new
for(i=0;i<nit && deltanew>(
 epsilon*epsilon*delta0);i++){
  /* q = Ad */
  matvecmul(aptr,m_dvec,qvecptr
   ,1,myrp,mycp);                      q = A.d
  /* compute d_transpose.q */
  dtransposeq=GA_Ddot(dvec,qvec);
  /* deltanew/(d_transpose.q) */       α = δ_new/d^T.q
  alpha = deltanew/dtransposeq;
  /* x = x+ alpha.d*/
  GA_Add(&d_one,xvec,&alpha,dvec,
   xvec);                              x = x + α.d
```

(a) the dot product, (b) the sparse matrix vector multiplication, and (c) vector operations such as addition and scale. (a) is trivial to realize – a simple tree-based dot-product kernel can accomplish it, alternatively, a call to native blas (e.g. `cublasDdot`) would compute the dot product on the GPU. For GPU-only and Mirrored address space extension, the result can completely be computed by a custom dot product kernel or the `cublasDdot` call. For Hybrid extension, the partial GPU result must be combined with the result computed on the host. (c) can similarly be accomplished with custom kernels or with native blas implementation for the GPU. (b), however, is distribution dependent and will require data transfers. GA does not support Compressed Row/Column formats for matrices. A compressed row/column format can still be allocated and stored in a distributed GA, however, GA data parallel operations such as GA Matrix Multiplication will not work for such arrays. This means that the multiplication that needs to be performed on the matrix cannot utilize the GA data parallel multiplication interface. The user is expected to manually code this multiplication by directly accessing sections of array using `GA_Access` calls. All the vectors in the CG solution can be directly allocated using GA and GA data parallel operations can directly be applied on them.

Our solution for sparse matrix vector multiplication involved assigning each row of the compressed matrix to a warp. The warp computes the dot product of a row of in the matrix with the vector, in parallel. This division of work implies that the compressed index and the matrix are accessed in a contiguous manner (but generally not aligned). Since an entire warp is assigned to each row, many threads will remain idle when their row contains a small number of elements. Here, again, we emphasize that our goal is not to implement an efficient CG solution on GPU but to show how a GAS model can be extended.

For our tests, we have chosen a sparse input matrix A is of size 28167*28167 with 186169 non-zero elements. The address space extension for the sparse matrix is GPU-only. The address space extension for all the vectors is mirrored and the mirrored synchronization points are at the dot products.

Program 1 shows the actual steps in CG and their imple-

mentation in the GA library. The objective behind utilizing GA data-parallel operations where ever possible is to minimize the amount of GPU-specific code a user needs to write in order to utilize th GPUs. Figure 8 shows the scaling and wall clock time (in seconds) of the benchmark for the traditional host address space and extended address space, Opteron system was used and we only ran one CPU process per node for our runs. For both GPU and CPU versions, we have hard-coded the number of iterations to 10000, this is a high iteration count chosen to dampen the impact from any outliers in per-iteration latency. Note that the problem size is small but it was chosen so we could keep the array on the GPU; however, doing this reduces the amount of computation per device. For example, on 32 processors the sparse-matrix-vector multiplication loop computes as few as 10000 elements per processor/GPU. (Fortunately, newer GPUs like NVIDIA's FERMI can offer up to 6 GB of onboard memory.) The performance advantage reduces over the CPU-only version for larger processor counts primarily due to the reduction in computation. Excluding the data transfer to and from the GPU, the latency of all steps of the CG computation involving 28167 rows is approximately 2.03 milliseconds while the same computation on 880 rows is 0.21 milliseconds; when the problem size is reduced by a factor of 32, the kernel time reduces by only a factor of 6. The CPU version takes 5 milliseconds for the same matrix.

4.3 NWChem Computational Chemistry Application

Ideally, our GA-GPU will support many real applications running on SHC clusters in the coming years. Our first effort focuses on NWChem: a software package for computational chemistry on massively parallel computing systems developed by the High Performance Computational Chemistry Group for the Environmental Molecular Sciences Laboratory. The software provides a variety of modules for quantum mechanical and classical mechanical simulation. The DFT module in NWChem package represents the workhorse of electronic structure for its balance between computational cost and accuracy.

Figure 9 shows the wall clock timings for the matrix evaluation of the XC potential of a zeolite fragment (SiOSi5) are reported as a function of the number of processors. The experiment has been run with 1 process per node for the CPU run and 1 CPU + 1 GPU per node for the CPU+GPU run. There are two main matrices in the DFT implementation

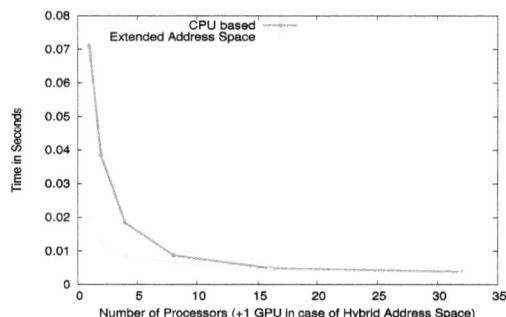

Figure 8: Conjugate Gradient Benchmark with traditional in comparison to extended address space

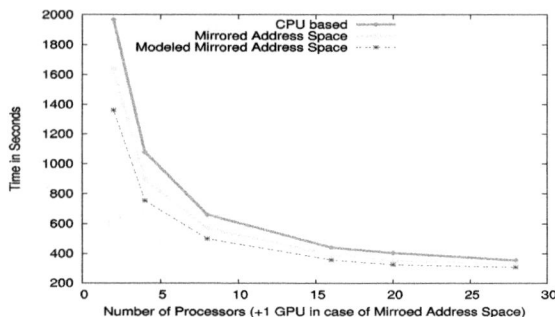

Figure 9: NWChem DFT benchmark, CPU based vs. mirrored address space

(see [21]): the input density matrix and the output Kohn-Sham (K) matrix. For the GPU case, the Density Matrix from a parallel matrix multiply is generated into a array that is mirrored on to the GPU. Subsequently, a Density Matrix block from the array is accessed for computation.

Note that the cost of data transfer has a significant impact on the overall time. On future systems, like AMD's HSA [3] and NVIDIA's Echelon [7], that will progressively integrate and unify the underlying memory models, we predict that either hardware or operating system support will effectively take care of coherently moving data between CPU caches, GPU memory, and main memory. We also predict that this will reduce data transfer latencies. When running on such hardware.

Figure 9 also shows a line that represents prediction of the performance when data transfer latency to/from GPU is a very small value (1 micro second). The extended address space variation benefits from the use of GPU; however, reducing the data transfer cost increases the attainable benefit.

5. CONCLUSIONS

We have demonstrated how a GAS model can improve the programmability of scalable heterogeneous computing systems. Efforts to extend the highly productive PGAS languages and libraries to SHC will reduce the programming burden in programming complex systems. In this paper, we have described how GPUs in SHC systems may be used implicitly and explicitly using an extension to an existing GAS programming model. We have proposed and evaluated three options for address space extensions to the GPU. Our extensions to GA in order to extend the address space to use the GPU, which was transparent to the user, has improved the performance of Accumulate operation for larger message sizes. Our experiments evaluated the latency of these operations in various scenarios. We have also implemented and tested a unoptimized, extended address space version, of the conjugate gradient benchmark and a small part of an NWChem DFT module. Our prototype infrastructure, GA-GPU, has the potential to be utilized by multiple GAS/PGAS languages and libraries. With the state of the art in GPU hardware/software today, there is a significant overhead from the latencies of communicating between the GPU and the host, due in part to the PCI-Express interface and the required host system intervention. Having an infrastructure and the interfaces in place allows us to utilize future hardware improvements with minimal modifi-

cations will allow us to improve programmer productivity, and possibly influence the course of the future GAS hardware features on SHC systems. As future work, we plan to implement optimized accumulate and GA data parallel operation kernels to be executed on GPUs. We will also implement and utilize our infrastructure in PGAS languages, such as Co-Array Fortran [25].

6. REFERENCES

[1] H. Attiya and R. Friedman. A Correctness Condition for High-Performance Multiprocessors (extended abstract). In *STOC '92: Proceedings of the twenty-fourth annual ACM symposium on Theory of computing*, pages 679–690, New York, NY, USA, 1992. ACM.

[2] C. Bell, W.-Y. Chen, D. Bonachea, and K. A. Yelick. Evaluating support for global address space languages on the cray x1. In P. Feautrier, J. R. Goodman, and A. Seznec, editors, *ICS*, pages 184–195. ACM, 2004.

[3] N. Brookwood. AMD Fusion family of APUs: enabling a superior, immersive PC experience. Mar 2010.

[4] R. Carvalho, C. Martins, R. Batalha, and A. Camargos. 3D Parallel Conjugate Gradient Solver Optimized for GPUs. In *Electromagnetic Field Computation (CEFC), 2010 14th Biennial IEEE Conference on*, page 1, may 2010.

[5] A. Cevahir, A. Nukada, and S. Matsuoka. Fast Conjugate Gradients with Multiple GPUs. In G. Allen, J. Nabrzyski, E. Seidel, G. van Albada, J. Dongarra, and P. Sloot, editors, *Computational Science âĂŞ ICCS 2009*, volume 5544 of *Lecture Notes in Computer Science*, pages 893–903. Springer Berlin / Heidelberg, 2009. 10.1007/978-3-642-01970-8_90.

[6] N. Corp. Compute Unified Device Architecture Programming Guide. *NVIDIA: Santa Clara, CA*, 83:129, 2007.

[7] B. Dally. Keynote presentation: Gpu computing to exascale and beyond. In *SC10: Proceedings of the Conference on High Performance Computing Networking, Storage and Analysis*. NVIDIA, 2010.

[8] M. Fatica. Accelerating linpack with cuda on heterogenous clusters. In *Proceedings of 2nd Workshop on General Purpose Processing on Graphics Processing Units*, GPGPU-2, pages 46–51, New York, NY, USA, 2009. ACM.

[9] M. Frumkin, H. Jin, and J. Yan. Implementation of nas parallel benchmarks in high performance fortran.

[10] G. Gao and V. Sarkar. Location consistency-a new memory model and cache consistency protocol. *Computers, IEEE Transactions on*, 49(8):798–813, Aug 2000.

[11] The Green500 List: Environmentally Responsible Supercomputing. http://www.green500.org, 2010.

[12] W. W. Gropp and E. L. Lusk. A taxonomy of programming models for symmetric multiprocessors and smp clusters. In *In Proceedings of 1995 Programming Models for Massively Parallel Computers*, pages 2–7, 1995.

[13] H.-J. Kim and W. Lee. Multi GPU Performance of Conjugate Gradient Algorithm with Staggered Fermions. *PoS*, LATTICE2010:028, 2010.

[14] P. Kogge, K. Bergman, S. Borkar, D. Campbell, W. Carlson, W. Dally, M. Denneau, P. Franzon, W. Harrod, K. Hill, J. Hiller, S. Karp, S. Keckler, D. Klein, R. Lucas, M. Richards, A. Scarpelli, S. Scott, A. Snavely, T. Sterling, R. S. Williams, and K. Yelick. Exascale computing study: Technology challenges in achieving exascale systems. Technical report, DARPA Information Processing Techniques Office, 2008.

[15] S. Krishnamoorthy, J. Canovas, V. Tipparaju, J. Nieplocha, and P. Sadayappan. Non-collective parallel i/o for global address space programming models. In *Cluster Computing, 2007 IEEE International Conference on*, pages 41–49, Sept. 2007.

[16] L. Lamport. How to make a multiprocessor computer that correctly executes multiprocess progranm. *IEEE Trans. Comput.*, 28(9):690–691, 1979.

[17] J. Lee, J. Lee, S. Seo, J. Kim, S. Kim, and Z. Sura. Comic++: A software svm system for heterogeneous multicore accelerator clusters. In M. T. Jacob, C. R. Das, and P. Bose, editors, *HPCA*, pages 1–12. IEEE Computer Society, 2010.

[18] S. Lee and R. Eigenmann. Openmpc: Extended openmp programming and tuning for gpus. In *2010 ACM/IEEE International Conference for High Performance Computing, Networking, Storage and Analysis*, pages 1–11. IEEE Computer Society, 2010.

[19] C. Lin, L. Snyder, R. E. Anderson, B. L. Chamberlain, S.-E. Choi, G. Forman, E. C. Lewis, and W. D. Weathersby. Hpf: A comparison of performance and programming style, 1994.

[20] H. Ltaief, S. Tomov, R. Nath, P. Du, and J. Dongarra. A scalable high performant cholesky factorization for multicore with gpu accelerators. *High Performance Computing for Computational Science (VECPAR 2010)*, pages 93–101, 2011.

[21] R. H. Martyn, R. J. Harrison, M. F. Guest, R. A. Kendall, D. E. Bernholdt, A. T. Wong, M. Stave, J. L. Anchell, A. C. Hess, R. J. Littlefield, G. L. Fann, J. Nieplocha, G. S. Thomas, D. Elwood, J. Tilson, R. L. Shepard, A. F. Wagner, I. T. Foster, E. Lusk, R. Stevens, and H. performance Comp Chem. High Performance Computational Chemistry:(II) A Scalable SCF Program, 1995.

[22] J. Nieplocha, B. Palmer, V. Tipparaju, M. Krishnan, H. Trease, and E. Apra. Advances, Applications and Performance of the Global Arrays Shared Memory Programming Toolkit. *International Journal of High Performance Computing Applications*, 20(2):203–231, 2006.

[23] J. Nieplocha, V. Tipparaju, M. Krishnan, and D. K. Panda. High Performance Remote Memory Access Communications: The ARMCI Approach. In *International Journal of High Performance Computing Applications*, volume 20(2), pages 233–253, 2006.

[24] A. Nukada and S. Matsuoka. Auto-tuning 3-d fft library for cuda gpus. In *SC09: Proceedings of the Conference on High Performance Computing Networking, Storage and Analysis*, page 30, Portland, 2009. ACM.

[25] R. Numrich and J. Reid. Co-Array Fortran for parallel programming. *ACM Fortran Forum*, 17(2):1–31, 1998.

[26] NVIDIA. Nvidia's next generation cuda compue archtiecture: Fermi. Technical report, 2010.

[27] B. Palmer, J. Nieplocha, and E. Apra. Shared Memory Mirroring for Reducing Communication Overhead on Commodity Networks. *Cluster Computing, IEEE International Conference on*, 0:420, 2003.

[28] A. Rahimian, I. Lashuk, S. Veerapaneni, A. Chandramowlishwaran, D. Malhotra, L. Moon, R. Sampath, A. Shringarpure, J. Vetter, R. Vuduc, D. Zorin, and G. Biros. Petascale direct numerical simulation of blood flow on 200k cores and heterogeneous architectures (gordon bell award winner). In *2010 ACM/IEEE International Conference for High Performance Computing, Networking, Storage and Analysis (SC10)*, pages 1–11, New Orleans, 2010. IEEE Computer Society.

[29] V. A. Saraswat, R. Jagadeesan, M. Michael, and C. von Praun. A theory of memory models. In *PPoPP '07: Proceedings of the 12th ACM SIGPLAN symposium on Principles and practice of parallel programming*, pages 161–172, New York, NY, USA, 2007. ACM.

[30] M. Snir, W. D. Gropp, S. Otto, S. Huss-Lederman, D. Walker, J. Dongarra, A. Lumsdaine, E. Lusk, B. Nitzberg, and W. Saphir. *MPI–the complete reference (2-volume set)*. Scientific and engineering computation. MIT Press, Cambridge, Mass., 2nd edition, 1998. Marc Snir ... [et al.]. MPI Message passing interface–the complete reference ill. ; 23 cm. v. 1. The MPI core – v. 2. The MPI-2 extentions.

[31] K. Spafford, J. Meredith, and J. Vetter. Maestro: Data orchestration and tuning for opencl devices. In P. D'Ambra, M. Guarracino, and D. Talia, editors, *Euro-Par 2010 - Parallel Processing*, volume 6272 of *Lecture Notes in Computer Science*, pages 275–286. Springer Berlin / Heidelberg, 2010.

[32] V. Tipparaju, E. Apra, W. Yu, and J. Vetter. Enabling a highly-scalable global address space model for petascale computing. In *CF '10: Proceedings of the 7th ACM conference on Computing frontiers*, New York, NY, USA, 2010. ACM.

[33] Top500 Supercomputing Sites. http://www.top500.org, 2010.

[34] UPC Consortium. UPC Specification, v1.2. Technical Report LBNL-59208.

[35] J. Vetter, R. Glassbrook, J. Dongarra, K. Schwan, B. Loftis, S. McNally, J. Meredith, J. Rogers, P. Roth, K. Spafford, and S. Yalamanchili. Keeneland: Bringing heterogeneous gpu computing to the computational science community. *IEEE Computing in Science and Engineering*, 13(5), 2011.

[36] K. Wilkinson, P. Sherwood, M. Guest, and K. Naidoo. Acceleration of the gamess-uk electronic structure package on graphical processing units. *JOURNAL OF COMPUTATIONAL CHEMISTRY*, 2011.

[37] M. Wolfe. Implementing the pgi accelerator model. In *Proceedings of the 3rd Workshop on General-Purpose Computation on Graphics Processing Units*, pages 43–50, Pittsburgh, Pennsylvania, 2010. ACM.

[38] N. Yamanaka, T. Ogita, S. M. Rump, and S. Oishi. A parallel algorithm for accurate dot product. *Parallel Comput.*, 34:392–410, July 2008.

SnCTM: Reducing False Transaction Aborts by Adaptively Changing the Source of Conflict Detection

Isuru Herath, Demian Rosas-Ham, Mikel Luján, Ian Watson
Advanced Processor Technologies Group
The University of Manchester
United Kingdom
{herathh, rosasd, mikel.lujan, watson}@cs.man.ac.uk

ABSTRACT

Optimistic concurrency provided by Transactional Memory (TM) makes it a good candidate for maintaining synchronization in future multi-core processors. Speculative execution and bulk level conflict detection enable TM to provide synchronization at fine grain without the complexity of managing fine grain locks. Early hardware TM systems proposed to store the information needed for checking conflicts in the Level 1 (L1) cache, thereby limiting the size of a transaction to the size of the L1 cache. The introduction of signatures to TM systems removed this limitation and allowed transactions to be of any size.

However signatures produce false positives which leads to performance degradation in TM systems. The objective of introducing signatures to TM is that the size of a transaction can be bigger than the L1 cache. Once signatures are integrated to a TM system, they are used to detect conflicts regardless of the size of a transaction. This means signatures are being used even for transactions that can store their read and write sets in the L1 cache.

Based on this observation we propose SnCTM, a TM system that adaptively changes the source used to detect conflicts. In our approach, when a transaction fits in the L1 cache, cache line information is used to detect conflicts and signatures are used otherwise. By adaptively changing the source, SnCTM achieved up to 4.62 and 2.93 times speed-up over a baseline TM using lazy versioning and lazy conflict detection with two commonly used signature configurations. We also show that our system, even with a smaller signature (64 bit), can achieve performance comparable to a system with a perfect signature (8k bit).

Categories and Subject Descriptors

B.3 [**Hardware**]: Memory Structures; C.1.4 [**Processor Architectures**]: Parallel Architectures

General Terms

Design, Experimentation, Performance

Keywords

Hardware transactional memory, Signatures, Bloom filters, False positives

1. INTRODUCTION

Commodity processors are now shipped with more than one processor core and in few years time we will have processors with hundreds (if not thousands) of processor cores [9]. It is inevitable that parallel programming becomes the mainstream in order to make use of those cores in the chip. With parallel programming, maintaining mutual exclusive access is one of the issues that programmers have to face. Even though this is achieved via locks in the past, Transactional Memory (TM) [8], a lock free solution based on database transactions [5], has gained attention over the last decade. In TM, during the execution of a critical section, operations are performed speculatively and atomically. All the memory locations that are read/written speculatively, are recorded in a read/write-set respectively. At the end of an atomic block, conflicts are checked using these read and write sets.

Initial hardware TM systems like TCC [6], LogTM [14] propose to keep this read and write set in the Level 1 (L1) cache by extending it with a R (read) and W (write) bit. However this requires the size of a transaction to be able to fit in the L1 cache. Following the proposal for bulk disambiguation of addresses by Ceze *et al.* [2], Yen *et al.* propose LogTM-SE [20] which suggest the use of hardware signatures to represent the read and write sets of a transaction. A hardware signature is a fixed set of bits, that can be implemented using SRAMs, in which certain bits are set according to the address being considered. The important aspect of using signatures in TM is that, transactions are no longer bounded by the size of the L1 cache. However the disadvantage of using signatures is that they produce false positives. In this context, a false positive refers to a situation where the signature mechanism asserts a conflict, but actually there is not any. False positives lead to false transaction aborts and this degrades the performance of a TM system.

Several proposals [3, 4, 10, 15, 16, 21] have been made to reduce the number of false positives that occur in a hardware TM system. All of these approaches focus on the design and the implementation of signatures in hardware. In this paper we aim to address the issue of reducing false positives from a different angle. To begin our discussion, we raise a question: *Can the usage of signatures, in detecting conflicts, be reduced ?* The reason we raise that question is, if we can reduce the use of signatures, then we can reduce the false positives. Then the obvious question is, if we are not using signatures what else can we use to detect conflicts. The answer is cache lines. So the proposal is to use both cache lines and signatures to maintain the read and write set of a transaction. Thereafter, if the size of a transaction fits in the L1 cache, then we use cache line information to detect conflicts. When this is not the case, we use signatures. To this end we propose SnCTM: a hardware transactional memory system that adaptively changes the source used for detecting conflicts.

In this paper we make following contributions.

- We introduce the concept of adaptively changing the source of information used to detect conflicts in a hardware TM system. We show how an existing TM architecture can be extended to support the SnCTM concept.

- The performance evaluation of SnCTM shows improvements of up to 4.62 and 2.93 times speed-up over a baseline TM using lazy versioning and lazy conflict detection (an improved TCC [6]) with two commonly used signature configurations.

- SnCTM gives the opportunity to reduce the size of the signature without compromising the performance of the signature. Our sensitivity analysis shows that SnCTM with a 64 bit signature can deliver performance comparable to a perfect system with a 8k bit signature.

The rest of the paper is organized as follows. Section 2 presents the background on hardware signatures and shows the motivation for our SnCTM with a preliminary experiment. The SnCTM concept is discussed in section 3 and the architecture to support our proposal is presented in section 4. Evaluation of SnCTM is presented in section 5 and the related work is discussed in section 6. Finally section 7 concludes the paper.

2. MOTIVATION

Most of the TM systems (eg: LogTM-SE [20], SigTM [13], VTM [17]) propose to use signatures to record read and write sets of a transaction. This facilitates a transaction to have an unbounded amount of speculative data. Here, the term 'unbounded' means that a transaction is not bounded by the size of its local cache. This is because most of the initial TM systems like TCC [6], LogTM [14] propose to keep the read and write set of a transaction in its Level 1 (L1) cache. Some of the TM systems like LogTM-SE [20] that support unbounded transactions, also support virtualizable transactions, meaning that they can even be longer than the scheduling quanta. However support for virtualizable transactions cannot be provided by only having signatures to record read set and write set of a transaction, thus requires support from the runtime system. Therefore we will be focusing our discussion only to TM systems that use signatures to support an unbounded amount of speculative data.

Early HTM system like TCC, LogTM propose to extend L1 cache with Read and Write (R and W) bits to record the

read and write sets of a transaction. This requires transactions to be bounded by the size of the L1 cache of a processor. Bulk [2] proposes to encode this information into a fixed sized hardware 'signature'. This approach allows the size of a transaction not to be bounded by the size of the L1 cache. Signatures have the disadvantage of producing false positives. That is, when tested for the membership of an address in a signature, it may assert positive even if the address is not present in the signature. False positives lead to false transaction aborts, thereby degrading the performance of a transactional memory system.

False transaction aborts which are caused by false positives can be reduced by optimising the implementation of a signature. A number of approaches to achieve this, is discussed in section 6. In this paper, we take a completely orthogonal approach to those and propose a simple hardware solution to reduce false transaction aborts.

To begin our discussion, we raise the question *"Does a HTM system require signatures all the time, to detect conflicts ?"*. The answer is *"No"*. This is because, not all the transactions exceed the size of the L1 cache. When transactions are small, the read and write sets can be kept in the L1 cache of the processor. For such transactions, there is no need to use signatures. To get an intuition of how many transactions actually needed a signature, we made a preliminary experiment with a lazy-lazy HTM system, similar to TCC [6], using 2-16 cores. The experiment was carried out with two signature bit widths (1024, 2048) which are the sizes generally used in hardware TM experiments.

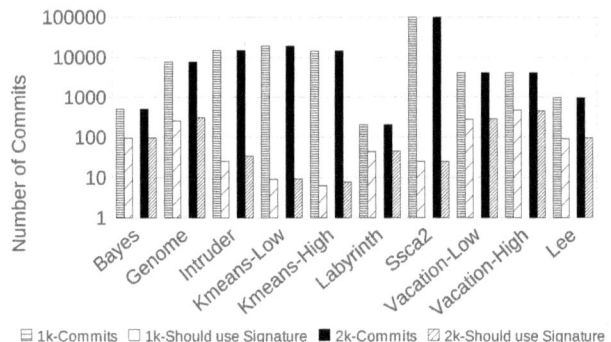

Figure 1: Signature Requirements for Transactions Committed (commits shown in the figure is the average of 2-16 cores)

Figure 1 shows the number of transactions committed and from those commits how many actually needed a signature. In the legend *1k-Commits* represents the number of commits made in the system with 1024 bit signature and *1k-Should use Signature* represents the number of commits that actually require a signature mechanism to detect conflicts in the same system. When the legend has *2k* instead of *1k*, the same definition applies to a system with 2048 bit signature.

For both signature configurations, we can see that the number of commits that require a signature is either low or negligible. The disadvantage of using signatures is that they produce false positives. In the above mentioned experiment, we also measured the amount of false positives that could have been avoided if we did not use signatures. The following mechanism is used for this measurement. Our simulator also has a monitor mode which we use to take certain statistics and it has no relation to the timing model of the simula-

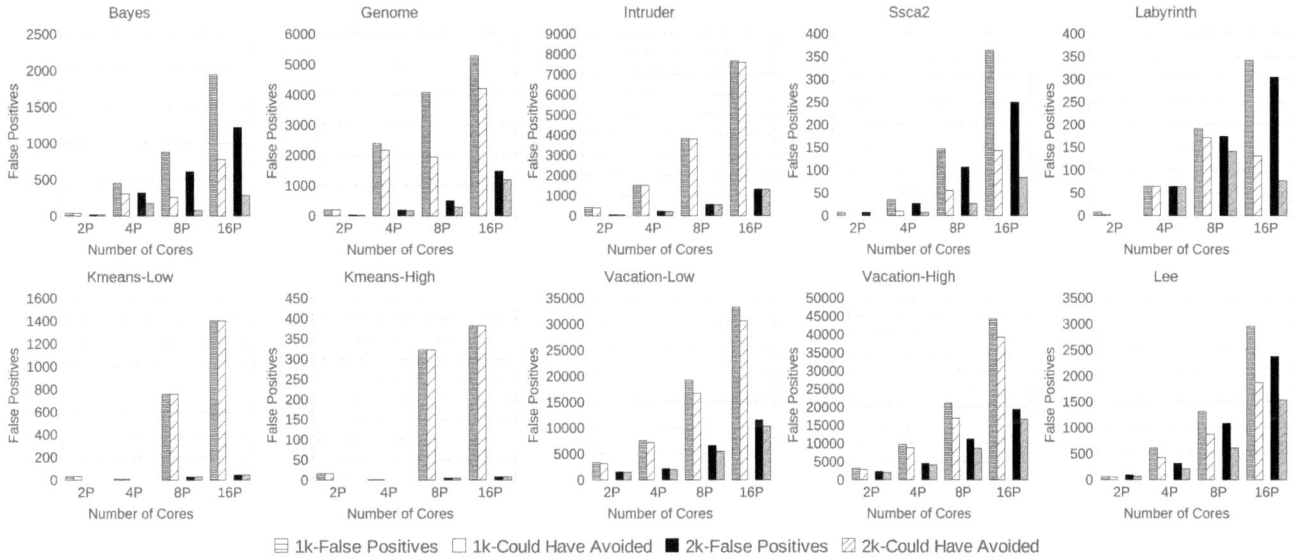

Figure 2: False Aborts that could have been avoided

Legend: ⊟ 1k-False Positives ☐ 1k-Could Have Avoided ■ 2k-False Positives ▨ 2k-Could Have Avoided

tion. When the conflict detection phase asserts an abort, the monitor mode uses its internal data structures to determine whether the abort is a true abort of a false abort. In the case of a false abort, monitor mode also checks whether a signature is required for this commit. If a signature is not required, it marks this abort as an abort that could have been avoided.

Figure 2 shows the number of false transaction aborts produced in the system and how many of them could have been avoided if we did not use signatures. Here in the legend *1k-False Positives* represents the number of false positives that occur in a system with 1024 bit signature and *1k-Could Have Avoided* shows the number of false positives that could have been avoided if signatures are not being used. Similarly when the legend has *2k* instead of *1k*, the same definition applies to a system with 2048 bit signature. In the same figure, the X axis represents the number of processors in the system (2P→2 processors, 4P→4 processors and so on). We can see from Figure 2 that majority of false positives could have been avoided if we use signatures only in cases where we have to do so.

To this end we form our hypothesis, that the execution time of a TM application can be reduced by reducing false aborts by means of changing the source of the information used to detect conflicts. By the term "changing the source of information" we mean adaptively using signatures or the 'R' and 'W' bits in the cache line, to detect conflicts.

3. SnCTM

With SnCTM, we propose to adaptively change the source of information used during the conflict detection phase in a Hardware Transactional Memory (HTM) system. The concept of our proposal is described in this section. When signatures are used to detect conflicts in HTM systems, they can produce false positives. However signatures are required for detecting conflicts, only if a particular transaction has speculative data that cannot be stored within its L1 cache.

In our approach, whether to use cache line information or signatures to detect conflicts is decided at the time of committing. This decision depends on the overflow status of currently running transactions. In this approach, when a transaction is going to commit, the committing processor needs to check whether any of the other processors have encountered a cache overflow during the speculative execution. If that is the case, the write signature of the committing processor is communicated to the others and they check their read signatures with the received one to detect conflicts. If none of the concurrently running transactions have encountered a cache overflow, then there is no need to use signatures to detect conflicts. Therefore the committing processor communicates its write-set to the other processors using the 'W' bit information in its cache line. When they receive this 'W' bit information, other processors check it with their 'R' bit information in the cache lines.

We need to generalise the communication of the commit message and the conflict detection phase to adaptively change between cache lines and signatures. This can be done by including a flag in the header of the commit message. When a processor is going to commit, it creates the commit message either using the signature or the cache line information and the flag is set accordingly. When a processor receives this commit message it first reads this flag and determines what source to use to detect conflict. Figure 3 (a) illustrates concept of SnCTM with respect to a committing processor and Figure 3 (b) shows it from the receiving processor's view.

In order to realise the SnCTM concept, a mechanism is needed to maintain the overflow status of the processors in the system. This can be done by having a local flag in each processor and setting it when a transaction overflows. In this approach the committing processor needs to communicate to all the other processors before initiating the commit phase, in order to decide whether to communicate cache line information or signature. We could also have a central bit map, in which each processor sets the corresponding bit when overflowing. Then the committing processor can check this bit map and decide what source to use to detect conflicts.

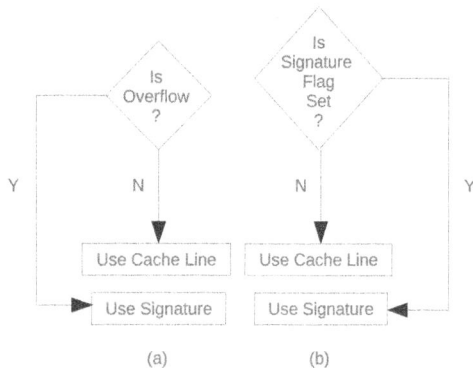

Figure 3: Concept of SnCTM

ture to all the other processors. Upon receiving this write-signature, each processor performs a bitwise AND operation with their read-signature. If all the hashes in the resulting signature are non-zero, then it is considered as a conflict and the processor aborts. Figure 4 shows signature operations used in the baseline architecture. Figure 4(a) shows performing an AND operation between two signatures and Figure 4(b) shows how to check whether all the resulting hashes are zero.

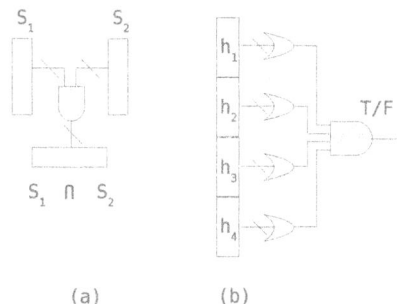

Figure 4: Signature Operations

Another aspect that needs to be considered when realising the SnCTM concept is, when to update signatures and 'R' and 'W' bits in cache lines. In the case of signatures the term "update" refers to, inserting an address to the signature. In the case of cache lines, it refers to setting 'R' and 'W' bits. The most simple approach is to maintain read/write sets and signatures simultaneously. That is when the 'R' bit is set in the cache line, that address is also inserted to the read signature and the same applies to writes that set the 'W' bit in the cache line. Another approach is to keep the read and write set in the cache line and to compose it to the corresponding signature only if the the committing processor asks to use signatures. Regardless of the method used to maintain signatures and cache line bits, the SnCTM approach guarantees that signatures are being used to detect conflicts only if it is necessary. In this manner SnCTM aims to keep the number of false transaction aborts to a minimum level, thereby reducing the execution time of an application.

4. SnCTM ARCHITECTURE

In this section we describe an architecture that supports the SnCTM concept. We start our discussion by describing the baseline architecture and later we show how this baseline can be extended to realise our proposal.

4.1 Baseline Architecture

We use an improved version of Transactional Memory Coherence and Consistency (TCC) [6] as the baseline architecture. The transactional memory implementation in the baseline is similar to any other lazy-lazy hardware TM system. In order to provide an unbounded amount of transactional data, the baseline uses hardware signatures [18] to maintain the read and write sets, using parallel bloom filters to increase accuracy. Since our baseline architecture is based on TCC which does not implement any coherence protocols, transactions are used to maintain coherence and consistency as well. Therefore at the end of a transaction, the next level memory copies are updated and local copies which are read/written are flushed. This is necessary because, local caches may end up keeping stale data due to the fact that no conventional coherence protocols are used.

When a processor needs to commit a transaction, it first requests commit permission from the centralised *commit-arbiter*. Commit permission is granted based on a least recently granted policy. Once the commit permission is granted, the committing processor broadcasts its write-signa-

After sending the write-signature to all the other processors, the committing processor updates the next level memory (either Level 2 (L2) cache or main memory) with all the speculatively modified values. During this commit phase, the communication arbiter denies any request to use the interconnect. Once the next level memory is updated with all the speculatively modified cache entries, all these entries need to be flushed and both read and write signatures need to be cleared as well.

When addressing cache overflows, our baseline serialises commits. That is, when a cache entry needs to be rejected while a processor is inside a transaction, permission is sought from the *overflow arbiter*. Overflow permission is also granted based on a least recently granted policy. Once the overflow permission is granted, the processor flushes the cache line from its L1 cache and updates the corresponding entry either in the L2 cache or the main memory. A processor needs to ask for overflow permission only if the cache line is modified during the current transaction. An extra 'W' bit is used to mark all the speculatively modified entries. A dirty bit is not sufficient for this purpose because the entry could have been dirty due to a write operation performed outside a transaction. Therefore the baseline architecture cannot eliminate both 'R' and 'W' bits that were present in the original TCC. It needs to keep the 'W' bit to indicate that this cache line has been modified during the transaction. If the 'W' bit is not set, there is no need to seek for overflow permission. If an overflow request is denied, the processor stalls until the request is granted.

Earlier in this section, we said that the *commit-arbiter* operates on a *least-recently-granted* policy. There is an exception to that for processors who have transactional cache overflows. That is, once the overflow permission is granted to a processor, all the commit requests from other processors are denied, until the overflowing processor commits. This is because once a speculatively modified entry is written back to the next level memory, either L2 cache or main memory, the old value is lost and this is a non-reversible action. Allowing cache overflows to speculatively modified entries, can be considered as violating the atomicity and isolation properties of the lazy-lazy transactional memory. This is because the overflowed cache entries can now be read by other processors before the current transaction commits. However we can maintain the consistency property by making the current transaction of the overflowing processor, an unabortable one. That is, as described earlier, by denying all the commit requests until the overflowing processor commits.

4.2 SnCTM Design

In this section we describe how we can extend the baseline architecture, described in section 4.1, to realise the SnCTM concept. As described in section 3, the basic idea of SnCTM is to adaptively change the source of information used to detect conflicts during the commit phase. Since the processor does not know in advance which source can be used to detect conflict, hardware should have the capability to store read and write sets in both formats, i.e 'R' and 'W' bits in cache lines and signatures. Since SnCTM does not use any cache coherence protocol, by reusing the the existing entry for the state field of the coherence protocol to keep 'R' and 'W' bits, area utilization of L1 cache can be kept unchanged.

When a processor is executing a transaction, all the read operations set the 'R' bit in the cache line and also it sets the corresponding bits in the read signature. The same applies to the write operations. In this way each processor keeps both the sources updated and one of them is used during the commit phase. Due to the nature of the baseline used, at any given time only one processor can be granted overflow permission. Also the commit protocol of the baseline prevents any other processors committing before the overflowing processor. When the commit permission is granted, without any communication to other processors, the committing processor itself can decide whether to use signature or cache lines. This is because if the committing processor is not the overflowing processor, there cannot be any other processor in the system which has granted overflow status. If there is any other processor which has granted overflow permission, then this processor cannot be granted the commit permission.

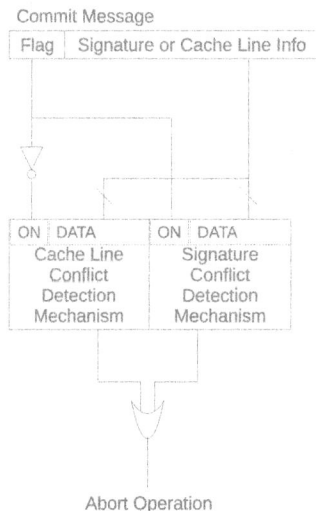

Figure 5: Adaptively Checking for Conflicts in a SnCTM Processor

Therefore, if the committing processor has granted overflow status, it broadcasts its write signature to other processors and they check it with their read signatures to detect conflicts. If the committing processor is not granted overflow status, this means the transaction was able to fit in the L1 cache. Therefore it can use the 'R' and 'W' bit information in the cache line to detect conflicts. In this case, the committing processor broadcasts its write set to other processors and they check it with their read set to detect conflicts. In order to adaptively decide which source to use in the conflict detection mechanism of the receiving processor, the commit message includes an extra flag called *Type* which notifies the receiving processor about the type of information it carries, i.e signature or cache line.

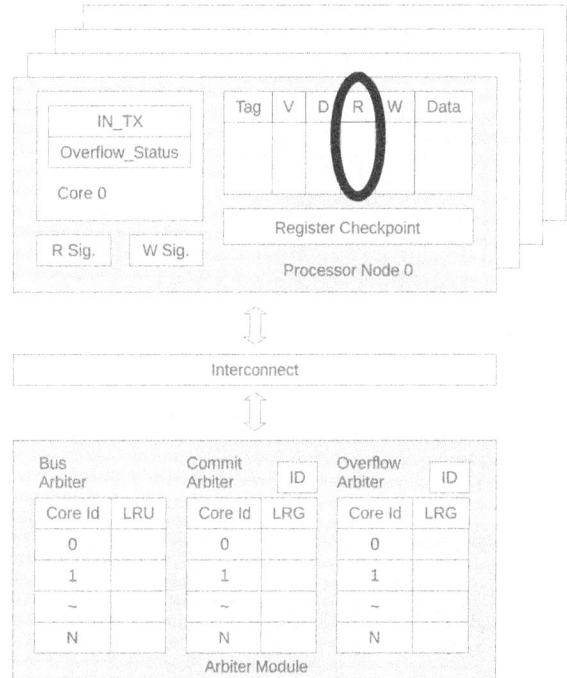

Figure 6: SnCTM System

In SnCTM when a processor is granted commit permission, it generates the commit message with signature or cache line information and the *Type* flag is set accordingly. Upon receiving the commit message, this *Type* flag is checked and the corresponding source for detecting conflicts is determined. In the baseline architecture each processor has a flag to indicate the overflow status of the processor. This is set when the overflow permission is granted and cleared when the overflowing transaction is committed. The purpose is, when a speculatively modified cache line needs to be rejected, the processor first checks this flag. If set, it does not need to ask for overflow permission, hence can be written back to the next level memory. If unset, overflow permission is sought and stalled until it is granted. This flag can also be used in SnCTM to determine whether to include signature or cache line information in the commit message. If set, signature is included in the commit message and the *Type* flag in the message is set. If unset, cache line bits are used and the *Type* flag of the commit message is kept unset as well. Figure 5 shows the mechanism used in a SnCTM processor when checking conflicts as a response to a commit message.

A complete SnCTM system is shown in Figure 6. The only thing we have added to the baseline, apart from the control logic, is the 'R' bit field in the cache lines.

5. EVALUATION

The evaluation of SnCTM is presented in this section. After discussing the evaluation setup in section 5.1, we show that SnCTM outperforms an improved version of TCC [6], with two commonly used signature configurations, in section 5.2. We characterise the results of SnCTM in section 5.3 and a sensitivity analysis of the signature length is presented in section 5.4.

5.1 Evaluation Setup

In order to evaluate the SnCTM architecture, we modelled a lazy-lazy hardware transactional memory system in Simics [11], a full system simulator running Linux kernel version 2.6.16. The SnCTM system is configured with the components shown in Table 1.

Component	Feature
Processors	1-16
L1 Data Cache	2 way assoc, 64 B line, 32 KB size, 2 cycle latency, private per core
Signature	1024, 2048 Bits, 4 Parallel H3 [1] Hash functions
L2 Data Cache	8 way assoc, 64 B line, 4 MB size, 20 cycle latency, shared
Interconnect	Split-transaction bus, 4 cycle latency, 64 B data width
Main Memory	100 cycle latency

Table 1: Components and Features

Lee's routing algorithm [19] and applications from the STAMP [12] benchmark suite were used to evaluate the SnCTM architecture. For comparison purposes, all the applications were also executed on the baseline architecture. However, due to the fact that no cache coherence protocol is implemented in baseline or SnCTM, none of these applications were able to execute without being modified. Since the baseline and SnCTM provide coherence using transactions, some of the applications were modified by adding extra transactions in places where they access shared data. No modification was required for Vacation, Labyrinth and Lee as they do not access shared data outside transactions. Smaller transactions similar to already existing ones have been added to Intruder, Genome and Kmeans. The only significant change has been made to Ssca2 by adding several large transactions as the majority of the non-transactional code accesses shared data.

The input configurations used for each benchmark are shown in Table 2. All the inputs for the STAMP suite are those suggested in [12]. All the evaluations are made on the parallel region of the applications.

5.2 Performance

Figure 7 shows the speedup of SnCTM over the baseline architecture. In the legend, 1024 refers to the case where the size of the signature of both baseline and SnCTM is 1024 bits and 2048 represents the situations where both systems

Application	Input
Genome	-g256 -s16 -n16384
Intruder	-a10 -l4 -n2038 -s1
Kmeans-Low	-m40 -n40 -t0.05 -i random-n2048-d16-c16.txt
Kmeans-High	-m15 -n15 -t0.05 -i random-n2048-d16-c16.txt
Labyrinth	-i random-x32-y32-z3-n96.txt
Ssca2	-s13 -i1.0 -u1.0 -l3 -p3
Vacation-Low	-n2 -q90 -u98 -r16384 -t4096
Vacation-High	-n4 -q60 -u90 -r16384 -t4096
Lee	75x75 Grid, 320 routes
Bayes	-v32 -r1024 -n2 -p20 -s0 -i2 -e2

Table 2: Benchmark applications and their inputs

use signatures of 2048 bits. In all the figures, the X axis represents the number of processors used for the experiment (2P→2 processors, 4P→4 processors and so on). The fist observation that can be made from the figure is that SnCTM outperforms the baseline in almost all the cases with an average of 1.51X (1024) and 1.23X (2048). The speedup varies from 1X (Ssca2, 2P) to 4.62X (Vacation-High, 16P) for the signatures of 1024 bit width. In the case of signatures of 2048 bit, the speedup varies from 0.99X (Kmeans-High, 16P) to 2.93X (Vacation-High, 16P). We can also observe that the speedup over baseline increases as we increase the number of processors. Table 3 shows the average speedup for each hardware configuration. There we can see that as the number of processors increases, the speedup increases and also baseline performs better with 2048 bit signature than 1024.

Processors	1024	2048
2P	1.16	1.10
4P	1.45	1.13
8P	1.56	1.25
16P	1.87	1.46

Table 3: Average Speedup over baseline for Each Configuration

As the number of processors increase, bus contention also increases. This can be aggravated by introducing false positives to the system. The number of false positives produced in SnCTM is less than those produced in the baseline. False positives cause a processor to flush its cache and bring data from the next level memory. Even though the operations involved in this process are the same for any processor configuration, the effect on the bus contention increase rapidly as the processor count increases. Therefore the relative bus contention of the baseline with higher number of processors is higher than the that of the baseline with lower number of processors. This makes the speedup of SnCTM over the baseline with higher number of processors to have a higher value than the speedup shown over the lower number of processors. Regarding the better performance of baseline with the signature size of 2048 bit, the accuracy of the signature increases as the size of it increases. Therefore the baseline performs better with a signature of 2048 bit size. However, SnCTM still performs better than the baseline.

5.3 Characterization of SnCTM

Since SnCTM is based on the principle of adaptively changing the source used for detecting conflicts, we first check the

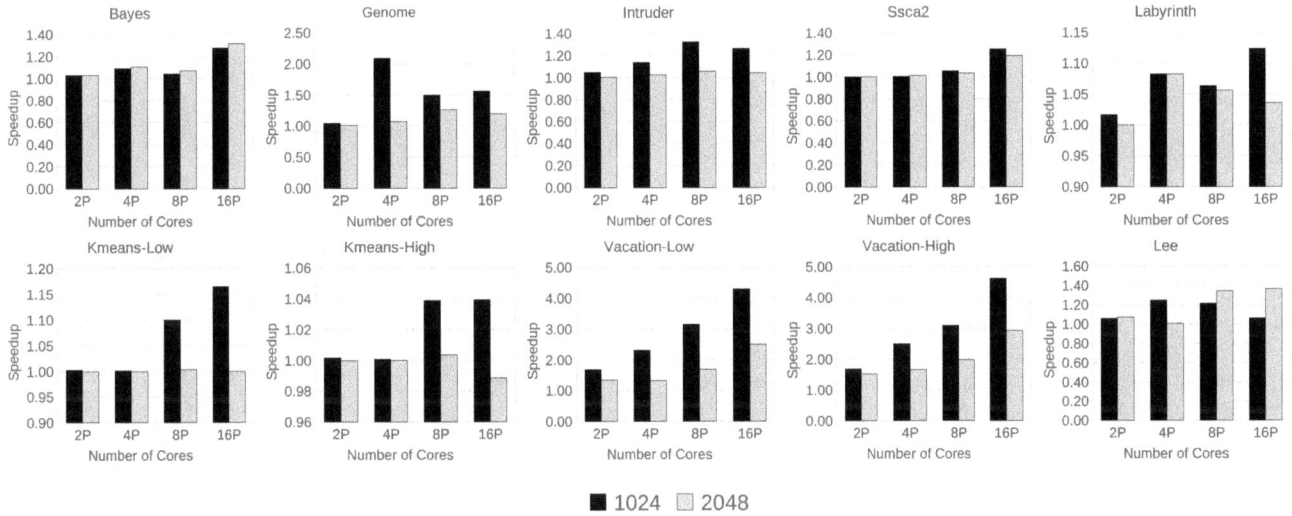

Figure 7: SnCTM speedup over baseline

effect of this on the number of transactions being aborted. Figure 8 shows the average number of transactions aborted in both signature configurations. In the legend, 1024 shows the statistics related to a system with 1024 bit signature and 2048 represents the system with 2048 bit signature. The values are normalised to their corresponding baseline configurations. With the SnCTM approach we are able to reduce the number of transaction aborts. However this reduction varies from 0% (Kmeans-High, 2024) to 92% (Vacation-Low, 1024).

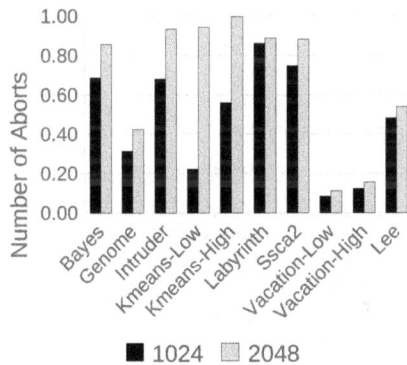

Figure 8: Transactions aborted normalised to baseline (aborts shown in the figure is the average of 2-16 cores)

The number of transactions aborted is mainly a characteristic of the application and also it depends on the the contention management policy used in the TM system. That said, false transaction aborts which can occur from cache line sharing or false positives in signatures, can count towards this as well. Since we used the number of false positive that could have been avoided as an motivating factor to our discussion in section 2, we also measured the false positives presented in SnCTM. Figure 9 shows the average number of false positives which occurred in SnCTM and baseline systems for both signature configurations. In addition to 1024 and 2048 bit widths, we also used a configuration with 8k

bits as the signature for this experiment. We consider this as a perfect system and the aim is to compare the number of false positives occurring in both baseline and SnCTM systems with a perfect system. In the legend *1k* corresponds to a system with 1024 bit signature and *2k* corresponds to a system with 2048 bit signature. As the name suggests *Baseline* represents the baseline architecture and *SnCTM* represents the SnCTM architecture.

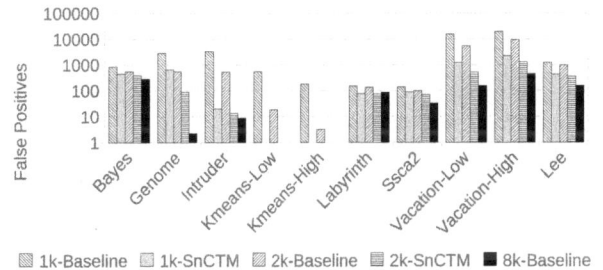

Figure 9: False positives (false positives shown in the figure is the average of 2-16 cores)

From Figure 9 we can see that, both SnCTM configurations report less false positives than their corresponding baseline systems. We can also see that in most of applications, the number of false positives in SnCTM is similar to that of the perfect system. A significant difference of false positives between baseline and SnCTM can be observed in Kmeans-low, Kmeans-high and Intruder. This is because these application have short transaction length, thus can be fit in the L1 cache. Therefore SnCTM can use cache lines to detect conflicts whereas baseline has to use signatures all the time. In the case of Ssca2, which is also categorised as an application having shorter transaction length in STAMP suite [12], does not show the similar behaviour in Figure 9. This is because, in our experiment we had to insert extra transactions to the Ssca2 application to maintain coherence, which causes it to have longer transactions. The reason we add extra transactions is because our architecture, which is fundamentally similar to TCC [6], does not use any conventional cache coherence protocols. Both SnCTM configurations report higher false positives than the perfect system (still less than baseline) in Vacation-low, Vacation-high and Genome. All these applications have medium transaction length and low contention. In these applications not all the transactions fit in the L1 cache. Therefore SnCTM has to use signatures for some transactions, which causes it to produce some false aborts. However, SnCTM manages to keep the number of false positives lower than the baseline by adaptively changing source used during conflict detection. In the cases of Lee, Labyrinth and Bayes all of them have long transaction length. Therefore SnCTM also has to use signatures for most of its conflict detection, thereby increasing the false positives. However our system was still able to produce less false positives than the baseline architecture.

5.4 Sensitivity Analysis

In this section we present a sensitivity analysis of the signature length in both baseline and SnCTM architectures. We used signatures of 64, 128, 256, 512, 1024, 2048 and 4096 bits for the experiment and a 8k bit signature as the perfect system. The execution times of both baseline and SnCTM systems, normalised to the perfect baseline, is shown in Figure 10. For each signature configuration, experiments are carried out with multi-core processors having 2, 4, 8 and 16 cores. We were not able to run Kmeans-low in a 16 core configuration with 64, 128 and 256 bits as the signature length. We believe this could be due to a limitation in the simulator.

From Figure 10 we can see that all the applications except Bayes, Labyrinth and Lee show a similar behaviour. That is the normalised execution time increases as the signature size reduces. However, in SnCTM this increase is either negligible or quite low in comparison to those of the baseline. The reason is, as the size of the signature decreases, the probability of producing false positive increases [18]. However SnCTM only uses signature for situations where a cache overflow happens within the transaction. According to Figure 1, shown in section 2, not many transactions fall into this category. Therefore the reduction in the signature size does not affect to SnCTM as it affects the baseline. This shows that with the SnCTM approach, we can use smaller signatures without compromising the performance of the system.

As the second observation we can see that for all the applications except Bayes, Labyrinth and Lee, the normalised execution time of the baseline increases significantly in comparison to the perfect system, as the number of processors increase. This is because, as the number of processors increase, the contention for the interconnect increases. When the contention increases, a processor has to wait longer to get access to the shared resources, thus the idle time increases. When processor idle time increases, transaction length increases. When a transaction takes longer time to finish, it becomes more susceptible to abort. Aborted transactions results in flushing all the modified cache entries and bringing in all the data, once the transaction is restarted. This also increase the contention for the interconnect, thus making it a cyclic problem.

In the case of Bayes, Labyrinth and Lee applications, firstly, they produced a high contention [12]. This increases the number of aborts produced. Secondly, all these applications have longer transactions. Therefore it is very likely that they overflow during atomic execution, requiring the use of signatures to detect conflicts. This makes these these

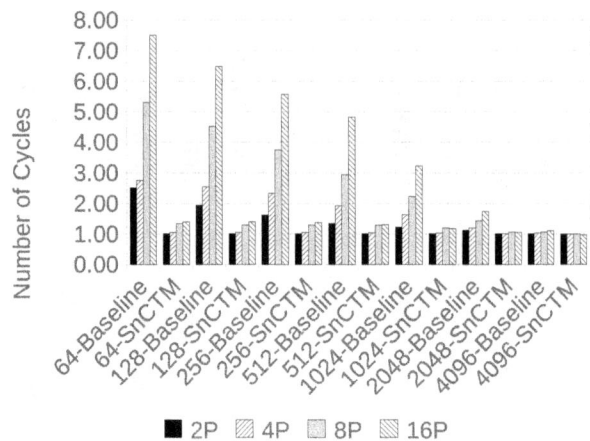

Figure 11: Processor idle time normalised to perfect

applications: (1) to have a lower speedup as the processor count increases; (2) to have less sensitivity to the signature length. Therefore they do not follow the same behaviour as others.

We also measure the processor idle time of both SnCTM and the baseline. Figure 11 shows the average of processor idle time for all benchmark applications (except Bayes, Labyrinth and Lee) for each hardware configuration. All the values are normalised to the perfect system. From Figure 11 we can see that for lower signature sizes as the processor count increases, the idle time of the baseline architecture increases significantly, where as in SnCTM it remains closer to the perfect system. Therefore the execution time of the SnCTM remains comparable to a perfect system even with a smaller signature, whilst the baseline suffers huge performance degradation.

6. RELATED WORK

Transactional memory (TM) [8] has been proposed as a way of achieving optimistic concurrency in parallel programming. In Transactional Memory Coherence and Consistency (TCC) [6] the authors propose to use transactions as the unit for maintaining coherence, consistency and synchronization. Since then, many TM approaches have been proposed and summarising them all is beyond the scope of this paper, but interested readers are directed to the book by Harris et al. [7].

Signatures were initially proposed by Ceze et al. [2] to represent the bulk of addresses. They propose the use of simple bit permutations of the address to generate the signature. LogTM-SE [20] also uses signatures to maintain read and write set of a transaction. Their signature implementation is based on selecting different bits of the address. SigTM [13] which is a hybrid TM system, also uses hardware support to maintain signatures. They use combination of permutation and bit shifting as their hash functions. Sanchez et al. concluded [18] that the H3 [1] class of hash functions should be used in signatures instead of bit selection as in previously proposed signature implementations [2, 13, 20]. The authors also showed that using k single ported SRAMs (parallel bllom filters) to implement signatures is an area efficient technique. Yen et al. [21] argue that H3

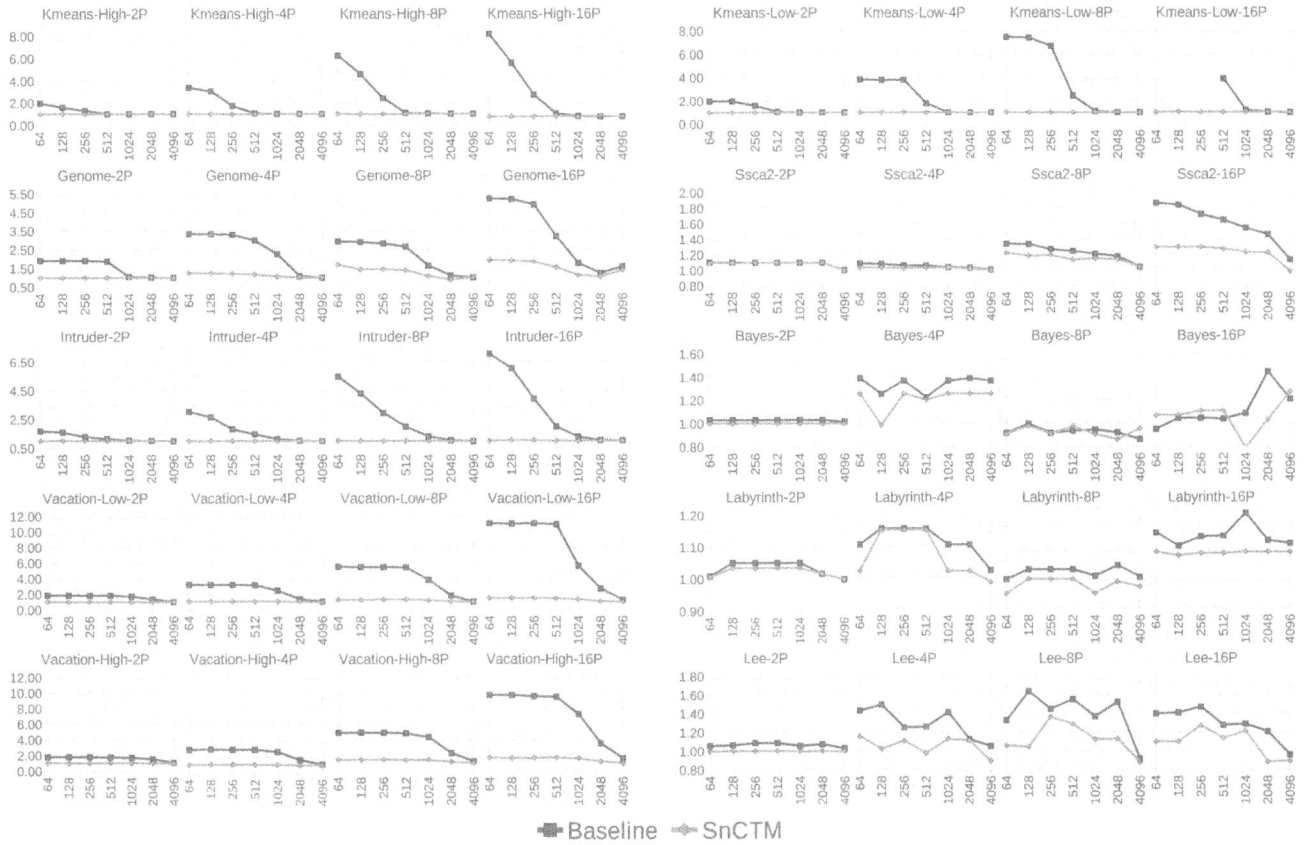

Figure 10: Execution time normalised to perfect (In each figure X-axis represents the signature configuration and Y-axis represents the normalised execution time)

implementations use many XOR gates, thus increasing the area and power overhead of the signatures. They proposed Page-Block-XOR (PBX) hash function that delivers performance similar to H3 hash function, but at a lesser hardware cost. They also proposed a filtering mechanism to reduce the numbers of address being inserted to signatures. By reducing the number of insertions made to the signature, Notary [21] was able to reduce false aborts thereby reducing the execution time of an application. Quislant *et al.* [15] propose to take the advantage of locality of memory references to design hardware signatures. With their approach, authors were able to reduce false aborts for transactions having spatial locality in their read and write sets.

Choi *et al.* [3] present an interesting fact, that is sometimes false positives in a signature based TM system can be helpful as well. They argue that, when a signature asserts an abort erroneously, it could also be the case that this transaction is meant to be aborted in future due to a real conflict. Therefore if the transaction aborts early because of the false abort, it could save the wasted work that it would have been doing from the false abort to the real abort. They categorise these false aborts as "good" and use this early conflict detection to improve the performance. They observed that there is a relation between the good/bad false positives and the granularity of bits used in the address. Based on this phenomenon they propose *Adaptive Grain Signature* which changes the granularity of the bit range input to the hash function. Their mechanism used a history table of aborts to

adaptively change the granularity. The same authors propose the use of single signature for both read and write sets [4]. With this approach of having a *unified-signature*, the authors aim to double the size of the signature by combining both read and write signature. By having a larger signature without any hardware cost, they were able to reduce the false positives, thereby increasing the performance. In order to reduce the impact on read-read dependencies signalling conflicts, they also proposed to use an small helper signature alongside the unified signature. Concurrently with work of Choi *et al.* [4], Quislant *et al.* proposed multiset signatures [16], which is also to combine read and write signatures into one. Their approach is enhanced using locality sensitive signatures [15] proposed by the same authors.

In addition to the above mentioned fixed signature implementations, Labrecque *et al.* [10] propose to use reconfigurable signatures. Their approach is to customise the signature to match with the access pattern of the application and to minimize the false conflicts.

Even though we have the same intention as many of the above, that is to reduce false aborts, we differ from all these approaches. Firstly because we do not propose another signature implementation, we propose to use it only when there is a need to do so. Secondly our approach is not tied to any signature implementation, therefore any of the above mentioned signature implementations can be used in our approach.

7. CONCLUSION

This paper presented the concept and the design of SnCTM, a novel way of reducing the false aborts by adaptively changing the source used during the conflict detection stage. The idea is to decide at the time of committing which source to use, i.e cache line or signature. This way the use of signatures are limited to situations where speculative data cannot be held in the local cache.

We evaluated SnCTM using the STAMP benchmark suite and Lee-TM. We showed that our proposal delivers better speed-ups (up to 4.62 and 2.93) over an optimized lazy-lazy TM system. We also performed a sensitivity analysis of the signature length and we compared both our system and the baseline against a perfect signature. We showed that even with a smaller signature (64 bit) SnCTM was able to deliver performance comparable to a perfect system where as the baseline suffers huge performance degradation. Another important aspect of our proposal is that it is independent of the underlying signature implementation. Therefore all the proposed techniques [3, 4, 10, 15, 16, 21] to improve the efficiency of a signatures can be used in SnCTM as well.

8. ACKNOWLEDGEMENTS

We would like to thank anonymous reviewers for their advice on the paper. Isuru Herath is supported by an Overseas Research Studentship and a School of Computer Science studentship from the University of Manchester. Demian Rosas-Ham is supported by the National Council of Science and Technology of Mexico. Dr. Luján is supported by a Royal Society University Research Fellowship.

9. REFERENCES

[1] J. L. Carter and M. N. Wegman. Universal classes of hash functions (extended abstract). In *Proceedings of the ninth annual ACM symposium on Theory of computing*, STOC '77, pages 106–112, New York, NY, USA, 1977. ACM.

[2] L. Ceze, J. Tuck, J. Torrellas, and C. Cascaval. Bulk disambiguation of speculative threads in multiprocessors. In *Proceedings of the 33rd annual international symposium on Computer Architecture*, ISCA '06, pages 227–238, Washington, DC, USA, 2006. IEEE Computer Society.

[3] W. Choi and J. Draper. Locality-aware adaptive grain signatures for transactional memories. In *Proceedings of the 24th International Parallel and Distributed Processing Symposium*, pages 1–10, Los Alamitos, CA, USA, 2010. IEEE Computer Society.

[4] W. Choi and J. Draper. Unified signatures for improving performance in transactional memory. In *Parallel Distributed Processing Symposium (IPDPS), 2011 IEEE International*, pages 817 –827, may 2011.

[5] J. Gray. The transaction concept: virtues and limitations (invited paper). In *Proceedings of the seventh international conference on Very Large Data Bases - Volume 7*, VLDB '1981, pages 144–154. VLDB Endowment, 1981.

[6] L. Hammond, V. Wong, M. Chen, B. D. Carlstrom, J. D. Davis, B. Hertzberg, M. K. Prabhu, H. Wijaya, C. Kozyrakis, and K. Olukotun. Transactional memory coherence and consistency. In *Proceedings of the 31st annual international symposium on Computer architecture*, ISCA '04, pages 102–, Washington, DC, USA, 2004. IEEE Computer Society.

[7] T. Harris, J. Larus, and R. Rajwar. Transactional memory, 2nd edition. *Synthesis Lectures on Computer Architecture*, 5(1):1–263, 2010.

[8] M. Herlihy and J. E. B. Moss. Transactional memory: architectural support for lock-free data structures. In *Proceedings of the 20th annual international symposium on Computer architecture*, ISCA '93, pages 289–300, New York, NY, USA, 1993. ACM.

[9] M. Hill and M. Marty. Amdahl's law in the multicore era. *Computer*, 41(7):33–38, 2008.

[10] M. Labrecque, M. C. Jeffrey, and J. G. Steffan. Application-specific signatures for transactional memory in soft processors. In *6th International Symposium on Applied Reconfigurable Computing (ARC'10)*, pages 42–54, 2010.

[11] P. Magnusson, M. Christensson, J. Eskilson, D. Forsgren, G. Hallberg, J. Hogberg, F. Larsson, A. Moestedt, and B. Werner. Simics: A full system simulation platform. *Computer*, 35:50–58, 2002.

[12] C. C. Minh, J. Chung, C. Kozyrakis, and K. Olukotun. Stamp: Stanford transactional applications for multi-processing. In *Workload Characterization, 2008. IISWC 2008. IEEE International Symposium on*, pages 35–46, 2008.

[13] C. C. Minh, M. Trautmann, J. Chung, A. McDonald, N. Bronson, J. Casper, C. Kozyrakis, and K. Olukotun. An effective hybrid transactional memory system with strong isolation guarantees. In *Proceedings of the 34th annual international symposium on Computer architecture*, ISCA '07, pages 69–80, New York, NY, USA, 2007. ACM.

[14] K. Moore, J. Bobba, M. Moravan, M. Hill, and D. Wood. Logtm: log-based transactional memory. In *High-Performance Computer Architecture, 2006. The Twelfth International Symposium on*, pages 254 – 265, 2006.

[15] R. Quislant, E. Gutierrez, O. Plata, and E. L. Zapata. Improving signatures by locality exploitation for transactional memory. In *Proceedings of the 2009 18th International Conference on Parallel Architectures and Compilation Techniques*, pages 303–312, Washington, DC, USA, 2009. IEEE Computer Society.

[16] R. Quislant, E. Gutierrez, O. Plata, and E. L. Zapata. Multiset signatures for transactional memory. In *Proceedings of the international conference on Supercomputing*, ICS '11, pages 43–52, New York, NY, USA, 2011. ACM.

[17] R. Rajwar, M. Herlihy, and K. Lai. Virtualizing transactional memory. In *Proceedings of the 32nd annual international symposium on Computer Architecture*, ISCA '05, pages 494–505, Washington, DC, USA, 2005. IEEE Computer Society.

[18] D. Sanchez, L. Yen, M. D. Hill, and K. Sankaralingam. Implementing signatures for transactional memory. In *Proceedings of the 40th Annual IEEE/ACM International Symposium on Microarchitecture*, MICRO 40, pages 123–133, Washington, DC, USA, 2007. IEEE Computer Society.

[19] I. Watson, C. Kirkham, and M. Lujan. A study of a transactional parallel routing algorithm. In *Proceedings of the 16th International Conference on Parallel Architecture and Compilation Techniques*, PACT '07, pages 388–398, Washington, DC, USA, 2007. IEEE Computer Society.

[20] L. Yen, J. Bobba, M. R. Marty, K. E. Moore, H. Volos, M. D. Hill, M. M. Swift, and D. A. Wood. Logtm-se: Decoupling hardware transactional memory from caches. In *Proceedings of the 2007 IEEE 13th International Symposium on High Performance Computer Architecture*, pages 261–272, Washington, DC, USA, 2007. IEEE Computer Society.

[21] L. Yen, S. C. Draper, and M. D. Hill. Notary: Hardware techniques to enhance signatures. In *MICRO '08: Proceedings of the 2008 41st IEEE/ACM International Symposium on Microarchitecture*, pages 234–245, Washington, DC, USA, 2008. IEEE Computer Society.

Architectural Support of Multiple Hypervisors over Single Platform for Enhancing Cloud Computing Security

Weidong Shi
University of Houston
Houston, TX 77004, USA
larryshi@ymail.com

JongHyuk Lee
University of Houston
Houston, TX 77004, USA
jonghyuk.lee@daum.net

Taeweon Suh
Korea University
Seoul, South Korea
suhtw@korea.ac.kr

Dong Hyuk Woo
Intel Labs
Santa Clara, CA 95054, USA
dong.hyuk.woo@intel.com

Xinwen Zhang
Huawei America R&D Center
Santa Clara, CA 95050, USA
xinwenzhang@gmail.com

ABSTRACT

This paper presents MultiHype, a novel architecture that supports multiple hypervisors (or virtual machine monitors) on a single physical platform by leveraging many-core based cloud-on-chip architecture. A MultiHype platform consists of a control plane and multiple hypervisors created on-demand, each can further create multiple guest virtual machines. Supported at architectural level, a single platform using MultiHype can behave as a distributed system with each hypervisor and its virtual machines running independently and concurrently. As a direct consequence, vulnerabilities of one hypervisor or its guest virtual machine can be confined within its own domain, which makes the platform more resilient to malicious attacks and failures in a cloud environment. Towards defending against resource exhaustion attacks, MultiHype further implements a new cache eviction policy and memory management scheme for preventing resource monopolization on shared cache, and defending against denial of resource exploits on physical memory resource launched from malicious virtual machines on shared platform. We use Bochs emulator and cycle based x86 simulation to evaluate the effectiveness and performance of MultiHype.

Categories and Subject Descriptors

D.4 [**Operating Systems**]

Keywords

Virtualization, Architecture, Security, Scalability

1. INTRODUCTION

Cloud computing is emerging as a viable alternative to premise-based deployment of hardware and software systems. The economy of scale and elasticity offered by cloud computing has garnered rapid adoption for increasingly dynamic and competitive business climate. As a consequence, cloud computing is quickly altering the landscape of the information technology service industry. Virtualization plays a critical role in cloud computing by multiplexing the resources and computing power of a single platform to mul-tiple logical platforms. The development of virtualization technology has turned traditional software into *irtual appliances* and allows software and their execution environment to be rapidly deployed and delivered as services in ways that are both massively scalable and elastic. According to IDC's analysis, cloud services will be in the order of $44.2bn in 2013 [8].

Virtualization has existed long before the emergence of cloud computing. However, with the light of recent advance on low cost many-core processors, virtualization has made cloud computing economically viable. Specifically, many-core processors have increased virtualization density to the point where large numbers of virtual servers can be ran concurrently on a single physical server. In foreseeable future, the number of processor cores in a single processor will continue to double steadily [11]. Therefore, we will reach the era of *hyperscale* virtual server consolidation where hundreds or even thousands of virtual servers can be packed on a single many-core based physical server. This will enable virtualization based computing at epic scale.

On the other side, although cloud computing holds great potential and promises, security is one of the main challenges and deficiencies in today's cloud environment. Not surprisingly, the characteristics of multi-tenancy and shared resources introduce new risks and threats to any resources on cloud platform. Potential risks include failure of separation mechanisms for storage, memory, routings between different tenants, and hypervisor subversion [30]. Further threats come from the possibilities of attacks that "escape" from a guest virtual machine (VM) and being able to inject codes into the host system or other VMs [16, 22]. Public consent and study [10, 17] have shown major security concerns, including the reluctance to deploy virtual machines on shared physical servers (which run against the fundamental cloud computing principles of resource sharing and on-demand provisioning), potential leak and disclosure of confidential and proprietary information to third parties, and compromising of co-located virtual machines. These concerns are well justified by identified and potential vulnerabilities associated with commodity hypervisors and virtual machine systems on shared platforms [25, 7, 16, 22, 30]. Due to those concerns, many data center customers demand their services be hosted by dedicated servers physically isolated from other customers' servers. In the near future, we can expect to see many new security exploitations on cloud environment towards platforms and user information.

In line with these trends and challenges, we propose *ulti-ype*, a poly-hypervisor architecture to improve the dependability, scalability, and security of many-core based cloud servers. Comparing with today's mono-hypervisor (Mono-Hype) based systems, MultiHype supports running multiple hypervisors or VMMs (virtual machine monitors) on a single physical platform, in turn, each of which can execute multiple VMs. By leveraging many-core based cloud-on-chip processor architecture, this extra abstraction provides strong isolation between physical resources managed by individual hypervisor *real s*. As a direct consequence, the vulnerabilities of one hypervisor or a VM within a hypervisor can be confined within its own domain, which makes platform-wide attacks much harder. With careful design on physical separation of CPUs, memory, storage, and I/O devices, MultiHype can achieve more dependable, secure, and scalable cloud server platform than today's MonoHype platform, which fits the requirement of hyper-scale virtual server consolidation.

Outline: Next section analyzes and summarizes security risks, threats, and attacks on existing cloud servers. In Section 3 we present the architecture and design of MultiHype. We then illustrate the evaluation methodology of MultiHype and result analysis in Section 4 and 5, respectively. Section 6 summarizes related work of this paper and Section 7 concludes this paper.

2. HYPERVISOR RELATED THREATS IN CLOUD COMPUTING

In cloud computing environment, virtual machines from different cloud customers share a single physical server and hypervisor. Virtualization offers "layered defense" for system security, usually by assuming that a malicious attacker who controls or penetrates one guest virtual machine cannot compromise the underlying system and other virtual machines. This should not always be taken for granted. Previous studies have demonstrated the vulnerabilities and real attacks that determined attackers can exploit hypervisor vulnerability, and consequently compromise services of co-located cloud users [25, 7, 16, 22, 30, 24]. We summarize several risks and threats of virtualized platform in cloud computing environment as follows.

2.1 Hypervisor Vulnerabilities

On a cloud server platform, virtual machines from different customers sit above a common hypervisor that manages both the physical hardware resources and customer resources. Like any other software layer, a hypervisor can have vulnerabilities and is prone to attacks or unexpected failure. Commodity hypervisor has significantly grown in functions and features, and thus in code size. These make them look closer to a real operating system (OS) with large trusted computing base (TCB), and increasing design and implementation vulnerabilities. Therefore their isolation and security functions might be compromised by attacks from guest OS [13]. An attacker can compromise a hypervisor by hacking it from inside a guest virtual machine and exploit all the guests. Hypervisor layer attacks are very attractive. In a MonoHype system, the hypervisor fully controls the physical resources and all guest virtual machines that run on top of it.

Past few years have seen a number of successful hypervisor subversions [25, 7, 16, 22, 30, 24]. King et al. [15] described the concept of a virtual machine-based rootkit and demonstrated the subversion of VMWare and VirtualPC using hypervisor rootkit SubVirt. Blue Pill [24] is a rootkit that can trap a running native OS into a guest virtual machine "on-the-fly" with hardware-assisted virtualization technology such as Intel VT-x or AMD Pacifica. In [22], the author investigated several popular x86 based virtual machine implementations and tested whether the assumed hypervisor security and virtual machine isolation can be taken for granted. The authors performed hypervisor stress tests by injecting random instructions and I/O activities to the hypervisor from a guest virtual machine. The results identified vulnerabilities in all popular virtual machine implementations for x86 architecture in use today. If exploited, a vulnerable VMM can be subverted to execute arbitrary code on the host with the privileges of the VMM process. In addition, an exploit from a virtual machine guest could cause VMM to terminate unexpectedly or trigger an infinite loop that prevents the host from performing normal administration operations for other virtual machines.

When a hypervisor is subverted, an attacker can escape the isolation between different customers. For example, a documented attack on VMWare [25] allows "guest to host escape". After a hypervisor is subverted, an attacker may take control of other virtual machines running on the same hypervisor or gain access to the data contained inside them. Furthermore, an attacker may manipulate resource allocation; reduce resources assigned to other virtual machines and as a consequence cause denial of service.

2.2 Weak Separation between VMs

Cloud computing infrastructures mostly rely on architectural designs to separate physical resources in a logical manner such as to share computing capacity, storage, and network among multiple virtual machines and therefore multiple customers. On a many-core computing platform, hundred or even thousand of virtual machines may share the same physical platform. Failure of resource separation between different tenants could lead to potential devastating results such as unauthorized access to shared resources, provoking denial of services by manipulating resources allocated to other customer's virtual machines or terminating other customer's running virtual machines, and side-channel data leakage. In [23], the authors illustrated the steps for accessing confidential information from running EC2 instances and demonstrated side-channel exploits.

2.3 Resource Exhaustion

Cloud services acquire resources in on-demand manner. In multi-tenancy working environment, malicious attackers may trigger resource exhaustion and cause denial-of-resources attacks to other users' virtual machines. Shared resources with capacity limitation include memory, storage, I/O bandwidth, networking buffers, CPU, etc. If an attacker can trigger the allocation of these limited resources, but the number or size of the resources is not controlled, the attacker could cause a denial of service by consuming all available resources on a physical platform. For example, a memory exhaustion attack against an application could slow down the application as well as its host OS. A malicious customer may run mischievous guest virtual machines that use certain resources intensively. For example, a virtual machine can deliberately trigger a lots of interrupts or generate switches between virtual machine and hypervisor at extremely high frequency.

3. ARCHITECTURE AND DESIGN

3.1 Requirements

Comparing with MonoHype systems [3, 19], a MultiHype system in ideal scenario should satisfy the following requirements.

- Multiple and separated hypervisors that can scale with large scale many-core based platform (e.g., hundreds of cores platform) and support of hyper-scale virtual server consolidation for multiple customers;

- Two-tiered resource allocation and isolation mechanism: resources such as CPUs and memory are first allocated and partitioned among hypervisors and then for each hypervisor, the resources are shared among guest virtual machines; and

- Security breach compartmentalization: an architecture capable of preventing security breach from spreading to other customer's hypervisors and virtual machines.

One desirable feature to support these requirements is that different hypervisors share minimal physical resources, thus the normal function of a hypervisor requires little or no interaction from other hypervisors. With this, an attack on one hypervisor by a malicious customer or attacker

Table 1: Comparison of Three Frameworks

	Multiple Hypervisors Single Physical Platform	Single Hypervisor Single Physical Platform	Distributed Hypevisors Multiple Physical Platforms
Hypervisor Vulnerabilities	Confined	Not confined	Not confined
Risks of Resource Monopolization	Low	High	High
Hypervisor Single Point-of-Failure	No or very limited	Yes	Yes
Shared Hypervisor States	Guests of the same realm/customer	All guests	Across physical servers
Hypervisor Creation	On-demand	Boot time	Boot time
Examples	MultiHype	All MonoHype based including [5]	3leaf systems [1]

may not affect other customers' hypervisors and guest virtual machines. Ideally, MultiHype achieves the same level of availability and dependability as running each hypervisor on a dedicated MonoHype platform using single physical server.

3.2 Advantages of MultiHype

Comparing with the existing Mono-hypervisor design, a MultiHype system has the following advantages,

First, MultiHype is well-positioned to be the virtualization platform for emerging large scale highly distributed platform. Future multi-processor multi-core sever platform that is armed with multiple memory controllers and multiple many-core processors (e.g., 32 independent cores per processor, and 128 cores per quad-processor platform in 2014 according to AMD) will behave more as a distributed system instead of a monolithic system. Such platform requires a scalable, decentralized hypervisor design to achieve its full potential. In a MonoHype system, all the virtual machine guests share the same hypervisor for handling page faults, exceptions, interrupts, and resource management. The monolithic hypervisor contains numerous mutexes, spinlocks, shared memory states, etc that hinder performance. Running multiple hypervisors with separated states is one of the solutions to address this challenge.

Second, MultiHype enhances cloud security and dependability by eliminating the reliance on shared hypervisor. In multi-tenancy cloud environment, a monolithic hypervisor exposed to virtual machine guests of different customers becomes a potential single-point-of-failure and is attractive to malicious attackers. MultiHype reduces the attack surface associated with shared monolithic hypervisor. In MultiHype, when a single server platform is shared among customers, a different hypervisor can be created for each customer. Virtual machine guests of the same customer are supported by separated hypervisor and, as a result hypervisor vulnerabilities are confined within each customer's own domain.

Table 1 compares three main concepts of cloud computing oriented virtualization environment, single hypervisor over single physical platform, multiple hypervisors over single physical platform, and single hypervisor over multiple platforms.

3.3 Hypervisor/Virtual Machine Realms

Figure 1 shows the concept of MultiHype platform. On a MultiHype server, a VM realm or hypervisor realm refers to all guest virtual machines supported by one VMM or hypervisor. A MultiHype server may constitute multiple concurrent virtual machine realms, and launch new VMMs in on-demand manner. A MultiHype server has a single control plane that administrates the physical machine and retains selective control of resources, including processor cores, physical memory, interrupt assignment, and I/O de-

vices. The control plane can be a virtual machine realm, aka manager realm, while others are regular realms. The manager realm does not run code from guest virtual machine for cloud customers; instead, it allocates physical resources to, bootstrap, and terminate a VMM. After being started, a VMM can function as a normal hypervisor and run independently, i.e., it can manage a number of guest virtual machines and act as a host for the guests. The control plane runs at the highest privilege level, higher than hypervisor's privilege level, therefore ensures isolation among VMMs by allocating or partitioning resources among them. The allocated resource can be physical or virtual. Within each hypervisor, virtual machine guests can be created with additional levels of privileges. For example, within each hypervisor, there can one or multiple administrative guests just like MonoHype system.

For strong isolation purpose, each realm comprises at least one physical processor core and allocated physical RAM space. There is no overlap on processor cores and RAM space for different realms. For a regular realm, its processor cores (one or more) run at lower privilege level than the manager realm. This prevents a regular hypervisor from changing resource allocation made by the control plane. After a hypervisor is started, the control plane delegates control of the allocated physical resources to the started hypervisor. In turn, the hypervisor can further create guest virtual machines and allocate assigned resources by the control plane to the guests.

When a hypervisor starts, it boots from a modified BIOS that bypasses physical RAM initialization. The control plane retains the control of certain physical resources such as physical memory allocation and I/O device discovery. Interrupts for each VM realm are routed and handled by the corresponding hypervisor for the realm. Page faults and exceptions caused by guest virtual machines of a realm are handled by the realm's hypervisor just like in normal MonoHype systems.

The whole system behaves like a distributed system with multiple concurrent virtual machine realms, each having its own hypervisor. Each hypervisor supports context switch between virtual machine mode and hypervisor mode using vm_enter and vm_exit. There is no such context switch between the management realm and a regular realm. The control plane and customer's hypervisor run concurrently using different cores. They communicate with one another through inter-core interrupts and messages. This makes MultiHype fundamentally different from other approaches such as supporting virtual machine creation inside a virtual machine.

3.4 Memory Mapping for Hypervisor/Virtual Machine Realms

To support strong memory partitioning between multiple hypervisors on a single platform, we propose a physical memory remapping mechanism. In particular, physical memory space is divided into chunks of equal size (e.g., 8MB). The control plane assigns physical memory chunks to each hypervisor realm. The remapping mechanism restricts memory access from a hypervisor realm to pre-assigned physical memory regions. This is achieved by a hardware physical memory remapping logic situated in the memory controller. The remapping logic creates a virtual continuous physical memory space for each hypervisor realm. It is programmed by the privileged control plane. A regular hypervisor running at lower privilege level cannot modify or program the remapping logic. For each memory access, e.g., read or write access from a hypervisor or its guest VMs, the memory remapping logic translates the address of the access request to its corresponding physical memory address. Therefore, it serves as a memory access reference monitor and performs access control based on configurations provided by the control plane. For translating memory addresses, the memory controller uses either a realm-to-memory remapping table managed by the control plane, or a local cache of the remapping table. The remapping table cache is part of the memory controller. It resembles TLB inside MMU and

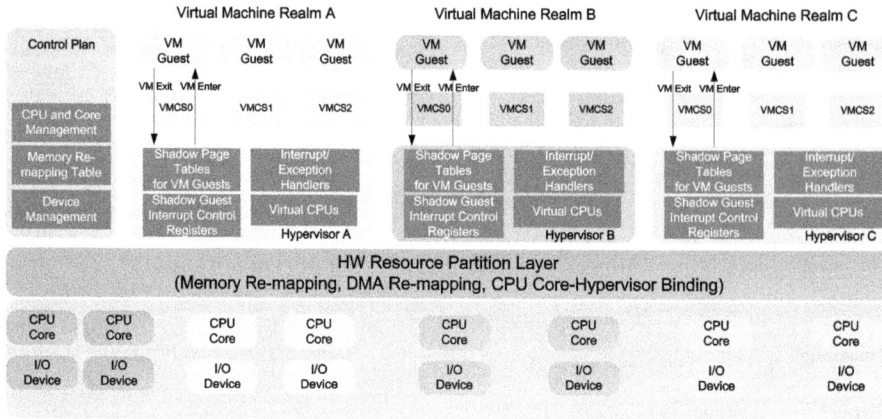

Figure 1: Concept of a MultiHype Platform

caches recently-used entries of the realm-to-physical memory remapping table.

Unlike a regular hypervisor, the control plane or privileged manager realm can access the entire physical memory space without using translation. However, only a portion of the physical memory space is allocated to the control plane. Operating systems or virtual machines within the control plane can use the physical memory space allocated to them freely for their own purposes. The rest physical memory space is reserved for other realms, while the control plane has read/write access rights to it. Overall, physical memory isolation for MultiHype is achieved by restricting memory access from hypervisor realm within the space that is assigned by the control plane, by using the remapping or the address-translation tables.

Figure 2 shows an example physical memory allocation for three VM realms: A, B, and C. When a hypervisor or a VM tries to access to a certain memory location, the remapping hardware looks up the address-translation tables for access permission of the realm to the specific location. If the hypervisor or VM realm tries to access outside of the memory range assigned to it by the control plane, the remapping hardware blocks the access and reports a fault to the control plane, which is achieved by raising exception to the processor core running the control plane. The described physical memory remapping is different from traditional virtual memory management in many aspects. Traditional memory paging and MMU are tied with process management, while our physical memory remapping mechanism is used for partitioning physical memory resources among multiple VM realms. It presents a "virtual" continuous physical memory space for each hypervisor.

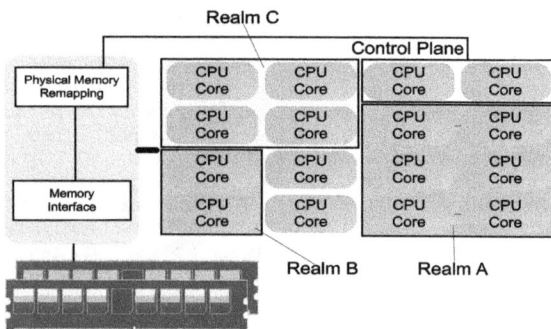

Figure 2: Physical Memory Re-mapping.

3.5 Memory Management

3.5.1 Weighted LRU for Shared L3

Onchip cache is shared by all cores in most today's many-core systems. As a critical hardware resource for achieving high performance, onchip cache becomes an attractive attacking point in multi-tenant computing environment. To address this issue, we design *eighted* U in MultiHype. The main idea is to manipulate LRU priorities in order to defend against resource exhaustion exploit of shared cache, which suits for large shared multi-way set associative cache.

Figure 3 provides an illustration of weighted LRU. For each cache block, in addition to tag, valid bit, and other necessary structures, there is a *real* and a LRU rank associated with it. For an 8-way cache, its LRU rank has three bits, which provides a rank of all eight cache blocks of a cache set (7 denotes the least recently accessed cache block and 0 denotes the most recently accessed cache block). Each time, when the cache block is accessed, the rank bits are updated using a map that implements LRU. Design of the map logic is relatively straightforward so we skip the details.

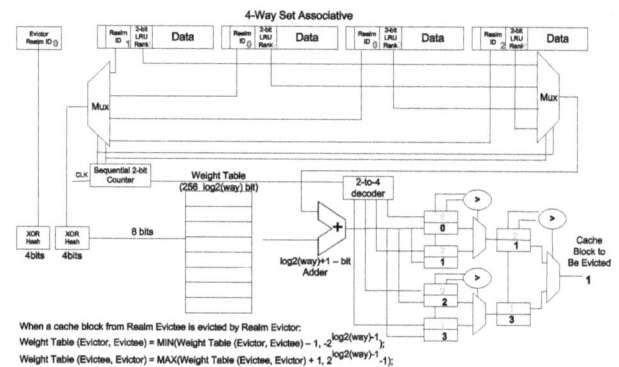

Figure 3: Weighted LRU in MultiHype.

The weight table shown in Figure 3 is used during cache block eviction. Consider that for a cache line, one cache block needs to be evicted to accommodate data from virtual machine realm 0 (evictor), and cache block 0 (candidate evictee) stores data of virtual machine realm 1 and has value 1 as LRU rank. For a pair of evictor and candidate evictee (for instance, realm 0 and realm 1), there is a weight value in the weight table, which can be added to the LRU rank. The summation result is a weighted LRU rank. The range of a weight value is from $-2^{log2(way)-1}$ to $2^{log2(way)-1} - 1$. For each block of a set, a weighted LRU rank can be computed based on the weights stored in the weight table. Using a comparison tree shown in Figure 3, the block with the highest weighted LRU rank can be found after $Log2(Way)$ steps. The block that emerges after the final comparison step will be replaced. After the replacement, the weight table is then updated. If a cache block from virtual machine realm 1 is evicted by virtual machine realm 0, the weight table entry corresponding to the realm pair $(0, 1)$ will decrement by 1, and the weight table entry corresponding to the realm pair $(1, 0)$ will increment by 1. The modified weights increase, in future cache replacements, the probability of evicting cache blocks of realm 0 by accesses from realm 1, and decrease the future probability of evicting cache blocks of realm 1 by accesses from realm 0.

Figure 4 shows one example that highlights the difference between LRU and weighted LRU. Assuming a 4-way set associative cache and two virtual machine realms, there are three write accesses from virtual machine realm 0, all mapped to the same cache line. For each way of the cache line, we use a pair of numbers for storing realm ID, and LRU rank. For example, way 0 stores cached data from realm 0 and its LRU rank is 0. Figure 4 also illustrates values of the weight table (2x2 for two virtual machine realms). For the three write accesses, Figure 4 compares the results of LRU vs. weighted LRU.

Weighted LRU has many attractive properties. First, weighted LRU reduces to standard LRU when there is only one virtual machine realm. This means that when a Mono-Hype based system is installed, weighted LRU behaves as LRU. Second, as a cache replacement policy, weighted LRU does not statically or dynamically change cache configuration. Consequently, it is orthogonal to and can be used in conjunction with other cache sharing techniques that statically or dynamically share cache among multiple virtual machines.

	Cache Line (4-way)				Weight Table	LRU	Weighted LRU
	Way 0	Way 1	Way 2	Way 3			
Initial Value	(0, 0)	(1,1)	(1,2)	(1,3)	0 1 / 0 0 0 / 1 0 0		
Write access from realm0	(0,1)	(1,2)	(1,3)	(0,0)	0 1 / 0 0 -1 / 1 1 0	Way 3 evicted	Way 3 evicted
Write access from ream 0	(0,2)	(1,3)	(0,0)	(0,1)	0 1 / 0 0 -2 / 1 1 0	Way 2 evicted	Way 2 evicted
Write access from realm 0	(0,0)	(1,3)	(0,1)	(0,2)	0 1 / 0 0 -2 / 1 1 0	Way 1 evicted	Way 0 evicted

Figure 4: Weighted LRU Example (4 Way Associative Cache and 2 VM Realms)

In the current design, MultiHype allocates physical cores to separated hypervisor realms. This eliminates possibilities of sharing L2 or L1 cache by multiple virtual machine realms. Therefore, we only need to consider the shared L3 cache. In weighted LRU, it takes multiple cycles to find out the cache block that should be replaced. There is no performance penalty because the delay is hidden by overlapping WLRU operations with memory fetch.

3.5.2 Per-realm Memory Throughput Management

Fair queuing is a technique that originally was designed for managing network bandwidth resources. It allows each flow of packets passing through a network device to have a fair share of network resources. Fair queuing has been demonstrated to help defend against network resource exhaustion attacks. The idea of using fair queuing in memory management was initially exploited in [20] under different application scenarios and CMP context.

The risks and threats of resource exhaustion exploit at system platform level are relatively new. The problem is exacerbated by the multi-tenancy nature of cloud computing. In MultiHype, we apply fair queuing to hypervisor realms to ensure that each of them can have its share of memory band-width resources in fair manner. Typically, implementing perfect fairness requires $O(log(n))$ to process each request. Deficit Round-Robin is an approximation of fair queuing that only requires $O(1)$ to process each request [26]. It is simple enough to be implemented in hardware. As shown in [26], Deficit Round-Robin can achieve near perfect fairness.

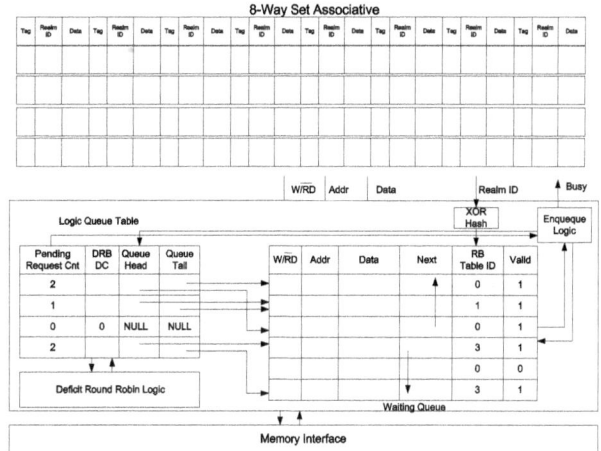

Figure 5: Deficit Round Robin in MultiHype.

Figure 5 illustrates the design of fair queuing in PolyHpye, where each memory access is tagged with its realm ID. There is a logic queue table with fixed number of entries (four in the example). If there are more realms than the queue table entries, an queue entry has to be shared by multiple realms (e.g., XOR the MSB and LSB bits of a realm ID). Each entry has a counter that counts the number of pending memory accesses for that queue, the pointer of queue head, and the pointer of queue tail. Each queue head or tail points to an entry of a memory access waiting queue. All pending memory accesses are buffered in the waiting queue. The waiting queue has only fixed number of entries (e.g., 32 or 64 entries). The waiting queue is shared by all logic queues using head and tail pointers. When the waiting queue is full, upstream logic units with new incoming memory access have to wait or stall until a new waiting queue entry becomes available. Each entry of the logic queue table will be visited by the Deficit Round-Robin Logic in round-robin fashion. For each visited logic queue entry (realm), if there are waiting memory accesses, the requests will be served using deficit Round-Robin, and then the Deficit Round-Robin Logic will visit the next logic queue entry.

3.5.3 Hardware Cost

The proposed micro-architectural features including weighted LRU and deficit Round-Robin have only small cost in size. For weighted LRU, each weight needs only three bits (for 8-way cache). The weight table uses only 96B. The largest hardware cost is caused by the realm ID associated with each cache block. Consider a 8-way set associative cache with 4096 sets, and 8 bit realm ID (256 realms), the cost is 32KB. For deficit Round-Robin, the hardware cost is also small. The waiting queue table can have 32 or 64 entries for buffering pending memory accesses. Each entry of the logical queue table has 32 bits. The logic table has variable number of entries with a range from 16 to 256. It costs from 64B to 1KB.

3.6 I/O Support

To virtualize I/O devices, the following operations need to be supported: (1) device discovery and configuration – query I/O devices on a hardware platform and set up the devices' configuration registers for initialization; (2) I/O transactions – transfer data to and from devices including DMA; and (3) interrupts – notify a hypervisor on state updates and events of a device.

I/O virtualization in MonoHype is typically implemented with one of three different approaches: emulation, para-virtualization, and hardware assisted virtualization (e.g., direct assignment on Intel VT-d [2] or single-root IOV where an I/O device can be shared by multiple VMs). Emulation implements I/O devices and hardware in software; para-virtualization requires modification of a guest OS; and hardware assisted I/O virtualization such as VT-d can allocate an I/O device to a VM using IOMMU, a memory address translation for I/O transactions. Single-root IOV enables virtual functions on I/O devices and allows an I/O device to be shared by multiple VMs. For I/O virtualization in Multi-Hype, we either use I/O proxy or leverage existing hardware assisted I/O virtualization such as device passthrough.

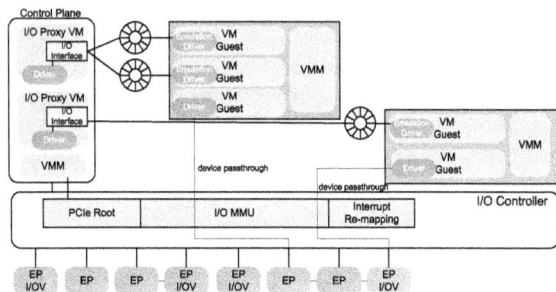

Figure 6: Support I/O Virtualization for MultiHype (I/O Proxy and Device Passthrough

IO Proxy: MultiHype uses device emulation for I/O virtualization, as Figure 6 shows. The control plane consists of a hypervisor and a number of I/O virtual machines, and has the full control of physical I/O resources. I/O devices are allocated to I/O virtual machines in control plane using hardware assisted I/O virtualization such as single-root IOV or VT-d. A regular hypervisor and its VMs can only access the physical I/O resources using the control plane services. In a VM realm, a guest virtual machine uses emulated device drivers, which communicate with the I/O virtual machines in control plane using physical shared memory. This is supported because the control plane has control of the entire physical memory space. Note that the control plane does not run virtual machines for cloud customers. Virtual machines on the control plane are executed by dedicated processor cores in parallel with customers' virtual machines in regular realms. At high level, the system functions like a distributed systems where the control plane and I/O virtual machines act as I/O proxies for the guest virtual machines of a regular realm, by performing I/O transactions and issuing DMA data transfer on behalf of the emulated device drivers. A drawback of this approach is that it does not scale well if there are numerous I/O transactions from multiple guests in a VM realm or VM realms since the control plane is one central place to process the transactions.

Using Existing Device Passthrough Support: Another approach is to leverage the existing hardware support for MonoHype I/O virtualization. It works as follows. The control plane retains the control of I/O devices and assigns I/O resources to guest virtual machines of a realm. This allows I/O virtualization on a MultiHype system using existing hardware I/O virtualization support. The control plane performs device discovery, manages the I/O devices, and assigns devices to guest virtual machines of a VM realm. One guest virtual machine can issue DMA data transfer using hardware I/O virtualization such as VT-d or IOMMU without involving the control plane. When it needs to access protected resources (such as I/O configuration and in-

terrupt management), it first exits into the hypervisor of its realm. The hypervisor then sends an interrupt (such as Inter-processor Interrupt (IPI)) to the processor cores running the control plane. The control plane handles the request and returns results to the hypervisor. For each regular VM realm, its hypervisor cannot perform these I/O controlling functions which are reserved for the control plane. It can only forward the requests from its guests to the control plane.

In our experimentation of MultiHype, both approaches were employed. Both approaches work with the existing I/O virtualization support in MonoHype based systems.

3.7 Interrupts

For the delivery of I/O interrupts to an appropriate VM realm, the current architecture can be minimally changed to support the hypervisor ID. In x86 systems, I/O interrupts are delivered using MSI either via I/O APIC or directly to Local APICs in cores. Destination is determined based on physical or logical IDs of Local APICs in a predefined memory address location. To support the interrupt delivery in MultiHype, an addition of only one register (Hypervisor ID register) is required in I/O APIC, Local APIC and PCIe devices as an extension of hardware virtualization support. Currently, MSI or MSI-x in PCIe 3.0 provides a plenty of space for address encoding. The procedure of interrupt generation and delivery is as follows with a NIC example; A realm requests a network packet to the NIC. Its device driver programs the requester realm ID to the device's hypervisor ID register along with other information. Upon receipt of the packet, the NIC sends an MSI message of which address field embeds the hypervisor ID (realm ID). The MSI message can be broadcasted to the entire realms or directed to the target realm if routers and/or switches in interconnection network inside many-core support the interrupt routing capability. Even simple broadcasting would not incur significant overhead in the interconnection bandwidth considering the intermittent nature of interrupts. The Local APICs compare their hypervisor IDs with the MSI message, and the target (requested) realm takes the interrupt.

4. IMPLEMENTATION & EVALUATION

4.1 Setup and Implementation

We use Bochs [12] – a full-system x86 emulator, and TAXI [29] – a compatible cycle based x86 architecture simulator, to evaluate MultiHype. Bochs models an entire platform including network device, hard drive, VGA, and other devices to support the execution of a complete OS and its applications. In addition, Bochs supports emulation of Intel VMX hardware support for virtualization. TAXI is a Simplescalar simulator with x86 front-end for our performance analysis. Architectural support for MultiHype and the associated resource management features such as weighted LRU, deficit Round-Robin memory bandwidth management, hypervisor realm memory remapping are implemented in both Bochs and TAXI.

We extended Bochs's VMX support and created an emulated hardware partition layer in Bochs. Our emulation framework emulates a multi-core platform. The framework supports configurable logic hardware partition. Multiple hypervisors can be started and executed on an emulated hardware platform using modified Bochs. The modification includes a thin layer of logic hardware partition. Processor cores are bound with hypervisors; that is, virtual machines supported by the same hypervisor can share processor cores, while different hypervisors and their virtual machines run over different processor cores. Each emulated hardware partition can boot a complete hypervisor (Xen 3.3) and run Ubuntu 8.04 Linux distribution.

Our implementation also includes physical memory management for hypervisor realms in Bochs. The performance simulator is extended to support realm based memory mapping, weighted LRU, and deficit Round-Robin. We also integrated an accurate DRAM model [9] to improve system memory modeling, where bank conflicts, page miss, and row miss are all modeled according to SDRAM specification. The processor parameters are listed in Table 2.

Table 2: Platform Parameters in Simulation

Parameters	Values
Frequency	2.0 GHz
Cores	4
Fetch/Decode width	8
Issue/Commit width	8
L1 I-Cache	DM, 16KB, 32B line
L1 D-Cache	DM, 16KB, 32B line
L2 Cache	4way, unified, 32B line, WB cache 256KB for each core
L1/L2 Latency	1 cycle / 6 cycles (256KB)
L3 Cache	8way, 128B line, WB cache, weighted LRU 4MB shared
L3 Latency	16 cycles 4MB
I-TLB	4-way, 128 entries
D-TLB	4-way, 256 entries
Weighted LRU	16 x 3bits table
Deficit Round Robin	16 queues, shared 64 entries
Memory Bus	200MHz, 8B wide
Memory Latency	X-5-5-5 (core clocks), X depends on page status
CAS latency	20 mem bus clocks
Precharge latency (RP)	7 mem bus clocks
RAS-to-CAS (RCD) latency	7 mem bus clocks

We use eight popular open source applications for our evaluation: ffmpeg (a complete cross-platform application to record, convert, and stream audio and video), bzip2 (a popular open-source data compressor), povray (a cross-platform ray tracer), gcc (free compiler for GNU system), pybench (a benchmark suite for python scripting language), octave (a high-level interpreted language for numerical computations, a clone of commercial Matlab), hmmer (an application for searching gene sequence databases), and xalan (an XSLT processor for transforming XML documents into HTML, text, or other XML document types). All applications are installed on Ubuntu 8.04 virtual machine guests and executed together with its host system.

4.2 Hypervisor Subversion Tests

The effectiveness of using multiple hypervisors to defend against attacking on MultiHype platform is evaluated using stress tests. We follow the approach in [22] where hypervisor vulnerability is evaluated by conducting several stress tests on main stream hypervisors. Since most revealed vulnerabilities have been patched, we use multiple older versions of hypervisors in our tests. Our experiments show that hypervisor failures induced by stress tests do not spread to other hypervisors. This confirms the validity of using MultiHype to fend off hypervisor based attacks. In addition, we also try to artificially inject faults into a hypervisor through Bochs. Boches emulates all executed x86 instructions. By altering instruction execution, we inject faults into the hypervisor running ontop. We have observed similar results with this approach. During the test we need to restart the failed hypervisor frequently. However, the fault did not spread to other hypervisors.

4.3 Denial of Resources Tests

We evaluate the strength of MultiHype against denial of resource attacks from co-located malicious virtual machines. We use a simple memory throughput exhaustion application as malicious denial of memory resource exploit. The application runs an infinite loop that walks through a large memory region (several times larger than L3 cache size) and tries to utilize maximum memory throughput by moving data around. The malicious application is executed inside a co-located virtual machine.

We test three collocation scenarios. The the first scenario (dual-hypervisor) includes two concurrently running hypervisors, each runs one guest virtual machine. One guest acts as attacker and is configured to execute the memory throughput exhaustion application. The other guest runs one of the eight benchmark applications. The second scenario (quad-hypervisor) include four concurrently running hypervisors, each runs one guest virtual machine. One guest acts as attacker and is configured to execute the memory throughput exhaustion application. The other three guests in different hypervisors run three of the eight benchmark applications. In the first quad-hypervisor setting (setting one), there are three guests of bzip2, hmmer, ffmpeg, one guest per hypervisor. In the second quad-hypervisor setting (setting two), there are three guests of xalan, gcc, and povray, one per hypervisor. The third scenario (quad dual-guest hypervisors) includes four hypervisors, each has two guests. One guest acts as attacker and is configured to execute the memory throughput exhaustion application. The rest guests are assigned to run bzip2, hmmer, ffmpeg, xalan, gcc, and povray.

5. PERFORMANCE ANALYSIS

Our quantitative performance study focuses on weighted LRU as a cache replacement policy for shared L3 cache, and deficit Round-Robin for memory access management. We evaluate how efficient they prevent memory exhaustion attacks under MultiHype architecture.

5.1 Weighted LRU

From our test results, we found that weighted LRU has three major effects defending against resource exhaustion attacks. First, it promotes fair sharing of cache resources. When there is malicious exploit on cache resources, weighted LRU can boost the amount of cache resources available to the legitimate realms. Second, compared with standard LRU, weighted LRU can significantly increase cache hit rates for guest realms under cache resource exhaustion attack. Third, weighted LRU reduces the likelihood that cached data from legitimate realms are evicted by bombarding cache access requests from resource exhaustion attacks.

Figure 7 shows percentage of L3 cache blocks occupied by legitimate realms and attack realms in the dual realm scenario. As shown in the figure, under the standard LRU, overwhelming amount of cache blocks is occupied by the attack realms. A legitimate realm only occupies insignificant amount of cache blocks – less than 5% in average. In contrast, under weighted LRU, for all the legitimate realms, their shares of L3 cache blocks increase to 12.5% in average. Similar effect of increased L3 occupancy is observed consistently in the other two test scenarios (Figure 9, 10, and 11).

With increased cache residence, the number of L3 cache misses decreases for the legitimate realms. Figure 8 shows L3 cache miss rates for all the tested realms. Compared with standard LRU, weighted LRU reduces L3 cache miss rate for all the legitimate realms from 60% to 41% in average. This effect can be found in the other two test scenarios as well (cf. Figure 9, 10, and 11).

Interestingly, as indicated by Figure 8, cache miss rate remains roughly the same under weighted LRU and standard LRU for the malicious realm. Though the malicious realm occupies less number of cache blocks under weighted LRU, its cache hit rate does not change much. The same effect is observed in all tested scenarios (see Figure 9, 10, and 11). This indicates that in terms of cache hit rate, weighted LRU does not improves cache performance for the legitimate realms at the expense of the attack realm.

Another effect of weighted LRU is that it increases the fairness in cache replacement across realms. Using weighted LRU, a malicious realm has less likelihood unilaterally evicting cache blocks of other hypervisor realms. In certain sense, weighted LRU bestows the legitimate realms power to resist cache evictions by the attack realm. The effect can be observed in Figure 12. When there are multiple realms (the third test scenario, four dual-guest hypervisors), under weighted LRU, cache replacements are more evenly distributed across the realms that have light memory access demand. The effect can be found in Figure 13.

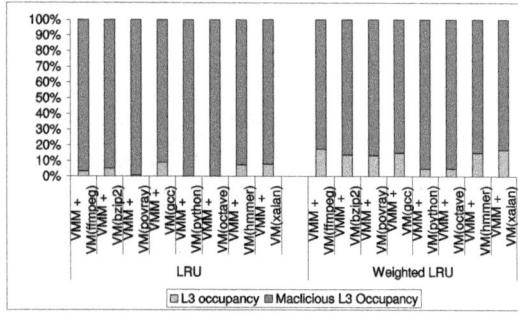

Figure 7: L3 Occupancy: One Legitimate Realm vs. One Malicious Realm.

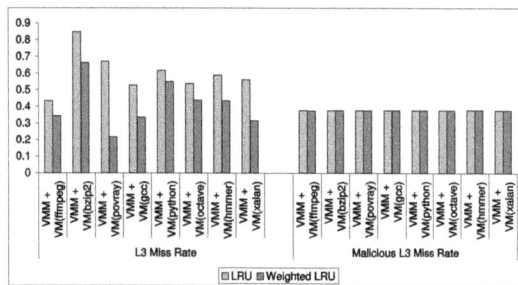

Figure 8: L3 Miss Rate: One Legitimate Realm vs. One Malicious Realm.

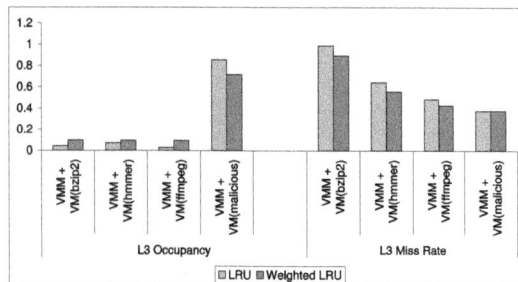

Figure 9: L3 Occupancy and L3 Miss Rate: Setting One of Four Realms.

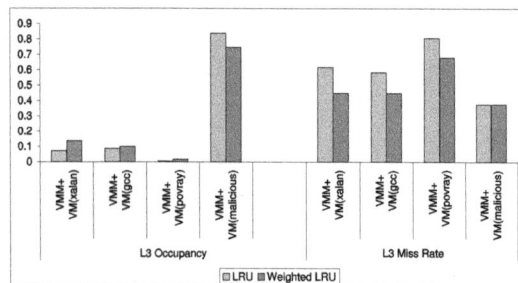

Figure 10: L3 Occupancy and L3 Miss Rate: Setting Two of Four Realms.

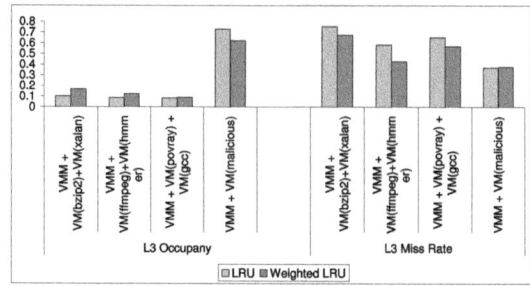

Figure 11: L3 Occupancy and L3 Miss Rate: Four Dual-Guest Realms.

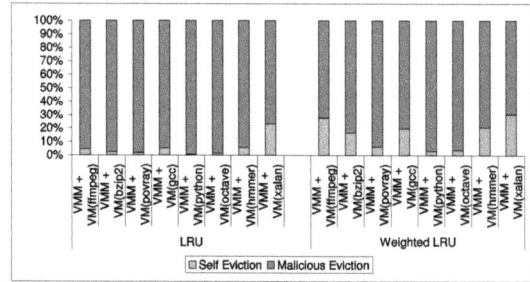

Figure 12: L3 Eviction Profile: One Legitimate Realm vs. One Malicious Realm.

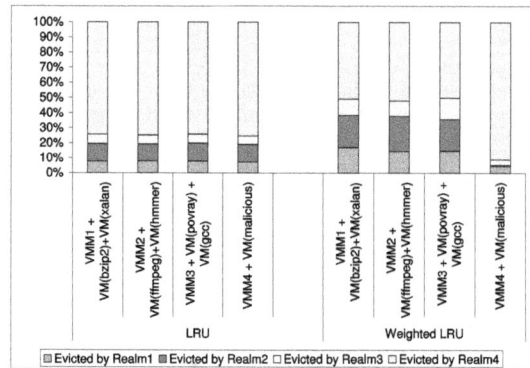

Figure 13: L3 Eviction Profile: Four Dual-Guest Realms.

5.2 Memory Utilization

Our next defense line against memory exhaustion attacks is at the memory interface using deficit Round-Robin. As aforementioned, deficit Round-Robin is a flavor of fair queueing, with the main advantage of simplicity over other fair queueing implementations. Deficit Round-Robin is easy to be implemented in hardware. In our test, we compare the memory utilization between deficit Round Robin and FIFO with a memory exhaustion attack application, which generates overwhelming amount of memory accesses. When FIFO is used for handling memory access requests, requests from the legitimate realms suffer because they have to wait for all outstanding memory requests from the malicious application to complete. Deficit Round-Robin iterates over all the memory request waiting queues and guarantees memory bandwidth allocation to all realms.

For each memory access, we measure its waiting time (time spent in the memory request queue or FIFO before memory bandwidth is allocated to the request). We calculate the average waiting time for all memory accesses under FIFO and deficit Round Robin. For each realm (legitimate and malicious), we compare the per-realm average waiting time against the overall waiting time across all realms. As shown in Figure 14, memory requests from the legitimate realms have much less relative waiting time under deficit Round Robin than that with the relative waiting time under FIFO. With deficit Round Robin, memory requests from the legitimate realms only need to wait 49% of the overall average waiting time. In contrast, with FIFO, memory requests from the legitimate realms need to wait 67% of the overall average waiting time. For the attacking realm, in both cases (FIFO and deficit Round Robin), the average waiting time is roughly the same as the overall average waiting time or slightly higher. This effect can be found in all other three test scenarios (see Figure 15 and 16). Our quantitative evaluation results show that both weighted LRU and deficit Round-Robin are effective against memory resource exhaustion attacks from a malicious realm and guest.

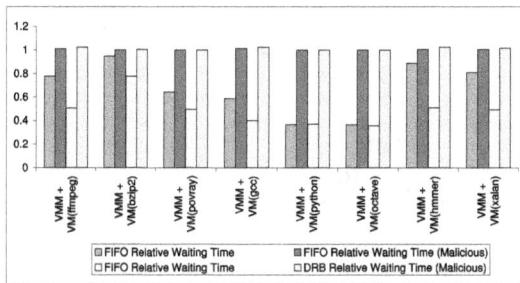

Figure 14: Relative Memory Access Waiting Time: One Legitimate Realm vs. One Malicious Realm.

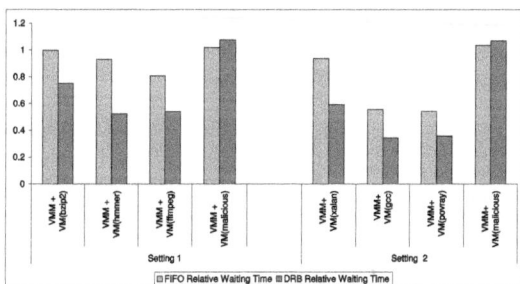

Figure 15: Relative Memory Access Waiting Time: Four Realms.

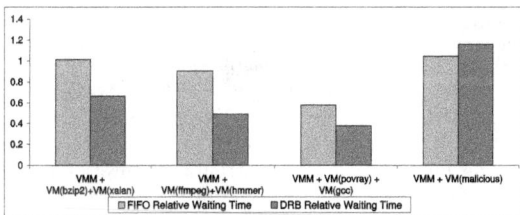

Figure 16: Relative Memory Access Waiting Time: Four Dual-Guest Realms.

6. RELATED WORK

Hardware and architectural support for CPU and I/O virtualization To our best knowledge, majority of the published studies and designs in this space focus on supporting single hypervisor based systems [2, 28]). In contrast to these systems, MultiHype is one of the first that employ new architectural features to support multi-hypervisor based platform. In [5], Ben Yehuda et al. propose a solution for

supporting nested virtual machines. Compared with MultiHype, this is a special type of mono hypervisor system as all nested virtual machines depend on a single bottom layer hypervisor. Thus, in many-core based environments, this cannot scale with a great many guest VMs because a single hypervisor should handle them. In addition, this has potential security problems because all guest VMs share the underlying raw hardware. NoHype [14] is an architecture that uses hardware virtualization extensions to remove any need for virtualization layer such as hypervisor. The architecture includes running one virtual machine per core, hardware enforced memory partitioning, dedicated (virtual) devices. However, NoHype cannot adjust resources partition between virtual machines dynamically because each guest virtual machine controls hardware directly.

Resource management in a multicore processor Many researchers in the last few years have explored the resource sharing problems of a multicore processor. These problems include fairness, QoS, or even DoS vulnerability in a shared cache [21, 6], memory bandwidth [20, 18], or both of them concurrently [31]. In contrast to the related studies that dynamically allocate cache and memory resources, MultiHype focuses on strong isolation between concurrently executed hypervisor realms over a single physical platform. Unlike related work that dynamically allocate cache and memory resources based on demand, our system does not give more cache and/or memory resources to any malicious application. The described weighted LRU cache replacement policy does not explicitly or directly manage cache resources (e.g., space and bandwidth); instead, it defends against malicious cache exploits indirectly by manipulating LRU weights of a shared cache. In a mono hypervisor environment, the policy reduces to standard LRU. Different from the related work, we use deficit Round-Robin to manage memory resources for each hypervisor realm, which introduces low cost and hardware efficient approximation to fair queuing, and is suited for independency of individual hypervisor realms. Furthermore, defending against resource exhaustion exploit is only one aspect of the strong isolation. Other aspect includes confining any fault or failure that occurs within a hypervisor realm.

Micro-kernel based hypervisor NOVA [27] is a micro-kernel based hypervisor that uses a thin and simple virtualization layer to reduce the attack surface and as a result improve system security. MultiHype is orthogonal and complementary to this approach. Comparing with this, MultiHype eliminates the necessity of sharing hypervisor among different cloud customers on a single platform and thereby improves platform reliability, scalability, and security.

Multi-kernel support Baumann et al. [4] proposed a new operating system, Barrelfish multikernel, which focuses on the scalability of heterogeneous multicore systems. Barrelfish treats each core as an independent entity as if each core is a node in a distributed system. In such a system, cores communicate using messages and do not share memory. In contrast, MultiHype intends to scale in a many-core platform running multiple hypervisors on a single physical server. Unlike Barrelfish, each hypervisor can manage multiple cores while running independently.

7. CONCLUSION

We present the design and evaluation of MultiHype, a platform architecture to support multiple hypervisors on a single physical platform by leveraging the emerging many-core based cloud-on-chip processor. Each hypervisor in MultiHype manages guest virtual machines like traditional virtualized platform. The strong isolation between hypervisors and their realms is achieved by the separation of physical resources provided by a control plane of the platform, which includes a new LRU based cache replacement policy for preventing cache exhaustion attacks, and efficient memory management approach for defending against denial of resource attacks on physical memory in multi-tenancy cloud environment. These micro-architectural features confines the vulnerabilities of one hypervisor or its virtual machine within its own domain, which makes the MultiHype platform more resilient to malicious attacks and failures in cloud computing environment. Our evaluations using Bochs emulator and cycle based x86 simulation show both qualitatively and quantitatively the effectiveness of MultiHype as a new platform architecture with improved security and dependability beyond legacy virtualization platform.

8. REFERENCES

[1] 3LEAF SYSTEMS. Next generation hybrid systems for hpc. http://www.3leafsystems.com/download/3leaf_wt_paper_Next_Gen_Hybrid_Sys\%tems_for_HPC.pdf, 2009.

[2] ABRAMSON, D., JACKSON, J., MUTHRASANALLUR, S., NEIGER, G., REGNIER, G., SANKARAN, R., SCHOINAS, I., UHLIG, R., VEMBU, B., AND WEIGERT, J. Intel Virtualization Technology for directed I/O. *ntel echnology Journal* , 3 (Aug. 2006), 179–192.

[3] BARHAM, P., DRAGOVIC, B., FRASER, K., HAND, S., HARRIS, T., HO, A., NEUGEBAUER, R., PRATT, I., AND WARFIELD, A. Virtual machine monitors: Xen and the art of virtualization. In *roceedings o the th Sy posiu on perating Syste s rinciples the Saga ore Bolton anding ake eorge Ne York US cto er — 3* (New York, NY 10036, USA, Dec. 2003), ACM, Ed., vol. 37(5) of *perating syste s re ie* , ACM Press, pp. 164–177. ACM order number 534030.

[4] BAUMANN, A., BARHAM, P., DAGAND, P., HARRIS, T., ISAACS, R., PETER, S., ROSCOE, T., SCH "UPBACH, A., AND SINGHANIA, A. The multikernel: a new os architecture for scalable multicore systems. In *S S* (2009), vol. 9, Citeseer, pp. 29–44.

[5] BEN-YEHUDA, M., DAY, M. D., DUBITZKY, Z., FACTOR, M., HAR'EL, N., GORDON, A., LIGUORI, A., WASSERMAN, O., AND YASSOUR, B.-A. The turtles project: design and implementation of nested virtualization. In *roceedings o the th US N X con erence on perating syste s design and i ple entation* (Berkeley, CA, USA, 2010), OSDI'10, USENIX Association, pp. 1–6.

[6] CHANG, J., AND SOHI, G. Cooperative cache partitioning for chip multiprocessors. In *roceedings o the st annual international con erence on Superco puting* (2007), ACM, pp. 242–252.

[7] FERRIE, P. Attacks on virtual machine emulators. *Sy antec Security esponse* (2006).

[8] FRANK GENS, ROBERT P MAHOWALD, R. L. V. An empirical study into the security exposure to hosts of hostile virtualized environments, 2007.

[9] GRIES, M., AND ROMER., A. Performance Evaluation of Recent DRAM Architectures for Embedded Systems. In *eport Nr o puting ngineering and Net orks a ( ) S iss ederal nstitute o echnology ( ) Zurich* (November 1999).

[10] HEISER, J., AND NICOLETT, M. Assessing the security risks of cloud computing. http://www.gartner.com/DisplayDocument?id=685308, 2009.

[11] HELD, J., BAUTISTA, J., AND KOEHL, S. White paper from a few cores to many: A tera-scale computing research review.

[12] K. LAWTON. Welcome to the Bochs x86 PC Emulation Software Home Page. http://www.bochs.com.

[13] KARGER, P. A., AND SAFFORD, D. I/O for virtual machine monitors: Security and performance issues. *Security ri acy 6*, 5 (2008), 16–23.

[14] KELLER, E., SZEFER, J., REXFORD, J., AND LEE, R. B. Nohype: virtualized cloud infrastructure without the virtualization. In *roceedings o the 3 th annual international sy posiu on o puter architecture* (New York, NY, USA, 2010), ISCA '10, ACM, pp. 350–361.

[15] KING, S. T., CHEN, P. M., MIN WANG, Y., VERBOWSKI, C., WANG, H. J., AND LORCH, J. R. Subvirt: Implementing malware with virtual machines. In *Sy posiu on Security and ri acy* (2006), pp. 314–327.

[16] KORTCHINSKY, K. Cloudburst – hacking 3D and breaking out of VMware. In *Black at US* (2009).

[17] MELL, P. Nist presentation on effectively and securely using the cloud computing paradigm v26. http://csrc.nist.gov/groups/SNS/cloud-computing/index.html, 2009.

[18] MOSCIBRODA, T., AND MUTLU, O. Memory performance attacks: Denial of memory service in multi-core systems. In *roceedings o 6th US N X Security Sy posiu on US N X Security Sy posiu* (2007), USENIX Association, p. 18.

[19] NEIGER, G., SANTONI, A., LEUNG, F., RODGERS, D., AND UHLIG, R. Intel Virtualization Technology: Hardware support for efficient processor virtualization. *ntel echnology Journal* , 3 (Aug. 2006), 167–177.

[20] NESBIT, K. J., AGGARWAL, N., LAUDON, J., AND SMITH, J. E. Fair queuing memory systems. In *roceedings o the 3 th nnual nternational Sy posiu on icroarchitecture* (Washington, DC, USA, 2006), MICRO 39, IEEE Computer Society, pp. 208–222.

[21] NESBIT, K. J., LAUDON, J., AND SMITH, J. E. Virtual private caches. In *roceedings o the 3 th annual international sy posiu on o puter architecture* (New York, NY, USA, 2007), ISCA '07, ACM, pp. 57–68.

[22] ORMANDY, T. An empirical study into the security exposure to hosts of hostile virtualized environments. In *anSecWest* (2007).

[23] RISTENPART, T., TROMER, E., SHACHAM, H., AND SAVAGE, S. Hey, you, get off of my cloud: exploring information leakage in third-party compute clouds. In *roceedings o the 6th con erence on o puter and co unications security* (New York, NY, USA, 2009), CCS '09, ACM, pp. 199–212.

[24] RUTKOWSKA, J. Blue pill. In *Black at US* (2006).

[25] SECUNIA. Advisory sa37081 - VMware ESX sever uodate for DHCP, kernel, and JRE. http://secunia.com/advisories/37081/.

[26] SHREEDHAR, M., AND VARGHESE, G. Efficient fair queuing using deficit round robin. *rans Net* (1996).

[27] STEINBERG, U., AND KAUER, B. NOVA: a microhypervisor-based secure virtualization architecture. In *roceedings o the th uropean con erence on o puter syste s* (New York, NY, USA, 2010), EuroSys '10, ACM, pp. 209–222.

[28] UHLIG, R. Forward: Intel Virtualization Technology: Taking virtualization mainstream on Intel architecture platforms. *ntel echnology Journal* , 3 (Aug. 2006), v-vi.

[29] VLAOVIC, S., AND DAVIDSON, E. S. TAXI: Trace Analysis for X86 Interpretation. In *roceedings o the nternational on erence on o puter esign* (2002).

[30] WOJTCZUK, R. Subverting the Xen hypervisor. In *Black at US* (2008).

[31] WOO, D. H., AND LEE, H.-H. Analyzing performance vulnerability due to resource denial of service attack on chip multiprocessors. In *Workshop on hip ultiprocessor e ory Syste s and nterconnects* (2007).

SuperCoP: A General, Correct, and Performance-efficient Supervised Memory System

Bharghava Rajaram, Vijay Nagarajan, Andrew J. McPherson and Marcelo Cintra
Institute for Computing Systems Architecture, University of Edinburgh
[r.bharghava, vijay.nagarajan, ajmcpherson]@ed.ac.uk , mc@staffmail.ed.ac.uk

ABSTRACT

Supervised memory systems maintain additional metadata for each memory address accessed by the program, to control and monitor accesses to the program data. Supervised systems find use in several applications including memory checking, synchronization, race detection, and transactional memory. Conventional memory instructions are replaced by supervised memory instructions (SMIs) which operate on both data and metadata atomically. Existing proposals for supervised memory systems assume sequential consistency. Recently, Bobba et al. [4] demonstrated the correctness issues (*imprecise exceptions* and *metadata read reordering*) in naively applying supervision to Total-Store-Order, and proposed two solutions – TSOall and TSOdata – for overcoming the correctness issues. TSOall solves correctness issues by forcing SMIs to perform in order, but performs similar to SC, since supervised writes cannot retire into the write-buffer. TSOdata, while allowing supervised writes to retire into the write-buffer, works correctly for only a subset of supervision schemes. In this paper we observe that correctness is ensured as long as SMIs read and process their metadata in order. We propose SuperCoP, a supervised memory system for relaxed memory models in which SMIs read and process metadata before retirement, while allowing data and metadata writes to retire into the write-buffer. Since SuperCoP separates metadata reads and their processing from the writes, we propose a simple mechanism – in the form of cache block level locking at the directory – to ensure atomicity. Our experimental results show that *SuperCoP* performs better than *TSOall* by 16.8%. SuperCoP also performs better than *TSOdata* by 6%, even though TSOdata is not general.

Categories and Subject Descriptors

C.0 [**General**]: System Architectures; D.2.5 [**Software Engineering**]: Testing and Debugging—*Monitors*

Keywords

Atomicity, Memory Ordering, Memory Trackers, Metadata, Supervised Memory

Supervised Memory Read (SMR)	Supervised Memory Write (SMW)

Atomic
{
    Read Data (R_d)
 	
    /* Read & process Metadata */
    Read Metadata (R_m)
    if (Metadata == ...)
        exception()
    Metadata = f(Metadata)
 	
    Write Metadata (W_m)
}
	Atomic
	{
	    /* Read & process Metadata */
	    Read Metadata (R_m)
	    if (Metadata == ...)
	        exception()
	    Metadata = f(Metadata)
	
	    Write Metadata (W_m)
	    Write Data (W_d)
	}

Figure 1: Supervised Memory Instructions

1. INTRODUCTION

In recent years, there has been renewed interest in memory systems which maintain additional data for each memory address accessed by the program. This additional data, or *metadata*, is used to store auxiliary information about the program memory, which is then used to control and monitor memory accesses issued by the program. Metadata is accessed and processed atomically with program data as shown in Figure 1. As we can see, each memory read (memory write) is associated with auxiliary memory operations which read metadata, process metadata (optionally) generating an exception, and (optionally) update metadata; furthermore, the entire sequence of data and metadata operations is performed atomically and is referred to as a supervised memory read - SMR (supervised memory write - SMW). Memory systems which support such supervised memory instructions (SMIs) are known as *supervised memory systems*. They serve as a foundation for important tasks such as enhancing security, reliability and programmability of applications – examples include memory trackers [2, 15, 17, 20, 21], transactional memory [3], fine-grained synchronization [22], and deterministic processing [7]. Supervised memory systems have become increasingly attractive with the emergence of multicore and manycore architectures which pose challenges in programmability and reliability.

(**Correctness issues in supervised memory systems**) Most current proposals for supervised memory systems, implicitly or explicitly, assume a sequentially consistent (SC) view of memory. Supervision can also be applied to Total-Store-Order (TSO) systems. While improving performance, supervision in TSO results in certain correctness issues. Bobba et al. [4] demonstrated the correctness issues in applying supervision to TSO consistency, resulting from retiring SMWs into the write buffer. An SMW that has retired into the write-buffer, performs its data and metadata operations only when the SMW reaches the head of the write buffer. The resulting correctness issues are twofold. First, *metadata read reordering* – where an SMR may read and process its metadata, before an earlier SMW in the write buffer can read and process its metadata. Second, *imprecise exceptions* – where the exception raised by an SMW (if any) is imprecise. Since an SMW processes its metadata (and generates exceptions) only when it reaches the head of the write-buffer, subsequent instructions (which follow the SMW) may have already retired when the exception is raised.

Bobba et al. proposed a solution in the form of two systems: *TSOall* and *TSOdata*. TSOall solves the correctness issues by performing *all SMIs in order*. Since SMIs are performed in order, metadata reads of SMIs cannot be reordered; this also ensures that the exceptions raised by SMIs will be precise. On the other hand, an SMW cannot simply retire into the write-buffer, and will have to be fully performed before instructions that follow it can retire. *Thus TSOall, while solving the correctness issues, performs similar to SC on programs with frequent SMIs.* In contrast to TSOall, TSOdata allows an SMW to retire into the write buffer, thereby improving performance over TSOall. *TSOdata*, however, works correctly only for a subset of supervision schemes – it suffers from imprecise exceptions and metadata reordering which affects correctness in supervision schemes such as deterministic processing [7], full-empty bits [2], and DIFT [15]. *Thus, TSOdata, while performing better than TSOall, is not a generic solution to the correctness problem.*

(Our approach) While TSOall requires all SMIs to perform (as a whole) in order, we make the observation that *correctness is ensured as long as SMIs merely read and process their metadata in order*. In other words, we reduce the correctness requirement of supervised memory systems from SMI ordering to metadata read ordering. We propose *SuperCoP*, a supervised memory system in which SMIs read their metadata (data) and process them (generating an exception if necessary) before retirement; SuperCoP allows the resulting writes to metadata (and data) to be retired into the write-buffer. Since SuperCoP ensures correctness without making any assumptions about the supervision scheme, it is a generic solution to the correctness problem. At the same time, since SuperCoP allows data and metadata writes to retire into the write-buffer, it is efficient.

Since SuperCoP separates metadata reads (data reads) and their processing from the metadata writes (data writes), i.e, breaks the atomicity of the SMI, we provide additional mechanisms to ensure that the SMI appears atomic. For this purpose, we propose a simple and efficient atomicity scheme in which each SMI which modifies metadata locks the corresponding cache block in the directory before it retires; the lock is subsequently released when the corresponding metadata write is issued from the write-buffer; this ensures that any intervening SMI which tries to access this cache block is denied access until the metadata write of the original SMI completes. This, in turn, ensures that the original SMI appears atomic.

We compare the performance of SuperCoP, TSOdata, and TSOall, using the HARD [21] supervision scheme to test the different supervised systems. Our experiments show that SuperCoP performs 16.8% better than TSOall, and 6% better than TSOdata. It is worth noting that SuperCoP performs better than TSOdata, even thought TSOdata is not applicable to all supervised systems.

In summary, this work makes the following contributions to supervised memory systems.

- We reduce the correctness requirement of supervised memory systems to be metadata read ordering, rather than supervised instruction ordering. This correctness requirement en-

ables the use of a write buffer, without compromising correctness.

- We propose SuperCoP a supervised memory system which reflects the above metadata read ordering requirement. Since SuperCoP separates reads and their processing from the writes, we propose a novel atomicity scheme to retain SMI atomicity.

- Since SuperCoP ensures correctness without making any assumptions about the supervision scheme, it is a generic solution to the correctness problem

- Our experiments show that SuperCoP is efficient, performing better than both TSOall (by 16.8%) and TSOdata (by 6%).

The rest of the paper is organized as follows. Section 2 provides some background information on supervised memory systems, and explains the working of a supervised system using the example of full-empty bits [2], including the issue of *metadata-data atomicity*. The correctness issues that manifest in supervised systems for TSO consistency are explained in section 3. We also provide our solution - SuperCoP - for these correctness issues in the same section. Our solution for the metadata-data atomicity issue is presented in section 4. Finally, section 5 presents the simulation results comparing the performance of SuperCoP, TSOall, and TSOdata.

2. BACKGROUND

2.1 Supervised Memory Systems

Supervised memory systems use metadata associated with each memory address to control and monitor access to those addresses. They make use of supervised memory instructions (SMI) to access and manipulate this metadata. The semantics of the metadata and the way it is used depends on the supervision scheme [1, 2, 3, 7, 15, 17, 20, 21, 22].

(Metadata, SMI) We use the full-empty bits supervision scheme [1, 2] throughout this paper in order to explain the working of supervised memory systems, and the issues associated with them. Full-empty bits is a supervision scheme which is typically used for word level producer-consumer synchronization. Here, each memory address is associated with a metabit (metadata with size 1 bit) which specifies whether the memory address is *full* (1) or *empty* (0). Processors make use of supervised memory writes (SMW) and supervised memory reads (SMR) to access data and metadata. A producer can write to the memory address only if the metabit is set to *empty*, and sets it to *full* once the write is complete. A consumer can read from a memory address only if the metabit is *full*, setting it to *empty* on completion. If an SMW encounters a *full* state, or if an SMR encounters an *empty* state, an exception is raised. An exception in the case of full-empty bits retries the memory access for a fixed number of times, and calls a trap handler if it still fails. The trap handler in turn decides to block the operation, retry the operation, or wake up the thread that is causing the exception to be raised in the first place.

(Metadata-data atomicity) One of the issues in supervised memory systems is that of metadata-data atomicity, which dictates that metadata operations should be atomic with respect to the corresponding data operations. Not observing this atomicity may lead to incorrect metadata values. Consider Figure 2, where both P_0 and P_2 perform an SMW to address A, while P_1 performs an SMR to the same address A. Assume that the initial metadata value for A is *empty*. If atomicity is preserved, the data and metadata operations

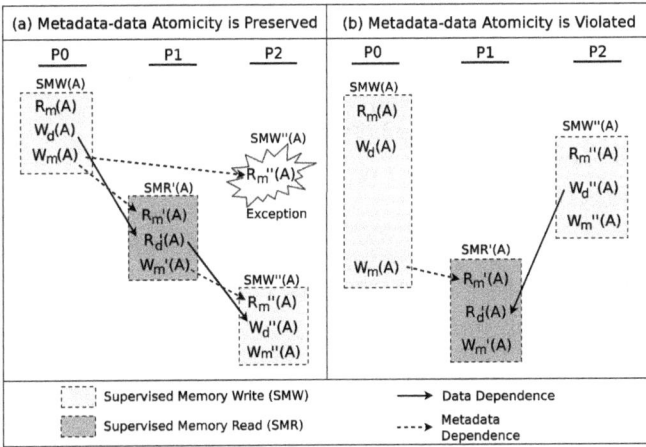

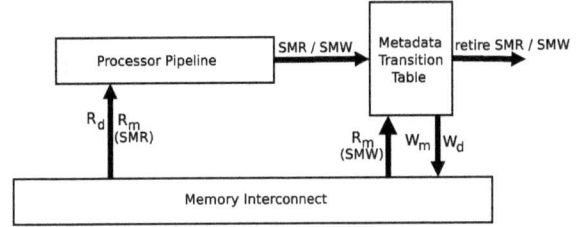

Figure 3: **Memtracker implementation of a supervised memory system. An SMI (SMR/SMW) can be retired only after its metadata and data operations are completed.**

Figure 2: **Metadata of A is initially** *empty*. **If metadata-data atomicity is preserved, SMR′(A) reads the value written by SMW(A). This is followed by SMW″(A), which updates A.** *The exception raised by SMW″(A) prevents SMR′(A) from reading an incorrect value.* **If metadata-data atomicity is violated, both SMW(A) and SMW″(A) are performed in an overlapped manner, and SMR′(A) ends up reading the data written by SMW″(A), instead of SMW(A).**

of SMW(A) and SMW"(A) cannot interleave with each other. This is illustrated in Figure 2(a), where SMW(A) completes first, following which P₂ tries to perform SMW"(A). But, the metadata of A at this point in time will be *full* which causes SMW"(A) to raise an exception. SMR'(A) from P₁, however, can be performed and reads the value written by SMW(A). Following this, SMW"(A) is allowed to perform as SMR'(A) would have restored the metadata state to *empty*. Thus, preserving atomicity results in an execution pattern where SMR'(A) reads the value written by SMW(A), following which SMW"(A) updates the data in address A and the final metadata state of A is *full*. If atomicity is not preserved, as shown in Fig. 2(b), both SMW(A) (from P₀) and SMW"(A) (from P₂) can potentially interleave with each other. Indeed, the figure shows the scenario where SMW"(A), which performs after SMW(A), does not see the metadata update of SMW(A) (*full*) and thus proceeds without any exceptions being raised. This causes SMR'(A) to read the value written by SMW"(A) (as opposed to SMW'(A)) and the final metadata state of A is *empty* (as opposed to *full*). This sequence is incorrect as it violates the full-empty bits supervision scheme by allowing two consecutive writes to a memory location.

2.2 Types of Supervised Memory Systems

Supervised memory systems can be software based, or hardware assisted – the two differ in how SMIs are performed, the way in which memory space is allocated for metadata, and the way in which metadata-data atomicity is ensured.

(Software based supervised memory systems) In software supervised systems[11, 13, 12], SMIs are executed along with program instructions using the same processor pipeline i.e. metadata read, its processing and metadata write are all performed as separate software instructions. Some software based supervised memory systems track the order of data coherence requests and mirror this order for metadata as well. This is called coupled coherence or shadow coherence [10]. Other atomicity schemes include the use of transactional memory [6], where supervised instructions occur

as part of transactions which are either committed or re-executed depending on whether metadata-data atomicity is intact or is violated. The fact that software supervised systems execute additional instructions to operate on metadata, results in a heavy performance overhead which sometimes exceeds 100% [11].

(Decoupled supervised memory systems) In decoupled systems described in [5, 8, 18], the application program and metadata processing are performed in separate processors, called *application core* and *metadata core* respectively. The application core feeds a stream of committed instructions to the metadata core, which then performs the metadata operations for those instructions. Decoupled systems are similar to software based supervision in the way SMIs are performed, metadata storage is allocated, and how atomicity is ensured. Decoupled systems, however, require one metadata core for every application core to provide the best performance [18].

(Hardware assisted supervised memory systems) The performance overhead of software based supervision and the fact that decoupled systems require an additional core, for every application core, to process metadata has led researchers to adopt hardware assisted supervised memory systems. We concentrate on such *hardware assisted supervised memory systems* [14, 15, 16, 17, 21], where SMIs are performed entirely in hardware by modifying the processor pipeline or adding extra hardware inside the processor itself. We consider the case of **Memtracker**[17], which is the state-of-the-art hardware assisted supervised memory system. Memtracker performs the metadata operations after the *commit* stage of the pipeline, as shown in Figure 3. *Here, the memory system is a tagged memory system, where the data width of each address is extended to store the metadata along with program data.* Thus, a read operation to the data address also fetches the metadata. Similarly, a data write operation can also write the metadata during the same access. An SMR instruction reads its data and metadata as part of the processor pipeline. Once the instruction is ready to retire, the *metadata transition table* operates on this metadata and generates an updated metadata value according to the supervision scheme. For an SMW instruction, the metadata read is performed after the instruction is ready to retire. Both data and metadata are written back once the metadata processing is complete. An instruction is retired only when both data and metadata operations associated with it have completed. This implementation does not incorporate a write buffer, which implies that all instructions are performed **in-order**. Thus Memtracker performs like an SC system.

For an SMI to be atomic in Memtracker, its metadata write should be atomic with respect to its metadata read. Memtracker uses load replay to ensure metadata read write atomicity. If the metadata value read by an SMI is modified by another processor before the write completes, the metadata read is replayed. This is typically done by observing the coherence requests from other processors.

(a)

The scenario below conisders the case where P1's execution is scheduled first

(b)   (c)

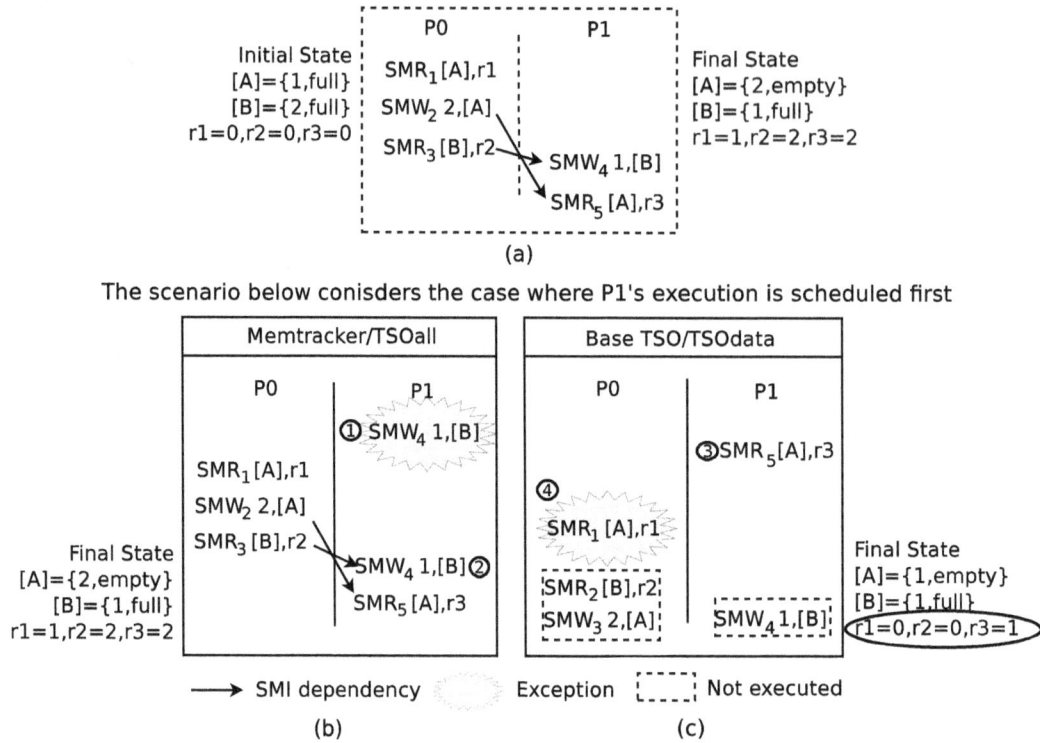

Figure 5: (a) shows the intended sequence of execution. **(b)** and **(c)** show the execution sequence in Memtracker and the base TSO model, when P_1's execution is scheduled before P_0. In Memtracker/TSOall, $SMW_4(B)$ results in an exception ① blocking the thread until $SMW_3(B)$ is performed. This results in $SMR_5(A)$ reading the value written by $SMW_2(A)$ ②. In the base TSO model/TSOdata $SMR_5(A)$ is ordered before $SMW_4(B)$ and reads the initial value of A ③, which is incorrect. Also, $SMR_1(A)$ raises an unnecessary exception ④

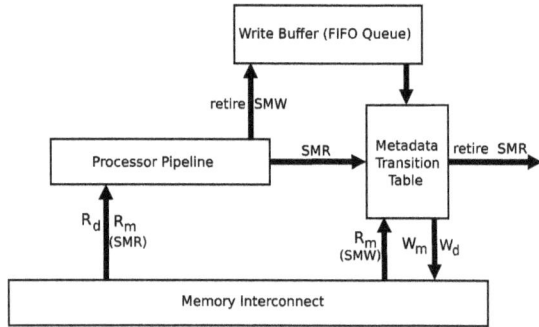

Figure 4: Base model for a TSO based supervised memory system. An SMR is retired after it has completed its data and metadata operations. An SMW is retired into the write buffer, and performs its data and metadata operations on reaching the head of the write buffer.

3. CORRECTNESS ISSUES IN TSO BASED SUPERVISED MEMORY SYSTEMS

(Base model) The TSO consistency model is widely used in present day systems, including Sun's SPARC, Intel's/AMD's x86 and its variants. The base system model considered in *Safe Supervised Memory* [4] is a TSO-based system, with a supervision mechanism similar to Memtracker [17]. The Memtracker proposal itself does not make use of a write buffer. The base TSO model for supervised systems, however, includes a write buffer into which all SMW instructions are retired. This results in an implementation where an SMW instruction reads its metadata only when it is issued from the write buffer i.e. when it reaches the head of the write buffer. Then, the metadata is processed and the resulting metadata (if any) and data are written back to memory. SMR instructions are processed in the same manner as in Memtracker. The resulting system model is described in Figure 4. Metadata-data atomicity is preserved in the same way as in Memtracker.

(Correctness issues) Bobba et al. [4] pointed out that retiring SMW instructions into the write buffer can causes correctness issues in the supervision scheme. It is possible that an SMR (that follows an SMW) can read its metadata before the preceding SMW in the write buffer can read its corresponding metadata. This is called *metadata read reordering* and can cause incorrectness in the supervision scheme. Furthermore, any exception caused by an SMW in the write buffer will not be raised until the SMW reaches the head of the write buffer. Thus the exception raised will be *late* or *imprecise*, since subsequent instructions (which follow the SMW) may have already retired when the exception is raised, again causing incorrectness in the supervision scheme. Since non-supervised writes do not read metadata

We use the full-empty bits supervision scheme to illustrate both these correctness issues. Consider the sequence of instructions shown in Figure 5(a). Here, $SMR_3(B)$ (from P_0) synchronizes with $SMW_4(B)$ (from P_1), to ensure that $SMR_5(A)$ (from P_1) reads the

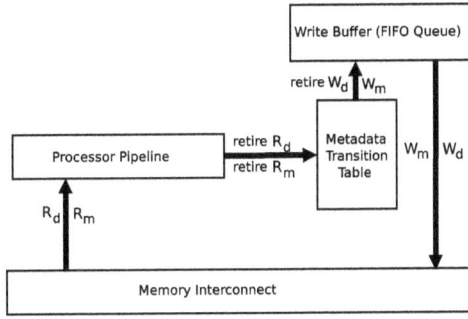

Figure 6: Implementation of SuperCoP. All SMIs are separated into their constituent operations and are retired separately. For an SMR, R_m/R_d are retired once they are completed, and W_m is retired into the write buffer. For an SMW, R_m is retired once the read is complete. W_d/W_m are retired into the write buffer.

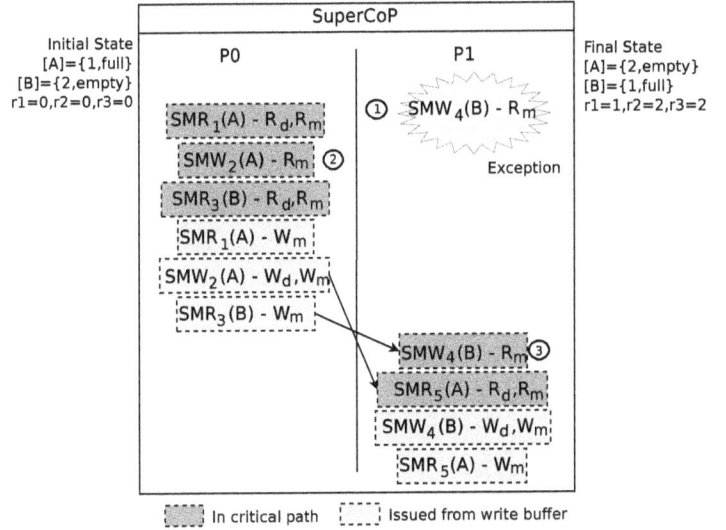

Figure 7: Resolving correctness issues in SuperCoP. If P_0 is scheduled before P_1, $SMW_4(B)$ performs its R_m first, which raises an exception ①. The thread is then blocked until this R_m can succeed. In P_0, $SMR_1(A)$ retires its metadata write to the write buffer, from which $SMW_2(A)$ reads its metadata ②. $SMW_4(B)$ can finally perform after $SMR_3(B)$ completes its metadata write ③. Now, when $SMR_5(A)$ is performed, it reads the value written by $SMW_2(A)$. Thus, there is no incorrectness.

value written by $SMW_2(A)$ (from P_0). Initially, both A and B are in the *full* state. In the expected execution sequence, P_0 performs $SMR_1(A)$ reading the initial value (1) into r_1. $SMR_1(A)$ also sets the metadata of A to *empty*. Then $SMW_2(A)$ writes the value 2 into A, reverting its metadata to *full*. P_0 then performs $SMR_3(B)$ which *empties* address B. This is followed by P_1 writing into B (SMW_4), and then reading from A (SMR_5). No exceptions are raised in this execution sequence. *The result of the execution is that $SMR_5(A)$ from P_1 reads the value written by $SMW_2(A)$ i.e. $r_3=2$.*

Now, it is possible that P_0 is stalled or blocked, resulting in P_1 executing its instructions first. In such a case, P_1 first tries to perform $SMW_4(B)$. In Memtracker (Figure 5(b)), this immediately raises an exception ① and P_1 is blocked until this instruction can successfully execute. P_1 can resume its execution only after $SMR_3(B)$ completes i.e $SMR_3(B)$ updates the metadata of B to *empty*. Once P_1 resumes, it performs $SMW_4(B)$ followed by $SMR_5(A)$. *This results in $SMR_5(A)$ reading the value written by $SMW_2(A)$, as in the expected execution sequence.*

In the base TSO model (Figure 5(c)), however, P_1 retires $SMW_4(B)$ into the write buffer, and proceeds to perform $SMR_5(A)$ ③. Since $SMR_5(A)$ reads a metadata state of *full*, it does not raise any exception and reads the value 1 into r_3 (setting metadata of A to *empty*). The exception on writing to B (which is in *full* state) is raised only when $SMW_4(B)$ is issued from the write buffer. This *imprecise exception* combined with the *metadata read reordering* that occurs when $SMR_5(A)$ reads its metadata before $SMW_4(B)$, *results in an incorrect value being read into r_3.* Also, with this execution sequence, when P_0 eventually performs $SMR_1(A)$, it reads a metadata value of *empty* resulting in an exception ④. Subsequent instructions are not performed till $SMR_1(A)$ is successful, which does not happen within this execution sequence.

Bobba et al. outline two systems, namely TSOall and TSOdata, to tackle these correctness issues. TSOall is the same as the Memtracker system model, with the only difference being that TSOall allows unsupervised write instructions to retire into the write buffer. Thus, TSOall does not suffer from any correctness issues, but has a high performance overhead as the write buffer is not used efficiently. TSOdata is the same as the base TSO model explained in Figure 4. Thus all correctness issues that afflict the base TSO model also manifest in TSOdata. Bobba et al. prescribe TSOdata, however, only for supervision schemes that tolerate metadata reordering, like HARD [21]. Unfortunately, not all supervision schemes tolerate metadata reordering, including full-empty bits. In sum-

mary, TSOall is correct but inefficient, and TSOdata is not applicable to all supervision schemes, even though it is efficient. We propose a general solution to the correctness issues in TSO based supervised systems without compromising on performance.

(Our Approach) Since Memtracker/TSOall does not suffer from correctness issues, we can conclude that inorder execution of SMIs is a sufficient condition to solve imprecise exceptions in TSO based supervised systems. This *inorder* execution of SMIs, however, results in a high performance overhead. We observe that inorder execution of SMIs is not a necessary condition for correctness. Intuitively, the necessary condition to avoid metadata read reordering is to guarantee that metadata reads (and processing) occur in program order. This will also ensure that metadata reads of SMW instructions will be performed before subsequent instructions retire. Thus, by enforcing metadata read ordering, both correctness issues that plague TSO based supervised memory systems can be solved. We, therefore, reduce the correctness requirement of a supervised system. The proposed correctness requirement is that metadata reads should be performed inorder, rather than entire SMIs being performed inorder. Since only metadata reads are to be performed inorder, metadata and data writes can be retired into the write buffer, which reduces the performance overhead as compared to Memtracker. Hence we propose SuperCoP - Supervision with Correctness and Performance, which ensures metadata read ordering by separating metadata reads from metadata writes.

The implementation of SuperCoP is illustrated in Figure 6. In SuperCoP, an SMR performs its data read (R_d) and metadata read (R_m) as part of the processor pipeline. Both read operations retire once they are completed. Then, the metadata is processed and the resultant metadata write (W_m), if any, is retired into the write buffer. Then the processor continues with its execution. This removes W_m from the critical path. An SMW also performs its R_m

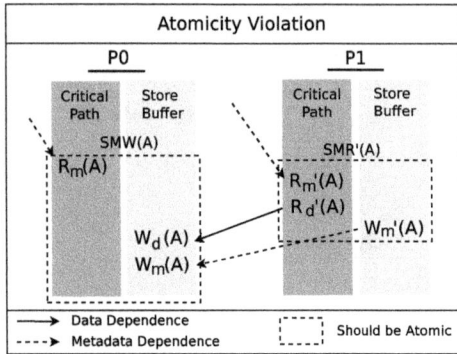

Figure 8: Atomicity Violation in SuperCoP. R_m (from P_0) retires and inserts W_m and W_d into the write buffer. Meanwhile, R'_m (from P_1) is performed and reads the same metadata value as R_m, instead of reading the metadata value written by W_m, as W_d is performed after R'_d.

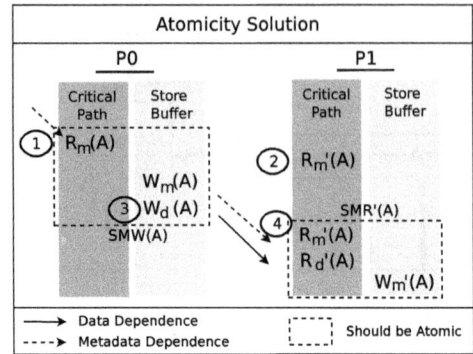

Figure 9: Solving Atomicity by fine grain locking. R_m locks address A ① prohibiting R'_m from being performed ②. W_m unlocks A ③ following which R'_m is performed successfully ④. Thus, R'_m correctly reads the metadata written by W_m.

as part of the pipeline, once address computation is complete. The metadata is then processed following which R_m retires. Then, both data write (W_d) and metadata write (W_m) are retired into the write buffer. As we can see, all metadata reads are performed in order, and instructions need only to wait for the metadata read and processing to be complete for them to be retired. Unlike TSOdata, we do not make any assumptions about the supervision scheme itself. This makes SuperCoP applicable to all supervised memory systems.

Consider the same sequence of instructions as in Figure 5. The execution order as per SuperCoP is shown in Figure 7. Assuming the same scenario (where P_0 has been stalled or blocked), P_1 begins with the execution of $SMW_4(B)$. Since SuperCoP performs metadata read of an SMW in the critical path, an exception is raised ① as the SMW is to a *full* location. This stalls P_1 until the metadata of B becomes *empty*. Now when P_0 eventually begins execution, it performs the metadata and data read for $SMR_1(A)$, and retires the metadata write to the write buffer. The next SMI being an SMW to A can read its metadata from the write buffer itself through a read bypass ②. The resulting metadata write and data write are retired into the write buffer. This is followed by $SMR_3(B)$. Once $SMR_3(B)$ completes its metadata write and updates the metadata of B to *empty*, P_1 is unblocked and proceeds with its execution ③. It is evident that SuperCoP's execution order is the same as Memtracker/TSOall. *It is worth noting that $SMR_5(A)$ in P_1 reads the value written by $SMW_2(A)$ which is the expected result.* This example shows how SuperCoP deals with the correctness issues that manifest in TSO based supervised systems.

4. ENSURING ATOMICITY

A consequence of separating metadata reads and writes in SuperCoP is that it can violate metadata-data atomicity which in turn leads to incorrectness in metadata. An example of this metadata-data atomicity violation is illustrated in Figure 8. For ease of explanation, we use a generic supervision scheme instead of the full-empty bits scenario.

Here, P_0 performs SMW(A), and P_1 performs SMR'(A). First, P_0 performs and retires R_m(A) in the critical path. Once the metadata processing is done, P_0 retires W_m(A) and W_d(A) into the write buffer, which may have other entries above it. Meanwhile, SMR'(A) is performed in P_1. R'_m(A) reads the same metadata

value read by R_m(A). The metadata is processed and W'_d(A) is retired into the write buffer and is immediately issued to the memory. W_d(A)-W_m(A) is then issued to memory. Here, even though W_m(A) is ordered after R'_d(A), R_m(A) does not read the metadata value written by W'_m(A). This violates metadata-data atomicity.

(Atomicity based on fine grain locking) To ensure atomicity, either SMR'(A) should be allowed to perform only after SMW(A) completes, or SMW(A) should be re-executed after SMR'(A) completes (similar to Memtracker). In case of the latter, R_m cannot be allowed to retire until its metadata write has completed. Since this obviates any performance gain in separating metadata read and write, we choose the former approach to implement atomicity. We ensure that an SMI can be performed in an uninterrupted fashion, by using a fine grain locking mechanism to lock the address accessed by an SMI when the metadata read is performed, and relinquish the lock when the metadata write is performed. All coherence requests to locked addresses will be denied/delayed until the unlock operation occurs. This will guarantee that no other SMI can access the metadata location locked by another SMI until it completes. An execution pattern for a generic fine grain locking based atomicity scheme is illustrated in Figure 9. ① First, address A is locked by R_m(A). ② Now, when R'_m(A) is issued, its coherence request is denied owing to the lock on A. ③ The lock on A is relinquished when W_m(A) is issued to memory. ④ Now, when R'_m(A) is issued to memory, it locks A. Here, SMR'(A) reads both its data and metadata from SMW(A), thus preserving metadata-data atomicity. A is later unlocked when W'_m(A) completes in the memory.

(Atomicity using local cache locking) In order to implement fine grain locking, all SMIs can be considered on the lines of conventional Read-Modify-Write (RMW) instructions. Conventional RMW instructions obtain write permissions to the cache block they address, and lock the cache block in the local cache. Similarly, an SMI instruction should obtain exclusive permissions to the cache block it addresses, lock the cache block locally, and then retire its write(s) into the write buffer. If a metadata write is not generated, the cache block is unlocked immediately. Otherwise, the lock is released when the metadata write is issued from the write buffer. Referring back to Figure 9, in ①, R_m(A) gets write permissions for A and locks the address in its local cache. R'_m(A)'s request for A is denied ②, until the lock is relinquished ③. Then R'_m(A) obtains write permissions for A by invalidating the copy in P_0. An SMI performs invalidations only when a metadata write is gener-

```
At the Processor:

When SMI(A) is performed:
1.      if A is modified/exclusive hit in L1
2.          lock A (in local cache)
3.          retire R_m
4.          if W_m is generated
5.              retire W_m (into write buffer)
6.          else
7.              unlock A
8.          end if
9.      else if A is shared hit in L1
10.         if W_m is generated or SMI=SMW
11.             request for directory lock for A
12.             wait for response
13.             retire R_m
14.         else
15.             retire R_m
16.         end if
17.     else            //miss in L1
18.         request for directory lock for A
19.         wait for response
20.         retire R_m
21.         if W_m not generated issue dummy W_m
22.     end if

At the Directory:

On receiving a request from SMI(A):
1.      if pending transaction on A
2.          insert request into directory queue
3.      else
4.          transition A into busy state
5.          acknowledge SMI(A)
6.      end if

On receiving W_m(A) / W_d(A):
1.      transition A into modified state
```

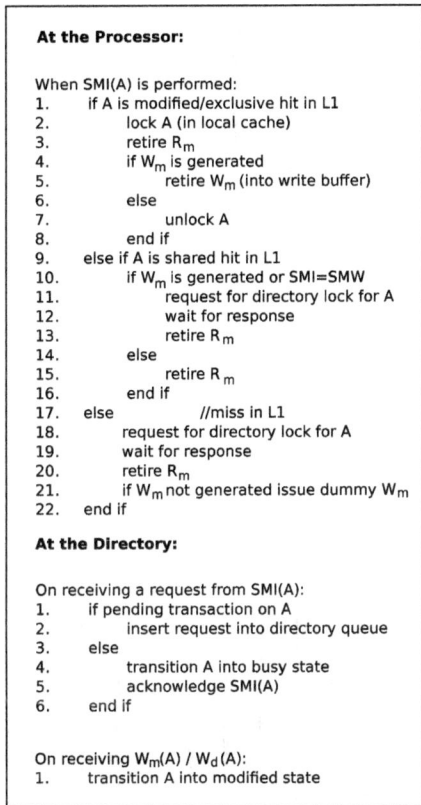

A request in the directory queue is serviced if there
are no requests to the same cache block ahead of it.

Figure 10: Protocol for the proposed Directory locking mechanism to preserve metadata-data atomicity.

ated. The invalidation, however, for both SMRs and SMWs occur in the critical path, owing to which the cache locking scheme will suffer a performance overheard similar to that of TSOall.

(Atomicity using directory locking) To address this drawback, we propose a novel atomicity scheme which reduces the number of invalidations and pushes the remaining invalidations out of the critical path. We make use of the underlying coherence protocol to implement this atomicity scheme, which in our case is the directory protocol. Invalidations occur when the metadata address is in the *shared* coherence state. If an SMI is issued to a *shared* address, then the cache block it addresses is locked in the directory instead of obtaining write permissions to it and locking it in the local cache. The lock is relinquished on completion of the SMI's metadata/data write. For an SMR, invalidations are carried out only if a metadata write is generated, thereby reducing the number of invalidations as compared to the local cache locking scheme. For both SMW/SMR, invalidations in the critical path are replaced by a directory access which is much cheaper. The invalidation itself is removed from the critical path and is performed as part of the write buffer logic.

The protocol followed for the directory locking mechanism is outlined in Figure 10. Let us assume an SMI to address A. If A is in modified/exclusive state in the local cache, the locking happens in the local cache (L1) itself. The corresponding metadata write unlocks the cache block. If no metadata write is generated, then the cache block is unblocked immediately. Like in local cache locking, all requests to a locked cache block are denied by the processor.

The request is forwarded to the directory if a) A is not present in

L1, or b) A is in *shared* state and the SMI is a read which generates a metadata write, or c) A is in *shared* state and the SMI is a write. The directory checks if there are any pending requests to A. If there are pending requests to A in the directory, the request is inserted into the directory queue and is serviced when there are no other requests to A ahead of it in the queue. When the request gets serviced the cache block is transitioned into a *busy* state, and an acknowledgement is sent to the requesting processor. The processor retires the read operation on receiving a response from the directory. If the directory receives a coherence request to a cache block in *busy* state, the request is queued in the directory. The cache block is transitioned out of the *busy* state when the directory receives a corresponding metadata write/data write. Thus, the *busy* state acts like a lock. If an SMI which has obtained a directory lock does not generate a metadata write (a miss in the local cache), a *dummy* write has to be issued to unlock the address in the directory. It is worth noting that this *dummy* write need not be issued in the critical path.

(Example) The working of the directory locking based atomicity scheme is illustrated in Figure 11, where P_0 performs SMW(A) and P_1 performs SMR′(A) (as shown in Figure 9). Assume that A is initially shared between P_0 and P_1. First, SMW(A) (from P_0) performs its metadata read. (1) Since, A is in *shared* state, the request is forwarded to the directory and (2) locks A (goes to *busy* state) in the directory. (3) The directory responds to the request so that R_m can be retired. (4) The metadata is then processed (in P_0) and the resulting metadata write is retired into the write buffer. It is worth noting that A is still in the *shared* state in the directory. (5) Now, when SMR′(A) (from P_1) sends a read request to the directory, (6) it is inserted into the directory queue, as A is in *busy* state. The metadata read of SMR′(A) is not retired as it does not receive a response from the directory. (7) When W_m is issued from P_0's write buffer, (8) P_1's copy of A is invalidated, and (9) the lock on A is relinquished by P_0. The directory transitions the cache block A to modified state owned by P_0. Now, (10) SMR′(A)'s request is serviced by the directory, which (11) (& (12)) obtains the updated copy of the data and metadata from P_0 and (13) locks A again, by transitioning it to the *busy* state. (14) The directory acknowledges SMR′(A), so that its metadata and data read can be retired. A is now again in *shared* state with both P_0 and P_1 having copies of it. (15) Eventually, SMR′(A) issues its metadata write to unlock A in the directory.

5. EXPERIMENTAL RESULTS

(System Specification) We built a hardware simulation infrastructure using the PIN tool [9], to simulate 16 processors connected in a mesh network. The interconnect has a link latency of 1 cycle and router latency of 4 cycles. Each processor has a 32-entry write buffer, and a private 4-way 32KB L1. A MESI-based directory protocol is used to keep all L1 caches coherent. The L2 cache (16-way 1MB/core) and the directory are static address interleaved. Each instruction takes 1 cycle to execute, and it takes a total of 4, 20, and 200 cycles to access the L1, L2, and main memory, respectively. As mentioned in previous sections, we use a *tagged* memory system to store metadata for the supervised system, where both metadata and data are stored together in the same address. All memory operations are considered as supervised memory operations. We evaluate the performance of TSOall, TSOdata, and SuperCoP using the SPLASH-2 [19] benchmark suite. The benchmarks and their respective input sizes are listed in Table 1. We evaluate SuperCoP with both cache based locking and directory based locking.

(HARD supervision scheme) We demonstrate the efficacy of SuperCoP as compared to TSOall and TSOdata using the HARD supervision scheme proposed by Zhou et al. [21]. HARD is used

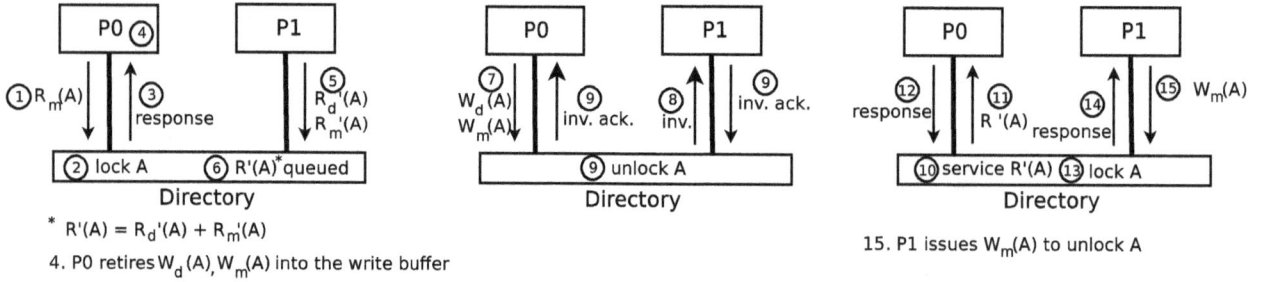

* $R'(A) = R_d'(A) + R_m'(A)$

4. P0 retires $W_d(A)$, $W_m(A)$ into the write buffer

15. P1 issues $W_m(A)$ to unlock A

Figure 11: Metadata-data atomicity with Directory locking. Here, P_0 performs SMW(A) and P_1 performs SMR$'$(A). The sequence of events are numbered in the ascending order. The figure on the left shows how SMW(A) locks address A, and SMR'(A) is queued in the directory. The figure in the center shows steps involved in unlocking A. In the figure on the left, SMR$'$(A) locks A, when it is serviced by the directory. Eventually, SMR$'$(A) issues its metadata write to unlock A.

Table 1: Splash-2 Benchmark Suite

Code	Problem Size
Barnes	16K particles
Cholesky	tk29.O
FFT	64K points
FMM	16K particles
LU (contiguous)	512x512 matrix, 16x16 blocks
LU (non-contiguous)	512x512 matrix, 16x16 blocks
Ocean (contiguous)	258 x 258 ocean
Ocean (non-contiguous)	258 x 258 ocean
Radiosity	room, -ae 5000.0 -en 0.050 -bf 0.10
Radix	1M integers, radix 1024
Raytrace	car
Volrend	head
Water-Nsq	512 molecules
Water-Sp	512 molecules

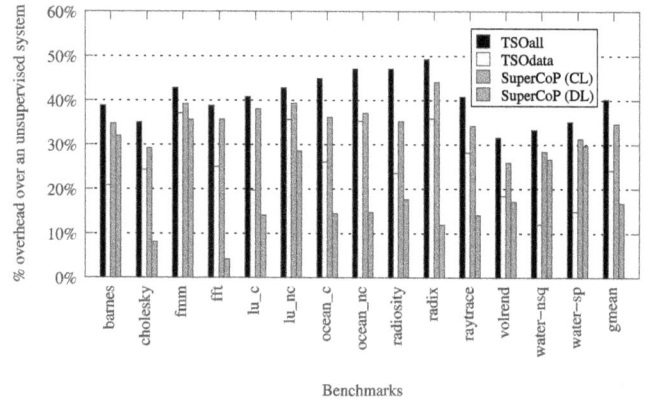

Figure 12: Performance comparison for the HARD supervision scheme. CL and DL represent the cache locking scheme and directory locking schemes, respectively.

for race detection in multi-threaded software. It ensures that all accesses to a shared variable are protected by at least one common lock. Each thread maintains a variable called LockSet which is the union of all the locks currently held by the thread. Each variable is protected by a Candidate Set which is the set of locks used to protect the variable thus far. On every memory access, the candidate set is updated to include the LockSet of the thread reading the variable. Candidate sets are written at cache-block granularity, and form the metadata in this system along with the state of the variable. A simple finite state machine is used to transition variable states, that initializes blocks in private states and transitions them to a shared state when they are accessed by multiple threads. On every data access, the LockSet, the CandidateSet, and the variable state are used to detect a race, and an exception is raised when a certain set of conditions are met. HARD uses Bloom filters to efficiently represent them in hardware. We chose the HARD supervision scheme to compare the various supervised systems as it is an example of a supervision scheme which reads processes and updates metadata. Also, the earlier work by Bobba et al. [4] uses HARD to compare TSOdata and TSOall.

(Simulation results for HARD) We compare the performance of TSOall, TSOdata, SuperCoP (with cache locking), and SuperCoP (with directory locking) for the HARD supervision scheme. The experimental results are shown in Figure 12. The percentage of SMIs which update metadata varies from 0.2% (*fmm*) to 57.8% (*lu-contiguous*) as shown in Table 2, with an average (geometric mean) of 4.5%. We observe from Figure 12 that TSOdata consistently performs better than TSOall as it retires SMWs to the write buffer,

while incurring the same latency for SMRs. On an average, TSOdata performs better than TSOall by 11.4%. With cache locking, SuperCoP performs worse than TSOdata for all benchmarks (average of 8.3%), as invalidations for SMRs and SMWs which update shared metadata are in the critical path. With directory locking, however, SuperCoP outperforms TSOdata by 6% across all benchmarks.

It is worth nothing that, TSOall performs invalidations for both SMRs which update metadata and SMWs in the critical path. TSOdata performs invalidations for SMRs which update metadata in the critical path, while SMWs are completely performed in the write buffer. With the cache locking scheme, SuperCoP performs invalidations for all SMIs which update shared metadata in the critical path. Since, invalidations of SMRs and SMWs are performed in the critical path, the cache locking scheme incurs a penalty close to TSOall. With the directory locking scheme, only SMRs which update metadata to shared locations, and SMWs to shared locations incur a directory access in the critical path, thereby providing better performance than even TSOdata.

We analyze the directory locking scheme in more detail. We observe that SuperCoP with the directory locking scheme performs much better than TSOdata for benchmarks which have a higher percentage of SMIs that update metadata (*fft* - 39.5%, *lu-contiguous* - 57.8%, *lu-noncontiguous* - 48.8%, *ocean-contiguous* - 14.5%,

Table 2: Characteristics of Supervised Instructions for HARD

Code	% of SMIs updating metadata
Barnes	8.5
Cholesky	0.7
FFT	39.5
FMM	0.2
LU contiguous	57.8
LU noncontiguous	48.8
Ocean contiguous	14.5
Ocean noncontiguous	20.9
Radiosity	7.2
Radix	5.6
Raytrace	11.3
Volrend	0.2
Water-Nsq	6.2
Water-Sp	2.1

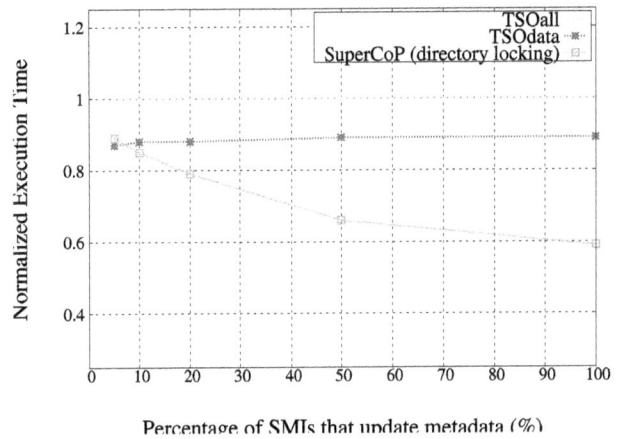

Figure 13: Scalability of supervised systems with respect to the number of SMIs which update metadata. The execution time is normalized to that of TSOall to better represent the scalability.

ocean-contiguous - 20.9%, *raytrace* - 11%). For *radix*, even though the percentage of SMIs which update metadata is comparatively less (5.5%), SuperCoP (with directory locking) performs much better than TSOdata as a larger percentage of SMIs which update metadata are shared SMRs (recall that shared SMRs which update metadata are more expensive in TSOdata than in SuperCoP) and the *number* of SMWs which update metadata to shared locations is negligible. Similarly, in *cholesky*, the *number* of SMRs updating metadata are much larger compared to SMWs which update shared metadata. SuperCoP (with directory locking) performs worse than TSOdata for *barnes, water-nsquared* and *water-spatial* as these applications issue a comparatively larger number of SMWs to shared locations. In case of *fmm*, even though the number of shared writes is large, the SMWs which update shared metadata is very few (0.06%) in number compared to the number of SMWs which update metadata in exclusive locations (21%). The overhead that these SMWs cause in SuperCoP is offset by the number of SMRs which update metadata, resulting in SuperCoP performing on par with TSOdata.

(Scalability with respect to metadata updates) It can be seen from the results for HARD that the percentage of SMIs that update metadata critically influences the performance of a supervised system. Thus, we can study the scalability of the supervised systems by implementing a generic supervision scheme, and varying the percentage of SMIs which update metadata. The cost associated with a metadata update depends on whether the SMI is an SMR or an SMW. Now, an SMR which updates metadata has a higher latency than an SMR which does not update metadata. This is evident from the implementations of TSOall and TSOdata where SMRs updating metadata result in an invalidation in the critical path. Also, in SuperCoP, an SMR updating shared metadata must access the directory. The cost of an SMW, however, depends on the coherence state rather than whether it updates metadata or not. Thus, the performance overhead of the supervision scheme increases proportionally with the percentage of SMRs updating metadata, which in turn depends on the supervision scheme. This means that scalability of a supervised system can be represented on the lines of *metadata update percentages*. In our experiments, we vary the percentage of SMIs which update metadata from 5% to 100% .

(Simulation results for scalability) Figure 13 shows how the performance of SuperCoP scales with percentage of SMIs updating metadata as compared with TSOdata. The execution time is averaged across all SPLASH-2 benchmarks and are normalized with respect to the execution time of TSOall. We have not represented

SuperCoP with the cache locking scheme as it is evident from the results of the HARD supervision scheme that the cache locking scheme performs as bad as TSOall.

Figure 13 shows that TSOdata provides the same performance improvement over TSOall as metadata update percentage increases. It is worth noting that the only performance improvement that TSOdata provides over TSOall is for SMWs, and even if these SMWs update metadata, performance improvement for TSOdata over TSOall will be the same. And SMRs are performed in the same manner for TSOall and TSOdata. Therefore, the only advantage that TSOdata provides over TSOall is the write buffer. In the case of SuperCoP, however, the latency of SMRs updating metadata is reduced as compared to TSOall and TSOdata. SMWs incur a small penalty of accessing the directory if it is to a shared location, which is constant across varying metadata update percentage. Thus, SuperCoP performs better than TSOall and TSOdata as the percentage of SMIs that update metadata increases.

6. CONCLUSION

Existing supervised memory systems, implicitly or explicitly, assume SC [4]. Bobba et al. proposed two systems; TSOall which has significant performance overhead, TSOdata which is not general and still suffers from correctness issues for certain supervision schemes. Bobba et al.'s work on safe supervised systems implicitly assumes that inorder execution of SMIs ensures correctness. We reduce this correctness requirement to *metadata read ordering*. To this end, we develop SuperCoP, which separates metadata reads and writes, and ensures *metadata read ordering* by performing the metadata reads in the critical path. We also propose a directory locking scheme to ensure metadata-data atomicity at a lower cost.

We demonstrate the efficiency of SuperCoP with respect to TSOall and TSOdata using the HARD supervision scheme. Our experimental results using HARD show that *SuperCoP* performs better than *TSOall* by 16.8% and *TSOdata* by 6%. We also analyze the scalability of supervised systems with respect to the percentage of SMIs which update metadata. It is evident from our experiments that SuperCoP scales better than TSOall or TSOdata. Thus we show that SuperCoP is a correct and performance efficient supervised memory system that is general, in that it is applicable to any supervision scheme.

7. ACKNOWLEDGEMENTS

We would like to thank the reviewers for their helpful comments. This work is supported by the Centre for Numerical Algorithms and Intelligent Software, funded by EPSRC grant EP/G036136/1 and the Scottish Funding Council.

8. REFERENCES

[1] A. Agarwal, R. Bianchini, D. Chaiken, K. L. Johnson, D. Kranz, J. Kubiatowicz, B.-H. Lim, K. Mackenzie, and D. Yeung. The mit alewife machine: architecture and performance. In *Proceedings of the 22nd annual international symposium on Computer architecture*, ISCA '95, pages 2–13, New York, NY, USA, 1995. ACM.

[2] R. Alverson, D. Callahan, D. Cummings, B. Koblenz, A. Porterfield, and B. Smith. The tera computer system. In *Proceedings of the 4th international conference on Supercomputing*, ICS '90, pages 1–6, New York, NY, USA, 1990. ACM.

[3] J. Bobba, N. Goyal, M. D. Hill, M. M. Swift, and D. A. Wood. Tokentm: Efficient execution of large transactions with hardware transactional memory. In *Proceedings of the 35th Annual International Symposium on Computer Architecture*, ISCA '08, pages 127–138, Washington, DC, USA, 2008. IEEE Computer Society.

[4] J. Bobba, M. Lupon, M. Hill, and D. Wood. Safe and efficient supervised memory systems. In *Proceedings of the 2011 IEEE 17th International Symposium on High Performance Computer Architecture*, pages 369–380, feb. 2011.

[5] S. Chen, B. Falsafi, P. B. Gibbons, M. Kozuch, T. C. Mowry, R. Teodorescu, A. Ailamaki, L. Fix, G. R. Ganger, B. Lin, and S. W. Schlosser. Log-based architectures for general-purpose monitoring of deployed code. In *Proceedings of the 1st workshop on Architectural and system support for improving software dependability*, ASID '06, pages 63–65, New York, NY, USA, 2006. ACM.

[6] J. Chung, M. Dalton, H. Kannan, and C. Kozyrakis. Thread-safe dynamic binary translation using transactional memory. In *Proceedings of the 2008 IEEE 14th International Symposium on High Performance Computer Architecture*, pages 279–289, feb. 2008.

[7] J. Devietti, B. Lucia, L. Ceze, and M. Oskin. Dmp: deterministic shared memory multiprocessing. In *Proceeding of the 14th international conference on Architectural support for programming languages and operating systems*, ASPLOS '09, pages 85–96, New York, NY, USA, 2009. ACM.

[8] H. Kannan. Ordering decoupled metadata accesses in multiprocessors. In *Proceedings of the 42nd Annual IEEE/ACM International Symposium on Microarchitecture*, MICRO 42, pages 381–390, New York, NY, USA, 2009. ACM.

[9] C.-K. Luk, R. Cohn, R. Muth, H. Patil, A. Klauser, G. Lowney, S. Wallace, V. J. Reddi, and K. Hazelwood. Pin: building customized program analysis tools with dynamic instrumentation. In *Proceedings of the 2005 ACM SIGPLAN conference on Programming language design and implementation*, PLDI '05, pages 190–200, New York, NY, USA, 2005. ACM.

[10] V. Nagarajan and R. Gupta. Architectural support for shadow memory in multiprocessors. In *Proceedings of the 5th international conference on Virtual execution environments*, VEE '09, pages 1–10, New York, NY, USA, 2009. ACM.

[11] N. Nethercote and J. Seward. How to shadow every byte of memory used by a program. In *Proceedings of the 3rd international conference on Virtual execution environments*, VEE '07, pages 65–74, New York, NY, USA, 2007. ACM.

[12] N. Nethercote and J. Seward. Valgrind: a framework for heavyweight dynamic binary instrumentation. In *Proceedings of the 2007 ACM SIGPLAN conference on Programming language design and implementation*, PLDI '07, pages 89–100, New York, NY, USA, 2007. ACM.

[13] J. Newsome and D. Song. Dynamic taint analysis for automatic detection, analysis, and signature generation of exploits on commodity software. In *Proceedings of the Network and Distributed System Security Symposium*, NDSS'05, 2005.

[14] F. Qin, C. Wang, Z. Li, H.-s. Kim, Y. Zhou, and Y. Wu. Lift: A low-overhead practical information flow tracking system for detecting security attacks. In *Proceedings of the 39th Annual IEEE/ACM International Symposium on Microarchitecture*, MICRO 39, pages 135–148, Washington, DC, USA, 2006. IEEE Computer Society.

[15] G. E. Suh, J. W. Lee, D. Zhang, and S. Devadas. Secure program execution via dynamic information flow tracking. In *Proceedings of the 11th international conference on Architectural support for programming languages and operating systems*, ASPLOS-XI, pages 85–96, New York, NY, USA, 2004. ACM.

[16] G. Venkataramani, I. Doudalis, Y. Solihin, and M. Prvulovic. Flexitaint: A programmable accelerator for dynamic taint propagation. In *Proceedings of the 2008 IEEE 14th International Symposium on High Performance Computer Architecture*, pages 173–184, feb. 2008.

[17] G. Venkataramani, I. Doudalis, Y. Solihin, and M. Prvulovic. Memtracker: An accelerator for memory debugging and monitoring. *ACM Trans. Archit. Code Optim.*, 6:5:1–5:33, July 2009.

[18] E. Vlachos, M. L. Goodstein, M. A. Kozuch, S. Chen, B. Falsafi, P. B. Gibbons, and T. C. Mowry. Paralog: enabling and accelerating online parallel monitoring of multithreaded applications. In *Proceeding of the 15th international conference on Architectural support for programming languages and operating systems*, ASPLOS '10, pages 271–284, New York, NY, USA, 2010. ACM.

[19] S. C. Woo, M. Ohara, E. Torrie, J. P. Singh, and A. Gupta. The splash-2 programs: characterization and methodological considerations. In *Proceedings of the 22nd annual international symposium on Computer architecture*, ISCA '95, pages 24–36, New York, NY, USA, 1995. ACM.

[20] P. Zhou, F. Qin, W. Liu, Y. Zhou, and J. Torrellas. iwatcher: Efficient architectural support for software debugging. In *Proceedings of the 31st annual international symposium on Computer architecture*, ISCA '04, pages 224–235, Washington, DC, USA, 2004. IEEE Computer Society.

[21] P. Zhou, R. Teodorescu, and Y. Zhou. Hard: Hardware-assisted lockset-based race detection. In *Proceedings of the 2007 IEEE 13th International Symposium on High Performance Computer Architecture*, pages 121–132, feb. 2007.

[22] W. Zhu, V. C. Sreedhar, Z. Hu, and G. R. Gao. Synchronization state buffer: supporting efficient fine-grain synchronization on many-core architectures. In *Proceedings of the 34th annual international symposium on Computer architecture*, ISCA '07, pages 35–45, New York, NY, USA, 2007. ACM.

Exploring Latency-Power Tradeoffs
in Deep Nonvolatile Memory Hierarchies

Doe Hyun Yoon
doe-hyun.yoon@hp.com

Tobin Gonzalez
tobin.gonzalez@hp.com

Parthasarathy Ranganathan
partha.ranganathan@hp.com

Robert S. Schreiber
rob.schreiber@hp.com

Intelligent Infrastructure Lab
Hewlett-Packard Labs
Palo Alto, CA, 94304

ABSTRACT

To handle the demand for very large main memory, we are likely to use nonvolatile memory (NVM) as main memory. NVM main memory will have higher latency than DRAM. To cope with this, we advocate a less-deep cache hierarchy based on a large last-level, NVM cache. We develop a model that estimates average memory access time and power of a cache hierarchy. The model is based on captured application behavior, an analytical power and performance model, and circuit-level memory models such as CACTI and NVSim. We use the model to explore the cache hierarchy design space and present latency-power tradeoffs for memory intensive SPEC benchmarks and scientific applications. The results indicate that a flattened hierarchy lowers power and improves average memory access time.

Categories and Subject Descriptors

B.3.3 [**Memory Structures**]: Performance Analysis and Design Aids; B.3.1 [**Memory Structures**]: Semiconductor Memories

General Terms

Design

Keywords

Nonvolatile memory, Memory hierarchy, Latency-power tradeoff

1 Introduction

A modern microprocessor has a private SRAM L1 cache (16-32KB); a private SRAM L2 cache (128-512KB); and a shared last-level cache (LLC) using SRAM or embedded DRAM, as large as 30MB in high-end processors. New technolo-gies such as 3D stacking and byte-addressable nonvolatile memory (NVM) are expected to bring even higher capacity caches. As a result, the cache hierarchy is becoming deeper, with L4 and L5 caches (3D-stacked, on-package, or off-chip DRAM caches, or all of them together).

Power and energy efficiency have become the number one design criterion; hence, designing a memory hierarchy should be an optimization procedure considering multiple objectives including performance and power. The key performance characteristic of cache is average memory access time (AMAT). Two factors dominate AMAT: hit rate, which is mostly determined by the size of LLC, and average latency for a hit. The traditional design strategy for reducing AMAT is a deep cache hierarchy, but this may lead to poor power efficiency. Increasing total capacity improves AMAT only slightly but at the cost of significant increase in power, and a deep hierarchy increases AMAT when the working set is bigger than the intermediate level caches.

NVM main memory changes the cache architecture problem; NVM main memory provides larger capacity but at the cost of higher latency than that of DRAM main memory. For NVM main memory systems, we advocate a 3-level cache hierarchy with an NVM LLC. A flat hierarchy burns less energy than a deeper hierarchy. An NVM LLC has near-zero standby power, and this allows a larger on-chip (or 3D-stacked) cache than a conventional SRAM or DRAM cache, increasing hit rate.

We first develop a latency-power tradeoff model in Section 2. With the model we undertake a co-design study of the optimal depth of a hierarchy in Section 3. Then, we expand the model to support new byte-addressable NVM and show latency-power tradeoffs of various designs. We discuss the limitations of the proposed approach and future work in Section 6 and conclude this paper in Section 7.

2 Latency-Power Tradeoff Model

In this section, we develop a latency-power tradeoff model. The main objective of this study is not to pinpoint a specific optimal configuration but to explore diverse design directions with potential future memory technologies and to identify which direction is most power efficient. The model is fast, so that we can practically explore a large design space.

Figure 1 delineates a high-level organization of the proposed model, which has a performance and power model

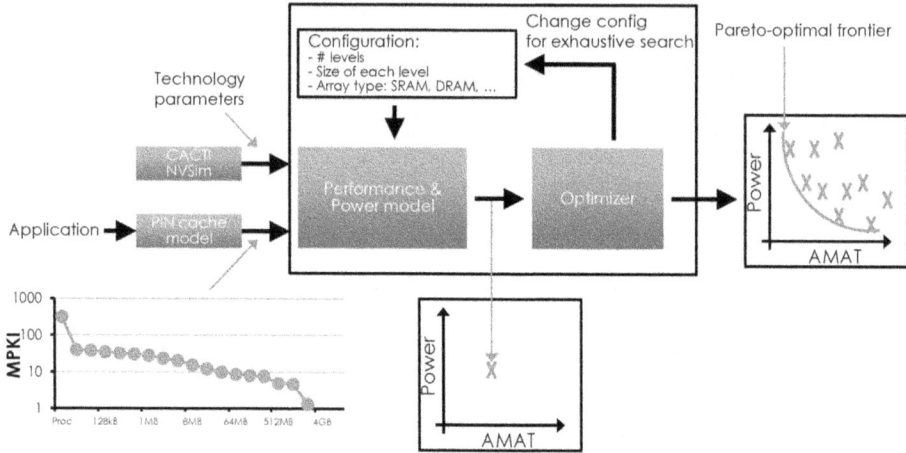

Figure 1: High-level overview of the proposed memory hierarchy analysis framework.

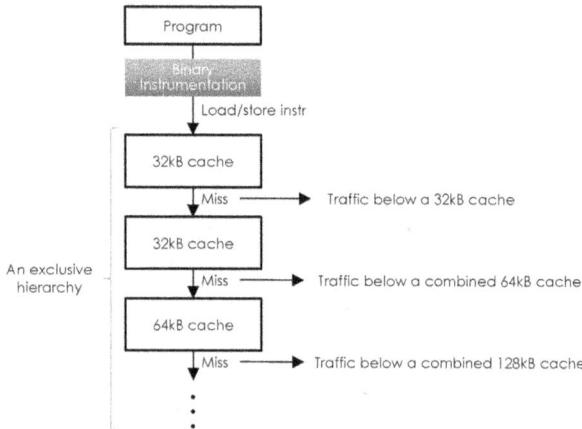

Figure 2: A cache model for PIN to profile MPKI vs. cache sizes.

and an optimizer. The performance and power model takes application characteristics and technology parameters and then estimates AMAT and power (including static and dynamic power) of the given memory hierarchy (the configuration). Each configuration can be represented as a point on a power-AMAT plane. The optimizer exhaustively explores a design space and identifies the Pareto-optimal frontier, presenting the latency-power tradeoff.

In the remainder of this section, we describe the details of the model: Section 2.1 and Section 2.2 discuss the inputs to the model; Section 2.3 describes the performance and power model; and Section 2.4 discusses the optimizer.

2.1 Application Characteristics

We capture application characteristic using a binary instrumentation tool, Pin [12]. We implement a hierarchical cache model as a pintool to profile $MPKI$ (misses per thousand instructions) for various cache sizes (from 32KB to $8GB$). Figure 2 illustrates how we profile traffic (MPKI) of each cache size. Each cache is 8-way set associative, and the number of sets is scaled accordingly to increase cache size: 64 sets in a 32kB cache, 128 sets in a 64kB cache, etc. This methodology is very similar to those of Lin et al. [10] and Murphy et al. [14].

The performance and power model in Section 2.3 uses the MPKI vs. cache size information to estimate AMAT and power. In this study, we use a subset of SPEC CPU 2006 benchmark suite [25] (we use mostly memory-intensive applications but include non-memory-intensive applications also) as well as scientific applications including Mantevo MiniApps [22] and Graph 500 [1]. Table 1 summarizes the applications in this study, and Figure 3 shows the profiled MPKI vs. cache size curves for SPEC CPU 2006 applications, Mantevo MiniApps, and Graph 500.

2.2 Technology Parameters

We leverage CACTI 6 [13] and NVSim [28] to draw technology parameters such as latency, energy per access, and static power. For each cache level, we allow 3 different technologies: SRAM, DRAM, and PCRAM (phase-change memory). We use PCRAM as an example NVM. SRAM and DRAM are modeled in CACTI, and PCRAM in NVSim.

2.3 Performance and Power Model

The performance and power model takes the application characteristics and technology parameters and estimates AMAT and power of a given configuration.

Configuration: The configuration (in Figure 1) specifies a cache hierarchy to be evaluated: n is the number of cache levels; $C(i)$ is cache capacity at level i ($1 \leq i \leq n$); and a cache memory at level i can be one of SRAM, DRAM or PCRAM. For a given configuration, we define MPKI, access latency, static power, energy per read, and energy per write at cache level i as $M(i)$, $L(i)$, $P_s(i)$, $E_r(i)$, and $E_w(i)$, respectively, where these values are from the profiled application characteristics (in Section 2.1) and technology parameters (in Section 2.2). In addition, we define $M(0)$, $L(n+1)$, and $E_r(n + 1)$ for easier formulation of equations: $M(0)$ is the number of load instructions per thousand instructions, and $L(n+1)$ and $E_r(n+1)$ are latency and energy per read of main memory (e.g., DRAM), respectively.

Performance model: We assume an in-order core and measure performance using AMAT as shown in Equation 1. While an aggressive out-of-order core or simultaneous multithreading can hide memory latency and leverage memory-level parallelism, lower AMAT, in general, indicates better performance as shown in [18].

Table 1: Workloads.

Benchmark Suite	Application	Description	Input
SPEC CPU 2006	mcf bzip2 hmmer omnetpp astar milc lbm	combinatorial optimization compression and decompression search a gene sequence database discrete event simulation 2D path finding physical and quantum chromodynamics - MIMD lattice computation computational fluid dynamics, lattice boltzmann model	SPEC reference input
Mantevo	MiniFE MiniMD	Unstructured implicit finite element codes Force computation in molecular dynamics	$160 \times 160 \times 160$ $80 \times 80 \times 80$
Graph 500	Graph 500	Breadth first search on a large graph	scale $= 22$

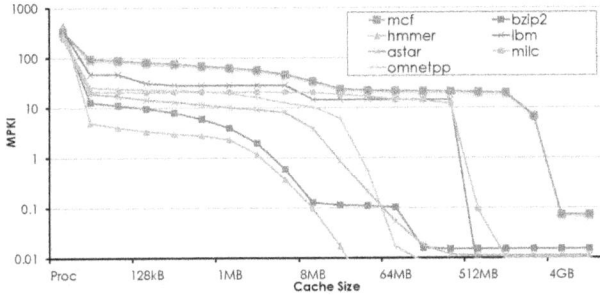

(a) SPEC CPU 2006

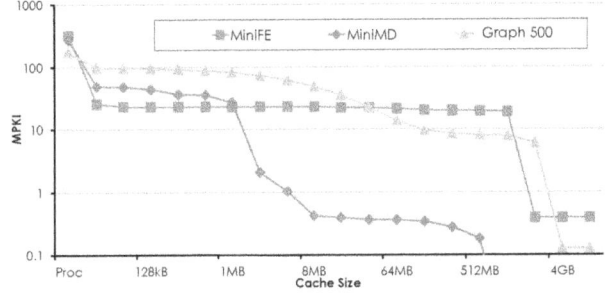

(b) MiniFE, MiniMD, and Graph 500

Figure 3: Traffic (MPKI) vs. cache sizes.

$$AMAT = L(1) + \sum_{i=1}^{n} M(i) \times L(i+1) \qquad (1)$$

Power model: We consider power only in caches and ignore power in wires across cache levels and other components in order to keep the model simple. Total power in a cache hierarchy, P_{total}, is a sum of static and dynamic power. Estimating static power consumption is straightforward as shown in Equation 2.

$$P_{static} = \sum_{i=1}^{n} P_s(i) \qquad (2)$$

Calculating dynamic power is a little bit tricky since we need to translate dynamic energy consumption into dynamic power. We first calculate total dynamic energy consumption for 1000 instructions as shown in Equation 3.

$$E_{dynamic} = M(0) \times E(1) + \sum_{i=1}^{n} M(i) \times (E_r(i+1) + E_w(i)) \qquad (3)$$

Then, we get total dynamic power in Equation 4. The denominator in Equation 4 is an estimated time to execute 1000 instructions, and we assume an in-order core with cycle time of T_{cyc} (1ns in our study).

$$P_{dynamic} = \frac{E_{dynamic}}{(1000 - M(0)) \times T_{cyc} + AMAT \times M(0)} \qquad (4)$$

2.4 Exploring the Design Space and Pareto-Optimal Frontier

As shown in Figure 1, the result of the performance and power model can be represented as a point on a power-AMAT plane. The optimizer runs the performance and power model iteratively, varying the configuration, and plots the operating points of all the possible configurations on a power-AMAT plane. Then it identifies the Pareto-optimal frontier, showing latency-power tradeoff.

We change the number of levels between 2 and 6. We evaluate SRAM caches up to 2GB in Section 3 to show negative impacts of a large SRAM cache. In Section 4, SRAM cache size is limited to 32MB, DRAM cache size is between 4MB and 64MB, and PCRAM cache size is between 16MB and 1GB. We apply these constraints to avoid unreasonably large SRAM caches or tiny PCRAM / DRAM caches.

Figure 4 shows an example running with the Graph 500 application. Red dots are Pareto-optimal, and blue dots are not. Among those optimal operating points, we annotate minimum latency, minimum power, and power-efficient configurations. All those configurations (red dots) are Pareto-optimal, the minimum latency configuration uses too much power, the minimum power configuration has poor performance, and the power-efficient configurations are balanced in both latency and power. From this, we argue for designing a power-efficient cache hierarchy rather than minimizing latency; designing a cache hierarchy to further minimize latency beyond the power-efficient point causes skyrocketing cache power.

3 Depth of a Cache Hierarchy

In this section, we use the latency-power model to study optimal depth of a cache hierarchy. We compare Pareto-

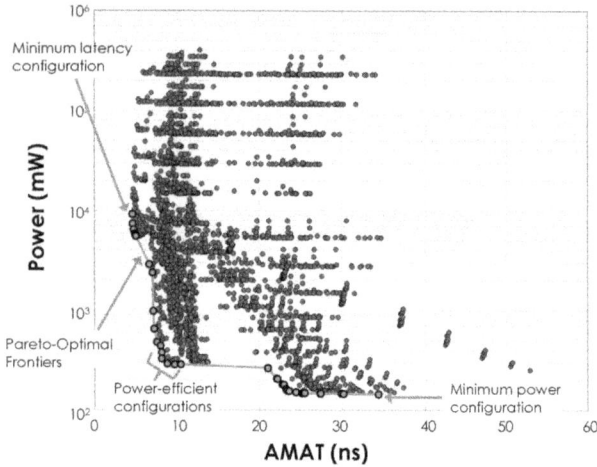

Figure 4: An example of exhaustive search and Pareto-optimal frontier.

optimal frontiers of cache hierarchies with different number of levels, from simple 2-level hierarchies to 6-level hierarchies.

Figure 5 shows latency-power tradeoffs of 2- to 6-level cache hierarchies for the Graph 500 application; As shown in Figure 5(a), the difference among the 3- to 6-level hierarchies is not critical. We evaluated more than 6 levels, but they were even worse, and we do not show them in Figure 5.

The rectangle in Figure 5(a) is magnified in Figure 5(b). The 2-level hierarchies achieve lower AMAT at low power, the 3-level hierarchies are better when higher power is allowed, and a hierarchy with 4 or more levels is worse than the a 3-level hierarchy.

Figure 6 shows the same latency-power tradeoffs for the MiniFE application. MiniFE has a flat traffic curve as shown in Figure 3(b) (streaming access pattern). This is due to sparse matrix vector multiplication (SpMV) in each iteration of the conjugate gradient solver in MiniFE. Hence, AMAT stays at around 7.5ns unless the largest cache is 2GB (top left operating points), which can hold the entire sparse matrix (around 1.5GB). Even a very large cache (e.g,. 1GB) cannot reduce AMAT effectively (top right operating points) but incurs orders of magnitude higher power.

We analyze other applications, and they show the same trend. Increasing the depth of a cache hierarchy beyond 3 levels does not reduce latency and often use more power. In general, a 3-level hierarchy balances latency and power. Large SRAM caches are not power efficient due to an order of magnitude higher power.

4 Cache Hierarchy for NVM Main Memory

Researchers have recently proposed new byte-addressable NVM such as PCRAM as a scalable substitute for DRAM as main memory [8, 21] The main advantage with NVM main memory is higher density and lower standby power than DRAM.

Previously, researchers also suggested a DRAM cache to compensate for high access time of NVM main memory [21, 11]. We analyze the latency-power tradeoffs of cache hierar-

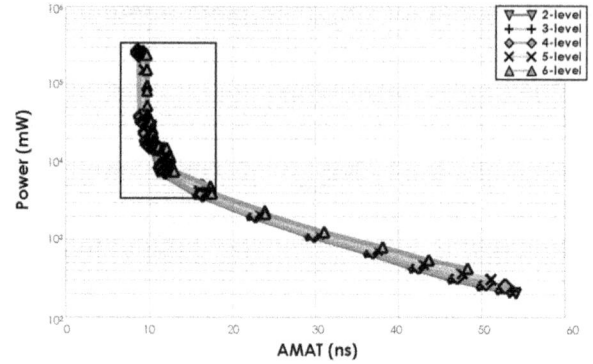

(a)

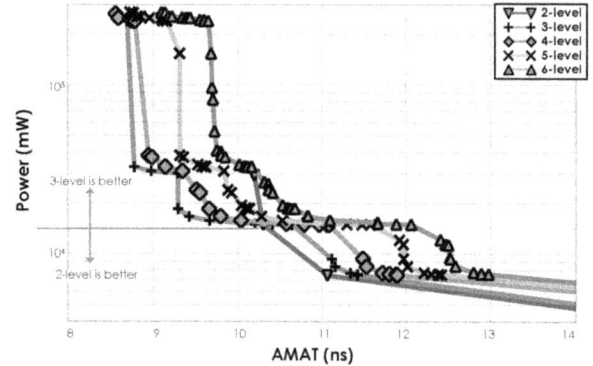

(b)

Figure 5: Graph 500 – power-performance tradeoffs of 2- to 6-level hierarchies. The rectangle in (a) is shown in (b).

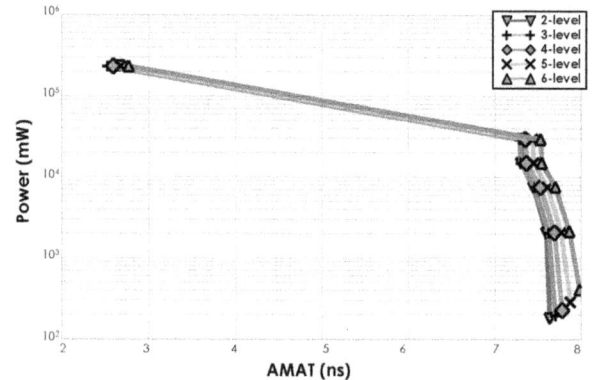

Figure 6: MiniFE – power-performance tradeoffs of 2- to 6-level hierarchies.

chies with heterogeneous technologies: SRAM, DRAM and PCRAM. We show that a large NVM LLC is power efficient. A large NVM LLC reduces costly off-chip traffic and does not increase power by much. An advanced cache management scheme can further improve the efficiency of NVM LLC for streaming applications.

4.1 Cache Hierarchy with Heterogeneous Technologies

Figure 7 shows latency-power tradeoffs of cache hierarchies with heterogeneous technologies for the Graph 500 application. *SRAM cache + DRAM main memory* denotes the

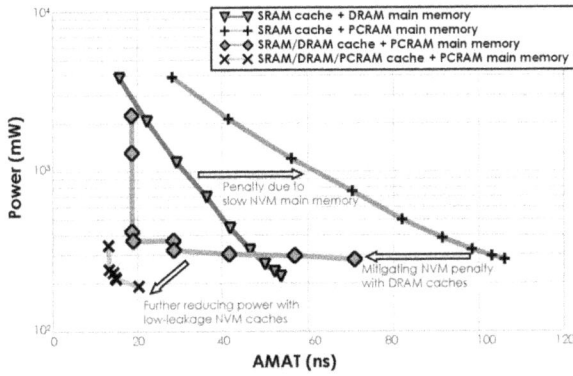

Figure 7: Effects of disparate technologies in main memory and a cache hierarchy (the Graph 500 application).

traditional SRAM-only cache hierarchies with DRAM main memory. When we replace DRAM main memory with PCRAM, the Pareto-optimal frontier moves away due to high access time of PCRAM (*SRAM cache + PCRAM main memory*). One of the advantages with PCRAM main memory is higher memory capacity than DRAM, reducing page fault rates, but our analysis does not show this benefit with PCRAM.

As prior work on a DRAM cache [21, 11], we use a DRAM cache to compensate for high PCRAM access time. We assume a 3D-stacked DRAM cache that leverages high TSV (through silicon via) bandwidth [27]. We present a latency-power tradeoff with mixed SRAM and DRAM caches (*SRAM/DRAM cache + PCRAM main memory*). We let the optimizer choose memory technology of each cache level, and the Pareto-optimal designs use SRAM for L1 and DRAM for L2 and L3. A DRAM cache uses lower power than an SRAM cache, so the SRAM/DRAM heterogeneous hierarchies allow a larger DRAM cache than SRAM, which reduces slow off-chip accesses.

We finally show a latency-power tradeoff with mixed SRAM, DRAM, and PCRAM caches (*SRAM/DRAM/PCRAM cache + PCRAM main memory*). PCRAM has very low leakage power; hence, it allows even larger 3D-stacked caches (e.g., 1GB) still at low power unlike SRAM and DRAM caches. Note that the best AMAT achieved with the mixed SRAM/DRAM/PCRAM cache hierarchies is only comparable to that of SRAM-only hierarchies. In fact, SRAM-only hierarchies can achieve even better performance if we allow larger than 32MB SRAM caches, but that incurs orders of magnitude higher power.

4.2 Cache Friendly Applications

Figure 8 shows the latency-power tradeoffs for cache friendly applications: astar and bzip2. Other cache friendly applications such as hmmer and MiniMD show similar behavior, and we do not present them here. Similar to Graph 500, a large DRAM cache makes up for the penalty with PCRAM main memory, and a PCRAM cache achieves superb power-efficiency.

4.3 Memory Intensive Applications

Figure 9 depicts the same analysis for memory intensive applications: mcf, milc, and lbm. These applications have MPKI bigger than 10 with a 1MB SRAM cache. Unlike the cache friendly applications, the SRAM/DRAM cache hierarchies cannot fully make up for the increased LLC miss

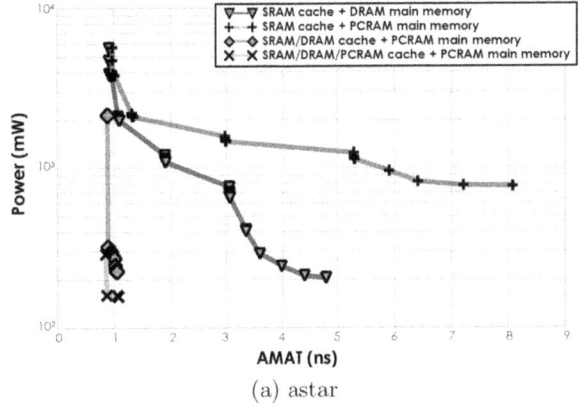

(a) astar

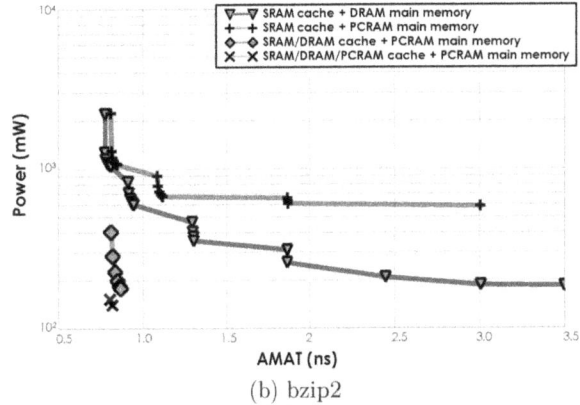

(b) bzip2

Figure 8: Power-performance tradeoffs with disparate technologies for astar and bzip2

penalty with PCRAM main memory, leading to less power efficiency than SRAM-only hierarchies with DRAM main memory. A PCRAM cache is effective in theses applications also. In lbm and milc, a 1GB PCRAM cache completely holds the whole working set, and in mcf, a 1GB PCRAM cache cuts off-chip traffic by half compared to the largest SRAM cache (32MB).

4.4 Streaming Access Patterns

A cache is not effective for streaming access patterns; a program scans a data array, which is much bigger than the largest cache. As discussed, SpMV in MiniFE has such an access pattern. The sparse matrix size is 1.5GB, and even the largest PCRAM cache, only 1GB in our study, cannot hold the whole working set. This results in the latency-power tradeoff in Figure 10(a); DRAM and PCRAM caches are worse than SRAM-only caches.

Recent research on cache management policies such as dynamic insertion policy (DIP) [19] and re-reference interval prediction (RRIP) [4] can preserve a fraction of working set in the cache for streaming access patterns. To incorporate such advanced cache designs in our model, we use an alternative replacement policy (instead of LRU) in the hierarchical cache model (Section 2.1). The alternative policy inserts a cache line only when there are empty slots. Once all the 8 ways of a set are filled with valid cache lines, those 8 lines are never replaced. This, relatively simple, policy does not work for most cases but lets a fraction of the sparse matrix stay in the cache hierarchy even if the whole sparse matrix

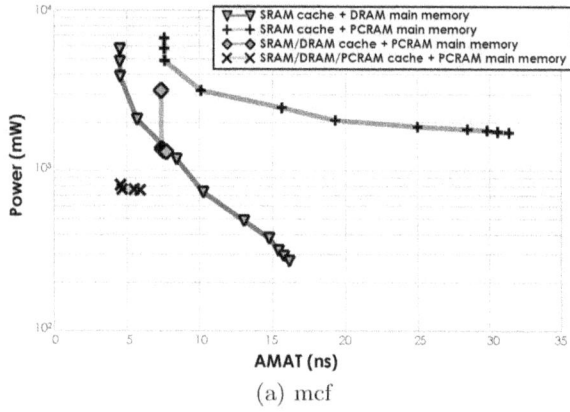

(a) mcf

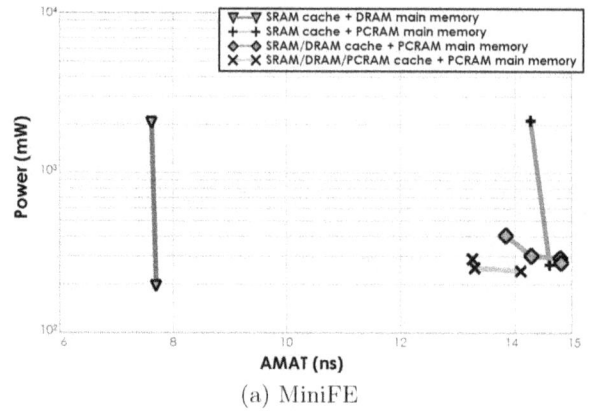

(b) milc

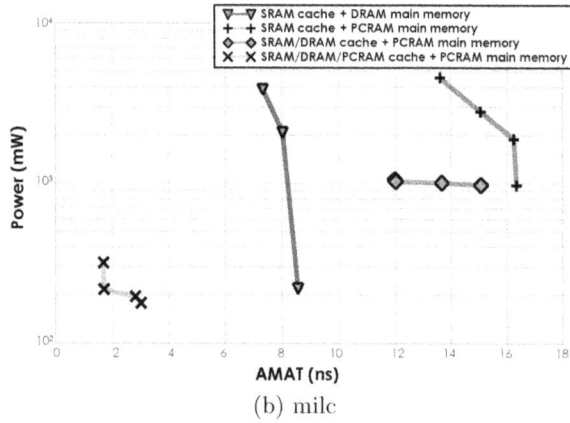

(c) lbm

Figure 9: Power-performance tradeoffs with disparate technologies for mcf, milc, and MiniFE.

is bigger than caches, mimicking DIP and RRIP. We apply the alternative policy only to caches larger than 32MB.

Figure 10(b) compares MPKI vs. cache sizes with a normal LRU replacement policy and the alternative policy. With LRU, traffic does not reduce unless cache size is bigger than the working set (1.5GB), whereas the alternative policy reduces traffic with caches ranging 128MB to 1GB.

We apply this traffic curve to the latency-power model (Figure 10(c)). A 1GB PCRAM cache effectively suppresses off-chip traffic; hence, the SRAM/DRAM/PCRAM cache hierarchies with PCRAM main memory achieves the most

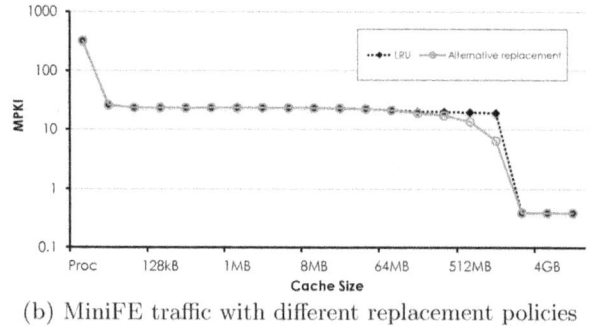

(a) MiniFE

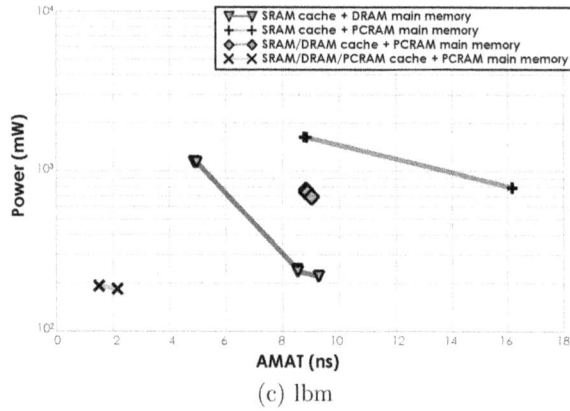

(b) MiniFE traffic with different replacement policies

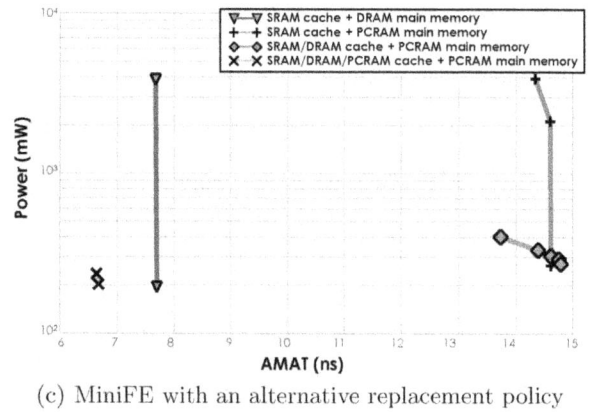

(c) MiniFE with an alternative replacement policy

Figure 10: MiniFE with an alternative replacement policy.

power efficient operating points and outperforms the SRAM-only hierarchies with DRAM main memory.

5 Related Work

Our work builds on an extensive amount of prior work. This includes research on analytical memory models and recent research on NVM-based systems.

Memory models: Multilevel cache hierarchy models [15, 6] are focused on average memory access time but do not consider power efficiency. They argue for two-level hierarchies as opposed to single-level cache. Our latency-power model is based on these models but is extended to support arbitrary number of cache levels and power estimation.

Jacob *et al.* developed a closed form solution for optimal size of each cache level and suggested that the cheapest memory level be increased in the first place [3]. This observation is in line with our analysis that incorporating a large PCRAM (3D-stacked) cache is effective.

Moguls [26] is another memory model that considers bandwidth and power (only dynamic power) in designing a memory hierarchy. Moguls uses the application-oblivious $\sqrt{2}$ model and do not analyze application-dependent behavior in detail.

New byte-addressable NVM: Nonvolatile memories such as PCRAM have been suggested as a scalable substitute for DRAM in many papers [8, 21, 17] since DRAM scaling is approaching its limit. Qureshi *et al.* proposed a DRAM cache to compensate for slow PCRAM main memory [21] and combining SLC and MLC PCRAM [17]. Studies on NVM main memory are focused on performance and reliability. Our work optimizes cache hierarchies (as opposed to optimizing a cache level), considering both performance and power.

A PCRAM-based cache is suggested by Joo *et al.* [5], focusing on PCRAM's finite write endurance. Dong *et al.* proposed 3D-stacked magnetic memory (MRAM) caches, claiming better power efficiency [2]. The approach is not thorough design space exploration including SRAM, DRAM, and NVRAM as in our work.

6 Limitations and Future Work

We developed a latency-power model that explores the design space exhaustively, but the model has limitations. We assumed an in-order core for performance and power estimation, but modern processors have latency-hiding techniques: out-of-order processing, non-blocking caches, simultaneous multi-threading, prefetching, etc. For a system that can hide memory latency, AMAT is not an adequate metric for performance. We leave developing a better performance model to future work.

We propose a PCRAM cache to increase cache capacity without increasing static power. PCRAM (and other NVM technologies) suffer from write endurance; a memory cell has limited lifetime. Most authors assume endurance of 10^8 write cycles, but recently developed fully-confined PCRAM cells have much longer lifetime (more than 10^{11} write cycles) [7]. We can also combine wear-leveling [20], failure tolerance [23, 29, 24, 16] and write buffers (SRAM or DRAM) to cope with write endurance.

Our estimate of poor power efficiency in SRAM-only hierarchies is based on CACTI 6. A recent study on circuit-level cache modeling revealed that SRAM leakage power can be reduced with power control mechanisms [9]. We believe that the big picture we present in this paper will not change significantly even with aggressive power control techniques. We leave incorporating various power reduction/control techniques to future work.

7 Conclusions

We develop a latency-power model of memory hierarchies; the proposed model reports both AMAT and power and is yet simple enough to enable exhaustive search for identifying latency-power tradeoffs.

We first use the model to compare cache hierarchies with different depths. Our analysis shows that deep hierarchies are less power efficient than flat hierarchies (2 or 3 levels) and that large SRAM caches demand a large amount of static power.

Then, we embrace new byte-addressable NVM technologies in our model. We corroborate prior work; NVM main memory degrades performance due to high NVM latency, and DRAM caches can make up for this penalty. But, large DRAM caches (similar to large SRAM caches) draw a large amount of static power, leading to poor power efficiency. We suggest a 3D-stacked NVM cache; an NVM cache can be even larger than SRAM or DRAM caches, while leakage power is much less. We also discuss streaming access patterns; combining NVM caches and advanced cache management schemes can potentially reduce costly off-chip traffic for streaming access patterns.

While there are several opportunities for refinement in the proposed approach, we believe the co-design by model-driven design space exploration is important and will lead to a more optimized system design.

8 Acknowledgment

This material is based upon work supported by the Department of Energy under Award Number DE - SC0005026.

9 Disclaimer

This report was prepared as an account of work sponsored by an agency of the United States Government. Neither the United States Government nor any agency thereof, nor any of their employees, makes any warranty, express or implied, or assumes any legal liability or responsibility for the accuracy, completeness, or usefulness of any information, apparatus, product, or process disclosed, or represents that its use would not infringe privately owned rights. Reference herein to any specific commercial product, process, or service by trade name, trademark, manufacturer, or otherwise does not necessarily constitute or imply its endorsement, recommendation, or favoring by the United States Government or any agency thereof. The views and opinions of authors expressed herein do not necessarily state or reflect those of the United States Government or any agency thereof.

10 References

[1] Graph 500. http://www.graph500.org/.

[2] X. Dong, X. Wu, Y. Xie, Y. Chen, and H. Li. Stacking MRAM atop microprocessors: An architecture-level evaluation. *IET Computers & Digital Techniques*, 5(3), 2011.

[3] B. L. Jacob, P. M. Chen, S. R. Silverman, and T. N. Mudge. An analytical model for designing memory hierarchies. *IEEE Transactions on Computers*, 45:1180–1194, Oct. 1996.

[4] A. Jaleel, K. Theobald, S. C. Steely Jr., and J. Emer. High performance cache replacement using re-reference interval prediction (RRIP). In *Proc. the 37th Ann. Int'l Symp. Computer Architecture (ISCA)*, Jun. 2010.

[5] Y. Joo, D. Niu, X. Dong, G. Sun, N. Chang, and Y. Xie. Energy- and endurance-aware design of phase change memory caches. In *Proc. the Conf. Design Automation and Test in Europe (DATE)*, Mar. 2010.

[6] N. P. Jouppi and S. J. E. Wilton. Tradeoffs in two-level on-chip caching In *Proc. the 21st Ann. Int'l Symp. Computer Architecture (ISCA)*, Apr. 1994.

[7] I. S. Kim, S. L. Cho, D. H. Im, E. H. Cho, D. H. Kim, G. H. Oh, D. H. Ahn, S. O. Park, S. W. Nam, J. T. Moon, and C. H. Chung. High performance PRAM cell scalable to sub-20nm technology with below $4F^2$ cell size, extendable to DRAM applications. In *Proc. the Symp. VLSI Technology (VLSIT)*, Jun.

[8] B. C. Lee, E. Ipek, O. Mutlu, and D. Burger. Architecting phase change memory as a scalable DRAM alternative. In *Proc. the 36th Ann. Int'l Symp. Computer Architecture (ISCA)*, Jun. 2009.

[9] S. Li, K. Chen, J. H. Ahn, J. B. Brockman, and N. P. Jouppi. CACTI-P: Architecture-level modeling for SRAM-based structures with advanced leakage reduction techniques. In *Proc.*

the *IEEE/ACM Int'l Conf. Computer-Aided Design (ICCAD)*, Nov. 2011.

[10] J. M. Lin, Y. Chen, W. Li, Z. Tang, and A. Jaleel. Memory characterization of SPEC CPU 2006 benchmark suite. In *Proc. the 11th Workshop for Computer Architecture Evaluation of Commercial Workloads (CAECW)*, Feb. 2008.

[11] G. H. Loh and M. D. Hill. Efficiently enabling conventional block sizes for very large die-stacked DRAM caches. In *Proc. the 44th Ann. IEEE/ACM Int'l Symp. Microarchitecture (MICRO)*, Dec. 2011.

[12] C.-K. Luk, R. Cohn, R. Muth, H. Patil, A. Klauser, G. Lowney, S. Wallace, V. J. Reddi, and K. Hazelwood. PIN: Building customized program analysis tools with dynamic instrumentation. In *Proc. the ACM Conf. Programming Language Design and Implementation (PLDI)*, Jun. 2005.

[13] N. Muralimanohar, R. Balasubramonian, and N. P. Jouppi. CACTI 6.0. Technical report, HP Labs., Apr. 2009.

[14] R. C. Murphy, A. Rodrigues, P. Kogge, and K. Underwood. The implications of working set analysis on supercomputing memory hierarchy design. In *Proc. the International Conference on Supercomputing (ICS)*, Jun. 2006.

[15] S. Przybylski, M. Horowitz, and J. Hennessy. Characteristics of performance-optimal multi-level cache hierarchies. In *Proc. the 16th Ann. Int'l Symp. Computer Architecture (ISCA)*, Jun. 1989.

[16] M. K. Qureshi. Pay-As-You-Go: Low overhead hard-error correction for phase change memories. In *Proc. the 44th IEEE/ACM Int'l Symp. Microarchitecture (MICRO)*, Dec. 2011.

[17] M. K. Qureshi, M. Fraceschini, L. Lastras, and J. Karidis. Morphable memory system: A robust architecture for exploiting multi-level phase change memories. In *Proc. the 37th Ann. Int'l Symp. Computer Architecture (ISCA)*, Jun. 2010.

[18] M. K. Qureshi, M. Franceschini, and L. Lastras. Improving read performance of phase change memories via write cancellation and write pausing. In *Proc. the 16th Int'l Symp. High-Performance Computer Architecture (HPCA)*, Jan. 2010.

[19] M. K. Qureshi, A. Jaleel, Y. N. Patt, S. C. Steely Jr., and J. Emer. Adaptive insertion policies for high-performance caching. In *Proc. the 34th Ann. Int'l Symp. Computer Architecture (ISCA)*, Jun. 2007.

[20] M. K. Qureshi, J. Karidis, M. Franceschini, V. Srinivasan, L. Lastras, and B. Abali. Enhancing lifetime and security of PCM-based main memory with start-gap wear leveling. In *Proc. the 42nd IEEE/ACM Int'l Symp. Microarchitecture (MICRO)*, Dec. 2009.

[21] M. K. Qureshi, V. Srinivasan, and J. A. Rivers. Scalable high-performance main memory system using phase-change memory technology. In *Proc. the 36th Ann. Int'l Symp. Computer Architecture (ISCA)*, Jun. 2009.

[22] Sandia National Laboratories. Mantevo project. https://software.sandia.gov/mantevo/index.html.

[23] S. Schechter, G. H. Loh, K. Strauss, and D. Burger. Use ECP, not ECC, for hard failures in resistive memories. In *Proc. the 37th Ann. Int'l Symp. Computer Architecture (ISCA)*, Jun. 2010.

[24] N. H. Seong, D. H. Woo, V. Srinivasan, J. A. Rivers, and H.-H. S. Lee. SAFER: Stuck-at-fault error recovery for memories. In *Proc. the 43rd IEEE/ACM Int'l Symp. Microarchitecture (MICRO)*, Dec. 2010.

[25] Standard Performance Evaluation Corporation. SPEC CPU 2006. http://www.spec.org/cpu2006/, 2006.

[26] G. Sun, C. J. Hughes, C. Kim, J. Zhao, C. Xu, Y. Xie, and Y.-K. Chen. Moguls: A model to explore the memory hierarchy for bandwidth improvements. In *Proc. the 38th Ann. Int'l Symp. Computer Architecture (ISCA)*, Jun. 2011.

[27] D. H. Woo, N. H. Seong, D. L. Lewis, and H.-H. S. Lee. An optimized 3D-stacked memory architecture by exploiting excessive, high-density TSV bandwidth. In *Proc. the 16th Int'l Symp. High-Performance Computer Architecture (HPCA)*, Jan. 2010.

[28] C. Xu, X. Dong, N. P. Jouppi, and Y. Xie. Design implications of memristor-based RRAM cross-point structures. In *Proc. the Design, Automation and Test in Europe (DATE)*, Mar. 2011.

[29] D. H. Yoon, N. Muralimanohar, J. Chang, P. Ranganathan, N. P. Jouppi, and M. Erez. FREE-p: Protecting non-volatile memory against both hard and soft errors. In *Proc. the 17th Int'l Symp. High-Performance Computer Architecture (HPCA)*, Feb. 2011.

The Tradeoffs of Fused Memory Hierarchies in Heterogeneous Computing Architectures

Kyle Spafford
Oak Ridge National
Laboratory
1 Bethel Valley Road
Oak Ridge, TN 37831
kys@ornl.gov

Jeremy S. Meredith
Oak Ridge National
Laboratory
1 Bethel Valley Road
Oak Ridge, TN 37831
jsmeredith@ornl.gov

Seyong Lee
Oak Ridge National
Laboratory
1 Bethel Valley Road
Oak Ridge, TN 37831
lees2@ornl.gov

Dong Li
Oak Ridge National
Laboratory
1 Bethel Valley Road
Oak Ridge, TN 37831
lid1@ornl.gov

Philip C. Roth
Oak Ridge National
Laboratory
1 Bethel Valley Road
Oak Ridge, TN 37831
rothpc@ornl.gov

Jeffrey S. Vetter
Oak Ridge National
Laboratory
1 Bethel Valley Road
Oak Ridge, TN 37831
vetter@ornl.gov

ABSTRACT

With the rise of general purpose computing on graphics processing units (GPGPU), the influence from consumer markets can now be seen across the spectrum of computer architectures. In fact, many of the high-ranking Top500 HPC systems now include these accelerators. Traditionally, GPUs have connected to the CPU via the PCIe bus, which has proved to be a significant bottleneck for scalable scientific applications. Now, a trend toward tighter integration between CPU and GPU has removed this bottleneck and unified the memory hierarchy for both CPU and GPU cores. We examine the impact of this trend for high performance scientific computing by investigating AMD's new Fusion Accelerated Processing Unit (APU) as a testbed. In particular, we evaluate the tradeoffs in performance, power consumption, and programmability when comparing this unified memory hierarchy with similar, but discrete GPUs.

Categories and Subject Descriptors

B.3.3 [**Memory Structures**]: Performance Analysis and Design Aids; C.1.3 [**Processor Architectures**]: Other Architecture Syltes—*heterogeneous (hybrid) systems*

Keywords

APU, hybrid memory, GPGPU, performance analysis, benchmarking

1. INTRODUCTION

1.1 GPUs and Heterogeneity

The demand for flexibility in advanced computer graphics has caused the GPU to evolve from a highly specialized, fixed-function pipeline to a more general processor. However, in its current form, there are still substantial differences between the GPU and a traditional multi-core CPU.

Perhaps the most salient difference is in the memory hierarchy: the GPU shuns high capacity, coherent caches in favor of a much larger number of functional units. This lack of coherent caches in the GPU is not surprising, given the low reuse of graphics data flowing through the frame buffer. Instead, GPUs have used wide memory busses and specialized texturing hardware (that provides a limited set of addressing and interpolation operations) for a high bandwidth, high latency connection to off-chip RAM. Because of these architectural differences, early GPGPU adopters observed that many data-parallel problems in scientific computing exhibited substantial performance improvements when run on a GPU.

Initially, achieving such speedups usually required that all operations be cast as graphics operations, comprising a "heroic" programming effort. This made the initial costs of GPGPU too high for mainstream scientific computing. However, with the advent of programming models like OpenCL and CUDA, which are very similar to standard C/C++, the barriers to entry have decreased and GPGPU now enjoys much wider adoption. Indeed, the low cost of the GPU hardware itself is one of GPGPU's main advantages.

Despite these improvements, most GPUs suffer from performance limitations due to the PCIe bus, and limited productivity to due an increasingly complex memory model. Both of these problems are direct consequences of the hardware architecture. Simply put, any data that moves between the CPU and a discrete GPU must traverse the PCIe bus, which has limited bandwidth (usually at least an order of magnitude less than GPU memory bandwidth). This archi-texture results in relatively slow transfers, and high latency synchronization between devices that applications should avoid when possible.

The complexity of the memory model for programming accelerated applications has also increased. The OpenCL memory model for a single GPU is already more complicated than the cache hierarchy of a traditional multicore. In fact, the OpenCL memory model contains five distinct memory spaces (global, local, constant, image, and private), each with its own coherency policy and optimal access pattern. Moreover, many of the address spaces only implement relaxed consistency, requiring the programmer to perform explicit synchronization. This model is further complicated by the PCIe bus, since the programmer is required to keep CPU and GPU memory consistent via explicit DMA transfers.

In an effort to address these difficulties, system architects and vendors are now focusing on designs which feature much tighter integration between the CPU and GPU, such as AMD's Fusion [4] (studied in this paper) and NVIDIA's Project Denver.

1.2 SoC and Tighter Integration

Another consumer trend that has motivated the design of the APU is the shift towards a system-on-a-chip (SoC). SoC design largely came about in the mobile and embedded spaces due to the desire for reuse of silicon designs, specifically reusing basic system blocks for wireless technologies, specialized media processing units, etc. Tighter integration also offers advantages in energy efficiency by enabling fine-grained dynamic voltage and frequency scaling (DVFS) across multiple system components. In DVFS, the clock speed and voltage of a processing element are raised or lowered by the operating system based on processor utilization and workload, resulting in higher performance under load and lower power consumption when cores are idle. This improved efficiency is increasingly appealing for HPC systems, due to the projections for the power requirements of an exascale computer [12], and the possibility of leveraging design trends in in the mobile and embedded markets, where the focus is on longer battery life.

1.3 Tradeoffs

Heterogeneity and SoC-like integration are both evident in the design of AMD's Fusion APU, shown in Figure 1; it replaces the PCIe connection between the CPU and GPU cores with a unified north bridge and two new busses, the Radeon Memory Bus (RMB) and the Fusion Compute Link (FCL), discussed further in Section 2.1. While integrated GPUs have existed for some time in the mobile market, AMD's fused GPU (fGPU) can snoop CPU cache transactions using the FCL, making Fusion the first mass-market architecture to support cache coherency between the CPU and GPU. This capability for cache coherency is the hallmark of a fused heterogeneous architecture.

Fusing these two distinct memory hierarchies results in numerous tradeoffs. For example, traditional GPU architectures support much higher memory bandwidth due to dedicated GDDR memory (see Section 4) than the Llano Fusion architecture. This paper explores five such tradeoffs using Llano as a forward-looking example of tightly-integrated CPU and GPU architectures:

1. In the multi-level cache hierarchy of fused designs, what is the set of caches that should be kept coherent in order to allow scalability to large core counts?

2. With fixed die space and transistor count, how should resources be allocated to improve serial performance (CPU cores) as opposed to parallel performance (GPU cores)?

3. Given a fixed power budget, should the memory be configured for higher capacity (e.g. DDR3) or higher bandwidth (e.g. GDDR5)?

4. Are fused designs more power efficient? Would power be better spent using discrete, specialized components?

5. Given a limited amount of programmer effort, what is the correct level of abstraction to use when programming APUs? Simple abstractions will require advanced runtime systems and middleware, while lower-level abstractions require more application programming effort.

2. CACHE COHERENCY VS. SCALABILITY

The specialization of the GPU memory hierarchy is also evident in its cache configuration, which has traditionally relied on a combination of simple, incoherent SRAM scratchpad memories with a specialized texturing unit. This texturing unit typically contains its own separate cache, targeted to regular access patterns on two dimensional data. It also implements a limited set of functions in hardware including several addressing computations and interpolation operations that are ubiquitous in graphics applications. Aside from the texture unit, the cache hierarchy of the GPU is remarkably flat compared to the CPU, largely due to the data parallelism of graphics operations. One of the benefits of this flat hierarchy is that it scales very well with the number of processor tiles (e.g. to sixteen hundred cores in Cypress, with only thirty-two kilobytes of scratchpad memory per tile). The disadvantage is that this hierarchy can only support relaxed consistency models for small groups of cores, which places a burden on the programmer which will be discussed more in Section 6.

On the other hand, CPUs have traditionally used multilevel, high capacity caches which are kept consistent using protocols like MESI. Such protocols provide strong consistency models for the programmer, but are much less scalable due to the rapid growth of coherency-related traffic. The key tradeoff, then, is in determining how the CPU and fGPU caches can be coupled to enforce coherency while preserving scalability to a large number of cores.

2.1 Fusion Memory Hierarchy

In Fusion, this coupling is accomplished via the addition of two new busses, the Fusion Compute Link (FCL) and the Radeon Memory Bus (RMB), depicted in Figure 1 as well as a unified north bridge which coordinates access to the different logical regions of physical memory. One of the goals of the Fusion memory hierarchy is to allow the CPU and GPU to share data while preserving performance for each processing element's predominant access pattern—the CPU should still support low latency access (optimized with caches) and the GPU should still have high bandwidth access (optimized

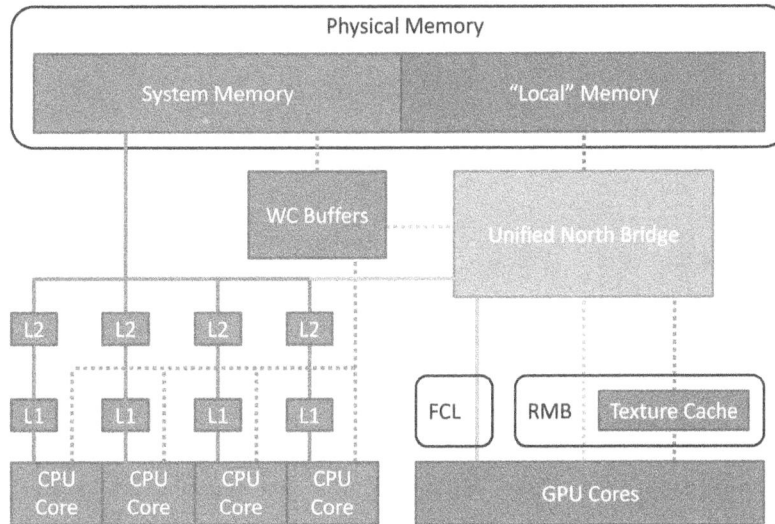

Figure 1: The Fusion Memory Hierarchy. The solid lines in this figure indicate cache coherent connections, and the dashed lines show lack of coherence. Blue indicates components of a traditional CPU memory hierarchy and red shows components of a traditional GPU hierarchy. For example, the CPU usually accesses System Memory through the L2 cache and the write-combining buffers. Orange indicates novel features and paths in Fusion. The familiar cache hierarchy of the CPUs is connected to the GPU cores by the FCL. The RMB preserves high bandwidth access from the GPU cores to the "Local" memory (optionally storing data in the texture cache). The CPU cores can access this same "Local" memory via the write-combining buffers through the Unified North Bridge.

via the RMB) to contiguous regions of memory. In order to understand the design at a high level, it is important to understand each of the components:

- **Physical Memory**. In Fusion, the same physical memory is shared between the CPU and GPU. The operating system maintains the partition between system memory (normal, pageable memory) and "local" memory, which is reserved for the GPU. Local memory is conceptually similar to the frame buffer or the onboard RAM on a discrete GPU.

- **Traditional CPU Cache Hierarchy**. The CPU cores are supplied with a standard cache hierarchy including private L1 data and instruction caches, and a 1MB private L2 cache (4MB total L2 capacity).

- **Write Combining Buffers**. Each CPU core in Llano has four uncached, write-combining buffers. Ideally, these buffers can provide relatively high write bandwidth (by merging memory transactions) but are typically avoided due to a lack of strict ordering and extremely high read latency. However, in Fusion, the WCBs are utilized when the CPU needs to write into "local" memory. In this case, they exploit the higher write bandwidth and avoid polluting the CPU cache with data that will be primarily used on the GPU cores.

- **Fusion Compute Link**. The FCL provides a high latency, low bandwidth from the GPU cores to the CPU cache. It's arbitrated by the UNB, and has the capability to snoop CPU cache transactions, providing for full coherency between the CPU and GPU. Due to

its low bandwidth (compared to other memory paths in the system), it should primarily be used for fine-grained data sharing between the CPU and GPU.

- **Radeon Memory Bus**. The RMB is a much wider bus that connects the GPU cores to the "local" partition of physical memory and mimics the performance of RAM access in a discrete GPU–high latency and high bandwidth. It bypasses all cache (except L1 and texture), and can saturate DRAM bandwidth.

Simply put, CPU-like accesses are supported by traditional caches, GPU access patterns are handled by the RMB, and the FCL enables cache coherency only when it is needed, with most of the pathways enabled through the address translation capabilities of the UNB.

3. LATENCY OPTIMIZED VS. THROUGHPUT OPTIMIZED CORES

Another distinction between the traditional CPU core and the GPU core is the marked difference in the allocation of transistors and die space. In CPUs, a substantial portion of these resources have been devoted to optimizing latency in single-threaded programs using caches, complex techniques for instruction-level parallelism including out-of-order execution, and other specialized units like branch predictors. In comparison to CPUs, GPUs have throughput-optimized cores that are much simpler, but GPUs tend to have far more cores. In addition, GPUs can schedule thousands of application threads onto these cores in order to hide memory access latency. For example, contemporary GPUs (e.g. Cypress and Llano's core counts) can have ten to one hundred times as many cores as CPUs. In these throughput-

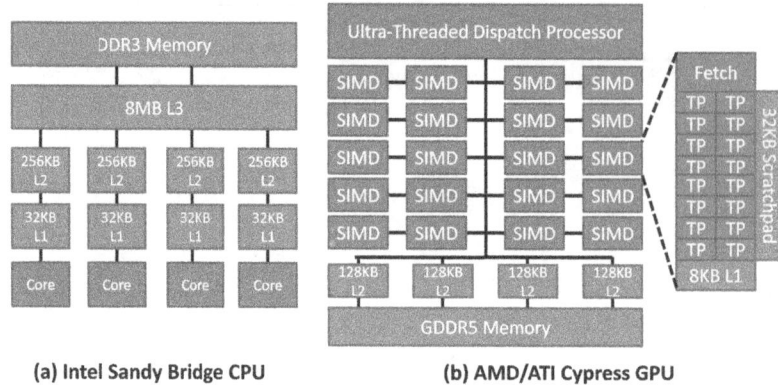

(a) Intel Sandy Bridge CPU   **(b) AMD/ATI Cypress GPU**

Figure 2: Block Diagram of Core i7-2600 (Sandy Bridge) and Cypress Architectures. Blue elements indicate memory or cache while red indicates processing elements. The dotted lines show that each SIMD engine in Cypress contains sixteen thread processors, each with five ALUs, a shared L1, and a shared scratchpad memory.

	Cores	Clock	Peak FLOPS	RAM	Bus Width	Mem. Clock	Bandwidth	TDP
Units	#	Mhz	GFLOPS (SP/DP)	GB	Bits	Mhz	GB/s	Watts
Core i7-2600	4	3400	108.8/54.4	8	128	1333	21	95
Llano's CPU	4	2900	46.4/23.2	8	128	1866	29.9	100
Llano's fGPU	400	600	480/0					
Redwood	400	775	620/0	0.5	128	1000	64	64
Cypress	1600	825	2640/528	2	256	1150	147.2	225

Table 1: Architecture Specifications. Note that Llano's CPU and fGPU cores share the same interface to physical memory and have a combined TDP of 100W.

oriented designs, performance is achieved through massive, fine-grained parallelism, and, particularly for HPC, a large number of floating-point units.

The question then, is how many resources should be devoted to serial performance (latency-optimized) compared to parallel performance (throughput-optimized). For instance, are wide SIMD units on the CPU cores still beneficial? Would those resources be better spent on more GPU cores, which would handle the majority of the floating point workload? This complex tradeoff has serious implications for sustained performance and depends on application characteristics like the fraction of parallel work, the instruction mix, and the requirements for synchronization.

It is difficult to characterize this tradeoff in a sense that will generalize well to any application. However, the amount of serial performance sacrificed to obtain parallel performance can be quantified by comparing an APU to a traditional CPU. This loss can then be weighed against increased parallel performance on an application-specific basis.

3.1 Experimental Platform

We compare a current APU architecture to a traditional CPU and discrete GPU can help illustrate some of the tradeoffs of fused designs. Specifically, we evaluate the concrete examples (shown in Figure 2) of AMD's A8-3850 Llano APU (with fGPU), the ATI Radeon HD5670 (codenamed Redwood), most similar to the fGPU of Llano, and the high-end ATI FirePro v8800 (Cypress). Also, any power or performance measurements involving the Redwood GPU use the Llano as a host system with the fGPU disabled to ensure

consistency. On some occasions, we also compare Llano to an Intel Core i7-2600 CPU (Sandy Bridge architecture). This CPU is similar in terms of core count and power envelope, but devotes far fewer resources to graphics operations. Its integrated graphics hardware does not support OpenCL and is not used in any of our tests. Table 1 gives a more detailed listing of the differences among Llano, Redwood, Cypress, and Sandy Bridge. None of the test configurations used ECC memory, which is not supported by these consumer versions of the architectures. For further introduction to GPU architectures, in general, we refer the reader to the overview from Owens [19] and the discussion of the AMD architecture by Daga et al [8].

Unless otherwise specified, all measurements were taken using the AMD APP SDK v2.4, SHOC [9] v1.1.2, GCC v4.4.5, and Scientific Linux v6.1.

3.2 CPU Performance

To evaluate Llano CPU performance, we compared the performance of a simple dense matrix-matrix multiply operation with another contemporary processor with similar power envelope, the Intel Core i7-2600 CPU (with Sandy Bridge microarchitecture). This benchmark is intended to show the processor's practical upper limit for computation rate. We also compared the performance of the High Performance Computing Challenge (HPCC) [10] benchmark suite on both processors. Because this benchmark suite measures the performance of several types of operations, it provides a more complete picture of CPU performance than the simple matrix-matrix multiply benchmark. The specifications of the systems used in this comparison are shown in Table 1. On the Sandy Bridge system, HyperThreading was disabled to avoid sharing floating point hardware between multiple threads within each core; thus, the Sandy Bridge test system supported four hardware threads total, like the Llano system. Turbo mode was enabled on the Sandy Bridge system, allowing the processor to increase the clock rate of a single core if it was performing a computationally intensive task while other cores on the chip were less busy. Also, the software stack for this system differs slightly from the listing in Section 3.1, with the Sandy Bridge tests using the Intel compiler v2011 SP1.8.274, MPI v4.0.3, and MKL math library v10.3.8 while the Llano was tested using the PGI compiler v11.10, ACML v4.4 and v5.0, and OpenMPI v1.5.4.

Llano and Sandy Bridge performance for the SGEMM and DGEMM benchmarks are shown in Figures 3 and 4, for several threading configurations and a range of matrix sizes. For DGEMM, the Core i7-2600 consistently outperforms the Llano CPU, more than doubling its peformance on the largest matrix. No results are shown from the Llano fGPU since it does not support double precision.

In contrast, the Llano's fGPU outperforms the Core i7-2600 on the SGEMM benchmark on large matrices, even when four threads are used. Note that the Llano benchmark used AMD's APPML math library v1.6, which is OpenCL-based.

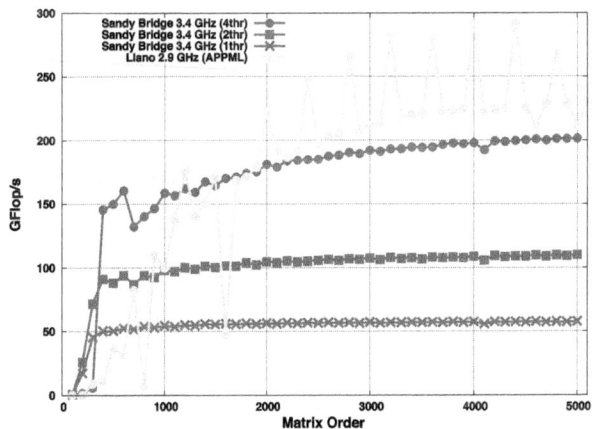

Figure 4: DGEMM CPU Performance for one, two, and four threads

tests, performance did not vary much under these different scenarios, but we did notice slightly better performance for the HPL and DGEMM subtests when pinning processes but not explicitly setting the number of OpenMP threads. Hence the Sandy Bridge numbers presented in Table 2 are for this scenario.

Benchmark	Units	AMD A8-3850	Intel i7-2600
HPL	TFlop/s	0.0290	0.0949
SingleDGEMM	GFlop/s	11.1037	24.7620
StarDGEMM	GFlop/s	10.9816	25.8956
PTRANS	GB/s	0.4093	2.3594
SingleRandomAccess	GUP/s	0.0363	0.0671
StarRandomAccess	GUP/s	0.0165	0.0253
MPIRandomAccess	GUP/s	0.0490	0.0912
SingleSTREAM_Triad	GB/s	5.4585	13.3438
StarSTREAM_Triad	GB/s	1.9530	3.5079
SingleFFT	GFlop/s	0.9810	2.8007
StarFFT	GFlop/s	0.6822	1.6154
MPIFFT	GFlop/s	1.6292	3.5563

Table 2: HPCC Performance

Figure 3: SGEMM Performance (one, two, and four CPU threads for Sandy Bridge and the OpenCL-based AMD APPML for Llano's fGPU)

Llano and Core i7-2600 performance on the HPCC benchmark suite is summarized in Table 2. The measurements from the table were obtained using four MPI processes (one per core) on each system. On the AMD system, we built HPCC with both the ACML 4.4 and 5.0 math libraries, and we tried explicitly setting the number of OpenMP threads to be used by the ACML library. We found slightly better performance from using ACML 4.4 on this system for the HPL and DGEMM subtests, without specifying the number of OpenMP threads, so the numbers presented in Table 2 reflect this scenario. On the Intel system, we ran HPCC under several scenarios. We tried pinning the each of the four HPCC processes to a specific processor core, and we tried explicitly setting the number of OpenMP threads to be used by the MKL math library. With these single node

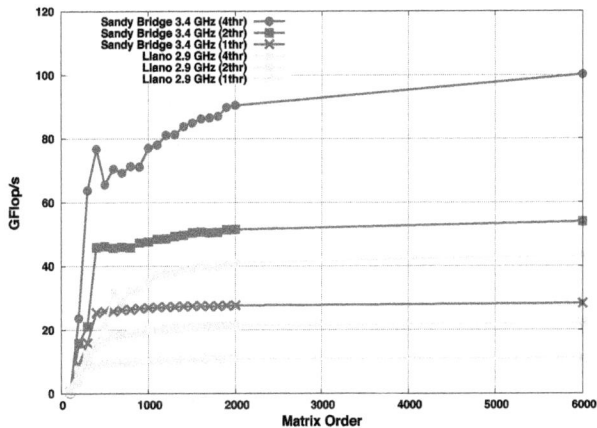

Llano's design reflects the perspective that the programmer will use the fGPU for floating point intensive work, thus the CPU microarchitecture is relatively simple, and the performance penalty for not following this distribution of work is substantial. In contrast, the Core i7-2600 design reflects the perspective that the CPU is the primary computational device in the system. These differing perspectives are evidenced in the HPCC measurements, where the Core i7-2600 outperformed the A8-3850 by a margin larger than would be expected based on clock speed differences alone. Interestingly, the gap was largest for the computationally intensive subtests, but narrowed significantly for subtests like RandomAccess that are more focused on memory hierarchy performance.

4. CAPACITY VS. BANDWIDTH

The next tradeoff is the type of physical memory used for the base of the fused memory hierarchy. Traditionally, CPUs have attempted to optimize latency to high capacity memory, like the DDR3 used in the Llano APU. Conversely, GPUs, which have traditionally been concerned with repeatedly streaming a fixed-size frame buffer, focus on achieving maximum bandwidth. In order to achieve this bandwidth, GDDR (*graphics* double data rate) standards began to diverge from their DDR counterparts to place an emphasis on wider memory busses and higher effective clock speeds. However, given a similar power budget, GDDR tends to have much less capacity than DDR. In a discrete architecture, each type of core can be paired with the most applicable memory, but in a fused architecture, the latency and throughput-oriented cores must use the same type of physical memory. In the near term, this is essentially a choice between DDR and GDDR memory. In the future, however, this tradeoff is likely to be become much more complex as the configuration of 3D stacked memories and advanced memory controllers may allow for increased flexibility in combining different types of memories in one node.

In our concrete examples, both the Redwood and Cypress discrete GPUs use GDDR5, while Llano's fGPU shares DDR3 with the CPU cores. As shown in Table 1, the gap in capacity is quite large, but the most salient difference is bandwidth. This is in large part due to the fact that GDDR5 is quad-pumped while DDR3 is double-pumped. That is, DDR3 delivers two bits of data per signal line per clock cycle (on the rising and falling edge of the clock) while GDDR5 transfers those two bits and an additional two bits at each midpoint using a second clock that is ninety degrees out of phase with the first. The difference in peak bandwidth illustrates the impact of these architectural differences—with the same bus width and a lower clock speed, Redwood has roughly twice the bandwidth of Llano's fGPU.

4.1 DDR3 vs. GDDR5 Memory

We evaluated how this difference translates to application performance using the Scalable Heterogeneous Computing (SHOC) benchmark suite [9]. SHOC includes synthetic benchmarks designed to measure bandwidth to each of the OpenCL memory spaces as well as real application kernels.

Figure 5 shows results from SHOC on the fGPU using DDR3 memory and the two discrete GPUs using GDDR5. Results are on a logarithmic scale and show the speedup of the discrete GPUs over Llano.

The HD5670 is the closest GDDR5-based discrete GPU to Llano's fGPU: the shader architecture is essentially the same, and it has only a 30% increase in clockspeed. Performance results from SHOC's MaxFlops benchmark reflect this, showing an approximately 25% improvement in pure floating point performance. Tests limited by global memory bandwidth show a much larger improvement, with the GDDR5 resulting in an approximate 3x speedup. The FirePro v8800 shows improvements of 2x to 8x, commensurate with or exceeding the increase in power consumption.

The lower half of Figure 5 shows much smaller speedups for the discrete GPUs. These lower results are benchmarks with a dependence on PCIe bus transfers, whether as an inherent part of the benchmark or as a GPU-centric benchmark with the CPU-GPU transfer of input and output data included. Although use of architecture-specific flags when creating buffers and special techniques when performing data transfers can allow somewhat higher bandwidths between System and Local memory in Fusion (see Section 2.1), the standard OpenCL mechanism for these transfers performs only slightly better than the discrete v8800 and is somewhat slower than transfer to the discrete HD5670. However, the tighter coupling of the fGPU with the CPU — seen, in part, in the faster Queue Delay performance due to the removal of PCIe latency — results in a net performance *increase* in the Llano, despite its slower shader clock and reduced memory bandwidth.

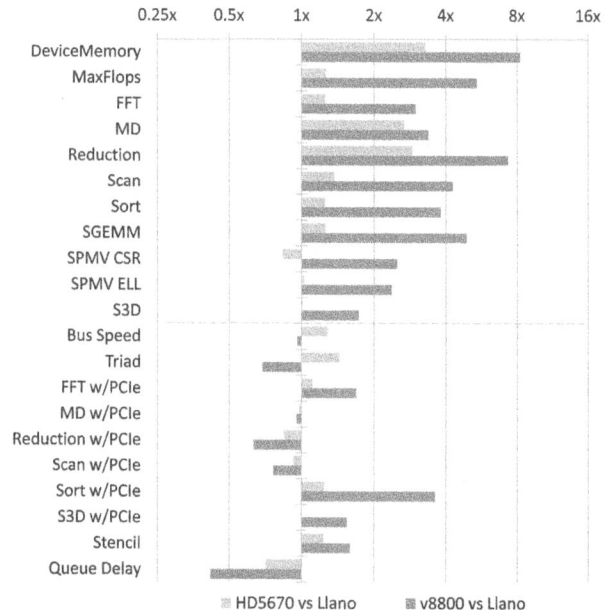

Figure 5: Speedup of a discrete Radeon HD5670 (Redwood, GDDR5) GPU and a discrete FirePro v8800 (Cypress, GDDR5), versus the fused GPU with DDR3 in Llano, on a logarithmic scale. Values greater than 1x indicate the discrete GPU outperforming Llano.

4.2 Contention

A performance model may be able to predict the preferred memory type for a given application based on its memory access characteristics. However, in a fused architecture, this tradeoff is complicated by contention effects between the CPU and GPU cores. For example, in the worst case, the throughput-optimized cores may generate enough memory requests to starve the latency-optimized cores, and, at a minimum, their traffic is likely to inject significant, unexpected latency. This type of resource exhaustion has traditionally been difficult to model.

To measure these contention effects on Llano we ran the SHOC benchmark suite on the fGPU under two conditions. First, we measured performance with the CPU cores idle and then with the CPU cores running a bandwidth-bound kernel which lasted for the duration of the benchmark suite. For the CPU kernel, we used JACOBI, a micro-kernel that solves Laplace equations using Jacobi iteration, available in any numerical analysis text [24]. The tested kernel uses two 12288 x 12288 matrices with one hundred iterations. Our hypothesis was that the increased memory traffic from the Jacobi kernel would saturate memory bandwidth and cause degraded performance in the fGPU. The results in Figure 6 show a penalty ranging from fifteen to twenty-two percent for bandwidth-bound benchmarks and smaller penalties for those that incorporate at least a modest floating point intensity.

We include results from the same experiment using the HD5670 to confirm that this penalty is unique to the fused memory hierarchy. That is, no contention should occur with the HD5670, and while the measurements show some minor noise, the magnitude of that noise is less than one percent.

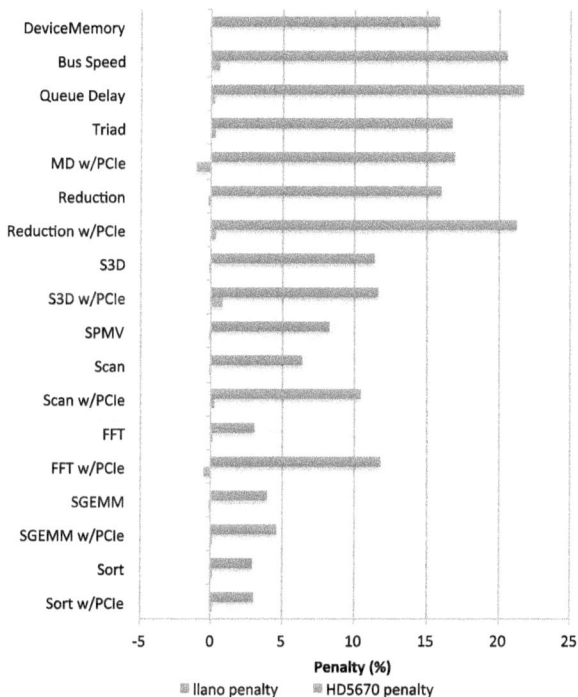

Figure 6: Performance penalty caused by memory contention between the CPU and the GPU.

The CPU performance under these same scenarios shows the average runtime of the Jacobi benchmark increasing under contention. As seen in Table 3, we observe almost no contention with the HD5670, but a 10% penalty when simultaneously using the fGPU.

	Average Runtime
No CPU/GPU Contention	22.3 s
Contention with HD5670 GPU	22.5 s
Contention with Llano fGPU	24.5 s

Table 3: Performance of the CPU Jacobi kernel under various contention scenarios.

5. POWER VS. PERFORMANCE

5.1 GPU Power Usage

Tighter integration of separate components like a GPU and CPU generally results in lower power usage. The reduction in redundant hardware requires less power, and when components are physically closer together, less energy is required for data movement across wires and board traces. This, in turn, can also lead to secondary reductions, such as lower requirements for cooling. We study the power usage of Llano fGPU and compare it with the discrete Radeon HD5670. We measure the whole system power with an in-line AC power meter and record the peak power consumption of the system. During the measurement, the default power saving features (i.e., employing appropriate power gating when possible) are enabled for both Llano and the discrete GPU.

Figure 7 displays system power consumption for specific GPU operations. We first notice that Llano using the fGPU has a lower power draw than the HD5670 in idle state by about 16.7%. We attribute this difference to the extra power consumption of global memory and peripheral circuitry on the HD5670. We further notice that the power difference is increased when the system is performing data transfers between the host and device (labeled 'Host/Dev Transfer' in the figure), floating point operations (labeled 'Compute FLOPS') and memory intensive operations (labeled 'Device Memory'). The lower power consumption of data transfer in Llano comes from the shorter data path and the elimination of the PCI bus and controller; the lower power consumption of floating point and memory operations comes from a lower shader clock on the Llano fGPU and from the simplified peripheral circuitry on the fGPU. Llano achieves an average power savings of approximately 20% compared to the HD5670 when running the computation kernels in the Level 1 tests from SHOC benchmark suite.

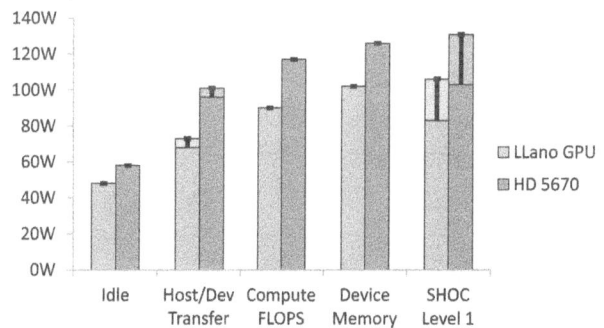

Figure 7: Full-system maximum power usage when using the integrated GPU in Llano and when using a discrete Radeon HD5670 GPU. The dark and light colors indicate the range of power usage across tests in each category.

5.2 Evaluation

Figure 8 shows the increase in power consumption versus the increase in performance when using the HD5670 compared to Llano for individual SHOC test results which do *not* depend on CPU-GPU data transfers. The vertical axis shows the best speedup obtained by using the discrete HD5670, and the horizontal axis shows the increase in peak power usage from the HD5670. We first notice that all points within the 2D performance-power plane are on the upper right side of the point (1.0x, 1.0x), which demonstrates better performance of HD5670 accompanied with greater power consumption.

The results in Figure 8 can be roughly clustered into three groups. The results above $y = 2.0x$, including DevMem-Read, DevMemWrite, MD, and Reduction show the largest performance speedup with a relatively small power increase. The benchmarks in this group are generally characterized as memory operation intensive. The groups on the right side of the line $x = 1.3\times$, including MaxFlops and S3D, represent those with the least speedup and the greatest power consumption. The benchmarks in this group are, in general, characterized as floating point operation intensive. The remaining benchmarks show a wider range of floating point and memory operation intensities; however, they do not approach either the performance improvement or the power increase of the other two groups.

Figure 9 shows similar results, this time for SHOC benchmarks which *do* include CPU-GPU data transfers. Note that some results are included in both Figures 8 and 9, but with different performance; in the latter, the data transfer times to GPU memory are incorporated. The relationship between power and performance is less straightforward in these results; the Llano fGPU performs relatively better once data transfers are included, often outperforming the HD5670, while power usage of the HD5670 is typically 30% higher than the Llano fGPU.

These results reveal that the high bandwidth of HD5670 brings performance benefit for memory intensive applications at the cost of small increase in power consumption, (i.e., the energy-delay product (EDP) is higher) while the tighter integration of Llano's fGPU may result in better energy efficiency for compute-intensive applications or those that require frequent CPU-GPU memory transfers.

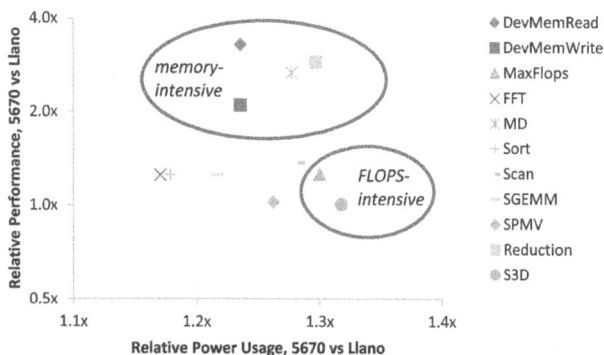

Figure 8: Performance and system power usage of the discrete HD5670 GPU on individual SHOC benchmarks relative to using the integrated GPU in Llano. This set of results does *not* include CPU-GPU transfers.

6. MODELS VS. RUNTIME SYSTEMS

One of the reasons for the success of GPGPU and, especially CUDA, is the effectiveness of the programming model.

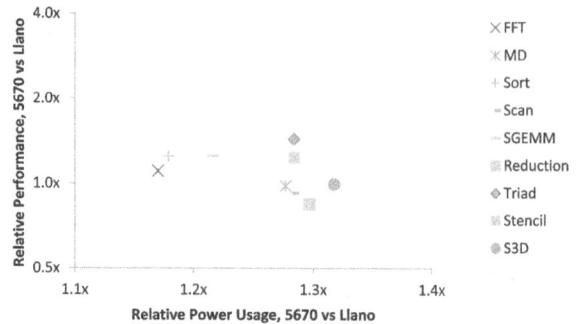

Figure 9: Performance and system power usage of the discrete HD5670 GPU on individual SHOC benchmarks relative to using the integrated GPU in Llano. This set of results *does* include CPU-GPU transfers.

CUDA's useful abstractions allowed access to the hardware resources of the GPU without having to learn graphics operations or very low-level device characteristics. For instance, the notion of a grid of thread blocks is easy to understand and hides many details about how the GPU actually schedules operations. The increased complexity of a fused heterogeneous architecture raises new questions for programming models. Which cores should a task run on? How does the programmer indicate that a task requires cache coherency among different cores? These questions begin to capture the next tradeoff, the contention between the desire for high-level abstractions and the complexity of the runtime systems required to support those abstractions.

Consider the problem of scheduling in more detail. Current capabilities in OpenCL allow the programmer to express a task that can run on the CPU or GPU cores. The programmer must then explicitly specify which device to use. The task may perform much better on one type of core, but it is the application's responsibility to track this and submit the task to the appropriate OpenCL device queue. Advanced scheduling features like preemption and task migration (from one core type to the other) are not yet available. However, the argument can be made that OpenCL is at a low-level of abstraction and the appropriate scheduling should be done by the application. At this extreme end of the tradeoff, maximal domain knowledge can be exploited, but the burden on application developers is large.

On the other hand, investment in a robust runtime system could significantly reduce this burden. Indeed, there have been several successes for these runtimes on CPUs including Cilk++ [15], with its work-stealing scheduler, and StarPU [2] for runtime scheduling on CPUs and discrete GPUs. These runtimes often outperform static scheduling strategies. It seems reasonable to assume that static scheduling will only become more difficult on the APU, as the scheduler will have to include task affinities for a given type of core, costs of moving memory between pageable and "local" memory partitions, and coscheduling requirements for deciding when to enable cache coherency between CPU and fGPU, which cannot be used in the general case for performance reasons. Also, it remains to be seen if the increased flexibility of the abstractions for an APU could be successfully incorporated into a distributed environment in a model similar to Charm++ [14] or Chapel [3].

Unfortunately, at the time of this writing, no such runtime systems were available for evaluation on the APU. Despite this, we believe the availability of an effective runtime will be an important factor in the success of any APU.

7. RELATED WORK

While the Fusion APU architecture [4] is the first of its kind, the trend toward increased heterogeneity (and specifically GPGPU) was recognized by Owens et al. in their review of heterogeneity in HPC, covering several successes in game physics and biophysics [19]. The trend towards tighter integration is mentioned by Kaeli and Akodes who document the movement of multicore processors and GPUs into mainstream consumer electronics like tablets and cellular phones [13] and identify the rapidly expanding class of problems which is amenable to GPGPU.

Prior to the release of the APU, several teams evaluated the performance of the ATI "Evergreen" GPU architecture, which includes two of the GPUs studied in this work, Cypress and Redwood. Both of these GPUs heavily influenced the GPU core architecture of Llano. These include a general study of performance and optimization techniques [16], a detailed characterization of the performance of atomic operations [17], and an evaluation of the energy efficiency of the architecture [26]. Others have also studied performance optimization on discrete NVIDIA GPUs [7, 20, 21, 22], some of which use a similar set of kernels to our experiments including GEMM [1, 11, 25], FFT [18], and molecular dynamics [5, 6].

There has also been an assessment of the Fusion architecture using the low power "Zacate" APU by Daga et al. [8] with a particular emphasis on absolute performance compared to a discrete GPU and the importance of the APU for scientific computing. Our results with the SHOC benchmark suite [9], also used by Daga, confirm the applicability of their findings at a different power scale. SHOC has also been used to study contention effects in previous work by Spafford et al. on NVIDIA-based platforms [23] with multiple GPUs that explores how PCIe contention becomes more complicated when traffic to the interconnect is considered.

8. CONCLUSIONS

We have identified five important tradeoffs for those designing or programming heterogeneous architectures with fused memory hierarchies. When constrained to a single type of physical memory, the choice between designs which focus on capacity and those that maximize bandwidth has a huge impact on GPU performance. So great, in fact, that this choice largely shaped the energy efficiency results in the last tradeoff, providing a fairly consistent method for grouping the mixed results of Figure 8. When system CPU-GPU data transfers become a more dominant portion of runtime (as seen in Figure 9), the efficiency benefits of tighter coupling do seem to overcome the specialized memory.

In the design of these fused memory hierarchies, the benefits of the tradeoff between cache coherency and scalability remains highly workload-specific and is not yet well understood. The addition of the FCL and the capability for cache coherency in Llano is an important first step. However, it will take time for this capability to make its way into mainstream programming models and scientific applications.

Furthermore, an APU-like design may only be beneficial if the application has a substantial parallel fraction and that fraction can be run on the throughput-oriented cores. The difference in performance of Llano's CPU cores and the Sandy Bridge CPU reflect the costs of not utilizing the appropriate core type or the potential penalty for devoting too many resources to a set of cores which won't be fully used by an application. When moving to a fused heterogeneous platform, an effective performance model and characterization of the instruction mix will be critical for choosing the correct core type for a kernel.

Finally, in the exploration of the tradeoff between simple abstractions and complex runtimes, we have identified a significant need for a robust APU runtime system. New concepts from the APU architecture impose additional complexity on programming models including kernel core affinity, coherence specification, and coscheduling requirements. While advanced applications may develop custom infrastructure to account for this complexity, the level of effort required to do so precludes many programmers from making this investment.

9. ACKNOWLEDGMENTS

This research is sponsored in part by the Office of Advanced Computing Research; U.S. Department of Energy. The work was performed at Oak Ridge National Laboratory, which is managed by UT-Battelle, LLC under Contract No.DE-AC05-00OR22725.

10. REFERENCES

[1] E. Agullo, J. Demmel, J. Dongarra, B. Hadri, J. Kurzak, J. Langou, H. Ltaief, P. Luszczek, and S. Tomov. Numerical Linear Algebra on Emerging Architectures: the PLASMA and MAGMA Projects. *Journal of Physics: Conference Series*, 180, 2009.

[2] C. Augonnet, S. Thibault, R. Namyst, and P.-A. Wacrenier. StarPU: A Unified Platform for Task Scheduling on Heterogeneous Multicore Architectures. In *Euro-Par 2009 Parallel Processing*, volume 5704 of *Lecture Notes in Computer Science*, pages 863–874. 2009.

[3] D. C. B. Chamberlain and H. P. Zima. Parallel Programmability and the Chapel Language. *The International Journal of High Performance Computing Applications*, 2007.

[4] N. Brookwood. AMD Fusion Family of APUs: Enabling a Superior, Immersive PC Experience. http://sites.amd.com/us/Documents/48423B_fusion_whitepaper_WEB.pdf, Mar 2010.

[5] W. M. Brown, A. Kohlmeyer, S. J. Plimpton, and A. N. Tharrington. Implementing Molecular Dynamics on Hybrid High Performance Computers — Particle–Particle Particle–Mesh. *Computer Physics Communications*, 183(3):449 – 459, 2012.

[6] W. M. Brown, P. Wang, S. J. Plimpton, and A. N. Tharrington. Implementing Molecular Dynamics on Hybrid High Performance Computers — Short Range Forces. *Computer Physics Communications*, 182(4):898 – 911, 2011.

[7] S. Carrillo, J. Siegel, and X. Li. A Control-Structure Splitting Optimization for GPGPU. In *Proceedings of the 6th ACM Conference on Computing Frontiers*, CF '09, pages 147–150, New York, NY, USA, 2009. ACM.

[8] M. Daga, A. Aji, and W. Feng. On the Efficacy of a Fused CPU+GPU Processor (or APU) for Parallel Computing. In *2011 Symposium on Application Accelerators in High-Performance Computing (SAAHPC)*, pages 141 –149, July 2011.

[9] A. Danalis, G. Marin, C. McCurdy, J. S. Meredith, P. C. Roth, K. Spafford, V. Tipparaju, and J. S. Vetter. The Scalable Heterogeneous Computing (SHOC) Benchmark Suite. In *Proceedings of the 3rd Workshop on General-Purpose Computation on Graphics Processing Units*, GPGPU '10, pages 63–74, New York, NY, USA, 2010. ACM.

[10] J. J. Dongarra and P. Luszczek. Introduction to the HPCChallenge Benchmark Suite. Technical Report ICL-UT-05-01, Innovative Computing Laboratory, University of Tennessee-Knoxville, 2005.

[11] T. Endo, A. Nukada, S. Matsuoka, and N. Maruyama. Linpack Evaluation on a Supercomputer with Heterogeneous Accelerators. In *2010 IEEE International Symposium on Parallel and Distributed Processing (IPDPS)*, pages 1 –8, 2010.

[12] J. Dongarra, P. Beckman et al. International exascale software roadmap. *International Journal of High Performance Computing Applications*, 25(1), 2011.

[13] D. Kaeli and D. Akodes. The Convergence of HPC and Embedded Systems in Our Heterogeneous Computing Future. In *2011 IEEE 29th International Conference on Computer Design (ICCD)*, pages 9 –11, oct. 2011.

[14] L. V. Kale and G. Zheng. Charm++ and AMPI: Adaptive Runtime Strategies via Migratable Objects. *Advanced Computational Infrastructures for Parallel and Distributed Adaptive Applications*, pages 265–282, 2009.

[15] C. Leiserson. The Cilk++ Concurrency Platform. *The Journal of Supercomputing*, 51:244–257, 2010.

[16] M. Daga, T. Scogland, and W. Feng. Performance Characterization and Optimization of Atomic Operations on AMD GPUs. In *Technical Report TR-11-08, Computer Science, Virginia Tech*, Retrieved from http://eprints.cs.vt.edu/archive/00001159/.

[17] M. Elteir, H. Lin, and W. Feng. Performance Characterization and Optimization of Atomic Operations on AMD GPUs. In *2011 IEEE International Conference on Cluster Computing (CLUSTER)*, pages 234 –243, sept. 2011.

[18] A. Nukada and S. Matsuoka. Auto-tuning 3-D FFT Library for CUDA GPUs. In *Proceedings of the Conference on High Performance Computing, Networking, Storage and Analysis*, SC '09, pages 30:1–30:10, New York, NY, USA, 2009. ACM.

[19] J. D. Owens, M. Houston, D. Luebke, S. Green, J. E. Stone, and J. C. Phillips. GPU Computing. *Proceedings of the IEEE*, 96(5):879–899, May 2008.

[20] S. Ryoo, C. I. Rodrigues, S. S. Stone, S. S. Baghsorkhi, S.-Z. Ueng, J. A. Stratton, and W. Hwu. Program Optimization Space Pruning for a Multithreaded GPU. In *Proceedings of the 6th Annual IEEE/ACM International Symposium on Code Generation and Optimization*, CGO '08, pages 195–204, New York, NY, USA, 2008. ACM.

[21] S. Ryoo, C. I. Rodrigues, S. S. Stone, S. S. Baghsorkhi, S. zee Ueng, and W. Hwu. Program Optimization Study on a 128-Core GPU. In *Proceedings of the First Workshop on General Purpose Processing on Graphics Processing Units*, 2007.

[22] S. Ryoo, C. I. Rodrigues, S. S. Stone, J. A. Stratton, S.-Z. Ueng, S. S. Baghsorkhi, and W. Hwu. Program Optimization Carving for GPU Computing. *Journal of Parallel and Distributed Computing*, 68(10):1389 –1401, 2008. General-Purpose Processing using Graphics Processing Units.

[23] K. Spafford, J. S. Meredith, and J. S. Vetter. Quantifying NUMA and Contention Effects in Multi-GPU Systems. In *Proceedings of The Fourth Workshop on General Purpose Processing on Graphics Processing Units*. ACM, 2011.

[24] J. Stoer and R. Bulirsch. *Introduction to Numerical Analysis*. Springer; 2nd edition, 1996.

[25] V. Volkov and J. W. Demmel. Benchmarking GPUs to Tune Dense Linear Algebra. In *Proceedings of the 2008 ACM/IEEE Conference on Supercomputing*, SC '08, pages –11, Piscataway, NJ, USA, 2008. IEEE Press.

[26] Y. Zhang, Y. Hu, B. Li, and L. Peng. Performance and Power Analysis of ATI GPU: A Statistical Approach. In *2011 6th IEEE International Conference on Networking, Architecture and Storage (NAS)*, pages 149 –158, July 2011.

DMA-circular: an Enhanced High Level Programmable DMA Controller for Optimized Management of On-chip Local Memories

Nikola Vujic[§], Lluc Alvarez[§‡], Marc Gonzalez[‡], Xavier Martorell[§‡], Eduard Ayguade[§‡]

[§]Barcelona Supercomputing Center
C/ Jordi Girona, 29
08034 Barcelona, Spain
{nvujic, xavim, eduard}@bsc.es

[‡]Universitat Politecnica de Catalunya
C/ Jordi Girona, 1-3
08034 Barcelona, Spain
{lluca, marc}@ac.upc.edu

ABSTRACT

This paper presents DMA-circular, a novel DMA controller for optimized memory management for on-chip local memories. DMA-circular embeds the functionality of caches into the DMA controller and applies aggressive optimizations using novel hardware. DMA-circular anticipates the computation requirements in terms of data transfers and performs buffer management for data that is mapped to the local memory. The explicit hardware support accelerates the most common actions related to the management of a local memory while the cache functionalities enable a high level of programmability for the DMA-circular. The evaluation is done on several high performance kernels from the NAS benchmark suite. Compared to traditional DMA controllers, results show speedups from 1.20x to 2x, keeping the control code overhead under 15% of the kernels' execution time and also reducing the energy consumption up to 40%.

Categories and Subject Descriptors

C.1.3 [**Processor Architectures**]: Other Architecture Styles; C.4 [**Performance of Systems**]: Design studies

Keywords

DMA, local memories, programmability

1. INTRODUCTION

Despite the fact that the most viable L1 memories in processors are caches, on-chip local memories (LMs) have been a great topic of consideration lately. LMs are an interesting design option due to their many benefits [3]: less area occupancy, reduced energy consumption and fast and constant access time. These benefits are especially interesting for the design of modern processors since power and latency are important assets in computer architecture nowadays. Unfortunately, LMs have not been well accepted in modern processors yet, mainly due to their poor programmability.

LMs impose programming difficulties since they are completely managed by software through programmable DMA engines. The best performance is obtained when LMs are managed manually by tuning every DMA transfer in conjunction with a good knowledge of the applications' behaviour. This option has been very successful in the High Performance Computing (HPC) and the embedded domain but is not viable in scenarios where programmability is important. Therefore, besides obtaining good performance, for the acceptance of LMs it is important to overcome the non-transparent/explicit memory management and to get closer to a level of programmability where little or no information about applications' behaviour is necessary to automatically adapt the context of LMs to the applications' needs.

So far, compilers have solved the programmability issues at the cost of performance penalties [8, 13, 11, 18, 2, 9]. In general, compilers select memory references to be mapped to the LM and generate code that manages the mapping. The essential action of the mapping is to program DMA transfers, but that is not all. Since DMA engines provide just basic operations to transfer data to/from the LM, the software takes care of the buffer management. Buffer management is a complex problem because it requires memory aliasing analyses [12, 7, 20]. Since even complex compiler analyses cannot reliably answer on the memory aliasing question, compilers have to emit code that checks aliasing conflicts to consistently do the buffer management, causing important overheads. The main reason for the overheads is the poor support in current DMA controllers for managing LMs.

This paper proposes the DMA-circular, an enhanced DMA controller tailored for reducing the overheads of managing LMs. The main contribution is the bringing of DMA controllers to a high level extension aimed for specific applications' needs at exactly appropriate places where LMs make sense but still end up in unacceptable overheads due to the need for the control code to substitute the lack of advanced data management support in DMA controllers. We show that DMA-circular is able to keep the control code under 15% of the execution time. Morever, speedups with respect to traditional DMA controllers range from 1.20x to 2x and the energy consumption is reduced from 5% to 40%.

The rest of the paper is organized as follows: Section

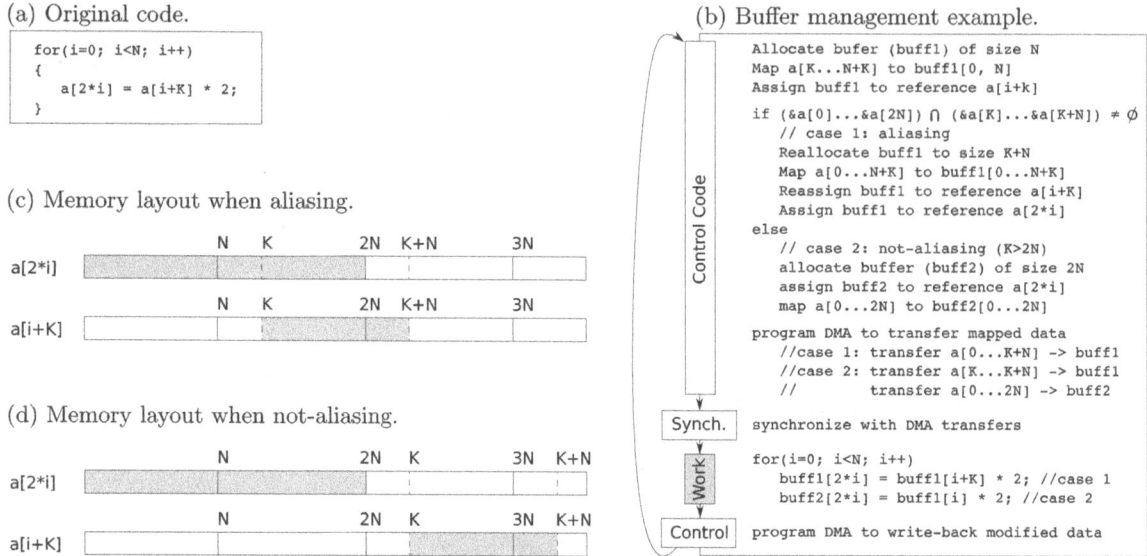

(a) Original code.

```
for(i=0; i<N; i++)
{
    a[2*i] = a[i+K] * 2;
}
```

(b) Buffer management example.

(c) Memory layout when aliasing.

```
                N   K        2N   K+N      3N
a[2*i]   [                        |            ]

                N   K        2N   K+N      3N
a[i+K]   [                        |            ]
```

(d) Memory layout when not-aliasing.

```
                N        2N   K      3N   K+N
a[2*i]   [                        |            ]

                N        2N   K      3N   K+N
a[i+K]   [                        |            ]
```

Control Code:
```
Allocate bufer (buff1) of size N
Map a[K...N+K] to buff1[0, N]
Assign buff1 to reference a[i+k]

if (&a[0]...&a[2N]) ∩ (&a[K]...&a[K+N]) ≠ ∅
    // case 1: aliasing
    Reallocate buff1 to size K+N
    Map a[0...N+K] to buff1[0...N+K]
    Reassign buff1 to reference a[i+K]
    Assign buff1 to reference a[2*i]
else
    // case 2: not-aliasing (K>2N)
    allocate buffer (buff2) of size 2N
    assign buff2 to reference a[2*i]
    map a[0...2N] to buff2[0...2N]

program DMA to transfer mapped data
    //case 1: transfer a[0...K+N] -> buff1
    //case 2: transfer a[K...K+N] -> buff1
    //        transfer a[0...2N] -> buff2
```

Synch. synchronize with DMA transfers

Work:
```
for(i=0; i<N; i++)
    buff1[2*i] = buff1[i+K] * 2; //case 1
    buff2[2*i] = buff1[i] * 2; //case 2
```

Control program DMA to write-back modified data
```

Figure 1: Buffer management. For simplicity, we assume $K > N$ in the given example.

2 presents some background about buffer management for LMs. Section 3 describes the DMA-circular design, while Section 4 evaluates the proposal. Section 5 discusses some related work and Section 6 concludes the paper.

## 2. BACKGROUND

This section explains the buffer management problems for LMs. We show the functionalities of a traditional DMA controller and we explain the execution model for LMs and its main challenges regarding buffer management.

### 2.1 DMA Controller

DMA controllers (or simply DMAs for short) are used to move data between the LM and the main memory. They offer three basic operations: *dma-put*, *dma-get*, and *dma-synch*. The *dma-get* command transfers data from the main memory to the LM while the *dma-put* does it in the opposite direction. The parameters of these two commands are a source address, a destination address, the size of the transfer and a tag to be assigned to the transfer. The *dma-synch* is used to synchronize with the data transfers associated to a particular set of tags.

### 2.2 Execution Model

The typical computation suitable for LMs is organized in a nest of loops that operate over array-like structures with predictable access patterns in the form of *strided memory references with constant strides* [15]. For such a computation, LMs impose an execution model organized in three different phases (repeated until the computation is over): control, synchronization, and work [8]. The control phase is responsible for all the buffer management actions, namely: *Buffer Allocation, Buffer Mapping, Buffer Assignment to references, Handling of aliasing, DMA programming, Write-back*, and *Prefetching*. The synchronization phase ensures the data transfers bringing data for the next work phase are finished, and the work phase does the actual computation. Figure 1 shows a code example (Figure 1a) and an example of a code transformation tailored to show buffer management actions for the mentioned execution model (Figure 1b).

**Buffer Allocation** is the first control action since, prior

to any data transfer, a buffer in the LM must be allocated. For instance, a buffer of size $N$ is allocated for the reference *a[i+K]*. Then the **Buffer Mapping** takes place to map data from the main memory to the buffer in the LM (e.g, mapping $a[K...N+K] \rightarrow buff1[0...N]$ for reference *a[i+K]*). This mapping determines the source and the destination address of a DMA transfer. The next action is the **Buffer Assignment** which assigns a buffer to a reference by means of translating the main memory address to the LM address (e.g., *a[i+K]* is translated to *buff1[i]*).

When more than one reference is managed, the **Handling of aliasing** is important. In Figure 1b, handling *a[2*i]* is conditioned by checking whether this reference is aliasing or not with some other reference. Figure 1d shows a memory layout with no aliasing between *a[i+K]* and *a[2*i]*. In this case, a new buffer is allocated and assigned to the reference *a[2*i]*. If the references are aliasing, as in Figure 1c, there is no need for a second buffer, since the already allocated buffer *buff1* can be reallocated to handle both references.

The next step is the **DMA programming**, that initiates the data transfers. Then the synchronization and work phases take place. At the end of the computation the DMA programming also appears in the form of **Write-back** actions, where modified data is flushed back to the main memory. All these buffer management actions can be more complex if double buffering techniques are introduced for data **prefetching** to overlap communication and computation.

All the mentioned control actions for buffer management cause an important overhead. The main contribution of this paper is the acceleration of the control code actions by allowing the DMA-circular to perform them in hardware.

## 3. DMA-CIRCULAR DESIGN

This section describes the design of the DMA-circular. Essentially, in every control phase the DMA-circular automatically manages the data in the LM to feed the next work phase. It does so by handling memory aliasing, buffer mapping and buffer assignment to references and by triggering data transfers. At the end of the control phase it provides outputs for the LM addresses resulting from the buffer assignments, the number of iterations that can be executed
```

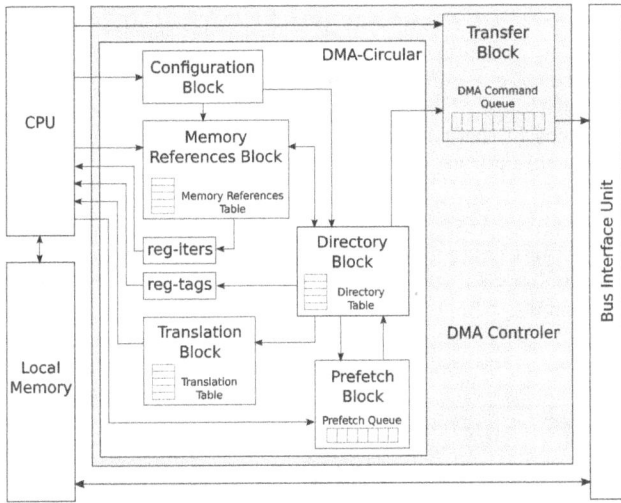

Figure 2: DMA-circular high level design.

in the next work phase and the set of tags to be used in the synchronization phase. Figure 2 shows a high level design of the DMA-circular, including the three main blocks: the Memory References Block, the Directory Block and the Translation Block.

The Memory References Block keeps the description of all the references that the DMA-circular handles. These descriptions are used by the other components of the DMA-circular to do the buffer management. The most important block for the buffer management is the Directory Block, which is a cache-like structure that keeps information (buffer descriptors) of all the buffers allocated in the LM and their mappings. Buffer allocation is addressed by splitting the whole LM space into equally sized buffers. Buffer descriptors are used to establish the mapping of data in the main memory to the buffers in the LM. Memory aliasing is simply addressed by doing an associative lookup in the table to check if some data is already mapped to the LM. In addition, the Directory Block is capable of triggering DMA transfers in a case of missing data in the LM or in a case of writing-back modified data. The buffer assignment is also done by the Directory Block, which notifies all the resulting LM addresses to the user through the Translation Block. Since the buffers in the LM cannot hold the whole workload, then in one shot the work phase can run only for a limited number of iterations (as long as the buffers in the LM can feed the computation). The Memory References Block is in charge of computing this number of iterations.

In the following sections we describe all the blocks of the DMA-circular in greater detail.

3.1 DMA-circular Structures

Traditional DMAs consist of the Transfer Block in Figure 2. The DMA-circular extends their design by adding the Memory References Block, the Directory Block, the Translation Block, the Configuration Block, the Prefetch Block and two registers named reg-tags and reg-iters.

3.1.1 Configuration Block

This block supports the configuration of the DMA-circular. It is used to specify the number of LM buffers, their size, and the address where they should be allocated. The number of buffers and buffer size determine the total size of the LM dedicated to the buffers, while the address determines

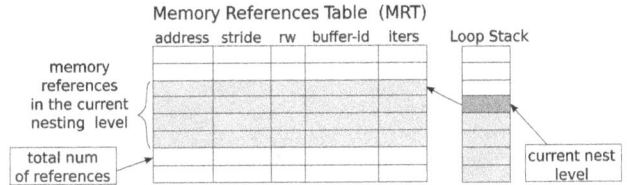

Figure 3: Memory References Block.

where that storage should start in the LM. For example, if we want to devote a half of the LM to the DMA-circular, it can be configured with these parameters.

3.1.2 Memory Reference Block

The Memory References Block (MRB) is shown in Figure 3. The main structure of the MRB is the Memory References Table (MRT), which contains descriptions for all the memory references to be treated by the DMA-circular. The DMA-circular handles references that appear in the loop bodies, but only those exposing *stride access pattern with constant strides* since only for this type of references it is possible to calculate the number of iterations a buffer in the LM can feed the computation. In the MRT, three fields are devoted for the description of references: (1) *address* - the address which is going to be accessed by a reference in the first iteration of the work phase, (2) *stride* - the size of the stride, and (3) *rw* - the read/write information of the reference. These three fields are provided by the software, while the other two fields (*buffer-id* and *iters*) are maintained by MRB. The *buffer-id* identifies the buffer in the LM that is assigned to the reference, while the *iters* corresponds to the number of iterations that can be executed within the assigned buffer. If *iters* is zero, there is no buffer assigned to the reference or the execution has reached the end of the currently assigned buffer. Both cases trigger actions in the Directory Block to bring new data for the reference.

The Loop Stack structure that appears in Figure 3 is used to identify what references have to be managed in a given control phase, which is essential to support nested loops. When a new loop is found its state is pushed to the Loop Stack by incrementing the current nest level and then by setting the top of the stack with the total number of references. When during the loop a reference is registered the total number of references is incremented. When the loop ends its state is popped from the Loop Stack by setting the total number of references to the number at the top of the stack and then by decrementing the current nest level.

3.1.3 Directory Block

The Directory Block (DB) is shown in Figure 4. This block is similar to the organization of standard caches, but extended with some specific features targeting buffer management for LMs. The main structure of the DB is the Directory Table (DT) which contains descriptors for all buffers in the LM. Each buffer is described by four fields in the DT: (1) *baddr* - a base address of the mapped chunk of data from the main memory, (2) *counter* - a counter that keeps track of the number of references that are assigned to this buffer, (3) *dirty* - describes whether the buffer is modified or not, and (4) *pf* - specifies if the buffer is under prefetching.

The main purpose of the DB is to provide correct buffer assignment to references by handling memory aliasing. An associative lookup is performed in the DT when a buffer is needed for a reference, as shown in Figure 4. If a hit occurs,

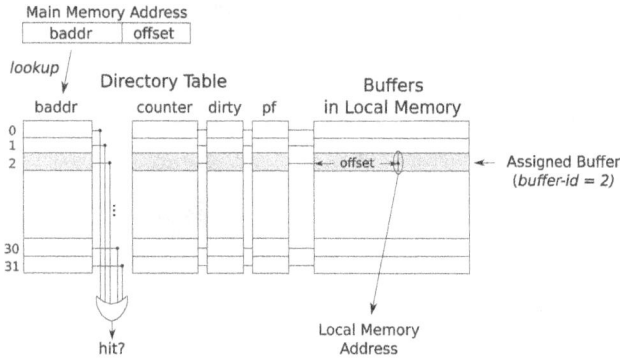

Figure 4: Directory Block.

the buffer is simply assigned to the reference by updating its *buffer-id* field in MRT. In the entry in the DT, the *counter* field of the buffer is incremented and the *dirty* field is updated using the reference's *rw* field from the MRT. In a case of a miss, an unused buffer in the LM is selected and the Directory Block automatically schedules a *dma_get* operation to transfer the mapped data to it.

The DB does not support replacement of a buffer. It is designed to maintain free and used buffers so that only free buffers can serve new references. The *counter* field is used for this purpose. If there are no free buffers, then no more references can be mapped to the LM. This constraint is necessary, since all buffers assigned to references must be resident in the LM during the work phase. It must not happen that a buffer gets replaced by another when both of them are needed. So, DMA-circular can handle as many references as there are entries in the DT. In this work we consider 32 entries. Loops using DMA-circular must be aware of this limitation, which is not a big problem for HPC kernels because it is very rare to find a loop with more than 32 references in its loop body and, in a case one was found, the exceeding references could be handled using traditional software techniques.

When a reference does not use a buffer anymore, its *counter* field is decremented. The MRB is responsible for notifying the DB when this happens. If the *iters* field in the MRT reaches zero because the reference reaches the end of the buffer, it is necessary to release the currently assigned buffer before requesting a new one. If the *counter* field of a dirty buffer reaches zero, the DB schedules a *dma_put* operation to transfer the buffer back to the main memory.

3.1.4 Prefetch Block

This block is responsible for prefetching actions. It uses a Prefetch Queue that stores the addresses to be prefetched. According to the sign of the stride of a reference, when the DB does a lookup of an address, it enqueues the base address of the next chunk of data in the Prefetch Queue. Once the prefetching is enabled by the software, the Prefetch Block invokes a lookup in the DB for every address in the Prefetch Queue. If the lookup misses, a free buffer is selected, the data is transferred to the LM with a *dma_get* operation and the *baddr* and the *pf* fields in the DT are set, without incrementing the *counter* field since the prefetched data is not assigned to any reference yet.

3.1.5 Translation Block

This component is an interface for the hardware to communicate to the software the translated addresses resulting

from the buffer assignment. When requesting a buffer for a reference, its main memory address is provided to the DB which does the buffer assignment and outputs the LM address within the assigned buffer. These LM addresses are preserved in the Translation Table so that the software can read them and use them in the work phase.

3.1.6 The reg-iters And reg-tags Registers

The reg-iters register is used to provide the software with the number of iterations that can be executed in the next work phase. This register is managed by the MRB.

The reg-tags register is used to provide the software with the tags to be used for the synchronization with the DMA transfers that bring the data needed in the next work phase. This register is managed by the DB.

3.2 Operational Model

In this section we describe how the DMA-circular works and how it interacts with the software. In Figure 5(a) we present how the computation in Figure 1a would look like when operating with the DMA-circular. The first thing to do is to configure the DMA-circular as described in Section 3.1.1. This is done with CONFIG_DMA, passing a given address, a given size and the number of buffers, 2 in this case. Then START_MEM_REF_REGISTRATION notifies the beginning of a new loop, that pushes a new loop in the Loop Stack of the MRT. Then the references are registered with REGISTER_MEM_REF, which places the descriptions of the references in the MRT. Each descriptor is stored in the row of the MRT pointed by the total number of references and then this value is incremented. In our example two references are registered, *a[i+K]* and *a[2*i]*, with their strides and read/write information. Figure 5(b) shows the MRT after the registration of these two references for their given footprint in the main memory.

The control code in software is reduced to two actions: START_UPDATE and WAIT_UPDATE. Figure 5(c) shows a flow diagram of the evolution of the MRT during the first two executions of the control code. START_UPDATE triggers lookups for the addresses of the active references in the MRT which *iters* field is zero. At the beginning, both references have no assigned buffer so two lookups (for addresses *16* and *0*) are triggered in the DT. Since these addresses are not mapped to any buffer in the LM, both lookups miss and the DB schedules two *dma_get* commands to bring the data. Additionally, two addresses (*32* and *16*) are placed in the Prefetch Queue in order to be used for prefetching later. In return, the DB updates the *buffer-id* entries in MRT for the references. One reference gets buffer *0* assigned, and the other gets buffer *1*. Along with this, the MRB updates the *iters* fields. In the given example in Figure 5(b), the two references can do four and two iterations. The minimum value of these two is placed in reg-iters, which denotes the maximum number of iterations to be executed in the next work phase. While the MRB and the DB are doing these actions, the CPU is waiting on WAIT_UPDATE. Once all updates are done, the control is returned to the CPU to proceed with the next actions: reading the LM addresses from the Translation Table with READ_TRANSLATION, reading the reg-iters register with READ_DMA_ITERS, adjusting the iteration boundaries of the loop, reading the reg-tags register with READ_DMA_TAGS, starting the prefetching with START_PREFETCH, synchronizing with the DMA

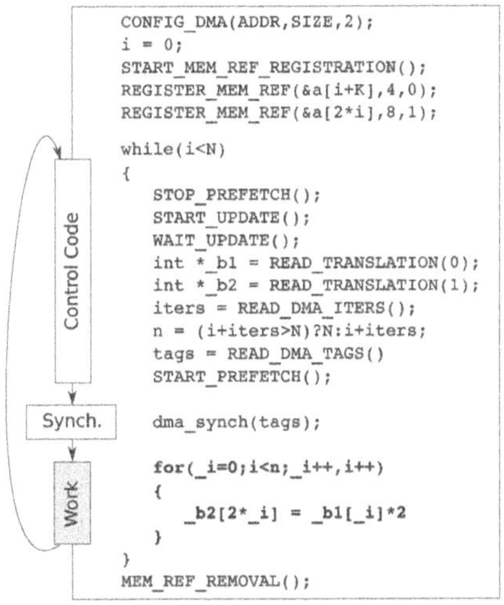

```
CONFIG_DMA(ADDR,SIZE,2);
i = 0;
START_MEM_REF_REGISTRATION();
REGISTER_MEM_REF(&a[i+K],4,0);
REGISTER_MEM_REF(&a[2*i],8,1);

while(i<N)
{
    STOP_PREFETCH();
    START_UPDATE();
    WAIT_UPDATE();
    int *_b1 = READ_TRANSLATION(0);
    int *_b2 = READ_TRANSLATION(1);
    iters = READ_DMA_ITERS();
    n = (i+iters>N)?N:i+iters;
    tags = READ_DMA_TAGS()
    START_PREFETCH();

    dma_synch(tags);

    for(_i=0;i<n;_i++,i++)
    {
        _b2[2*_i] = _b1[_i]*2
    }
}
MEM_REF_REMOVAL();
```

(a) A code example that operates with DMA-circular.

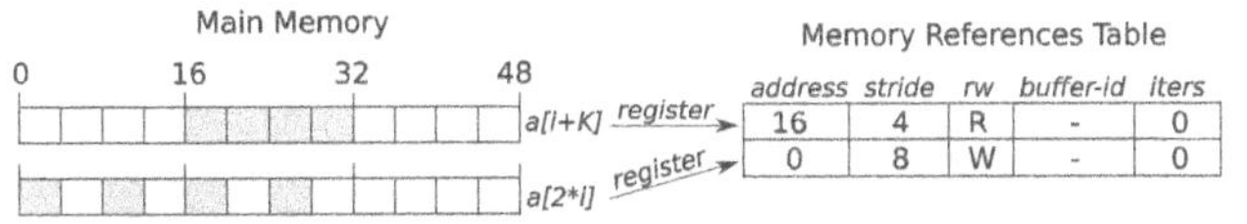

(b) Memory footprint example (K=16, Buffer size 16B) and registration of references.

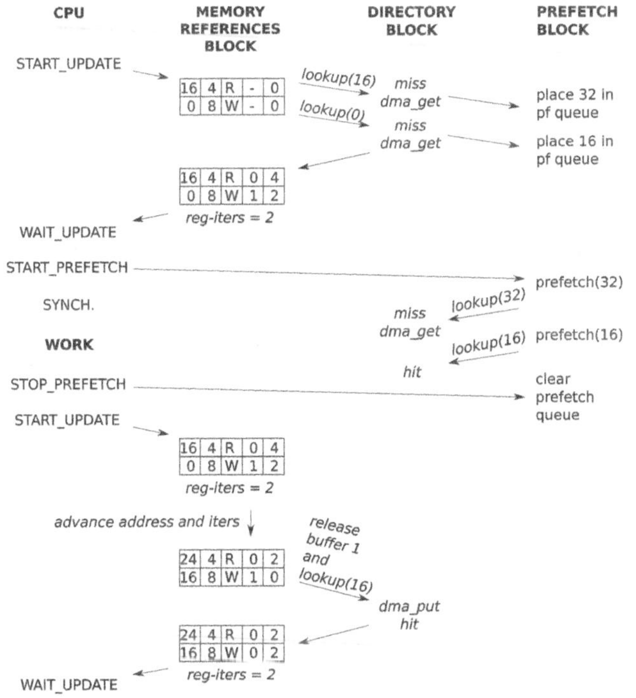

(c) Flow diagram with the evolution of the MRT for the first two executions of the control code.

Figure 5: Operational Model.

transfers using the read tags and finally executing the work phase. The prefetching is started prior to the synchronization. Figure 5(c) shows that while the CPU executes the synchronization and work phases, the Prefetch Block triggers lookups in DB for the addresses found in the Prefetch Queue, *32* and *16*. The former will miss in the DB and a

dma_get operation will be programmed, while the latter will hit.

After the work phase, the control phase is repeated since the whole workload has not been executed. In the second control phase, the first action to be taken is to stop prefetching (with STOP_PREFETCH) and START_UPDATE in the MRB again. Now, the MRB first updates the *address* and *iters* fields in the MRT. The *address* field is updated to the next address to be accessed ($address = address + stride \times reg\text{-}iters$), and the *iters* field is decremented by *reg-iters*. Since now *iters* is zero for the *a[2*i]* reference then, prior to invoking a lookup for the new address (address *16*), it is necessary first to release the old buffer (buffer *1*). Since *a[2*i]* is a write access reference then, when releasing buffer *1*, the DB schedules a *dma_put* command to transfer back the modified data to the main memory.

This execution model continues until the whole original iteration space of the loop is executed. At the end of the loop MEM_REF_REMOVAL is used to release all buffers assigned to references from the current nesting level and to notify the MRB that we are exiting from the loop so that Loop Stack can be popped in order to switch the MRB to work with the references from the previous nesting level.

At the end, one particular constraint regarding the usage of the DMA-circular is imposed. The DMA-circular writes back whole buffers of data, even if only a portion of the buffer is modified. In Figure 5(c), a *dma_put* is scheduled to transfer a buffer where actually every second element is modified. This can be a problem in multicore systems if buffer sharing appears, so that at least two cores work concurrently with the same buffer from the global memory but modifying different elements in the buffer. Even if this is not a common situation, the user must be aware of it in order to ensure that the kernels treated by the DMA-circular do not expose this behaviour.

4. EVALUATION

For the evaluation of the DMA-circular we use all the loops from CG, IS, FT, and MG applications of the NAS benchmark suite [1]. The evaluation covers the executions on a single-core in order to study the effect of offloading the control code from the software to the new hardware. Evaluating parallel executions is out of the scope of this paper since the DMA-circular is aimed to accelerate per core executions. The selected loops are typical HPC workloads that contain plenty of strided access references with constant strides, which are the only references addressed by our proposal. All loops are coded to use a traditional DMA and the DMA-circular. The baseline architecture is the implementation that uses a traditional DMA, and this implementation is based on the hybrid-access specific software cache [11] - an optimised buffer management runtime system for traditional DMAs and local memories. We use the PTLsim [22] simulation infrastructure, extending the simulator with a local memory, a traditional DMA and the DMA-circular. In addition, we embed the Wattch [4] library in PTLsim in order to gather power and energy results from the simulations. Table 1 shows the used configuration parameters.

The evaluation is divided in four parts. First, we measure the control code overheads with a traditional DMA. Second, we measure the effect of the DMA-circular in the control code. Third, we show the overall impact in performance, and finally we study the power and energy consumption.

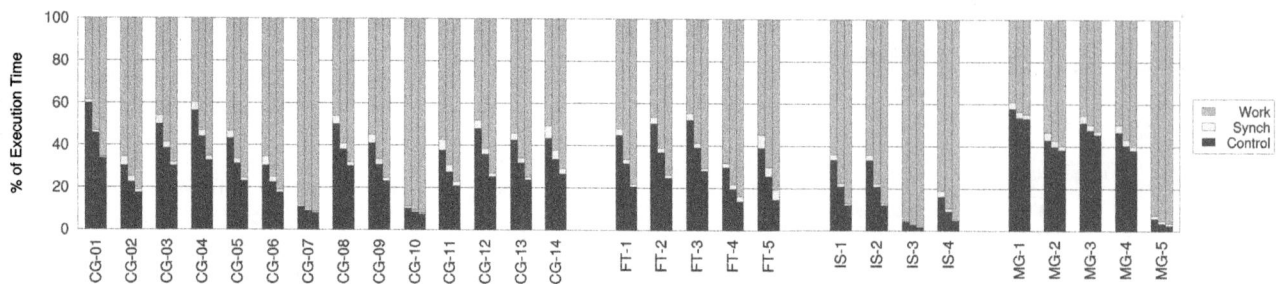

Figure 6: Control code overheads with a traditional DMA.

Table 1: PTLsim configuration parameters.

Parameter	Description
Issue scheme	Out-of-order (Fetch, Decode, Rename, Issue and Commit width of 4 instructions)
Branch predictor	Hybrid 4K selector, 4K G-share, 4K Bimodal, 4K BTB 4-way, and RAS 32 entries
Functional units	3 integer ALUs, 3 floating point ALUs, and 2 load/store units
Register file	256 integer registers 256 floating point registers
L1 I-cache	32 KB, 8-way set-associative 64-byte lines, 2 cycles latency
L1 D-cache	32 KB, 8-way set-associative 64-byte lines, 2 cycles latency
L2 cache	256 KB, 24-way set-associative 64-byte lines, 15 cycles latency
L3 cache	4 MB, 32-way set-associative 64-byte lines, 40 cycles latency
Local memory	size = 32 x studied buffer size 2 cycles latency
DMA-circular	1 cycle latency: loop stack operations, accessing an entry in MRB, lookup in DT, prefetch in DT, releasing a buffer in DB, writing to Translation Table, and queuing an address in to Prefetch Queue 4 cycles latency to calculate iters in MRB, with maintaining the minimum iters value. 3 cycles latency to update address and iters fields in MRB with maintaining the minimum iters value.
I/O mapped load and store	6 cycles latency

4.1 Control Code Overheads

The main aim of this section is to analyse the control code overheads of traditional DMAs and to determine an upper bound for the acceleration effect. Figure 6 shows the time distribution of the selected loops. The total execution time is broken down into control, synchronization and work. For each loop the figure shows three bars corresponding to three buffer sizes - left to right: 1KB, 2KB, and 4KB. We observe that the control code overheads vary a lot. Some loops have small overheads, less than 20% of the execution time, and some others have huge overheads of up to 60%.

This first thing to notice is that the size of the buffers has a huge effect on the control code overheads. The reason is that, with a given workload, the size of the buffers determine the length of the work phases and the number of control bursts. If the workload fits in the buffer size, the execution will go through one control phase and one work phase. If the size of the buffer is half the workload then two control phases and two work phases will take place. Splitting the computation in several work phases is not a problem because, at the end, the same amount of work is done. Contrariwise, having two times more control bursts means doubling the control code overhead, since all the operations involved in the control code are done twice and their costs

do not depend on the buffer size. This is the reason why the control code overheads decrease as the buffer size increases, as can be observed in the three bars of any loop in Figure 6.

The loops that suffer less overheads are CG-07, CG-10, IS-3, IS-4, and MG-5. These loops are computation bounded, and only a small percentage of time is spent in the control code because few references are handled. IS-4 handles two references that alias, so they share the same buffer. Only 5% of its execution time is control code overhead when working with 4KB buffers, increasing to 20% with 1KB buffers. In addition, loops CG-07, CG-10, IS-3 and MG-5 contain an irregular reference that dominates the whole execution time. Due to its unpredictability, this reference cannot be easily handled with traditional DMAs and causes important performance penalties, making the weight of the work phase much bigger than any other phase in the loop. So, for this set of loops, the DMA-circular is trying to accelerate 5%-20% of the total execution time.

In the rest of CG and IS loops the overheads range from 15% to 60%. Loops CG-02, CG-05, CG-06, CG-09, and CG-13 do a reduction operation on one or two arrays. IS-1, IS-2 and the rest of CG loops consist of very simple computations over one or two arrays, namely vector initializations, vector copies and vector additions. Due to the fast computation in the work phases, the control code takes a significant part of the execution time: 15% to 35% with big buffers, 20% to 45% with 2KB buffers and 35% to 60% with 1KB buffers.

FT loops are computationally complex kernels with many references to be handled. In FT-1, FT-2 and FT-3, 20% of the execution time is spent on control code when 4KB buffers are used. With 2KB buffers, the overhead is around 35%, while with 1KB buffers it is around 50%. FT-4 and FT-5 treat less references than FT-1, FT-2, and FT-3, which translates to overheads ranging from 15% to 40%.

The MG loops are interesting examples where the control code overhead is high, around 40% or 50%, for all tested buffer sizes. MG-4 (the most time consuming loop in MG) is a case of 3 nested loops where the innermost loop has a short iteration space and a considerable number of references, 18. Due to the short iteration space, the majority of iterations of the innermost loop fit in 1KB buffers. This means that, after the innermost loop is sub-chunked in very few work bursts, the outermost loops are executed and then the control code for the new instance of the innermost loop is executed again. So, when bigger buffers are used, instead of having a significant reduction of control code phases due to the sub-chunking of the innermost loop, here the number of control code instances in the innermost loop is barely the same because it is dictated by the iteration space of the outer loops. The acceleration opportunities in this case are high, since 50% of the execution time can be optimized.

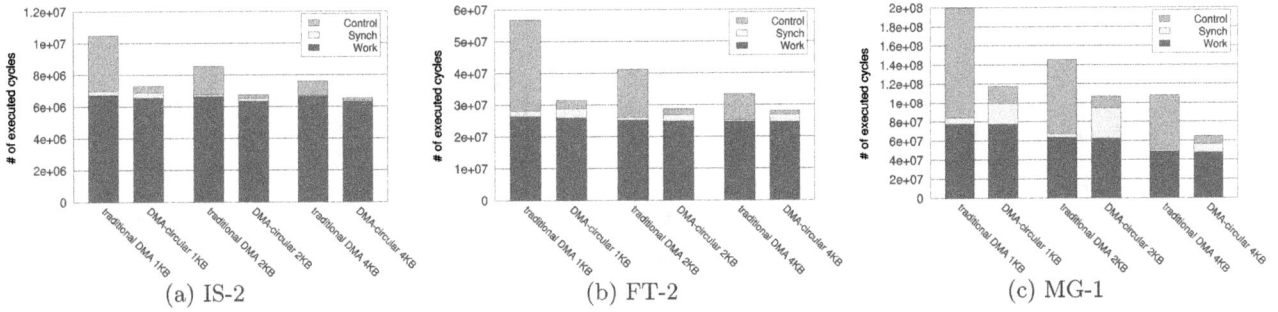

(a) IS-2   (b) FT-2   (c) MG-1

Figure 7: Execution time for some loops using a traditional DMA and the DMA-circular.

In conclusion, the DMA-circular addresses to optimize from 5% to 50% of the loops execution time, depending on the loop type and the buffer size. Loops that are computation bounded with very few references offer low optimization opportunities, between 5% and 20%. The other loops offer bigger optimization opportunities, with overheads between 20% to 60%. These loops are: loops which are not computation bounded so that more weight is pushed on the control code side (many CG and IS loops), nested loops with short innermost loops (all MG loops but MG-5), and any type of loop where the number of references to be handled is very high (FT loops).

4.2 Control Code Acceleration

This section shows the effectiveness of the DMA-circular. The acceleration on the control code depends on two factors: the number of references that are treated and the number of times the control phase is executed. Because of that we select three representative loops (IS-2, FT-2 and MG-1) to explain the acceleration effect in detail. Figure 7 shows the execution of the selected loops, each one executed using a traditional DMA and the DMA-circular. Execution time is decomposed into actual work, control overhead, and synchronization. Each loop is executed using three different buffer sizes: 1KB, 2KB, and 4KB.

IS-2 is a non-nested loop that has very few references. All CG and IS loops fall in this category. Figure 7(a) shows the time distribution for the loop. We can see that control code is around 30% when buffers of 1KB are used, while it is a bit less for bigger buffers: 20% for 2KB buffers and 15 % for 4KB buffers. Even in this case where control phases handle few references, the DMA-circular successfully accelerates the control code, reaching a speedup of 9x with 1KB buffers. The execution time of the work component remains flat in all versions, which is expected since the DMA-circular has no effect on the work phase. Finally, the synchronization time increases a bit due to the much shorter control phases, that are not long enough to completely overlap communication and computation when the DMA-circular is used.

FT loops have high overheads because they use many references. An example is the FT-2, shown in Figure 7(b). The DMA-circular achieves speedups of 7x, 8x and 12x in the control code, using buffers of 4KB, 2KB and 1KB, respectively. This means the smaller the buffers the bigger the speedup. This is because the control code handles a big number of references, so the cost of a control phase is highly reduced by the DMA-circular no matter the buffer size. Since smaller buffers imply executing more control phases, the effect of the acceleration is more noticeable with small buffers.

The case of MG-1 in Figure 7(c) is representative of loops dominated by the control code because of nested loops with short innermost loops. The speedup in the control code is significant, around 7x, but the total number of cycles spent in the control phase is not as low as in the previous situations. The reason is that, even after optimizing the control code, it still needs a small number of cycles to be executed. This small number of cycles multiplied by the iteration spaces of the outermost loops result in a non-negligible control code overhead. In any case, the overhead is still greatly reduced. Another interesting observation is the drastic increase in the synchronization time, especially for 1KB and 2KB buffers, when the DMA-circular is used. This is because MG-1 suffers from wrong prefetching when 1KB and 2KB buffers are used, while with 4KB buffers the prefetching works fine. That is also why the synchronization time with 1KB and 2KB buffers is much higher than with 4KB buffers. However, the increase in the synchronization time is not that drastic to diminish the effects of the acceleration and thus speedups in the total execution time are observed. Moreover, the execution time of the work phase depends on the size of the buffer in this case. This is not caused by the DMA-circular but by the sub-chunking of the iteration space of the innermost loop: it is faster to execute the whole iteration space in one burst than to break it down in a few bursts because in the latter case more jump instructions are involved. For non nested loops with long iteration spaces the increase of jump instructions has a negligible impact on the total number of executed instructions but, for short iteration spaces in the innermost loop of a nest of loops, it has a significant impact.

In conclusion, the DMA-circular succeeds in diminishing the control code overheads without incurring an unacceptable increase in the other components of the execution time. The degree of success depends on the number of references to be treated and in the number of control phase executions, but in any case the acceleration is significant. The synchronization time usually increases with the DMA-circular since the new control code is not long enough to overlap all data transfers, but that increase is not big enough to overcome the effect of the acceleration. We observe that the speedups in the control code range from 6x to 12x, usually being more efficient for smaller buffers than for bigger buffers.

4.3 Overall Loop Performance

In this section we evaluate the overall loop performance of the DMA-circular against a traditional DMA. Figure 8 shows the speedups in execution time obtained in the tested loops. For each loop three bars are plotted, one per buffer size - left to right: 1KB, 2KB and 4KB.

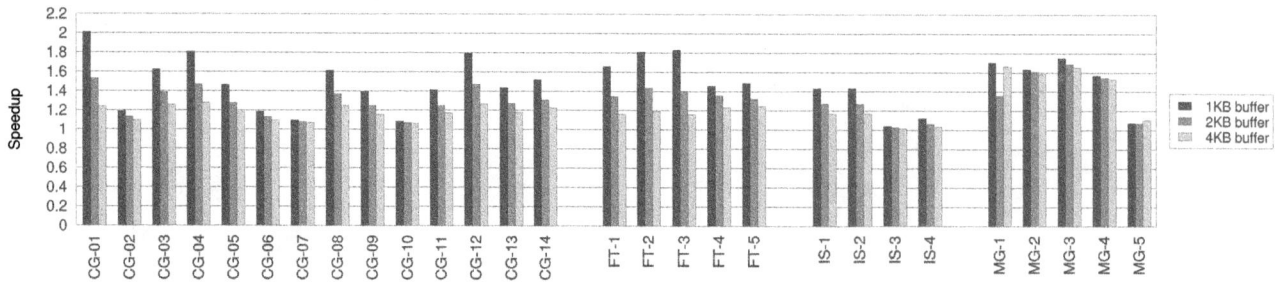

Figure 8: Speedup of the DMA-circular against a traditional DMA.

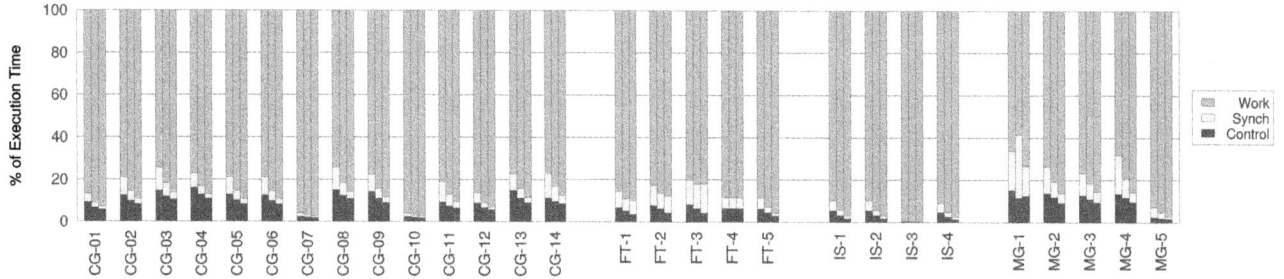

Figure 9: Control code overheads with the DMA-circular.

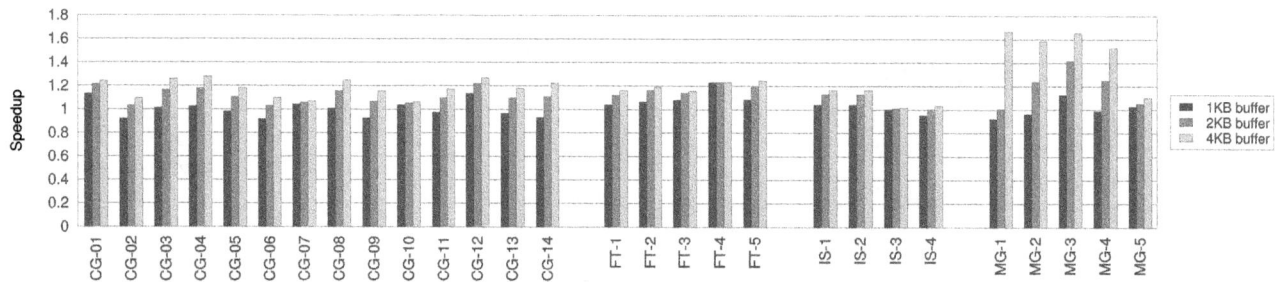

Figure 10: Speedup of the DMA-circular against a traditional DMA with 4KB buffers.

There is a direct relation between the control code overheads with a traditional DMA (Figure 6) and the speedup obtained by the DMA-circular. The loops, that present less overheads (CG-07, CG-10, IS-3, IS-4, and MG-5), obtain low speedups, less than 1.1x. Besides in these loops there are very little room for optimization, some speedup is obtained. Other loops that have higher overheads benefit more from the DMA-circular. On example, FT-2 have overheads of 50%, 40%, and 20% for 1KB, 2KB and 4KB buffers, respectively, and the obtained speedups in this loop for 1KB, 2KB, and 4KB buffers are 1.8x, 1.4x, and 1.2x, respectively. The same trend is observed in the other loops.

In general, the speedups are higher when small buffers are used. This is because small buffers introduce high overheads which are successfully accelerated with the DMA-circular. The obtained speedups for 2KB and 4KB buffers are lower than the ones obtained with 1KB buffers in CG, FT and IS loops. In the MG loops, the trend is a bit different. The overheads in all MG loops but MG-5 are more or less the same no matter the buffer size. As expected, the speedup is similar for all the tested buffer sizes. We can see that MG-1, MG-2, MG-3, and MG-4 have speedups ranging between 1.5x and 1.8x. Only MG-1 has a bit lower speedup for 2KB buffer, caused by the increased synchronization time due to wrong prefetching.

Figure 9 shows the control code overhead when the DMA-circular is used. Compared to a traditional DMA (Figure 6)

it is noticeable that the DMA-circular reduces the overheads significantly. We can see the resulting control code overhead almost never exceeds 15% of the execution time while in the baseline it was going up to 60% in some loops.

In conclusion, the DMA-circular obtains speedups of 1.2x to 2x with 1KB buffers and a little bit less with 2KB and 4KB buffers, from 1.1x to 1.6x. Moreover, the control code overheads are reduced to less than 15% in all cases.

4.4 Impact On The Local Memory Size

This section shows that the DMA-circular working with small buffers can be as efficient as a traditional DMA working with big buffers. In Figure 10 we show the speedup of the DMA-circular working with 1KB, 2KB and 4KB buffers against a traditional DMA working with 4KB buffers. The main observation is that the DMA-circular with 1KB buffers almost always outperforms a traditional DMA with 4KB buffers, except in some loops which present a slowdown of up to 10%. However, when the DMA-circular works with 2KB buffers, it outperforms a traditional DMA with two times bigger buffers in all cases, reaching even higher speedups when 4KB buffers are used.

This is an important advantage of DMA-circular. Being able to achieve good performance with small buffers, which is not possible with a traditional DMA, has tremendous benefits, especially in area and power. With a traditional DMA, the smaller the buffer, the more control bursts have to be

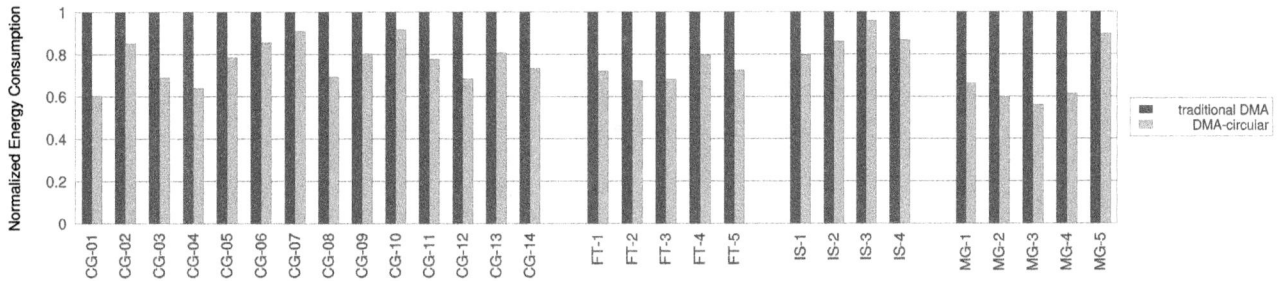

Figure 11: Energy consumption of the DMA-circular normalized against a traditional DMA.

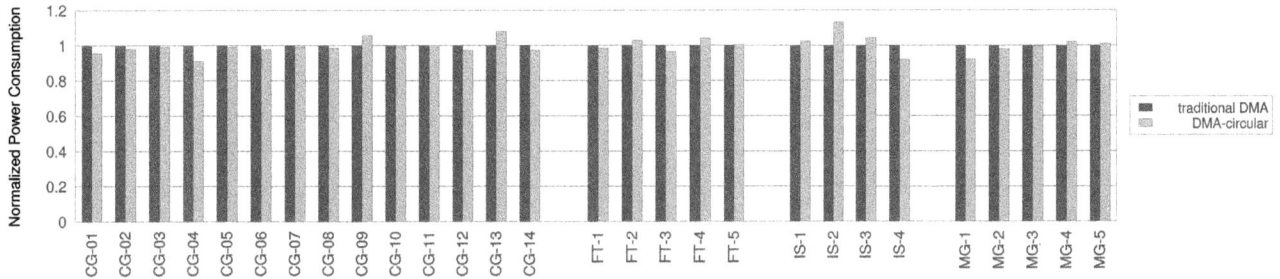

Figure 12: Power consumption of the DMA-circular normalized against a traditional DMA.

executed and, since they are costly, a big overhead is introduced. With the DMA-circular the execution of the control code has a very low cost so the increase of control burst executions becomes affordable. Being able to efficiently work with small buffers translates to being able to have smaller local memories, saving a lot of area in the chip and also reducing the power consumption.

4.5 Energy And Power Consumption

This section discusses the implication in energy and power consumption of the DMA-circular.

Figure 11 shows the energy consumption of a core equipped with the DMA-circular normalized to the energy consumption of a core with a traditional DMA, taking into consideration the energy consumed by a traditional DMA and the DMA-circular. The presented numbers are for a buffer size of 2KB. We observe that the energy consumed by a core with the DMA-circular is always lower than with a traditional DMA. The reason is that, even though the DMA-circular consumes more than a traditional DMA, the energy savings coming from executing less instructions in the control code are much bigger. On the one hand, the hardware structures of the DMA-circular increase the energy consumption for about 4%. The increase is little because the additional hardware structures are not very frequently triggered, just during the control phases, which now represent 15% of the execution time at most. The remaining 85% of the time, the hardware structures can be clock-gated, so to consume very little energy (we assume 10% of the maximum energy per cycle when off [4]). On the other hand, the number of instructions in the control code is drastically reduced: from hundreds of instructions per reference per control phase to just a load per reference per control phase. All these instructions that do not traverse the pipeline anymore (with its many power-hungry hardware structures) produce very important energy savings, from 10% to 40% in general, and up to 50% in MG-3.

The DMA-circular does not change the power consumption significantly, as shown in Figure 12. Since the benefits

in both performance and energy consumption are directly related to the decrease in instructions of the control code and the weight it has in the loops' execution time, when the average power is calculated, these two metrics compensate each other and the resulting power consumption is barely the same. In almost all loops the power consumption of the DMA-circular is similar to the baseline's power consumption, observing just loops CG-04, IS-4 and MG-1 with power savings of about 10% and loops CG-13 and IS-2 with power overheads of also about 10%.

5. RELATED WORK

Previous research works targeting the management of an on-chip local memory mainly differ on the existing hardware support for the actual management and how this hardware interacts with the software execution. In the case where no specific hardware support is available, explicit buffer allocation and a DMA programming style totally based on loop tiling techniques [8, 5] is the solution. This approach, however, requires precise information about memory aliasing of regular memory references at compile time which is not a case in our proposal.

S. Seo et al [18], propose a pure software cache architecture, with a configurable cache line size, a fast and adaptive placement and replacement mechanism for accelerator-based architectures with local memories. In general, this solution defines simple mechanisms and compiler code transformations to smooth the overhead related to the local memory management. The proposal in this paper is a natural hardware design that accelerates several aspects of the software-based solutions. The proposed DMA engine is general enough to support and accelerate most of the mechanisms in this work.

Software caching techniques have been also applied to reduce the amount of power consumption associated to cache management. These proposals face similar problems as the ones addressed in this work and introduce explicit hardware support that could be adopted for the management of a lo-

121

cal memory. For instance, Direct Addressed Caches [21] propose the elimination of the tag checks by making the hardware to remember the exact location of a cache line, so that hardware can access data directly. This proposal requires the definition of new registers in the architecture to relate load/store operation to specific cache lines, leaving to the compiler the decision of what memory references have to be associated to the additional registers.

In Osman Unsal et al. [19], a tag-less cache architecture for scratchpad memories is described. The miss handler is implemented in software but there is specific hardware to notify the program there has been a cache miss. New registers are introduced implementing the hotcachelines, associated to memory references that their access pattern can be easily predicted at compile time. The main aim of this approach is to reduce the energy consumption related to the tag checking. The scratchpad memory is totally managed by software, so there is no support for buffer allocation and memory disambiguation between buffers, and the eviction process of modified data is also under software control with no acceleration given by the hardware. All these points are addressed in the DMA-circular with dedicated hardware to accelerate these mechanisms.

Other works coming from embedded systems [16, 6] also address the management of a local memory. In general, these works target energy savings in the cache subsystem. The cache architecture is partitioned and fine grain placement mechanisms to skip the tag checks are introduced. The compiler generates enhanced load and stores operations that directly access to a specific partition. It is needed complex compiler analysis to appropriately map memory references to partitions. In general, this solution requires profile information, something very usual in embedded systems, but not so accepted for programming general purpose cores.

In this last context, similar ideas have been explored [10, 14, 17] but implemented on top of dynamic mechanisms supported in hardware at the cache logic level. These works define cache partitions to adapt to the observed locality at runtime. In general, all these works define two trends: first, place the control of the cache events at software level, and second, dynamically accommodate the cache mechanisms to the access patterns in the computation. The proposal in this paper mixes both strategies, and in particular takes the first strategy up to a limit where the DMA-circular is mostly controlled by software.

6. CONCLUSIONS

This paper proposes the DMA-circular, a new DMA controller that operates with on-chip local memories. The motivation of the design is to accelerate control code overheads of managing buffers in the local memories while not imposing programmability issues. The two key features of the new design are: the introduction of cache functionalities within the DMA controller and the addition of specific hardware blocks that accelerate the common control actions and events associated to the operability of a local memory.

The DMA-circular is evaluated with several high performance computational kernels of the NAS benchmark suite. The results indicate that the design reduces the control code overheads under 15% of the execution time. The overall performance of the tested kernels is improved between 1.2x to 2x when DMA-circular is used. Also, energy consumption is reduced from 5% to 40% respect the energy consumption when old DMA is used. Reduced energy consumption is proportional to the obtained improvement in the execution time which turns the power disipation to be comparable to the power disipation of the systems using a traditional DMA.

7. ACKNOWLEDGMENTS

We thankfully acknowledge the support of the European Commission through the HiPEAC-2 Network of Excellence (FP7/IST 217068), the support of the Spanish Ministry of Education (TIN2007-60625, and CSD2007-00050), the Generalitat de Catalunya (2009-SGR-980), FPI scholarship (BES-2008-008885) and the BSC-IBM MareIncognito project.

8. REFERENCES

[1] D. Bailey et al. The nas parallel benchmarks. In *SC'91*, pages 158–165, 1991.

[2] J. Balart et al. A novel asynchronous software cache implementation for the cell-be processor. In *LCPC'07*, pages 125–140, 2007.

[3] R. Banakar et al. Scratchpad memory: design alternative for cache on-chip memory in embedded systems. In *CODES'02*, pages 73–78, 2002.

[4] D. Brooks, V. Tiwari, and M. Martonosi. Wattch: a framework for architectural-level power analysis and optimizations. In *ISCA'00*, pages 83–94. ACM, 2000.

[5] T. Chen et al. Optimizing the use of static buffers for dma on a cell chip. In *LCPC'07*, pages 314–329, 2007.

[6] H. Cho et al. Dynamic data scratchpad memory management for a memory subsystem with an MMU. In *LCTES'07*, pages 195–206, 2007.

[7] A. Deutsch. Interprocedural may-alias analysis for pointers: beyond k-limiting. In *PLDI'94*, 1994.

[8] A. E. Eichenberger et al. Optimizing compiler for the cell processor. In *PACT'05*, pages 161–172, 2005.

[9] A. E. Eichenberger et al. Using advanced compiler technology to exploit the performance of the cell broadband engine™ architecture. *IBM Systems Journal*, 2006.

[10] A. Gonzalez et al. A data cache with multiple caching strategies tuned to different types of locality. In *ICS'95*, pages 338–347, 1995.

[11] M. Gonzalez et al. Hybrid access-specific software cache techniques for the cell be architecture. In *PACT'08*, pages 292–302, 2008.

[12] W. Landi et al. A safe approximate algorithm for interprocedural aliasing. In *PLDI'92*, 1992.

[13] T. Liu et al. DBDB: optimizing DMATransfer for the cell be architecture. In *ICS'09*, pages 36–45, 2009.

[14] V. Milutinovic et al. The Split Spatial/Non-Spatial Cache: A Performance and Complexity Evaluation. *Newsletter of TCCA*, pages 3–10, 1999.

[15] Y. Paek et al. Efficient and precise array access analysis. *TOPLAS'02*, 24(1):65–109, 2002.

[16] R. Ravindran et al. Compiler-managed partitioned data caches for low power. In *LCTES'07*, pages 237–247, 2007.

[17] J. Rivers et al. Reducing conflicts in direct-mapped caches with a temporality-based design. In *ICPP'02*, pages 154–163, 2002.

[18] S. Seo et al. Design and implementation of software-managed caches for multicores with local memory. In *HPCA'09*, pages 55–66, 2009.

[19] O. S. Unsal et al. Cool-cache for hot multimedia. In *MICRO'01*, pages 274–283, 2001.

[20] R. P. Wilson et al. Efficient context-sensitive pointer analysis for c programs. In *PLDI'95*, 1995.

[21] E. Witchel et al. Direct addressed caches for reduced power consumption. In *MICRO'01*, pages 124–133, 2001.

[22] M. T. Yourst. PTLsim: A Cycle Accurate Full System x86-64 Microarchitectural Simulator. In *ISPASS'07*, pages 23–34, 2007.

Studying The Impact Of Application-level Optimizations On The Power Consumption Of Multi-Core Architectures *

S M Faizur Rahman
Univ Of Texas At San Antonio
srahman@cs.utsa.edu

Jichi Guo
Univ Of Texas At San Antonio
jguo@cs.utsa.edu

Akshatha Bhat
Univ Of Texas At San Antonio
abhat@cs.utsa.edu

Carlos Garcia
Univ Of Texas At San Antonio
carlosg@cs.utsa.edu

Majedul Haque Sujon
Univ Of Texas At San Antonio
msujon@cs.utsa.edu

Qing Yi
Univ Of Texas At San Antonio
qingyi@cs.utsa.edu

Chunhua Liao
Lawrence Livermore Nat. Lab
liach@llnl.gov

Daniel Quinlan
Lawrence Livermore Nat. Lab
dquinlan@llnl.gov

ABSTRACT

This paper studies the overall system power variations of two multi-core architectures, an 8-core Intel and a 32-core AMD workstation, while using these machines to execute a wide variety of sequential and multi-threaded benchmarks using varying compiler optimization settings and runtime configurations. Our extensive experimental study provides insights for answering two questions: 1) what degrees of impact can application level optimizations have on reducing the overall system power consumption of modern CMP architectures; and 2) what strategies can compilers and application developers adopt to achieve a balanced performance and power efficiency for applications from a variety of science and embedded systems domains.

Categories and Subject Descriptors

D.3.4 [**Software**]: Programming Languages—*Processors* [Optimization, Compilers]; C.1.4 [**Computer System Organization**]: Processor Architectures—*Parallel Architectures*

Keywords

Power consumption, energy efficiency, application level optimization, compiler optimization

1. INTRODUCTION

Power consumption and dissipation is a primary concern in the design and deployment of modern architectures, from high-end supercomputers, to multi-core desktops, to energy efficient laptops, and to embedded chips in cell phones and MP3s. Since it critically determines the operating costs,

*This research was supported in part by the National Science Foundation under Grants 0833203, 0747357, 0855247, and by the Department of Energy under Grant DE-SC0001770

cooling requirements, and failure rates of key architectural components, software should be made energy-aware and use the full power of computers only when necessary. Most Operating Systems can automatically scale down the voltage or frequency of microprocessors when they are idle. However, it is less clear how compilers and application developers can effectively optimize the energy efficiency of their applications while preserving a satisfactory level of performance.

This paper conducts an extensive experimental study to help compilers and developers make informed decisions when optimizing their applications for energy efficient computing. Based on an existing infrastructure for empirical tuning of application performance [18], we studied the variation of the overall system power consumption of multi-core architectures when using the machines to evaluate a wide variety of different applications using varying optimization and runtime configurations. The study has produced insightful answers to the following important questions.

- How much impact can application level optimizations make in terms of reducing the overall system power and energy consumption of modern CMP architectures?

- What strategies can compilers and application developers adopt to achieve a balanced performance and power efficiency?

The results are significant and can be used to guide future compilers and developers to effectively reduce the power consumption of their applications while achieving a balanced level of performance and energy efficiency. In particular, we found that for most benchmarks, while the variations in performance are much more dramatic than those in power consumption, there seems to be no direct correlation between the performance attained and the power consumption incurred by application-level optimizations. Similar levels of performance can often be attained while incurring dramatically different power consumptions. As a result, collectively optimizing both the performance and power efficiency of applications is not only possible, but also immensely profitable.

The rest of the paper is organized as follows. Section 2 summarizes related work. Section 3 presents the benchmarks used in the evaluation and our experimental methodology. Section 4 presents the overall variations of power consumptions when running the benchmarks with different optimization and runtime configurations. Sections 5 through 7

id	name	suite	parallel.	description
1	jacobi7	kernel	pthread	7 point jacobi stencil kernel
2	jacobi27	kernel	pthread	27 point jacobi stencil kernel
3	gauss7	kernel	pthread	7 point gaussian stencil kernel
4	gemm	kernel	openmp	Matrix-matrix multiplication
5	gemv	kernel	openmp	Matrix-vector multiplication
6	ger	kernel	openmp	Vector-vector multiplication
7	BT	NPB	openmp	Block Tridiagonal PDE solver
8	CG	NPB	openmp	Conjugate Gradient
9	DC	NPB	openmp	Data Cube operator
10	EP	NPB	openmp	Embarrassingly Parallel
11	FT	NPB	openmp	Fast Fourier Transform
12	IS	NPB	openmp	Integer Sort
13	LU	NPB	openmp	non-linear PDE solver
14	LU-hp	NPB	openmp	The hyperplane version of LU
15	MG	NPB	openmp	MultiGrid solver
16	SP	NPB	openmp	Scalar Pentadiagonal PDE solver
17	Black-scholes	PARSEC	openmp, pthread, tbb	Computational Financial Application
18	Bodytrack	PARSEC	openmp, pthread, tbb	Realtime Computer Vision Application
19	Stream-cluster	PARSEC	pthread, tbb	Machine Learning Application
20	Swaptions	PARSEC	pthread, tbb	Computational Financial Application
21	Dedup	PARSEC	pthread	Enterprise Storage Kernel
22	Freqmine	PARSEC	openmp	Data-mining Application
23	Fluid-animate	PARSEC	pthread, tbb	Animation Application
24	Canneal	PARSEC	pthread	Engineering Application
25	Raytrace	PARSEC	pthread	Rendering 3D Graphics
26	Vips	PARSEC	pthread	Multimedia Application
27	x264	PARSEC	pthread	Multimedia Application
28	Facesim	PARSEC	pthread	Animation Application
29	DMR	LoneStar	Galois	Mesh Refinement Application
30	DT	LoneStar	Galois	Mesh Generation Application
31	SP	LoneStar	Galois	Heuristic SAT-solver
32	adpcm	MiBench	Serial	Adaptive Differential Pulse Code Modulation
33	basicmath	MiBench	Serial	Mathematical calculations
34	bitcount	MiBench	Serial	Bit manipulation
35	CRC32	MiBench	Serial	Cyclic Redundancy Check
36	djkstr	MiBench	Serial	shortest path algorithm
37	FFT	MiBench	Serial	Digital signal processing
38	jpeg	MiBench	Serial	Image compression
39	patricia	MiBench	Serial	Traverse sparse leaf trees
40	qsort	MiBench	Serial	Sorting of large arrays
41	sha	MiBench	Serial	Secure hash algorithm
42	susan	MiBench	Serial	Image recognition package

Table 1: Benchmarks used for experiments

study the impact of varying groups of optimizations. Finally, Section 8 presents our conclusions.

2. RELATED WORK

Power consumption and dissipation has long been an important concern in CPU design, especially for embedded systems [14, 4]. Optimizations for power management have traditionally focused on *dynamic voltage and frequency scaling* (DVFS) by operating systems [8, 5]. Compiler optimizations to enhance power efficiency of applications have mostly focused on varying instruction scheduling schemes [13, 16, 22, 26] and thread-allocation and scheduling strategies [2, 1, 23]. Power consumption has been estimated using architectural simulation [4, 16, 2], offline profiling [6], and real time monitoring of hardware counters [23, 18]. This paper investigates the impact of a wide variety of compiler optimization and runtime configurations on the overall system level power with DVFS turned-off to minimize OS interferences.

Valluri and John [24] studied the impact of different com-

piler optimization levels on processor power/energy on a Dec Alpha 21064 CPU. Kandemir et al [11] studied the power/energy impact of both low-level compiler optimizations (instruction scheduling and register assignments) and three loop reordering optimizations (loop interchange, tiling, and unrolling) on both the CPU and the memory system using a matrix multiplication computation. Seng and Tullsen [21] studied the power/energy effects of different compiler optimization levels and three specific optimizations (loop unrolling, vectorization, and function inlining) on an Intel Pentium 4 Processor. In contrast, our work uses a much more extensive collection of benchmarks to empirically study the impact of both compiler optimization and runtime configurations on the overall system power consumption and dissipation of modern CMP architectures. Our objective focuses on providing insights to guide future compiler and application-level optimizations, with supporting compiler-architecture co-design only as a secondary goal.

3. EXPERIMENTAL DESIGN

We have studied 42 benchmarks, summarized in Table 1, by evaluating these benchmarks under varying compiler optimization and runtime configurations on two multi-core architectures. The following first presents details of the benchmarks and then summarizes our tuning infrastructure and methodology of data collection.

3.1 Benchmarks

Table 1 summarizes the 42 benchmarks we used in our evaluation, where each benchmark is given a unique integer identifier. Some benchmarks, e.g., those in rows 1-16, include both multi-threaded and sequential implementations, while others include only sequential implementations (e.g., rows 32-42) or only multi-threaded implementations (e.g. lines 17-31). The following further categorizes these benchmarks into five groups.

3.1.1 Matrix And Stencil Kernels

We have selected six scientific kernels: three dense matrix computations (rows 4-6) and three stencil codes (rows 1-3), to study the impact of finely parameterized loop optimizations. Using POET [28], an interpreted program transformation language designed to support the fine-grained parameterization of compiler optimizations, a specialized optimization script is built for each kernel so that the configurations of these optimizations can be empirically tuned [19, 27]. Each matrix kernel is optimized with 6 optimizations: OpenMP loop parallezation, loop blocking, array copying, loop unroll-jam, scalar replacement, and innermost loop unrolling [27]. Each stencil kernel is parallelized with three strategies, single time step parallelization, pipelining, and wavefront parallelization, with the locality within each thread enhanced with loop blocking combined with time-skewing [19]. Each POET script can be reconfigured via command-line options so that the blocking and unrolling factor of each loop can be arbitrarily adjusted, and each optimization can be optionally turned off.

3.1.2 NAS Parallel Benchmarks (NPB) [10]

This is a set of programs derived from computational fluid dynamics applications (rows 7-16 of Table 1), and we have selected their OpenMP [7] implementations in NPB version 3.2 [10]. We have compiled each of these benchmarks with-

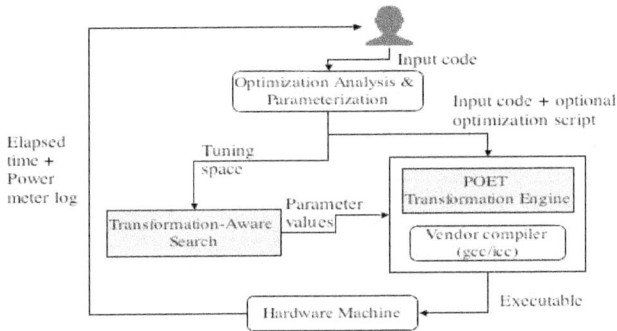

Figure 1: Empirical Tuning Workflow

out any source level modification, using vendor compilers with varying optimization levels, and have evaluated them with different thread allocation and scheduling policies.

3.1.3 PARSEC benchmarks [3]

The Princeton Application Repository for Shared-Memory Computers (PARSEC) is a benchmark suite focusing on next generation shared-memory programs for chip-multiporcessors. It includes applications in recognition, mining and synthesis (RMS), and the applications mimic large-scale multithreaded commercial programs using POSIX threads [15], OpenMP [7], and Intel Threading Building Blocks (TBB) [20]. We used all available parallel implementations and compiled them with no modification using vendor compilers with different optimization flags.

3.1.4 LoneStar benchmarks [12]

The LoneStar suite includes C++ applications which use pointer-based irregular data structures (e.g. graphs, trees) and amorphous data-parallelism, where an initial set of tasks which process composite data structures dynamically create additional tasks during execution. We selected three of these benchmarks (rows 29-31 of Table 1) which have been parallelized using the Galois system [17], which provide runtime support for speculative execution of tasks. We used the POET transformation engine, shown in Figure 1, to parameterize their invocations to the Galois library with varying runtime task scheduling policies (e.g., global and distributed task queues and stacks with different chunk sizes).

3.1.5 MiBench benchmarks [9]

This is a set of commercially representative embedded programs of six categories: Automotive and Industrial Control, Netowrk, Security, Consumer Devices, Office Automation, and Telecommuncations. We selected 11 applications from this suite (rows 32-42 of Table 1). All benchmarks are serial, and we have compiled them using vendor compilers with varying optimization flags.

3.2 Tuning Infrastructure

Figure 1 shows the workflow of our empirical tuning infrastructure, which we use to collect runtime statistics of the 42 benchmarks shown in Table 1. For each benchmark, we have determined its tuning space based on the underlying runtime model (i.e., sequential vs. multi-threaded) and the varying runtime configurations that are applicable (e.g., using different numbers of threads and different task scheduling policies). We compiled the NAS, PARSEC, and MiBench benchmarks only using vendor compilers with varying optimization flags. For the matrix and stencil kernels and the

LoneStar benchmarks, however, we have used POET [28], an interpreted program transformation language, to support the fine-grained parameterization and tuning of optimizations. As shown in Figure 1, an optional POET optimization script was developed, either manually [19] or automatically via an optimizing compiler [27], for each of these benchmarks, and an optional POET transformation engine was invoked to apply additional source-level optimizations before invoking the vendor compilers.

3.3 Empirical Data Collection

We performed our experiments on two multi-core machines: an 8-core Dell Precision T7500n workstation with two 2.27GHz Intel Xeon quad-core processors (each with 4*256KB L2 and 4MB shared L3 cache) and 4GB memory; and a 32-core HPX workstation with four 2.0GHz eight-core AMD Opteron processors (each with 8*512KB L2 and 12MB shared L3 cache) and 16*4GB memory. For each machine, we connected a *Watts Up PRO 99333* power meter [25] with its power supply to log down the overall system power consumption per second of the machine while evaluating each benchmark in Table 1 with varying compiler optimizations and runtime configurations.

To ensure the accuracy of measurement, our scripts ran each benchmark continuously for at least 5-6 seconds so that the power meter can accurately log down power consumption of the duration. While using the machines to compile and run each benchmark, each machine is left completely idle otherwise. After each evaluation, we let the machine cool down until the power meter reading goes back to the lowest threshold before starting the next evaluation, to ensure statistics of different runs are completely independent of each other. Besides the power meter readings, while evaluating each benchmark, we collected both the elapsed time and the number of floating point and integer operations performed during each evaluation.

All benchmarks were compiled using gcc 4.4.4 and icc 11.1 on the 8-core Intel machine, and were compiled using gcc 4.6.1 on the 32-core AMD machine. For each runtime configuration, we repeated the evaluation three times and report the average of the measurements. The variations among repetitive evaluations are very minor as the machines were kept free of external interferences during the evaluations.

3.4 Terminologies

We use the following terminologies throughout the rest of the paper in discussion of our experimental results.

- *Peak Power*: the highest power consumption rate, in terms of *Watts*, attained at any moment across all evaluations of each benchmark;

- *Max (or Min) Average Power*: here the power consumption rates attained throughout the evaluation of each configuration are averaged for the duration, and the highest (or lowest) average rate among all configurations of the same benchmark is reported;

- *Max (or Min) MFLOPS*, the highest (or lowest) MFLOPS (Millions of floating point operations per second) rate attained among all configurations of each benchmark; For benchmarks 29-31, MIPS (Millions of integer operations per second) rates are used instead;

- *MFLOPS on max (or min) average power*, MFLOPS of

125

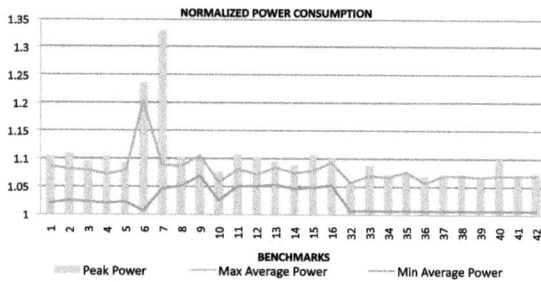

(a) Power normalized against machine idle power(154W)

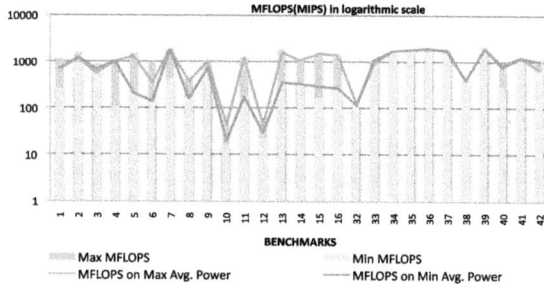

(b) *MFLOPS* of benchmarks

Figure 2: Sequential benchmark on 8-core Intel

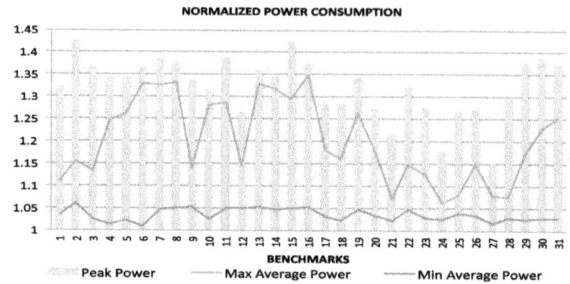

(a) Power normalized against machine idle power(154W)

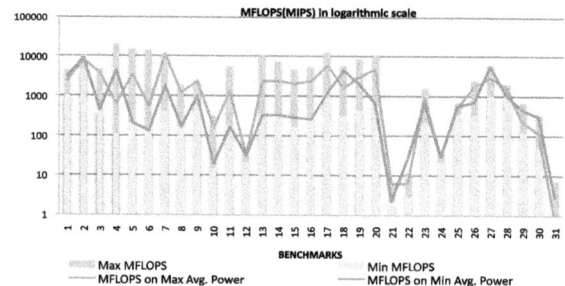

(b) *MFLOPS* of benchmarks (benchmarks 29-31 use *MIPS*)

Figure 3: Parallel benchmark on 8-core Intel

the corresponding configuration that attained the *Max* (or *Min*) average power for each benchmark.

4. POWER CONSUMPTION VARIATION

Figures 2-4 show the overall variations of performance and power efficiencies when evaluating different benchmarks with varying compilation and runtime configurations.

From Figure 2(a), for sequential benchmarks, the power consumption peaks at 133% of the baseline on the 8-core Intel (we omitted evaluating sequential codes on the AMD machine as their runtime configurations are similar to those on the 8-core Intel), and the *average power consumption* are between 101%-120% of the machine idle power baseline. When running multi-threaded implementations of the benchmarks, the power consumption peaks at 143% of the machine idle power consumption baseline on the 8-core Intel machine in Figure 3(a) and at 170% of the baseline on the 32-core AMD in Figure 4(a). The *average power consumption* range between 101%-135% of the baseline on the 8-core Intel and between 101-165% on the 32-core AMD.

From Figures 2-4(b), the variations in performance are much more dramatic, ranging from 1% (benchmark 41 in Figure 2(b)) to orders of magnitude (e.g., benchmarks 19 and 20 in Figures 3-4(b)). So optimizing for performance naturally lead to better overall energy savings in most cases, as energy consumed = average power consumption * execution time. However, for some benchmarks, e.g., 32-39 and 41 in Figure 2, where compiler optimizations makes little difference in performance, the optimizations can instead focus on reducing the power consumption of the benchmarks, where up to 10% of energy saving may be resulted.

In Figures 2-4(b), on top of max and min MFLOPS (MIPS) rates attained for each benchmark, we plotted the corresponding MFLOPS (MIPS) rates when incurring the max and min average power consumptions. On the 8-core Intel, two parallel benchmarks (7, 9) in Figure 3(b) and eight se-

quential benchmarks (8-11, 12-16) in Figure 2(b) attained max MFLOPS rates while incurring the max average power consumptions. On the other hand, two parallel benchmarks (18, 27) in Figure 3(b) and eight sequential benchmarks (4, 7, 33-36, 39, 41) in Figure 2(b) attained max MFLOPS rates while incurring the least average power consumption. Further, for many benchmarks, incurring the min average power has attained comparable performance as that attained while incurring max power. In Figure 4(b), on the 32-core AMD, although incurring max power consumption has resulted in significantly better performance by employing a larger number of threads, the performance difference is insignificant for a number of benchmarks (e.g., 20, 24, 27, 29), and min average power has resulted in the best performance for 2 of the benchmarks (30, 31).

Therefore, when the inherit amount of concurrency within an application is limited, there seems to be little direct correlation between the performance levels attained and the power consumptions incurred by application-level optimizations. A pattern can be observed that when performance optimizations are ineffective (i.e., when performance enhancement is difficult), the optimization can instead focus on reducing the power consumption to achieve significant energy savings. Further, similar levels of performance can often be attained while incurring dramatically different power consumption, so collectively optimizing both the performance and power efficiencies of applications is not only possible, but also profitable, for a majority of the applications.

5. COMPILER OPTIMIZATION LEVELS

To investigate the overall trend of how applications are impacted by the aggressiveness of compiler optimizations, Figures 5-6 compare the MFLOPS and average power consumption attained when compiling the sequential and parallel implementations of each benchmark using the Intel *icc* compiler on the 8-core Intel machine with -O0, -O1, -O2, and -O3 optimization flags, which instruct the compiler to

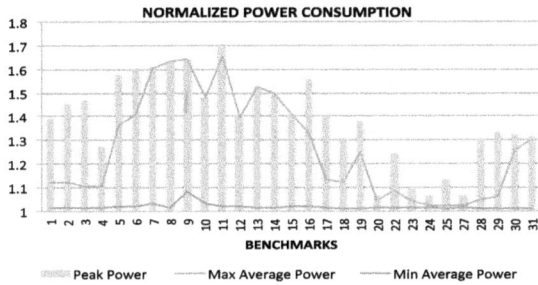

(a) Power normalized against machine idle power(360W)

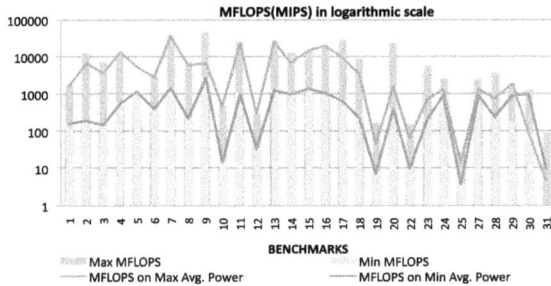

(b) *MFLOPS* of benchmarks (benchmarks 29-31 use *MIPS*)

Figure 4: Parallel benchmark on 32-core AMD

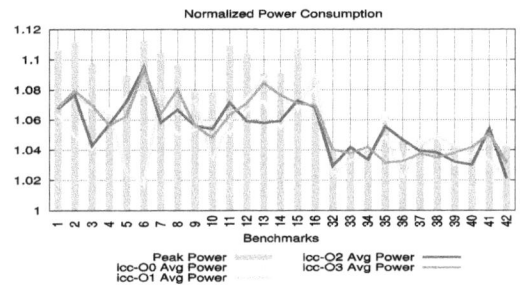

(a) Power normalized against machine idle power(154W)

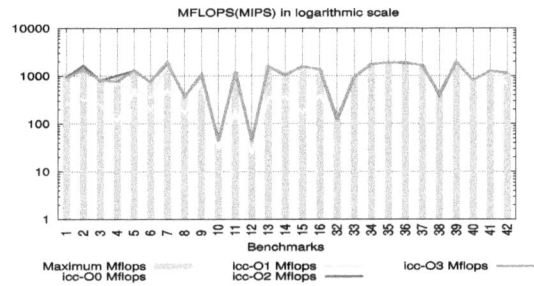

(b) *MFLOPS* of benchmarks

Figure 5: Impact of compiler optimization levels on Sequential benchmark in 8-core Intel

apply no optimizations, to optimize for speed (-O1 disables some optimizations that increase code size), and to apply additional loop transformations and data prefetching for improved memory-usage efficiency respectively. We study optimization levels of *icc* because of its known effectiveness in optimizing for Intel processors. The 32-core AMD machine uses only *gcc*, so its statistics are omitted here. To isolate the impact of vendor compiler optimizations, for the matrix and stencil kernels, we have disabled all the POET optimizations except OpenMP parallelization. For all benchmarks, we have used 8 threads with the default runtime thread scheduling policy to evaluate their parallel implementations.

From Figures 5-6(b), compiling using icc with O1- O3 flags makes little difference in the performance levels achieved, although all of them are able to significantly improve the performance levels attained by -O0 by a large margin for about half of the benchmarks. For the other half (benchmarks 1-3, 21-31,32-41), all the optimization levels attained similar performance as icc failed to decipher the complex data flow within these codes. Overall, the different optimization levels are fairly consistent in terms of affecting the performance levels of different benchmarks.

However, when looking at their impact on the average power consumption in Figures 5-6(a), the trend is rather mystic. In particular, in Figure 5(a), the average power consumption of differently optimized sequential codes vary by up to 5% (benchmark 35), but there does not seem to be any correlation between the relative performance and power efficiencies of the differently optimized code. In Figure 6(a), for the multithreaded implementations, the power variation is slightly bigger, by up to 11% (benchmark 6). While neither -O2 nor -O3 has a clear advantage over each other, they triggered similar or lower power consumption than -O0 for a majority of cases. Their better power efficiency is likely a benefit of the reduction of synchronization overhead by the OpenMP optimizations which are disabled by -O0.

Although the performance levels attained by icc -O2 and

-O3 flags are almost identical, the optimized codes in many cases differ by a nontrivial margin in their average power consumptions, both for sequential and multithreaded implementations. This again indicates that reordering optimizations such as loop transformations and data prefetching can often be used to reduce power consumption of applications without sacrificing performance.

6. IMPACT OF MULTI-THREADING

Multi-threaded applications typically consume more power than sequential codes as they make more CPU cores busy. The performance and power consumption of their evaluations are directly impacted by the varying numbers of threads being used as well the the allocation and scheduling policies for the concurrent threads.

6.1 Varying Numbers Of Threads

Figures 7-8 compare the performance and power efficiencies of evaluating the multithreaded benchmarks using varying numbers of threads on the 8-core Intel and the 32-core AMD machines. Within each figure, the average power consumption and MFLOPS rates when evaluating each benchmark using different numbers of threads are plotted on top of the highest power and MFLOPS rates across all different configurations.

From Figures 7-8(a), on both machines, the average power consumption are relatively sorted in increasing order as the number of threads used to evaluate each benchmark increases. In Figure 7 (a), the ordering is violated only in two cases for benchmarks 5 and 16, where using two threads had incurred higher average power consumption than using four threads. In Figure 8(a), four similar cases (benchmark 15, 17, 25 and 28) exist on the 32-core AMD, where using 32 threads has incurred less power consumption than the other configurations. The power consumption variations range from 1% - 25% on the 8-core Intel in Figure 7(a) and

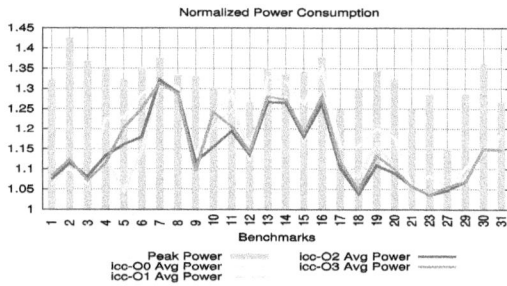

(a) Power normalized against machine idle power(154W)

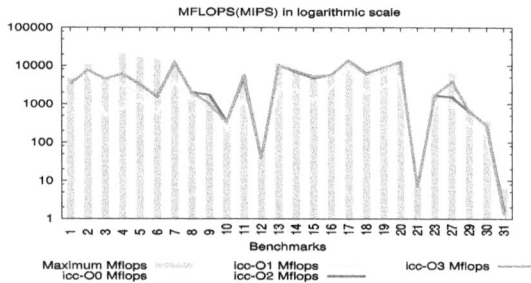

(b) *MFLOPS* of benchmarks (benchmarks 29-31 use *MIPS*)

Figure 6: Impact of compiler optimization levels on Parallel benchmark in 8-core Intel

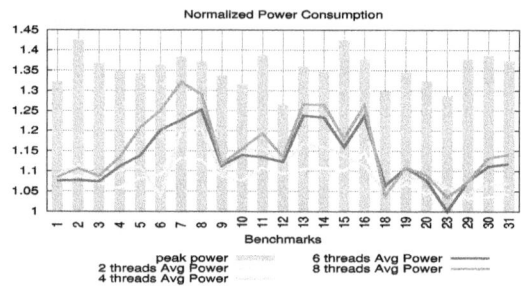

(a) Power normalized against machine idle power(154W)

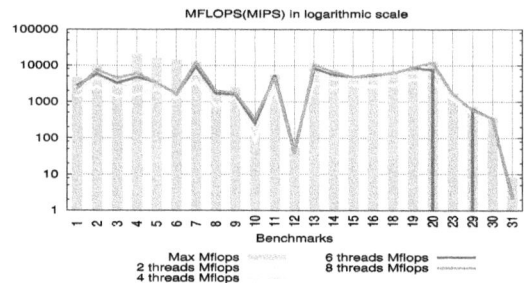

(b) *MFLOPS* of benchmarks

*There is no data for benchmark 23 using 6 threads because the benchmark requires the total number of threads to be a power of 2.

Figure 7: Impact of varying numbers of threads on 8-core Intel

from 1% - 40% on the 32-core AMD in Figure 8(a). From Figures 7-8(b), using more threads has resulted in better overall performance in most cases on both machines in a consistent fashion.

We believe the small number of anomalies in Figures 7-8(a) are due to the default thread scheduling policies on the machines failing to group related threads on the same sockets. As discussed in the following, the overhead of the extra data movement across the sockets could be prohibitive when using inefficient thread scheduling schemes.

6.2 Varying Scheduling Policies

The efficiencies of multithreaded applications are often affected by how their concurrent tasks are distributed to different threads and how the threads are scheduled on different CPU cores. Figures 9-10 show their impact on the performance and average power consumption of 16 selected benchmarks on both the 8-core Intel and the 32-core AMD machines. These selected benchmarks are parallelized either through OpenMP, where we used the OMP_SCHEDULE environment variable to specify both a scheduling policy (STATIC, DYNAMIC or GUIDED) and a chunk size for the GUIDED policy, or through amorphous data parallelism, where we used POET scripts to vary the dynamic task scheduling policies using ChunkedFIFO, ChunkedLIFO, dChunked-FIFO or dChunkedLIFO and associated chunk sizes for the three LoneStar benchmarks (29-31). The other parallel benchmarks are not selected as it is more difficult to modify their scheduling policies. For each selected benchmark, *Max (or Min) average power* stands for the highest (or lowest) average power consumption rate across different scheduling policies and associated chunk sizes, and *MFLOPS on max (or min) average power* stand for their MFLOPS rates when attaining the corresponding power consumption.

From Figure 9(b), on the 8-core Intel, the varying schedule policies made little difference in the overall performance of

the benchmarks, as the Max and Min *MFLOPS* are within 1-2% of each other for all benchmarks. Their impact on the average power consumption in Figure 9(a), however, is more significant, where the variation is up to 8% of the machine idle power for two OpenMP NAS benchmarks and is close to 20% for the three LoneStar benchmarks. Since the 8-core Intel machine has only two sockets, and 8 threads are used to evaluate each benchmark, the dynamic scheduling of tasks may not significantly impact the performance. However, the movement of data resulted from different scheduling policies can significantly impact the power/energy consumption of applications, even on a machine with only two sockets.

From Figure 10(a), a similar degree of variation on the average power consumption can be observed on the 32-core AMD machine, where 5%-28% of variation is observed for the NAS and LoneStar benchmarks. However, as the number of CPU cores increase, the performance of applications can also be dramatically impacted by the scheduling policies, by up to factors of 7 (benchmark 9) in Figure 10(b).

An interesting trend is that when incurring the highest average power consumption, the corresponding MFLOPS rates are either the best among all other scheduling policies, or the worst. A natural speculation from this trend is that when the extra data movements among the CPU cores are necessary and productive, they lead to the best performance. But when they are unnecessary, they clog the communication channels of other useful data movements and lead to the worst performance. Note that in many cases the best performance is attained while incurring the lowest power consumption. Therefore adapting scheduling policies to minimize unnecessary data movements can dramatically improve both the performance and power efficiencies of multithreaded applications on many-core architectures and should be exploited whenever possible.

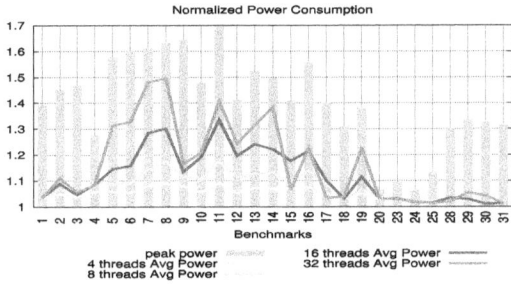

(a) Power normalized against machine idle power(360W)

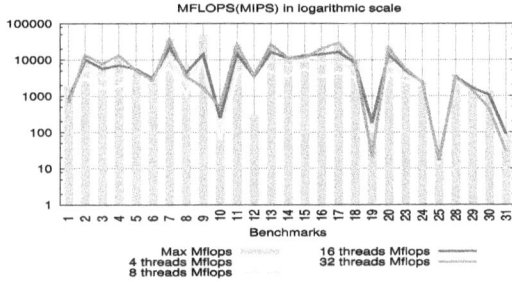

(b) *MFLOPS* of benchmarks (benchmarks 29-31 use *MIPS*)

Figure 8: Impact of varying numbers of threads on 32-core AMD

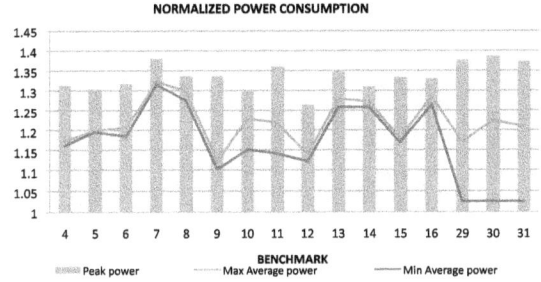

(a) Power normalized against machine idle power(154W)

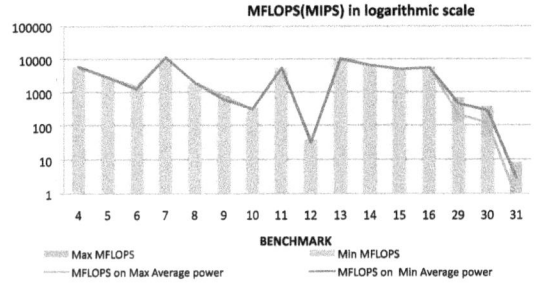

(b) *MFLOPS* of benchmarks (benchmarks 29-31 use *MIPS*)

Figure 9: Impact of scheduling policies on 8-core Intel

6.3 Thread Affinity

Data locality is an important factor that often critically determines the overall performance of multi-threaded applications. Our 32-core AMD and 8-core intel machines have 4 and 2 sockets respectively. To investigate the impact of placing related threads on different sockets, we pinned down each thread to a specific core using environment variables (e.g., GOMP_CPU_AFFINITY for the gcc compiler) for OpenMP applications and using library calls for applications parallelized with Pthread.

Figures 11-12 show the impact of evaluating the selected benchmarks with varying thread affinity configurations on the 8-core intel and 32-core AMD machines, where *Max (or Min) average power* stand for the highest (or lowest) average power consumption across different affinity configurations, *MFLOPS on max (or min) average power* plot their MFLOPS rates when incurring the corresponding power consumption, *Max (or Min) MFLOPS* stand for the highest and lowest MFLOPS rates achieved across different affinity configurations, and *Average power on max (or min) MFLOPS* plot their corresponding average power consumption.

From Figures 11-12(a), different thread affinity configurations have resulted in significant variations in the average power consumption of these benchmarks, ranging from 2%-15% on the 8-core intel and up to 25% on the 32-core AMD. The variation in performance (MFLOPS rates) in Figures 11-12(b) is more sporadic. On the 8-core Intel, variation of up to 120% in performance can be observed for benchmark 6 in Figure 11(b). In Figure12(b), on the 32-core Intel, a variation by factors of 6 is observed for benchmark 7 but the variation is small otherwise.

Therefore, thread affinities seem to significantly affect the power consumption of applications in a majority of cases but makes a significant difference in performance only occasionally. Therefore it should definitely be exploited for collective optimization of performance and power efficiency.

There does not seem to be any direct correlation between the performance and the power efficiency of the different configurations, which indicates empirical tuning may be required.

7. SEQUENTIAL OPTIMIZATIONS

We have isolated five optimizations, cache blocking, unroll&jam, scalar replacement, loop unrolling, and SSE vectorization, which aim to enhance the efficiency of memory, register and instruction scheduling within individual CPU cores, to study their respective impact on the performance and power efficiencies of the sequential implementations of our benchmarks. The following presents our results of using the 8-core Intel machine to evaluate the sequential benchmarks compiled with the icc compiler using *-O2*, combined with POET optimization scripts when appropriate.

7.1 Cache Blocking

For the six matrix/stencil kernels (benchmarks 1-6) and the three LoneStar benchmarks (29-31), we used POET optimization scripts to either apply loop blocking (for the matrix and stencil kernels) or automatically revise the chunk sizes of task scheduling (for the LoneStar benchmarks) to enhance cache reuse. All benchmarks are evaluated using only a single thread. Note that although the LoneStar benchmarks use amorphous data parallelism, evaluating them using one thread with different chunk sizes for task scheduling would effectively serve the purpose of cache blocking.

Figure 13 shows the impact of applying cache blocking to the sequential implementations of these benchmarks with varying blocking factors, where *Max (or min) average power* stand for the highest (or lowest) average power consumption across different blocking factors, *MFLOPS on max (or min) average power* plot the MFLOPS rates when incurring the corresponding power consumption, *Max (or min) MFLOPS* stand for the highest (or lowest) MFLOPS rates achieved across different blocking factors, and *Average power on max*

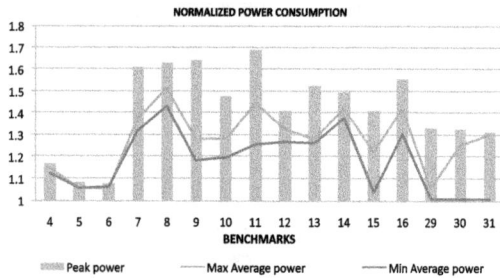

(a) Power normalized against machine idle power(360W)

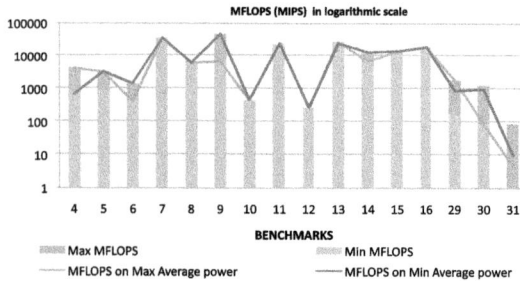

(b) *MFLOPS* of benchmarks (benchmarks 29-31 use *MIPS*)

Figure 10: Impact of scheduling policies on 32-core AMD

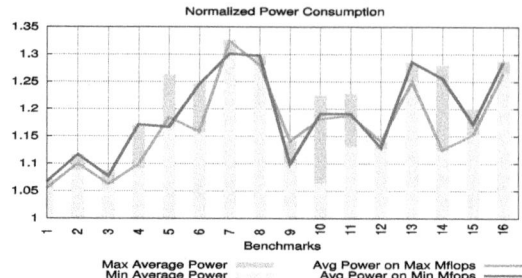

(a) Power normalized against machine idle power(154W)

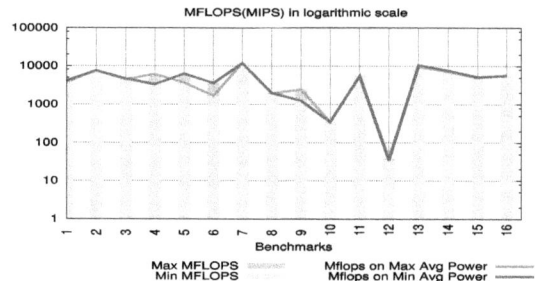

(b) *MFLOPS* of benchmarks

Figure 11: Impact of different thread affinites on 8-core Intel

(or min) MFLOPS plot their corresponding average power consumption rates.

From the graphs, different cache blocking factors have resulted in significant variations in both performance and power consumptions of these benchmarks. In particular, the variations are 5-18% in power consumption and 15-60% in performance (MFLOPS rates). Further, attaining max MFLOPS has required higher power consumption than that required by attaining min MFLOPS for all benchmarks except benchmark 4 (the matrix multiplication kernel), where close to max MFLOPS performance can be achieved while incurring the min average power consumption.

Since a high degree of cache reuse can be made possible via cache blocking for the matrix multiplication kernel (benchmark 4), the high degree of cache reuse has resulted in both low power consumption (less memory traffic) and high performance. For the other benchmarks, as the degree of reuse within cache cannot fully compensate the underlying memory traffic resulted from blocking, relatively high power consumption may be required. Note that incurring max power consumption does not necessarily lead to better performance, as manifested by *MFLOPS on max average power* in Figure 13(b), as efficient use of memory traffic is required to convert the extra Watts consumed into meaningful MFLOPS.

7.2 Utilization Of Registers

We have used POET scripts to parameterize the application of unroll&jam and scalar replacement optimizations to the three matrix computation kernels (rows 4-6 in Table 1). Figure 14 shows the attained performance and power consumption when optimizing these kernels with different unroll&jam factors and selectively replacing different array references with scalar variables to promote the use of registers. In particular, *Max (or Min) average power* shows the highest (or lowest) average power consumption across all the

tuning evaluations, and *MFLOPS on max (or min) average power* show the MFLOPS rates attained when incurring the corresponding average power consumption.

From Figure 14(a), the register level optimizations are able to effect 5-10% of difference in average power consumption. From Figure 14(b), the optimized code that achieves the lowest power consumption had simultaneously achieved the highest MFLOPS across all tuning evaluations.

The results in Figure 14 confirm our belief that efficient utilization of registers not only improves application performance but also reduces overall power and energy consumption, since fewer memory references naturally result in both higher speed of execution and lower power consumption in the caches and memories. Therefore reducing memory usage is an effective optimization strategy to simultaneously enhance both performance and power efficiency.

7.3 Loop Unrolling And SSE Vectorization

The Intel icc compiler provides two command-line options, *funroll-loops* and *msse4.1*, which instruct the compiler to apply loop unrolling and SSE vectorization respectively to optimize a given input file. To investigate the impact of these two optimizations, both of which aim to enhance the concurrency of instruction scheduling within a single CPU core, we combined them with the *-O2* flag (which includes neither of the optimizations) to compile all the serial benchmark implementations.

Figure 15 shows the resulting performance and power efficiencies of the differently optimized codes, where *Peak Power* shows the highest peak power consumption across all combinations of compilation flags, and *Max MFLOPS* shows the highest MFLOPS attained. For each combination of the *icc* compilation flags, the average power consumption and MFLOPS rates attained for each benchmark are additionally plotted. Note that the *-funroll-loops* and *-msse4.1* flags seem to frequently interfere with each other when both are

(a) Power normalized against machine idle power(360W)

(b) *MFLOPS* of benchmarks

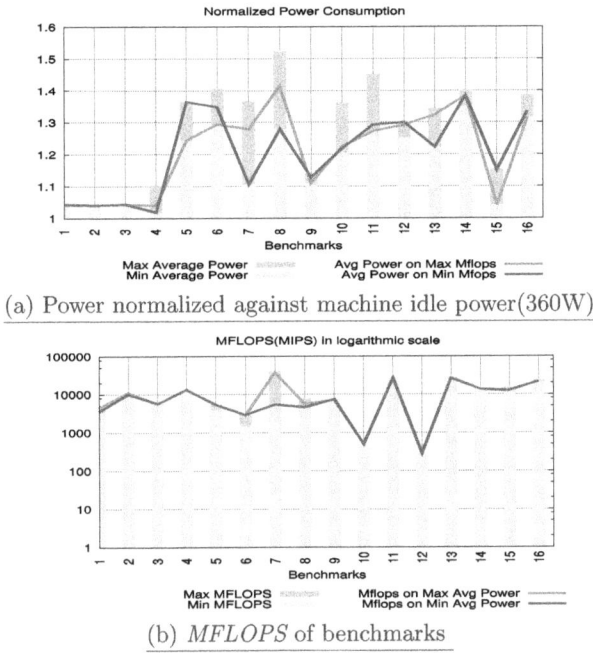

Figure 12: Impact of different thread affinites on 32-core AMD

specified, and we removed this combination to avoid obfuscation of the individual impact of each optimization flag.

From the graphs, applying loop unrolling in addition to -*O2* in *icc* made little difference in performance in Figure 15(b) while incurring up to 4% of variation (benchmark 4) in average power consumption in Figure 15(a) for the sequential benchmarks. For a majority of benchmarks, the average power consumption increases when loop unrolling is additionally applied, although a reduction in power is resulted in a few cases (benchmarks 5, 11, 40). We suspect that the lack of speedup by loop unrolling may have resulted in extra activities within the CPU nonetheless, which contributed to its negative impact in the power consumption.

On the other hand, SSE vectorization makes slightly more significant impact in performance for several MiBench applications. Further, it increases power consumption by up to 2% for 6 benchmarks but reduces power consumption by up to 2% for 7 other benchmarks. Therefore, it seems to have a positive impact on both the performance and power efficiencies on our benchmarks. This is expected as SSE vectorization, when applied successfully, allows a single instruction stream to operate on a number of data items simultaneously, reducing both activities inside the CPU and references to the memory or cache.

8. CONCLUSIONS

This paper presents an extensive study of the impact of application level optimizations on both the performance and power efficiencies of applications from a wide variety of scientific and embedded systems domains. We observe that application-level optimizations often have a much bigger impact on performance than on power consumption. However, optimizing for performance does not necessarily lead to better power consumption, and vice versa. Compared to sequential applications, multithreaded applications give more

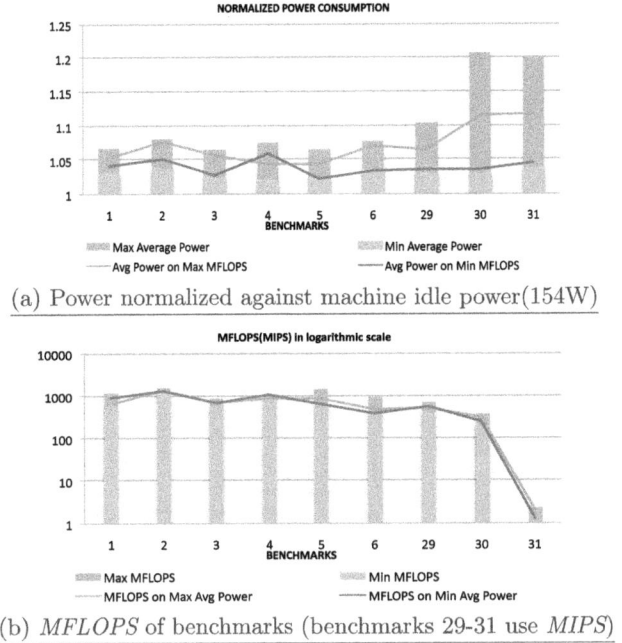

(a) Power normalized against machine idle power(154W)

(b) *MFLOPS* of benchmarks (benchmarks 29-31 use *MIPS*)

* All benchmarks are optimized with default configurations using POET and compiled with icc -O2.

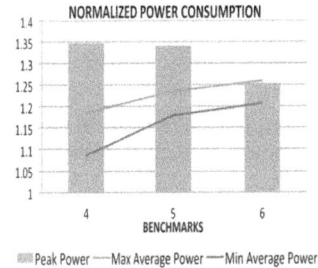

Figure 13: Impact of loop blocking on 8-Core Intel

(a) Power normalized against machine idle power(154W)

(b) MFLOPS of benchmarks

* For each kernel, the default configurations are used for other POET optimizations that are not being tuned, and OpenMP parallelization is disabled. The POET optimized codes are then compiled using icc with -O2 flag.

Figure 14: Result of tuning register optimizations on 8-core Intel

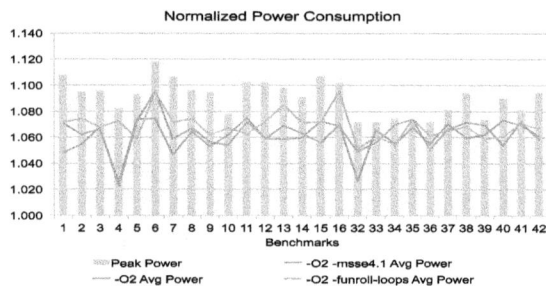

(a) Power normalized against machine idle power(154W)

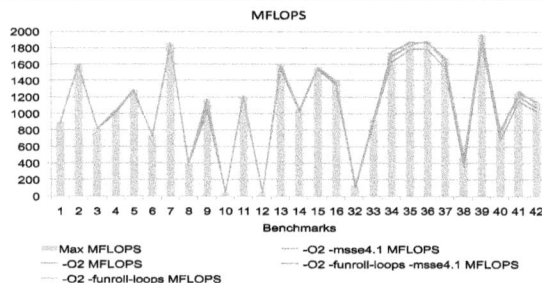

(b) MFLOPS of benchmarks

Figure 15: Impact of CPU optimizations on 8-core Intel

room for both performance and power improvements. Additionally, a number of optimizations, including both loop and thread affinity optimizations, have shown great potential in supporting collective enhancement of both performance and power efficiency. Our experimental results provide several insights to help exploit these optimizations effectively.

9. REFERENCES

[1] D. Bautista, J. Sahuquillo, H. Hassan, S. Petit, and J. Duato. A simple power-aware scheduling for multicore systems when running real-time applications. In *IPDPS '08*.

[2] Y. Ben-Itzhak, I. Cidon, and A. Kolodny. Performance and power aware cmp thread allocation modeling. In *HIPEAC*, pages 232–246, Jan. 2010.

[3] C. Bienia. *Benchmarking Modern Multiprocessors*. PhD thesis, Princeton University, January 2011.

[4] D. Brooks, V. Tiwari, and M. Martonosi. Wattch: a framework for architectural-level power analysis and optimizations. In *ISCA '00*.

[5] D. J. Brown and C. Reams. Toward energy-efficient computing. *Commun. ACM*, 53:50–58, March 2010.

[6] G. Contreras and M. Martonosi. Power prediction for intel xscale®processors using performance monitoring unit events. In *ISPLED*, pages 221–226, New York, NY, USA, 2005. ACM.

[7] L. Dagum and R. Menon. Openmp: an industry standard api for shared-memory programming. *Computational Science & Engineering, IEEE*, 1998.

[8] V. W. Freeh, D. K. Lowenthal, F. Pan, N. Kappiah, R. Springer, B. L. Rountree, and M. E. Femal. Analyzing the energy-time trade-off in high-performance computing applications. *TPDS '07*.

[9] M. R. Guthaus, J. S. Ringenberg, D. Ernst, T. M. Austin, T. Mudge, and R. B. Brown. Mibench: A free,

[10] H. Jin, M. Frumkin, , and J. Yan. The OpenMP Implementation of NAS Parallel Benchmarks and its Performance. Technical report, 1999.

[11] M. Kandemir, N. Vijaykrishnan, and M. J. Irwin. Compiler optimizations for low power systems. *Power aware computing*, pages 191–210, 2002.

[12] M. Kulkarni, M. Burtscher, C. Casçaval, and K. Pingali. Lonestar: A suite of parallel irregular programs. In *ISPASS '09*, 2009.

[13] C. Lee, J. K. Lee, T. Hwang, and S.-C. Tsai. Compiler optimization on instruction scheduling for low power. In *ISSS '00*, 2000.

[14] M. T.-C. Lee, V. Tiwari, S. Malik, and M. Fujita. Power analysis and low-power scheduling techniques for embedded dsp software. In *ISSS '95*.

[15] B. Nichols, D. Buttlar, and J. P. Farrell. *Pthreads Programming*. O'Reilly Media, Inc., 1996.

[16] A. Parikh, S. K. Kim, M. Vijaykrishnan, and M. J. N. Irwin. Instruction scheduling for low power. *Journal of VLSI Signal Processing Systems For Signal Image And Video Technology*, (1):129–149, 2004.

[17] K. Pingali, D. Nguyen, M. Kulkarni, M. Burtscher, M. A. Hassaan, R. Kaleem, T.-H. Lee, A. Lenharth, R. Manevich, M. Méndez-Lojo, D. Prountzos, and X. Sui. The tao of parallelism in algorithms. In *PLDI*, 2011.

[18] S. F. Rahman, J. Guo, and Q. Yi. Automated empirical tuning of scientific codes for performance and power consumption. In *HIPEAC '11*.

[19] S. F. Rahman, Q. Yi, and A. Qasem. Understanding stencil code performance on multicore architectures. In *CF'11: ACM International Conference on Computing Frontiers*, Ischia, Italy, May 2011.

[20] J. Reinders. *Intel threading building blocks*. O'Reilly & Associates, Inc., Sebastopol, CA, USA, 2007.

[21] J. S. Seng and D. M. Tullsen. The effect of compiler optimizations on pentium 4 power consumption. INTERACT '03, Washington, DC, USA, 2003.

[22] W.-T. Shiue. Retargetable compilation for low power. In *CODES '01*.

[23] K. Singh, M. Bhadauria, and S. A. McKee. Real time power estimation and thread scheduling via performance counters. In *dasCMP*, 2008.

[24] M. Valluri and L. John. Is compiling for performance == compiling for power? INTERACT, 2001.

[25] wattsup? Power meters. https://www.wattsupmeters.com.

[26] H. Yang, G. R. Gao, and C. Leung. On achieving balanced power consumption in software pipelined loops. In *CASES '02*, pages 210–217, 2002.

[27] Q. Yi. Automated programmable control and parameterization of compiler optimizations. In *CGO*, Apr. 2011.

[28] Q. Yi. POET: A scripting language for applying parameterized source-to-source program transformations. *Software: Practice & Experience*, 2011.

commercially representative embedded benchmark suite. In *WWC '01*, 2001.

Improving Energy Efficiency for Mobile Platforms by Exploiting Low-power Sleep States

Alexander W. Min, Ren Wang, James Tsai, Mesut A. Ergin, Tsung-Yuan Charlie Tai

Circuits and Systems Research, Intel Labs
2111 N.E. 25th Avenue, Hillsboro, OR 97124
{alexander.w.min, ren.wang, james.tsai, mesut.a.ergin, charlie.tai}@intel.com

ABSTRACT

Reducing energy consumption is one of the most important design aspects for small form-factor mobile platforms, such as smartphones and tablets. Despite its potential for power savings, optimally leveraging system low-power sleep states during *active* mobile workloads, such as video streaming and web browsing, has not been fully explored. One major challenge is to make intelligent power management decisions based on, among other things, accurate system idle duration prediction, which is difficult due to the non-deterministic system interrupt behavior. In this paper, we propose a novel framework, called E2S3 (Energy Efficient Sleep-State Selection), that dynamically enters the optimal low-power sleep state to minimize the system power consumption. In particular, E2S3 detects and exploits short idle durations during active mobile workloads by, (i) finding optimal thresholds (i.e., energy break-even times) for multiple low-power sleep states, (ii) predicting the sleep-state selection error probabilities heuristically, and by (iii) selecting the optimal sleep state based on the expected *reward*, e.g., power consumption, which incorporates the risks of making a wrong decision We implemented and evaluated E2S3 on Android-based smartphones, demonstrating the effectiveness of the algorithm. The evaluation results show that E2S3 significantly reduces the platform energy consumption, by up to 50 % (hence extending battery life), without compromising system performance.

Categories and Subject Descriptors

D.4.1 [**Operating System**]: Process Management—*scheduling*

General Terms

Design, Experimentation, Measurement, Performance, Algorithms

Keywords

Energy efficiency, mobile platform, low-power sleep states, idle duration prediction, reward-based sleep-state selection.

1. INTRODUCTION

Today's mobile devices, such as smartphones and tablets, are equipped with high-end, power-intensive resources, such as faster (and higher core-count) CPUs, more memory, multiple network interfaces, various sensors, in order to provide a richer user experience by enabling more sophisticated features and capabilities [37, 1]. However, advances in battery technology continue to lag behind performance demands, especially given the slim and compact form-factor devices [40, 24]. As a result, improving energy efficiency and extending battery life for mobile devices has become an increasingly important design consideration, especially for active usages. For many capable and interactive uses, energy-efficient operation is essential to provide smooth user experience, e.g., video calls (e.g., Apple FaceTime [2]), content sharing (e.g., Intel WiDi [3]), and cloud gaming.

Unlike some typical server workloads that are generated and processed back-to-back in a batch-mode without pauses (or relatively long idle durations) in between jobs [35], most mobile workloads, especially network-driven ones, exhibit bursty and random behaviors. This results in frequent idle durations during execution, which cannot easily be exploited to utilize the low-power states of the system by the existing power management mechanisms [45, 46]. These idle durations are often long enough for the mobile platform to enter a low-power sleep state, providing fine-grained power management opportunities [42]. Moreover, advances in SoC design allow for a multitude of ultra low-power states and very small state transition latencies, further encouraging aggressive use of low-power states [10] for mobile workloads. We thus can improve the energy-efficiency of mobile devices significantly by exploiting such brief idle durations during active workloads to transition into an appropriate sleep state.

Despite its great potential for saving power, extensive use of system low-power states under active mobile workloads has not been fully explored. Based on our experimental observations, the state-of-the-art sleep-state selection mechanisms, e.g., the idle governor in Linux OS [4], work reasonably well for relatively idle systems. However, they often perform worse when the system is active, primarily due to their inaccuracy in idle duration prediction. For this reason, the mobile system operates far from being *energy proportional* [14]—i.e., consumes power that is not proportional to its utilization, even with low CPU usage. Although the topic of mobile platform energy efficiency has been studied extensively in various aspects, e.g., [41, 44, 20, 39], existing solutions are not applicable to active mobile workloads, due to their inability in (i) tracking system idle durations, and (ii) incorporating the risk of making an erroneous sleep-state decision. For example, in the Linux idle governor [4], the idle duration prediction algorithm is based on simple heuristics (e.g., moving average filter), and the sleep-state selection algorithm are designed without consideration of making erroneous decisions and resulting power implications.

In this paper, we propose to maximally utilize system low-power sleep states under active workloads for mobile platforms, thus reducing system energy consumption and eventually extending battery life. Specifically, we design an E2S3 (Energy Efficient Sleep-State Selection) framework, motivated by the observation that the interrupt patterns are harder to predict with network-driven mobile applications, and the system low-power states are very difficult to utilize efficiently, even for light workloads. E2S3 predicts the short idle durations observed during active workloads more accurately, by handling the interrupts that affect these idle durations under deterministic and stochastic (random) categories, separately. E2S3 also calculates the expected *reward*, e.g., power consumption, for each sleep state. The reward metric incorporates the risk of making an incorrect decision, which is inevitable for active mobile workloads. The optimal sleep state is then selected to maximize the reward metric. More accurate prediction and a better decision-making mechanism enable the system to select the most appropriate low-power state among multiple available states. As a result, E2S3 reduces power consumption even under very active mobile workloads, without undermining system performance.

We have implemented E2S3 on an Android running smartphone and evaluated the schemes using mobile workloads under various settings. In addition, we have conducted a simulation study based on real mobile workload traces captured from smartphone use cases with Wi-Fi network access. Our experimental results show that E2S3 reduces mobile platform power consumption by up to 50 % for active mobile workloads, while preserving high system performance.

This paper makes the following five contributions:

- We propose a novel low-power sleep-state selection framework for mobile platforms, called E2S3, providing more accurate idle duration prediction and flexible sleep-state selection methods for optimal power savings.

- We introduce a new metric, called *relative energy break-even time* (R-EBT), that allows a system to select the most energy efficient sleep state for a given idle duration and platform power characteristics. The concept of R-EBT is generic and can be applied to any device/system with multiple low-power states.

- We design mechanisms to accurately predict sleep-state selection probabilities. For this, we propose exploiting the periodicity of deterministic interrupts, and modeling random interrupts using a stochastic process.

- We develop a reward-based sleep-state selection algorithm, which allows a mobile platform to enter the state that maximizes the expected reward, e.g., power saving, by incorporating the probability of making a wrong decision. This is very different from the existing methods, as they solely rely on idle duration prediction.

The remainder of this paper is organized as follows. Section 2 motivates our problem by identifying the three key challenges in achieving platform energy-efficiency. Section 3 introduces the concept of relative energy break-even time to find an optimal sleep-state selection. Section 4 describes algorithms for run-time estimation of system idle durations. Section 5 proposes a reward-based sleep-state selection algorithm. Section 6 presents a detailed evaluation of the proposed approaches. Section 7 summarizes the research related to our work. Section 8 concludes the paper and discusses future research directions.

2. MOTIVATION

In this section, we first advocate the necessity of leveraging low-power sleep states for active power management in mobile platforms. We then discuss the key requirements of active power management and identify the limitations of the existing techniques, followed by a brief overview of the proposed E2S3 framework.

2.1 Why Leverage Low-power Sleep States During Active Mobile Workload?

System idle durations are difficult to predict due to random interrupts from various subsystems, such as communications and graphics. Under network-driven active mobile workloads, such as video streaming/conferencing and web browsing, it becomes more difficult to predict upcoming idle durations with high accuracy because of the volume of interrupts driven by the packets arriving from the Internet.. Thus, idle-duration prediction-based selection algorithms (e.g., the idle governor in Linux kernel) often perform sub-optimal in terms of energy efficiency and performance.

Optimal selection and use of low-power sleep-states are essential to improving energy efficiency for active mobile workloads, motivated by the following practical considerations.

- *Improving user experience & satisfaction:* Energy-efficient operation of mobile devices can improve user experience by allowing users to enjoy their applications longer with less worry of limited battery life. Cloud computing allows the mobile workload to be offloaded, however, the battery life implication of this to the end-user device is not trivial, as network interfaces consume significant power and impose a profound power impact on the whole platform [12]. Recent market survey results indicated that only 8 % of mobile users are satisfied with the battery performance of their smartphones [5]. Moreover, the majority of mobile users picked the battery performance among the most important factors in their future mobile device purchase decisions.

- *Achieving energy proportionality:* Mobile platform power consumption is often not scalable with respect to the CPU utilization [14], even for light workloads. This is because certain subsystems are not efficiently power managed, e.g., stay active even when the CPU becomes idle. To achieve energy proportionality, and thus to reduce the energy consumption, mobile platforms must be capable of utilizing available low-power states very efficiently by taking advantage of all idle durations—especially the short ones, in addition to the long ones.

- *Reduced performance implications:* So far, the potential of losing energy and performance by entering a low-power sleep state discouraged its aggressive use. This is especially true under active workloads, where probability of making an incorrect sleep-state decision is high. Fortunately, however, recent advances in power management techniques continuously reduce state-transition latencies, encouraging mobile platforms to opportunistically enter deep sleep states without noticeably affecting system performance and user experience. For example, our measurement study on Android-based smartphones has shown that the average inter-interrupt arrival time for YouTube 1080p video streaming is roughly 2 ms, which is long enough to enter most of the CPU (i.e., Cx) and platform (i.e., S0ix) sleep states [4].

Motivated by the practical considerations discussed above, we will address the problem of selecting the optimal low-power state that best suits the users' energy and perfor-

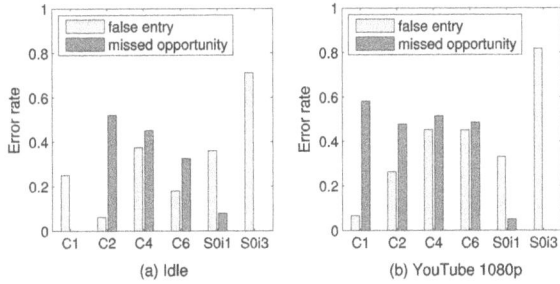

(a) Idle   (b) YouTube 1080p

Figure 1: Inaccuracy of sleep-state selection: False-entry and missed-opportunities for CPU (i.e., Cx) and platform (i.e., S0ix) sleep states are very high in both cases where the system is: (a) idle and (b) streaming a YouTube 1080p HD video. The total error rates are up to 97%.

mance needs. A reward-based sleep-state selection algorithm for improving the energy efficiency will be described and evaluated in the following sections.

2.2 Requirements of Sleep-State Selection for Active Mobile Workloads

Due to the unique characteristics of mobile workloads—e.g., bursty and random interrupt patterns—and the performance implications of using low-power states, the following requirements need consideration when designing a good active power management framework.

Idle duration prediction accuracy. A system idle-duration prediction technique should provide reasonably accurate results for efficient sleep-state selection. However, it is not a trivial task to predict very short idle durations embedded in active mobile workloads. To assess the accuracy of the existing idle-duration prediction-based sleep-state selection schemes, we measured sleep-state selection error rates on an Android-based smartphone, while streaming an HD YouTube video. We measured the sleep-state selection accuracy in terms of false-entry and missed-opportunity rates. False-entry happens when the actual idle duration is shorter than the energy break-even time (EBT) of the target sleep state, whereas missed-opportunity happens when the actual idle duration is longer than the EBT of the next deeper sleep-state. That is, false-entry and missed-opportunity indicate the over- and under-estimation of the idle durations, respectively, both resulting in a waste of energy. Here, EBT of a given low power state is defined to be the minimum amount of time the system needs reside in the state to amortize the transition costs in power (refer to Section 3 for more details on EBT).

Fig. 1 plots the false-entry and missed-opportunity rates when the system is (a) idle and (b) streaming a YouTube video.[1] The figure shows that the error rates are very high for most sleep states (up to 97%), demonstrating the poor idle-duration prediction performance. We observed that such high inaccuracy stems partially from the inherently random nature of the interrupt events. Without a reasonably accurate idle-duration prediction, it is difficult to benefit from the low-power states during active workloads. In the remainder of the paper, we will introduce novel methods to

---

[1]The error rates represent the ratio of the total number of false-entry/missed-opportunity counts and the total number of entrances to the target sleep state during the measurement period (i.e., 1 min).

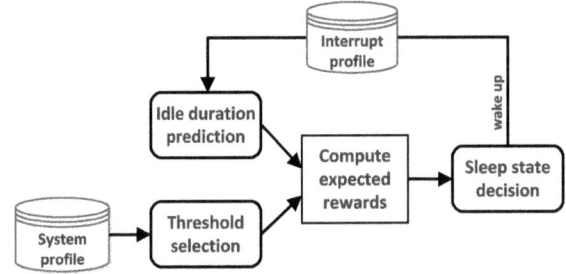

Figure 2: E2S3 Framework.

better predict the system interrupts, improving the sleep-state selection process (see Section 4 for details).

Minimum performance impact. Low-power sleep-state selection algorithms must consider the inherent tradeoff between energy efficiency and performance. Overly aggressive access to deep sleep states may not only affect the user experience adversely, but also might result in higher energy consumption. One naive solution to guaranteeing the performance is to be conservative in entering deep sleep states. For example, Microsoft Windows can choose to completely disable deep sleep states based on system requirements [6]. While this approach is simple and safe, it is also suboptimal and may yield poor energy efficiency. Moreover, sleep-state selection algorithms must allow mobile platforms to fine-tune their selection behavior—instead of relying solely on idle-duration prediction—because each low-power state may have different power-saving or performance-overhead implications.

Implementation feasibility. The idle-duration prediction and sleep-state selection algorithms must be feasible to implement in the OS or platform firmware, depending on the design requirements. For active mobile workloads, a platform may need to make the sleep-state decisions very frequently, and thus a lightweight algorithm is highly desired. Some of the advanced prediction algorithms, e.g., using adaptive filters or machine learning, may incur prohibitive computational overhead in predicting idle durations, therefore it may not be desirable to implement them, especially in firmware or hardware because of the large code footprint.

2.3 The E2S3 Framework

E2S3 is a low-overhead, energy efficient sleep-state selection framework that fully leverages a plurality of low-power sleep states, while preserving the system performance. E2S3 consists of the following three main building blocks:

- *Threshold selector* finds the optimal thresholds based on the sleep-state characteristics, such as power level, state transition latency, and system power profile (see Section 3).

- *Idle duration estimator* predicts the next system idle duration, with reasonable accuracy, based on recent history (see Section 4).

- *Sleep-state decision maker* selects the optimal low-power sleep state that maximizes the expected reward, e.g., power consumption (see Section 5).

E2S3's high level operation is illustrated in Fig. 2. Note that, although the design of E2S3 is tailored to CPU (i.e., Cx) and platform (i.e., S0ix) sleep-state selection, the methods introduced in E2S3 are generic and can be easily applied to the sleep-state selection of various devices. In the following

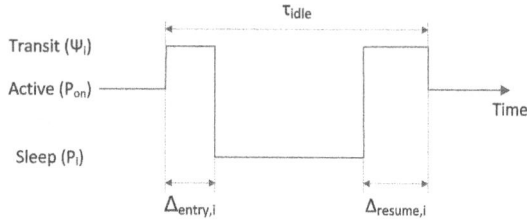

Figure 3: An illustration of sleep-state transition: Sleep-state decisions must consider the associated state entry/resume latency overhead.

sections, we will elaborate on each component of the E2S3 framework.

3. THRESHOLD DESIGN FOR LOW-POWER SLEEP STATES

In this section, we first describe the system sleep-state model and Energy Break-even Time (EBT), and then we introduce a new concept called Relative Energy Break-even Time (R-EBT), which is designed to be discriminant in selecting the best energy-saving state among multiple states.

3.1 System Sleep State Model

Modern mobile devices support multiple system low-power sleep states, offering a wide spectrum of energy saving opportunities [29]. However, switching to/from these sleep states incurs associated state transition latencies; in general, deeper sleep states introduce longer delay, which reduces performance.

We consider a system that supports a set of CPU/platform sleep states, where each sleep state i can be described by the following five attributes:

- Δ_i: The state transition latency, which includes both entry and resume latencies.
- P_{on}: Power consumption in the active state.
- P_{tr}: Power consumption in the transition state.
- P_i: Power consumption in the sleep state.
- Φ_i: Energy break-even time (EBT).

While the system consumes less power in a sleep state, compared to the active state, the power consumption during a state transition period is usually higher than the active state power consumption (i.e., $P_{tr} > P_{on} > P_i$) [17, 44]. Therefore, a system must remain in state i for a certain amount of time to offset the energy cost associated with state transition. We refer to this as Energy Break-even Time (EBT).

3.2 Derivation of Energy Break-even Time

Conventionally, EBT for sleep state i (denoted as Φ_i) is defined as the minimum time duration (including the state entry/resume latencies), during which a system must stay in the lower-power state i, to amortize the energy cost in state transitions [34, 16, 33, 21]. Fig. 3 illustrates the process of switching to and from sleep state i, while the platform was initially in the active state. The system can save energy by entering state i, if idle duration τ_{idle} is larger than the EBT of the target state, i.e., $\tau_{idle} \geq \Phi_i$; otherwise, entering the sleep state results in higher energy consumption than staying in the active state. Hence, EBT for sleep state i can be derived as:

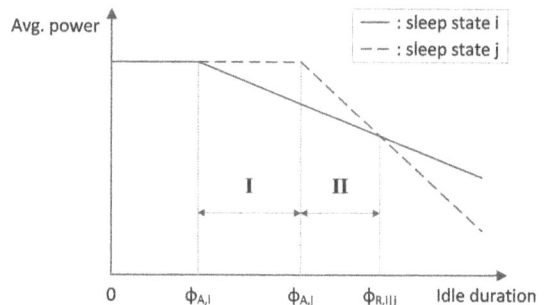

Figure 4: An illustration of platform power consumption with A-EBT and R-EBT. A system should consider R-EBT ($\Phi_{R,i|j}$ in Eq. (2)) rather than A-EBT (Φ_A in Eq. (1)) to enter the optimal sleep state that maximizes power savings.

$$\Delta_i \cdot P_{tr} + (\Phi_i - \Delta_i) \cdot P_i = \Phi_i \cdot P_{on}$$
$$\implies \Phi_i = \left(\frac{P_{tr} - P_i}{P_{on} - P_i} \right)^+ \cdot \Delta_i. \qquad (1)$$

Note that the transition power P_{tr} represents the average measured value during the transition periods[2] Eq. (1) indicates that EBT is proportional to the state transition latency, Δ_i, and dependent on power consumption in the active, transition, and target sleep states.

The derivation of EBT implicitly assumes that deeper sleep states are more energy efficient as long as the platform can save power compared to the active state. As we will show later, this assumption does not hold true for systems with multiple sleep states, and EBT values need to be derived by comparing the power saving opportunities among all available states for optimal energy efficiency. Henceforth, we refer to the EBT in Eq. (1) as the *absolute* EBT (A-EBT) (denoted as $\Phi_{A,i}$), to differentiate it from *relative* EBT (R-EBT), which we discuss next.

3.3 Relative Energy Break-even Time

For a system with multiple low-power states, the optimal sleep state should be chosen by comparing the potential energy savings among all the available sleep states. This constitutes the basic design principle for R-EBT, and here we describe how to calculate R-EBT, denoted as $\Phi_{R,i|j}$.

For a given upcoming idle duration of τ_{idle}, a system can save more power by entering state i rather than entering its adjacent shallower state j (i.e., $P_i < P_j$), if the following two conditions hold:

1) $\tau_{idle} \geq \Phi_{A,i}$.
2) $\Phi_{A,i} \cdot P_{on} + (\tau_{idle} - \Phi_{A,i}) \cdot P_i < \Phi_{A,j} \cdot P_{on} + (\tau_{idle} - \Phi_{A,j}) \cdot P_j$.

We defined R-EBT as the minimum amount of time the system must enter and stay in state i, so that the expected power consumption from states i and j become equal. Then, R-EBT, $\Phi_{R,i|j}$, for state i can be derived as:

$$\Phi_{R,i|j} = \frac{P_{on}(\Phi_{A,i} - \Phi_{A,j}) + (\Phi_{A,j}P_j - \Phi_{A,i}P_i)}{P_j - P_i}. \qquad (2)$$

Eqs. (1) and (2) indicate that A-EBT and R-EBT could be quite different in practice. Note that the R-EBT values

---

[2]Note that in cases where $P_{tr} \approx P_{on}$ (i.e., the transition power is the same as the active power), Φ_i is equivalent to transition latency Δ_i.

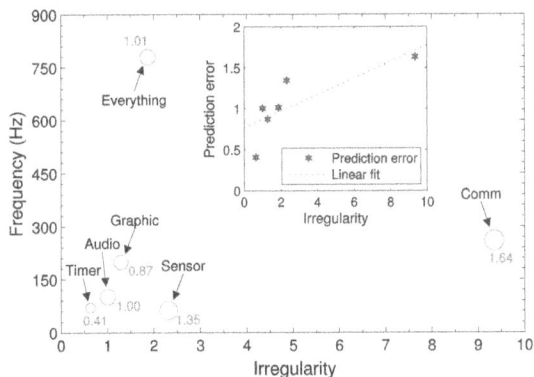

Figure 5: **Relationship between interrupt characteristics (i.e., irregularity and frequency) and the predictability of the interrupt arrivals.**

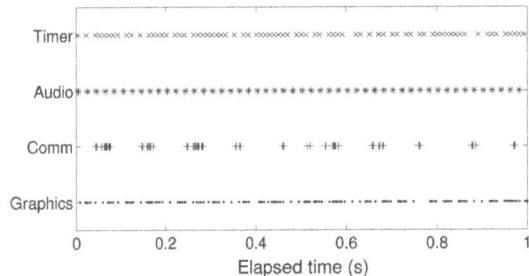

Figure 6: **Two classes of interrupts: (pseudo) deterministic (i.e., timer and audio) vs. stochastic (i.e., communications and graphics).**

in Eq. (2) can be calculated off-line and used via a look-up table based approach.

Fig. 4 illustrates average platform power consumption as a function of idle duration. The solid and dotted lines represent the power consumption of sleep states i and j, respectively, where $i < j$, hence $\Phi_{A,i} < \Phi_{A,j}$. The figure clearly shows that R-EBT is different from A-EBT. For example, in **region II**, the platform should enter state i for better power savings, even though the idle duration is long enough to enter the next deeper state j, in the A-EBT sense. The slope depends on the difference in active and idle state power, i.e., $P_{on} - P_i$; the greater the difference, the steeper the slope.

Ideally, assuming perfect idle duration prediction, sleep-states can be chosen by simply comparing the predicted idle duration and the R-EBT values described above. However, it is difficult to accurately predict idle durations, especially for active mobile workloads, resulting in frequent sub-optimal decisions, as we observed in Fig. 1

In the following sections, we first propose new methods to predict system idle durations at run-time, and we then introduce the notion of "reward" to incorporate the power implications of incorrect idle-duration predictions, which can severely undermine energy efficiency of mobile platforms.

4. RUN-TIME IDLE DURATION ESTIMATION

In this section, we first investigate the key characteristics of the system interrupts for active mobile workloads, and then propose a systematic approach to improve the prediction of idle durations.

4.1 Characterization of Mobile Workload Interrupts

It is important to understand the interrupt dynamics since they determine the behavior of system idle durations. For this, we collected interrupt information from typical mobile workloads and analyzed the distributions. In Fig. 5, we plot the interrupt behavior of an HD video (1080p) streaming session over the Internet as an example. The figure shows interrupt frequency, irregularity, and resulting prediction error (indicated by the size of the circles in the figure) if a simple weighted moving average estimator is used. The sources of the plotted interrupts include timer, audio, graphics, sensor, and communications (over Wi-Fi) subsystems. The *frequency* represents the number of interrupts per second, and *irregularity* is the ratio of the standard deviation to the aver-

age of the interrupt inter-arrival time. The *prediction error* is the ratio of the average prediction error (i.e., the difference between the expected and the actual idle durations) to the average interrupt inter-interval time.

We observe that the timer and audio subsystems exhibit relatively regular interrupt patterns, and therefore can be considered under a *deterministic* source category (see Fig. 6). These deterministic interrupts can be identified either at the design time (e.g., by consulting to the device tree) or at the run-time via estimation. Treatment of the other interrupt sources (i.e., graphics, sensor, and communication subsystems) would fall under the *stochastic* category as they exhibit a relatively irregular behavior. Such classification can be based on the design-time system information or the information in the firmware/driver configurations. The figure embedded in Fig. 5 shows positive correlation between the irregularity and prediction error for the interrupt sources; it is very difficult to predict inter-interrupt times as the irregularity increase for a given source.

Based on above observations, we first classify all interrupts into (pseudo) deterministic and stochastic categories so as to treat them differently in the prediction process. The prediction of the next interrupt employs more precise tracking of deterministic ones, and incorporation of the stochastic/random ones via probabilistic methods. In the following subsections, we will describe the details of the prediction methods proposed for each of the classes.

4.2 Prediction of Deterministic Interrupts

We propose the following three approaches for the treatment of interrupts with deterministic patterns.

Decomposition. Certain subsystems may share a single interrupt line to address the needs of multiple internal functional blocks. This results in the composite interrupt to exhibit a seemingly more random behavior and makes the idle duration estimation more difficult, even though each of the functional blocks behave highly predictable. We thus propose to decompose the composite interrupt sources and consider their forming blocks individually.[3]

Grouping. Some interrupt sources may generate a consistent burst of interrupts with very small inter-arrival times within the burst. We propose to group this known burst as a single system event, and introduce a holding period, during which prediction pauses until the rest of the interrupt burst is complete, saving computation cycles for estimating and increasing accuracy.

Dependency. Some of the interrupts from certain devices or subsystems may depend on others. For example,

---

[3]Information pertaining to interrupt sources is generally available in platform/system firmware as well as in OS device drivers.

most slave device controller interrupts (e.g., SDIO controller) are likely to be followed by an interrupt from the controlled device (e.g., SDIO Wi-Fi radio). We exploit such dependency among interrupt sources to improve prediction accuracy while minimizing overhead. A holding period similar to the one mentioned above can be applied here.

The three design approaches outlined above form the basis of better prediction of the (pseudo) deterministic interrupts. Then, the next expected interrupt arrival time for deterministic interrupts can be calculated as:

$$\widehat{T}_d = \min\left\{ \hat{t}_1, \hat{t}_2, \ldots, \hat{t}_n \right\} - \epsilon, \qquad (3)$$

where $\hat{t}_k$ is the expected arrival time of deterministic interrupt source k, and n is the total number of deterministic interrupt sources. ϵ is a small positive value to compensate for the prediction error.

4.3 Prediction of Stochastic Interrupts

Unlike pseudo deterministic interrupts, stochastic interrupts are more difficult to predict due to their inherent randomness. Therefore, the approaches used for deterministic interrupt prediction may not apply. Here, we model the random interrupt arrivals from each such source as a stochastic process. In particular, we observed that the random interrupt arrivals can be accurately approximated as a heavy-tailed Pareto distribution, as shown in Fig. 7. Then, the probability of occurrence for at least one interrupt during the next time period τ can be estimated as:

$$P_s(\tau) \approx 1 - \left(\frac{\widehat{x}_m}{x}\right)^{\widehat{\alpha}}, \qquad (4)$$

where $\widehat{x}_m > 0$ and $\widehat{\alpha} > 0$ are scale and shape parameters, which can be estimated using the Maximum Likelihood (ML) estimator at run-time based on previous history.

The model can be used in two ways. One is to predict the next interrupt arrival time (e.g., T_s in Eq. (5)). The other is to evaluate the probability of a false-entry and a missed-opportunity for each possible sleep state. The latter will be used in the proposed reward-based sleep-state selection algorithm (see Section 5 for details).

4.4 Idle Duration Prediction based Sleep-state Selection

Based on the proposed mechanisms to predict deterministic and stochastic interrupts in Eqs. (3) and (4), the next system idle duration—the time duration until the next deterministic or stochastic interrupt occurs—can be computed as:

$$\widehat{T}_{idle} = \min\left\{ \widehat{T}_d, t_{s,last} + \mathbb{E}[T_s] - t_o \right\}, \qquad (5)$$

where $t_{s,last}$ is the most recent stochastic interrupt arrival time, $\mathbb{E}[T_s]$ is the expected inter-interrupt arrival time of random interrupts (calculated based on Eq. (4)), and t_o is the current time.

Ideally, for a given estimated idle duration of $\widehat{T}_{idle}$, a system should enter sleep state i if the following condition holds:

$$\Phi_{R,i|i-1} < \widehat{T}_{idle} < \Phi_{R,i+1|i} \quad \forall i, \qquad (6)$$

where $\Phi_{R,i|i-1}$ is the R-EBT for state i and $\Phi_{R,i|i-1} = \Phi_{A,i}$ when $i = 1$.

The idle-duration prediction in Eq. (5) has two main benefits: It (i) fully exploits the (pseudo) periodic nature of deterministic interrupts, and (ii) models random interrupt arrivals as a stochastic process with heavy-tailed inter-interrupt arrival distributions (see Section 6 for detailed evaluation results).

Despite these improvements over the conventional prediction algorithms, our prediction method may still not be sufficient to

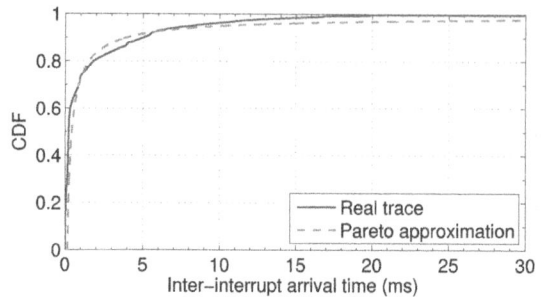

Figure 7: An empirical CDF of interrupt arrival times for stochastic interrupts while streaming an HD YouTube 720p video.

produce optimal results for active mobile workloads. The resident error in prediction needs to be compensated for in order to keep the sleep-state error rates at their minimum. This motivates our design of a reward-based sleep-state selection approach, which we discuss next.

5. REWARD-BASED SLEEP STATE SELECTION

In this section, we introduce a reward-based low-power sleep-state selection algorithm. We first explain the design rationale behind the reward-based sleep-state decision, and then we describe an exemplary algorithm design that maximizes the energy efficiency.

5.1 Design Rationale

For active mobile workloads where idle durations often vary rapidly and/or unpredictably, there is a high likelihood of making an incorrect sleep-state decision due to erroneous idle-duration prediction, as we observed in Fig. 1. As a result, conventional idle-duration based energy-conservation mechanisms (e.g., the idle governor in Linux OS) may perform sub-optimally because inaccurate idle duration prediction can severely undermine their effectiveness. Therefore, we propose a reward-based sleep-state selection algorithm, in which the reward incorporates the potential energy/performance loss of making suboptimal sleep-state decisions into the decision process.

5.2 Reward Definition

A reward may represent any measure of performance/energy of particular interest to the system designer. False-entry or missed-opportunity metrics that we presented earlier can be proxies for potential losses in energy or performance. For example, when false-entry occurs, the platform may consume more power than it would have at the active or shallower state. Once the reward metric is defined, the selection algorithm will choose the sleep state that maximizes the expected reward.

In this paper, as an example, we define the reward for entering state i as follows:

$$\mathbb{E}[R_i] = (1 - \widehat{P}_{FE,i} - \widehat{P}_{MO,i}) \cdot G_i + \widehat{P}_{FE,i} \cdot L_{FE,i} + \widehat{P}_{MO,i} \cdot L_{MO,i}, \qquad (7)$$

where G_i is the expected gain (e.g., energy/performance) from entering the state. $\widehat{P}_{FE,i}$ and $\widehat{P}_{MO,i}$ are the estimated false-entry and missed-opportunity probabilities, respectively, and $L_{FE,i}$ and $L_{MO,i}$ are the associated potential energy/performance losses (or penalties).

Here the "gain" from entering a sleep state and the "loss" due to false-entry and missed-opportunity for each sleep state are design parameters, which can be adapted to best suit users needs, e.g., power consumption, latency and throughput. Thus, reward-based sleep-state selection is highly flexible compared to conventional sleep-state selection based on idle duration prediction.

Table 1: Estimated Sleep-state Selection Error Probabilities.

	C1	C2	C3
$P_{FE,i}$	1	$1 - \left(\frac{\widehat{x}_m}{\Phi_{A,i}}\right)^{\widehat{\alpha}}$	$1 - \left(\frac{\widehat{x}_m}{\Phi_{A,i}}\right)^{\widehat{\alpha}}$
$P_{MO,i}$	0	0	$\left(\frac{\widehat{x}_m}{\Phi_{R,i+1|i}}\right)^{\widehat{\alpha}}$

5.3 Sleep-state Selection Error Probabilities

Now we describe how to estimate sleep-state selection error rates, i.e., $\widehat{P}_{FE}$ and $\widehat{P}_{MO}$, in Eq. (7). In order to calculate the selection error probabilities for sleep state i, we need to consider the following three cases based on (i) how soon in the future the deterministic interrupt will occur (i.e., $\widehat{T}_d$), and (ii) absolute and relative sleep-state selection thresholds (i.e., $\Phi_{A,i}$ and $\Phi_{R,i}$):

C1. $0 \leq \widehat{T}_d < \Phi_{A,i}$: If the platform knows that at least one deterministic interrupt (e.g., timer) will happen before the A-EBT of state i, then $\widehat{P}_{FE,i} = 1$ and $\widehat{P}_{MO,i} = 0$. Hence, there is no need to consider stochastic interrupts.

C2. $\Phi_{A,i} \leq \widehat{T}_d < \Phi_{R,i+1|i}$: If the platform knows that deterministic interrupts will happen in between the A-EBT of i and R-EBT of $i+1$, then it should consider stochastic interrupts. In this case, $\widehat{P}_{MO,i} = 0$, and $\widehat{P}_{FE,i}$ is the probability that at least one stochastic interrupts will occur before the A-EBT expires.

C3. $\Phi_{R,i+1|i} \leq \widehat{T}_d$: If the platform knows that the next deterministic interrupt will happen after the R-EBT of the next sleep state, then $\widehat{P}_{FE,i}$ is the same as in **C2**, and $\widehat{P}_{MO,i}$ is the probability that no stochastic interrupt will occur until the R-EBT of $i+1$ expires.

Table 1 summarizes the error probabilities for the three cases discussed above, assuming that the stochastic interrupt arrivals follow a Pareto distribution, as discussed in Section 4.3. Note however, that our proposed method is generic, and other stochastic processes can be used to estimate sleep-state error probabilities.

5.4 Reward-based Algorithm Description

While the "reward" metric is general enough to incorporate any meaningful performance measure, in this section, we specifically use expected power consumption as the reward. Thus, we need to consider only the following two cases:

C1$'$. $\widehat{T}_d < \Phi_{A,i}$: In this case, the system will waste energy compared to staying at the active state (i.e., C0) regardless of the behavior of stochastic interrupts. Assuming a uniform distribution of interrupt arrivals in $[t_o, t_o + \Phi_{A,i}]$, we have:

$$\mathbb{E}[R_i] \approx \frac{\Phi_{A,i} \cdot P_{on}}{\frac{\Phi_{A,i}}{2}} = 2 P_{on},$$

where t_o is the time of decision making, $\Phi_{A,i}$ is the A-EBT of state i, and P_{on} is the active state power consumption.

C2$'$. $\Phi_{A,i} < \widehat{T}_d$: In this case, the system may save power depending on the arrival of stochastic interrupts, i.e.,

$$\mathbb{E}[R_i] = (1 - \widehat{P}_{FE,i}) \cdot \left[\frac{(\widehat{T}_{idle} - \Phi_{A,i}) P_i + \Phi_{A,i} P_{on}}{\widehat{T}_{idle}} \right]$$
$$+ 2 \widehat{P}_{FE,i} P_{on},$$

where $\widehat{T}_{idle}$ is the expected idle duration calculated using Eq. (5) and P_i is the power consumption in state i.

Then, a system must enter the most rewarding state for the next idle duration, i.e.,

$$i^* = \arg\min \left\{ \mathbb{E}[R_i] \right\}_{i=1}^{n}. \qquad (8)$$

Algorithm 1 REWARD-BASED SLEEP-STATE SELECTION

For each system idle period, E2S3:

(1) Calculates expected reward
  1: **for** $i=1$ to n **do** /* n is the # of sleep states */
  2:     estimate deterministic interrupt arrival time $\widehat{T}_d$
  3:     update parameters for stochastic interrupt process
  4:     estimate $\widehat{P}_{FE,i}$ and $\widehat{P}_{MO,i}$
  5:     calculate expected reward $\mathbb{E}[R_i]$
  6: **end for**
(2) Selects the best sleep state
  7: **return** $i^* = \arg\min \left\{ \mathbb{E}[R_i] \right\}_{i=1}^{n}$

Note that this selection rule includes the possibility of staying at the normal operating state (i.e., C0), if switching to sleep states do not provide any energy saving opportunities. **Algorithm 1** describes the overall procedure of the proposed reward-based sleep-state selection algorithm.

5.5 Threshold-based Adaptation

In practice, the overhead involved in calculating the reward metric can be avoided under two typical conditions dependent on the arrival rate of the stochastic interrupts. If the stochastic interrupts are arriving rarely (w.r.t. the deepest sleep-state R-EBT), then they won't affect sleep-state selection significantly. This is also true if the stochastic interrupts are arriving very fast one after the other (w.r.t. the shallowest sleep state R-EBT). Therefore, we propose to adaptively enable the stochastic prediction based on stochastic interrupt frequency, as shown in Fig. 8. When the frequency is below the lower threshold, TH_L, (Region 1) the interrupts rarely occur, and thus the system can ignore their effects in expected reward (or power consumption). When the frequency is above the upper threshold, TH_U, (Region 3) interrupts are too frequent, preventing the system from entering sleep states; hence there is no need to predict idle durations. If the frequency is in between (Region 2), the interrupts are monitored to update sleep state error rates.

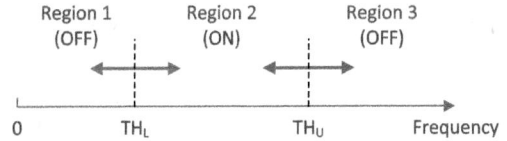

Figure 8: Threshold-based adaptation for interrupt prediction.

6. EVALUATION

In this section, we first describe our evaluation methodology, and then evaluate E2S3's energy efficiency and performance impact with detailed experimentation. In summary, E2S3 provides up to 50 % platform energy savings and improves responsiveness on average by avoiding erroneous deep sleep-state selection.

6.1 Experimental Setup

6.1.1 Testing Schemes and Workloads

To facilitate comparisons of the performance of the idle-duration prediction and sleep-state selection algorithms introduced for E2S3, we evaluate below five schemes:

- **Idle Governor:** the stock algorithm in Linux kernel 2.6.3x.
- **Prediction w/ A-EBT:** the proposed idle-duration prediction-based sleep-state selection using A-EBT.
- **Prediction w/ R-EBT:** the proposed idle-duration prediction-based sleep-state selection using R-EBT.
- **Reward-based w/ R-EBT:** the proposed reward-based sleep-state selection using R-EBT.
- **Oracle:** the ideal case, where always perfect decisions are assumed.

The proposed prediction-based scheme uses Eq. (5) for idle duration prediction and sleep-state decisions. It is different from the stock Linux idle governor because it handles deterministic and stochastic interrupts separately, and leverages their interrupt characteristics, i.e., the periodicity for deterministic ones and the heavy-tailed distribution for stochastic ones. For the `Oracle` scheme, we assume that the algorithm has *a priori* information about the upcoming system idle duration, hence always makes the optimal sleep-state decision. We use this as an upper bound for energy savings.

We implemented the threshold selector (i.e., R-EBT) in E2S3 on an Android-based smartphone with Linux kernel 2.6.3x. We also implemented `Oracle` by observing the actual system idle durations and mapping them into appropriate sleep states. To comparatively evaluate the proposed idle-duration prediction and sleep-state selection algorithms, we conducted interrupt-trace-based simulations using MATLAB partly due to the limited information available in the OS., such as interrupt characteristics etc. We used `pyTimechart` [7] to collect system interrupt traces.

We evaluate the schemes using custom synthetic workloads and also with Iperf network testing tool [8], in order to control and repeat experiments (e.g., file download) in various throughput ranges. The synthetic workload we customized can be modeled as a two-state `on`/`off` renewal process; `off`→`on` state transition occurs when the system receives an interrupt (e.g., audio, graphic, timer, etc.), whereas `on`→`off` state transition occurs when CPU completes the execution of a given set of instructions. We refer to the time period between two consecutive `off`→`on` transition as *cycle*. The average fraction of time spent in the state `on` represents CPU utilization. Our synthetic workload represents the bursty packet-arrival behavior of network-driven mobile workloads, such as file downloading [46].

In the experiments, we assume the arrival of the stochastic interrupts follow a Poisson process, mainly because of its simplicity and implementation feasibility. It also performs reasonably well for the scenarios we tested. A more accurate model, e.g., Pareto, can also be used at the cost of increased computational overhead.[4] Each test is run for 120 s, unless otherwise specified, and multiple tests are performed for each scenario. The averages are reported as the performance measure.

6.1.2 Performance Metrics

To evaluate the performance of the proposed algorithms, we use the following three performance metrics:

- **Platform power/energy consumption**: we project the total platform power consumption of the testing schemes using our platform power model.[5] We normalize the calculated platform power consumption to that of all active state (i.e., C0). For the network driven mobile workload, the energy consumption is proportional to the power consumption, since the total execution time, determined by the network input rate, is roughly the same.

- **Sleep-state selection error rates**: we measure the sleep-state selection error rates, i.e., false-entry and missed-opportunity, by comparing the realized idle duration (by looking back after waking up from the sleep state) and the EBT of the respective sleep states.

- **Sleep-state transition latency**: we evaluate the total sleep-state resume latencies (for both correct and false entries) to understand the performance implications of the testing schemes. We normalize the resume latency to the total measurement duration.

---

[4] It is very important to reduce the computational complexity of idle-duration prediction and sleep-state selection algorithms because a system has to make sleep-state decision very frequently, e.g., durations in the order of tens of micro seconds for active workloads.

[5] We use a spreadsheet power projection model based on `Cx`/`SOix` residency distribution, state-specific power numbers, sleep-state false-entry and missed-opportunity rates, etc., and it has been validated on the target platform. We omit the description of the detailed platform power model due to space limitations.

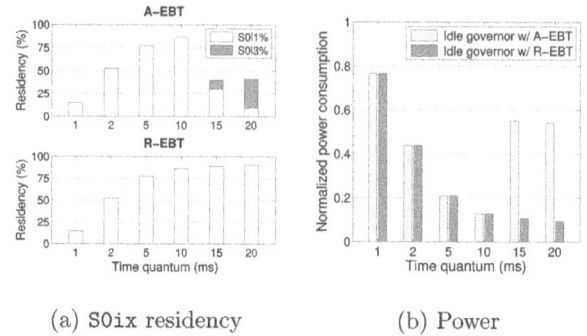

(a) `SOix` residency (b) Power

Figure 9: Comparison of A-EBT vs. R-EBT.

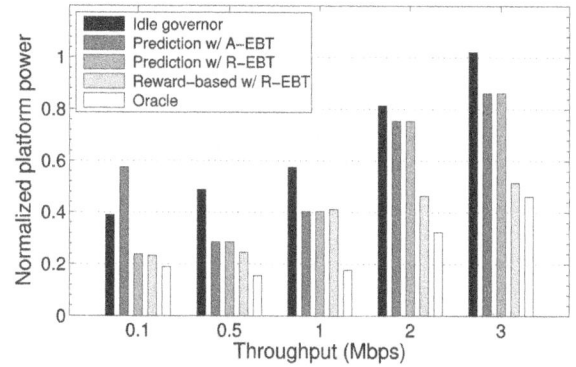

Figure 10: Platform power consumption of the idle-duration prediction-based vs. reward-based sleep-state selection algorithms.

6.2 Effects of Relative Energy Break-even Time

To demonstrate the efficacy of R-EBT, we compare the Linux idle governor's platform sleep state (i.e., `SOix`) selection behavior and its total platform power consumption with A-EBT and R-EBT. In this experiment, we use a CPU-bound synthetic workload with periodic active (i.e., `on`) and idle (i.e., `off`) windows to highlight the effects of R-EBT. The length of one cycle (denoted as time quantum) is chosen between 1 ms and 20 ms for each experiment. The CPU utilization is fixed at a typical 10 % level. The A-EBT of the platform sleep states, `SOi1` and `SOi3`, are 0.8 ms and 12 ms, respectively, which are assumed default system parameters. R-EBT values are calculated based on Eq. (2) in Section 3. Note that the platform power is *normalized* by the full active state platform power consumption.

Fig. 9(a) compares the platform sleep-state residency with A-EBT and R-EBT. With A-EBT (the upper figure), the platform starts to enter `SOi3` as the time quantum (and thus idle duration) exceeds the A-EBT of `SOi3` (i.e., 12 ms). In contrast, R-EBT (the lower figure) refrains from entering `SOi3` until the expected idle duration exceeds the R-EBT of `SOi3`. As a result, R-EBT consumes less power by better utilizing the sleep states for the cases when the time quantum is 15 ms and beyond.

Fig. 9(b) compares the normalized platform power consumption. using the idle governor with A-EBT and R-EBT. The figure shows that, with R-EBT, platform power consumption monotonically decreases with increasing time quantum; with A-EBT, the platform power starts to increase beyond a time quantum of 15 ms as it starts to enter `SOi3`, which is sub-optimal. The figure shows that when the time quantum is 20 ms, R-EBT reduces the platform power consumption by 83 % compared to that of A-EBT, demonstrating the efficacy of R-EBT and its potential for significant power saving, especially for light workloads with relatively long idle durations.

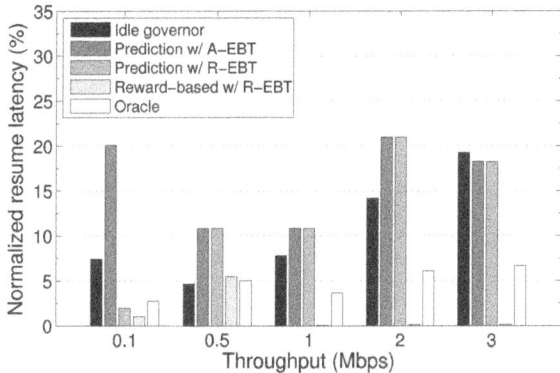

Figure 11: Performance impact of the idle-duration prediction-based vs. reward-based sleep-state selection algorithms.

6.3 Effects of Reward-based Sleep-state Selection

Fig. 10 shows the normalized platform power consumption for the tested schemes. Results demonstrate that the reward-based algorithm outperforms the idle-duration prediction-based schemes (i.e., idle governor and prediction), because of its ability to consider the risk of making an erroneous sleep-state decision and the associated energy costs.

We also make the following two observations. First, for a very light workload (i.e., 1 Mbps), the idle duration prediction-based algorithm using A-EBT consumes more power than the ones using R-EBT. This is because A-EBT encourages the system to aggressively enter deeper platform sleep states (i.e., S0i3), resulting in energy loss due to frequent false entries. Second, the power consumption of the reward-based algorithm saturates as the throughput increases. This is because it can assess the risks of entering a sub-optimal state, and refrains from doing so. The figure shows that the power consumption of the reward-based algorithm becomes close to the ideal case, i.e., `Oracle`, at 3 Mbps. On the other hand, the power consumption of the idle-duration prediction-based algorithms increases with throughput, because they suffer from increasingly frequent false-entries in the high throughput regime. In summary, use of the reward-based algorithm reduces the platform power consumption by up to 50 % compared to the prediction-based algorithms, thus significantly expending battery life.

To evaluate the performance implications, we compared the normalized sleep-state transition latencies of the testing schemes; the higher the resume latency, the greater the potential of performance impact. Fig. 11 shows that the reward-based algorithm significantly lowers the resume latency compared to the idle-duration prediction based algorithms. This is because, the reward-based algorithm prefers to enter shallow states when the system becomes busier, thus avoiding potential power loss due to false entries. This conservative behavior makes the algorithm to even outperform the ideal-power case (`Oracle`) in terms of latency, at the cost of increased power consumption, as we observed in Fig. 10.

Table 2 shows that the reward-based selection algorithm maintains relatively low sleep-state false-entry rates (i.e., < 35 %), thus avoiding the introduction of unnecessary sleep-state transition latencies, which might negatively affect system performance. For testing scenarios with a throughput of 1 Mbps or higher, the false-entry rate is extremely low (< 1 %), corroborating our observations made from Fig. 11. In summary, the proposed reward-based sleep-state selection algorithm reduces platform power and energy consumption significantly without degrading system performance.

7. RELATED WORK

In this section, we briefly summarize the approaches to improve energy efficiency in mobile platforms first. We then review the work related to the system-level power management.

Power management for mobile platforms. Much effort has been made to extend the battery life of mobile platforms. Previous work can be classified into the following four categories:

Table 2: Sleep-state Selection False-entry Rates (%) w/ R-EBT.

Throughput (Mbps)	0.1	0.5	1	2	3
Prediction (%)	24.6	55.2	71.9	72.6	76.5
Reward-based (%)	13.8	35.1	< 1.0	< 1.0	< 1.0

(i) platform and component leakage power reduction [23]; (ii) component active power reduction, e.g., CPU DVFS [41, 44, 36, 20], and display active power reduction [39, 11]; (iii) coarse grain system and device power management, e.g., timeout based sleep-state selection [26, 31] and device runtime PM, etc. (iv) fine grained power management, e.g., [4]. We consider that our work falls in this last category.

Idle-duration prediction & sleep-state selection. The problem of accurate run-time estimation of system idle durations is of critical importance for power management. Hence it has been studied extensively, e.g., [13, 43, 27, 18, 15], and we discuss some of the work closely related to ours. Pallipadi *et al.* [38] introduced a simple moving-average-based idle-duration prediction algorithm, which is used in the current Linux idle governor [4]. Benini *et al.* [15] modeled the system active and idle states as a two-state Markov model. Diao *et al.* [22] proposed to use machine learning algorithms to predict the next idle durations for a multi-core CPU package. Chung *et al.* [18] developed a learning-tree-based idle-prediction mechanism based on previous idle duration history. Gniady *et al.* [25] proposed to use program counters to learn and predict I/O activities. Devasdas *et al.* [19] devised a Kalman-Filter-based idle-duration prediction scheme.

While these sophisticated algorithms help improve idle duration prediction accuracy, they incur prohibitively high computational overheads for active mobile workloads, which require the system to make sleep-state decisions very frequently (e.g., sub-millisecond scales). Moreover, such high computation complexity limits their hardware and firmware implementation feasibility.

Interrupt manipulation Another promising approach to improving energy efficiency is to directly manipulate the interrupts. For example, by merging/coalescing and/or aligning the interrupts, a system can create longer and predictable idle durations [42, 30, 46, 32, 28]. For example, many Network Interface Cards (NICs) employ Interrupt Modulation (IM) [9] to reduce the number of interrupts. With the IM technique, NIC may choose to wait for more packets or a time-out before generating an interrupt, instead of issuing each interrupt immediately after receiving a packet. This feature is mainly used to reduce the interrupt processing overhead when the interrupt rate is very high. Wang *et al.* [46] proposed a mechanism, called `ATC`, that opportunistically coalesces communications interrupts and sends them in bursts to create longer and more deterministic idle duration for the system, without affecting the performance. Liu *et al.* [32] introduced the idea of batching correlated interrupts to reduce whole system wake-up events. In a similar vein, Huang *et al.* [28] proposed to create long-idle durations in memory access patterns by coalescing existing short-idle durations. Our proposed approaches are orthogonal and complementary, to the above-mentioned interrupt manipulation methods. Interrupt manipulation techniques can augment E2S3 to better exploit low-power sleep states.

8. CONCLUSION

In this paper, we proposed a novel low-power sleep-state selection framework, E2S3, that improves energy efficiency by leveraging short-idle durations observed during active workloads for mobile platforms. We have shown that current idle-duration prediction algorithms may not work well for active mobile workloads, hindering a full realization of the potential benefits in multiple low-power states. To address this problem, we (i) proposed the notion of relative energy break-even time to fully exploit the benefit of multiple low-power sleep states, (ii) developed methods to calculate sleep-state selection error rates by modeling random interrupts as a stochastic process, and (iii) introduced a reward-based sleep-state selection algorithm that incorporates the risk of making an incorrect sleep-state decision. We implemented E2S3 algorithms in Android-based smartphones and our experimental results showed that the proposed reward-based sleep-state selection algorithm in E2S3 significantly reduces the platform energy consumption and extend battery life, while conserving system performance.

9. REFERENCES

[1] Intel Ultrabook, http://www.intel.com/content/www/us/en/sponsors-of-tomorrow/ultrabook.html.

[2] Apple FaceTime, http://www.apple.com/mac/facetime/.

[3] Intel Wireless Display (WiDi), http://www.intel.com/content/www/us/en/architecture-and-technology/intel-wireless-display.html.

[4] The idle governor in Linux kernel, http://www.kernel.org.

[5] 2011 U.S. Wireless Handset Customer Satisfaction Studies, http://www.jdpower.com/news/pressRelease.aspx?ID=2011146/.

[6] Windows 7 Power Management, http://www.supertalent.com/datasheets/Windows7.pdf.

[7] pyTimechart, http://packages.python.org/pytimechart/.

[8] Iperf, http://iperf.sourceforge.net.

[9] Interrupt Moderation Using Intel GbE Controllers, http://www.intel.com/content/dam/doc/application-note/gbe-controllers-interrupt-moderation-appl-note.pdf/.

[10] H. Amur, R. Nathuji, M. Ghosh, K. Schwan, and H.-H. S. Lee. Idle power: Application-aware management of processor idle states. In *ACM MMCS*, June 2008.

[11] B. Anand, K. Thirugnanam, J. Sebastian, P. G. Kannan, A. L. Ananda, M. C. Chan, and R. K. Balan. Adaptive display power management for mobile games. In *ACM MobiSys*, June/July 2011.

[12] M. Armbrust, A. Fox, R. Griffith, A. D. Joseph, R. Katz, A. Konwinski, G. Lee, D. Patterson, A. Rabkin, I. Stoica, and M. Zaharia. Above the clouds: A berkeley view of cloud computing. In *Technical Report. UCB/EECS-2009-28. EECS Department, University of California, Berkeley*, February 2009.

[13] S.-Y. Bang, K. Bang, S. Yoon, and E.-Y. Chung. Run-time adaptive workload estimation for dynamic voltage scaling. *IEEE Transactions on Computer-Aided Design of Integrated Circuits and Systems*, 28(9):1334–1347, September 2009.

[14] L. A. Barroso and U. Hölzl. The case for energy-proportional computing. *IEEE Computer*, 40(12):33–37, December 2007.

[15] L. Benini, A. Bogliolo, G. A. Paleologo, and G. D. Micheli. Policy optimization for dynamic power management. *IEEE Transactions on Computer-Aided Design of Integrated Circuits and Systems*, 18(6):813–833, June 1999.

[16] L. Benini and G. D. Michel. System-level power optimization: Techniques and tools. *ACM Transactions on Design Automation of Electronic Systems*, 5(2):115–192, April 2000.

[17] T. D. Burd, T. A. Pering, A. J. Stratakos, and R. W. Brodersen. A dynamic voltage scaled microprocessor system. *IEEE Journal of Solid-State Circuits*, 35(11):1571–1580, November 2000.

[18] E.-Y. Chung, L. Benini, and G. D. Micheli. Dynamic power management using adaptive learning tree. In *ACM ICCAD*, November 1999.

[19] V. Devadas and H. Aydin. On the interplay of voltage/frequency scaling and device power management for frame-based real-time embedded applications. *IEEE Transactions on Computers*, 61(1):31–44, January 2011.

[20] G. Dhiman, K. K. Pusukuri, and T. Rosing. Analysis of dynamic voltage scaling for system level energy management. In *ACM HotPower*, December 2008.

[21] G. Dhiman and T. S. Rosing. Dynamic power management using machine learning. In *ACM ICCAD*, November 2006.

[22] Q. Diao and J. Song. Prediction of CPU idle-busy activity pattern. In *IEEE HPCA*, February 2008.

[23] K. Flautner, N. S. Kim, S. Martin, D. Blaauw, and T. Mudge. Drowsey caches: Simple techniques for reducing leakage power. In *IEEE Computer Architecture*, August 2002.

[24] J. Flinn and M. Satyanarayanan. Energy-aware adaptation for mobile applications. In *ACM SOSP*, December 1999.

[25] C. Gniady, Y. C. Hu, , and Y.-H. Lu. Program counter based techniques for dynamic power management. In *IEE Software*, February 2004.

[26] R. Golding, P. Bosch, and J. Wilke. Idlness is not sloth. In *ACM USENIX*, September 1995.

[27] M. Hayenga, C. Sudanthi, M. Ghosh, P. Ramrakhyani, and N. Paver. Accurate system-level performance modeling and workload characterization for mobile internet devices. In *ACM MEDEA*, October 2008.

[28] H. Huang, K. G. Shin, C. Lefurgy, and T. Keller. Improving energy efficiency by making DRAM less randomly accessed. In *ACM ISLPED*, August 2005.

[29] S. Irani, S. Shukla, and R. Gupta. Competitive analysis of dynamic power management strategies for systems with multiple power saving states. In *ACM DATE*, March 2002.

[30] A. Kulkarni, R. Wang, C. Maciocco, S. Bakshi, and J. Tsai. IDC: An energy efficient communication scheme for connected mobile platforms. In *IEEE ICC*, June 2009.

[31] K. Li, R. Kumpf, P. Horton, and T. Anderson. A quantitative analysis of disk drive power management in portable computers. In *ACM USENIX*, December 1994.

[32] J. Liu and P. H. Chou. Optimizing mode transition sequences in idle intervals for component-level and system-level energy minimization. In *IEEE/ACM ICCAD*, January 2005.

[33] Y.-H. Lu, E.-Y. Chung, T. Šimunić, L. Benini, and G. D. Micheli. Server workload analysis for power minimization using consolidation. In *ACM USENIX*, September 2009.

[34] Y.-H. Lu and G. De Micheli. Comparing system level power management policies. *IEEE Design Test of Computers*, 18(2):10–19, March/April 2001.

[35] D. Meisner, B. T. Gold, and T. F. Wenisch. Powernap: Eliminating server idle power. In *ACM ASPLOS*, March 2009.

[36] A. Miyoshi, C. Lefurgy, E. V. Hensbergen, R. Rajamony, and R. Rajkumar. Critical power slope: Understanding the rumtime effects of frequency scaling. In *ACM ICS*, June 2002.

[37] NVIDIA, September 2001. The Benefits of Quad Core CPUs in Mobile Devices, http://www.nvidia.com/content/PDF/tegra_white_papers/tegra-whitepaper-0911a.pdf.

[38] V. Pallipadi, S. Li, and A. Belay. cpuidle—do nothing, efficiently... In *The Linux Symposium*, June 2006.

[39] K. Patel, E. Macii, and M. Poncino. Frame buffer energy optimization by pixel prediction. In *ACM ICCD*, October 2005.

[40] K. Pentikousis. In search of energy-efficient mobile networking. *IEEE Communications Magazine*, 48(1):95–103, January 2010.

[41] P. Pillai and K. G. Shin. Real-time dynamic voltage scaling for low-power embedded operating systems. In *ACM SOSP*, October 2001.

[42] P. Ranganathan. Recipe for efficiency: Principles of power-aware computing. *ACM Communications*, 53(4):60–67, April 2010.

[43] K. D. Ryu and J. K. Hollingsworth. Exploiting fine-grained idle periods in networks of workstations. *IEEE Transactions on Parallel and Distributed Systems*, 11(7):683–698, July 2000.

[44] T. Simunic, L. Benini, A. Acquaviva, P. Glynn, and G. D. Michieli. Dynamic voltage scaling and power management for portable systems. In *ACM DAC*, June 2001.

[45] A. Verma, G. Dasgupta, T. K. Nayak, P. De, and R. Kothari. Server workload analysis for power minimization using consolidation. In *ACM USENIX*, September 2009.

[46] R. Wang, J. Tsai, C. Maciocco, T.-Y. C. Tai, and J. Wu. Reducing power consumption for mobile platforms via adaptive traffic coalescing. *IEEE Journal on Selected Areas in Communications*, 29(8):1618–1629, September 2011.

Improving Coherence Protocol Reactiveness by Trading Bandwidth for Latency

Lucía G. Menezo   Valentin Puente   Pablo Abad   José Ángel Gregorio

University of Cantabria
Los Castros Ave. s/n 39005 Santander (Spain)
{gregoriol, vpuente, abadp, monaster}@unican.es

ABSTRACT

This paper describes how on-chip network particularities could be used to improve coherence protocol responsiveness. In order to achieve this, a new coherence protocol, named LOCKE, is proposed. LOCKE successfully exploits large on-chip bandwidth availability to improve cache-coherent chip multiprocessor performance and energy efficiency. Provided that the interconnection network is designed to support multicast traffic and the protocol maximizes the potential advantages that direct coherence brings, we demonstrate that a multicast-based coherence protocol could reduce energy requirements in the CMP memory hierarchy. The key idea presented is to establish a suitable level of on-chip network throughput to accelerate synchronization by two means: avoiding the protocol serialization, inherent to directory-based coherence protocol, and reducing average access time more than in other snoop-based coherence protocols, when shared data is truly contended. LOCKE is developed on top of a Token coherence performance substrate, with a new set of simple proactive policies that speeds up data synchronization and eliminates the passive token starvation avoidance mechanism. Using a full-system simulator that faithfully models on-chip interconnection, aggressive core architecture and precise memory hierarchy details, while running a broad spectrum of workloads, our proposal can improve both directory-based and token-based coherence protocols both in terms of energy and performance, at least in systems with up to 16 aggressive out-of-order processors in the chip.

Categories and Subject Descriptors

B.3.2 [**Memory structures**]: Design Styles – *cache memories*

Keywords CMP, coherence protocol, memory hierarchy.

1. INTRODUCTION

Chip multiprocessors (CMPs) represent a major milestone in computing system evolution. Adding more processors per chip seems to be the most reasonable approach to keep translating the continuous enhancement in technological integration into performance improvements. Given the challenge involved in parallel software development, the hardware has to assist the programmer's productivity [4] as much as possible. The consensus is that it is much easier to perform this task by providing all chip cores with a unified memory view. From the

hardware point of view, in CMP systems one of the major challenges is the off-chip bandwidth wall. Among other solutions, it is essential to provide complex on-chip cache hierarchies to minimize off-chip interface pressure.

If we combine the above-mentioned facts, it seems that cache coherent CMP will become the dominant class of systems, at least in general purpose computing. Today, many commercial products that target this market implement this approach [28][18][7]. However, this statement does not negate the suitability of non-cache coherent CMPs, such as [13], in some specialized markets.

In a CMP system, the computing elements are so intricate that hardware-enforced cache coherence is the easiest way to support the shared memory model and so, the coherence protocol has a fundamental role to play. Many architectural solutions used in CMP systems are borrowed from the off-chip realm without substantial alterations. In particular, many of the cache coherence protocols used or proposed take advantage of premises from System-Multiprocessors. Some of them are very cautious about bandwidth utilization at the expense of increasing latency. In an off-chip interconnection network, bandwidth is scarce because of the discrete nature of the communication system elements. In contrast, in on-chip interconnection networks bandwidth availability is greater. In this type of systems, communication link width is much greater and the delay allows much faster data rates with lower energy cost. 3D stacked systems [37] and utilization of low-swing links [20] substantially increase the excess in bandwidth and reduce the energy cost of moving data.

The coherence protocol should, at all costs, use on-chip network bandwidth availability to avoid adding extra latency in the form of indirections. Currently there are a substantial number of CMP coherence protocol proposals that share our view [2][22][26][30]. Most of these ideas use broadcasting as the mechanism to overcome indirection at intermediate ordering points. Nevertheless, bandwidth demand is still a concern in most of these works and they allow some performance to be lost in exchange for saving bandwidth consumption.

With a suitable interconnection network design it could be possible to increase the whole system performance by improving the coherence protocol behavior. Following this premise, we introduce the LOCKE Coherence Protocol in this work. This protocol uses the token coherence framework [22] as its starting point, but enhancing responsiveness and stability in several ways. First, token coherence deals with concurrent requests coming from different processors to shared blocks using a passive approach called "Persistent Request". This mechanism uses a time-out-based triggering policy to address the aforementioned situation. Consequently, critical operations, such as contended synchronizations, could be artificially delayed. This negatively affects system performance. Second, the mechanism could overreact when the network is heavily loaded, potentially turning most of the processor memory accesses into persistent requests. Contention is hard to manage and adds unpredictable and non-depreciable delays in latency. On top of that, persistent request increases contention due to the extra traffic generated. In extreme situations, some applications could render the system useless due to the chain-reaction produced by persistent request explosion and contention. Neither static nor dynamic time-out estimation is sufficient to avoid such unstable behavior, because they cannot capture the diverse and complex situation that contention produces.

In order to identify where each token position is, LOCKE uses explicit acknowledgments for each token movement. Thus, each memory request will locate either tokens or pending acknowledgments. In this way, we can quickly forward requests to in-flight tokens' destinations, which would improve latency when accessing contended data. Applying a correct ordering between true racing requests, eventually any pending operation will locate the data and all the tokens needed to complete the transaction. No starvation avoidance mechanism, such as persistent request, is required. It might appear that acknowledgment traffic will increase bandwidth utilization and added contention could potentially increase network latency or network energy consumption, however, using state-of-the-art network design we will demonstrate that this is not the case. The effectiveness of the token location mechanism compensates for its extra bandwidth consumption, improving the energy-performance tradeoff of both token coherence and directory-based coherence protocols.

We have evaluated the effectiveness of the idea using a state-of-the-art full-system simulator which includes a very precise interconnection network simulator with a wide variety of workloads ranging from multithreaded server applications, through multithreaded numerical applications to multi-programmed workloads. LOCKE outperforms, on average, a conventional Directory and a Token Coherence protocol by 16% and 28% respectively for 16-core CMP with Nehalem-like cores. Additionally, LOCKE exhibits lower susceptibility to workload characteristics, having six times less performance variance than Token Coherence.

The rest of the paper is organized as follows: Section 2 explains the motivation for the introduction of LOCKE. Section 3 describes the proposal itself, explaining the foundations of the coherence protocol. Section 4 describes the experimental methodology employed. Section 5 presents performance results and provides insight into LOCKE responsiveness. Section 6 summarizes the related work and, finally, Section 7 states the main conclusions of the paper.

2. MOTIVATION

2.1 Trading Bandwidth for Latency

Bandwidth availability is profuse in CMP environments because of the utilization of scalable point-to-point interconnection networks, scalable cache hierarchies such as NUCA, and ultra-wide short links. In contrast, the portion of the chip reachable per clock cycle is shrinking as the technology advances. Under this scenario, it seems inadequate to maintain coherence in a CMP using protocols originally conceived for off-chip systems, such as directory-based ones [21], especially if their utilization increases data access latency due to the burden of multiple indirections across the chip. Therefore, taking advantage of bandwidth availability to avoid adding extra delay makes sense. As stated before, snoop-based protocols running on top of scalable interconnection networks provide the best design choice for CMP systems. Currently most commercial aggressive CMPs, such as [28][18], use this approach. Nevertheless, it is commonly accepted that those protocols are not free of shortcomings, namely: 1) The multicast traffic required for on-chip cache requests will increase power consumption; 2) An excessive network and cache bandwidth consumption could increase contention and increase on-chip latency, potentially ruining the rationale of snoop-based coherence protocols, and 3) The extra cache tag lookups produced in such protocols will increase cache energy consumption.

Although these considerations are pertinent, their impact can be much smaller than is commonly believed. First, power consumption is affected by this multicast traffic in a different way depending on the network characteristics. If the network has hardware support for multicast [10], its impact is highly reduced. In this case, each network resource is used at most once per request instead of many times as occurs when no support is provided. According to [1], using multicast support could save up to 70% in the Energy Delay Square Product (ED2P)[1] . Second, a correctly dimensioned design for the cache hierarchy capable of decoupling the number of cores and the on-chip cache bandwidth will oblige the use of NUCAs [14], as [28][18] are already doing. Under these circumstances, on-chip communication bandwidth will scale in proportion to core count. Third and finally, if we take into account the growing leakage in each technological advance [15], the area devoted to cache, and the substantial benefit in terms of performance obtained by snoop-based coherence, increased tag snoop energy is quickly amortized by the reduction in static energy.

2.2 Token Coherence Responsiveness

Conceptually the Token Coherence protocol deals with racing requests by counting tokens. This way, data races are avoided by forcing different ongoing memory operations to require an incompatible number of tokens in order to be performed. For example, performing a simultaneous read (GETS) and write (GETX) over the same cache block requires more than the maximum number of tokens available in the system. In starvation-prone circumstances, each contending processor eventually issues a persistent request, which will statically determine the winner and force the losers to return the tokens to the frontrunner processor. When this one finishes its operation, the next processor obtains the tokens required to perform its pending memory transaction. Assuming that under realistic working conditions racing requests are not frequent, this serialization will have a negligible impact on performance.

However, synchronization is a key operation in multithreaded workloads [35], which in most cases will involve racing requests. The passive approach used by token coherence to resolve that situation, which is bounded by the time established to issue the persistent request, could delay synchronization resolution unnecessarily. Additionally, persistent requests not only serialize potential data races, but also address temporary lack of knowledge about token location. This problem situation arises when some of the tokens required to perform a specific memory transaction are unavailable at the end point of all multicast messages issued by the request. For example, this happens when a block is evicted from the cache and the request overtakes the in-flight data block

---

[1] ED2P is the most suitable energy-performance tradeoff for high-performance systems [38], such as the scenario assumed in this paper.

in the interconnection network. In these circumstances, the request will not be fulfilled because the destination of the tokens being evicted will never be located by the original request. The outcome of this situation is similar to a temporary racing request, denoted as "false racing request". By contraposition, we denote concurrent and simultaneously incompatible operations issued over the same block by different processors as "true racing requests". When interconnection network contention is considered, this situation might not be as negligible as it was with true racing requests, especially in highly contended situations.

2.3 Token Coherence Stability

The persistent request method is a starvation avoidance mechanism that solves true or false request races by keeping track of the time involved in each pending memory request. If the time is greater than a fixed time threshold, a persistent request is sent. In order to maintain the scalability of the hardware, structures are required to perform persistent requests and to provide a distributed and fair arbitration scheme. Token coherence assumes that only one ongoing persistent request per core is supported. To minimize performance impact in processors with multiple outstanding memory operations, the original request is reissued one or more times before sending a persistent request.

The timeout chosen to trigger this process can be established statically, looking at the on-chip miss access latency, or dynamically, averaging the average latency of recent memory transactions. If the time of a particular ongoing memory transaction is above this limit, it seems reasonable to suppose that there might be another core accessing the same block. The request is reissued and if the timeout is once again exceeded then a persistent request is sent. Although this mechanism seems to be very simple, contention effects are ignored. For example, when the load applied over the network is significant, the communication latency of each individual message increases as a result of the unavailability of resources in use by other messages. At medium loads the total latency could increase by a few cycles, but when the load is higher this variation could be substantially larger and, worst of all, highly dependent on the applied load and on the interconnection network implementation.

In a low contention situation, network latency is closer to the base latency and persistent requests work as expected. Nevertheless, if a spike of traffic suddenly appears, contention increases and so does the latency of all pending memory transactions. If the effect of the contention is over the persistent request timeout, a chain reaction is triggered. The positive feedback between reissues and persistent request and network contention creates a storm of these types of requests in which almost any memory operation is reissued or even resolved by a persistent request. Under this unstable situation, the system performance drops dramatically. To illustrate this phenomenon, we will focus our interest on two particular applications (NUMERICAL and SERVER) running in 16 aggressive cores in the CMP, described in subsection 4.1. All of the parameters of the system, including the network, are correctly dimensioned, i.e. they are chosen in order to obtain an optimal cost/performance ratio over a large set of applications. The sharing degree of the two applications is quite different, in the SERVER it is high and in the NUMERICAL it is low. However, for an optimal time-out threshold and one reissue before sending a persistent request, the proportion of memory transactions resolved by persistent request is less than 0.1% for SERVER and more than 10% for NUMERICAL.

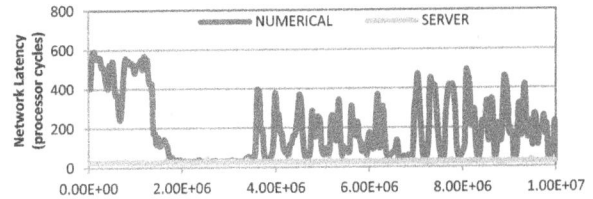

(a)

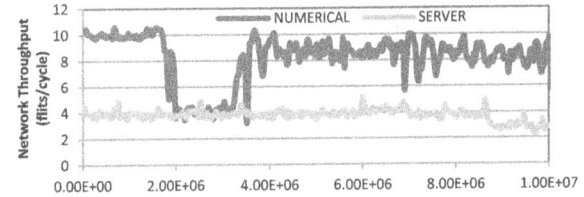

(b)

Figure 1. Network dynamic evolution with a 16-processor system (a) Average latency (includes injection queue delay), (b) Throughput.

This behavior, which is apparently contradictory according to the sharing degree of each application, is easily explained looking at Figure 1. It shows the network latency (a) and the applied load (b) during 10 million processor cycles for both applications. In contrast to the SERVER, the NUMERICAL application is very interconnection network demanding during short intervals due to the access to highly contended blocks. During these phases, the latency spikes due to on-network contention effects. These effects are exacerbated by the one-to-all traffic pattern of the application. During these spikes, reissue and persistent request frequency increases, not because of true racing requests but because packets are delayed within the network. This triggers more reissues and persistent requests, which further increases contention. Even using dynamically predicted thresholds, we are unable to predict any sudden variations in latency. In fact, dynamic estimations could accelerate system instabilities even preventing the complete execution of the workload. The described effect is not a rare anomaly and similar behavior could also be observed if off-chip bandwidth is saturated. All in all, without a solution for this problem, employing this protocol in a general purpose machine would be highly risky.

3. LOCKE COHERENCE PROTOCOL

LOCKE will use token counting to maintain coherence invariants, but it introduces a smart mechanism to actively resolve true racing requests, making a passive starvation avoidance mechanism unnecessary. In order to do this, LOCKE is based on precise knowledge of where any token is or will be located in the near future. If the protocol is able to track all the tokens, no false racing requests are possible. True racing requests are solved with a starvation-free self-inhibition mechanism that serializes data access of simultaneous incompatible memory transactions. Next, we will detail how false racing requests are avoided and true racing requests are dealt with. For readers interested in a more detailed specification of the protocol, a table-based state-transition table of cache controllers can be seen at [27].

3.1 False Racing Requests: Token location

In order to determine token location, any block movement is monitored at the originating location, keeping a label of the destination of the block. The label information is kept until a message reception acknowledgement is received from that destination. Thus, when a coherence controller generates a request, all the tokens needed or the flag of some pending acknowledgement will be found. Note that, in contrast to directory-based protocols, LOCKE's acknowledgement messaging is outside the critical data access path.

If the request corresponds to a write operation (Get Exclusive or GETX) every token will be forwarded to the requestor. On the contrary, if the request corresponds to a read operation (Get not exclusive or GETS) only the controller with the owner token will reply. If a request arrives when the tokens required are in-flight the requestor is notified with the final destination of the tokens. In this way, the requestor may reissue a unicast request to the one holding the necessary tokens. The intermediate node always notifies the requestor if the transaction is a GETX, but only notifies that the owner token is in-flight when the request is a GETS. Note that this is the situation depicted in the example in Figure 2, where simultaneously, processors P0 and P2 try to perform a GETS operation for the same block, and P1 holds only the owner token for that block. This situation in Token Coherence Protocol implies a false racing request. The side effect of this mechanism is the generation of extra unicast traffic for acknowledgement packets and reissuing the GETS. As we said before, in contrast to directory-based coherence protocols, acknowledgments operate outside the critical path of any memory transaction. In this example, the hit latency of processor P2 will not be increased because of the mechanism.

Unfortunately, the previous scheme is starvation prone. To exemplify this, Figure 3 shows the same initial situation as in Figure 2. This time, P0's request is delayed long enough so that it arrives at P1 when the acknowledgement message from P2 has already been received. In this situation, P1 does not notify P0 that P2 has the block and the owner token. Moreover, P2 is unaware of P0 being interested in that block because P0's request arrived at P2 before this processor issued the GETS. If both of these things happen, P0's transaction starves.

In order to prevent this anomalous situation, we need an approach to order both requests on the interconnection network. The most scalable way to perform such ordering is to use the same multicast routing tree for each set of addresses. If we force all the requests to a specific address to follow that routing tree, then no request or acknowledgment race is possible because the messages involved cannot be overtaken. To balance network resource utilization we could define different multicast trees per address. Routers should include the mechanism to use the right routing tree according to the address accessed. Using the least significant bits in the address we could select which one to follow. Figure 4 shows a possible distribution in an 8-processor CMP with non-uniform cache architecture using a 4×4 mesh interconnection network and four multicast trees. We will denote the multicast trees as I-trees. To minimize base latency effects, each I-tree trunk can pass through the last level (LLC) slice where the address could be located. Note that one of the destinations for the request multicast will be an L2 slice. For example, addresses mapped in slice 0, 4, 8 and 12 will use the I-tree for addresses %XXX00.

---

[2] The shadowing in the lines reflects the block state: Inv (Invalid state), O (Owner State), OI (Owner to Invalid), IS (Invalid to Shared). The line in the arrows reflects the nature of the message: dashed lines correspond to multicast, solid lines correspond to unicast.

Any multicast-capable network requires a multicast routing tree [11]. For example, in Figure 4, if core 0 requests data that is located in core 1 L1 cache, it will take only one hop in the network to reach it. In the worst case, if data is located in core 4 L1 cache using the I-tree in the figure it will take 7 network hops to reach it when in an optimal multicast tree it will take 3 hops. Although the average impact on on-chip latency overhead will depend on data distribution and network contention, the average distance increment for multicast messages is less than 10%. Moreover, the rest of the traffic (no requests or acks) always follows minimal paths.

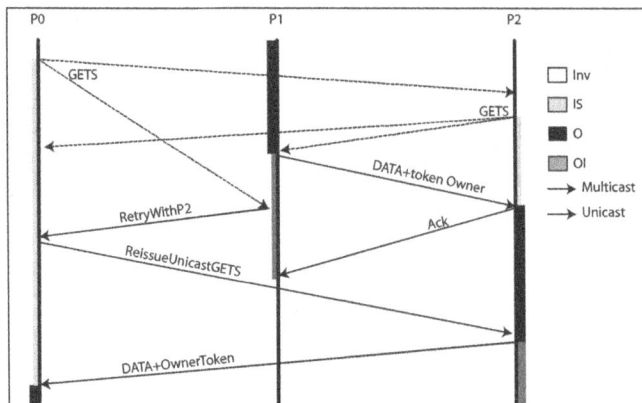

Figure 2. Token location with explicit acknowledgement: P0 issues a GETS operation transitioning the block to IS[2], P2 issues another GETS operation for the same block. The request from P2 arrives first at P1, which has only the owner token. P1 sends the data with the owner token to P2, transitioning its own block to OI. This state will be maintained until the explicit reception acknowledgement from P2 arrives at P1. When the block is received at P2, the block goes to the stable state O and the acknowledgement message is sent. In the meantime, the request from P0 arrives at P1 which informs it that P2 has the owner token. P0 reissues a unicast to P2 demanding a copy of the data.

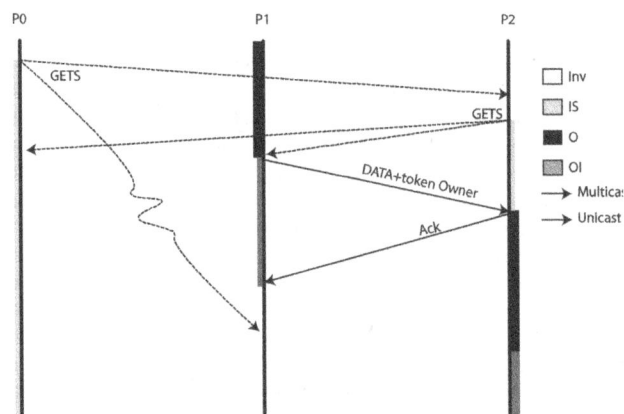

Figure 3. Starvation with request overtaking: With the same initial state depicted previously, the P0 multicast request message arrives at P2 before it issues its own GETS and arrives at P1 after the acknowledgement reception from P2. Both processors P1 and P2 ignore P0's request.

146

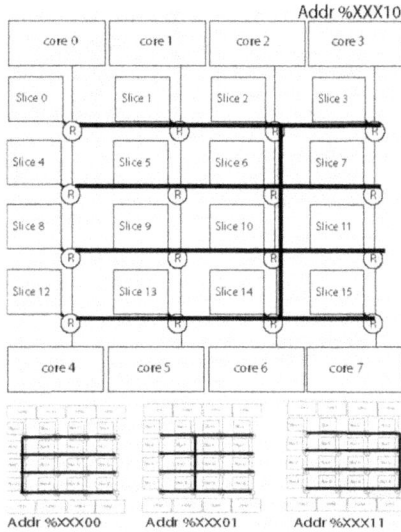

Addr %XXX10

Figure 4. Ordering I-tree in an S-NUCA architecture.

3.2 True Racing Requests: Arbitration

3.2.1 Self-inhibition

If the location of all tokens needed to complete a transaction is known then only true racing requests have to be dealt with. When two or more processors are trying to perform simultaneous but incompatible operations, LOCKE solves the situation using scalable self-regulated arbitration. The solution adopted is to assign a priority order to each processor and operation and to allow the resolution of the race without breaking the coherency invariants. The different coherency controllers apply this policy in a fully distributed way, so guaranteeing system scalability.

Two or more simultaneous operations over the same block are incompatible if the total number of required tokens is greater than the number of processors P. If one coherence controller detects the possibility of such a situation arising, it must choose whether to keep going with the operation or to give up. For example if it wants to perform a write operation in a cache block and sees an incoming write request from another processor trying to write in the same cache block, it has to check each request priority. Initially and for the sake of simplicity we will assume that the priority is determined by the processor index. If the current controller has an index smaller than the incoming request, the controller goes ahead with its operation or, if not, it self-freezes the operation.

If the controller decides to temporarily inhibit the outgoing transaction, due to its inferior priority with respect to the remote incoming request, it changes the block state to "frozen" and annotates the winner controller for that block. When a block is frozen, any incoming token will be forwarded to the annotated winner controller. The block will remain in a frozen state until the winner notifies the completion of the operation, via a complete multicast message. If this happens, the inhibited operation is reissued from the beginning. Figure 5 presents an example of this situation.

---

[3] The shadowing in the lines reflects block state: Inv (Invalid state), M (Modified State), MI (Modified to Invalid), IM (Invalid to Modified), Frozen (frozen memory operation).

When a block is frozen, any other write request from another controller, no matter what its priority is, will be ignored. Thus, according to the timing of the reception of requests an implicit tree of pending operations is formed. This tree has a tendency to follow the address I-tree shape. Usually, independently of the number of controllers that are trying to perform the operation concurrently, the ordering tree shape is deep. Therefore, the request reissue after reordering is lazy; only one pending memory transaction is reissued after the completion of a write in most cases.

3.2.2 Priority Ordering with Out-of-order processors

Statically assigned priorities could provoke pathological situations because contended blocks will be obtained most often by the same processor. Nevertheless, assuming multiple outstanding requests per core, there is an easy and scalable solution to deal with this if we are capable of guaranteeing that: (a) Two different processors cannot issue an operation to the same block with the same priority; (b) The probability of having a different priority ordering at two contended blocks from two different processors has to be non zero.

The first condition guarantees that two different processors will never simultaneously grab a subset of tokens from the same block, i.e. avoiding starvation. The second condition guarantees that, on average, there will not be any memory operation favored over others. The most straightforward way to achieve this is to construct the priority of each request as the combination of the processor ID (LSB bits) used to achieve condition one, and a small random number (MSB bits) to achieve condition two. Experimentally, it is observed that this approach provides similar performance to an age-based priority (which requires a complex coordinated timestamp-based mechanism) at a fraction of the cost.

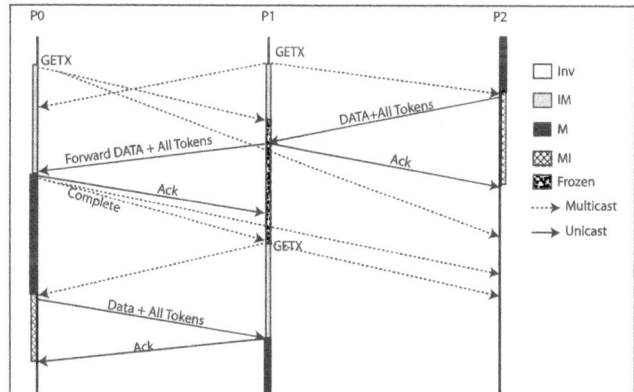

Figure 5. Example of write serialization: P0 and P1 simultaneously issue a GETX over a block in M^3 state at P2 (i.e., all the tokens are located there). Let's assume P0 has higher priority than P1. P1's request arrives at P2 first, so P2 sends data and all tokens, changing its state block to transitory state MI until the acknowledgement from P1 is received. Before receiving the data and the tokens, P1 sees a request from processor P0 which has more priority than its own priority, so it self-freezes its operation and annotates P0 as the winner at the MSHR. When data and tokens from P2 arrive, they are immediately forwarded to the winner P0, annotating the in-flight tokens. When P0 receives the data and tokens it sends an acknowledgement to P1 and finalizes its operation. When P0's GETX operation ends, it broadcasts a complete message. P1's MSHR hit unfreezes the operation and reissues it.

The performance reduction observed for a four-bit random number compared to an idealized fully age-based approach is less than 1%.

4. EVALUATION METHODOLOGY

4.1 Target System Configuration

In order to validate the advantages of our proposal, we have used two coherence protocols for the given system architecture with the configuration parameters shown in Table 1. The main parameters of the target system mimic state-of-the-art high-end CMPs such as [6][28][18]. The baseline coherence protocol used is an optimized directory protocol similar to the one used to compare the token coherence protocol in [25], but adapted to NUCA. Directory information is distributed across all slices and full mapping. Optimistically, null storage overhead is assumed for this protocol. Broadcast-based token coherence protocol variation [22] is considered, as a representative counterpart to snoop-based protocols. A fixed timeout to reissue the request is used. Only one reissue is tolerated before triggering a persistent request. This timeout has been selected measuring all the benchmarks with different timeouts and choosing the one with best average performance. Dynamically estimated time-out does not provide performance benefits.

For the cache hierarchy we will assume NUCA [14] for the last level cache. Although LOCKE is also applicable for a tiled system, NUCA architecture is a better approach because it decouples the number of LLC cache slices from the number of cores, providing much more flexibility to scale on-chip bandwidth. This cache architecture is currently a mainstream choice in high-end CMPs.

As far as the interconnection network is concerned, we will add the minimum variation over a commonly used router microarchitecture and network topology. As for the router microarchitecture used, it will be similar to the proposal described in [10], using on-network multicast support when required. We use dynamic buffering allocation per virtual channel and 1-cycle pipeline pass-through latency. In each protocol we use the required number of virtual channels to avoid message-dependent deadlock [31] and network deadlock [9].

In order to observe the scalability of the proposal we chose two different system sizes composed of 8 and 16 processors. The eight-processor system layout is similar to the one shown in Figure 4. For 16 cores, although the processor, L1 and router remain unchanged, the LLC capacity and bandwidth are scaled up in accordance with the larger number of processors [28].

In all configurations, instead of using in-order cores, we opted for aggressive out-of-order processors to mimic [18][28]. Although a large number of small cores could make sense for cloud-computing workloads, in general purpose computing, an aggressive processor microarchitecture still matters [12]. Additionally, medium size systems with a large number of outstanding memory transactions per processor will be much more demanding for the coherence protocol than many simple cores.

4.2 Simulation Stack

We work with a framework that allows us to perform full-system evaluation, i.e. user and system level code are accurately simulated. The main strategy of the proposal is that network bandwidth can be used cleverly to boost system performance; therefore, careful interconnection network modeling is essential. In order to achieve this requirement, SICOSYS [29] replaces the original interconnection network simulator of the full-system

Table 1. Basic system configuration, 32 nm. technology assumed for energy estimations

Processor Config.	Number of cores	8 @3GHz(config1) *16 @3GHz(config2)*
	Functional Units	4xI-ALU/4xFP-ALU/ 4xD-MEM
	IWin size/Issue Width	128, 4-way
	Fetch-to-Dispatch	7 cycles
L1 Cache	Size/Associativity/ BlockSize/Access Time	128KB I/D, 4-way, 64B, 2 cycles
	Max. Outstanding Mem. Operations	16
L2 Cache	Size/Associativity/ BlockSize	8MB, 16×512KB, 16-way, 64B (config1) *16MB, 32×512KB, 16-way, 64B (config2)*
	NUCA Mapping	Static, interleaved across slices
	Slice Access Time	5 cycles
Memory	Capacity/Access Time/ Memory Controllers/ BW	4GB, 240 cycles,2 centered / 32GBs (config 1) *4GB, 240 cycles, 4 centered/64GBs (config 2)*
Network	Topology / Link Latency/ Link Width	4×4 Mesh, 1 cycle, 16B (config 1) *6×6 Mesh,1cycle, 16B (config 2)*
	Router Latency/ Flow Control/ Buffering Size / Routing	1 cycle/ Wormhole/ 5.4KB/DOR

simulation tool GEMS [23]. SICOSYS models router microarchitecture very precisely. Therefore, network contention effects induced by extra traffic will be precisely modeled in the simulations. SICOSYS is augmented with Orion [17] in order to estimate the network energy consumption with each protocol. Power consumption in other components of the memory hierarchy is computed using CACTI [36]. The energy required by the cores will be assumed, pessimistically for performance leaders, to be constant across the different coherence protocols. The energy of each event is estimated assuming 32 nm technology.

4.3 Workloads

Fifteen workloads (see Table 2) are considered in this study, including both multi-programmed and multi-threaded applications (numerical and server) running on top of the OpenSolaris 10 OS.

Table 2. Evaluated workloads

Multithreaded Workloads	Wisconsin Commercial Workload [3]	Apache (1000 Surge dynamic)	Zeus (1000 Surge Static)
		Jbb (4000 SpecJbb)	OLTP (500 TPC-C alike)
	NAS Parallel Bench. [16]	FT (Class W)	CG (Class A)
		LU (Class A)	IS (Class A)
	PARSEC [5]	blackscholes (native)	
		canneal (native)	
		fluidanimate (native)	
Multiprogrammed Workloads	Spec 2006 [32] (Rate Mode)	astar (reference)	hmmer (reference)
		lbm (reference)	ommetpp (reference)

The server benchmarks correspond to the whole Wisconsin Commercial Workload suite [3], released by the authors of GEMS in version 2.1. The remaining class corresponds to multi-programmed workloads using part of the SPEC CPU2006 suite [32] running in rate mode (where one core is reserved to run OS services. Each application is simulated multiple times with random perturbations in memory access time in order to reach 95% confidence intervals. The number of applications enables the sweeping of a broad spectrum of usage scenarios, with diverse sharing degree, sharing contention, working set size, etc.

5. EVALUATION

5.1 Performance and Efficiency

Figure 6 shows the performance with the basic 8-processor CMP (*config1* in Table 1). On average, DIRECTORY is outperformed by LOCKE and TOKEN. As expected, some workloads are insensitive, which attenuates the average performance impact of coherence protocol. In contrast, in applications with highly contended blocks, such as NAS benchmarks, coherence is very relevant. In those cases, LOCKE outperforms other protocols by up to almost 30%. In applications with high sharing degree but limited contention, such as server workloads, LOCKE outperforms the other counterparts by a smaller but noticeable margin. Although, on average, TOKEN performs better than DIRECTORY some noticeable results such as IS or FT, even in a modest size system like this one, show its performance is poor for the reasons explained in Section 2.3. In contrast, LOCKE exhibits a consistent performance across all the workloads.

End-point traffic comparison of different protocols may not reflect a direct impact in performance or energy profile. First, when the network uses capable routers, as in our case, a multicast packet with n destinations will not use the same effective bandwidth as n unicast packets for the same destination [10]. This issue will be considered again later in subsection 5.4. Second, network energy

is only a part of the on-chip memory hierarchy which is dominated by cache. Third, Energy Delay Square Product (ED2P) is the most suitable metric to estimate energy-performance tradeoff in high-performance systems such as ours [38]. Therefore, we provide this metric, grouped for each suite of benchmarks and protocols in Figure 6 (b). As we can see, the cubic influence of performance in ED2P has a major effect, meaning that the ED2P of the network, in spite of producing more traffic, is even smaller for broadcast-based protocols. Additionally, for 32nm technology and a large cache footprint (8MB in this configuration), leakage power, which is constant across coherence protocols, causes the ED2P leakage proportion to grow significantly when the performance is worse. Therefore, and contrary to common belief, snoop-based broadcast coherence protocols have lower average ED2P than the one based on directories. Due to the more consistent LOCKE performance, on average it requires 19% less ED2P than DIRECTORY. In contrast, due to performance instabilities, TOKEN is only capable of saving 7%.

5.2 System Scalability

To explore the scalability of each protocol, system size has been increased to 16 cores (*config2* in Table 1). Using a higher number of processors, given their architectural complexity, would imply an unattainable computational cost for the simulations. Additionally, most of the benchmarks do not scale well beyond sixteen cores. In any case, given that each processor can have up to 16 pending memory transactions, the system could have up to 512 simultaneous coherence actions, including L1 misses and write-backs. This could be four times more demanding for the coherence protocol than having 64 in-order cores.

The performance observed in Figure 7 (a) indicates that LOCKE is able to increase its advantage in comparison to DIRECTORY. Scaling up the network size to accommodate NUCA slices would increase the cost of DIRECTORY indirections. Nevertheless, the

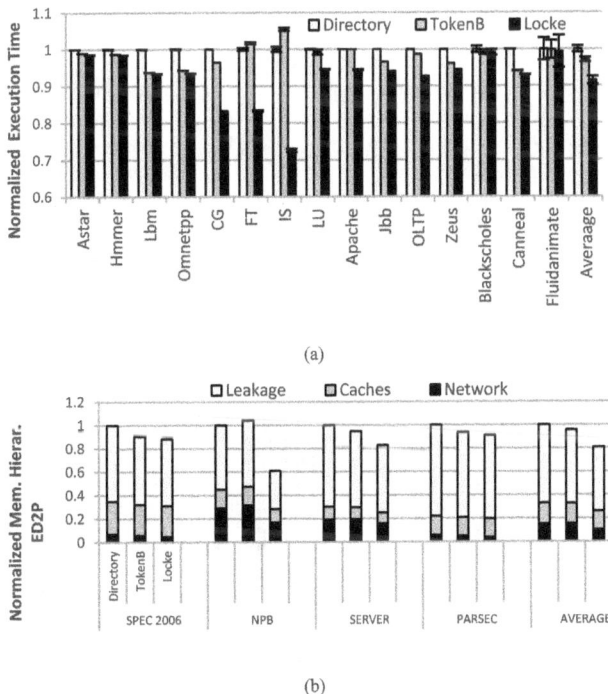

(a)

(b)

Figure 6. Directory normalized 8-processor CMP.
(a) Execution Time. (b) Memory Hierarchy ED2P.

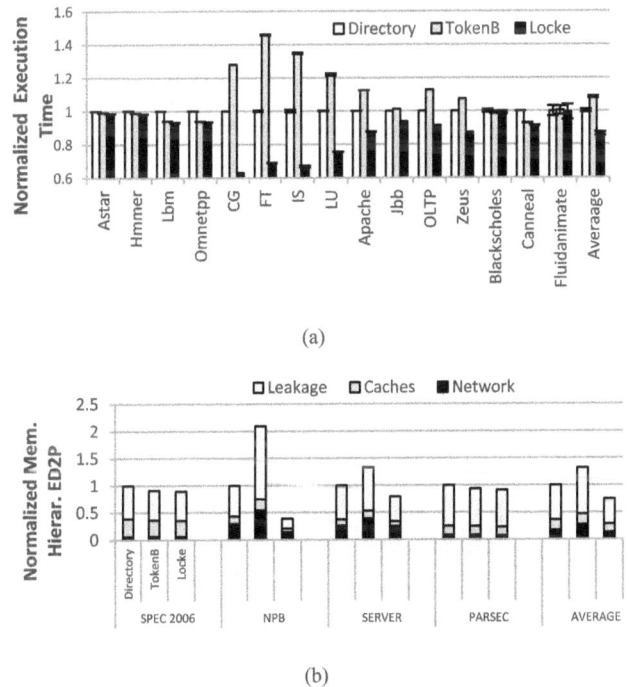

(a)

(b)

Figure 7. Directory Normalized 16-Processor CMP.
(a) Execution Time. (b) Memory Hierarchy ED2P.

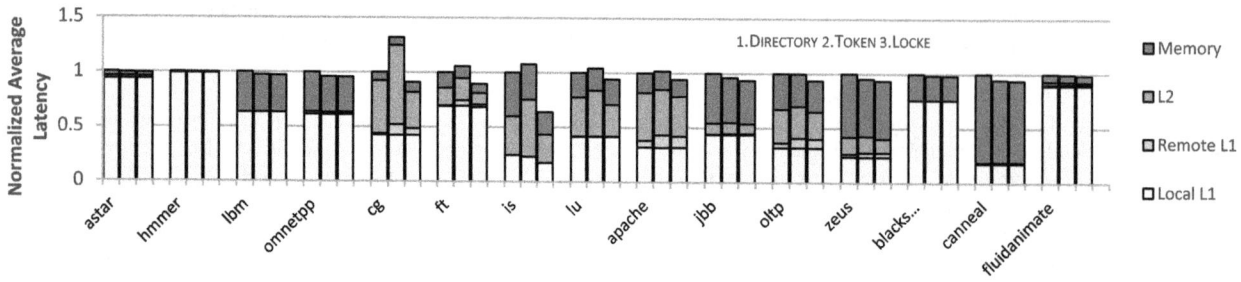

Figure 8. Directory Normalized Average Latency for 8-Processor system.

increased contention due to larger numbers of multicast destinations seems not to increase the latency in the network significantly for LOCKE. Therefore, the performance advantage of LOCKE over the directory is now greater than in 8-core CMP (16%). In contrast, TOKEN performs poorly, being noticeably slower than DIRECTORY.

5.3 Coherence Protocol Responsiveness

In order to provide insight into protocol effectiveness, Figure 8 shows the average latency perceived by the processor with each protocol for an 8-processor system.

As can be appreciated in both systems, the DIRECTORY-based protocol has a larger memory contribution in some applications. This is a direct consequence of inclusiveness. Whereas snoop-based protocols do not need inclusiveness to track on-chip block sharers, DIRECTORY requires an entry in LLC for all L1 cached blocks. Consequently, the effective cache capacity is larger in the former protocols, raising LLC miss rate. This problem is acknowledged as a serious drawback of directory coherence protocols [7]. Serialization with directory reduces on-chip hit latency in applications where network contention is not significant. TOKEN coherence introduces pressure on the network in some applications and the starvation avoidance mechanism increases the on-chip hit latency significantly, making the average access time up to 40% slower in applications such as IS. In contrast, LOCKE seems to consistently outperform other protocols in most applications.

Although, on-chip hit latency provides a good idea about protocol efficiency, it might be interesting to isolate how the protocol reacts when multiple coherence events arise simultaneously for the same block. In these situations, the effectiveness of the protocol is the key to prompt resolution of the situation. Figure 9 shows how effective each protocol is when dealing with true racing requests in eight processor systems. As we can see, in most cases LOCKE is the fastest one, being on average 10% faster than

DIRECTORY and 60% faster than TOKEN. Token's persistent mechanism to resolve those situations makes it the slowest one, being on average 40% slower than DIRECTORY. Although not shown, for sixteen-core systems the advantage of LOCKE is even greater. With non-conflicting coherence events broadcast-based coherence protocols are faster than directory due to inclusiveness, which increases on-chip miss rate, as can be appreciated in the memory contribution in Figure 8.

5.4 Network Energy Impact of Multicast Traffic

As stated before, it is commonly assumed that multicast traffic has a large impact on network power consumption. This assumption is based on the large increment in control traffic observed at the end-point, i.e. consumers. Nevertheless, when a network has multicast support, i.e. on-network packet replication, this is completely wrong because multicast packets use network resources only once before replication [10][1]. Therefore, unlike unicast-only networks, energy consumption is not proportional to end-point traffic, but to average link utilization. For example, Figure 10 shows the directory normalized network link utilization for LOCKE and TOKEN for eight- and sixteen-processor CMPs. All the links in the interconnection networks have been considered, including the connections from routers to L1 caches, L2 slices and memory controllers.

As we can appreciate, and contrary to common belief, network activity in snoop-based protocols is not much higher than directory protocols. Multicast capable routers have an identical data-path to conventional ones [10][1], so normalized link utilization differences will be translated into energy consumption (and negligible implementation cost). In all cases, LOCKE has lower link activity because the multicast tree used is much deeper than the one used in TOKEN, which tries to reach all the destinations as soon as possible. As indicated in Section 3.1

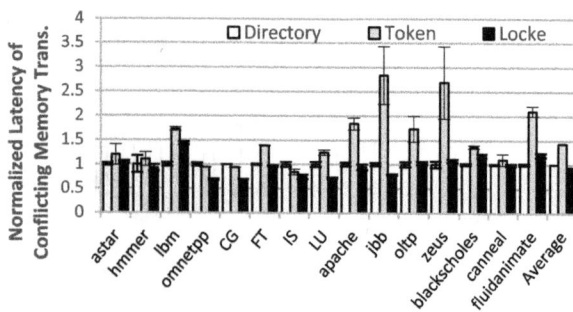

Figure 9. Normalized time to resolve conflicting memory accesses for an 8-processor CMP.

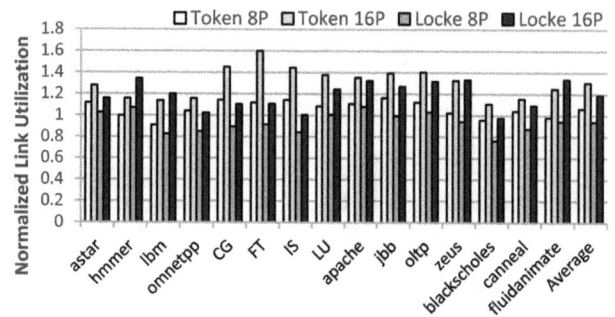

Figure 10. Directory Normalized Average Network link utilization.

LOCKE ordering I-trees delay packet replication, which increases request base latency, but reduces network activity. With particularly demanding applications, such as most NPB benchmarks, or bigger system sizes, TOKEN starvation avoidance increases the amount of activity. Even in the largest system, network system activity is only 15% greater in LOCKE than in DIRECTORY. Performance benefits offset this, making LOCKE the most efficient coherence protocol. With small size, the system DIRECTORY generates more network activity than snoop-based protocols due to protocol indirections and the larger number of on-cache misses.

6. RELATED WORK

There are numerous proposals for snoop-based on-chip coherence protocols over unordered networks in both academic [2][22][30][33] and commercial architectures [28][19]. In our proposal, two main characteristics can be seen. On the one hand, our method fulfills its main aim: to maintain all the advantages of token counting while eliminating the drawbacks of the persistent request method. Working in the same direction, the authors of the original token coherence protocol proposed PATCH [30]. This work extends a standard directory protocol to track tokens and uses token counting rules for enforcing coherence permissions. Token counting allows PATCH to support direct requests on an unordered interconnect, while a mechanism called "token tenure" uses local processor timeouts and the directory's per-block point of ordering at the home node to guarantee forward progress without relying on broadcasting. Nevertheless, this solution still depends on a suitable choice of the timeout used. Our proposal, offers the advantage of not needing fixed delays in order to take coherence decisions, which improves protocol responsiveness and stability. We believe that no quantitative performance comparison with PATCH is strictly necessary, because according to its authors, PATCH performance is between TOKEN and DIRECTORY, and LOCKE is better than both. It should be noted that the main motivation of PATCH is to reduce end-point traffic, which it successfully achieves. Nevertheless, as background motivation and according to the results presented in this paper, for on-chip systems it does not seem to be a fundamental issue.

On the other hand, to maintain system scalability, unordered networks are essential, but coherence protocols should provide a method to offer some kind of ordering of requests. There are many proposals where different solutions are provided. One of the possibilities is to establish this order by adding information to the requests sent to facilitate their ordering at their destination. In Timestamp Snooping [24], a coherence protocol is proposed in which a logical timestamp is added to all requests. These requests are sent out-of-order and put back into order at their destination.

Ordered requests may also be accomplished by using a physical structure through which requests may travel. One of the most simple and low-cost approaches is to embed a ring in the network and use it to transfer snoop messages. In order to address possible long response latencies or too many snoop operations, adaptive snooping algorithms are proposed in Flexible Snooping [34]. In these algorithms, depending on the chance of providing the line, a node receiving a snoop request will snoop first and then forward the request, or forward first and then snoop the operation. Moreover, if the node can prove that it will not be able to provide the line, it will skip the snoop operation, forwarding the request directly to the next node in the ring. However, any protocol using a ring as an interconnection network (either logical or physical) needs to send its snoop requests through it, forcing all requests to visit every node, which obviously means the loss of any possibility of parallelism with the snoop requests, thus increasing transaction latency. Trying to solve this problem, Unconstrained Snoop Request Delivery (UNCORQ) was proposed [33]. While requests are delivered using any network path, responses use the logical ring. A similar ring-approach, but inspired by token coherence, was used in [26].

Similarly to LOCKE, Virtual Tree Coherence [11] uses a tree to maintain ordering. This coherence protocol keeps track of sharers of a coarse-grained region, and multicasts them through a virtual tree to enforce ordering. Virtual trees are embedded inside a physical network of the topology. The root of the virtual tree provides an ordering point needed to order requests. Note that other works, such as [8], use trees with Token coherence, however, not for ordering but to avoid deactivations in persistent requests. Therefore, the lack of responsiveness and potential instabilities that persistent requests incur are still present.

7. CONCLUSIONS

This work presents a new coherence protocol suitable for CMP on-chip interconnection network characteristics. The protocol augments token coherence protocol, avoiding potential instabilities induced by workloads or system configuration. The increased robustness is accompanied by a performance benefit. LOCKE can proactively separate true data sharing and synchronization among cores from spurious data movements. Clearly LOCKE's benefits compensate its shortcomings, achieving a great scalability with aggressive out-of-order processors. In conclusion, LOCKE is competitive in terms of performance and energy footprint, not only with token but also with directory. LOCKE clearly demonstrates that the utilization of snoop-based coherence protocols is a suitable choice for managing CMP coherence, at least in systems with up to 16 aggressive out-of-order processors in the chip.

8. ACKNOWLEDGMENTS

The authors would like to thank José Ángel Herrero for his invaluable assistance with the computing environment, and the anonymous reviewers for many useful suggestions. This work has been supported by the MICCIN (Spain) under contract TIN2010-18159 and the HiPEAC European Network of Excellence.

9. REFERENCES

[1] P. Abad, V. Puente, and J.-A. Gregorio. MRR: Enabling fully adaptive multicast routing for CMP interconnection networks. In *15th Int S High Perf Comp (HPCA)*, 355-366, 2009.

[2] N. Agarwal, L.-S. Peh, and N. K. Jha. In-Network Snoop Ordering (INSO): Snoopy coherence on unordered interconnects. In *15th Int S High Perf Comp (HPCA)*, 67-78, 2009.

[3] A. R. Alameldeen et al. Simulating a $2M Commercial Server on a $2K PC. *Computer*, vol. 36, 50-57, 2003.

[4] K. Asanovic et al. *The Landscape of Parallel Computing Research: A View from Berkeley*. Technical Report. EECS Dept. U. of California Berkeley, vol. 18, no. UCB/EECS-2006-183, 2006.

[5] C. Bienia and K. Li. PARSEC 2.0: A New Benchmark Suite for Chip-Multiprocessors. In *MoBS*, 2009.

[6] M. Butler. AMD 'Bulldozer' Core - a new approach to multithreaded compute. In *HOT Chips* 22, 2010.

[7] P. Conway et al. Cache Hierarchy and Memory Subsystem of the AMD Opteron Processor. *IEEE Micro*, vol. 30, no. 2, 16-29, 2010.

[8] B. Cuesta, A. Robles, and J. Duato. An effective starvation avoidance mechanism to enhance the token coherence protocol. In *15th Euromicro Conf Proc*, 47-54, 2007.

[9] J. Duato. A theory of deadlock-free adaptive multicast routing in wormhole networks. *IEEE Transactions on Parallel and Distributed Systems*, vol. 6, no. 9, 976-987, 1995.

[10] N. D. Enright Jerger, L.-S. Peh, and M. Lipasti. Virtual Circuit Tree Multicasting: A Case for On-Chip Hardware Multicast Support. In *Int S Comp Arch (ISCA)*, 229-240, 2008.

[11] N. D. Enright Jerger, L.-S. Peh, and M. H. Lipasti. Virtual tree coherence: Leveraging regions and in-network multicast trees for scalable cache coherence. In *41st Int Symp Microarch*, 35-46, Nov. 2008.

[12] M. D. Hill and M. R. Marty. Amdahl's Law in the Multicore Era. *Computer*, vol. 41, no. 7, 33-38, Jul. 2008.

[13] H. P. Hofstee. Power Efficient Processor Architecture and The Cell Processor. In *Int S High Perf Comp (HPCA)*, 258-262, 2005.

[14] J. Huh, C. Kim, H. Shafi, L. Zhang, D. Burger, and S. W. Keckler. A NUCA substrate for flexible CMP cache sharing. In *19th Int Conf Supercomputing (ICS)*, 31-40, 2005.

[15] ITRS. Roadmap 2010.

[16] H. Jin, M. Frumkin, and J. Yan. *The OpenMP Implementation of NAS Parallel Benchmarks and its Performance*. NAS Technical Report NAS-99-011, NASA Ames Research Center, Moffett Field, CA, 1999.

[17] A. B. Kahng et al. ORION 2.0: A Fast and Accurate NoC Power and Area Model for Early-Stage Design Space Exploration. In *Design, Automation & Test*, 423-428, 2009.

[18] R. Kalla, B. Sinharoy, W. J. Starke, and M. Floyd. Power7: IBM's Next-Generation Server Processor. *IEEE Micro*, vol. 30, no. 2, 7-15, 2010.

[19] C. N. Keltcher, K. J. McGrath, A. Ahmed, and P. Conway. The AMD Opteron processor for multiprocessor servers. *IEEE Micro*, vol. 23, no. 2, 66-76, 2003.

[20] K. Lee, S.-joong Lee, and H.-jun Yoo. Low-power network-on-chip for high-performance SoC design. In *IEEE Trans. on Very Large Scale Int. (VLSI) Systems*, vol. 14, no. 2, 148-160, 2006.

[21] D. Lenoski et al. The Stanford Dash multiprocessor. *Computer*, vol. 25, no. 3, 63-79, Mar. 1992.

[22] M. M. K. Martin, M. D. Hill, and D. A. Wood. Token Coherence: a new framework for shared-memory multiprocessors. *IEEE Micro*, vol. 23, no. 6, 108-116, 2003.

[23] M. M. K. Martin et al. Multifacet's General Execution-driven Multiprocessor Simulator (GEMS) Toolset. *Computer Architecture News*, vol. 33, 4, Nov. 2005.

[24] M. M. K. Martin et al. Timestamp Snooping: An Approach for Extending SMPs. In *Architectural Support for Prog. Lang. and O. Systems (ASPLOS)*, vol. 1, no. 212, 1-12, 2000.

[25] M. R. Marty, J. D. Bingham, M. D. Hill, A. J. Hu, M. M. K. Martin, and D. A. Wood. Improving Multiple-CMP Systems Using Token Coherence. In *11th Int S High Perf Comp (HPCA)*, 328-339, Feb 2005.

[26] M. Marty and M. Hill. Coherence Ordering for Ring-based Chip Multiprocessors. In *39th Int Symp Microarch (MICRO)*, 309-320, 2006.

[27] L.G. Menezo, V. Puente, JA. Gregorio. *Locke Formal Specification Tables*. Technical Report. Available online: http://sg.sg/GPGFef. 2011.

[28] C. Park et al. A 1.2 TB/s on-chip ring interconnect for 45nm 8-core enterprise Xeon® processor. In *2010 IEEE International SolidState Circuits Conference(ISSCC)*, 180-181, 2010.

[29] V. Puente, J. A. Gregorio, and R. Beivide. SICOSYS: An Integrated Framework for Studying Interconnection Network Performance in Multiprocessor Systems. *IEEE Comput. Soc*, pp. 15-22, 2002.

[30] A. Raghavan, C. Blundell, and M. M. K. Martin. Token tenure: PATCHing token counting using directory-based cache coherence. In *41st Intl S Microarch*, 47–58, Nov. 2008.

[31] Y. H. Song and T. M. Pinkston. Efficient handling of message-dependent deadlock. In *15th Int Parallel & Distributed Proc Symp (IPDPS)*, 2001.

[32] SPEC Standard Performance Evaluation Corporation. *SPEC 2006*. [Online]. Available: http://www.spec.org.

[33] K. Strauss, X. Shen, and J. Torrellas. Uncorq: Unconstrained Snoop Request Delivery in Embedded-Ring Multiprocessors. In *40th Int S Microarch (MICRO)*, 327-342. 2007.

[34] K. Strauss, X. Shen, and J. Torrellas. Flexible Snooping: Adaptive Forwarding and Filtering of Snoops in Embedded-Ring Multiprocessors. In *33rd Int S Comp Arch (ISCA)*, 327-338, 2006.

[35] M. Suleman, O. Mutlu, M. Qureshi, and Y. N. Patt. Accelerating critical section execution with asymmetric multi-core architectures. In *14th Intl. Conf. on Architectural Support for Progr. Lang. and OS (ASPLOS)*, 253–264, 2009.

[36] D. Tarjan, S. Thoziyoor, and N. P. Jouppi, *CACTI 4.0*. 2006.

[37] A. W. Topol et al. Three-dimensional integrated circuits. IBM J. of Research and Development, vol. 50, no. 4, 491-506, Jul. 2006.

[38] V. Zyuban, and P. Kogge. Optimization of high-performance superscalar architectures for energy efficiency. In *Intl S on Low Power Electronics & Design*, 84-89, 2000.

A Programmable Processing Array Architecture Supporting Dynamic Task Scheduling and Module-Level Prefetching

Junghee Lee
Georgia Institute of
Technology
777 Atlantic Dr NW
Atlanta, GA 30332, USA
junghee.lee@gatech.edu

Hyung Gyu Lee
Georgia Institute of
Technology
777 Atlantic Dr NW
Atlanta, GA 30332, USA
hyunggyu@gatech.edu

Soonhoi Ha
Seoul National University
1 Gwanak-ro, Gwanak-gu
Seoul 151-742, Korea
sha@iris.snu.ac.kr

Jongman Kim
Georgia Institute of
Technology
777 Atlantic Dr NW
Atlanta, GA 30332, USA
jkim@ece.gatech.edu

Chrysostomos Nicopoulos
University of Cyprus
75 Kallipoleos Avenue
P.O. Box 20537
1678 Nicosia, Cyprus
nicopoulos@ucy.ac.cy

ABSTRACT

Massively Parallel Processing Arrays (MPPA) constitute programmable hardware accelerators that excel in the execution of applications exhibiting Data-Level Parallelism (DLP). The concept of employing such programmable accelerators as sidekicks to the more traditional, general-purpose processing cores has very recently entered the mainstream; both Intel and AMD have introduced processor architectures integrating a Graphics Processing Unit (GPU) alongside the main CPU cores. These GPU engines are expected to play a pivotal role in the espousal of General-Purpose computing on GPUs (GPGPU). However, the widespread adoption of MPPAs, in general, as hardware accelerators entails the effective tackling of some fundamental obstacles: the expressiveness of the programming model, the debugging capabilities, and the memory hierarchy design. Toward this end, this paper proposes a hardware architecture for MPPA that adopts an *event-driven execution model*. It supports dynamic task scheduling, which offers better expressiveness to the execution model and improves the utilization of processing elements. Moreover, a novel module-level prefetching mechanism – enabled by the specification of the execution model – hides the access time to memory and the scheduler. The execution model also ensures complete *encapsulation* of the modules, which greatly facilitates debugging. Finally, the fact that all associated inputs of a module are explicitly known can be exploited by the hardware to hide memory access latency without having to resort to caches and a cache

coherence protocol. Results using a *cycle-level simulator* of the proposed architecture and a variety of *real application benchmarks* demonstrate the efficacy and efficiency of the proposed paradigm.

Categories and Subject Descriptors

C.1.4 [**Processor Architectures**]: Parallel Architectures; D.1.3 [**Programming Techniques**]: Concurrent Programming; B.2.1 [**Arithmetic and Logic Structures**]: Design Styles

General Terms

Design, Performance

Keywords

Dynamic scheduling, Prefetch, Reconfigurable, Programmable

1. INTRODUCTION

As the further development of single-core architectures faces seemingly insurmountable physical and technological limitations, computer designers have turned their attention to alternative approaches. One such promising alternative is the utilization of several smaller cores working in unison as a programmable hardware accelerator. The most popular and widely used embodiment of this concept is the Graphics Processing Unit (GPU). While initially devised as a graphics-only coprocessor, it is now envisioned as a powerful processor that can undertake much more diverse duties. This realization has given rise to the emerging paradigm of General-Purpose computing on GPUs (GPGPU). A programmer may now use the GPU as a general-purpose accelerator. Intel's latest Sandy Bridge micro-architecture [7] and AMD's Fusion (Llano) [1] architecture both integrate a GPU engine on the same die as the general-purpose CPU cores.

This move signals the introduction of *heterogeneous* Chip Multi-Processors (CMP), which amalgamate cores with disparate capabilities in a unified setting. It is clear that the vast – and, as yet, largely untapped – potential of hardware accelerators (such as the GPU) is coming to the forefront of computer architecture. To be more general, in this paper we refer to the accelerator consisting of many small cores as a Massively Parallel Processing Array (MPPA) [2].

The widespread adoption of MPPAs as general-purpose hardware accelerators faces several challenges. One of them is the *expressiveness* of the execution model. Both GPUs and the latest Accelerated Processing Units (APU, a term coined by AMD for their CPU/GPU Fusion line of products) currently employ the venerable Single-Instruction Multiple-Data (SIMD) model. While this is a powerful model, it is suitable only for certain applications with regular computational kernels, such as graphics applications. Moreover, within the context of parallel programming, *debugging* is an often forgotten challenge that is very important in real-world applications. Finally, from the hardware perspective, the *memory hierarchy* is one of the most challenging design decisions. For relatively small numbers of cores, the cache is adequate, but for large numbers of cores, the cache coherence protocol becomes a bottleneck, as it does *not* scale well [10].

This paper aims to address all three of the aforementioned challenges that impede the consolidation of MPPAs as the de facto processing archetype of the future. We hereby propose a hardware architecture for MPPAs, which supports an event-driven execution model. The combination of said event-driven execution model and appropriate support from the hardware architecture enables us to overcome these challenges.

The key contributions of the proposed architecture are *dynamic task scheduling* and *module-level prefetching*. While previous architectures supporting a similar execution model determine task mapping at compile-time, our proposed architecture allows *run-time dynamic scheduling*. This attribute allows for better expressiveness. At the same time, the execution model imposes sufficient limitations on the semantics for a better debugging environment. In order to overcome the run-time overhead incurred by the dynamic task scheduling, we employ *module-level prefetching*, which also hides the memory access latency. By exploiting the fact that the execution model forces the input data of a module to be explicit, the hardware can prefetch instructions and data while other modules are running. Since prefetching is performed at the module level, it works accurately regardless of any data dependencies and branches. Finally, the proposed execution model does not assume a global shared memory, thus eliminating the need for a cache coherence protocol and offering markedly better scalability.

Extensive simulations using a cycle-level simulator of the proposed architecture running real application benchmarks demonstrate the capabilities and effectiveness of the new processing paradigm. Our results are extremely promising and clearly highlight the vast potential of such architectures.

The rest of the paper is organized as follows: Section 2 discusses and analyzes prior related work. Section 3 gives a motivational example that is also used as an illustrative example throughout the paper. Section 4 defines the utilized execution model. The proposed hardware MPPA architecture and its architectural support for the execution model

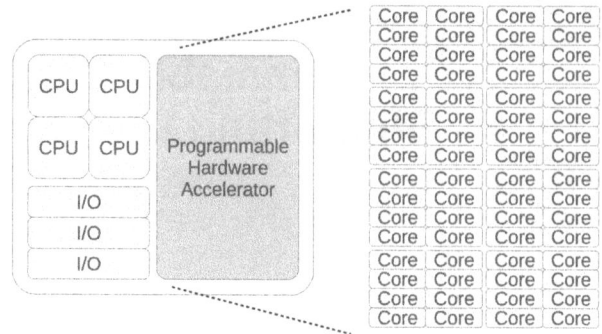

Figure 1: A high-level overview of a processor architecture employing a Massively Parallel Processing Array (MPPA) as a programmable hardware accelerator.

are introduced in Sections 5 and 6, respectively. Section 7 presents the employed evaluation framework, the various experiments, and accompanying analysis. Finally, Section 8 concludes the paper.

2. RELATED WORK

Figure 1 shows a high-level overview of a typical microprocessor architecture employing MPPA as a programmable hardware accelerator. The assumption is that the main CPUs and the MPPA are integrated on the same die (akin to the latest trends in the industry). The MPPA comprises a multitude of small cores and supporting logic. The latter includes the interconnection network, a memory sub-system, and hardware support for the programming model.

Coarse-Grain Reconfigurable Architectures (CGRA) [17] share a similar concept. However, the basic building block of CGRAs is an Arithmetic and Logic Unit (ALU), while that of MPPAs is a whole CPU core. The target architecture of CGRAs consists of ALUs and a reconfigurable interconnection infrastructure. The designer can modify the functionality of the system by reconfiguring the interconnections among the various ALUs. Since CGRAs have ALUs – not generic processors – as their primary primitive, they are only amenable to the implementation of data-path-dominated algorithms, not control-oriented algorithms.

A similar architecture can also be found in the Cell microprocessor [8] architecture. It consists of a Power Processor Element (PPE) as a main CPU and eight Synergistic Processing Elements (SPEs) acting as an accelerator. If the number of SPEs were tens, or hundreds, we could classify this architecture as MPPA.

As previously mentioned, commercialized MPPAs – including GPGPUs [15] and AMD's APU [1] – adopt the SIMD model. In academia, the stream processor [9] is a well-known SIMD-type processor. The SIMD model is effective for applications with regular computational kernels, whereby the same kernel is replicated on a number of cores. All the cores execute the same job, with different data. However, as modern algorithms are getting more complex and irregular (in order to accommodate more functionality), the need for a more flexible programming model is growing.

Tilera [20] and Rigel [10] support a standard multithreading programming model, thus providing the programmer with the maximum (known) flexibility. This programming model can be applied to any kind of parallel algorithm. However, the same model also imposes significant burden on the process of debugging, and the hardware itself. Maximum flexibility makes debugging very difficult, because there are too many possible causes for unexpected behavior. Without careful synchronization and protection, the program is likely to be unreliable and unpredictable. As for the hardware, a cache coherence protocol must be implemented, in order to support the shared memory assumption of the multithreading programming model. Tilera [20] employs a Dynamic Distributed Cache (DDC), but its scalability is still not proven for the 1000-core systems similar to Rigel [10]. Rigel implements a 1000-core accelerator, but the coherency of its caches is maintained by software.

The Ambric architecture [3] is the MPPA implementation that is most relevant to our work, because it adopts a similar execution model, i.e., a Kahn Process Network (KPN) with bounded queues. Mapping tasks on processing elements is determined at compile-time. At run-time, it does not allow *dynamic task scheduling*. This restriction limits the expressiveness of its execution model, because new tasks cannot be instantiated and their interconnection cannot be modified at run-time. Moreover, if there are dependencies among tasks, there may exist idle processing elements that are waiting for results from other tasks. Instead, dynamic task scheduling offers better expressiveness and yields higher utilization.

Our dynamic task scheduling policy follows a simple first-come, first-serve algorithm. However, task scheduling should consider resource constraints, communication cost, and performance issues, among others. There has been significant prior work in this domain, especially aimed at Multi-Processor Systems-on-Chip (MPSoC) [5, 16]. We believe that the specific algorithm employed by the dynamic task scheduler is orthogonal to this work, so we leave this analysis for future work.

It is true that dynamic task scheduling incurs run-time overhead. If the size of tasks is small and the number of processing elements is large, the overhead can be excessive [14]. To overcome this overhead, and to hide memory access latency, we adopt *prefetching* in this paper. For GPGPUs, an inter-thread prefetching technique has been proposed [13]. The authors exploit the common memory accesses among threads and devise a throttling mechanism to avoid performance degradation from mis-predictions. Our approach is to exploit the execution model itself and take advantage of the fact that all input data should be explicitly declared for every task. While a task is running, a hardware prefetcher prefetches all the data for the next task. Since input data is explicitly associated with the task, prefetching is always accurate.

The *execution model* can be derived from various programming models. Our event-driven execution model can support various models of computation, including KPN, synchronous data-flow graphs, finite state machines, etc. StreamIt [19] adopts the data-flow model, which can also be supported by our event-driven execution model. Previous work on programming models [12] is complementary to our work.

3. MOTIVATIONAL EXAMPLE

The *quicksort algorithm* [6] is used throughout this paper as an illustrative example. Figure 2 illustrates the parallelism exhibited in the quicksort algorithm. Given an array of values to be sorted, a pivot is selected, which is usually

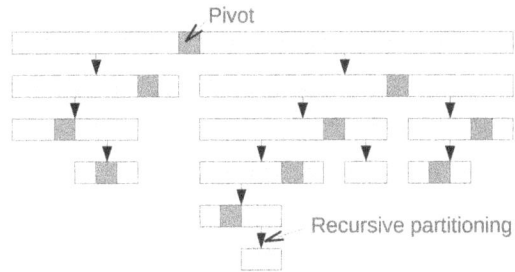

Figure 2: Illustration of the parallelism exhibited in the quicksort algorithm.

the first element in the array. The array is partitioned so that the left side of the pivot contains smaller elements than the pivot, while the right side contains larger elements than the pivot. Subsequently, the same partitioning is done recursively and independently on each side.

Once the partitioning of a segment finishes, its sub-segments can commence partitioning. However, the partitioning of the individual segments of the array can be done independently and simultaneously. Given a large array size, the quicksort algorithm exhibits abundant parallelism, as illustrated in Figure 2.

Although partitioning can be done independently, it does not mean that all the partitioning processes take exactly the same code path. Depending on the elements in the array, each partitioning may take a different path of the code. Moreover, one does not know at compile-time how many times recursive partitioning is needed. This information is dependent on the input data and is determined at run-time. If a multithreading programming model is used, we can create new threads for the partitioning of the sub-segments. In contrast, GPGPU does not allow spawning of new threads at run-time. In such a case, we may employ *job queueing* instead of spawning new threads [14]. Using this approach, the threads are created at initialization. Every thread fetches a job from a centralized (or distributed) job queue(s). If there is no job in the queue, some threads may become idle. When a new job is created, it is pushed into the queue, thus obviating the need to create a new thread.

Algorithmic nuances render the SIMD implementation of quicksort inefficient. Figure 3 shows the execution time of quicksort when varying the number of threads. The execution time is measured on NVIDIA's Quadro NVS 295 GPU, which has 8 CUDA cores per multiprocessor. In a GPU context, a *multiprocessor* consists of multiple CUDA cores and a memory that is shared by the cores within the multiprocessor. A thread block is mapped to a multiprocessor and threads in the block are executed by the cores in the mapped multiprocessor. In this experiment, the number of blocks is fixed to one and only the number of threads per block is varied. Hence, in this setting, all the threads are executed in a single multiprocessor. Assuming all the cores within the multiprocessor are fully utilized, one would expect the execution time to decrease proportionally to the number of threads at least up to 8 threads, since there are 8 cores in a multiprocessor. Instead, Figure 3 shows a different result for quicksort (*QS on GPGPU* curve).

As seen in Figure 3, the execution time of quicksort does not benefit from an increasing number of threads (*QS on*

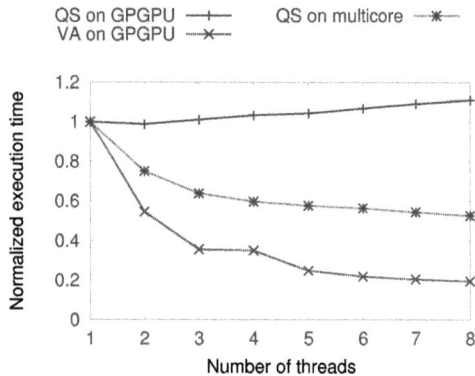

Figure 3: Inefficiency of the SIMD model for applications with irregular computation kernels.

GPGPU curve). In contrast, the execution time of vector addition does (*VA on GPGPU* curve). Vector addition adds two vectors by adding each corresponding element in the vectors. This algorithm is a typical example that is suitable for the SIMD model. It is obvious that the performance of vector addition is improved, even with a small number of threads.

To provide another reference for comparison, we conducted the same experiments on a multicore CPU machine, which employs the multithreading execution model. The execution time on the multicore machine is measured using the Simics full-system simulator [21]. Eight x86 processors are assumed, and the operating system on the simulated machine is Fedora 12 (Linux kernel 2.6.33). It is evident that the execution time of quicksort (*QS on multicore* curve) scales well up to 8 threads. However, as discussed in Section 2, the multithreading model faces scalability issues because of the cache coherence protocol. We may not be able to sustain any performance improvement beyond tens of processors.

Note that this experiment demonstrates an inefficiency of the SIMD model, *not* of the GPGPU paradigm. When the number of blocks and the number of threads increase far beyond 8, the performance of quicksort may benefit from various aspects of GPGPU support, including multiple number of multiprocessors, warp scheduling, thread multiplexing to hide memory latency, and so on. Regardless, what this experiment shows is that the hardware resources are not fully utilized, because of the limitations of the SIMD model.

One more alternative method to implement the quicksort algorithm is by using KPN, as in Ambric [3]. Unfortunately, it is very hard to express the dynamic nature of quicksort by using KPN, because we do not know how many times we need the recursive partitioning process, while the task mapping and the interconnections are required to be determined at compile-time.

It should be noted that it is always possible to tailor a specific algorithm for a particular model, just like GPU-Quicksort [4] does. However, what is discussed in this paper is a *general* way to implement algorithms.

4. THE EXECUTION MODEL OF THE PROPOSED MPPA ARCHITECTURE

This section provides the definition and details of the *execution model* of our proposed architecture.

4.1 Specification

The execution model consists of a set of modules M, a set of signals S, and a net list N. A module $m \in M$ is defined as a tuple of behavior b, an input port list P_i, an output port list P_o, a sensitivity list C, and a prefetch list F.

$$m = (b, P_i, P_o, C, F) \in M \qquad (1)$$

b is a set of instructions that specifies the behavior of the module. In fact, b can be viewed as a program including computation, memory access, function calls, etc. C and F are a subset of P_i ($C \subseteq P_i$, $F \subseteq P_i$). C indicates when this module should be executed, and F determines the prerequisite data before running this module. The *internal state* of a module can be represented by a feedback signal from the output to the input of the same module.

N defines the connectivity of ports and signals. Each signal $s \in S$ should have a corresponding unique entry $n(s)$ in N. $n(s)$ is defined as a tuple of a driver port d and a set of sink ports K.

$$n(s) = (d, K) \in N \qquad (2)$$

$n(s)$ indicates a signal s is connected to ports d and $\forall k \in K$. Data is written only through port d and broadcast to all the ports in K.

4.2 Semantics

A module is triggered when any signal connected to the ports in C changes. To execute the module, the instructions (b) and signals connected to ports in F should be prefetched. Once they are ready, a module is executed. The execution of a module is atomic, i.e., a module cannot be stopped until it finishes its execution. The atomic execution semantics eliminate the need for explicit synchronization primitives, such as locks and barriers. Instead, the communication channel serves as the synchronization primitive [2].

Function calls and memory accesses are strictly limited to within a module. b can access only functions within its own module boundaries (i.e., b) and signals connected to P_i and P_o. There is no global shared memory. These features ensure *encapsulation*. As highlighted in [3], encapsulation facilitates efficient *debugging*, since it limits the possible causes of errors within its own code body (i.e., b) and input signals.

The communication semantics follow non-blocking writes and blocking reads. In practice, since the depth of FIFOs cannot be infinite, the write may be blocked when the FIFO is full. There should only be one driver for a channel, but multiple sinkers can read data from the channel. Written data is broadcast to all sinkers connected to that signal.

Since the hardware architecture supports *dynamic task scheduling*, the descriptions of M, S, and N are allowed to be reconfigured at run-time. This feature offers more expressiveness to the execution model, and it improves the utilization of hardware resources.

A module can be instantiated and destroyed at run-time. The sensitivity list (C) and the prefetch list (F) can also be modified at run-time. Moreover, signals may be instantiated and destroyed at run-time, which implies that the addition and removal of nets from N are allowed. Finally, the model also allows the modification of d and K in $n(s)$.

4.3 Using the Event-Driven Execution Model

This subsection illustrates how the quicksort algorithm may be specified with the event-driven execution model.

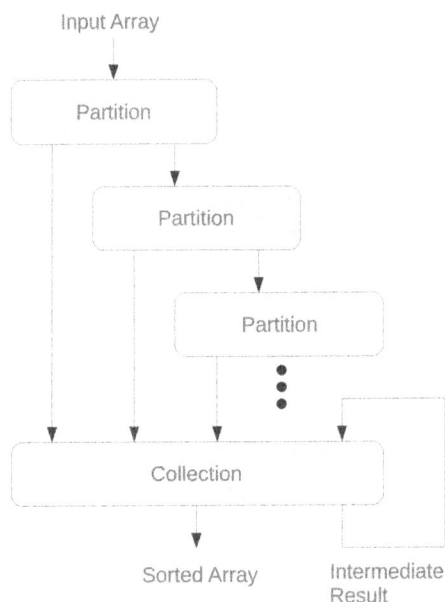

Figure 4: Module diagram of the quicksort algorithm, as specified using the proposed event-driven execution model.

The algorithm would consist of two modules: `partition` and `collection`, as illustrated in Figure 4. The `partition` module partitions the given array into two sub-arrays. It partitions one of these again and passes the other to a new module. It instantiates another `partition` module and a signal, it connects the signal to the new module, and it sends the sub-array to the new module. If partitioning is finished, the final output is sent to the `collection` module that collects all the sorted segments of the array. The `collection` module generates the final output when all the segments are collected.

The `partition` module has one input port (P_i) and two output ports (P_o). The input port is included both in the sensitivity list (C) and the prefetch list (P), which means that whenever the signal connected to the input port changes, the `partition` module is triggered, and – before the module is executed – the input signal is prefetched.

The input port consists of *start* and *end* positions, as well as the actual array of elements to be sorted. The *start* and *end* positions are necessary to inform the `collection` module which segment of the input array is to be sorted. The *start* and *end* positions do not need to be sent through separate ports, because the semantics of the port comprise a stream of bytes with variable length. As long as the sender and the receiver agree, any aggregated type of data can be carried through the port.

The input ports of the `collection` module are ports for the `partition` modules to send their outputs, and an extra port for the intermediate result. The two output ports are for the final output and for the intermediate result. The intermediate result stores the collected sorted segments so far. It can be considered as the state of the `collection` module. This input port should be included in the prefetch list, but not in the sensitivity list, since the intermediate result needs to be prefetched before the module is executed, but its change does not need to trigger the module.

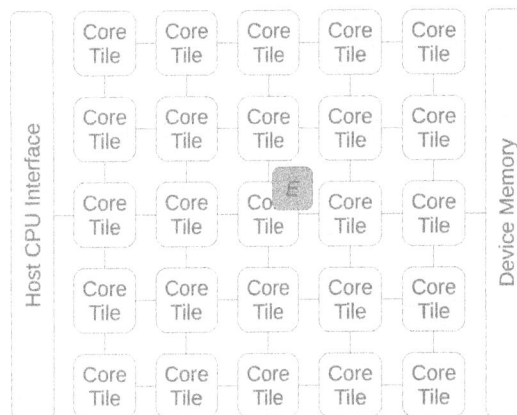

Figure 5: The proposed MPPA microarchitecture consists of several identical *tiles* interconnected using an on-chip interconnection network.

5. THE HARDWARE ARCHITECTURE

Our proposed MPPA architecture consists of several identical *tiles*, as shown in Figure 5. A conventional Network-on-Chip (NoC) is used to interconnect the nodes (core tiles). Although core tiles are identical, we designate one of them as the *execution engine* (denoted as 'E' in Figure 5). The execution engine is implemented in software, which runs on the μCPU of the particular core tile. The execution engine is placed in the middle of the MPPA, so as to minimize the average distance to/from the other nodes. The execution engine consists of a *scheduler*, *signal storage*, and *interconnect directory*. All data managed by the execution engine is stored in the device memory. The scratch-pad memory of the execution engine node is used as a software-managed cache memory. Recall that the execution model consists of modules (M), signals (S), and a net list (N). The scheduler manages and schedules the states of modules. The signal storage stores signal values and the locations of signals (if the signals are fetched by nodes). The interconnect directory keeps track of the connections of ports and signals.

The host CPU interface facilitates interaction with the system's main CPU(s). From the viewpoint of the execution model, a host CPU is treated as a module. The core tile connected to the host CPU interface is dedicated to handling the interactions with the host CPU(s).

The MPPA also makes use of *device memories*. The device memories have larger capacity – but longer access latency – than the scratch-pad memory of the core tile shown in Figure 6. Only execution engines can *directly* access the device memories. Other nodes are required to place a request to the execution engine. The device memory is separated into multiple banks for concurrent accesses by various execution engines. This segregation aims to eliminate conflicts on the device memory by accesses from different execution engines.

A detailed block diagram of one core tile is depicted in Figure 6. A core tile consists of a scratch-pad memory, a context manager, input/output queues, a message queue, a prefetcher, a message handler, and a network interface. Only nodes serving as execution engines have their memory, message queue, and network interface enabled.

The scratch-pad memory is, essentially, a double buffer. Half of the buffer is dedicated to the current module and the

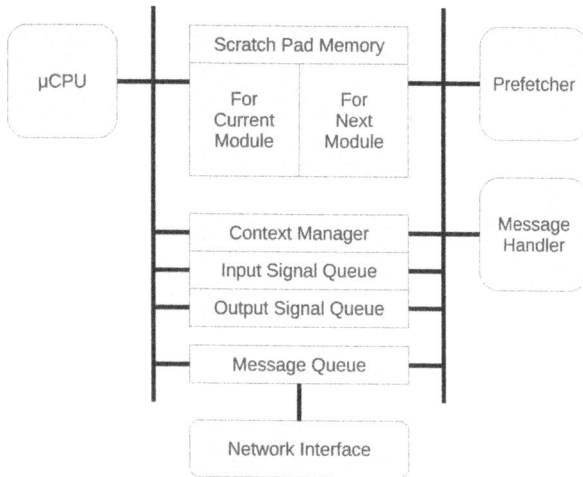

Figure 6: Block diagram of a *single* core tile of the many-core MPPA architecture shown in Figure 5.

other half is reserved for the next module. While the μCPU accesses the current module's half, the prefetcher prefetches code and variables to the next module's half. The two buffer halves switch their roles upon receiving a control signal from the context manager.

The context manager is accessed when the current module completes its execution. If there is no other available module to run, the context manager disables the μCPU. Otherwise, it sends control signals to the memory and peripherals to switch to the next module, and then it restarts the μCPU so as to run the next module.

The input queue retains input signals for the current module and the next module. The input signals for the next module are prefetched by the prefetcher. Input signals for the current module are discarded when control signals from the context manager indicate a context switch.

The output queue stores the output signals. When an output signal is updated, a control message is sent to the interconnect directory to trigger those modules whose sensitivity list includes the updated signal. The actual data is kept in the output queue until the context manager triggers a context switch. When context switching is triggered, the output queue flushes the output signals to the signal storage.

The message queue is used to send and receive control messages. Although a complete list of control messages is not given in this paper (see next section), it is assumed that all control messages are defined by the system. Signals are carried within control messages.

The prefetcher is responsible for prefetching all the necessary inputs and instructions. When a control signal arrives from the context manager, the prefetcher commences operation.

The message handler is a counterpart to the prefetcher. Some input signals of a particular module may be stored in *other nodes*, instead of the signal storage. In such a case, the signal storage forwards a request message to those nodes. When such requests arrive at the requested nodes, the message handler reads the requested signal from the output signal queue and forwards it to the requester.

Finally, the network interface is a typical NoC router/switch.

It supports multiple outstanding requests for the concurrent prefetching of multiple input signals.

6. ARCHITECTURAL SUPPORT FOR THE EXECUTION MODEL

This section explains how the hardware architecture supports the execution model.

6.1 Execution Engine

The heart of the architectural support is the execution engine. While the hardware facilitates communication, most of its functionality is implemented in software running on the μCPU. Implementation in software gives us flexibility in the number and location of execution engines, which will be demonstrated shortly.

One possible way to visualize our MPPA is to regard the execution engine as an event-driven simulation kernel and the specification of an algorithm as a Hardware Description Language (HDL). The execution model described in Section 4.1 is, essentially, an extension of HDL. The execution engine executes the specification in a similar way as an event-driven simulation kernel.

The execution engine interacts with modules running on other μCPUs through messages. Table 1 summarizes the various messages. Note that this table only shows the portion of the supported message set that is needed to understand the rest of this paper.

For example, any module can instantiate another module by sending a request message `REQ_INST_MODULE` to the scheduler. Recall that the execution engine consists of a scheduler, signal storage, and interconnect directory. After the scheduler instantiates a new module, it sends a response message `RES_INST_MODULE` to the requester. Similarly, a signal can be instantiated by exchanging `REQ_INST_SIGNAL` and `RES_INST_SIGNAL` with the signal storage. A module is allowed to change its own or other modules' sensitivity list and prefetch list by sending corresponding messages. The remaining messages will be explained in the following subsections.

The scheduler keeps track of the state of modules and their location. The states of a module can be `wait`, `ready`, and `run`. There are three queues, and modules are stored in a corresponding queue according to their state. Initially, the state of a module is `wait`. When a signal connected to the port in the sensitivity list changes, the module is triggered and its state is changed to `ready`. Once the module is fetched by a node, its state becomes `run` until it finishes. Unless another signal triggers this module again, its state returns to `wait`. In addition, the scheduler stores instances of modules in the device memory. When a module is fetched by a node, it reads its instance from the memory and sends it to the node.

The signal storage stores values of signals in the device memory. Sometimes, the latest value resides in the output queue of a node. When an output of a module is updated, its new value is stored in the output queue of that node. The signal storage and the scheduler are notified of the fact that the output has been updated. The signal storage invalidate its copy and keeps track of the signal's location. The scheduler triggers the modules (i.e., it moves modules from the wait queue to the ready queue) whose sensitivity lists include that signal.

Table 1: Message types supported by the proposed MPPA architecture

Category	Type	From	To	Payload
Instantiation	REQ_INST_MODULE	Module	Scheduler	Arguments for the constructor
	RES_INST_MODULE	Scheduler	Module	Module instance ID
	REQ_INST_SIGNAL	Module	Signal storage	None
	RES_INST_SIGNAL	Signal storage	Module	Signal instance ID
Reconfiguration	ADD_SENSITIVITY	Module	Interconnect directory	Module instance ID, port ID
	REMOVE_SENSITIVITY	Module	Interconnect directory	Module instance ID, port ID
	ADD_PREFETCH	Module	Scheduler	Module instance ID, port ID
	REMOVE_PREFETCH	Module	Scheduler	Module instance ID, port ID
Prefetching	REQ_FETCH_MODULE	Prefetcher	Scheduler	None
	RES_FETCH_MODULE	Scheduler	Prefetcher	List of input ports to be prefetched
	MODULE_INSTANCE	Scheduler	Prefetcher	Module instance
	REQ_SIGNAL	Prefetcher	Interconnect directory	Port ID, destination node
	RES_SIGNAL	Signal storage or node	Prefetcher	Signal data
Execution	NOTIFY_SIGNAL_UPDATE	Module	Interconnect directory	Signal instance ID
	TRIGGER_MODULE	Interconnect directory	Scheduler	List of modules

The interconnect directory keeps track of the connectivity of signals and ports. A module accesses its input and output through ports. It is unaware of which signal is connected to its ports. To access a signal, the module sends a request to the interconnect directory in order to find which signal is connected to the port. Then, the interconnect directory forwards the request to the signal storage, and the signal storage responds to the module. The interconnect directory also keeps track of the sensitivity list. If a signal is updated, the list of its associated modules is sent to the scheduler.

6.2 Module-Level Prefetching

Dynamic scheduling incurs run-time overhead. The preferching mechanism is employed to hide the overhead, as well as the memory access latency. Hiding memory access latency is not demonstrated in detail in this paper.

The execution model enables accurate prefetching by forcing a module to only access the code within its boundaries and to only access its explicitly associated inputs and outputs.

Figure 7 shows a sequence diagram of the prefetching process. While a module is executed within a μCPU, the prefetcher prefetches *instructions* and *data* for the next module. The fetching of *instructions* involves the scheduling process within the scheduler and memory accesses to the device memory. The fetching of *data* involves accessing of the signal storage and memory accesses to the device memory. Therefore, prefetching hides both the overhead of the execution engines and the access latency to the device memory.

As soon as a module starts running on a μCPU, the prefetcher starts prefetching the next module to run. It gets a module instance ID to run by exchanging REQ_FETCH_MODULE and RES_FETCH_MODULE messages with the scheduler. If the module to run is not the same module currently running, the scheduler provides the prefetcher with the code of a module via a MODULE_INSTANCE message, after reading it from the device memory. Otherwise, the prefetcher keeps the current module and fetches only input signals. The prefetcher may get none, which indicates that no module is ready to run. Subsequently, the node goes into a *sleep mode* as soon as the current module finishes, unless it receives a module to run from the scheduler by another RES_FETCH_MODULE.

RES_FETCH_MODULE contains the list of input ports to be prefetched for the module. The prefetcher sends request messages REQ_SIGNAL to the interconnect directory. The interconnect directory fills the signal ID field of the message by looking up its port-to-signal mapping table and forwards

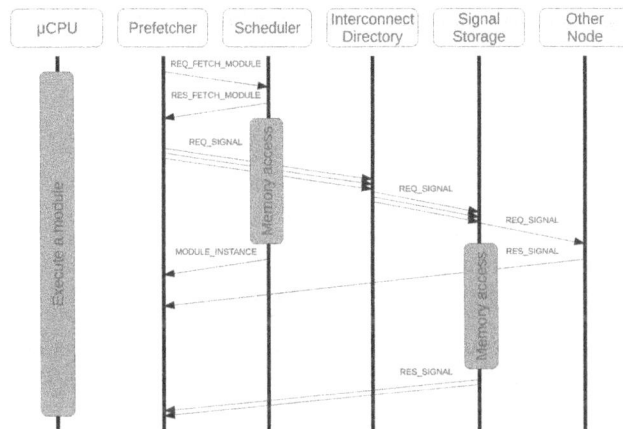

Figure 7: Sequence diagram of the prefetching process of the proposed MPPA architecture. Notice how prefetching can hide both the overhead of the execution engine and the access latency to the device memory.

the message to the signal storage. The signal storage returns the signals through a RES_SIGNAL message. If other nodes hold the requested signals, the request messages are forwarded to them.

If the execution of the module takes longer than prefetching, the latter can hide the memory access latency, as well as the scheduling overhead. If there is only one task per μCPU, instructions do not need to be fetched again. Inputs need to be fetched only when they are changed, just as the semantics of the programming model dictates. Even though a cache may be used, this cache latency cannot be hidden. If an input is changed, the corresponding cache line would be invalidated by the coherence protocol. The cache line would then be re-fetched. The benefit of the proposed method over a cache is scalability. To the best of our knowledge, there is no cache coherence protocol that can scale efficiently to more than one hundred cores. In our proposed method, the programming model eliminates the need for a coherence protocol.

6.3 An Event-Driven Execution Example

Figure 8 illustrates how the proposed MPPA executes an event-driven model of our quicksort algorithm example. The figure shows three core tiles and the execution engine. There

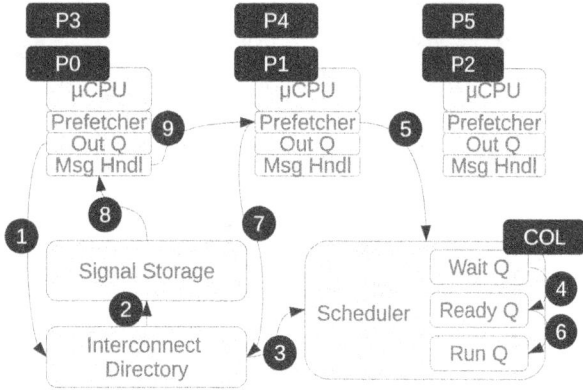

Figure 8: Illustrative example of an event-driven execution of the quicksort algorithm.

Table 2: Simulated system parameters

Parameter	Value
Number of Core Tiles	32
Memory access time	1 cycle for scratch-pad memory 100 cycles for device memories
Memory size	8 KB scratch-pad memory per core 32 MB device memory
Communication delay	4 cycles per hop

Table 3: Module execution times for the benchmark applications used

Benchmark	Execution time in cycles		
	Min	Max	Average
Forward Solve (FS)	26	646	336.00
Backward Solve (BS)	42	569	305.50
Cholesky Factorization (CF)	151	11800	789.35
Canny Edge Detection (CED)	330	5011	669.68
Binomial Tree (BT)	117	4506	462.71
Octree Partitioning (OP)	1441	6679	2678.70
Quick Sort (QS)	88	47027	683.70

are six instances of the `partition` module (P0–P5). P0, P1, and P2 are running on the μCPU and P3, P4, and P5 are prefetched and waiting for execution. One instance of the `collection` module is in the wait queue (COL).

Suppose that P0 generates an output. The output is stored in the output queue and the fact that the output signal has been updated is signified via `NOTIFY_SIGNAL_UPDATE` (1). The output is actually written to a port. Which signal is connected to that port is determined at run-time and managed by the interconnect directory. `NOTIFY_SIGNAL_UPDATE` is sent to the interconnect directory, which looks up the connected signal, augments the signal ID, and forwards the message to the signal storage (2). `NOTIFY_SIGNAL_UPDATE` indicates only that the signal is updated and the actual data is still stored in the output queue. The signal storage changes the location of the signal to point to the first core tile. The interconnect directory also keeps track of the sensitivity list. It looks up which module should be triggered by the updated signal and sends `TRIGGER_MODULE` to the scheduler (3). The scheduler moves the module (in this example, COL) from the wait queue to the ready queue.

Right after this, suppose that P1 finishes. Since P4 has been prefetched, the second core tile immediately switches to run P4. At the same time, the prefetcher starts prefetching the next module. It requests the next module from the scheduler by sending `REQ_FETCH_MODULE` (5). The scheduler looks up the ready queue to check if there is any available module. In this example, COL is in the ready queue. The scheduler moves COL to the run queue (6) and sends the module and the list of its associated input ports to the requester via `RES_FETCH_MODULE`. Then, the prefetcher starts prefetching the input signals. It sends `REQ_SIGNAL` to the interconnect directory, where its connected signals can be looked up (7). The interconnect directory augments the signal ID and forwards the message to the signal storage. The signal storage looks up the entry of the signal and finds that its data is stored in the first core tile. The signal storage forwards `REQ_SIGNAL` to the first core tile (8). The message handler in the first core tile sends the data to the second core tile via `RES_SIGNAL` (9). Although it is not shown in this example, the output queue of the second core tile flushes the signals associated with P1 while the prefetcher is working. As long as the prefetching process explained in this paragraph finishes before P4 finishes, the second core tile can

continue to work on COL without any delay, as soon as P4 finishes.

7. EXPERIMENTAL EVALUATION

To evaluate the proposed MPPA architecture, we employ a detailed, cycle-level simulator to model the entire MPPA and associated devices. Table 2 summarizes the simulated architectural parameters. In terms of benchmark applications, we use the task-level parallel benchmarks of the Recognition, Mining and Synthesis (RMS) benchmark suite [11]. Specifically, the applications are Forward Solve (FS), Backward Solve (BS), Cholesky Factorization (CF), Canny Edge Detection (CED), and Binomial Tree (BT). In addition, we use Octree Partitioning (OP) [18] and Quick Sort (QS) [6]. Table 3 shows the module execution times for all simulated benchmarks. Note that these execution times do not account for the memory access latency. If the prefetching finishes in time, the memory access latency can be hidden, as previously explained.

The chosen applications have abundant parallelism, which makes them suitable for MPPA. However, they exhibit heavy *dependencies among tasks*, which are not efficiently supported by existing MPPAs, like GPUs (as used for GPGPU), because the latter adopt a SIMD-based programming model whose efficiency is maximized only when *all cores run the same code*. Moreover, all chosen applications are dominated by *short tasks*, whereby the execution time of each task is very short and the overhead of dynamic scheduling becomes quite significant [11]. This attribute will help us evaluate the efficiency of our proposed prefetching mechanism. Since the chosen benchmarks are dominated by short tasks, their memory requirement is at most 4 KB. Hence, an 8 KB scratch-pad memory is enough for double-buffering purposes. In the case of the execution engine, the full size of the scratch-pad memory can be utilized as a cache.

The applications are efficiently implemented in the proposed MPPA, because its execution model allows dynamic instantiation of modules and run-time reconfiguration of their interconnections. More importantly, the prefetching mechanism hides the run-time overhead of dynamic task scheduling, as will be demonstrated shortly.

Figure 9 shows the average access time of the scheduler (denoted by the line graph and the right y-axis), normalized

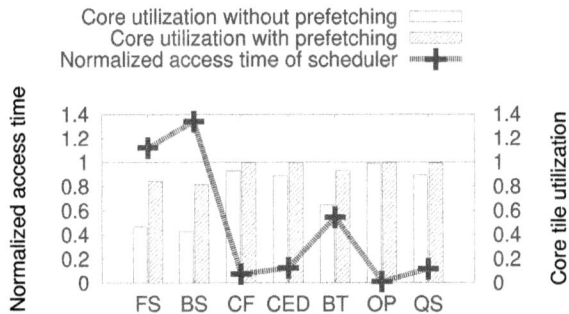

Figure 9: Average access times of the scheduler (normalized to the average execution time of the modules), and average utilization of the processing elements (i.e., the core tiles).

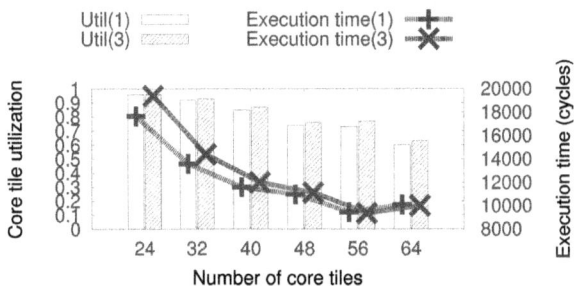

Figure 10: The impact on performance of the number of core tiles designated to serve as part of the *execution engine*. "Util(k)" and "Execution time(k)" denote the tile utilization and the total execution time, respectively, when the number of core tiles devoted to the execution engine is k. The benchmark used is CED.

to the average execution time of the modules. A normalized access time below 1 indicates that the access time is completely hidden by the prefetching mechanism, because the accessing of the scheduler is complete before the module execution finishes. Since the memory requirements of the chosen benchmarks are not particularly high, most device memory access time is hidden by the execution engine's cache in this experiment. Remember, the scratch-pad memory in the *execution engine* core tile is used as a cache for the device memory. The access time of the scheduler shown in Figure 9 is, in fact, dominated by the queuing latency.

By juxtaposing Table 3 and Figure 9, we can observe that the shorter the average execution time of an application is, the longer the scheduler access time becomes. Shorter execution times lead to more frequent accesses to the scheduler, which result in longer queuing delays [14]. This is the reason why short-task dominated benchmarks suffer from excessive overhead incurred by dynamic scheduling.

However, prefetching may be used to alleviate the issue. Prefetching hides the dynamic scheduling overhead by fetching modules *simultaneously* with the execution of other modules. As a result, the prefetching mechanism improves the utilization of core tiles, as demonstrated by the dark-colored bars in Figure 9 (the bars refer to the left y-axis). Since the average execution times of FS, BS, and BT are very

short, even prefetching cannot hide the entire scheduler access time. However, prefetching still improves the utilization substantially.

The execution engine may need to be split up to support a growing number of core tiles. The optimal number of execution engines is dependent on the characteristics of the applications. Determining such an optimal number is left as future work. To evaluate the impact of the number of execution engines, we performed an experiment whereby the execution engine is split into a *distinct* scheduler, signal storage, and interconnect directory, with each component assigned to a separate core tile. Thus, *three* tiles are dedicated to the execution engine in total, while the others are used solely for compute purposes. Figure 10 compares this setup to the conventional case, where only one core tile is devoted to the execution engine. Although dedicating three core tiles to the execution engine always exhibits better *utilization* than dedicating one tile, the latter offers better *performance* up to 48 cores, because there are more *processing* tiles (as opposed to execution-engine tiles). This is the reason why the experiments of Figure 9 assume a single-tile execution engine. When the number of core tiles becomes larger than 48, the higher utilization of the system with a three-tile execution engine starts to compensate for the smaller number of working core tiles. Of course, dedicating three tiles to the execution engine of a 56-tile system only yields a 0.89% improvement in execution time. However, this is expected to increase as the number of core tiles increases. Overall, this experiment demonstrates that the proposed MPPA architecture scales well up to 56 cores, even for an application with heavy data dependencies, such as CED. This is because the overhead of dynamic scheduling is hidden by the prefetching mechanism. As a point of reference, when the entire CED benchmark is executed on a *single core* (i.e., serially), its execution time is 395,791 cycles.

The experiments of this section demonstrate the improvements obtained through the use of prefetching. It is demonstrated that the proposed MPPA scales well up to 56 cores, even for applications dominated by short tasks, where the overhead of the dynamic scheduling could be excessive. Further studies on the splitting of the execution engines would enable even larger-scale MPPAs with tens, or hundreds, of cores.

8. CONCLUSIONS

The last few years have witnessed the emergence of the powerful computational paradigm of Massively Parallel Processing Arrays (MPPA), employed as general-purpose hardware accelerators. Graphics Processing Units (GPU) constitute a prime example of this concept, as manifested by the increasing popularity of GPGPU. However, the widespread adoption of MPPAs as general-purpose hardware accelerators faces three fundamental challenges: the expressiveness of the programming model, the debugging capabilities, and the memory hierarchy.

This paper proposes an MPPA hardware architecture that effectively addresses these issues through the intelligent interplay between the *execution model* and the *hardware architecture*. The presented design employs an *event-driven* execution model that facilitates efficient debugging. Our execution model offers better expressiveness than existing GPGPU practices by allowing hardware-supported run-time reconfigurability and *dynamic task scheduling*, which greatly improves the utilization of processing elements. The execution model also ensures *encapsulation* of the modules. All the accesses to data and function calls are limited within the module and no global shared memory is assumed. Encapsulation facilitates debugging by limiting possible causes of erroneous behavior, while the absence of a shared memory *eliminates the need for a cache coherence protocol*. Finally, the explicit declaration of all input signals enables accurate *module-level prefetching*, which is demonstrated – through simulation experiments – to hide the access latency to both the device memory and the execution engine's scheduler.

The work presented in this paper serves as an initial proof of concept. Important issues, such as scheduling policies and splitting of the execution engine, are critical and form part of our ongoing and future work.

9. ACKNOWLEDGMENTS

This work is partially supported by KORUSTECH(KT)-2008-DC-AP-FS0-0003 and the MKE(The Ministry of Knowledge Economy), Korea, under the ITRC support program supervised by the NIPA (NIPA-2012-H0301-12-1011). It also falls under the Cyprus Research Promotion Foundation's Framework Programme for Research, Technological Development and Innovation 2009-10 (DESMI 2009-10), co-funded by the Republic of Cyprus and the European Regional Development Fund, and specially under Grant ΤΠΕ/ΠΛΗΡΟ/0609(ΒΙΕ)/09.

10. REFERENCES

[1] N. Brookwood. AMD Fusion family of APUs: enabling a superior, immersive, PC experience, 2010.

[2] M. Butts. Synchronization through communication in a massively parallel processor array. *IEEE Micro*, 27:32–40, September 2007.

[3] M. Butts, A. M. Jones, and P. Wasson. A structural object programming model, architecture, chip and tools for reconfigurable computing. In *Proceedings of the 15th Annual IEEE Symposium on Field-Programmable Custom Computing Machines*, pages 55–64, Washington, DC, USA, 2007. IEEE Computer Society.

[4] D. Cederman and P. Tsigas. Gpu-quicksort: A practical quicksort algorithm for graphics processors. *J. Exp. Algorithmics*, 14:4:1.4–4:1.24, January 2010.

[5] E. de Souza Carvalho, N. Calazans, and F. Moraes. Dynamic task mapping for MPSoCs. *IEEE Design Test of Computers*, 27(5):26 –35, sept.-oct. 2010.

[6] C. A. R. Hoare. Algorithm 64: Quicksort. *ACM Communication*, 4(7):321, 1961.

[7] Intel. Product specification of Intel Core i5-2540M Processor, 2011. http://www.intel.com/SandyBridge.

[8] J. A. Kahle, M. N. Day, H. P. Hofstee, C. R. Johns, T. R. Maeurer, and D. Shippy. Introduction to the cell multiprocessor. *IBM J. Res. Dev.*, 49:589–604, July 2005.

[9] U. J. Kapasi, S. Rixner, W. J. Dally, B. Khailany, J. H. Ahn, P. Mattson, and J. D. Owens. Programmable stream processors. *IEEE Computer*, pages 54–62, 2003.

[10] J. H. Kelm, D. R. Johnson, M. R. Johnson, N. C. Crago, W. Tuohy, A. Mahesri, S. S. Lumetta, M. I. Frank, and S. J. Patel. Rigel: an architecture and scalable programming interface for a 1000-core accelerator. In *Proceedings of the 36th annual international symposium on Computer architecture*, ISCA '09, pages 140–151, New York, NY, USA, 2009. ACM.

[11] S. Kumar, C. Hughes, and A. Nguyen. Carbon: Architectural support for fine-grained parallelism on chip multiprocessors. In *ISCA '07: Proceedings of the 34th annual International Symposium on Computer Architecture*, pages 162–173, 2007.

[12] S. Kwon, Y. Kim, W.-C. Jeun, S. Ha, and Y. Paek. A retargetable parallel-programming framework for MPSoC. *ACM Trans. Des. Autom. Electron. Syst.*, 13:39:1–39:18, July 2008.

[13] J. Lee, N. Lakshminarayana, H. Kim, and R. Vuduc. Many-thread aware prefetching mechanisms for GPGPU applications. In *Proceedings of the 43rd Annual IEEE/ACM International Symposium on Microarchitecture*, pages 213 –224, dec. 2010.

[14] J. Lee, C. Nicopoulos, Y. Lee, H. G. Lee, and J. Kim. Hardware-based job queue management for manycore architectures and OpenMP environments. In *IPDPS '11: Proceedings of IEEE International Parallel and Distributed Processing Symposium*, 2011.

[15] NVIDIA. NVIDIA CUDA C programming guide version 4.0, 2011.

[16] A. Shabbir, A. Kumar, B. Mesman, and H. Corporaal. Distributed resource management for concurrent execution of multimedia applications on MPSoC platforms. In *Proceedings of the International Symposium on Systems, Architectures, MOdeling and Simulation (SAMOS)*, 2011.

[17] M. Sima, M. McGuire, and J. Lamoureux. Coarse-grain reconfigurable architectures - taxonomy -. In *PacRim 2009: Proceedings of IEEE Pacific Rim Conference on Communications, Computers and Signal Processing*, pages 975–978, 2009.

[18] L. Soares, C. Menier, B. Raffin, and J. L. Roch. Work stealing for time-constrained octree exploration: Application to real-time 3d modeling. In *Proceedings of Eurographics Symposium on Parallel Graphics and Visualization*, 2007.

[19] W. Thies, M. Karczmarek, M. I. Gordon, D. Z. Maze, J. Wong, H. Hoffman, M. Brown, and S. Amarasinghe. Streamit: A compiler for streaming applications. Technical Report MIT/LCS Technical Memo LCS-TM-622, Massachusetts Institute of Technology, Cambridge, MA, Dec 2001.

[20] Tilera. TILE-Gx processor family overview, 2010.

[21] Wind River Systems. http://www.windriver.com/.

Adaptive Task Duplication Using On-line Bottleneck Detection For Streaming Applications

Yoonseo Choi, Cheng-Hong Li[*], Dilma Da Silva, Alan Bivens, Eugen Schenfeld

IBM Research

Yorktown Heights, NY, United States

{yoonseo.choi, chenghong.li}@gmail.com, {dilmasilva,jbivens,eugen}@us.ibm.com

ABSTRACT

In this paper we describe an approach to dynamically improve the progress of streaming applications on SMP multicore systems. We show that run-time task duplication is an effective method for maximizing application throughput in face of changes in available computing resources. Such changes can not be fully handled by static optimizations. We derive a theoretical performance model to identify tasks in need of more computing resources. We propose two online algorithms that use indications from the performance model to detect computation bottlenecks. In these algorithms, a task can identify itself as a bottleneck using only its local data. The proposed technique is transparent to end programmers and portable to systems with fair scheduling. Our on-line detection algorithms can be applied to other dynamic scenarios, for example, involving run-time variation of workload.

Our experiments using the StreamIt benchmarks [5] show that the proposed run-time task duplication achieves considerable speed-ups over the multi-threaded baseline on a 16-core machine and on the scenarios with dynamically changing number of processing cores. We also show that our algorithms achieve better application throughput than alternative approaches for task duplication.

Categories and Subject Descriptors

J.0 [**Computer Applications**]: General; D.3.4 [**Programming Languages**]: Processors—*Code generation, Run-time environments*

General Terms

Performance

Keywords

Streaming application, runtime bottleneck detection, parallelization

---

[*]Cheng-Hong Li is currently working at NEC Laboratories America.

1. INTRODUCTION

Stream computing is an increasingly important area. In this programming paradigm an application is represented as a directed graph in which a node represents an actor and an edge represents data transfer from one actor to another. Streams of data constantly flow from upstream actors to downstream actors. Since computation and communication are separated, the parallelism within the application is explicit. This style of programming has been used for different application domains such as financial systems, manufacturing, video/audio applications, and high-performance data-intensive applications comprising scientific programs with regular or irregular data accessing patterns.

Many research efforts have exploited task, data, and pipeline parallelism in streaming applications. One important approach is the fission and fusion of actors and hardware/software pipelining using partitioning of stream graphs in compile-time [5, 10, 4]. A partition is a set of computation actors grouped into a task. A partition can be implemented as a software thread, for example. Most of the partition-based work rely on two assumptions. First, actors have a fixed workload that can be known statically or by executing a profiling phase. Second, the number of available physical cores is fixed. Based on the workload, actors can be evenly partitioned into a number of groups so that the load for each processor can be balanced with all other processors. These techniques have been evaluated on streaming multi-core architectures with distributed memory address spaces like the IBM CELL [10] or on many-core architectures such as RAW [5] and Merrimac [3], where the compiler orchestrates the execution of actors on each processor and the data transfers between processors.

However, in many streaming applications workloads can change at runtime in response to input data values or the external environment. For example, for some software-based radio streaming applications a filter may need to carry out more computation for weaker input signals than for normal or strong input signals in order to obtain similar quality outputs. In addition, in many general purpose multi-core systems, the available computing resources to a stream program can be dynamic depending on the degree of the multiprogramming or on the presence of higher priority applications that reserve some cpu resources. With static partitioning, applications are not able to make use of additional resources made available to them during run-time. Our work achieves run-time load balancing that can cope with changing computing resources. Instead of adhering to a static workload partition, our approach is to achieve balance by identifying actors with heavier loads and splitting their work during run-time. We call actors with the maximum load *computation bottlenecks.* We propose a method for identifying computation bottlenecks on the fly and relieving them by splitting their loads. This workload splitting is realized by employing additional software threads that will share the workload with the original master thread for the actor. Our run-time task duplication mechanism is applicable to general purpose SMP multi-core architectures.

We derived a performance model to characterize the throughput improvements introduced by task duplication. Further, we provide a set of algorithms for on-line identification of computation bottlenecks based on the indications from the performance model. These algorithms work locally within the scope of each actor; no global data structures are needed either.

Our run-time task duplication framework embeds the bottleneck detection algorithms into streaming applications during the code generation phase of their compilations. No application changes or user intervention are required.

The contributions in this paper are as follows.

- We introduce a run-time task duplication method for maximizing the throughput of a stream program. It is equipped with low overhead run-time computation bottleneck detection algorithms. Each actor is able to identify itself as a bottleneck without any centralized process or control system monitoring global program behavior. Our technique operates in the application level and is decoupled from any specific operating system, assuming only a fair scheduler of tasks/processes. Our run-time task duplication technique is transparent to end-users: task duplication mechanisms are automatically embedded into the application by compile-time code generation.

- We define a performance analysis and prediction model for run-time task duplication on SMP multi-core environments. We present experimental results that confirm the validity of our model.

The remainder of this paper is organized as follows: Section 2 presents an overview of our run-time task duplication. Section 3 introduces the performance model of the run-time task duplication. Section 4 describes a set of on-line computation bottleneck detection algorithms for adaptive run-time task duplication. Section 5 provides the experimental results. Finally, Section 6 reviews related work and Section 7 concludes the paper.

2. ON-THE-FLY TASK DUPLICATION

2.1 Streaming Computing Model

In this paper we focus on streaming applications that can be described as directed acyclic graphs (DAG) where a node represents an actor and an edge between nodes represents the communication between them. An actor is an autonomous unit of computation that works on the incoming data and generates output data. We call the unit of data an actor works on a data item or an item. The transfer of data items from a producer actor to a consumer actor can be done in FIFO fashion. There is a constant flow of incoming data to a set of source actors of a graph, or the source actors constantly produce items for their downstreams. A firing of an actor is an execution of the actor's body. For one firing of an actor, the actor requires a certain number of input data items. Similarly, for one firing, an actor produces a certain number of output data items. These numbers are called

pop and push counts of the actor and denoted as *popcnt* and *pushcnt*, respectively. Our main interests are in streaming applications with fixed push and pop counts. The *popcnt* and *pushcnt* values are either known at the compile time. The *workload* of an actor is defined as the CPU cycles spent by the actor for one firing.

In this paper, we take the following baseline execution model. Each actor is implemented as a user-level software thread. Each edge, a communication channel, is implemented as a fixed-size, blocking FIFO queue. The consumer actor of an input queue waits until there are at least *popcnt* data items in the queue. The producer actor of an output queue also waits until there are sufficient available space for storing *pushcnt* data items in the output queue. By making each actor a thread and using multiple entries in communication queues, pipeline parallelism between different iterations of a stream graph is exploited.

The data items should be executed in order and are not allowed to be omitted. We also assume that the operating system is equipped with a scheduler that attempts to distribute the available CPU cycles equally to all user-level tasks.

2.2 Benefits Of Task Duplication

We present an example how task-duplication increases the throughput of a stream program, in which each actor and each edge are implemented as one thread and one fixed-size blocking queue, respectively. For the sake of simplicity, we assume there is only one stream program to be scheduled in the system. Figure 1(a) shows a simple stream program with three actors. The workload of an actor i is denoted by w_i. In this example, the *popcnt* of all actors except the source, and *pushcnt* of all actors except the sink, are one. A possible schedule of the stream program on two cores is shown on the right hand side of the stream program. Each square box denotes a scheduling slot, where a scheduling slot is defined as a pair of a core and a time unit, i.e. $sl(core\_id, timeunit\_id)$. A circle in scheduling slot $sl(i, j)$ represents a thread corresponding to an actor that is assigned to core i at time unit j. For example, a thread for actor B is taking up three consecutive scheduling slots $sl(1, 2)$, $sl(1, 3)$, and $sl(1, 4)$ on core 1 to denote that the workload of B is 3 time units. A superscript over an actor represents an iteration index (e.g. B^0 and B^1 are B in the first and second iterations of the given stream graph, respectively). The pipelining effect of two different iterations of stream graph is shown. Both threads B^0 for the first iteration and A^1 for the second iteration are running in parallel in time slot 4. The throughput of this schedule is $1/3$, meaning one output is produced at the sink every 3 time units as designated by one solid C^i within the interval of three time slots.

The impact of the task duplication is shown in Figure 1(b). Actor B is duplicated into two separate threads, $B0$ and $B1$. The producer actor A needs to repeat twice to feed both $B0$ and $B1$ as shown by $\times 2$ *repetitions*. Likewise, actor C needs two repetitions.

The possible schedule of this duplicated stream program is shown in the right hand side of Figure 1(b). The superscripts denoting iteration indices are given in the granularity of the duplicated stream graph. Thus, one iteration of the duplicated graph generates two outputs from C. Now the throughput is $2/5$, meaning two outputs over 5 time units. The throughput is increased from $1/3$ of Figure 1(a).

Why does the duplication in Figure 1(b) increase the throughput of the original stream program in Figure 1(a)? More scheduling slots are contributing to the throughput in Figure 1(b) than in Figure 1(a). In Figure 1(a), some scheduling slots, for example, $sl(1,6)$, $sl(2,9)$ and $sl(1,12)$ are idle because one thread representing an actor can not be scheduled into two cores at the same time slot. Even filling $sl(1,6)$ with A^2 would not increase the throughput because it will only shift the idle slots ahead. On the other hand, in Figure 1(b), all scheduling slots in the figure are contributing to throughput. We notice that both schedules in Figure 1(a) and (b) are valid though the actual assignment of a thread to a core can be different from the ones in the figure depending on the decisions of the scheduler in the system. The validity of the schedule arises from the fact that the probability of actor n occupies a scheduling slot among all actors within one iteration of stream graph G is preserved in both schedules. The probability is defined as shown in Eq. (1) based on two assumptions 1) we implement each actor in stream program G as a thread and each edge as a fixed-size blocking queue and 2) we are assuming the scheduler in the system is fair in that every thread in G is given the same opportunity to be scheduled [1].

$$p(n) = \frac{w_n}{\sum_{\forall m \in \text{set of actors in } G} w_m} \qquad (1)$$

For example, in Figure 1(a), $p(A) = 1/(1+3+1)$ and $p(B) = 3/(1+3+1)$. In Figure 1(b), $p(B0) = p(B1) = 3/(2+3+3+2) = 3/10$ and $p(A) = p(C) = 2/10$. The workloads of A and C are doubled due to the repetitions after duplication of B.

It is important to duplicate the actor with a maximum workload, to improve the performance. Duplicating a non-bottleneck without duplicating a bottleneck does not improve the throughput. The performance model that predicts the usefulness of task duplication will be described later on in Section 3.

The above task duplication can be applied to *stateless* actors. Consecutive firings of a stateless actor can be executed concurrently. On the other hand, a firing of a *stateful* actor is dependent on its previous firings. The consecutive firings cannot be parallelized. However, our baseline computing model takes advantage of pipeline parallelism even for stateful actors by implementing each actor as a thread and queues with multiple entries.

2.3 The Framework of Run-time Task Duplication

To facilitate the run-time task duplication we implement an actor not with a single thread but with one master thread and a pool of sibling threads. The master thread activates a certain number of sibling threads in the pool. The remaining inactivated sibling threads are put to sleep. For example, the implementation of actor B using a master and a pool of sibling threads is illustrated in Figure 2(b) given a stream program in Figure 2(a). Each sibling thread directly writes its output to the designated entry of the output queue of actor B. Upon the completion of all sibling threads the master thread updates the status of the actor's output queue. Thus, consumer actor C of actor B only sees the consecutively filled input queue. We currently make the

[1] The second assumption seems to be opposite to Eq. (1), but the fact that a thread is to be blocked without taking up CPU cycles whenever there are not enough data items or spaces causes Eq. (1)

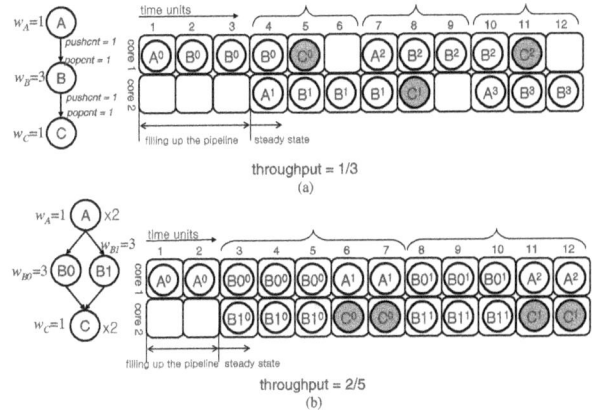

Figure 1: The impact of the task duplication with two physical cores: (a) the original stream program and its probable schedule, (b) the duplication of actor B and the resulting possible schedule. w_i represents workload of the actor i in terms of time units.

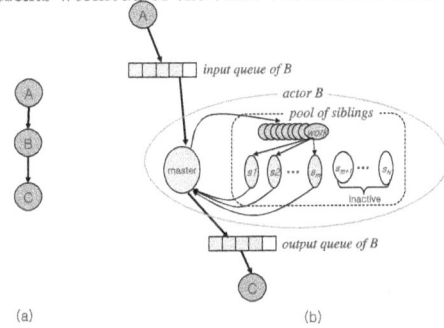

Figure 2: Master thread and sibling threads of actor B are exemplified.

master thread to wait for all siblings so that all data items are executed in order. In-order execution of data items is one of the assumptions in our current streaming model. This assumption, however, does not limit the applicability of our run-time task duplication through bottleneck detections.

The pseudo code for the master thread is shown in Algorithms 1 and 2. The master thread also does useful work as shown in line 5 in Algorithm 2.

The bottleneck detection algorithms on top of Algorithms 1 and 2 will be described later on in Section 4. Notice that this adaptive workload splitting mechanism through the collaboration among a master and sibling threads is transparent to the end-users. End-users can focus on the Work($\cdot$) function of each actor, and the flow of data. The load balancing scheme using sibling threads and bottleneck detection is embedded into the program through the code generation phase.

3. PERFORMANCE MODELING

Our framework provides useful insights to the performance optimization of stream programs using task duplication. It models the throughput of a stream program with given workloads and computing resources for a steady state. We assume in one phase the workload of a stream program and the number of available cores are stable. Transitions in workload and computing resources will lead to another phase. We aim to capture the effectiveness of task duplication in a stable phase because we are considering stream programs that spend most of their execution time in stable phases than in transitions.

Our modeling framework models a stream program as a *timed marked graph* (TMG) [2, 15]. The inverse of the minimum cycle time of the proposed TMG model bounds the

Input: *inQs, outQs, sibThread, workQForSibs, maxThreads*
/* *sibThread* is a pool of sibling threads for this actor. */

1 *curThreads* ← size(*sibThread*)+1;
2 **while** *true* **do**
3 $\quad$ WaitOnInputs(*inQs*);
4 $\quad$ WaitOnOutSpaces(*outQs*);
5 $\quad$ *numFirings* ← CalcNumFirings(*inQs, outQs*);
6 $\quad$ WorkAndHireSiblings(*numFirings, curThreads, inQs, outQs, sibThread*);
7 $\quad$ UpdateHeadsAndTails(*inQs, outQs, numFirings*);

Algorithm 2: WorkAndHireSiblings: the master does its own work and also distributes work among siblings

---

Input: *numFirings, curThreads, inQs, outQs, sibThread*
1 *myQuota* ← *numFirings* / *curThreads*;
2 **for** $i = 1$ **to** *curThreads* − 1 **do**
3 $\quad$ activate(*sibThread*[*i*]);
4 *workQForSibs* ←
   FillWorkQueueOfSiblings(*numFirings* − *myQuota, inQs, outQs*);
5 Work(*myQuota, inQs, outQs*);
6 WaitForAllOtherFirings(*numFirings* − *myQuota*);

---

maximum throughput of the modeled stream program. The evaluation of the minimum cycle time of the TMG reveals the limiting factors of the throughput. We analyze these limiting factors to derive general principles used by the proposed on-line bottleneck detection and task duplication algorithms.

Timed marked graph. A *marked graph* is a 4-tuple $\mathcal{M} = \{P, T, F, M_0\}$, where $P = \{p_1, \ldots, p_n\}$ is the set of *places*, $T = \{t_1, \ldots, t_m\}$ the set of *transitions*, $F : (P \times T) \cup (T \times P)$ the set of *edges*, and $M_0 : P \to \mathbb{N}$ assigns an initial number of tokens to each place. In a marked graph each place has at most one input transition and at most one output transition. A transition is *enabled* if all of its input places have at least one token. An enabled transition can fire, and its firing removes one token from each of its input place and deposits one token to each of its output place. In a loop of a marked graph the total number of tokens remains constant regardless of the firing of the transitions [12]. This property will be used later to model the available resources, e.g., the number of processor cores and the size of the data channel queues.

In a *timed* marked graph (TMG) each transition is associated with a non-negative firing time. When a transition of firing delay δ fires at time t, its enabling tokens become unavailable for other transitions during the time interval $[t, t + \delta)$. The transition then removes the enabling tokens and deposits new tokens at $t + \delta$. The transition can continue to fire during the time interval $[t, t + \delta)$, as long as there is a sufficient number of tokens still available to enable the transition. This "infinite server" firing semantics is crucial for modeling task duplication.[2] Figure 3(b)–3(d) show some TMG examples, modeling the stream program in Figure 3(a). The workload w_i of actor A_i is translated into

---

[2] The firing semantics of TMG given here is from Sifakis in [15].

firing time w_i of transition T_i. In the figures transitions are horizontal bars, places large circles, and tokens solid dots.

The *minimum cycle time* of a TMG is the minimum time interval between two consecutive firings of any transition. It has been shown that the minimum cycle time of a TMG is

$$\max_k \frac{D_k}{N_k}, \qquad (2)$$

where k is a loop of transitions interleaved with places in the TMG, D_k the sum of the firing time of the transitions on loop k, and N_K the sum of the number of initial tokens on loop k [12]. A loop k is *critical* if it gives the highest ratio of $\frac{D_k}{N_k}$.

Modeling stream programs as TMGs. Our modeling of a stream program as a TMG consists of multiple steps. A basic TMG model is first constructed and then is refined in the subsequent steps. For simplicity we assume the stream program is a homogeneous synchronous data flow [3], and the communication cost between each pair of adjacent actors through the in-memory channel is negligible. These two assumptions do not limit the applicability of our model. Non-homogeneous data flow programs can be converted to homogeneous ones before being modeled as TMGs [11, 16]. Further communication channels with non-negligible delay can be converted to one-input-one-output actors with certain workload.

The transformation of a stream program to its basic TMG model follows the topology of the stream program. The transformation creates a transition T_i for each actor A_i of the stream program. For each data channel (A_i, A_j) of the stream program, two places P_{ij} and P'_{ij} and four edges (T_i, P_{ij}), (P_{ij}, T_j), (T_j, P'_{ij}), and (P'_{ij}, T_i) are added to the TMG model. The firing time of a transition T_i is the same as the workload of its corresponding actor A_i. To model the finite buffering capacity of channel (A_i, A_j), we assign a number of initial tokens to P'_{ij} that is the same as the size of the channel queue [17]. Figure 3(b) reports the basic TMG model of the simple stream program in Figure 3(a), assuming each channel can store up to 5 data items. Notice that our TMG model is always strongly connected because of places like P'_{ij} modeling the queues size.

The second modeling step considers the *auto-concurrency* of actors, defined as the maximum possible number of concurrent firings of the actor [17]. A stateful actor cannot have more than one firing at a time, while a stateless actor can have many concurrent firings. In practice the number of a stateless actor's concurrent firings is limited by the number of software threads assigned to it. To capture this limitation in the TMG, for each transition T_i we create a "self-loop" attached to the transition by adding a place P_i and edges (T_i, P_i) and (P_i, T_i), as shown in Figure 3(c). If actor A_i is stateful, P_i has exactly one initial token, limiting the number of the concurrent firings of transition T_i to one. On the other hand, if A_i is stateless, P_i has S_i initial tokens, where S_i is the number of A_i's software threads.

The final step in our modeling framework considers the limited number of processor cores. We assume a fair scheduling policy for the software threads in the stream program. This step introduces an additional simple loop in the TMG consisting of all of the transitions and some extra places. For the entire TMG we add one special place P''_{CPU}. Let

---

[3] *pushcnt* and *popcnt* of all actors are 1. See [12] for more details.

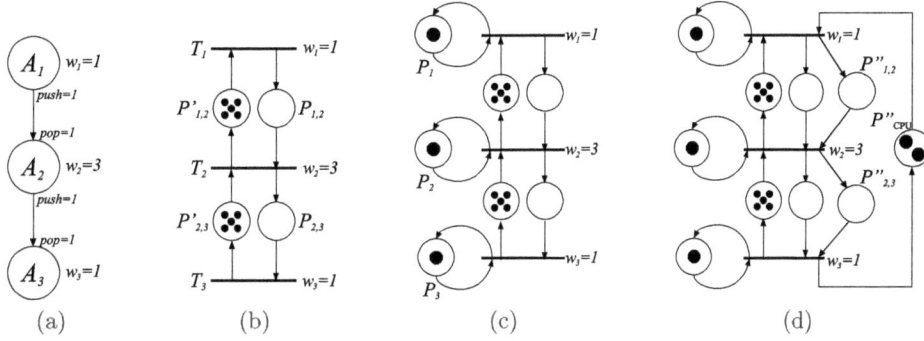

Figure 3: A stream program and its timed marked graph (TMG) models.

$\{A_1, \ldots, A_n\}$ be a feasible activation sequence of the actors from the program's initial state.[4] We add $(n-1)$ of places $P''_{1,2}, P''_{2,3}, \ldots, P''_{n-1,n}$ between each pair of the actors in the sequence. These places are connected to transitions by edges (P''_{CPU}, T_1), $(T_1, P''_{1,2})$, $(P''_{1,2}, T_2)$, $\ldots$, $(P''_{n-1,n}, T_n)$, and (T_n, P''_{CPU}). The number of initial tokens at place P''_{CPU} is the same as the number of processor cores. The distribution of the tokens among places like $P''_{i-1,i}$ in the new simple loop represents a possible snapshot of the scheduling of the actors: if place $P''_{i-1,i}$ holds a token, actor A_i is selected for execution pending the presence of its input data and output buffering capacity. The final TMG of the stream program in Figure 3(a), run by 2 processor cores, is reported in Figure 3(d).

Bottleneck analysis. According to Eq. (2) each loop in a TMG imposes a lower bound on the TMG's minimum cycle time and thus an upper bound on the throughput of the modeled stream program. We classify the loops in the TMG resulted from our modeling framework into three types. Define w_i and S_i as the workload and the number of the software threads of actor A_i, respectively, and C as the number of the processor cores.

1. The self-loop at each transition T_i ($T_i \to P_i \to T_i$) imposes a throughput upper bound S_i/w_i caused by the auto-concurrency of actor A_i.

2. The simple loop consisting of places P''_{CPU}, $P''_{i-1,i}$, and all of the transitions in the TMG imposes a throughput upper bound $C/\sum_i w_i$ caused by the number of processor cores. This bound coincides with the inverse of the *resource constrained minimum initiation interval* [13].

3. Any loop involving places like P'_{ij} imposes a throughput upper bound resulted from the size of channel (A_i, A_j)'s queue.

This work focuses on the throughput bounds imposed by the first two types of loops modeling the effects of the number of software threads and the processor cores. We assume that all of the queues have enough capacity such that the third type of loops does not limit the throughput of a stream program. Under these assumptions the maximum throughput of the stream program is bounded by

$$\min \{C/\sum_i w_i, S_1/w_1, \ldots, S_n/w_n\}. \qquad (3)$$

Based on the TMG modeling and Eq. (3) we derive some useful principles that will be used to develop adaptive task duplication algorithms. First, if the auto-concurrency of a

stateless actor A_i is the limiting factor of the throughput, S_i/w_i is the minimum value in Eq. (3). Second, we conjecture that the tokens in a critical loop are always busy, i.e., these tokens are always used by certain transitions in the loop. Notice that it also suggests that for addition of software threads to be useful the number of the processor cores is not the limiting factor, that is, $C/\sum_i w_i$ is not the minimum value of Eq. (3).

Example. We can decide if the throughput of the stream program of Figure 3(a) can be improved by the addition of software threads to the stateless actor A_2 based on Eq. (3). The throughput of the stream program is bounded by $\min\{2/5, 1/1, 1/3, 1/1\} = 1/3$, and thus is constrained by A_2's auto-concurrency. Adding one more software thread to A_2 the throughput can be improved to $\min\{2/5, 1/1, 2/3, 1/1\} = 2/5$. After this addition the number of the processor cores becomes the new limiting factor, and adding more software threads to A_2 does not help.

4. ADAPTIVE TASK DUPLICATION USING RUN-TIME BOTTLENECK DETECTION

In this section, we propose two different runtime computation bottleneck detection algorithms utilizing the indicators provided by the performance model to identify which tasks are in need of more computing resources. Both of the algorithms are executed locally at each actor to work without the intervention of a central agent that has the global knowledge of a streaming application such as the topology of the graph and the delays of all actors.

4.1 Delay Propagation Method

According to Eq.(3) in Section 3, the maximum achievable throughput is approached as the auto-concurrency of an actor with the maximum workload increases. Based on this observation we attempt to identify the actor with the largest workload by propagating delays of actors and to increase the number of threads for that actor. The term delay simply means the measured workload of an actor at run-time.

An actor measures its delay whenever it executes its body of work and compares the delay against the incoming delays from the upstreams. An actor also forwards the result of the comparison to its downstream actors. As the local measurement and propagation continually occur, every actor comes to observe the maximum effective delay of the stream program and finally identifies itself either as a bottleneck or not.

A dedicated delay channel is used to forward delay information between two actors. Different from the main data queue for data items, a delay channel has non-blocking

[4]For example, if the stream program is a DAG, the sequence can be the topological order of the actors.

167

read/write policies to minimize their impact on performance. Delay channels are built at compile time tracing the topology of data channels in the stream graph. For each data channel (i, j), a parallel delay channel from actor i to j is added. In addition, a channel from the sink t to the source s is added for the reachability to all actors in the graph. A single *source* actor s and a *sink* actor t is assumed because we are considering acyclic graphs in this paper.

Algorithm 3 describes the master thread of an actor with the bottleneck detection. In addition to the basic functionality of the master thread in Algorithm 1, the execution delay is measured, and the bottleneck detection routine is called (line 13). The sibling threads are used for the next execution only if the actor is identified as a bottleneck (lines 14 through 17). Given incoming delays and its own measured delays, an actor individually runs a bottleneck detection algorithm, which is a simple two-state algorithm as described in Algorithm 4. If its own measured delay is smaller than the incoming delay, the actor decides that it is a bottleneck. Otherwise, the actor decides that it is not a bottleneck. If an actor identifies itself as a bottleneck, it forwards its measured delay to downstream actors. Notice that two different measured delays are used for the comparison to the incoming delays (*faceDelay* at line 2) and for the propagation to the downstream actors (*effectiveDelay* at line 7). *faceDelay* is a delay per firing by one thread while *effectiveDelay* is an effective delay per firing. For example, suppose a master thread and an additional sibling thread (two threads in total) are used for an actor. Further, suppose both master and sibling threads spend w time units for one firing, respectively. The delay per firing by one thread (i.e. *faceDelay*) is w. If the total time of the two threads is also w assuming the both threads run concurrently, *effectiveDelay* is $w/2$. *faceDelay* is calculated from the measured delay of the work time of the master thread, *masterDelay* (lines 8 and 11 in Algorithm 3). *masterDelay* is the elapsed time in the master's work (line 5 in Algorithm 2). On the other hand, *effectiveDelay* is measure over all threads (line 12 in Algorithm 3). We use *faceDelay* to minimize the oscillation between states S_B (i.e. *isBottleneck*) and S_{NB} (i.e. *!isBottleneck*) and *effectiveDelay* to resolve the next bottlenecks that are emerging after the resolution of one bottleneck. The larger *faceDelay* of an actor, the sooner the actor converges to the state S_B than other actors. An actor with the smaller *faceDelay* can oscillate between S_B and S_{NB} until all other actors with larger *faceDelay* converge to state S_B. We allow these initial temporary changes to enable sibling threads as soon as possible.

4.2 Work-Ratio Based Method

Another method can be derived by using a hypothesis observed from the proposed TMG model: the tokens on the loop that contributes to the tightest throughput bound in Eq. (3) will always be used by transitions on the loop. Therefore if the number of threads used for an actor is limiting the throughput, the actor's threads will be constantly active in doing useful work. This observation is used to determine if an actor is a bottleneck and to dynamically adjust the number of the actor's sibling threads.

The overall degree of busyness of the master and the sibling threads is quantified by the *work ratio*. The work ratio is the proportion of time the actor's threads spend on computation instead of being blocked, defined as (*work time*) / (*total time*). The total time is the time during which the

---

Algorithm 3: Master thread using on-line bottleneck detection based on propagating delays.

Input: $inQs$, $outQs$, $sibThread$, $workQForSibs$, $maxThreads$, $inDelayChs$, $outDelayChs$

1   $curThreads \leftarrow maxThreads$;
2   $isBottleneck \leftarrow false$;
3   **while** *true* **do**
4   WaitOnInputs($inQs$);
5   WaitOnOutSpaces($outQs$);
6     $numFirings \leftarrow$ CalcNumFirings($inQs$, $outQs$);
7     $tStart \leftarrow$ GetTime();
8     $masterDelay \leftarrow$ WorkAndHireSiblings($numFirings$, $curThreads$, $inQs$, $outQs$, $sibThread$) /* Algorithm 2 */;
9     $tEnd \leftarrow$ GetTime();
10    $allDelay \leftarrow tEnd - tStart$;
11    $faceDelay \leftarrow masterDelay/ (numFirings/ curThreads)$;
12    $effectiveDelay \leftarrow allDelay/ numFirings$;
13    $isBottleneck \leftarrow$ PropagateDelay($inDelayChs$, $outDelayChs$, $faceDelay$, $effectiveDelay$, $isBottleneck$, $numFirings$);
14   **if** *isBottleneck* **then**
15      $curThreads \leftarrow maxThreads$;
16   **else**
17      $curThreads \leftarrow 1$;

Algorithm 4: PropagateDelay identifies bottlenecks

Input : $inDelayChs$, $outDelayChs$, $faceDelay$, $effectiveDelay$, $isBottleneck$, $numFirings$
Output: Whether this actor is a bottleneck or not

1   $maxDelay \leftarrow$ CalcMaxDelay($inDelayChs$);
2   $smaller \leftarrow$ IsSmaller($faceDelay$, $maxDelay$);
3   **if** IsSmaller **then**
4     $isBottleneck \leftarrow$ false;
5   **else**
6     $isBottleneck \leftarrow$ true ;
7     $maxDelay \leftarrow effectiveDelay$;
8   UpdateOutDelays($outDelayChs$, $maxDelay$);
9   **return** $isBottleneck$;

---

stream program is active,[5] while the work time is the sum of the time each thread spends on computation. In each execution the master thread computes the work ratio and uses it to adjust the number of sibling threads to use in the subsequent executions. Algorithms 5 and 6 show the measurement of total and work times, and computation of work ratio, respectively.

Two types of work ratios are calculated according to the current number of threads. If only the master thread is active without any sibling thread, the following ratio

$$R1 = masterWorkDelay/totalDelay$$

is used (line 2 in Algorithm 6). If value $R1$ exceeds a certain threshold, the actor identifies itself as a bottleneck and increases the number of sibling threads for the next execution by the amount of *step* (line 3). On the other hand, if the master thread is working along with the sibling threads, the work ratio of the second type is used to account for the usefulness of the sibling threads.

$$R2 = \left\lceil \frac{masterWorkDelay + \sum_{i=1}^{curThreads - 1} siblingDelays[i]}{totalDelay} \right\rceil$$

[5]In our current implementation the total time is approximated by the elapsed run time of the stream program and is measured by each actor.

Algorithm 5: Master thread using on-line bottleneck detection based on work ratios

Input: $inQs$, $outQs$, $sibThread$, $workQForSibs$, $maxThreads$

1   $curThreads \leftarrow maxThreads$;
2   $masterWorkDelay \leftarrow 0$;
3   $tInit \leftarrow \texttt{GetTime()}$;
4   **while** $true$ **do**
5     $\texttt{WaitOnInputs}(inQs)$;
6     $\texttt{WaitOnOutSpaces}(outQs)$;
7     $numFirings \leftarrow \texttt{CalcNumFirings}(inQs, outQs)$;
8     $tStart \leftarrow \texttt{GetTime()}$;
9     $\texttt{WorkAndHireSiblings}(numFirings, curThreads, inQs, outQs, sibThread)$;
10    $tEnd \leftarrow \texttt{GetTime()}$;
11    $masterWorkDelay \leftarrow masterWorkDelay + (tEnd - tStart)$;
12    $totalDelay \leftarrow tEnd\text{-} tInit$;
13    $\texttt{UpdateHeadsAndTails}(inQs, outQs, numFirings)$;
14    $sibDelays \leftarrow$ measured delay from each sibling thread ;
15    $curThreads \leftarrow \texttt{WorkRatioBasedAdjustThreads}(masterWorkDelay, totalDelay, sibDelays, curThreads, maxThreads)$;

The work time of each sibling thread $siblingDelays[]$ is measured and also accumulated at each sibling thread. The value of $R2$ indicates the effective number of threads that are spending most of their time in useful work instead of being blocked. If $R2$ is equal to the current number of threads, it suggests that *almost* all of the current threads are busy working. Thus the number of threads is increased for the next execution (lines 6 and 7). In contrast, if $R2$ is smaller than the current number of threads, it suggests that at least one or more threads do not have enough input data and thus start to be idling. In such a case the number of threads is decreased for the next firing (lines 8 through 11).

Comparison to the delay propagation method. Unlike the previous one, this bottleneck detection algorithm is purely *local* since it depends only on the local measurement without communicating delay information with other actors. Further it dynamically adjusts the number of sibling threads to the right level proportionally to the computed work ratios rather than activating and deactivating all sibling threads. This dynamic adjustment feature based on the work ratio enables it to be highly adaptive to changing resources.

5. EXPERIMENTS

We used stream programs in the StreamIt benchmarks [5] for our experiments. Using the StreamIt compiler, we generated streamit benchmarks with synthetic workloads. To evaluate how well our run-time task duplication algorithms can work with different amount of bottlenecks, we applied different synthetic workloads to the stream programs. Table 1 presents the list of programs we used with their numbers of actors and edges in stream graphs.

We ran our experiments on a four-socket quad-core Intel Xeon 1.6 GHZ machine, which has 16 cores in total. We used GNU/Linux kernel version 2.6 (RHEL 6.2) as our operating system.

We made a comparison among the following different approaches to demonstrate the effectiveness of run-time task duplication and the usefulness of our run-time bottleneck detection algorithms.

- For the baseline, **baseline**, we implement each actor in a stream graph as a single master thread. No additional sibling thread per actor is used so that run-time duplication

Algorithm 6: `WorkRatioBasedAdjustThreads` adjusts the thread number using work ratios.

Input : $masterWorkDelay$, $totalDelay$, $siblingDelays$, $curThreads$, $maxThreads$, $threshold$, $step$; /* $threshold$ and $step$ are given as predefined parameters */
Output: A new number of threads which are to be activated in the next kernel firing.

1   $newThreads \leftarrow curThreads$;
2   **if** $curThreads = 1$ and $masterWorkDelay/totalDelay \geq threshold$ **then**
3     $newThreads \leftarrow newThreads + step$;
4   **else if** $curThreads > 1$ **then**
5     $activeThreads \leftarrow \left\lceil \frac{masterWorkDelay + \sum_{i=1}^{curThreads-1} siblingDelays[i]}{totalDelay} \right\rceil$;
6   **if** $activeThreads \geq curThreads$ **then**
7       $newThreads \leftarrow curThreads + 1$;
8   **else**
9   **if** $activeThreads = 1$ **then**
10        $newThreads \leftarrow 1$;
11   **else**
12        $newThreads \leftarrow curThreads$;

13   **return** $\min\{newThreads, maxThreads\}$;

Table 1: Number of actors and edges for each benchmark.

benchmark	number of actors	number of edges
FMRADIO	31	37
AUDIOBEAM	22	35
FFT2	26	26
FILTERBANK	53	59
MATMUL	43	62
TDE	55	56
SAR	44	44
BITONIC-SORT	370	594
DES	423	598
MP3	180	294
SERPENT	234	266

does not occur. Only the master thread works as worker thread. Notice, however, that our baseline is already a multi-threaded program that exploits task and pipeline parallelism on multiple cores. All speedup numbers we report are against this multi-threaded baseline program. According to Table 1, the number of actors in stream graphs we used ranges from 20 to 600. The baseline is already using more software threads than the available 16 hardware threads. Thus, we show that our run-time duplication is capable of increasing the performance of a multi-threaded stream program even when the number of software threads deployed in the program already exceeds the number of physical cores.

- The approach **no-detect** enables as many sibling threads as the number of hardware threads (denoted as C) minus one for an actor all the time. For example, it activates 15 sibling threads for each actor on a machine with sixteen hardware threads. As a result C threads in total are used for an actor. No run-time bottleneck detection algorithm is used.
- The approach **manual** uses the knowledge of the exact bottlenecks. It uses $C - 1$ sibling threads only for each of the exact bottleneck actors, i.e. actors with the maximum workloads, w_{max}. all other actors use only a master thread without using any sibling threads. This configuration is maintained throughout the whole execution. No run-time bottleneck detection algorithm is used. This approach is not applicable when the exact bottleneck are not known before run-time. Thus, **manual** is mainly for evaluating how well our proposed algorithms perform in detecting bottlenecks during run-time. Theoretically, **manual** can achieve

the maximum achievable throughput, $\frac{C}{\sum_i w_i}$, in Eq. (3) because $\frac{C}{w_{max}}$ is not greater than $\frac{C}{\sum_i w_i}$.

- The approaches delay-prpg and work-rt refer to our run-time task duplication methods using the two run-time bottleneck detection algorithms proposed in Sections 4.1 and 4.2, respectively. Recall that work-rt adaptively changes the number of sibling threads activated per actor during run-time whereas delay-prpg enables $C - 1$ sibling threads whenever an actor is determined as a bottleneck.

- Finally, elastic is a variant of the approach proposed in [14]. By monitoring run-time performance for different numbers of threads per actor, the one that achieved the best performance so far is selected. In [14] bottleneck actors were identified before run-time and the degree of the multi-threading for each bottleneck is adjusted at run-time by a machine learning algorithm based on monitored performance. Whereas, in our experiment we apply this performance monitoring approach to all actors to see if the bottleneck detection can be attained in this way. Thus, our purpose is rather adopting the performance monitoring approach in [14] as a bottleneck detection method, not providing a direct performance comparison.

Table 2 summarizes the above approaches. For a fair comparison, for all approaches we used the same queue sizes, which are large enough to avoid communication bottleneck.

Table 2: Descriptions of different approaches: C denotes the number of hardware threads (cores).

Name	Description
baseline	No sibling threads, but only a master thread as a worker, for each actor.
no-detect	The $C - 1$ sibling threads are added to all actors without any detection of bottlenecks. The number of sibling threads does not change.
manual	The $C - 1$ sibling threads are added only to the bottlenecks known before the run-time. The number of sibling threads per bottleneck doesn't change during run-time.
delay-prpg	A run-time bottleneck detection based on delay propagation. On detected bottlenecks $C - 1$ siblings are used.
work-rt	A run-time bottleneck detection: the number of sibling threads is adjusted between 0 and $C - 1$ based on the work ratio of threads at run-time.
elastic [14]	A run-time bottleneck detection: the number of sibling threads is adjusted between 0 and $C - 1$ based on monitoring of the performance at run-time.

The effect on a small number of bottlenecks. In this experiment, we inject only one bottleneck actor in each application. The purpose of adding only one bottleneck is twofold. First, we conduct a sanity test of our run-time bottleneck detection algorithms. Second, we evaluate how much additional performance gain can be achieved when only a small portion of an application serves as a bottleneck. The bottleneck is given the workload of w_{max} where as all the other actors are given the same workload w. We set w_{max} to nine when w is one. For work-rt, the parameter step is given as $C - 1$ as a result of testing various configurations.

Figure 4 illustrates the speed-ups of different approaches on the 16-core machine. As mentioned above, the speed-up numbers are against the performance of the multi-threaded baseline.

One of our bottleneck detection approaches, work-rt works almost as well as manual for the first 7 benchmarking programs. Recall that manual is near-optimal in that its throughput draws near the maximum achievable throughput, $\frac{C}{\sum_i w_i}$, since $\frac{C}{\sum_i w_i} \leq \frac{C}{w_{max}}$ and $\frac{C}{\sum_i w_i} \leq \frac{1}{w}$. The performance of work-rt closely follows that of manual. This trend demon-

strates the effectiveness of our run-time bottleneck detection algorithm.

The usefulness of the bottleneck detection on top of the naive run-time task duplication is evaluated through the comparison to no-detect. Our work-rt performs better than no-detect up to 8%, and 4% on average. Notice that no-detect is also theoretically near-optimal in that from Eq. (3) $\min\{\frac{C}{\sum_i w_i}, \frac{C}{w_{max}}\}$ is $\frac{C}{\sum_i w_i}$. It means the maximum cpu utilization is achieved. However, as shown from our experiment, the performance of no-detect is less than that of work-rt and manual due to the overhead of managing a larger number of threads. As the applications and the number of processor cores become bigger, no-detect becomes unpractical. For example, even 500 actors on 128 cores already lead to a very large number of threads (500×128).

Between our two bottleneck detection algorithms, work-rt performs better. By using local work ratio as an indication of the need of a raise or a drop in the number of threads work-rt quickly adjusts to the right number of threads. The source of the less desirable performance of delay-prpg is mainly from the latency for propagating delays over the whole graph.

Both our algorithms perform better than the elastic approach adopted from [14], the performance monitoring method. It takes long for elastic to activate a sufficient number of sibling threads for bottlenecks. In order to increase or decrease the current number of threads, an application should run for a while with a couple of adjacent numbers of threads for monitoring performance. In addition, elastic starts each actor with only a small initial number of threads, 1. Exploring the space between 1 and C takes a fair amount of time. In our experiment, elastic ends up with using only a few threads for a bottleneck, and the number of sibling threads per actor oscillated in many cases. In contrast, our algorithms quickly employ as many threads as the number of hardware threads per bottleneck using the observation from the performance model.

Comparing different benchmarks, FMRADIO, AUDIOBEAM, and FFT2 tend to perform better than others. This is as predicted by the derived performance model. The number of physical threads, i.e. the number of cores, should be at least $\frac{\sum_i w_i}{w_{max}}$ to see any performance gain through task duplication. The second column (i.e. the one with *with a single bottlenck*) of Table 3 shows these minimum required numbers of hardware threads to expect any gain over the baseline with a single 9x bottleneck. It is clear that we see more gains in the benchmarks with smaller minimum required numbers of hardware threads.

Table 3: The calculated minimum required physical threads

benchmark	with a single bottleneck	with multiple(10%) bottlenecks
FMRADIO	3.33	5.89
AUDIOBEAM	2.88	5.55
FFT2	3.55	7.11
FILTERBANK	6.55	10.11
MATMUL	4.11	6.78
TDE	6.55	10.11
SAR	5.55	8.22
BITONIC-SORT	27.78	52.67
DES	11.48	55.00
MP3	15.77	26.44
SERPENT	19.55	33.78

The effect on a multiple bottlenecks. In this experiment around 10% among all actors are picked as bottleneck actors for each application. Workload w_{max} is assigned for

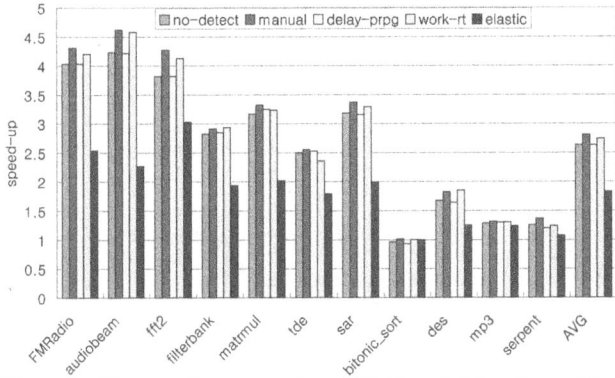

Figure 4: The speed-ups over the multi-threaded baseline with a single bottleneck on a 16-core machine.

each bottleneck whereas workload w is assigned to each of the remaining actors. Again, we set w_{max} to nine and w to one. In the third column, Table 3 shows the theoretical minimum required physical number of threads to see performance gain using task duplication when 10% of all actors are bottlenecks.

Figure 5 illustrates the performance comparisons on the 16-core machine. In many cases, no-detect works best. It is not unexpected. The maximum achievable throughputs of no-detect and of manual are the same as $\frac{C}{\sum_i w_i}$ from Eq. (3) as described before. In addition, generally speaking, as the number of bottlenecks increases it is more difficult to detect all the bottlenecks accurately during run-time. At the same time, the difference in the total numbers of activated threads for an application for the different approaches no-detect, manual, and work-rt gets smaller as the number of bottleneck increases. This implies the relative overhead in multi-threading management in no-detect drops as the number of bottleneck increases. With the above reasons no-detect tends to work better with multiple bottlenecks. Still, our algorithms work-rt and delay-prpg perform better than elastic. Notice that for the last four benchmarks, most of the duplicating approaches performs worse than baseline. Considering the minimum required numbers of cores for achieving gain over baseline in the third column of Table 3, this is as expected.

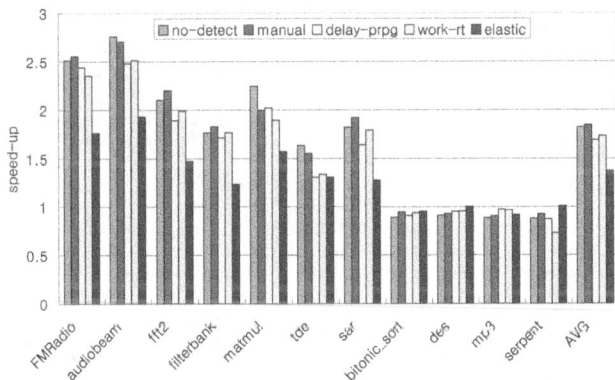

Figure 5: The speed-ups over the multi-threaded baseline with multiple bottlenecks on a 16-core machines.

Adaptation to the changing computing resources. In this experiment, we evaluate the capability of our algorithms to adapt to a dynamically changing run-time environment. For this purpose, we change the number of available CPU cores for an application during run-time by periodically updating the cpu affinity mask via a system call. More specifically, for the machine with 16 cores, the numbers of available

CPU cores are iterated among 16, 8, and 4 every one second. The workload of a bottleneck (9x) and the ratio of multiple bottlenecks (10%) for an application are the same as described before.

The same value 16 is used for configuration parameter C in all approaches in Table 2 even when the resources change among 4, 8, and 16 during run-time. This is reasonable since the number of cores available at one point during run-time (denoted by $C_{current}$) is not known when resources dynamically change but the total number of cores ($C = 16$) in the system is usually known. Notice that 16 is the best performing C configuration for no-detect even when $C_{current}$ is less than C. It draws the maximum achievable throughput, $\frac{C_{current}}{\sum_i w_i}$ from Eq. (3) because $\frac{C_{current}}{\sum_i w_i} \leq \frac{C}{\sum_i w_i}$ for all $C_{current}$. On the other hand, if the parameter is set to a value less than C for no-detect, the maximum throughput will not be achievable when $C_{current} = C$. With the similar reasoning, we also used the same C for manual.

The parameter step for work-rt is also set to C as before. The parameter step is the increasing granularity of the sibling threads in the algorithm. When the computing resources change we found using a value smaller than $C - 1$ for step is often more beneficial. However, we still use $C - 1$ to make a fair comparison to other approaches.

Figures 6 and 7 show the results when a single bottleneck and multiple bottlenecks exist(s) in an application, respectively. Both with a single bottleneck and multiple bottlenecks, work-rt works very well. It performs as well as manual which has the knowledge of the exact bottlenecks and outperforms no-detect in many cases. For a single bottleneck, work-rt performs better than no-detect by up to 39% and 23% on average. For multiple bottlenecks, work-rt performs better than no-detect by up to 20% and 10% on average. The reason why work-rt works better than no-detect even with multiple bottlenecks when the CPU resources dynamically change is twofold. Now the relative overhead in managing multi-threads for no-detect is higher than when there is no change in the availability of the computing resources. Even when 8 cores are available out of 16, no-detect still manages 16 threads per actor. In addition, this applies to every actor in an application. In contrast, work-rt manages a smaller number of threads that are close to current available cores and it also strives to apply sibling threads only to the bottlenecks, not to every actor in an application. Secondly, as the set of available CPUs changes the newly introduced cost of migrating threads is more expensive in no-detect with more threads to migrate than in work-rt. Again, for the last four benchmarks, duplicating approaches are hardly useful as expected from Table 3.

6. RELATED WORK

There has been much work on load balancing of stream applications based on the statically estimated workload. Replicating, clustering of actors and software-pipelining of dataflow graphs during compile time have been utilized to maximize the throughput in the context of stream processors [5, 10, 4]. Also the optimal throughput-latency trade-off in dataflow applications was investigated using static time task duplications [18, 19]. Our work is complementary to the work above in that the load balancing can be achieved further at run-time on top of the static result.

There has been some recent work on dynamic adaptation of dataflow applications. The adaptation to the resource availability in multicore streaming architecture like IBM CELL [9] was proposed [8]. They assume fixed workload and only regroup the workloads for a new resource budget at runtime. For a similar architecture the idea of embedding a helper actor that is acti-

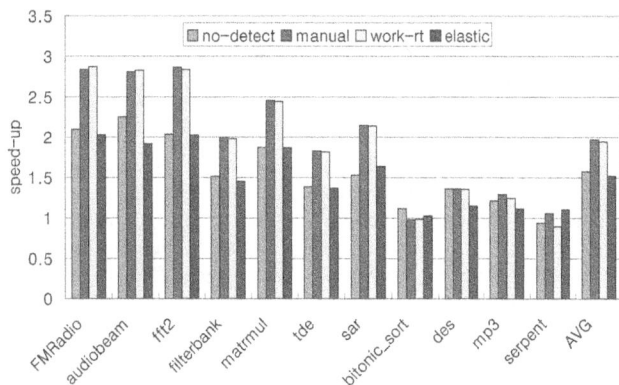

Figure 6: The speed-ups over the multi-threaded baseline with a single bottleneck when availability of CPU resources.

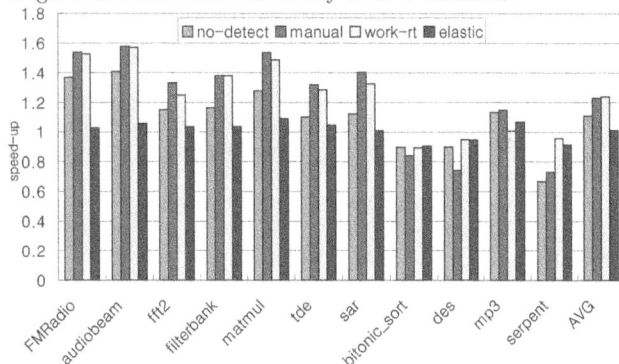

Figure 7: The speed-ups over the multi-threaded baseline with with multiple bottlenecks when availability of CPU resources.

vated by the back-pressure was proposed [1]. The number and assignment of helper actors to cores are predetermined at static time. A dynamic adaptation of data analytic actors to incoming workload and resource budget on SMP multi-core systems has been proposed [14]. It builds a performance history as the thread number changes, and attempts to use the number of threads that gives the best performance so far. Our work is distinguished by the explicit bottleneck detection algorithm.

The method of detecting CPU and I/O bottlenecks in DAG-based data flow applications in cluster or cloud computing environments is recently proposed [20]. The bottlenecks are identified by the traversal of the graph with the knowledge of the whole graph topology. In contrast, our bottleneck detection algorithms are locally performed by each actor at runtime.

Executing streaming applications on general-purpose multi-core SMP machines has been also proposed [7, 6]. The dynamic load balancing between the kernel operations and memory operations is handled by separated work queues with dependency information. The focus of these methods is not on the relieving of the computation bottlenecks.

7. CONCLUSION

We proposed a runtime load balancing mechanism for streaming applications targeting SMP multi-core systems. We showed that our proposed runtime computation bottleneck detection algorithms can achieve considerable speed-ups over already multi-threaded baseline streaming application on a 16-core machine. When the available computing resources dynamically change during run-time, our on-line bottleneck algorithms not only achieves speed-ups over the baseline but also noticeably outperforms other task duplication methods. Our run-time bottleneck detection algorithm may have other useful applications in other domains such as on-line task migrations, scheduling, and resource allocations.

Acknowledgement

This research was partially supported by an Enterprise Partnership Scheme grant co-funded by IBM, the Irish Research Council for Science, Engineering & Technology (IRCSET), and the Industrial Development Agency (IDA) Ireland.

8. REFERENCES

[1] R. L. Collins and L. P. Carloni. Flexible filters: load balancing through backpressure for stream programs. In *EMSOFT '09: Proceedings of the seventh ACM international conference on Embedded software*, pages 205–214, New York, NY, USA, 2009. ACM.

[2] F. Commoner, A. W. Holt, S. Even, and A. Pnueli. Marked directed graphs. *Journal of Computer and System Sciences*, 5(5):511 – 523, 1971.

[3] W. Dally et al. Merrimac: Supercomputing with streams. In *Proc. of the 2003 ACM/IEEE Conf. on Supercomputing*, pages 35–42, 2003.

[4] A. Das, W. J. Dally, and P. Mattson. Compiling for stream processing. In *Proc. of Intl. Conf. on Parallel architectures and compilation techniques*, pages 33–42. ACM, 2006.

[5] M. I. Gordon, W. Thies, and S. Amarasinghe. Exploiting coarse-grained task, data, and pipeline parallelism in stream programs. In *Proc. of Intl. Conf. on Architectural support for programming languages and operating systems*, pages 151–162, 2006.

[6] J. Gummaraju, J. Coburn, Y. Turner, and M. Rosenblum. Streamware: programming general-purpose multicore processors using streams. In *Proceedings of the 13th international conference on Architectural support for programming languages and operating systems*, pages 297–308. ACM, 2008.

[7] J. Gummaraju and M. Rosenblum. Stream programming on general-purpose processors. In *Proc. of the annual IEEE/ACM Intl. Symposium on Microarchitecture*, pages 343–354, 2005.

[8] A. Hormati, Y. Choi, M. Kudlur, R. Rabbah, T. Mudge, and S. Mahlke. Flextream: Adaptive compilation of streaming applications for heterogeneous architectures. In *Proceedings of the 2009 18th International Conference on Parallel Architectures and Compilation Techniques*, pages 214–223. ACM, sep 2009.

[9] IBM. *Cell Broadband Engine Architecture*, Mar. 2006.

[10] M. Kudlur and S. Mahlke. Orchestrating the execution of stream programs on multicore platforms. In *Proc. of the 2008 ACM Conf. on Programming Language Design and Implementation*, pages 114–124, jun 2008.

[11] E. A. Lee. *A Coupled Hardware and Software Architecture for Programmable Digital Signal Processors*. PhD thesis, EECS Department, University of California, Berkeley, 1986.

[12] C. V. Ramamoorthy and G. S. Ho. Performance evaluation of asynchronous concurrent systems using Petri nets. *IEEE Tran. on Software Engineering*, 6(5):440–449, Sept. 1980.

[13] B. R. Rau, M. S. Schlansker, and P. P. Tirumalai. Code generation schemas for modulo scheduled do-loops and while-loops. In *Hewlett-Packard Company Techinical Report*, pages 1–35, 1992.

[14] S. Schneider, H. Andrade, B. Gedik, A. Biem, and K.-L. Wu. Elastic scaling of data parallel operators in stream processing. In *IPDPS '09: Proceedings of the IEEE International Symposium on Parallel and Distributed Processing*, pages 1–12. IEEE, 2009.

[15] J. Sifakis. *Performance evaluation of systems using nets*, volume 84 of *Lecture Notes in Computer Science*, pages 307–319. Springer Berlin, 1980.

[16] S. Sriram and S. S. Bhattacharyya. *Embedded multiprocessors: Scheduling and synchronization*. CRC, 2009.

[17] S. Stuijk, M. Geilen, and T. Basten. Exploring trade-offs in buffer requirements and throughput constraints for synchronous dataflow graphs. In *Proc. of the Design Automation Conf. (DAC)*, pages 899–904, 2006.

[18] J. Subhlok and G. Vondran. Optimal latency-throughput tradeoffs for data parallel pipelines. In *the eighth annual ACM symposium on Parallel algorithms and architectures*. ACM, 1996.

[19] N. Vydyanathan, U. Catalyurek, T. Kurc, P. Sadayappan, and J. Saltz. Optimizing latency and throughput of applicationworkflows on clusters. *Technical Report OSU-CISRC-4/08-TR17, Ohio State University*, pages 1–25, 2007.

[20] D. Warneke, B. Lohrmann, D. Battre, A. Stanik, and M. Hovestadt. Detecting bottlenecks in parallel dag-based data flow programs. In *MTAGS10: 3rd IEEE Workshop on Many-Task Computing on Grids and Supercomputers*, pages 1–10. IEEE, 2010.

Concurrent Hybrid Switching for Massively Parallel Systems-on-Chip: The CYBER architecture

Francesca Palumbo, Danilo Pani, Andrea Congiu, Luigi Raffo
Dept. of Electrical and Electronics Engineering, University of Cagliari
Via Marengo 3, 09123 Cagliari, Italy
francesca.palumbo@diee.unica.it

ABSTRACT

Massively Parallel Systems-on-chip represent the new frontier of integrated computing systems for general purpose computing. The integration of a huge number of cores poses several issues such as the efficiency and flexibility of the interconnection network in order to serve in the best way the different traffic patterns that can arise.

In this paper we present the CYBER architecture, an advanced Network-on-Chip (NoC) for concurrent hybrid switching with prioritized best effort Quality of Service. Compared to similar architectures, CYBER allows the simultaneous exploitation of packet switching and circuit switching, providing two different priorities to packets in order to be able to transmit urgent messages (e.g. signalling) while long-lasting transactions and huge packets congestion are present. In terms of the typical NoC metrics, evaluated on synthetic traffic representative of several application categories, their standard trend is degraded while serving both circuit and packet switching simultaneously but the architecture preserves a predictable behaviour. A CMOS 90nm implementation reveals a maximum operating frequency of about 1GHz.

Categories and Subject Descriptors

C.1.2 [**Multiple Data Stream Architectures (Multiprocessors)**]: Interconnection architectures

Keywords

NoC, Hybrid Switching, Prioritized Best Effort, MPSoC, QoS

1. INTRODUCTION

The Massively Parallel Systems-on-chip (MPSoc) era is already begun. A large number of cores are efficiently adopted in streaming digital signal processing (up to 273 for the PicoArray PC 205 architecture by Picochip Ltd.), where parallelism is inherent in the applications and the communications can be scheduled at design time. Conversely, general purpose architectures still use a few cores (4 or 8) for multitasking and, in this case, either traditional or ad-hoc solutions at the interconnect level can be conceived for performance optimization (e.g. for the Cell multiprocessor). However, with the cores number growth, scalability problems arise and more general approaches based on advanced Network-on-chip (NoC) models are required to cope with the communication demands of the MPSoCs.

Oppositely to streaming processing, common MPSoC workloads lead to possibly concurrent heterogeneous traffic patterns demanding flexibility at the interconnect level [15]. Different parallel applications may coexist on the same computing platform and both inter/intra-application communications must be served. Wiring optimizations impose exploiting short local connections rather than long links, so that when a long-distance transaction of considerable size must be accomplished, the interconnect appears prone to stalls hampering the establishment of other communications. This could happen either when large data structures have to be moved from a processor to another one for the application purposes or when task migration policies are implemented. In order to mitigate such a communication interference side effect within a NoC, traffic segregation is usually exploited [2], allocating to different clusters of (possibly contiguous) nodes different applications [28]. However some communication-critical applications, where different levels of message priority and size can be identified (such as advanced modeling simulations, event-driven simulations, etc.), require also novel approaches at the architectural level to be able to provide a proper communication layer.

This paper introduces the Concurrent hYBrid Enhanced Router (CYBER), a flexible NoC architecture implementing several interesting features for future MPSoCs. CYBER main characteristic is concurrent hybrid switching, allowing the instantiation of both circuit switching (CS) and packet switching (PS) communications, simultaneously on separate channels. In this way, time consuming long-distance communications have no effect on the other traffic composed of packets with different priorities. From this point of view the architecture is autonomously able to decide whether to exploit PS or CS depending on the transaction size. The user can choose the priority of short messages: high priority ones can be sent with the same priority reserved to the circuit instantiation packets, which is higher than that of the normal packets. This feature is supported by two virtual channels (VC) exploiting a different control flow policy. For this reason we can say that CYBER is capable of managing three different virtual switching levels. Due to the concurrency in PS and CS, this NoC presents peculiar characteristics which are difficult to analyse in terms of standard evaluation metrics. Nevertheless we propose at first a preliminary functional analysis highlighting the features of robustness and predictability of the approach, relying on a cycle accurate SystemC simulation of an 8×8 nodes implementation. Then we present the typical NoC metrics exploiting an optimized RTL Verilog implementation of a 4×4 nodes system. In both cases, advanced traffic generators are used to feed the network with an exactly parametrized traffic, mimicking real applications communication workload. Syntheses on standard cell 90nm technology are also presented in order to evaluate some implementation metrics.

2. RELATED WORKS

At the state of the art, the Quality of Service (QoS) problem has been addressed at different levels in NoC architectures for MPSoCs. A first issue on the stack is network topology. Typical 2D meshes suffer increasing communication latencies when the diameter of the network grows. This led to the so called *express topology*, either *physical* or *virtual* [7]. In the same direction the kilo-NoC [13] implements an heterogeneous infrastructure employing QoS-enabled routers with conventional buffering just in some predefined parts of the network and light-weight elastic buffered nodes elsewhere. Topology-based solutions are mainly related to PS NoCs, thus potentially suffering intrinsic limitations in heterogeneous multi-threaded environments [15].

At the architectural level, VCs represent the conventional way to manage different QoS strategies. The QNoC[5] provides statistical QoS guarantees, 4 dedicated (signalling messages, real-time traffic, read/write traffic and block transfers) input VCs are used. Nevertheless some approaches have been proposed to maximize link utilization overcoming the limitations of VCs [3]. In [10], switch replication is used to improve the channel bandwidth utilization of the ×pipes NoC with respect to a VC-based approach.

At the switching policy level (with a necessary reflection on the architectural level), dual mode routers have been conceived to tackle heterogeneous traffic scenarios improving bandwidth utilization. Many different works have been proposed in the past such as NOSTRUM [17], MANGO [4], SoCBUS [24], HCS [15], the NoC presented in [20] and the Philips Research Labs NoC named Æthereal [11, 12]. In particular the proposed work presents several common points with the last two architectures:

- the router presented in [20] supports both PS and CS implementing them in a non-exclusive way, meaning that the router-to-router available bandwidth is used to serve in parallel packets and circuits;

- Æthereal implements not concurrent hybrid switching so that packets traversal is affected by the presence of established circuits along the path.

3. THE CYBER NOC

The CYBER architecture has been specifically conceived for MPSoCs requiring to support highly heterogeneous traffic workloads. The chosen name directly descends from its features. It is not only an hybrid switching NoC supporting both soft Guaranteed Throughput (GT) and Best-Effort

(BE) communications but it also implements them concurrently: all the links are designed to manage in parallel both PS and CS transactions, without any interference among them. Therefore, CYBER implements by construction two physical switching levels. Moreover, as its name says, those two physical switching levels have been enhanced. CYBER is capable of managing three different virtual switching levels due to the fact that, at the PS level, the proposed interconnect is capable of guaranteeing prioritized BE communications. This feature is implemented exploiting the *Wormhole* and the *credit-based Virtual Cut Through* flow control techniques serving two different priority packets.

As for the largest part of MPSoCs, [22, 27] a standard 2D mesh direct topology has been adopted in order to ensure high scalability while preserving a simple floor-planning. Each node of the NoC is composed of two main modules: the Network Interface (NI) and CYBER. The NI manages packets creation and injection, being responsible of protocol conversion and QoS negotiation. The interconnect of CYBER nodes is responsible of the communication flow from source to destination. Each router has 5 I/O channels, 4 connected to the neighbouring nodes and 1 dedicated to the NI. Each I/O port is composed of a bidirectional link carrying concurrently PS and CS communications.

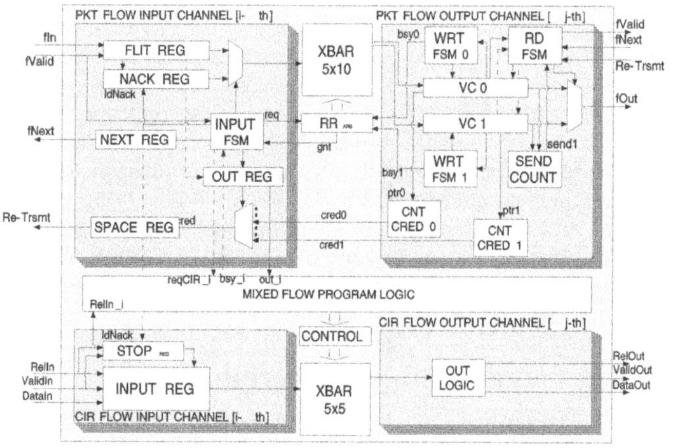

Figure 1: CYBER architecture block diagram.

Providing concurrent hybrid enhanced switching implies an increase in hardware complexity, compared to simpler single-switching routers [8], due to the fact that it is necessary to guarantee that higher priority communications do not prevent lower priority ones to complete. An overview of our implementation is depicted in Fig. 1. Two parallel sections sharing control signals and logic have been designed: the packets flow logic (*PFL*) and the circuits flow logic (*CFL*).

Packets travel along the NoC subdivided into 16-bit flits. Input channels in the *PFL* section are responsible of handling their traversal, decoding the control information stored in the first flit (header) and dispatching them to the proper output channel through the crossbar. An output buffering strategy based on two different VCs has been implemented to avoid the head-of-the-line blocking phenomenon. VCs are also exploited to handle the prioritized BE support (detailed in Sect. 3.3).

3.1 QoS Negotiation and Transactions Management

In the CYBER switching strategy, the computational layer is totally unaware of the switching techniques adopted at the NoC level. To initiate a communication, the NI receives control information from the processing core on top of it, converting the end-to-end protocol signals into different types of CYBER packets. According to both the transaction size and end-to-end priority, the NI creates a different header carrying the control directives. Such headers are locally decoded in the routers that will then handle a simple PS transaction or a CS management one. In this way, great flexibility and optimal performance can be guaranteed when a large variety of applications is running on the same system, relieving the computational layer from the selection of the proper communication type.

At design time it is possible to choose a threshold T for the transactions size. For a long streaming data transfer ($size \geq T$) the implemented NI instantiates a circuits set-up request (REQ), whereas for a shorter transaction ($size < T$) a simple PS communications is initiated. In this way long vectorial transactions, requiring a certain guaranteed bandwidth, or task migrations, will be served using connection-oriented GT in order to avoid congesting the interconnect, whereas small bursty transactions will traverse the NoC according to connection-less BE services. Also a control field ($CTRL$) is encoded in each CYBER header to identify:

- in case of CS: (a) CS set-up packets (REQ) => $CTRL = 00$; (b) positive CS acknowledgement packets (ACK) => $CTRL = 01$; (c) negative CS acknowledgement packets ($NACK$) => $CTRL = 10$;

- in case of PS (priority information are taken into account): (a) High, Level 0 (L0) packets => $CTRL = 00$; (b) Low, Level 1 (L1) packets => $CTRL = 11$.

In the proposed implementation, the PFL section in Fig. 1 is responsible of managing both simple BE transactions (generic PS packets) and GT communications establishment (REQ, ACK and $NACK$ packets). Therefore, soft GT is provided: CS transactions throughput and latency are predictable only since the circuit establishment phase is successfully accomplished. As soon as an ACK is received by the source node, the circuit switched data will effectively flow along the reserved path, in the CFL section, in parallel to the regular BE traffic and not interfering with it. The circuits tearing-down phase is also handled by the CFL section not interfering with PS transactions.

3.2 Hybrid Switching Overhead

In order to handle hybrid switching, a dedicated packet related logic, PFL section, and a circuit related one, CFL section, are required. Nevertheless these different hardware sections are not conceived to implement two disjointed couples of data/control paths. They are tightly coupled through a dedicated mixed flow program logic (MFL) to guarantee contemporary circuits establishment and packets flow.

Apparently, due to such hardware duplication, the increased architectural complexity seems to have a great impact on silicon area. Nevertheless, the adoption of two smaller crossbars, a 16-bit one in the PFL section and a 18-bit one ($\{DataIn[15:0], ValidIn, RelIn\}$) in the CFL section, is not more costly than having a single 34 bits crossbar since hardware complexity is of order $N^2 \times W$ (N is the number of ports in a square crossbar, W is the width of the datapath [6]). According to this formula, adding the contributions of the two crossbars leads to the same cost of a single crossbar providing the same bandwidth. Thus, considering of sharing the same amount of bandwidth to serve in parallel CS and PS communications, the circuit dedicated crossbar in the CFL section will affect the area occupation simply due to the logic necessary to drive it.

With area-saving purposes in mind, to cut down any extra area overhead, CS has not been implemented using the traditional time division multiplexing, which would have implied recording or slot tables [11, 1, 14], but exploiting a programmable shared 5-bit register placed in the MFL. This register can be read/written by all the input channels of the PFL, checking for the availability of a certain link in the CFL, and written by all the release signals travelling along the CFL section, tearing down already established circuits. Higher priority has been accorded to the tear-down signals to provide the possibility of re-assigning the same j-th circuit output channel in two subsequent clock cycles.

3.3 Prioritized BE Support

CYBER has been conceived to guarantee three different virtual switching levels. Two of them are actually also physical due to the concurrent hybrid switching support while the third one is implemented leveraging the VCs located in the output channels of the PFL section of each router. Switching virtualization at the packet level allows to satisfy end-to-end QoS requirements implementing prioritized BE support through the combination of *Wormhole* and *credit-based Virtual Cut Through* control flow strategies. The highest priority L0, the same assigned to CS management packets (REQ, ACK, $NACK$), can also be used for extremely urgent signalling transactions (e.g. in event-based systems). The lowest priority L1 is used for generic data packets. L0 packets flow along the interconnect according to the *Wormhole* strategy, thus "reserving" the encountered resources along their path while flowing. L1 packets instead cannot occupy more than one router at the same time and, prior to leave the current node, they need to check if the downstream one has enough room in its VCs to store them. This prioritized BE support allows having higher priority packets flowing quite undisturbed along the network. Therefore, their latency is minimal in absence of congestion since they cannot be stalled by lower priority packets uselessly occupying any link. On the contrary, a situation like the one presented in Fig. 2 could take place when the only *Wormhole* strategy is implemented. In this example, Tile_10 is waiting for an answer from Tile_02, which is delayed because of a saturation condition occurred in the lower priority VC ($VC1$). If L1 packets are handled using *Wormhole*, even if the $VC1$ in Tile_00 has room just for the header of a L1 packet, this last will be accepted, keeping busy the link between T_00 and T_01 until its tail is not written in $VC1$. Thus the ACK from Tile_02 is stacked waiting for the link to be released. This situation cannot take place in a CYBER based interconnect, because L1 packets obeys to the *credit-based Virtual Cut Through* strategy, meaning that if an L1 packet cannot be entirely stored in the destination $VC1$ of the downstream router, neither its header will be accepted. Therefore, this avoids that lower priority packets stall higher priority ones, keeping busy any link if not effectively used. Obviously other solutions could have been adopted to overcome this stalling

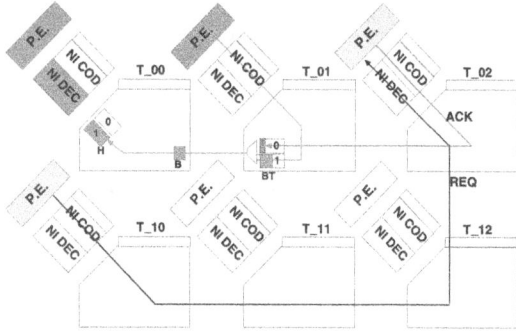

Figure 2: Example of wormhole switching lower priority packets stalling higher priority ones.

problem limitation, e.g. multiplexing in time over the same physical link the two adopted VCs (though such a strategy would have required higher area and power overhead [3], unacceptable in the proposed architecture due to the overhead already present caused by the hybrid switching).

In any router, the combination of the two flow control mechanisms is implemented in the read FSMs (RD FSM in Fig.1) placed in the output channels of the *PFL*, responsible of properly reading packets from one of the two VCs and of interacting with the downstream input channels to determine whether the communication can take place or not.

3.4 Semi-Adaptive Routing Scheme

Packets are routed according to the X-Y routing algorithm. In order to reduce as much as possible the overhead required to establish a CS communication, *REQ* packets exploit a simple form of adaptive routing to have a second chance to proceed to destination prior to send a *NACK* back to the source. If the requested VC in the X (or Y) direction has been already reserved, the complementary channel in the Y-X scheme (or X-Y) is used, provided that both it is available and the minimal path condition is still verified (to avoid livelocks). Deadlock avoidance is guaranteed since:

- the end-to-end consumption assumption paradigm is ensured and separated buffers per message type are provided [25];

- having implemented this mechanism just for the *REQ* packets leads to remove one of the four conditions, *mutual exclusion*, *hold and wait*, *no preemption* and *circular wait*, that bring to deadlocks [26]. In fact if both the directions have been already reserved, the current *REQ* receives a *NACK* that is sent back to the source and the *REQ* is cancelled from the upstream output channel implementing *preemption*.

Fig. 3 provides an example of this mechanism. A circuit is connecting T_01 to T_02 and, at the same time, T_00 attempts to establish a CS communication with T_12. This latter is prohibited, due to the fact that in T_01 the requested west channel is already reserved (Phase 1). Nevertheless, the input channel east of T_01 can still try to serve the *REQ* from T_00, checking for the availability of the south link and, since it is free, that *REQ* can continue its path toward destination, where it can be acknowledged (Phase 2).

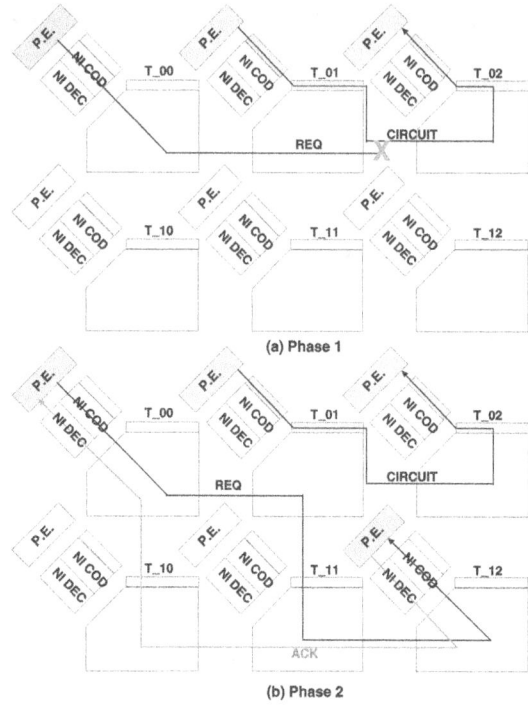

(a) Phase 1

(b) Phase 2

Figure 3: Semi-adaptive Minimal Path Routing Scheme.

4. HIGH-LEVEL FUNCTIONAL ASSESSMENT

The results that are going to be presented in this section are meant to demonstrate the potentialities of the proposed approach in terms of offered functionalities. To this aim, all the explorations that will be discussed are going to compare the CYBER switching approach to a more traditional non-concurrent hybrid one (such as the one in [11, 12, 1, 14, 9]) for the heterogeneous traffic support. This latter has been obtained from CYBER removing the possibility of handling the concurrency: the overall data bandwidth (which is 32 bits, {$fOut, DataOut$} in Fig. 1) is accorded entirely either to PS or to CS transactions. The adopted designs under test (DUTs) are composed of a homogeneous tile-based infrastructure such as the one presented in Fig. 4. An 8×8 2D mesh has been assembled using in each tile: (a) a synthetic traffic generator, which is responsible of initiating and receiving data transactions as a core would do; (b) a DMA; (c) the NI; (d) the router.

Compared to real traffic, that could be strongly application-dependent, testing with several synthetic traffic patterns could stress the interconnect allowing to evaluate the behaviour in response to diverse possible requirements. In [8] a mathematical formalization of synthetic traffic patterns descending from real applications is presented, e.g. Transpose for matrix transpose operations, Nearest Neighbour for fluid dynamics simulations, etc.

The emulated MPSoC environment, described in SystemC for both the DUTs, has been validated through several cycle accurate simulations. Simulations have been performed customizing for the DUTs the SysCgrid simulation environment presented in [21], in order to automatically generate different large sets of multi-parametric simulations, executed on supercomputing infrastructures. The adoption of such an

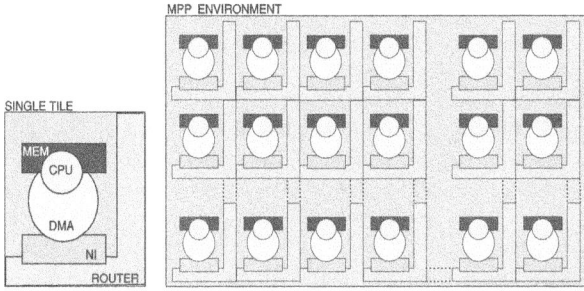

Figure 4: 2D mesh of tiles forming the reference MPSoC environment.

high level exploration methodology allowed us to deeply explore the behaviour of the proposed architecture before any low-level optimization.

During this first assessment phase all the simulations were intended to stress the DUTs to explore their responses to specific stimuli. Mainly dynamic features related to the traffic characterization [18], such as injection time and/or transfer sizes, have been varied since the focus of the exploration is the behaviour of the two different switching policies implemented on the DUTs.

The following metrics have been used in the comparisons:

- *Injection Packets Time Delay (IPTD)*: the time that lasts between the theoretical scheduled time for a packet to be injected in the NoC and its actual injection time during execution.

- *Intrinsic NoC Latency (INL)*: for each packet it is the difference between the injection and the arrival times (referred to routers traversal).

- *Transaction Completion Time (TCT)*: it is the time necessary to complete a transaction and takes into account the contributions of both the delay experienced by each packet prior to be delivered to the NoC (IPTD) and the one necessary to traverse the NoC (INL).

4.1 Comparison on Robustness

The first set of simulations, presented in Fig. 5, shows the impact of changing the volume and the transaction size of the injected circuits. The represented cost function considers the INL versus the IPTD. Fig. 5(a) has been obtained running the CIR_SWEEP[1] multi-parametric simulation type [21]. Even changing the circuits population from 1000 to 5000, the CYBER cost function scatter does not vary and all the points are crowded in a small area, meaning that this NoC model is quite insensitive to the variation of the circuits population volume. On the contrary, adopting the non-concurrent hybrid switching approach, the more circuits are injected the more INL and IPTD increase. Fig. 5(b) shows the same analysis varying the distribution of the size of the injected circuits. A CIR_LASTING_U[2] multi-parametric simulation has been run [21]. As in the previous case, CYBER is robust also to the variation of the transaction size for the circuit switched communications: its

[1] The number of the circuits in the traffic distribution is linearly increased within an arbitrary interval.
[2] The transaction size of the circuits in the traffic distribution is varied according to a Gaussian distribution.

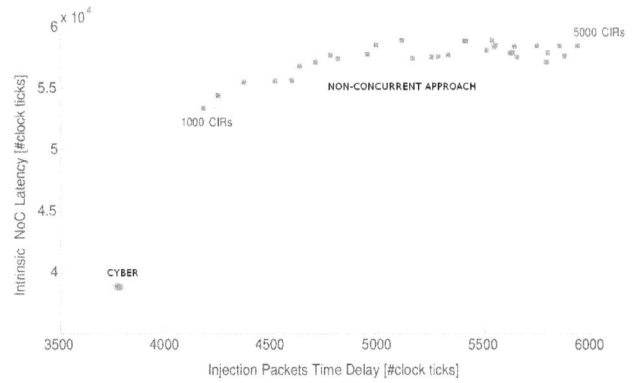

(a) CIR_SWEEP

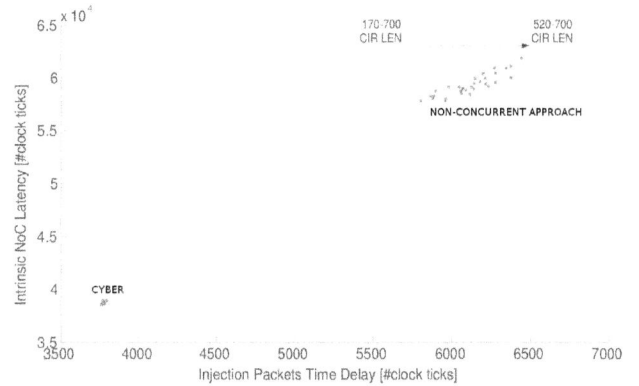

(b) CIR_LASTING_U

Figure 5: Scatter plot of the INL versus the IPTD. a) CIR_SWEEP: Robustness of the proposed approach to the CS transactions volume variation. b) CIR_LASTING_U: Robustness of the proposed approach to the CS transactions size variation.

scatter plot is again localized in a small area. That is not the case for the non-concurrent solution, still presenting the same trend as before.

4.2 Comparison on Predictability

Fig. 6(a) represents the scatter plot of the INL versus the IPTD obtained running a SWEEP multi-parametric simulation [21]. In this kind of simulation, circuits density is linearly increased from 1000 to 5000 dividing the simulation set in 8 subsets with constant circuits density, whereas packets density is linearly increased in each subset from 50000 to 200000. This simulation confirms CYBER robustness to circuits injection, already discussed in Sect. 4.1, since the 8 different curves of the 8 subsets simply overlap with each other. These 8 overlapping curves also demonstrate that it is possible to achieve a predictable behaviour with respect to packets injection since all the simulation points lay on very well shaped curves. On the opposite, dealing with the curves obtained adopting the non-concurrent hybrid switching approach, less regularity, less predictability and higher absolute values are obtained: the cost function is worsened as the number of injected circuits is increased. These aspects

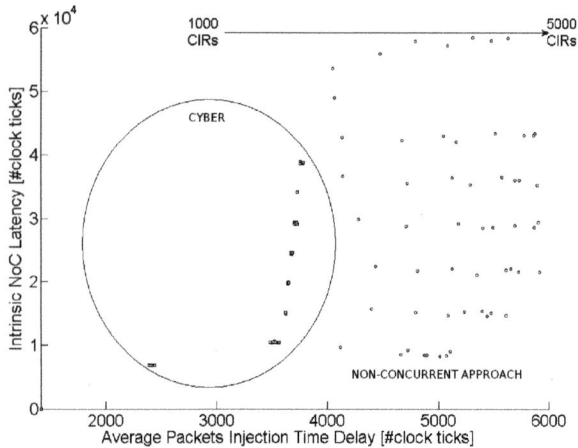

(a) SWEEP

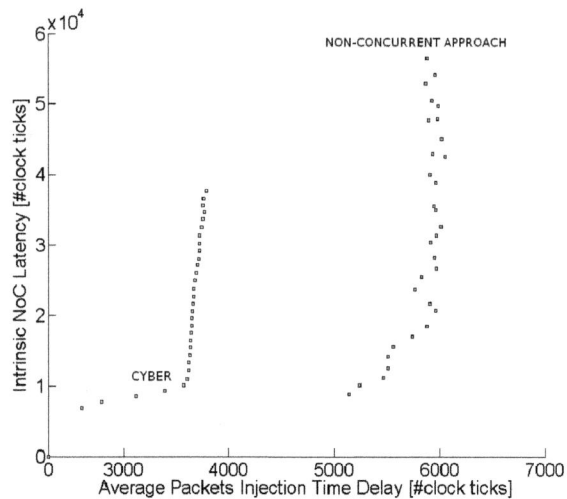

(b) PKT_SWEEP

Figure 6: Scatter plot of the INL versus the IPTD. a) SWEEP over 64 cores: Predictability of the proposed approach to the PKTs and CIRs volume variation. b) PKT_SWEEP over 32 cores: Predictability of the proposed approach to the PKTs volume variation.

are better clarified in Fig. 6b where a PKT_SWEEP[3] multi-parametric simulation is performed [21]. Here the packets density is increased linearly from 50000 to 200000 and the number of circuits is kept constant to 5000. A clear breakdown point, much more evident dealing with the proposed approach, can be highlighted. Below this point the INL is quite unaffected by the increase in packets injection. This is not the case for the IPTD: small packets volume increments create considerable variations, since it is measured not inside the NoC but at the source prior the injection. Above the breakdown point the situation reverses: INL variations dominate the scatter plot and the IPTD is somehow saturated. In this second example it is much more clear that

---

[3]The volume of the packet in the traffic distribution is linearly increased.

the proposed solution is able to lead to considerably more predictable results, despite traffic heterogeneity.

4.3 VCs Assessment

It has been shown that the proposed solution can guarantee not only better general behaviours but also better performance in terms of absolute values. Here we show also the response of the DUTs to the VCs depth variation, in heterogeneous traffic scenarios, in terms of TCT when a FIFO[4] multi-parametric simulation is run [21].

To assess the behaviour of the two approaches, different traffic distributions have been adopted modifying their spatial and temporal characteristics. The concept of spatial distribution deals with the mapping of different tasks on different nodes in an MPSoC, and it is of paramount importance. A static mapping of seven different clusters for both approaches has been adopted. The final allocation patterns depicted in Fig. 7 are the result of the allocation/deallocation of about 100 clusters using three different allocation algorithms in literature: a regular contiguous one [16] (RC), an irregular contiguous one [19] (IC) one and an irregular non-contiguous one [29] (RNC). Gaussian, Poisson and Uniform injection time distributions of the CS and PS transactions have been adopted. Figure 8 depicts the results obtained

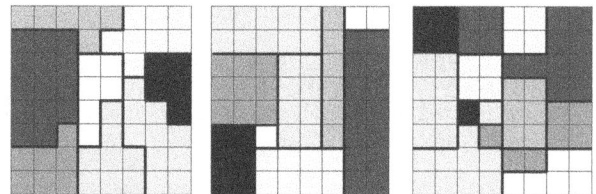

Figure 7: Clusters allocation schemes: from left to right, irregular contiguous, regular contiguous, irregular non contiguous.

where it is evident that CYBER is able to guarantee a better completion time than its non-concurrent counterpart, no matter the spatial or temporal traffic configuration. Moreover, in terms of robustness to the FIFOs depth variation, the CYBER boxplots remain quite identical as the FIFOs depth increases, which is not true for the non-concurrent approach. Therefore, it is confirmed that our concurrent hybrid switching better withstands traffic heterogeneity, allowing PS data to flow towards their destinations without experiencing long stalls along their path due to bandwidth reservation for CS communications.

5. LOW LEVEL EXPLORATION

The previous section was intended to prove the functional effectiveness of the approach followed in this work to implement hybrid switching. It has been shown that robustness, predictability and better absolute indexes are reachable with respect to a non-concurrent approach. Therefore, having demonstrated that very good results can be achieved from the functional point of view, it is necessary to explore the proposed architecture also at a lower level of abstraction. To this aim, the architecture has been implemented in RTL Verilog.

---

[4]The size of the FIFOs in the routers is varied.

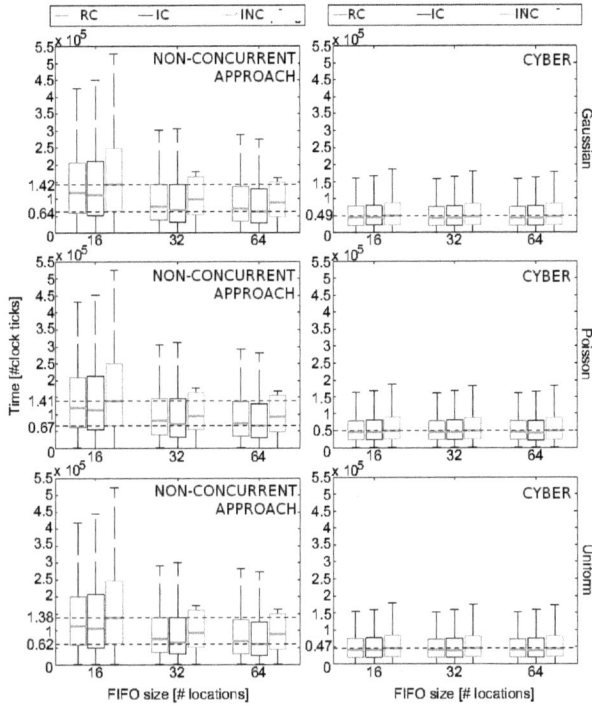

Figure 8: FIFO multi-parametric simulation: box-plots of the TCT.

The new DUT resembles the one shown in Fig. 4, but a smaller 4 × 4 2D mesh has been used and a different traffic generator created. The adopted traffic patterns are highly representative to define the low level functional indexes hereafter introduced and widely adopted to characterize PS NoCs [8].

- *Latency* - It is defined as the time required for a packet to traverse the NoC from source to destination. It is depicted as Latency vs. the Offered Traffic.

- *Throughput* - It is defined as the rate at which packets are delivered by the NoC for a particular traffic pattern. It is depicted as Throughput vs. the Offered Traffic.

Table 1 is representative of the simulation setup. The VCs depth of each router has been fixed to 16 slots since, as it has been demonstrated discussing Fig. 8, CYBER guarantees robustness with respect to the FIFO depth variation. It has to be noticed that the FIFO depth in the NIs, in order to isolate the traffic injection from the actual traffic flowing on the network [8], has been ideally fixed to an infinite value. Obviously such an infinite depth that, according to the traffic to be injected, has been reproduced using 4096 slots, has been used only during the low level simulation phase (Sect. 5.1); whereas for synthesis purposes the FIFO depth in the NIs has been set to 16 slots.

5.1 BE Traffic Evaluation and Hybrid Switching Degradation

Figure 9 is representative of purely BE simulation results, obtained for three different traffic injection patterns (Tornado, Bit Complement and Transpose), when the DUT is

Table 1: Low Level Simulation Setup.

Parameter	Value
Topology	2-D mesh 4 × 4
NI FIFO Depth	∞
Routers FIFO Depth	16
Traffic Type	Bit Compl., Random, Transp., Tornado, Near Neigh.
Total PKTs Injected	16000
Total CIRs Injected	[0;100;200;..;900;1000]
PKTs Inj. Rate[PIR]	[10-300]
Tot. Conf.	**1600**

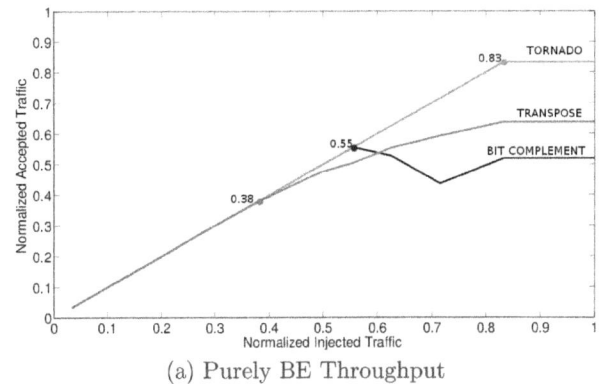

(a) Purely BE Throughput

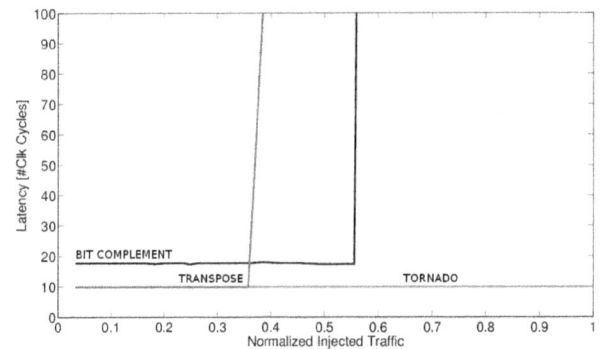

(b) Purely BE Latency

Figure 9: Purely BE simulation results for the Bit Complement, the Tornado and the Transpose traffic patterns. a) Throughput vs. Normalized Injected Traffic. b) Latency vs. Normalized Injected Traffic.

stimulated with PS transactions only. As it can be noticed Tornado does not stress the network, since on a 4 × 4 NoC it is equivalent to a Nearest Neighbour traffic. This absence of congestion allows guaranteeing a maximum Throughput of 1 packet every 12 cycles, which is nearly the 0.83% of the Normalized Injected Traffic, and the possibility of preserving a constant Latency of nearly 10 cycles to transfer 1 single packet (notice that each packet is composed of 4 flits) among two neighbouring nodes. The Bit Complement pattern by definition tends to concentrate several communications in the centre of the mesh, resulting in a more severe congestion of that region. In this trial the maximum achieved Throughput is 1 packet every 16 cycles (nearly the 0.55% of the Normalized Injected Traffic), whereas the Latency, before the saturation point, is on average 16 cycles. The Transpose

(a) BE Transpose Throughput, with GT superimposed

(b) BE Transpose Latency, with GT superimposed

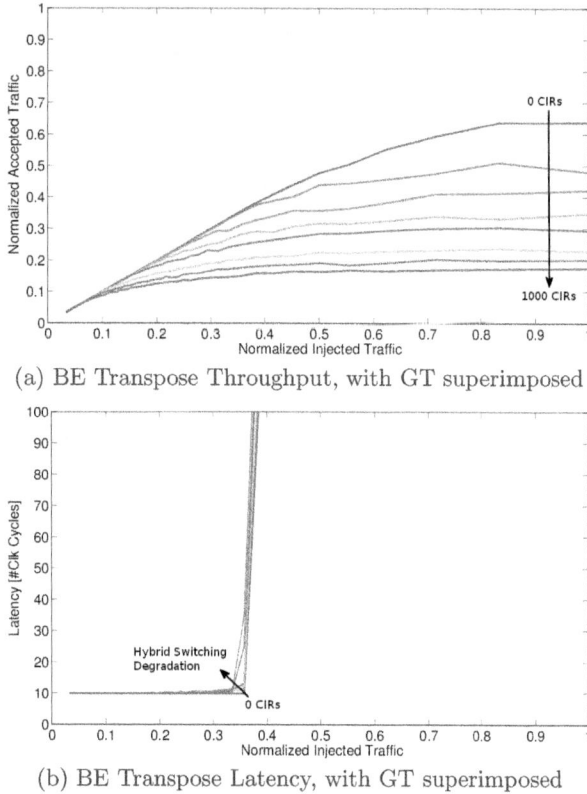

Figure 10: Degradation of the BE simulation results when CS transactions are superimposed to the BE ones. a)Throughput vs. Normalized Injected Traffic, Transpose traffic pattern. b) Latency vs. Normalized Injected Traffic, Transpose traffic pattern.

pattern, while presenting the worst maximum Throughput (1 packet every 26 cycles, nearly the 0.38% of the Normalized Injected Traffic), still enables NoC to guarantee a better Latency, before the saturation point, with respect to the Bit Complement pattern.

At the state of the art a formal definition of the expected metrics for hybrid switching NoCs does not exist. During our analysis we have observed that the ideal Throughput and Latency curves are generally degraded by the presence of the GT traffic, as the curves shown in Fig. 10. Circuits injection obviously changes the ideal set up environment defined in [8], therefore both Throughput and Latency cannot maintain the ideal shape. Nevertheless, the concurrent proposed approach is able to ensure that those curves are not completely altered. You should consider also that degradation is not caused just by the interconnect. In fact, in this use case, while a node is busy in receiving/sending a circuit it is not enabled to receive/send any packet. This characteristic limits the implemented traffic management. Therefore it is possible to assume that implementing a smart end-to-end strategy (e.g. a multi channel DMA) could lead to better match the ideal Throughput and Latency curves, taking a more effective advantage of the concurrent hybrid switching.

5.2 Synthesis Results

Preliminary synthesis results have been achieved using the Synopsys 2009 Design Compiler. A 4×4 NoC (node =

CYBER+NI) network has been synthesized using a 90 nm CMOS technology by TSMC. The chosen technology enabled the adoption of Multi-Vt technology libraries instead of standard single Vt ones, reducing the static power consumption of the interconnect. All the results presented here are representative of the overall 16-node architecture.

First of all, our synthesis trials have been focused on defining the maximum achievable operating frequency. Figure 11 depicts the variation of the area occupancy and the static power dissipation as the operating frequency is increased. This figure highlights that the synthesized architecture can reach a maximum frequency of 1 GHz. Other synthesis trials

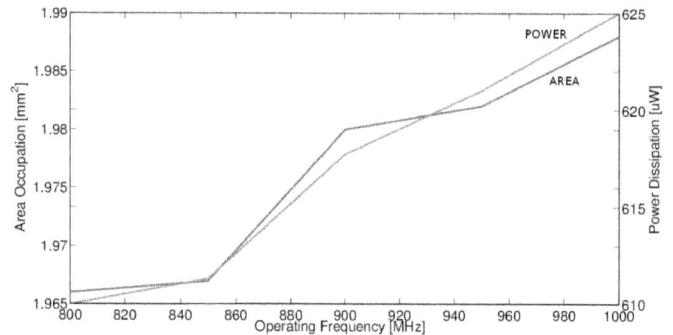

Figure 11: Area occupation (blue curve) and static power dissipation (red curve) for the 4×4 2D mesh [synthesis flow with Multi-Vt technology libraries].

have been performed focusing on the dynamic power optimization. This contribution to the power dissipation is determined according to the switching activity observed during simulations and mapped onto the synthesized design. All the results in Tab. 2 are referred to the maximum achievable operating frequency (1GHz). In this second synthesis trial we optimized the dynamic power consumption therefore, keeping the operating frequency at the maximum value, the area and the static power consumption are degraded with respect to the results presented in Fig. 11. Such a degradation for the 4×4 network is in the range 0.05-1% for the area $(1.99mm^2/(2.00-2.01)mm^2)$ and between 7.7-14.4% for the static power consumption $(625.00\mu W/(673.19-714.96)\mu W)$.

6. COMPARISON WITH RELATED HYBRID SWITCHING NOC

QNoC [5], despite implementing prioritized BE support at the PS level, does not provide any specific support for long streaming transactions. NOSTRUM [17] uses a PS NoC to support both BE and GT transactions. Similarly, the MANGO network [4] exploits a PS NoC to implement hybrid switching: eight VCs are used to handle GT and one to handle BE traffic. CYBER does not handle CS leveraging on VCs. SoCBUS [24] provides only soft GT, BE communications are used just for circuits management purposes. Therefore, since CS is the only type of switching allowed, the risk is that small packets will undergo an high overhead due to circuits establishment.

The HCS [15] approach exploits piggy-backing to overcome the circuit set-up time overhead; therefore, CS data do not wait for any acknowledge to traverse the network. The problem is that, in case of contention, CS communications can be tagged as PS ones, flowing in this way until

Table 2: Dynamic power optimization results for the 4×4 2D mesh. Synthesis trials performed at 1GHz.

CIRs	PIR [%]	Transpose, 16 nodes			Bit Complement, 16 nodes			Tornado, 16 nodes		
		Dyn. Pw. [mW]	St. Pw. [μW]	Area [mm^2]	Dyn. Pw. [mW]	St. Pw. [μW]	Area [mm^2]	Dyn. Pw. [mW]	St. Pw. [μW]	Area [mm^2]
0	0.38	130.57	714.96	2.00	135.86	678.02	2.00	134.34	683.52	2.00
	0.55	-	-	-	134.80	693.06	2.01	135.77	673.19	2.00
	0.83	-	-	-	-	-	-	135.82	673.89	2.00
600	0.38	135.14	696.66	2.00	132.24	709.70	2.01	134.76	685.42	2.00
	0.55	-	-	-	134.97	686.37	2.00	134.91	685.17	2.00
	0.83	-	-	-	-	-	-	133.01	707.51	2.01

their destinations. CYBER implements soft GT, suffering circuit set-up time overhead but, when started, CS communications have their throughput guaranteed, since they will never be interrupted nor downgraded to PS transactions.

The approach presented in [20] is close to the proposed one since, in both cases, hybrid switching is realized leveraging on a parallel usage of the available bandwidth. The main limit of that solution is that CS is always privileged with respect to PS: in fact, any packet that is not a circuit management one traverses the interconnect at the lower possible priority. Leveraging the three virtual switching levels, CYBER is capable of offering prioritized BE support exploiting a combination of *Wormhole* and *credit-based Virtual Cut Through* control flow strategies.

Æthereal is able to provide both GT and BE services, tackling GT traffic with CS. In earlier Æthereal router releases [11], circuits did not have any header, as the next hop was determined by local slot tables. In more recent implementations [12], slot tables have been removed to save area and a header has been introduced to carry path information. BE traffic makes use of non-reserved or unused slots and is mainly exploited to program the GT slots of the routers. Similar architectures have been proposed in [14] and [1]. In all these approaches a mutual exclusive usage of the bandwidth is adopted and GT data are served with an higher priority: PS data are penalized by already established circuits and the overall completion time is delayed. These drawbacks are completely avoided adopting the CYBER approach.

7. CONCLUSIONS

MPSoCs probably represent the next frontier for mainstream computers and, at the time being, they are carefully considered as potential embedded platforms targeting several advanced simulation problems. Such platforms are intrinsically communication-centric and the interconnect cannot be relegated to the role of a simple component of the system. In this evolving scenario, it is necessary to define advanced communication infrastructures able to serve in the best way all the possible traffic patterns that could arise at run time.

In this paper we presented and evaluated a novel advanced NoC able to provide up to three virtual switching levels over two coupled physical links normally able to concurrently serve both circuit and packet switching. In this way, long-lasting CS communications required for instance to transmit long data streams or for task migration, are not obstructive for the other shorter communications, which can be used in turn also for solving data dependencies or for signalling purposes. Concurrency allows to achieve more robust and predictable performance despite traffic heterogeneity compared

to other not concurrent solutions. A priority mechanism introduced at packet switching level, exploiting two virtual channels and different control flow strategies, enables a fast dispatching of important messages (useful, for instance, in event-driven systems) while preserving the possibility to dispatch normal messages too.

The results clearly show the potentialities of the approach. The NoC is able to run at 1GHz (90nm CMOS technology) and the typical quality indexes reveal good performance. Goossens et al. for the Æthereal case in [12] argued that, in their implementation, *"the inclusion of BE traffic was a mistake"* since BE traffic has a lower priority than GT one and then it is not possible to offer a low latency to BE communications, despite the extra cost ratio. Using a 65 nm CMOS technology, having GT and BE implemented on the same architecture, an 8×8 Æthereal router with 4-flit BE buffers reaches a cost ratio of $0.6GHz/0.07mm^2$ versus that of a GT-only router of $1.9GHz/0.022mm^2$. A 5×5 CYBER node with 16-flit VCs, adopting a 90 nm CMOS technology, provides a cost ratio per node of $1GHz/0.12mm^2$. Therefore CYBER synthesis results, combined with the functionality potentials demonstrated in Sect. 4, brought us to the conclusion that in our case the overhead can be considered more affordable. For these reasons, CYBER is going to be integrated into a research MPSoC for advanced testing with real benchmarks, in particular for advanced simulations in neuroengineering. In fact, in large spiking neural network simulations, different traffic patterns coexist in the MPSoC: the typical event-driven simulation approach could require the dispatch of signalling packets (related to neuronal firing events) with high priority, whereas the import of the synaptic weights (large tables of data) in a processing node requires long data transfer from non-local memories [23]. In such a scenario, the key functional/architectural features of CYBER could help in providing an efficient communication substrate.

8. ACKNOWLEDGMENTS

The research leading to these results has received funding from the European Community's Seventh Framework Programme (FP7/2007-2013) under grant agreement no. 248424, MADNESS Project, and by the Region of Sardinia, Young Researchers Grant, PO Sardegna FSE 2007-2013, L.R.7/2007 "Promotion of the scientific research and technological innovation in Sardinia".

9. REFERENCES

[1] B. Ahamad, A. Erdogan, and S. Khawarm. Architecture of a dynamically reconfigurable NoC for adaptive reconfigurable MPSoC. In *Proc. of the first*

NASA/ESA Conf. on Adaptive Hardware and Systems (AHS'06), 2006.

[2] F. Angiolini and S. Murali. *Communication Architectures for Systems-on-Chip*, chapter 4 - Quality-of-Service in NoCs, pages 127Ū–157. CRC Press, 2011.

[3] N. Banerjee, P. Vellanki, and K. S. Chatha. A power and performance model for network-on-chip architectures. In *DATE '04: Proceedings of the conference on Design, automation and test in Europe*, 2004.

[4] T. Bjerregaard and J. Sparsø. A router architecture for connection-oriented service guarantees in the MANGO clockless network-on-chip. In *Proceedings of Design, Automation and Testing in Europe Conference 2005 (DATE05)*. IEEE, 2005.

[5] E. Bolotin, I. Cidon, R. Ginosar, and A. Kolodny. QNoC: QoS architecture and design process for network on chip. *Journal of Systems Architecture, special issue on Network on Chip*, 50:105–128, 2004.

[6] T. Caohuu, T. T. Le, M. Glesner, and J. Becker. Dynamically reconfigurable reduced crossbar: A novel approach to large scale switching. In *FPL '99: Proceedings of the 9th International Workshop on Field-Programmable Logic and Applications*, pages 507–513, London, UK, 1999. Springer-Verlag.

[7] C.-H. O. Chen, N. Agarwal, T. Krishna, K.-H. Koo, L.-S. Peh, and K. C. Saraswat. Physical vs. virtual express topologies with low-swing links for future many-core nocs. *Networks-on-Chip, International Symposium on*, pages 173–180, 2010.

[8] W. Dally and B. Towles. *Principles and Practices of Interconnection Networks*. Morgan Kaufmann Publishers Inc., San Francisco, CA, USA, 2003.

[9] J. Diemer and R. Ernst. Back suction: Service guarantees for latency-sensitive on-chip networks. *Networks-on-Chip, International Symposium on*, pages 155–162, 2010.

[10] F. Gilabert, M. E. Gomez, S. Medardoni, and D. Bertozzi. Improved utilization of noc channel bandwidth by switch replication for cost-effective multi-processor systems-on-chip. *Networks-on-Chip, International Symposium on*, pages 165–172, 2010.

[11] K. Goossens, J. Dielissen, and A. Radulescu. The Æthereal network on chip: Concepts, architectures, and implementations. *IEEE Design and Test of Computers*, 22(5):21–31, 2005.

[12] K. Goossens and A. Hansson. The Æthereal network on chip after ten years: Goals, evolution, lessons, and future. In *Proc. Design Automation Conference (DAC)*, June 2010.

[13] B. Grot, J. Hestness, S. W. Keckler, and O. Mutlu. Kilo-noc: a heterogeneous network-on-chip architecture for scalability and service guarantees. In *Proceedings of the 38th annual international symposium on Computer architecture*, ISCA '11, pages 401–412, New York, NY, USA, 2011. ACM.

[14] S. Hsu, Y. Lin, and J. Jou. Design of a dual-mode noc router integrated with network interface for amba-based ips. In *Proc. IEEE Asian Solid-State Circuits Conf.*, pages 211–214, 2006.

[15] N. D. E. Jerger, L.-S. Peh, and M. H. Lipasti.

Circuit-switched coherence. In *NOCS '08: Proc. of the Second International Symposium on Networks-on-Chip*, pages 193–202, 2008.

[16] M. Livingston and Q. Stout. Parallel allocation algorithms for hypercubes and meshes. In *Proc. 4th Conf. Hypercube Concurrent Comput. Applications*, pages 59–66, 1989.

[17] M. Millberg, E. Nilsson, R. Thid, S. Kumar, and A. Jantsch. The nostrum backbone-a communication protocol stack for networks on chip. In *VLSI Design, 2004. Proceedings. 17th International Conference on*, pages 693 – 696, 2004.

[18] U. Y. Ogras, J. Hu, and R. Marculescu. Key research problems in noc design: A holistic perspective. In *International Conference on Hardware - Software Codesign and System Synthesis*, September 2005.

[19] F. Palumbo, D. Pani, L. Raffo, and S. Secchi. A surface tension and coalescence model for dynamic distributed resources allocation in massively parallel processors on-chip. In *NICSO '07: Proc of the International Workshop on Nature Inspired Cooperative Strategies for Optimization*, pages 335–345. 2007.

[20] F. Palumbo, S. Secchi, D. Pani, and L. Raffo. A novel non-exclusive dual-mode architecture for mpsocs-oriented network on chip designs. In *SAMOS08: Proc. of the 8th international workshop on Embedded Computer Systems*, pages 96–105, Berlin, Heidelberg, 2008. Springer-Verlag.

[21] D. Pani, F. Palumbo, and L. Raffo. A fast mpi-based parallel framework for cycle-accurate HDL multi-parametric simulations. *Int. J. High Perform. Syst. Archit.*, 2:187–202, August 2010.

[22] picoArray. picoChip company. http://www.picochip.com/, web.

[23] A. D. Rast, X. Jin, F. Galluppi, L. A. Plana, C. Patterson, and S. Furber. Scalable event-driven native parallel processing: the SpiNNaker neuromimetic system. In *Proceedings of the 7th ACM international conference on Computing frontiers*, pages 21–30, 2010.

[24] S. Sathe, D. Wiklund, and D. Liu. Design of a switching node (router) for on-chip networks. *Proceedings of the 5th International Conference on ASIC*, pages 75–78, 2003.

[25] Y. H. Song and T. M. Pinkston. A progressive approach to handling message-dependent deadlock in parallel computer systems. *IEEE Transactions on Parallel and Distributed Systems*, 14(3):259–275, 2003.

[26] W. Stallings. *Operating Systems (5th Edition)*. 2004.

[27] Tilera. The tile64 chip. http://www.tilera.com/, web.

[28] F. Triviño, J. L. Sánchez, F. J. Alfaro, and J. Flich. Virtualizing network-on-chip resources in chip-multiprocessors. *Microprocessors and Microsystems*, In Press, 2010.

[29] F. Wu, C.-C. Hsu, and L.-P. Chou. Processor allocation in the mesh multiprocessors using the leapfrog method. *IEEE Trans. Parallel Distrib. Syst.*, 14(3):276–289, 2003.

A Hierachical Configuration System for a Massively Parallel Neural Hardware Platform

Francesco Galluppi[*]
APT group
School of Computer Science
The University of Manchester
Manchester, U.K.

Sergio Davies
APT group
School of Computer Science
The University of Manchester
Manchester, U.K.

Alexander D. Rast
APT group
School of Computer Science
The University of Manchester
Manchester, U.K.

Thomas Sharp
APT group
School of Computer Science
The University of Manchester
Manchester, U.K.

Luis A. Plana
APT group
School of Computer Science
The University of Manchester
Manchester, U.K.

Steve B. Furber
APT group
School of Computer Science
The University of Manchester
Manchester, U.K.

ABSTRACT

Simulation of large networks of neurons is a powerful and increasingly prominent methodology for investigate brain functions and structures. Dedicated parallel hardware is a natural candidate for simulating the dynamic activity of many non-linear units communicating asynchronously. It is only scientifically useful, however, if the simulation tools can be configured and run easily and quickly. We present a method to map network models to computational nodes on the SpiNNaker system, a programmable parallel neurally-inspired hardware architecture, by exploiting the hierarchies built in the model. This PArtitioning and Configuration MANager (PACMAN) system supports arbitrary network topologies and arbitrary membrane potential and synapse dynamics, and (most importantly) decouples the model from the device, allowing a variety of languages (PyNN, Nengo, etc.) to drive the simulation hardware. Model representation operates on a *Population/Projection* level rather than a single-neuron and connection level, exploiting hierarchical properties to lower the complexity of allocating resources and mapping the model onto the system. PACMAN can be thus be used to generate structures coming from different models and front-ends, either with a host-based process, or by parallelising it on the SpiNNaker machine itself to speed up the generation process greatly. We describe the approach with a first implementation of the framework used to configure the current generation of SpiNNaker machines and present results from a set of key benchmarks. The system allows researchers to exploit dedicated simulation hardware which may otherwise be difficult to program. In effect, PACMAN provides automated hardware acceleration for some commonly used network simulators while also pointing towards the advantages of hierarchical configuration for large, domain-specific hardware systems.

Categories and Subject Descriptors

C.1.3 [**Processor Architectures**]: Other Architecture Styles— *Neural networks*; D.2.11 [**General**]: Software Architectures— *Domain-specific architectures*

Keywords

Spiking Neural Networks, Neuromorphic Hardware, Parallel Hardware, SpiNNaker

1. INTRODUCTION

Large-scale models of spiking neural networks are an essential tool to test hypotheses regarding the mechanisms of information processing in the brain [33] [12] or to exploit the computational capabilities of networks of neurons [15] [31]. An improved knowledge in this are would lead to more accurate understanding of brain-related diseases and of the functions that robotics and machine learning are trying to mimic with cognitive computing [2]. The brain is composed of numerous non-linear units (neurons) communicating asynchronously and organised in a hierarchical fashion [28]. This makes simulation on standard parallel hardware challenging due to synchronization and communication overheads [39]; dedicated hardware emerges then as a natural candidate simulation substrate. While a variety of modelling tools make neural modelling easier from a user point of view, they introduce technological challenges [5]. Study of efficient modelling technologies is therefore a key requirement for computational neuroscientists [35]. Various hardware architectures try to exploit parallelism to circumvent software limitations [34] [2]. However, to be a generic platform for neural exploration, both atomic elements (neurons and synapses) and connection topologies must be easily configurable and extensible so some approaches focus on a software abstraction layer which can easily reconfigure the hardware and make it accessible to non-hardware experts [36] [14] [6] [19].

In this context we present an approach to decouple the

[*]francesco.galluppi@cs.man.ac.uk

model specification stage and the generation of data structures representing the model on a parallel system. This approach can be used to configure different types of computational nodes (neurons) connected in an arbitrary way and map them to a dedicated architecture. By organising neurons into homogeneous populations, the system maintains hierarchical information about the model, using it to drive the allocation on the system in a simpler way than by considering single neurons. We begin by reviewing most popular neural simulation strategies in software and hardware in section 2, in order to introduce the SpiNNaker system, a massively parallel digital architecture oriented to the simulation of large networks of spiking neurons in section 3. To demonstrate the proposed approach we present an implementation of the abstraction layer which translates a model from different front-ends and allocates it on the SpiNNaker machine in section 4. Results obtained using this configuration approach are in 5. Finally, we discuss the challenges and potential in such an approach and overall implications in the last two sections.

2. NEURAL NETWORK SIMULATORS

Simulation of neural network models can be done either on dedicated hardware or with general purpose hardware running software simulators. While the first offers more efficiency and higher speeds, the latter offers more flexibility in the neural model and the interconnectivity.

2.1 Hardware

The large number of nodes (neurons) and interconnections (synapses) required to simulate neural networks has led to different hardware solutions. Each tries to exploit the intrinsic parallelism of neural networks directly in hardware. Efficiently mapping a neural network onto a hardware substrate is a nontrivial task, due to the massive parallelism and communication bandwidth required by the high connectivity. Different approaches have been proposed to circumvent this problem:

Supercomputers, notably the IBM Blue Gene, have been used in brain modelling at different levels of abstraction, from the ion-channel level [33] to point neurons [2]. Such a use of supercomputers is generally tightly optimised to the model simulated, and accessibility to such computational resources is not widespread. Finally, the power requirements make scaling of the model challenging.

Graphical Processing Units (GPUs) are more mass-market devices, and with their inherent parallelism they offer a reasonable alternative for medium-scale neural modelling. GPUs can also easily be configured to run arbitrary models by interfacing them with PyNN [14] or PyNN-like interfaces [36], making them accessible to non hardware experts. As the limiting factor is the access to memory [36], however, GPUs are primarily suited for high computation-to-communication-ratio models [3]; in fact the maximum available bandwidth can be accessed only using highly idealised memory access patterns [14]. The other major limiting factor is power, which affects scalability, a typical GPU consuming ~250W/chip.

Neuromorphic Hardware: ASICs (Application Specific Integrated Circuits) can be used to effect a specific neural model in circuitry [27]. While such an approach is very power- and compute- efficient [41] [26], it comes at the price of reconfigurability, since the neural model or the connectivity [9] is hard-wired. Some systems [34] [6] use an FPGA-like lookup to overcome connectivity limitations, combining analogue neural simulation with digital packet-based spike communication to support more general connectivity patterns, albeit at lower density. Another way to enhance reconfigurability of such hardware is to use an FPGA for storing connectivity information in multi-chip analogue SNN system [49]. Nonetheless flexibility remains the principal challenge.

Field-Programmable Gate Arrays (FPGA) are used standalone as exploratory tools since their reconfigurability softens the low flexibility of neural models cast into silicon [8]. However mapping very high connection densities in FPGAs is challenging due to the circuit-switched architecture, and cost, power consumption and performance scales poorly [32].

2.2 Software

Simulation on dedicated hardware offers an efficient way of modelling, but data exchange between hardware models is difficult since lack of standards means that the data organisation is typically proprietary. Simulation in software makes flexible and exploratory modelling accessible to a wide community. According to a survey conduced by NeuroDebian [24] the most popular tools for neural modelling are[1]:

NEURON [7], a modelling and simulation tool oriented to the simulation of finely detailed neurons which can be connected in complex networks. It is a very popular instrument for neuroscientists as it helps model the physical properties of the neurons, but also for network modelling by expansion through python bindings. As of today more than 1000 publications have used NEURON[2].

Brian [22], a neural network simulator entirely written in Python, oriented to the simulation of large networks of point neurons. In addition to standard neuron models, powerfully, using Brian the user can input the equations to be solved by the simulator directly in a standard notation. The choice of Python as a native language, which has "turnkey" packages for numeric and vector-based computation as Scipy and Numpy, rather than using C/C++ like GENESIS and NEST, lets the user run the simulations, plot and analyse data all in the same environment.

PyNN [11], a Python-based standard description language able to run a model on a chosen supported back-end simulator (most of the ones mentioned here). The declared objective of the language is to *"write the code for a model once, run it on any supported simulator without modification"* [11]. It is composed of a standardised set of neuron, synaptic, plasticity and connector models.

Nengo [44], the tool used to implement the Neural Engineering Framework principles [12]. In this respect it is a tool which is specific to a modelling framework rather then a general purpose system, requiring specific implementation strategies. It affords the user the possibility to map a wide range of neuro-computational dynamics to spiking neural networks.

---

[1]http://neuro.debian.net/survey/2011/results.html
[2]http://www.neuron.yale.edu/neuron/static/bib/usednrn.html

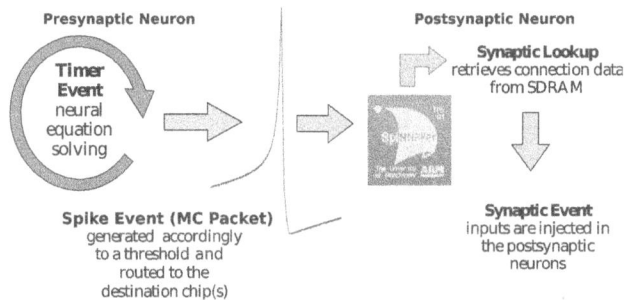

Figure 1: Neural Simulation Events

GENESIS (the GEneral NEural SImulation System) [4], a tool for realistic simulation based on physical structures and biological properties. Using an object oriented scripting language, users configure abstract objects and can interact with the simulation through a GUI, while the computation is carried out in the underlying Script Language Interpreter (SLI) written in C.

NEST (NEural Simulation Tool) [20] can be used to simulate large networks composed of standard neuron models efficiently. It is able to model Leaky Integrate-and-Fire and Hudgkin-Huxley neurons, along with various synaptic models and plasticity methods. Initially based on a proprietary core language, it now supports interaction with Python through PyNest [13]. NEST supports parallelisation through multithreading and message passing [39].

3. SPINNAKER SYSTEM

3.1 Architecture

The SpiNNaker System is a programmable asynchronous massively parallel multi-core system oriented to the simulation of heterogeneous large-scale models of spiking neural networks [17]. Each SpiNNaker chip contains 18 ARM968 cores embedded in a programmable, packet based, network on chip [38]. Spikes are encoded as source-based AER [30] event packets and transmitted through a Multicast (MC) Router capable of handling one packet per clock cycle. Every core has a local Tightly-Coupled Memory (TCM - 32Kb for instruction and 64Kb for data), while each core has access through a dedicated DMA controller to a 1Gb SDRAM shared by the 18 ARM cores within a single chip, with an aggregate memory bandwidth of 5.6 Gb/s. SDRAM is partitioned into regions containing core-specific synaptic information, eliminating the issue of memory sharing across the system. The memory system is thus local to every chip, circumventing the challenges needed on, e.g. GPUs to access memory [3] and maintain process coherency [36], while keeping power consumption lower than on such systems. Each chip can be connected to 6 adjacent neighbours in a toroidal mesh using bi-directional asynchronous links for an aggregate spiking bandwidth of 1.5 Gb/s [37], supporting reconfigurable arbitrary connectivity [16]. Arguably a MC mesh NoC is the most suitable interconnect architecture for reconfigurable neural network implementations [46]. The custom packet-switching network [38] is easily reconfigurable by changing the MC routing tables and more wire-efficient than a circuit-switched architecture [32] [8].

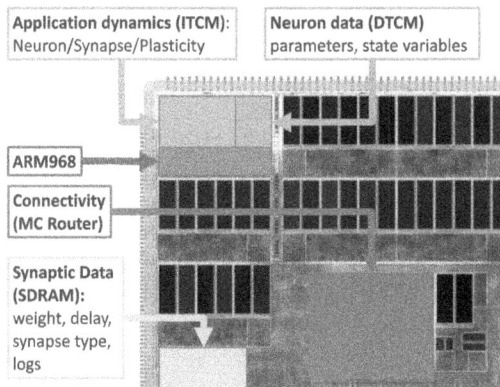

Figure 2: Functional blocks on a section of a SpiN-Naker Chip

The SpiNNaker System offers an alternative set of trade-offs to neuromorphic chips [26] and programmable, standard computing systems [2]. While being outperformed in absolute power consumption [27] or speed [41] by dedicated analog hardware, and in representational flexibility by general-purpose computers, SpiNNaker offers a scalable and completely reconfigurable platform for exploration of a wide range of network models, within a low power budget of 1 W/Chip [15]. The full system is designed to contain up to 65,536 chips and more than a million cores [15].

3.2 Hardware Reconfigurability

From a computational and communication point of view each ARM core offers flexibility in the complexity and number of neurons and the way they are embedded in a configurable network based on the Multicast Router. The number of neurons which can be modelled on a single core depends on factors including the activity of the neurons, the computational power needed to solve the neurodynamic equations in real time, the number of synapses and the memory occupancy. The software that allocates neurons on board must facilitate exploring such trade-offs so as to be able to experiment with different configurations. As introduced in the previous section, the SpiNNaker system is an architecture with multiple dimensions of configurability, in particular:

Application reconfigurability: single cores in the system can be configured to run different applications, for instance different neural, synaptic or plasticity kernels, or non-neural applications like data collection and on-board analysis. Each application needs to be configured with its parameters (eg. governing the neural equations). Seamless integration of new applications into the existing framework is critical, so to have them as available resources in system deployment.

Connection reconfigurability: the MC router system permits arbitrary network topologies to be mapped through a 2-stage routing and lookup system which is able to route a spike efficiently to many different destination neurons placed anywhere in the system. Spikes are encoded as source-based AER events: The MC routers manage the first stage through the leading field of the routing key (processor coordinates in the system), while the lookup phase deals with the second field of the routing key (neuron id within a processor). The

	nodes	connections
Model Level	Populations	Projections
System Level	partPopulations	partProjections
Device Level	Neurons	Synapses

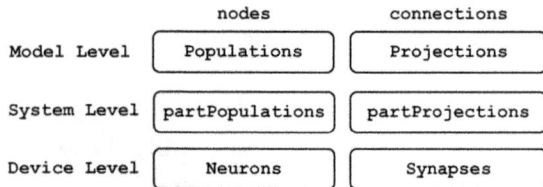

Figure 3: Hierarchical Approach

field definitions themselves are not fixed but programmable through mask bits in the router.

3.3 Neural Applications

While the SpiNNaker system is a general purpose scalable parallel machine, its architecture is designed for simulation of large networks of spiking neurons, as they can be modelled efficiently by representing spikes as stereotypical events encoded in an MC packet. Neural applications (or kernels) are based on a set of APIs [43] written in C which expose the event-driven nature of the system. From a user perspective we distinguish 2 events (fig. 1):

Timer Event (Neural Event): each core contains a programmable timer generating interrupts at configurable time steps (eg. every msec). At each time step, for each neuron, the equations are solved and spikes generated as required.

DMA Done (Synaptic Event): once a spike arrives to its destinations, DMA retrieves the relative synaptic information from SDRAM and the input is injected into the post-synaptic neurons.

Figure 1 shows how events interact: each time step produces a timer event. Neural equations are solved (according to the neural application, parameters and state variables) and a Spike Event is produced if a condition is met (eg. the membrane potential crosses a threshold). Spikes are encoded as source-based AER packets and are routed to their destination cores by the MC routers. On the post-synaptic chip synapses are retrieved locally using a source-based lookup to access SDRAM; synaptic inputs are then injected into the target neurons according to the synaptic model used.

Neural applications use run-time, model-dependent data to configure neural dynamics and connectivity. These need to be compiled for the system, translating the model (neurons and synapses with associated parameters) into SpiNNaker data structures. Such data structures are presented in fig. 2 and include the individual neural parameters, the routing tables to route spikes from source to destinations, the lookup table to retrieve synaptic data from memory and the synaptic data itself. To configure the entire system, several data structures need to be created after having allocated and mapped the model on the architecture.

To reconfigure and expand a system of thousands of chips and up to about a million cores rapidly, data structure creation needs to be as flexible and efficient as possible. The next section presents the proposed approach.

4. MODEL TO HARDWARE

By introducing a translation level (*map* or system level) from one to the other layer, the approach effectively decouples the device from the neural network model level. This

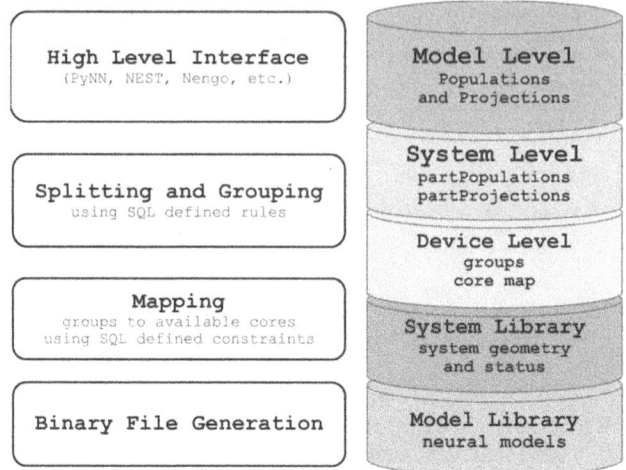

Figure 4: PACMAN structure

layer needs to reflect the availability of a variety of models (neural, synaptic, plasticity), their allocation on the system, and the configuration of the connections between neurons, in order to transform the high-level representation into an on-chip representation. It also needs to be able to represent the resources present in the system, both from a software and hardware point of view. This layer then becomes central to any model-to-machine interaction: at boot time for configuring the system, at runtime for real-time interaction and for data analysis. Therefore it needs to be efficient, as the potential of a real-time configurable device is wasted if the time or complexity to configure and interact with it becomes unmanageable. It also needs to scale up to configure networks with millions of neurons and billions of connections. Finally, it must be compatible with different programming languages or modelling front-ends and approaches to leverage the hardware reconfigurability fully.

We represent information at the *Population* (group of neurons) and *Projection* (bundle of single connections between Populations) level, as most of the languages considered use this representation natively [11] [44] [20]. This greatly simplifies the allocation, mapping and generation processes as against flattening out the whole network at a neuron level, using hierarchical information to effect the translation from the model and place it on the device. Atomic reconfigurability (single neurons and synapses) is maintained, but is pushed to the data file generation step in a way which can easily be ported on-chip and parallelised. The 2-stage routing/lookup system lets the router deal only with Populations, greatly saving routing entries and lowering the complexity through interval routing [47] (where a routing interval can be considered as either the set of routing keys in a Population or in a core, depending on the granularity of the mapping algorithm). This approach simplifies reconfigurability both for arbitrary connectivity between Populations and for easy integration of new cell types constituting Populations. To maximise system scalability, we choose to represent all the data of this layer in SQL format, taking advantage of a "language agnostic" representation which can be easily be accessed from different languages with high performance database technologies. The following sections explain the structure and function of this layer by presenting an im-

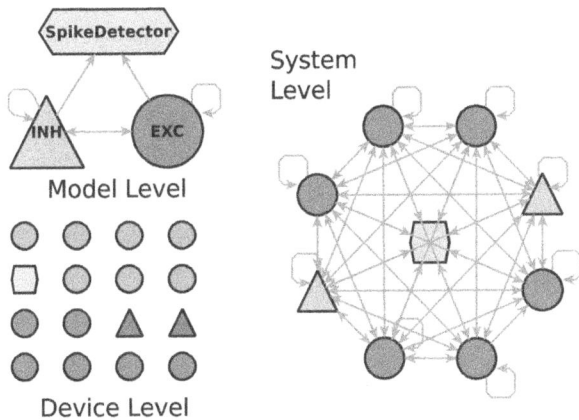

Figure 5: Example network composed of 2 Populations and a Spike Detector interconnected

plementation which is able to translate models from different front-ends and drive data structure generation.

4.1 General Structure

The function of PACMAN - the PArtitioning and Configuration MANager, is to transform the high-level representation of a neural network into a physical on-chip implementation. PACMAN is based on a database that holds three representations of the neural network (fig.4): **Model Level**, the network as specified in the high-level language (PyNN, Nengo, etc.); **System Level**, the network as partitioned into *partPopulations* that can be fit into a single computing core, Projections, probes and inputs being split accordingly; and **Device Level**, a map linking groups of *partPopulations* that can fit into a single core with a particular core (identified by its coordinates) in the system. These representations are specific for every network instantiated, while the *Model and System Libraries* are imported to represent information about the system resources and geometry and the models available. Such translations enable the network to be mapped and deployed on the SpiNNaker system, by generating the binaries needed to configure the simulation components and topology, implementing the hierarchical approach described in figure 3. PACMAN itself (fig.4) is divided into 4 different steps:

Splitting, responsible for splitting neural *Populations* which will not fit in a single core (because of memory or computational complexity limitations) into *partPopulations* that will fit in a core.

Grouping, responsible for collating *partPopulations* which can be run using the same application code in order to fit more of them onto a single core. The result of this operation is a *group*, a collection of neurons which may belong to one or more *partPopulations* and that can fit in a single core.

Mapping, responsible for allocating neural groups to processors and calculating routing. At this stage the model is placed onto the device.

Binary file generation, which creates the actual data binaries from the partitioned and mapped network.

Figure 5 illustrates an example, showing a common scenario where one excitatory (red circle) and one inhibitory (blue triangle) population of neurons is interconnected [5]. A spike detector device is placed to record spike activity. PACMAN splits Populations into *partPopulations* according to their size (in the example the result is 6 excitatory and 2 inhibitory *partPopulations*), and *Projections* between them into *partProjections*, maintaining connectivity unaltered. Finally, it maps *partPopulations* to physical cores at the Device level.

Rules for Splitting and Grouping can be defined in SQL format so as to represent arbitrary rules, which can be easily incorporated in the framework. For example, splitting can be done on the basis of the maximum number of a certain neural type a core can model in real time, while grouping can be applied to neurons using the same neural/plasticity model and having compatible mapping constraints. This information can be passed to the Mapper stage along with model-specific data provided by the high-level generation tool, giving it all the information needed to generate each portion of the network locally. The Mapping stage can take into account constraints, also defined in SQL on a Population basis. This makes interaction with external tools and user-entered constraints simple; if none are specified, groups are assigned to available cores on a first-come first-serve basis. The *System Library* (fig. 4) represents available resources of the system, holding a representation of the system size, geometry and functional status so to map around malfunctioning resources. This process can also differentiate between multiple users accessing separate parts of the machine independently. When a user requests resources, PACMAN will grant only chips allocated to him.

Output from the Mapper is a hierarchical physical description of the entire network. At this point the description still contains abstract objects rather than single neurons or synapses. The mapper organises this information in a way such that binary file generation can be easily parallelised, evaluating the table produced by the mapper core by core. This in turn passed to an Object File generator (which for the moment resides on the Host but could eventually be migrated to an on-SpiNNaker implementation) which flattens the network and generates the actual data binaries for the system. The neural and connectivity structures are computed by retrieving the translation, size and position of the parameters in the neural structure from the Model Library. Parameters can be defined as single values, random distributions or lists explicitly defining the parameter values for each neuron or synapse.

4.2 Introducing new types

The previous section presented how cells can be divided into populations and placed on the system according to their connectivity. Within this framework, new neural, synaptic, plasticity and connectors can easily be implemented. All these elements have a representation in the *Model Library* which contains the translation methods for those objects into SpiNNaker data structure. Using this approach, new models based on the event-driven API can easily be incorporated in a neural application framework [43] and generated using the approach described. PACMAN can be used to specify the translations (order, data types, size) of the parameters describing the neural model. This makes integration of new models onto the machine rapid, exploiting the ARM cores' reconfigurability [18].

4.3 Compatible Frontends

Typically dedicated hardware platforms have their own proprietary font-end [36], or offer compatibility with a single standard one [6] [14] or don't address compatibility with a standard description language [3] [8]. We have proposed an intermediate model-to-system translation layer which effectively decouples the front-end model language from the hardware back-end configuration. As a result of this operation it is possible to plug different front-ends, analysis or representation tools to the system by interfacing with PACMAN, as the process of configuring and compiling the data structures is the same regardless of the language used. The Population/Projection abstraction is already built into many of the front-ends considered, making the integration seamless. The *Model Library* stores the neuron, synapse, plasticity and connector models, containing language-neutral translation methods for the models available on the system. Most of the tools also make native use of Python or Python bindings [13] [11] [1] [44] [25], motivating the choice of Python as an implementation language.

PyNN: as an emerging standard, PyNN is a central tool that can be used to exchange and validate models and results between different groups or compare neuromorphic hardware [14] [36] [6]. We implement the High Level API as a natural extension of the *Population* and *Projection* objects used in the language. *OneToOne*, *AllToAll*, *FixedProbability* and *FromList* connectors are supported (which subsumes the remaining connector types, e.g. *DistanceDependent*). As discussed PyNN supports standard cells and plasticity methods; we extended it to incorporate the Izhikevich neural model and to test novel plasticity algorithms [10].

Nengo: in contrast to all the other front-ends considered, Nengo [44] is specific to the Neural Engineering Framework, which computes connection and weights between groups of neurons to achieve a desired neural computation [12]. It demonstrates the flexibility of the system, in that it proves possible to translate a model from Nengo to PACMAN and generate the correct structures for the model, by implementing an *encoding* and a *decoding* cell type [18].

NEST: a preliminary NEST plugin based on PyNEST [13] has been developed which can be used to create neural populations and connections. The *Device* object in NEST nicely map to a generic application core doing parallel data collection and analysis rather than neural simulation.

Different type of tools can also been integrated within the current framework:

I/O mapping: other than being used at a model generation time, PACMAN can be used to translate information flowing from/to the system at run time. It also makes the mapping of AER devices [30] in the system manageable as another system resource. This lets the end user work exclusively with the model level, PACMAN managing the translation to the Device level when sending/retrieving information to specific populations or neurons when, for example, interfacing with a data visualisation software or with a peripheral.

Network Analysis tools: it is possible to consider *Populations* and *Projections* (or their *part* versions) as nodes and edges of a graph. A weight can then be introduced on the edges, representing the connection density between two

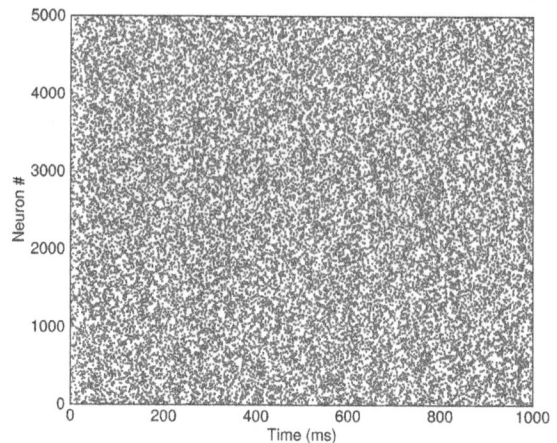

Figure 6: Example Benchmark Network Dynamics

populations. It is also possible to represent the Device level in this way, considering cores and routes between cores as nodes and edges, and using the connection density metric to optimize the placement of the cores on the system for example by clustering the most connected cores or by using existing graph representation/analysis tools (as Networkx or GraphML). Those can directly be interfaced with the Mapping stage at SQL level in order to improve placement of the model on the device.

5. RESULTS

We present a set of models having different structures and characteristics. All models run in real-time on a 2x2-chip SpiNNaker board; each core models 500 LIF neurons; all models are written in PyNN. Results have been obtained running PACMAN on an Intel Core 2 Duo T6600 with 4Gb of RAM. We first present results for the configuration of existing SpiNNaker machines (4 chip boards equipped with a total of 72 cores) and we then explore the challenges of configuring larger machines.

5.1 4 chip board results

5.1.1 Example Benchmark Network

The network presented as an example in section 4 (fig. 5) can be used to study the balance of excitation and inhibition in a neural network, and is commonly considered a spiking neural network benchmark [5], as it can easily be scaled up while maintaining the network dynamics intact. The model [48] consists of a network of excitatory and inhibitory neurons, connected via current-based first order synapses (injected current with instantaneous rise and exponential decay) with a 2% probability of interconnection. Figure 6 presents the dynamics for a 5000-neuron instantiation of the network: neurons are driven by their internal dynamics and settle to a state in which they fire in the 5-10Hz range. Figures 9 and 8 presents the performance of PACMAN with different network sizes. This network represents a worst-case scenario, as every partPopulation (and consequently every core in the system) is interconnected and every partProjection is probabilistic. The overhead of creating partProjections is maximal as they are then utilised with only 2% connection density.

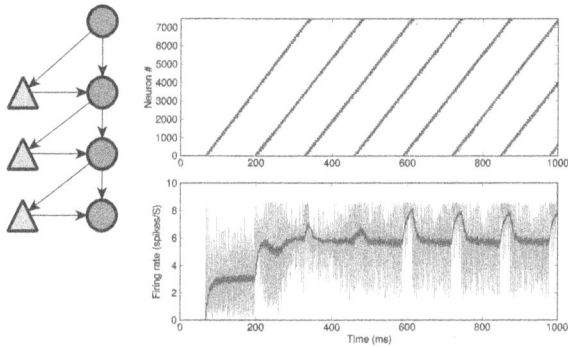

Figure 7: Results from a synfire chain of 60 nodes of 100+25 neurons each

5.1.2 Synfire Chain

Synfire chains are well-studied systems of accurate signal propagation in networks of spiking neurons [48] and they offer an ideal mapping benchmark, since scaling the number of units while keeping the network dynamics intact is a relatively easy task. As the network is scaled up the interconnection probability is scaled down so as not to change the dynamics [6]. Figure 7 shows the general connectivity pattern of the synfire chain: each layer is composed of a population of excitatory neurons (red circles) and a population of inhibitory neurons (blue triangles); each excitatory population is interconnected with both the inhibitory and excitatory population in the next layer in a feed-forward inhibition fashion [29] to make it stable; the inhibitory population suppresses the corresponding excitatory population. Figure 7 presents the results for a run of a synfire chain composed of 60 nodes of 100 excitatory + 25 inhibitory neurons each. The first population stimulates the single propagation through the chain. Figure 9 summarises build times for different nodes/network sizes. The placing process (splitting, grouping and mapping populations and projections to the system) is fast for every experiment, with a maximum in Synfire #2 since it contains more nodes and populations.

5.1.3 Randomly Connected Network

The previous two examples have dealt with very different interconnectivity patterns: in the first any given neuron has finite probability to connect to any other neuron in the network. In the second there is a fixed feed-forward connection topology, where each population projects to the next level or receives projections from the inhibitory cells in the same layer. In order to study intermediate classes of topologies we introduce a network where populations are randomly interconnected; neurons are injected with random currents so to sustain activity. While neural dynamics are of limited interest, this model can be used to explore different mappings on the system as the number of populations and their interconnections varies, and it can, for instance, represent how signals from a group of functionally specialized neural populations are integrated [45]. This network topology takes advantage of fewer (but denser) partProjections between cores and can therefore be considered as an intermediate case. Results in figure 8 and 9 demonstrate that as the indexing overhead is reduced (few partProjections) and

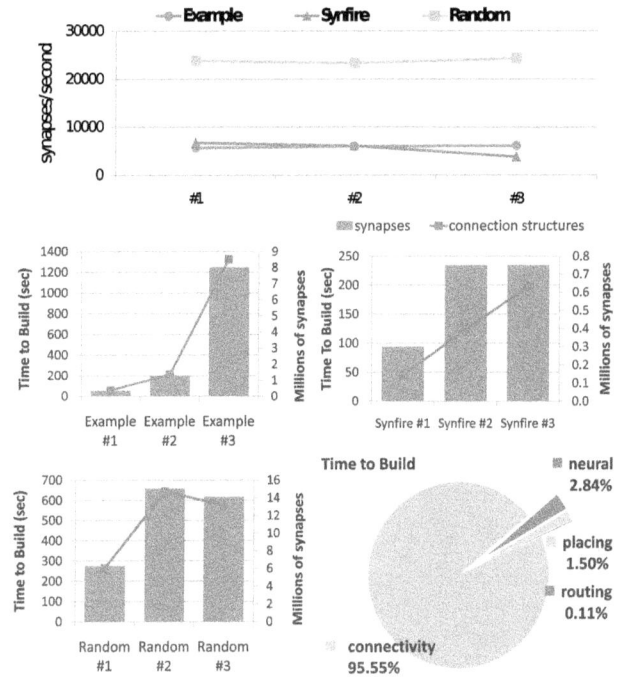

Figure 8: 2x2 results analysis

the probability of synaptic connection is high (50%, making dense Projections), synapse generation is considerably faster than the Example Benchmark Network. It is worth noting that for a given model topology the number of synapses created per second is constant (see fig. 9), leading to a linear scaling up of execution time when adding more synapses.

5.2 PACMAN for larger systems

In the previous sections we have used an approach for configuring 2x2 systems that shows that the limiting factor for large systems is the generation of complex data structures (see fig. 8) that need to be indexed by every core in every chip. We can use the same approach to test bigger systems without simulating the data structure creation. As we have chosen models that maintain their dynamics under scaling, we can simply increase the number of neurons per population so as to fill a much larger system. System size and geometry can be easily modified by adding entries in the *Model Library* representing new chips: PACMAN will then consider them in the mapping phase as available resources. In order to test how the population-based placing approach works on bigger systems, we simulate a network of 16x16 SpiNNaker chips; assuming 16 cores available for neural modelling per chip we model a total of 4,096 cores available for neural simulation.

5.2.1 Results

Figure 10 presents build times for each PACMAN stage and model specifications. As in the previous section, cores model 500 LIF neurons each. The Splitting stage is the one which is in charge of re-indexing Projections into partProjections, and as their number increases the process takes longer, as does the routing which needs to route such partProjections. This is evident from last plot: the time to build is directly proportional to the number of partProjections in

189

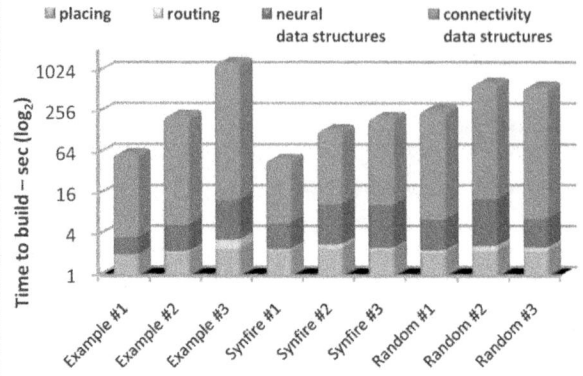

	Model Specifications			PACMAN			
	neurons	synapses	cores	placing	routing	connectivity	neural
Example Network #1	4,000	320,000	8	1.98	0.04	56.43	1.56
Example Network #2	8,000	1,280,000	16	2.13	0.14	215	3.22
Example Network #3	20,000	8,000,000	40	2.46	0.91	1323	9.6
Synfire #1 40 nodes, 250 neurons/node	10,000	292,500	20	2.3	0.14	44.7	3.4
Synfire #2 100 nodes, 250 neurons/node	25,000	742,500	50	2.5	0.37	123.79	8.35
Synfire #3 10 nodes, 2500 neurons/node	25,000	675,000	50	2.36	0.16	198	8.34
Random Network #1 50 populations, 5 projections	12,500	6,262,500	25	2.17	0.17	262.9	4.25
Random Network #2 120 populations, 5 projections	30,000	15,030,000	60	2.29	0.43	643.9	10.29
Random Network #3 50 populations, 10 projections	12,500	14,075,000	25	2.28	0.3	577.7	4.26

Figure 9: Time building results for models run on a 2x2 system

the system. As the previous section discusses, the example benchmark network is worst-case, both for the placing strategy and for the system itself. It is no surprise then that, regardless of the neuron and synapse count, this is the model that takes most time to build. A model with fewer but more dense Projections (such as the Random Network) takes less time to be built despite having 4× more neurons and twice as many synapses as the Example Network. The Synfire Chain Network is the fastest to build, as it has fewer Projections/synapses, but stresses the Grouper, since inhibitory Populations can be grouped in pairs together in a core. The Mapping stage is trivial in all cases as no constraints are provided, and hence it just needs to allocate groups to cores serially. This results show the potential of the system with different connectivity patterns, and hint at the ones that are easier to model on the machine.

6. DISCUSSION

The software infrastructure presented can be used to configure parallel digital hardware system for simulation of spiking neural networks by exploiting its arbitrary remapping capability, both on a single computational node and a connectivity level. The approach takes advantage of hierarchical information embedded in the model at a neural *Population* level to drive the configuration of the system in an efficient way, by deferring the data file compilation stage until after the resource mapping on the system, simplifying its parallelisation (and hence the generation of the configuration data structures on the machine itself). This is a key result of the paper: by using a hierarchical approach and considering Populations and Projections rather than flattening single neurons and synapses all the mapping and placing algorithms have lower complexity, while still maintaining a full low-level representation at the device level. The results presented in the previous section show interesting aspects of the problem and of the approach proposed to solve it. It is evident that for the scale of systems considered in this section the most complex task is compiling the data structures, especially for synaptic data. Indeed, the allocation and mapping on this system sizes is trivial, as is routing, since they work on a core/partPopulation basis rather than on a single neuron/synapse level. We have identified the bottleneck of the actual system - the generation of complex synaptic structures that must be indexed by every core in every chip. While optimization techniques at a DB level

	cores	part populations	part projections	splitting	grouping	mapping	routing
Example Network 500K neurons 5.000M synapses (2%interconn probability)	1,000	1,000	1,000,000	337	24	0.66	1378
Synfire Chain 1600 nodes 1000+250 neurons each 60M synapses	4,000	4,800	12,792	17	53	0.91	40
Random Network 2000 Populations 1000 neurons/10 Projections 2M neurons 9.000M synapses	4,000	4,000	80,000	72	38	0.92	213

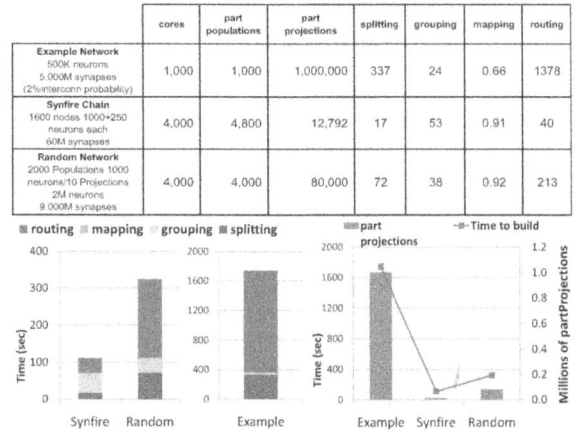

Figure 10: Results from models on a 16x16 system

(proper indexing, using prepared statements, partitioning of large tables) or at a Python level (using fast numerical libraries as Numpy) could be used to improve performance, data structure creation is an "embarrassingly parallel" problem (each core needs only to configure is local portion of memory independently) and thus we propose to implement this stage of PACMAN on-chip.

Another key result of this approach is that at the end of the Mapping stage information is already represented in a local, core-based way and can therefore be parallelised and distribute on the machine itself, greatly speeding up the most critical processes and exploiting the system architecture in the configuration phase. At this point each neuron has been allocated to a core, and it is possible to route the network, associating neurons to routing keys, even though the data structures do not as yet exist. Therefore, this part of the process can be done on the host machine, and the hierarchical representation permits the use of interval routing [47], simplifying the problem greatly. Allocating neurons to system resources can be done by sending the Population parameters to the corresponding core. Each core can then receive information about the incoming partProjections (parameters, range of routing keys considered, connectivity pattern) from PACMAN, and initialise, compile, organize and index its own synaptic data structures in SDRAM, having all the necessary information represented locally. Hence the host

190

system only needs to send abstract information to the machine which self-configures by populating its local portion of memory.

The proposed approach has already been used to map models which explore new plasticity models [10] or structural biological models of the cortex micro-circuitry [42]. Creating new neural applications which can then be seamlessly used as computational resource nodes is an approach that greatly exploits the reconfigurability of a digital architecture [43] and can be used to introduce new computational frameworks rapidly for the architecture [18]. For general purpose use, a user will in future be able to create his own neural model specifying dynamical equations as done with Brian [1]. As the system is completely event-driven, this neural model creation tool will map dynamics to events [40], making use of code generation techniques [23] either from the modelling language or from a standard XML format [21].

7. CONCLUSIONS

We have presented a hierarchical approach for configuring large parallel systems. The layer proposed effectively decouples the model, written in a user-selected front-end language, and the device level, abstracting the hardware to the end user and letting non-hardware experts exploit the reconfigurability of the architecture in a seamless way. We have tested the proposed method by configuring the current generation of SpiNNaker systems in a variety of networks of thousands of neurons and millions of synapses. We indicate the current limitations and propose solutions, discussing the capabilities of an approach which promises to be able to scale up to configure systems of millions of neurons and thousands of processors. A system which combines off-hardware hierarchical decomposition of the application with on-board generation of the data binaries is a compelling and efficient model for very large-scale parallel applications that maximises the utilisation of available hardware resources. This approach is a natural one whenever the application, like networks of neurons, has its own internal structure which naturally suggests the on-hardware mapping.

8. ACKNOWLEDGEMENTS

We would like to thank Chris Eliasmith and Terry Stewart for their contribution in the Nengo/SpiNNaker interface. The SpiNNaker project is supported by the Engineering and Physical Science Research Council (EPSRC), grant EP/4015740/1, and also by ARM and Silistix. We appreciate the support of these sponsors and industrial partners.

9. REFERENCES

[1] http://www.briansimulator.org/.

[2] R. Ananthanarayanan, S. K. Esser, H. D. Simon, and D. S. Modha. The cat is out of the bag: cortical simulations with 10^9 neurons, 10^{13} synapses. In *Proceedings of the Conference on High Performance Computing Networking, Storage and Analysis*, SC '09, pages 63:1–63:12, New York, NY, USA, 2009. ACM.

[3] M. Bhuiyan, V. Pallipuram, and M. Smith. Acceleration of spiking neural networks in emerging multi-core and GPU architectures. In *Parallel & Distributed Processing, Workshops and Phd Forum (IPDPSW), 2010 IEEE International Symposium on*, pages 1–8. IEEE, 2010.

[4] J. M. Bower and D. Beeman. The book of GENESIS (2nd ed.): exploring realistic neural models with the GEneral NEural SImulation System. 1998.

[5] R. Brette, M. Rudolph, T. Carnevale, M. Hines, D. Beeman, J. Bower, M. Diesmann, A. Morrison, P. Goodman, F. Harris, and Others. Simulation of networks of spiking neurons: a review of tools and strategies. *Journal of computational neuroscience*, 23(3):349–398, Dec. 2007.

[6] D. Brüderle, M. Petrovici, B. Vogginger, M. Ehrlich, T. Pfeil, S. Millner, A. Grübl, K. Wendt, E. Müller, M. Schwartz, and Others. A comprehensive workflow for general-purpose neural modeling with highly configurable neuromorphic hardware systems. *Biological cybernetics*, 104(4-5):1–34, May 2011.

[7] T. Carnevale. Neuron simulation environment. *Scholarpedia*, 2(6):1378, 2007.

[8] A. Cassidy, A. Andreou, and J. Georgiou. Design of a one million neuron single FPGA neuromorphic system for real-time multimodal scene analysis. In *Information Sciences and Systems (CISS), 2011 45th Annual Conference on*, pages 1–6. IEEE, 2011.

[9] T. Choi, B. Shi, and K. Boahen. An ON-OFF Orientation Selective Address Event Representation Image Transceiver Chip. *IEEE Transactions on Circuits and Systems I: Fundamental Theory and Applications*, 51(2):342–353, Feb. 2004.

[10] S. Davies, F. Galluppi, and A. Rast. A forecast-based STDP rule suitable for neuromorphic implementation. *Neural Networks*, 2012.

[11] A. P. Davison, D. Brüderle, J. Eppler, J. Kremkow, E. Muller, D. Pecevski, L. Perrinet, and P. Yger. PyNN: A Common Interface for Neuronal Network Simulators. *Front Neuroinformatics*, 2:11, 2008.

[12] C. Eliasmith and C. H. Anderson. *Neural engineering: Computation, representation, and dynamics in neurobiological systems*. MIT Press, Cambridge, MA, 2003.

[13] J. M. Eppler, M. Helias, E. Muller, M. Diesmann, and M.-O. Gewaltig. PyNEST: A Convenient Interface to the NEST Simulator. *Front Neuroinformatics*, 2:12, 2008.

[14] A. K. Fidjeland, E. B. Roesch, M. P. Shanahan, and W. Luk. NeMo: A Platform for Neural Modelling of Spiking Neurons Using GPUs. In *2009 20th IEEE International Conference on Application-specific Systems, Architectures and Processors*, pages 137–144. IEEE, July 2009.

[15] S. Furber and A. Brown. Biologically-Inspired Massively-Parallel Architectures - Computing Beyond a Million Processors. In *Proceedings of the 2009 Ninth International Conference on Application of Concurrency to System Design*, ACSD '09, pages 3–12, Washington, DC, USA, 2009. IEEE Computer Society.

[16] S. B. Furber, S. Temple, and A. D. Brown. High-Performance Computing for Systems of Spiking Neurons. *The AISB06 workshop on GC5: Architecture of Brain and Mind*, 2006.

[17] S. B. Furber, S. Temple, and A. D. Brown. On-chip and Inter-Chip Networks for Modelling Large-Scale Neural Systems, 2006.

[18] F. Galluppi, S. Davies, T. Stewart, C. Eliasmith, and

S. Furber. Real Time On-Chip Implementation of Dynamical Systems with Spiking Neurons. In *Neural Networks (IJCNN), The 2012 International Joint Conference on*. IEEE, 2012.

[19] F. Galluppi, A. Rast, S. Davies, and S. Furber. A general-purpose model translation system for a universal neural chip. In *Neural Information Processing. Theory and Algorithms*, pages 58–65. Springer, 2010.

[20] O. Gewaltig, M. Diesmann, and M.-O. Gewaltig. NEST (NEural Simulation Tool). *Scholarpedia*, 2(4):1430, 2007.

[21] N. H. Goddard, M. Hucka, F. Howell, H. Cornelis, K. Shankar, and D. Beeman. Towards NeuroML: model description methods for collaborative modelling in neuroscience. *Philos Trans R Soc Lond B Biol Sci*, 356(1412):1209–1228, Aug. 2001.

[22] D. Goodman. Brian: a simulator for spiking neural networks in Python. *Frontiers in Neuroinformatics*, 2, 2008.

[23] D. Goodman. Code generation: a strategy for neural network simulators. *Neuroinformatics*, 8(3):183–96, Oct. 2010.

[24] M. Hanke and Y. Halchenko. Neuroscience runs on GNU/Linux. *Frontiers in neuroinformatics*, 5, 2011.

[25] M. L. Hines and N. T. Carnevale. The NEURON Simulation Environment. *Neural Computation*, 9(6):1179–1209, Aug. 1997.

[26] K. M. Hynna and K. Boahen. Neuronal Ion-Channel Dynamics in Silicon. In *Proc. 2006 Int'l Symp. Circuits and Systems (ISCAS 2006)*, pages 3614–3617, 2006.

[27] G. Indiveri, E. Chicca, and R. Douglas. A VLSI array of low-power spiking neurons and bistable synapses with spike-timing dependent plasticity. *IEEE Transactions on Neural Networks*, 17:211–221, 2006.

[28] C. Johansson and A. Lansner. Towards cortex sized artificial neural systems. *Neural Networks*, 20(1):48–61, 2007.

[29] J. Kremkow, A. Aertsen, and A. Kumar. Gating of Signal Propagation in Spiking Neural Networks by Balanced and Correlated Excitation and Inhibition. *Journal of Neuroscience*, 30(47):15760–15768, 2010.

[30] J. Lazzaro, J. Wawrzynek, M. Mahowald, M. Silviotti, and D. Gillespie. Silicon Auditory Processors as Computer Peripherals. *IEEE Transactions on Neural Networks*, 4(3):523–528, May 1993.

[31] W. Maass, T. Natschläger, T. U. Graz, and H. Markram. On the computational power of circuits of spiking neurons. *J. of Physiology (Paris*, 2005, 2003.

[32] L. P. Maguire, T. M. McGinnity, B. Glackin, A. Ghani, A. Belatreche, and J. Harkin. Challenges for Large-Scale Implementations of Spiking Neural Networks on FPGAs. *Neurocomputing*, 71, Dec. 2007.

[33] H. Markram. The blue brain project. *Nat Rev Neurosci.*, 7:153–160, 2006.

[34] P. A. Merolla, J. V. Arthur, B. E. Shi, and K. A. Boahen. Expandable Networks for Neuromorphic Chips. *IEEE Transactions on Circuits and Systems I: Regular Papers*, 54(2):301–311, Feb. 2007.

[35] A. Morrison, C. Mehring, T. Geisel, A. D. Aertsen, and M. Diesmann. Advancing the boundaries of high-connectivity network simulation with distributed computing. *Neural computation*, 17(8):1776–801, Aug. 2005.

[36] J. M. Nageswaran, N. Dutt, J. L. Krichmar, A. Nicolau, and A. V. Veidenbaum. A configurable simulation environment for the efficient simulation of large-scale spiking neural networks on graphics processors. *Neural Networks*, 22(5–6):791–800, 2009.

[37] C. Patterson, J. Garside, E. Painkras, S. Temple, L. Plana, J. Navaridas, T. Sharp, and S. Furber. Scalable Communications for a Million-Core Neural Processing Architecture. *Accepted by the Journal of Distributed Computing*.

[38] L. Plana, S. Furber, S. Temple, M. Khan, Y. Shi, J. Wu, and S. Yang. A GALS Infrastructure for a Massively Parallel Multiprocessor. *IEEE Design & Test of Computers*, 24(5):454–463, 2007.

[39] H. Plesser, J. Eppler, A. Morrison, M. Diesmann, and M. Gewaltig. Efficient parallel simulation of large-scale neuronal networks on clusters of multiprocessor computers. *Euro-Par 2007 parallel processing*, pages 672–681, 2007.

[40] A. Rast, F. Galluppi, X. Jin, and S. Furber. The leaky integrate-and-fire neuron: A platform for synaptic model exploration on the spinnaker chip. In *Neural Networks (IJCNN), The 2010 International Joint Conference on*, pages 1–8. IEEE, 2010.

[41] J. Schemmel, D. Brüderle, A. Grübl, M. Hock, K. Meier, and S. Millner. A wafer-scale neuromorphic hardware system for large-scale neural modeling. In *Proc. 2010 Int'l Symp. Circuits and Systems (ISCAS 2010)*, pages 1947–1950, 2010.

[42] T. Sharp, F. Galluppi, A. Rast, and S. Furber. Power-efficient simulation of detailed cortical microcircuits on SpiNNaker. *Journal of Neuroscience Methods*, 2012.

[43] T. Sharp, L. A. Plana, F. Galluppi, and S. Furber. Event-Driven Simulation of Arbitrary Spiking Neural Networks on SpiNNaker. In *ICONIP 2011*, volume 2011, pages 424–430. Springer, 2011.

[44] T. C. Stewart, B. Tripp, and C. Eliasmith. Python scripting in the Nengo simulator. *Frontiers in Neuroinformatics*, 3(0), 2009.

[45] G. Tononi, G. M. Edelman, and O. Sporns. Complexity and coherency: integrating information in the brain. *Trends in cognivitve sciences*, 2(12):474–484, 1998.

[46] D. Vainbrand and R. Ginosar. Scalable network-on-chip architecture for configurable neural networks. *Microprocessors and Microsystems*, 35(2):152–166, Mar. 2011.

[47] J. Van Leeuwen. Interval Routing. *The Computer Journal*, 30(4):298–307, Apr. 1987.

[48] T. P. Vogels and L. F. Abbott. Signal propagation and logic gating in networks of integrate-and-fire neurons. *J Neurosci*, 25(46):10786–10795, Nov. 2005.

[49] R. J. Vogelstein, U. Mallik, E. Culurciello, G. Cauwenberghs, and R. Etienne-Cummings. A multichip neuromorphic system for spike-based visual information processing. *Neural computation*, 19(9):2281–300, Sept. 2007.

Reuse Distance Based Performance Modeling and Workload Mapping

Sai Prashanth Muralidhara, Mahmut Kandemir, Orhan Kislal
{smuralid, kandemir, omk103}@cse.psu.edu
Pennsylvania State University

ABSTRACT

Modern multicore architectures have multiple cores connected to a hierarchical cache structure resulting in heterogeneity in cache sharing across different subsets of cores. In these systems, overall throughput and efficiency depends heavily on a careful mapping of applications to available cores. In this paper, we study the problem of application-to-core mapping with the goal of trying to improve the overall cache performance in the presence of a hierarchical multi-level cache structure. We propose to sample the memory access patterns of individual applications and build their reuse distance distributions. Further, we propose to use these reuse distance distributions to compute an application-to-core mapping that tries to improve the overall cache performance, and consequently, the overall throughput. We show that our proposed mapping scheme is very effective in practice yielding throughput benefits of about 39% over the worst case mapping and about 30% over the default operating system based mapping. We believe, as larger chip multiprocessors with deeper cache hierarchies are projected to be the norm in the future, efficient mapping of applications to cores will become a vital requirement to extract the maximum possible performance from these systems.

Categories and Subject Descriptors

C.1.0 [**Processor Architectures**]: General

General Terms

Performance, Design, Measurement

Keywords

Multicores, memory, shared caches, reuse distance

1. INTRODUCTION

Many current chip multiprocessors (CMPs) support on-chip hierarchical caches. For instance, Intel Xeon 7400 processor (previously code-named Intel Dunnington) [?] has six on-chip cores with each pair of cores sharing a level two (L2) cache and all cores sharing a level three (L3) cache. A Dell

R900 server rack contains two such Dunnington chips [?] making it twelve cores with three levels of cache topology, L1, L2 and L3. Although these hierarchical cache structures have only recently emerged in commercial CMPs, shared L2 caches have been prevalent for quite some time in dual core and quad core CMPs. In such CMPs, multiple cores sharing an L2 cache leads to a situation where applications running on these cores contend for the shared cache space. This contention can have varying effects on the performance of the simultaneously-executing applications. For instance, an application's performance can be adversely impacted by sharing a cache with another application, whereas the same application can experience minimal adverse impact when running together with some other application. The cache performance of an application is affected by its co-runners that share a cache with it, and further, degree to which the application's cache performance is affected depends not only on its own cache behavior but also on that of its co-runner's. Therefore, co-scheduling threads that have lower contention and hence run well together at the same time is beneficial [?, ?, ?]. This problem gets more complicated in the presence of multi-level cache hierarchies.

In this paper, we address the problem of mapping a workload (a set of single-threaded applications) to the cores of a CMP in the presence of a hierarchical cache structure, and present a mapping algorithm. The presence of different degrees of cache sharing among the subsets of cores introduces different levels of cache contention at different levels of the cache hierarchy. A direct consequence of this contention is the non-triviality of finding an application-to-core mapping which minimizes the overall cache contention effects and improves the overall cache performance.

Our proposed workload mapping scheme starts out by sampling the memory accesses of all applications. The reuse distance distributions are built for all applications in the workload individually using their memory access samples. The performance effects of possible cache contention at different levels of the cache hierarchy are modeled. These reuse distance based models estimate two types of performance effects for each application. The first of these is a measure of the extent to which an application's performance can be adversely affected by other contending applications, and the second measure is the extent to which an application can adversely affect the performance of other (simultaneously executing) contending applications. We present two variants of the reuse distance based models. We then propose a hierarchical grouping technique that uses the reuse-distribution based models to obtain a good application-to-core mapping for a given cache hierarchy and a workload. "Good" in this context means a mapping that reduces the overall cache contention effects (at all cache levels). The grouping algorithm considers all levels of the cache hierarchy progressively and, as a result, the varying degrees of cache sharing among cores

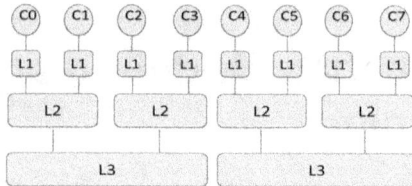

Figure 1: A three-level hierarchical cache architecture.

are taken into account to reduce the contention effects at all levels.

There have been past studies that analyze the effect of cache contention in the presence of a co-runner [?, ?]. There have also been some online efforts to characterize application behavior [?]. Also, recently, there have been scheduling techniques proposed to address the shared resource contention problem [?] and, algorithms targeted at finding the optimal schedule when the contention between applications is known [?]. *ur ork is distinguished ro prior efforts in that e take into account ultiple le els o the on-chip cache hierarchy and odel in detail the per or ance effects o applications using reuse distance analysis at different cache le els* We then use these reuse distance based performance models to group and schedule the target workload on to the cores. Therefore, we propose a complete end-to-end scheme to efficiently map a given workload.To summarize, we make the following contributions:

• In order to motivate the problem, we start out by measuring the performance effects of contention at different levels of a given on-chip cache hierarchy and its effect on overall system throughput.

• We propose *reuse distri ution ased odels* to estimate the cache performance effects of applications due to contention at different cache levels.

• A *cache hierarchy-a are application grouping algorith* is proposed that tries to find an application-to-core mapping with minimal predicted overall cache-contention-effects.

• We evaluate our proposed mapping scheme on an eight-core and a twelve-core system. In 90% of the cases tested, our scheme computes the best possible mapping, and, the mappings produced by our proposed scheme are within 4% of the best case mappings in all cases. Application-to-core mappings produced by our scheme perform up to 39% better in terms of throughput over a worst-case mapping and up to 30% over the default operating system (OS) based mapping.

2. BACKGROUND AND SETUP

Hierarchical Caches. Caches and cache hierarchies in CMPs have evolved over the years and span purely private cache organizations, totally shared cache structures and hybrid cache organizations comprising elements of both private and shared cache components. As an example, consider Figure **??** which depicts an eight core machine with a three-level hierarchical cache structure. We use this hierarchical cache architecture for the evaluations in this paper.

Cache Hierarchy Representation. A hierarchical cache structure can potentially have multiple levels with multiple caches at each level, depending on the underlying topology. Such a hierarchical cache structure can be represented as a tree called the *ache ierarchy ree*. Root of a cache hierarchy tree will be the last level cache if there exists a single last level cache shared by all the cores. If there are more than one last level caches, root of the cache hierarchy tree will be a dummy node, representing the shared off-chip memory. We also define a parameter $C_{i,j}$ to be the number of caches at level i connected to each cache at level j. Therefore, if $C_{i,j} = \delta$, then a total of δ level i caches are connected to each level j cache. Also, level 0 represents the level of the cores. Therefore, a core connected to a private

L1 cache is represented by $C_{0,1} = 1$. Figure **??** shows the cache hierarchy tree and the $C_{i,j}$ values for the multicore architecture in Figure **??**.

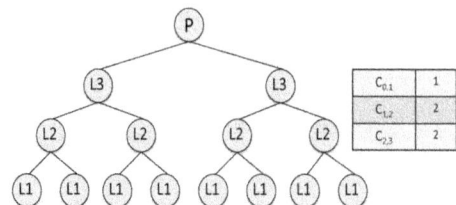

Figure 2: Representation of the cache hierarchy shown in Figure **??**.

Degree of Sharing. In CMP architectures with a hierarchical cache structure, depending on the number of levels of the cache, different subsets of cores can have different *degrees o cache sharing*. Therefore, a hierarchical cache structure creates heterogeneous subsets of cores in terms of cache sharing. The cores present in a CMP can be represented by a set $Cores = \{c_0, c_1, ..., c_m\}$, where m is the number of cores in the system. For every core subset, $S \in Cores$, we define a bit vector called the "sharing degree". *Sharing degree* of a core subset S will be $SD(S) = (sd_1, sd_2, ...sd_n)$, where n is the number of levels in the cache hierarchy, and a particular bit sd_j is 1 if all the cores in S share the level j cache, and 0 otherwise. Consequently, there is a bit for each level of the cache which indicates the cache sharing among the subset of cores at that level. Consider the architecture depicted in Figure **??**. The set of all cores in this architecture can be represented by $Cores = \{c0, c1, ..., c7\}$. We can identify three degrees of cache sharing in this particular topology:

• *igh sharing*. Consider the core subset $S \in Cores$. If the cores in S share all levels of the hierarchy except the L1 cache, then S is classified as a *highly sharing*[1] subset of cores. For instance, $S_0 = \{c0, c1\}$ (in Figure **??**) is a highly sharing subset of cores. The sharing degree vector of core subset S, $SD(S_0)$ is (011). The above subset of cores can experience contention at multiple cache levels (L2 and L3).

• *ediu sharing*: If the cores in the subset $S \in Cores$ share the L3 cache but not the L1 and L2 caches, then the subset, S, is classified as a *ediu sharing* subset. An example of this is subset $S_1 = \{c1, c2\}$. In this case, the sharing degree vector is $SD(S_1) = (001)$, and, cores in S_1 experience contention at only the L3 cache level.

• *No sharing*: Core subset $S \in Cores$ is classified as a subset with no sharing if the cores in S do not share any cache. $S2 = \{c3, c4\}$ is an example of this case. Here, the sharing degree vector is $SD(S2) = (000)$. Since no cache is shared, there will be no contention in this case.

The degree of sharing and the corresponding subsets of cores depend on the number of levels in the target cache hierarchy and the way the caches in this hierarchy are connected to each other. For example, in Figure **??**, there are three different degrees of cache sharing possible, resulting in corresponding contention issues at multiple levels. It is expected that future multicore systems will have deeper cache hierarchies [?], thereby leading to more diverse degrees of cache sharing.

Experimental Methodology and Setup. All experiments and evaluations presented in this paper are carried out using Simics [?], which is a full system simulator. Multicore architectures with different number of cores are simulated on Simics. All of the cores simulated in this study are alike and are based on the UltraSparc 3 architecture [?]. The important features of the simulated system are given in Figure **??**

---

[1]"Sharing" in this context refers to whether the cores in a subset share a cache or not and has nothing to do with data sharing, which is an application execution characteristic.

(in Section ??). The cache sizes vary with the different cache architectures we tested. However, in the default architecture (shown in Figure ??) used in most of our experiments, the L1 cache is 16KB (4 way associative), each L2 cache (shared by two cores) is 512KB (8 way associative), and each L3 cache (shared by four cores) is 3MB (16 way associative). We also use Simics to obtain the memory access traces of the applications. To map and bind applications to a particular core, we use the Solaris shell command *p ind*. All experiments are performed using applications from the SPEC 2006 benchmark suite [?] with reference inputs. There are a large number of combinations possible while evaluating a workload mapping scheme. For instance, if there are eight applications to be run on eight cores, the number of mappings possible can be as high as 8!, although not all of the mappings are unique as mentioned in Section ??. In this paper, for each application mix, we evaluate all possible mappings, unless otherwise stated. However, due to space constraints, we present results from only a representative sample of the evaluated combinations.

3. MOTIVATION

In order to motivate our application-to-core mapping problem, we quantify the differences in performance when different application-to-core mappings are used. Also, we repeat this experiment on architectures with different cache structures. In other words, we present the differences in performance when different mappings are employed, and study how these differences vary when different cache structures are used. We conduct experiments on three eight-core architectures with different cache structures: a purely shared (all cores share the last level L2 cache), pairwise shared, and the hierarchical three-level cache architecture shown in Figure ??.

The overall throughput of the system in terms for all application-to-core mappings on all three of the above mentioned cache hierarchies is plotted in Figure ??. The throughput values are normalized to the highest throughput value in each configuration. Firstly, not surprisingly, all mappings result in very similar system throughput on a purely shared cache architecture. This is because there is only one possible degree of sharing among subsets of cores. When a pairwise shared cache hierarchy is used, however, some mappings do much better than the others. More interestingly, when the cache hierarchy shown in Figure ?? is used, the mappings which performed very well in the second case do not necessarily perform well now. Also, the variation in performance between different mappings is very high. This is due to the fact that this cache hierarchy has the maximum number of sharing degrees, which is three. This is an important observation since an additional level of shared cache leads to three possible degrees of cache sharing among subsets of cores and, consequently, an additional level of contention, and the combinations of different contention levels result in very high variation among different mappings. The two takeaway points from this set of experiments are:

• In hierarchical multilevel cache structures, performance difference between the best mapping and the worst mapping can be very high. For example, there is about 30% degradation from the best case to the worst case for the three-level hierarchy in Figure ??. Therefore, the importance of finding a good mapping is critical.

• Considering cache sharing at one level is not sufficient. *egree o sharing*, which indicates cache sharing and contention at multiple levels, needs to be considered when determining a good mapping. For example, a mapping which is good on a pairwise shared cache architecture may not be so good for the architecture in Figure ??.

The next question we address here is whether all applications are affected or affect other contending applications differently. To quantitatively answer this question, we select a single application (*Bzip*) and compare its performance when it is executed under different scenarios. The two scenarios we studied are:

• One companion. *Bzip* runs on core 0 on a pairwise shared cache architecture with another application executing on core 1. We repeat the experiment with different applications on core 1. What runs on the other cores is irrelevant to this experiment (since there is no L3 cache shared across cores 0-3).

• Multiple companions. *Bzip* runs on core 0 of the architecture shown in Figure ?? with three other applications on core 1, core 2 and core 3. We repeat the experiment with different combinations of other applications on core1, core2 and core3.

We plot the performance of *Bzip* in each of the above two scenarios in Figure ??. As with the system throughput, the performance of *Bzip* depends on not only its immediate companion that shares the L2 cache but also on the other relatively distant companions that share the L3 cache with it. Therefore, any attempt to find a good application-to-core mapping for Bzip should consider the contention effects at *oth* L2 and L3 caches (which is indicated by the *degree o sharing*). To check whether other applications behave similarly, we repeated the same experiment with and plotted the results in Figure ??. As we can observe from this figure, the performance of does not change much with different mappings. We can conclude that the performance of an application and the performance effects of the application on other contending applications depends on the following three factors: (a) *egree o sharing* of the subset of cores on which the application and other contending applications are executing, (b) Memory access behavior of the application, and (c) Memory access behavior of the contending applications.

Therefore, in order to find a good mapping, we need to consider the following two metrics for each application: (a) Extent to which an application's performance is negatively affected by the other contending applications, and (b) Extent to which an application impacts the performance of the other applications.

4. PROBLEM DEFINITION AND ROADMAP

Computing an application-to-core mapping is akin to finding a good permutation of the given set of applications.

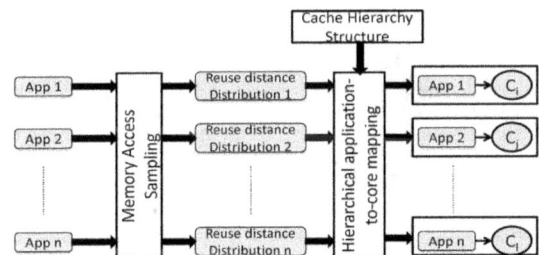

Figure 7: High level description of our approach to application-to-core mapping.

Figure ?? depicts a high-level view of our approach. The first step of our approach is to sample the memory access patterns of each individual application. The second step is to build reuse distance distributions of individual applications. Section ?? describes the proposed reuse-distance based modeling of performance effects of applications, when they execute in contention with other applications. Section ?? proposes a hierarchical workload mapping scheme. This mapping scheme is implemented as an apriori profiling

Core architecture	UltraSparc 3+
Core frequency	1 GHz
Operating system	Sun Solaris
L1 cache latency	3 cycles
L2 cache latency	10 cycles
L3 cache latency	40 cycles
Memory latency	260 cycles

Figure 3: Major system parameters and their values.

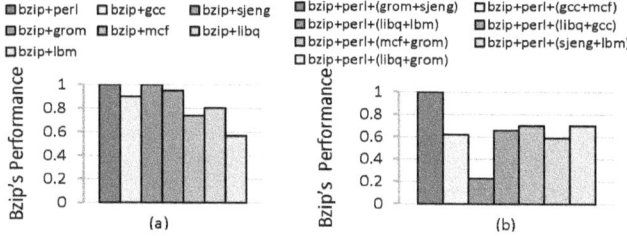

Figure 4: Throughput of different application-to-core mappings when executed on three architectures: a purely shared, pairwise shared and the three-level hierarchical cache architecture shown in Figures ??. Note here that, throughput is normalized with respect to the one with the highest throughput value in each architecture case.

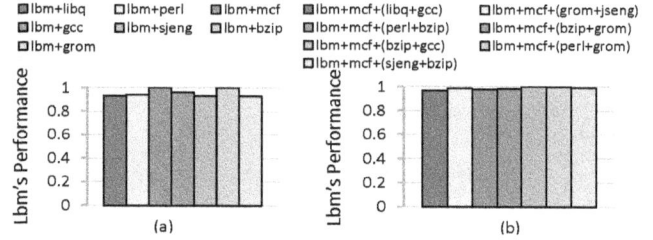

Figure 5: (a) shows the performance of Bzip on a pairwise shared cache architecture with different companion applications. (b) shows the performance of Bzip on the architecture shown in Figure ?? with different combinations of companion applications. Performance is normalized with respect to the highest performance case.

Figure 6: (a) shows the performance of Lbm on a pairwise shared cache architecture with different companion applications. (b) shows the performance of Lbm on Figure ?? with different combinations of companion applications. Performance is normalized with respect to the highest performance case.

scheme.The memory accesses of individual applications are sampled, their reuse distance profiles are built, and the workload mapping is determined and applied apriori before the execution begins. Since the sampling and computation are not performed at runtime, the sampling can be performed for longer periods and at multiple points with no runtime overhead.

5. MODELING PERFORMANCE EFFECTS

In this section, we characterize the performance effects of running a given application with other contending applications on a subset of cores with a given degree of sharing. The mentioned performance effects are of two kinds: the first one is the extent to which a given application's performance can be adversely affected by other contending applications, and the second one is the extent to which the given application adversely affects the performance of other contending applications. We define various parameters derived from the reuse distance distribution of an application. These different parameters are essential to characterize the aforementioned performance effects of an application. Reuse distance analysis is a technique that can be employed to predict the cache performance of an application execution in isolation (without other contending applications). Reuse distance analysis is explained in greater detail in Section ??.

5.1 Reuse Distance Analysis

Reuse distance is defined as the number of other "unique" cache lines accessed between two contiguous accesses to a particular cache line. A frequency distribution of the reuse distance occurrences is a good indicator of data locality and is called the *reuse distri ution* [?]. Figure ?? shows a part of the reuse distance distribution of a particular phase of execution of application *Bzip*. Reuse distance is particularly useful since most caches use a variant of the least recently used (LRU) cache replacement policy. In a fully-associative

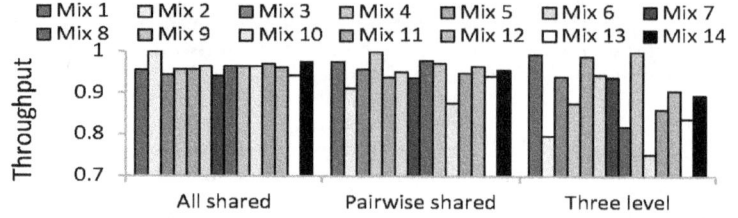

cache with the LRU replacement policy, reuse distance accurately predicts whether an access is a hit or a miss. If the reuse distance is greater than the total number of cache lines in the cache, then the access is a miss; otherwise, the cache access is a hit. Therefore, computing a histogram of reuse distances can accurately predict the miss rate for a fully-associative cache of a given size. This is done by classifying all the frequencies in the reuse distribution histogram with the reuse distance value less than the total number of cache lines as hits and the rest as misses. This reuse distance analysis predicts the cache performance even in the case of associative caches with a small margin of error. Figure ?? indicates the hit-miss threshold barrier marked for an L1 cache of size 128 cache lines. All the accesses with reuse distance below the threshold barrier of 128 are estimated to be hits and those with reuse distance higher than 128 are predicted to be misses as shown in Figure ??. For instance, using the distribution in Figure ??, the cache performance predicted in terms of miss rate is 35.1%, while the actual value on a 4-way set associative cache was 34.3%. Therefore, reuse distance analysis is an accurate way of predicting the cache performance even in the presence of set associativity.

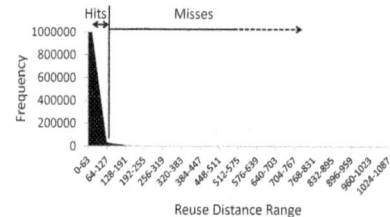

Figure 8: A part of the reuse distance distribution of Bzip with the hit-miss threshold barrier marked.

5.2 Reuse Distribution Based Parameters

The reuse distance based characterization described in the Section **??** holds only when the application runs alone with no other applications contending for the cache. More specifically, this characterization is targeted at a scenario where the application runs on a single core processor with no shared caches. However, as described earlier, in the case of multicore architectures with hierarchical cache structures, there will be subsets of cores with different degrees of sharing and hence with different degrees of contention. We now extend this characterization to multicores with hierarchical caches by accounting for these in our modeling. Figure **??** shows the reuse distribution of a sample application for illustrative purposes. We define four parameters that can be derived using the reuse distance distribution of an application. These parameters capture the different regions of reuse distance distribution defined by different intervals, are defined for a given level of the target cache hierarchy, and their values will vary with different levels of cache. Let k be the level of the cache considered. Now, consider an application app_a running on core c_i and let Figure **??** be its reuse distance distribution. In this plot, $f(R)$ is the frequency of reuse distance R. Let $S \in Cores$ be a subset of cores such that $c_i \in S$ and the kth bit of the "sharing degree vector" of subset S is set to 1; i.e., $S = \{c_l, c_m...\} \in Cores$, such that $c_i \in S$ and $SD(S)[k] = 1$. Let n be the total number cores sharing the cache at level k, i.e., $n = |S|$. Further, let $totalcache$ be the total number of cache lines. We now define the following metrics for a given cache size $totalcache$ and for a given cache level k:

- *ower level cache hits (LCH).* This parameter estimates the fraction of the reuse distances that will be hits in the lower level of the cache hierarchy and, consequently, will not reach the level k cache. We define "lower level cache hits" as: $LCH_k = \frac{\Sigma_{R=0}^{T_1} f(R)}{\Sigma_{R=0}^{T_\infty} f(R)}$. In this equation, if the lower level cache is the private L1 cache, then the threshold T_1 (shown in Figure **??**) will be set to the total number of cache lines in the private L1 cache. However, if the lower level cache is a shared cache, our hierarchical application-to-core mapping algorithm sets the value of threshold T_1 as follows: $T_1 = (\frac{1}{n_{low}} + \alpha \times \frac{1}{n_{low}}) \times totalcache_{low}$, where n_{low} is the number of cores sharing the cache at level $k-1$ and $totalcache_{low}$ is the total number of cache lines in the level $k-1$ cache. It is to be noted that, we are determining the threshold T_1 in a conservative manner, i.e., the probability of accesses with reuse distance less than T_1 being a hit in the lower level cache is very high. T_1's value is computed with the insight that shared cache contention is proportional to the number of contending cores. However, the effect of contention can be quite non-uniform at extreme reuse distances, thereby, creating a band of values where T_1 might lie. The tunable parameter α is used to fix the value of T_1 using a very conservative estimation as mentioned above. We later present the chosen value and a sensitivity analysis on α.

- *ow reuse distance (LRD).* We characterize the fraction of the level k cache accesses that have a relatively low reuse distance and therefore have a high possibility of being hits in the level k cache as the "low reuse distance" accesses, $LRD_k = \frac{\Sigma_{R=T_1}^{T_2} f(R)}{\Sigma_{R=T_1}^{T_\infty} f(R)}$, where T_1 is defined as before and $T_2 = (\frac{1}{n} - \beta \times \frac{1}{n}) \times totalcache$. It is highly likely that the accesses with reuse distance between T_1 and T_2 are going to be hits in the current level (level k). Applications with very high LRD values exhibit very good locality due to a high percentage of low reuse accesses which are likely to be hits even in the presence of high contention. T_1 and T_2 are shown in Figure **??**. Again, β is a parameter similar

to α that helps tune T_2 conservatively based on the effects of contention at reuse distance extremes.

- *edium reuse distance (MRD).* Medium reuse distance (MRD) parameter estimates the fraction of level k cache accesses that can be either hits or misses depending on other contending applications (i.e., applications running on cores belonging to core subset S). We define MRD as:

$$MRD_k = \frac{\Sigma_{R=T_2}^{T_3} f(R)}{\Sigma_{R=T_1}^{T_\infty} f(R)}, \text{ where } T_2 = (\frac{1}{n} - \beta \times \frac{1}{n}) \times totalcache$$

and $T_3 = (\frac{1}{n} + \alpha \times \frac{1}{n}) \times totalcache$. Note here that, MRD is an estimation of the extent to which an application can be affected by contention from other applications. When contention from other applications running on core subset S is high, these accesses are likely to be misses. On the flipside, when the contention is low, these will likely be cache hits at cache level k. Again, this is a conservative estimate, and T_2 and T_3 are shown in Figure **??**.

- *igh reuse distance (HRD).* When the reuse distance of an access is very high, it is likely going to result in a cache miss. High reuse distance (HRD) parameter estimates the fraction of level k cache accesses that fall under this category. We define HRD as: $HRD_k = \frac{\Sigma_{R=T_3}^{T_\infty} f(R)}{\Sigma_{R=T_1}^{T_\infty} f(R)}$, where $T_3 = (\frac{1}{n} + \alpha \times \frac{1}{n}) \times totalcache$. HRD includes all the accesses which are going to be cold misses and also accesses that have very high reuse distance. When an application runs alone on core c_i with no other contending applications running on other $cores \in S$, then an access with a reuse distance greater than $totalcache$ will very likely be a miss. In the presence of other contending applications, instead of $totalcache$, we use a threshold T_3, which conservatively estimates the fraction of the effective cache space available to this application.

- *otal k le el accesses (TotAcc).* This is the total number of accesses to the kth level cache. Therefore, $TotAcc$ for the kth level cache is defined as: $TotAcc_k = \Sigma_{R=T_1}^{T_\infty} f(R)$.

5.3 Performance Effects

We now use the above defined parameters to characterize the cache performance of an application in the context of a multicore environment. We present two kinds of characterizations, namely, a "fixed threshold" characterization and a "probabilistic threshold estimation" scheme.

5.3.1 Fixed Thresholds

In this approach, we consider the reuse distance distribution of an application in isolation and estimate its performance effects when it executes in a multicore environment with a shared cache hierarchy. To that end, we define two metrics, namely, *Hindrance Factor* and *Susceptibility Factor*, for each application. Since both these metrics are defined using the parameters defined in Section **??**, they are for a particular level and size of cache.

- **Hindrance Factor.** Hindrance factor of an application estimates the extent to which an application might adversely affect the performance of other contending companion applications. For instance, consider two applications, app_a and app_b, running on two cores with a shared L2 cache. Hindrance factor of application app_a measures the extent to which the cache performance of application app_b is adversely affected due to the contention created by application app_a. We define the hindrance factor of an application (HF) at level k as: $HF_k = HRD_k \times \frac{TotAcc_k}{time}$, where HRD_k and $TotAcc$ are obtained from the reuse distance distribution of an application (as described in Section **??**) and, $time$ is the memory access sampling duration in terms of cycles. If the time of sampling is t sec and frequency of the cores is f Hz, then $time = t \times f$. The hindrance factor measures the number of cache accesses with very high reuse distance

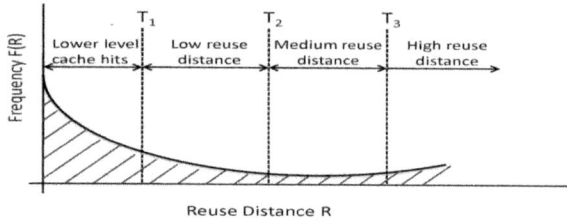

Figure 9: Reuse distance distribution of a sample application epoch with different thresholds.

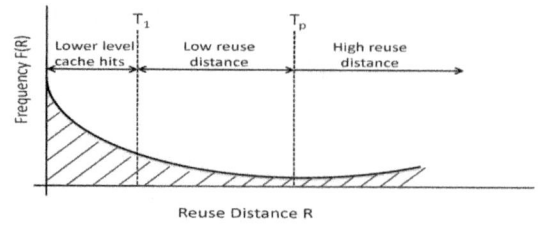

Figure 10: Reuse distance distribution and the probabilistic threshold T_p.

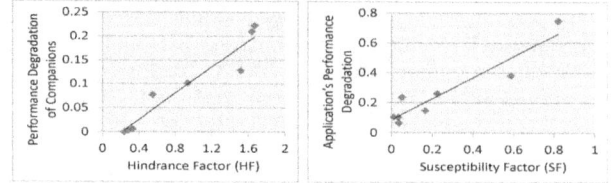

Figure 11: (a) shows the correlation of HF with the performance degradation of the companion applications, and (b) shows the correlation of SF with the application's own performance degradation. The data points represent different applications.

per cycle. Therefore, it approximates the number of misses possible per cycle. *HF is actually an esti ate o the rate at hich an application rings in ne data cache lines into the cache* An application with very high HF value is likely to bring in a large number of cache lines to the cache and, therefore, is likely to occupy more space in the shared cache. Also, such an application can interfere and kick out cache lines that belong to other contending applications. Therefore, a high HF value application is likely to adversely affect other applications due to high contention. Interestingly, an application with very high HF value has relatively lower SF (defined shortly) value and, therefore, is not likely to display good behavior (high performance) in presence of low contention from other applications. However, the actual values of HF and SF are necessary for the performance models, and therefore, we consider both HF and SF metrics.

- **Susceptability Factor.** Susceptability factor of an application estimates the extent to which the application's performance can be adversely affected by other contending applications. For instance, as before, consider two applications, app_a and app_b, executing on a pair of cores with a shared L2 cache. Susceptability factor of application app_a measures the extent to which application app_a's performance can be adversely affected by the contending application app_b. More specifically, the susceptability factor of an application (SF) at cache level k is defined as: $SF_k = MRD_k \times \frac{TotAcc_k}{time}$, where MRD_k and $TotAcc$ are obtained from the reuse distance distribution as described in Section **??**, and *time* is defined as in the case of hindrance factor. Recall that, medium reuse distance (MRD) is defined in Section **??** as the accesses with reuse distance which is not very high and therefore can be hits if the contention for the cache is low and could turn out to be misses in the presence of high cache contention. Susceptability factor of an application is a good estimate of how much an application's cache performance can potentially be affected. Therefore, it is important to note that, performance of applications with very high SF values is prone to contention and can easily deteriorate in the presence of high contention. To summarize, our fixed threshold scheme characterizes an application's cache behavior in terms of how much its own performance can be adversely impacted (SF) and how much it can affect the performance of other contending applications (HF).

HF and SF Correlation. We conducted experiments with applications *erl Bzip ro acs Sjeng cc c and i quantu* in order to measure the effectiveness of HF and SF in capturing the performance effects. To compute the correlation of HF with the performance degradation of contending applications, we plot the HF values of different applications versus the performance degradation experienced by the contending applications in Figure **??**(a) (each data point represents an application). The performance degradation is calculated as the percentage degradation from the best case performance and the performance degradation values are averaged over all the applications. We can observe that, the HF metric reflects the trend of performance degradation of the contending applications very

well, with a correlation coefficient of 0.96. Figure **??**(b) plots the SF values of different applications against their own performance degradation due to contending applications. Applications with high SF values suffer a higher performance degradation due to contention than those with lower SF values. The correlation coefficient in this case is 0.94.

5.3.2 Probabilistic Threshold Estimation

The fixed threshold scheme explained above considers an application's reuse distance distribution in *isolation* and estimates its performance effects in the presence of cache contention. To obtain more precise and accurate estimates of the cache performance in presence of contention, we next introduce the "probabilistic threshold estimation" scheme. The probabilistic scheme considers an application's reuse distance distribution and computes a single threshold value using the reuse distance distributions of other contending applications. This new threshold T_p can be used to estimate the cache performance in presence of other contending applications. All accesses with reuse distances below T_p can be classified as hits and those with reuse distances above T_p as misses. Therefore, T_p (shown in Figure **??**) is a single threshold which can predict the cache performance in presence of other contending applications.

Estimation of T_p. Consider an instance of reuse distance n from application app_a. To calculate T_p, we try to estimate the length by which the reuse distance instance of length n gets incremented due to contention from other applications. Although reuse distance is independent of the underlying cache, the reuse distance seen by a particular shared cache is dependent on the other contending applications. Suppose app_a is running on core 0, while another application, app_b, is executing on core 1. Assume further that core 0 and core 1 share a cache at level k. Two accesses by app_a to an element in the shared cache separated by n unique cache line accesses by app_a (reuse distance of n) can be interjected by additional unique cache line accesses by the contending application app_b. Therefore, the actual reuse distance of app_a at the shared cache can be higher than n due to these intervening accesses by app_b. Note that there can be multiple contending applications and this procedure is repeated for each contending application. Using a probabilistic approach, we measure the *expected alue* of the number of such

198

intervening accesses between each pair of unique cache line accesses within the reuse distance of length n. These intervening cache accesses are illustrated in Figure **??**, where we consider two accesses from app_a to cache lines c_i and c_{i+1}. Now, we define the expected value for the number of intervening unique cache accesses from app_b as:

$$I_{c_i,c_{i+1}} = \frac{Total_{app_b}}{Total_{app_a}} \times P(R_b > (i + I_{c_{i-1},c_i}), \text{ where}$$
$$Total_{app_b} = \Sigma_{R=T_1}^{T\infty} f_b(R_b), \ Total_{app_a} = \Sigma_{R=T_1}^{T\infty} f_a(R_a),$$
$$\text{and,} \quad P(R_b > (i + I_{c_{i-1},c_i})) = \frac{\Sigma_{R_b=(i+I_{c_{i-1},c_i})}^{T\infty} f_b(R_b)}{\Sigma_{R_b=T_1}^{T\infty} f_b(R_b)}.$$

Here, $P(R_b > (i + I_{c_{i-1},c_i})$ is the probability of there being an intervening access from app_b with a reuse distance greater than $i + I_{c_{i-1},c_i}$. If the reuse distance is less than $i + I_{c_{i-1},c_i}$, then it will not be a unique access and will not increase the reuse distance of app_a. $\frac{Total_{app_b}}{Total_{app_a}}$, which is the ratio of memory access rates of app_a and app_b, is the total number of probable intervening memory accesses (including non-unique accesses) by app_b. Using the above formulation, we now obtain the new updated reuse distance corresponding to the original reuse distance of length n as $n_{new} = n + \Sigma_1^n I_{c_{i-1},c_i}$. Also, threshold T_p can now be calculated as $T_p = \frac{n}{n_{new}} \times Totalcache_k$, where $Totalcache_k$ is the total number of cache lines at the kth level cache. We next use the threshold value, T_p, to define two metrics:

- *redicted lo reuse hits (PLRH).* The fraction of the accesses that have reuse distances lower than the T_p and hence are predicted to be cache hits at cache level k: $PLRH_k = \frac{\Sigma_{R=T_1}^{T_p} f(R)}{\Sigma_{R=T_1}^{T\infty} f(R)}$.

- *redicted high reuse isses (PHRM).* This is the fraction of the total accesses that have reuse distances greater than T_p. $PHRM$ is the fraction of the accesses that are predicted to be misses: $PHRM_k = \frac{\Sigma_{R=T_p}^{T\infty} f(R)}{\Sigma_{R=T_1}^{T\infty} f(R)}$. As with the case of fixed thresholds, the values of $PLRH$ and $PHRM$ are different for different cache levels and sizes. $PLRH$ and $PHRM$ are used later in the probabilistic application grouping scheme as a basis for grouping the applications.

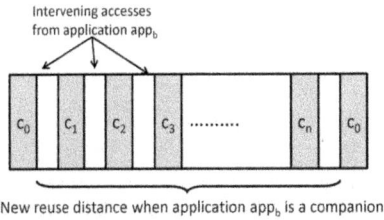

Figure 12: Reuse distance instance of app_a with intervening accesses from app_b.

6. REUSE DISTANCE BASED WORKLOAD MAPPING

Our application-to-core mapping strategy is carried out in two stages. The first stage, called *"application grouping"*, creates groups of applications based on the cache hierarchy tree. The second stage, called the *"group apping"*, maps these groups of applications to subsets of cores available in the target system.

Application Grouping. This stage computes application groups based on the cache hierarchy tree (see Figure **??**). The groups are formed hierarchically by considering each level of the cache hierarchy tree. "Single Level Grouping" algorithm groups the applications into groups considering a given level of cache. The "Hierarchical Grouping" algorithm

---

```
Single_Level_Grouping
  Inputs: k - cache level; T - cache hierarchy tree
    IS - set of elements to be divided into groups
    mem_limit - threshold to characterize cache behavior
  Output: groups - set of groups computed
        //groups is set of subsets of IS, such that,
        g_i, g_j ∈ groups, g_i ∩ g_j = ∅
        and, g_0 ∪ g_1 ∪ ... g_n = IS, where, n = |groups|
  Initialization:
        m - |IS|; num_nodes = number of nodes in T at level k
        group_size = m/num_nodes; groups = {}
  Grouping:
        while (IS ≠ ∅) //until all elements are grouped
            curr_group = {}
            if ∃elem_x ∈ IS, such that,
            HF_k(elem_x) > mem_limit // HF_k- hindrance factor
                first_elem = elem_x
            else
                select elem_y ∈ IS, such that SF_k(elem_x) is max
                where, SF_k is the susceptibility factor.
                first_elem = elem_y
            curr_group = {first_elem},IS = IS - first_elem
            for num ← 1 to group_size:
                if (HF_k(first_elem) > mem_limit)
                    if ∃elem_j ∈ IS,
                    such that, HF_k(elem_j) > mem_limit
                    curr_group = curr_group + elem_j,
                    IS = IS - elem_j
                else:
                    select elem_k ∈ IS, such that, SF_k(elem_k) is min
                    curr_group = curr_group + elem_k,
                    IS = IS - elem_k
                else
                    select elem_j ∈ IS with minimum SF_k(elem_j)
                    curr_group = curr_group + elem_j,
                    IS = IS - elem_j
            end for
            groups = groups + curr_group
        end while
        return groups
```

Figure 13: Single-level grouping algorithm using *fixed thresholds*.

```
Hierarchical_Grouping
  Inputs: AS = {app_0, app_1, .., app_m}, T - cache hierarchy tree
  Output: hgroups - set of groups after hierarchical grouping
        //each hg_i ∈ hgroups can be a set of groups
  Initialization:
        level= k, such that, C_{k-1,k} > 1 and C_{k-2,k-1} = 1
        // level is the lowest shared level in T
        top = root level of the cache hierarchy tree, m = |AS|
  Hierarchical Grouping:
        hgroups_old = IS; hgroups_new = ∅
        while (level < top)
            hgroups_new =
            Single_Level_Grouping(level, hgroups_old, T)
            hgroups_old = hgroups_new; level = parent(level)
            //update level to the parent of the current level in the T
        end while; return hgroups
```

Figure 14: Hierarchical application grouping algorithm.

---

goes through all levels of the cache hierarchy, in the process invoking the single-level-grouping algorithm at each level.

Single Level Grouping. Single-level-grouping algorithm shown in Figure **??** takes an input set, IS, of ele ents and groups the elements into p groups. p is the total number of caches at the cache level k. In other words, p is the number of nodes at level k of the cache hierarchy tree T. The elements in the input set, IS, can be either applications or groups of applications. This is because, before the hierarchical group algorithm invokes the single-level-grouping at some level j, it would have invoked the single-level-grouping at the previous level $j-1$, which would have created groups at level $j-1$. Therefore, at level j, the set of these groups are further clustered into larger groups. We use a heuristic that prunes the search space to a very small space. Our algorithm uses *indrance actor* and *Suscepti ility actor* of applications derived from the reuse distance based parameters (see Section ??) to make grouping decisions. Note that, HF and SF values for the kth level cache are used here (i.e., HF_k and SF_k). This is important because different invocations of the algorithm for different cache levels use different HF and SF values of applications.

The goal of our single level grouping algorithm is to group applications such that the adverse effects of cache contention are mitigated and performance is improved at runtime compared to other possible groupings. The size of the groups to be formed is determined by considering the total number of caches at level k and computing the number of applications per level k cache assuming an equal division of applications.[2] The algorithm starts out by choosing and grouping elements with very high HF value together. For an application, app_a, its HF value, $HF(app_a)$, is classified as "very high" if $HF(app_a) > mem\_limit$. Here, mem_limit is a threshold value chosen such that, applications with $HF > mem\_limit$ adversely affects the performance of the contending applications, especially if the contending applications have a high SF (*suscepti ility actor*). This however is a tunable parameter. The reasoning behind grouping all these "badly behaving" applications together is twofold. Firstly, by quarantining these applications together in a different group, other applications with high SF value and low HF value are not adversely impacted by these applications. The second reason is that these applications have such high HF values that their cache performance will be poor even if they are running alone. In other words, even in case of lesser or no contention, these applications achieve very little performance gain compared to the applications with high SF and low HF values. Therefore, it may make sense to group and schedule them together. Note that, the algorithm may run out of other similar high HF value applications. This is because of the fixed size of groups as mentioned before. In that case, the high HF value application is grouped with an application with the minimum SF value. This is done with the intention that the high HF value application with high contention impacts a low SF value application lesser than a high SF value application. After all the high HF values are grouped, our algorithm starts grouping applications with relatively low HF values. The strategy employed by the algorithm to group these applications is different from that of the very high HF applications. The algorithm tries to group an application with high SF with another application with a low SF value, because a high SF value means that an application has a lot of accesses which can potentially be hits under low contention but can be misses under high contention environment. Therefore, the high SF value application has a higher number of cache hits due to low contention from the other application since it has a lower SF value. Also, the other application with lower SF value anyway has very few accesses, which can be affected by contention and hence is not affected too much by the high SF application. Computation and usage of HF and SF values are a key step in the above algorithm. As we mentioned before, an element of the input set (IS) can be an application or a group of applications. The HF and SF values have an additive property in our algorithm, that is, the HF and SF values of a group of elements will be equal to the sum of the HF and SF values of the elements present in the group.

---

[2]"Size" in this context refers to the number of applications in a group.

7. SINGLE LEVEL GROUPING USING THE PROBABILISTIC SCHEME

This scheme works similar to that shown in Figure ??, except that it uses the *pro a ilistic single threshold esti ation* scheme presented in Section ?? to make grouping decisions. One of the main advantages of this scheme is the fact that it uses a more accurate threshold (see Section ??) to estimate the performance effects in the presence of contention, instead of conservative fixed thresholds.

Hierarchical Grouping. The previous section described the grouping of applications in a cache-sharing aware manner but considering cache sharing at a given single level in the cache hierarchy. Figure ?? describes our approach that computes application groupings based on all levels of the cache hierarchy. This algorithm hierarchically groups applications by calling single level grouping algorithm (Figure ??) at each level of the cache hierarchy tree. This grouping scheme starts from the first shared level of cache and hierarchically groups the applications at each level until the root of the hierarchy tree, T, is reached.

Mapping Groups to Cores. Once the hierarchical application groups have been created, the applications in these groups are mapped to cores based on their groups and the sharing degree of the subsets of cores. This mapping algorithm takes the grouping determined by the hierarchical grouping algorithm as input and starts assigning these groups to cache nodes at each level of the hierarchy. The mapping begins with the root node of the cache hierarchy tree and proceeds downwards till the leaf node level, at which point the determined grouping is assigned to the cores.

8. ILLUSTRATION

Figure ?? shows an illustration of how our mapping approach works in practice. The hierarchical grouping algorithm starts out at the bottom level (leaf node level) and moves to towards the root, calling the single-level-grouping algorithm at each level on the way. The grouping returned by our single-level-grouping algorithm at each level is shown in Figure ??. The mapping algorithm takes the generated grouping as input and traverses from the root to the leaf node level of the tree, assigning groups to cache nodes at each level. When the private cache level is reached, the assignment is complete.

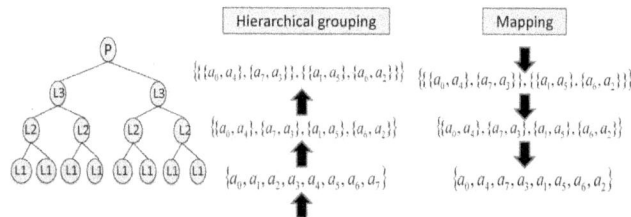

Figure 18: Illustration of the grouping and mapping steps.

9. EXPERIMENTAL EVALUATION

The experimental setup and the methodology described in Section ?? are used in all of the experiments. In order to build the reuse distance profiles, the applications were sampled for 100 million instructions. After preliminary experiments, we selected the values of α and β parameters (mentioned in Section ??) to be 0.3 and 0.2, respectively, and set the value of mem_limit (mentioned in Section ??) to 1.

Average Results. We evaluated the performance of our proposed hierarchical mapping scheme using 12 randomly

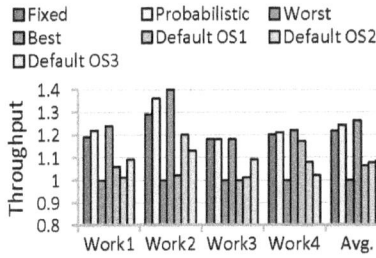

Figure 15: Throughput comparison for four representative workloads and the average case (over all 12 workloads) on the eight-core CMP shown in Figure ??.

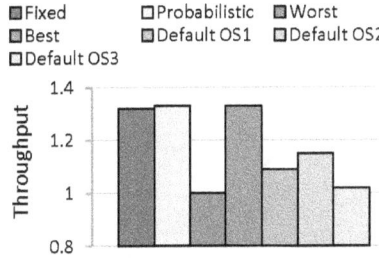

Figure 16: Throughput comparison on the eight-core CMP shown in Figure ??, when different combinations of perl, bzip, gromacs, sjeng, gcc, mcf, lbm and libq are executed.

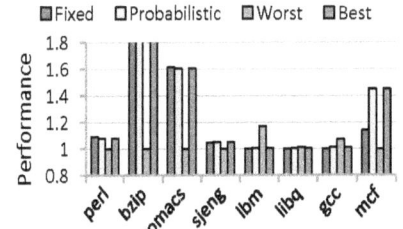

Figure 17: Performance comparison of applications on the eight-core CMP shown in Figure ??, when different combinations of perl, bzip, gromacs, sjeng, gcc, mcf, lbm and libq are executed.

selected workloads built using applications from the SPEC 2006 benchmark suite [?]. Figure ?? presents the throughput comparison of our proposed schemes over the best case mapping, worst case mapping and three different runs of the default OS scheduling scheme for four representative workloads. In this paper, by throughput, we always refer to IPC throughput unless otherwise mentioned. Figure ?? also plots the average throughput comparison (averaged over all 12 workloads). The workloads considered here are $Work1=\{Sphinx \quad ilc \quad i \quad quantu \quad o \quad k \quad - er \quad Bzip \quad erl\}$, $Work2=\{ \quad ro \quad acs \quad 6 \quad er \quad c \quad Sphinx \quad o \quad k \quad erl\}$, $Work3=\{Sjeng \quad o \quad k \quad cc \quad c \quad i \quad quantu \quad erl \quad Bzip\}$ and $Work4=\{ \quad er \quad Sphinx \quad Sjeng \quad erl \quad i \quad quantu \quad Bzip \quad o \quad k\}$. The probabilistic scheme finds a better mapping than the fixed threshold scheme in the case of $Work1$ and $Work2$, while they find the same mapping for the other workloads. For $Work3$ and $Work4$, our proposed scheme finds the best possible mapping, while in the case of the other sets, mapping computed by our proposed scheme is within 4% of the best case mapping. Also, mappings computed by our scheme are up to about 40% (average of 25%) better than the worst case mapping in terms of system throughput. In the above experiment, the best case and worst case mappings are determined by trying out all possible combinations of mappings. For the default OS based scheme, we run the applications on the eight-core system and do not bind the applications to cores. Interestingly, since the OS does not consider the cache hierarchy and schedules applications randomly (with respect to cache hierarchy awareness), different runs of the OS based scheme yield different mappings and hence, different results. In order to demonstrate this, we run the default OS based scheme multiple times.

Workload Instance. In order to analyze the performance impact of our proposed scheme on both the workload throughput and the individual application performance, we consider a single workload comprised of $erl \quad Bzip \quad ro- acs \quad Sjeng \quad cc \quad c$ and $i \quad quantu$ applications. Figure ?? shows the throughput achieved by the fixed threshold scheme and the probabilistic threshold scheme alongside the best case mapping, the worst case mapping, and the default OS based mapping. One can observe from these results that, the fixed threshold scheme achieves performance benefits of about 32% over the worst case mapping and up to 30% over the default OS mapping. The probabilistic scheme finds the best possible mapping, which yields performance benefits of about 33% over the worst case mapping. In Figure ??, we show the performance of the individual applications under different schemes. Note that, we do not show the individual application performances in the OS based scheme.

This is because, since in the OS based scheme we do not bind the applications to cores, it is hard to determine which application runs on which core. One can see from Figure ?? that, $Bzip$ and ro acs can significantly improve their performance when a good application-to-core mapping is employed. This is because they have a very high SF values. erl and $Sjeng$ can also perform better when the mapping is good. An important point to note here is that, in this case, both the fixed threshold and the probabilistic threshold schemes find the best possible mapping.

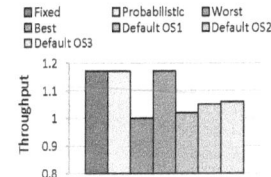

Figure 19: Throughput comparison on a 12-core CMP.

10. SENSITIVITY EXPERIMENTS

We conducted experiments on a twelve core CMP, where each pair of cores share an L2 cache and each group of six cores share an L3 cache. Each L2 cache is 512 KB (8 way associative) and each L3 cache (shared by 6 cores) is 6 MB in size. The twelve applications run in this experiment are $erl \quad Bzip \quad ro \quad acs \quad o \quad k \quad Sjeng \quad er \quad Sphinx \quad cc \quad c \quad ilc \quad i \quad quantu$ and . Figure ?? present the throughput results in this case. Our scheme outperforms the worst case mapping by about 17% in terms of the overall system throughput.

We then repeated the eight-core experiments mentioned above with larger on-chip caches (1MB L2s and 4MB L3s). Our scheme outperformed the worst case mapping by about 17% and the default OS mappings by around 7%.

11. DISCUSSION OF RELATED WORK

There have been research efforts aimed at predicting cache contention in terms of performance degradation due to cache contention [?, ?]. Song et al. model the L2 cache behavior for a set of scientific applications on CMPs [?]. Federova et al. propose an L2 cache aware scheduling algorithm based on metrics such as missrate [?]. Xie et al. aim to make a broad characterization of programs at runtime using metrics such as miss rate [?]. Gang scheduling of threads of parallel jobs concurrently provides performance benefits as proposed by

Jette et al [?]. Bulpin et al. propose to use hardware performance counters to bind threads to processors. [?] and [?] aim to find a symbiotic job schedule which runs well together after trying out different combinations. DeVuyst and Tullsen propose an unbalanced scheduling scheme that yields power and performance benefits [?]. Federova et al. propose a scheduling algorithm to improve performance isolation [?]. [?] proposes OS enhancements that use hardware monitors to improve the capabilities of OS to manage CMP resources. In [?], performance degradation among different combinations of applications is estimated and a co-scheduling scheme is proposed using these estimated degradation values. Tam et al. propose to cluster threads based on the data sharing between them [?] when the threads of a single application can share data. Chen et al. also propose to schedule threads for constructive cache sharing [?]. In [?], Zhang et al argue that when threads belong to the same application, alternate schedules do not enhance cache sharing. Reuse distance analysis has been studied extensively in the context of single, sequential execution [?, ?, ?]. In [?], Beyls et al. show that reuse distance analysis of a sequential execution can reflect its cache performance in terms of miss rate very accurately even in the presence of associativity. There have also been proposals to efficiently calculate reuse distance distributions [?]. In [?], authors try to maintain multiple reuse stacks in the case of CMPs to gather reuse distances. Some of the prior works mentioned above try to measure cache contention when there are two cores sharing a cache [?], while others try to compute contention aware schedules [?]. There has been *no* prior work however to model the performance effects in detail when there are *multiple levels in the cache hierarchy* and multiple associated cores, where different subsets of cores can have different degrees of sharing. There have been efforts to find near-optimal schedules which assume the knowledge of performance degradation between different combinations of applications [?]. The problem with such schemes is that, not only is computing such performance degradation values difficult but also the fact that these performance degradation values depend on the cache structure. For a given architecture with a particular hierarchical cache-structure, our work models in detail the effect of cache contention and cache interference at different levels of the cache hierarchy using the reuse distance profiles of the individual applications. Our scheme then uses these models to compute a smart workload mapping.

12. CONCLUSION AND FUTURE WORK

In this paper, we showed that the reuse distance analysis is very effective in predicting the performance effects of an application when it is executed with other contending applications. Based on our reuse distance based performance modeling, we then studied a workload mapping strategy targeting CMPs with hierarchical caches. This strategy is very effective in choosing a good mapping with performance benefits of up to 39% over the worst-case mapping and up to 30% over the default OS based mapping. As part of our future work, we intend to study a runtime scheme that can perform our workload mapping scheme dynamically during execution.

13. REFERENCES

[1] http://www.intel.com/p/en_US/products/server/processor/xeon7000?iid=servproc+body_xeon7400subtitle
[2] http://www.dell.com/us/en/enterprise/servers/server-poweredge-r900/pd.aspx?refid=server-poweredge-r900&cs=555&s=biz
[3] http://www.spec.org/spec2006.
[4] G. Almasi et al. Calculating Stack Distances Efficiently. In *Workshop on emory System erformance*, 2002.
[5] R. Azimi et al. Enhancing operating system support for multicore processors by using hardware performance monitoring. In *S S per Syst e*, 2009.
[6] K. Beyls et al. Reuse distance as a metric for cache behavior. In *S*, 2001.
[7] J. R. Bulpin et al. Hyper-threading aware process scheduling heuristics. In *Usenix nnual echnical on erence*, 2005.
[8] G. Cascaval et al. Estimating Cache Misses and Locality Using Stack Distances. In *S*, 2003.
[9] D. Chandra et al. Predicting Inter-Thread Cache Contention on a Chip Multi-Processor Architecture. In *, 2005.
[10] S. Chen et al. Scheduling threads for constructive cache sharing on CMPs. In *S*, 2007.
[11] M. DeVuyst et al. Exploiting unbalanced thread scheduling for energy and performance on a CMP of SMT processors. In *S*, 2006.
[12] A. Fedorova et al. CASC: A Cache-Aware Scheduler For Multithreaded Chip Multiprocessors. In *Sun echnical eport*, 2005.
[13] A. Fedorova et al. Improving performance isolation on chip multiprocessors via an operating system scheduler. In *, 2007.
[14] R. Hetherington. In *he UltraSparc processor*. SUN, 2005.
[15] M. A. Jette et al. Performance characteristics of gang scheduling in multiprogrammed environments. In *Super o puting*, 1997.
[16] Y. Jiang et al. Analysis and approximation of optimal co-scheduling on chip multiprocessors. In *, 2008.
[17] P. S. Magnusson and et al. Simics : A full system simulation platform. In *o puter 3 ( ) - , 2002.
[18] E. P. Markatos et al. Locality-Based Scheduling for Shared-Memory Multiprocessors. In *arallel o puting aradig s and pplications*, 1993.
[19] F. Song et al. L2 Cache Modeling for Scientific Applications on Chip Multi-Processors. In *, 2007.
[20] D. Schuff et al. Multicore aware reuse distance analysis. In *urdue echnical eport*, 2009.
[21] A. Snavely. Symbiotic jobscheduling for a simultaneous multithreaded processor. In *S S*, 2000.
[22] A. Snavely. Symbiotic jobscheduling with priorities for a simultaneous multithreaded processor. In *S S er or al e*, 2002.
[23] D. Tam et al. Thread clustering: sharing-aware scheduling on SMP-CMP-SMT multiprocessors. In *uroSys*, 2007.
[24] C. Wu et al. Characterization and Dynamic Mitigation of Intra-Application Cache Interference. In *S SS*, 2011.
[25] Y. Xie et al. Dynamic classification of program memory behaviors in CMPs. In *- S (in conjunction ith S)*, 2008.
[26] S. Zhuravlev et al. Addressing shared resource contention in multicore processors via scheduling. In *S S*, 2010.
[27] E.Z. Zhang et al. Does cache sharing on modern CMP matter to the performance of contemporary multithreaded programs? In *o*, 2010.
[28] Platform 2015: Intel Processor and Platform Evolution for the Next Decade. *ntel White aper*, 2005.

The Boat Hull Model: Enabling Performance Prediction for Parallel Computing Prior to Code Development

Cedric Nugteren   Henk Corporaal
Eindhoven University of Technology, The Netherlands
http://parse.ele.tue.nl/
{c.nugteren, h.corporaal}@tue.nl

ABSTRACT

Multi-core and many-core were already major trends for the past six years and are expected to continue for the next decade. With these trends of parallel computing, it becomes increasingly difficult to decide on which processor to run a given application, mainly because the programming of these processors has become increasingly challenging.

In this work, we present a model to predict the performance of a given application on a multi-core or many-core processor. Since programming these processors can be challenging and time consuming, our model does not require source code to be available for the target processor. This is in contrast to existing performance prediction techniques such as mathematical models and simulators, which require code to be available and optimized for the target architecture.

To enable performance prediction prior to algorithm implementation, we classify algorithms using an existing *algorithm classification*. For each class, we create a specific instance of the *roofline model*, resulting in a new class-specific model. This new model, named the *boat hull model*, enables performance prediction and processor selection prior to the development of architecture specific code.

We demonstrate the boat hull model using GPUs and CPUs as target architectures. We show that performance is accurately predicted for an example real-life application.

Categories and Subject Descriptors

C.1.4 [**Processor Architectures**]: Parallel Architectures;
C.4 [**Performance of Systems**]: Modeling Techniques

General Terms

Performance

Keywords

Parallel Computing, Performance Prediction, The Roofline Model, GPU, CPU

CF'12, May 15–17, 2012, Cagliari, Italy.
Copyright 2012 ACM 978-1-4503-1215-8/12/05 ...$10.00.

1. INTRODUCTION

For the past five decades, single-processor performance has shown an exponential growth, enabling technology to become pervasive and ubiquitous in our society. This exponential growth ended in 2004, limited by two aspects: 1) it became unfeasible to increase clock frequencies because of power dissipation problems, and 2), processor architecture improvements have seen a diminishing impact [9]. To re-enable performance growth, parallelism is exploited. Enabled by Moore's law, more processors per chip (i.e. multicore) was already a major trend for the past six years and is expected to continue for the next decades [7]. While multicore is expected to enable 100-core processors by 2020 [7], another trend (many-core) already yields more than 2000 cores per chip, enabled by using much simpler processing elements. An example of such a many-core processor is the Graphics Processing Unit (GPU).

These trends (multi-core and many-core) make processor selection increasingly challenging. Which processor to use for a given application set is far from trivial. It is simply not feasible anymore to port an application to all target candidate processors. This is caused by two factors. Firstly, the search space has expanded, as both multi-core and many-core processors co-exist in one system or even on a single chip [12]. Secondly, it has become increasingly challenging and time consuming to program such processors [12].

To solve this problem of processor selection, we argue that a performance prediction method which does not require code to be available is desirable. This is in contrast to existing performance prediction techniques such as mathematical models or simulators, which do require code to be available and optimized for a target processor.

In this work we present the *boat hull model*. We use an existing *algorithm classification* to classify algorithms. Then, for each class, we adapt the *roofline model* [21] to include class information. In this way, we generate multiple rooflines, each specific for an algorithm class. We present an example application to demonstrate the new model. Although we focus in this work on the domains of image processing and computer vision, we believe that the concepts of the boat hull model can be extended to other domains.

The remainder of this paper is organized as follows. First, in sections 2 and 3, we present related work and background information respectively. Following, in section 4, we introduce the boat hull model. In section 5, we evaluate the work by predicting the performance of an example real-life application with the new model. Finally, we discuss future work in section 6 and conclude in section 7.

2. RELATED WORK

In this work, we present a new method to perform performance prediction. In this section we therefore discuss related work on performance prediction techniques. Additionally, since we base our work on an algorithm classification, we discuss existing algorithm classification methods.

2.1 Performance prediction methods

Traditionally, performance prediction is achieved using analytical performance models or detailed hardware simulators. For many-core architectures such as the GPU, multiple detailed performance models (e.g. [2], [11] and [19]) and hardware simulators (e.g. [3]) exist. These performance prediction techniques are both based on detailed knowledge of the hardware architecture and on the presence of optimized code for the target architecture, both of which we assume not to be present in our work.

In recent work, performance was predicted for a Convey HC-1 processor using an idiom recognizer tool [6]. This tool analyzes reference source code to find *idioms* and predicts performance based on the presence of these idioms. Similar to the goals of our work, their tool does not require code to be available for the target architecture. However, in contrast to our work, their work does not target multi-core CPUs and GPUs, is based on limited algorithm classes (or: idioms), does not provide an insightful visual model, and does require the presence of reference code.

2.2 Algorithm classification methods

Many variations of algorithm classifications have been introduced as part of work on *algorithmic skeletons* [8], for example [4]. In [5], a survey of 10 different classifications is presented. They include on average 4 classes, with *divide and conquer*, *pipeline*, and *farm* being the most common among all 10 classifications. These types of classes distinguish algorithms at a coarse-grained level, while we use a much finer-grained classification in this work.

Classifications for other purposes exist, such as *dwarfs*, *computational patterns* [1], and *design patterns* [13]. These even less detailed classifications introduce classes as a scheme to capture solutions for recurring design problems in systematic ways. They are intended to be used in natural language rather than with automated tools.

Another existing algorithm classification intended to be used for algorithmic skeletons is the classification presented in [15]. This classification does distinguish algorithms at a fine granularity, and is therefore used in this work. An overview of this classification is presented in section 3.2.

3. BACKGROUND AND MOTIVATION

We base our work on the *roofline model* an on an existing algorithm classification, which we both introduce in this section as background information. Additionally, we motivate the approach taken in this work.

3.1 The roofline model

Performance prediction and bottleneck analysis are two topics that have become increasingly important for heterogeneous and parallel computing. The roofline model was introduced as an easy to understand performance model capable of identifying performance bottlenecks [21]. This model gives a rough performance estimate based on the assumption

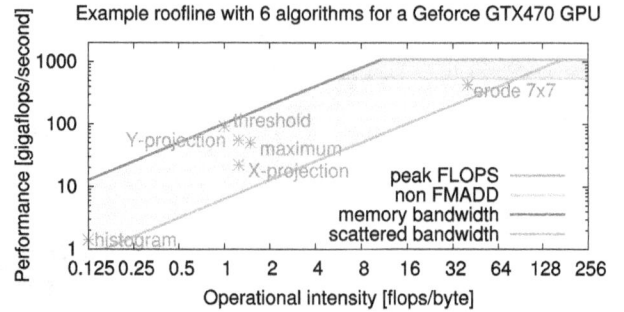

Figure 1: Applying the roofline model to an example GPU. The red stars represent the measured performance of example algorithms.

that performance is limited either by peak memory bandwidth or by peak ALU throughput. The roofline model is processor specific: for each processor there is a specific instance of the model.

In the roofline model, performance is measured in operations per second, which will either be memory bound or compute bound, dependent on an application's operational intensity (given in operations per byte). Because not every application will reach the peak performance (and thus the *roof* of the model), multiple *ceilings* can be added, denoted by properties such as limited instruction level parallelism or scattered memory accesses. These properties make the model suitable for bottleneck analysis and guidance during application development.

To illustrate the use of the roofline model, we map 6 example algorithms onto the roofline model for a GeForce GTX470 GPU. The results are shown in figure 1. The location of each algorithm is based on two aspects: 1) the performance of a CUDA implementation executed on the GPU, and 2), the operational intensity in ALU operations per off-chip load/store.

We observe two obstacles if we want to use this model to predict performance: 1) the execution time is not directly visible, and 2), the range of the predicted performance is very wide. For example, as shown in figure 1, the performance of the X-projection algorithm is a factor 7 beneath the memory bandwidth roof.

3.2 Algorithm classification

In [15], a well-defined fine-grained algorithm classification is introduced. The granularity of such a classification is of high importance for the applicability. When using the classification for performance prediction, a finer-grained classification might yield a more accurate prediction. On the other hand, if the classification is coarser-grained, it can be easier to use and to understand. The classification presented in [15] finds a solution to this trade-off by introducing a modular and parameterisable classification. This enables a fine-grained classification, while using a limited vocabulary.

We briefly illustrate the classification by giving four example code snippets and their corresponding classes. These examples, shown in listing 1, are classified as follows:

- In lines 1-2 a vector of size K is element-wise multiplied, incremented, and stored as another vector. Since every *element* of the input corresponds to an *element* of the output and the vector size is K, we classify this code snippet as 'K|element → K|element'.

- The for-loop in lines 4-5 performs a similar operation, but now also requires two *neighbours* to compute one output *element*. The classification becomes 'K|neighbourhood(3) → K|element', since the neighbourhood is of size 3 (including the element itself).

- Similar to the code snippet in lines 1-2, the code in lines 7-12 performs an *element* to *element* computation. However, in this case, we process two dimensional matrices of size 10 by 10. The code is therefore classified as '10x10|element → 10x10|element'.

- The final snippet (lines 14-15) processes the input per *element*, but stores the result in a *shared* output. It is therefore classified as 'K|element → 1|shared', with 1 being the size of the output.

The algorithm classification captures both the parallelism as well as the data access dependencies. Further details and more code examples can be found in [15].

```
1   for(i=0; i<K; i=i+1)
2     B[i] = 2 * A[i] + 5;
3
4   for(i=0; i<K; i=i+1)
5     B[i] = 0.3*A[i-1] + 0.4*A[i] + 0.3*A[i+1];
6
7   for(a=0; a<10; a=a+1)
8     for(b=0; b<10; b=b+1)
9       value = A[a][b];
10      if(value > 255)
11        value = 255;
12      B[a][b] = value;
13
14  for(i=0; i<K; i=i+1)
15    B = B + A[i];
```

Listing 1: Four example code snippets of different algorithm classes.

4. THE BOAT HULL MODEL

Selecting which processor architecture is best suited for a given application can be done using architecture models or hardware simulators. These methods do however require the presence of optimized target architecture code, which is often not available before selecting a processor. Although not designed for this purpose, the roofline model does give an indication of the expected performance without requiring code, but falls short when an application's compute or data-access patterns are non-ideal. To enable performance prediction prior to algorithm implementation, we introduce a modified version of the roofline model based on the algorithm classification presented in [15].

The modified model, referred to as the boat hull model, makes the following changes to the roofline model in order to enable performance prediction:

- With use of the classification, the roofs and the ceilings of the roofline model can be fine-tuned to match the properties of a specific class. Because the amount of off-chip data accesses is inherent to a class-architecture combination, the metric on the horizontal axis of the model can be changed from 'operations per byte' into 'complexity': the number of operations given for a class' operator $f()$ (see [15]).

- Since application developers are primarily concerned about execution time, the metric on the vertical axis of the model is changed from 'flops per second' into 'execution time', as is also briefly mentioned in [20]. In combination with the change of the metric on the horizontal axis, we create an inverse view of the roofline model, resembling the cross section of a boat's hull.

Furthermore, for accelerators such as the GPU, data transfer time between the accelerator and a host processor can influence whether or not to run an application on such an accelerator. Therefore, the boat hull model is extended to include data transfer cost between different processors. Moreover, we can now enable performance prediction of a complete application by combining multiple computational parts of an application with host-accelerator data transfer.

In this section, we discuss the boat hull model. We first give two toy examples to illustrate the model. Following, we introduce and validate the boat hull model for both NVIDIA GPUs and Intel CPUs. We shortly discuss our corresponding tool, and finally evaluate the new model. In this section, we use the notation *primitive* to refer to a computational intensive part of an algorithm (i.e. *kernel*).

4.1 Code examples

To get an intuitive feel for the boat hull model, we discuss two toy examples. We take two out of the four examples from listing 1 and use an NVIDIA GPU as a target processor architecture. We set up two bounds for these code snippets: the memory bound and the compute bound. The largest of these will set the performance bound in terms of execution time. In these examples, we use the notation $P_{compute}$ to denote the theoretical peak architecture limitation for ALU performance in operations per second, and $P_{coalesced}$ and $P_{uncoalesced}$ to denote the practical peak memory performance in bytes per second, for respectively sequential and scattered memory accesses. We assume individual data elements to be 32-bit (4 byte) large in these examples.

- In lines 1-2, K elements are read and as many are written to background memory in a coalesced fashion. If we divide the amount of bytes accessed by the peak bandwidth, we obtain the execution time in the case that the snippet is memory bound: $\frac{2 \cdot K \cdot 4}{P_{coalesced}}$. To obtain the compute bound, we divide the amount of operations by the peak compute rate. Implementing every iteration of the loop as a thread, we perform 2 operations per thread, plus an offset to calculate among others the array index. With K iterations, this results in: $\frac{K \cdot (2 + offset)}{P_{compute}}$.

- The example in lines 14-15 reads K elements coalesced, but writes the result uncoalesced. The memory bound becomes in this case: $\frac{K \cdot 4}{P_{coalesced}} + \frac{1 \cdot 4}{P_{uncoalesced}}$. The compute bound is similar to the snippet from lines 1-2, but now performs only 1 operation. On a GPU, a parallel reduction tree is used, which causes a certain overhead. This is taken into account using the *offset* variable: $\frac{K \cdot (1 + offset)}{P_{compute}}$.

In order to determine whether the code snippet is compute or memory bound and to find the predicted execution time, we evaluate both equations and identify the one that gives us the highest execution time.

Table 1: Example classes and their corresponding parameters for a GPU boat hull model. The table lists for each class an example from the domain of image processing. The expressions for α_i and β_i for neighbourhood-based classes are left out for readability.

class	example primitive	w	m	o	d	c	u	floors
AxB|element $\rightarrow$ AxB|element	binarization	A·B	1	16	2·A·B	d	0	c_1
unordered AxB|element $\rightarrow$ AxB|element	xy-mirroring	A·B	1	16	2·A·B	d	0	c_1 and m_1
AxB|tile(1xB) $\rightarrow$ A|element	x-projection	A	B	$4 \cdot m$	A·B+A	d	0	c_1 and m_1
AxB|tile(UxV) $\rightarrow \frac{A}{U}x\frac{B}{V}$|element	scale down	$\frac{A}{U}x\frac{B}{V}$	U·V	$4 \cdot m$	2·A·B	d	0	c_1
AxB|tile(UxV) $\rightarrow$ AxB|tile(UxV)	2D-DCT	$\frac{A}{U}x\frac{B}{V}$	U·V	$4 \cdot m$	2·A·B	A·B	A·B	c_1
AxB|element $\rightarrow$ A·UxB·V|tile(UxV)	enlarge	$\frac{A}{U}x\frac{B}{V}$	U·V	$4 \cdot m$	2·A·B	d	0	c_1
AxB|neighbourhood(NxM) $\rightarrow$ AxB|element	2D-convolution	A·B	N·M	64	2·A·B	$d+\alpha_1$	β_1	c_1
AxB|neighbourhood(N) $\rightarrow$ AxB|element	1D-convolution	A·B	N	64	2·A·B	$d+\alpha_2$	β_2	c_1
AxB|element $\rightarrow$ 1|shared	sum	A·B	1	16	A·B+1	A·B	1	c_1
AxB|element $\rightarrow$ C|shared	histogram	A·B	1	64	A·B+N	N	A·B	c_1
AxB|element $\wedge$ AxB|element $\rightarrow$ AxB|element	differencing	A·B	1	32	3·A·B	d	0	c_1

4.2 The boat hull model for example classes

In this section, we introduce the boat hull model for 11 example classes, which we present in table 1. These classes are taken from [15] and are defined in more detail in [15]. To introduce the boat hull model, we take NVIDIA GPUs as example target processors. A similar approach can be taken for other processors.

Analogous to the roofline model, we define a compute equation (c_0) and a memory equation (m_0). While these equations represented theoretical roofs in the roofline model, they represent performance predictions in terms of execution time in the boat hull model. These equations additionally contain class-dependent variables (w, m, o, c, and u) in order to create a distinguished model per class. The equations further depend on the amount of operations performed on input data, defined as the complexity of the operator $f()$, which in turn is defined as part of the classification. For an NVIDIA GPU, we define these equations as:

$$c_0 = \frac{w \cdot (f_{complexity} \cdot m + o)}{P_{compute}} \quad \text{(Compute equation)}$$

$$m_0 = \frac{c}{P_{coalesced}} + \frac{u}{P_{uncoalesced}} \quad \text{(Memory equation)}$$

Similar to the roofline model, performance is either compute bound (by c_0) or memory bound (by m_0). Therefore, to find the execution time, we take the maximum value of these equations. The complexity of the operator ($f_{complexity}$) remains variable in these equations, while $P_{compute}$, $P_{coalesced}$ and $P_{uncoalesced}$ represent peak limits of the processor and are constant for a given GPU model. The class-dependent variables (w, m, o, c, and u) are set as shown in table 1 for a number of example classes and are defined as:

w: This represents the amount of parallel **work-units**. For a large number of classes, this is equal to the input data size. In the case of a GPU, w reflects the number of worker-threads which can be spawned and possibly be executed in parallel.

m: A **modifier** for the amount of computations per work-unit. This is used for example for tile and neighbourhood based computations, for which the operator $f()$ is applied multiple times per work-unit. For other classes, m equals 1.

o: The **offset** per work-unit. In the context of GPUs, this can be seen as the class-specific initialization per thread, such as index computation and pre-loading data into on-chip memory. The values for o are estimates obtained experimentally and are rounded to powers of two. The prediction is not very sensitive for this variable: for large values of $f_{complexity}$ o is insignificant (equation c_0) and for small values it is likely that equation c_0 is not used at all (memory bound). The offset is responsible for the curve in the compute equations, as seen later on in figures 2, 3 and 7.

d: The total amount of input plus output **data** to be accessed.

c: Amount of compulsory off-chip memory accesses in a **coalesced** manner (i.e. sequential).

u: The amount of compulsory off-chip memory accesses in an **uncoalesced** manner (i.e. scattered).

For the variables d, c and u, we consider only compulsory memory accesses. Any accesses to local memories in case of data re-use are not added to these variables.

Not all relevant characteristics can be captured by classes, some are still dependent on the operation $f()$ performed. Therefore, we add floors to the boat hull model (similar to ceilings in the roofline model). For a GPU, we define a compute floor (c_1) and a memory floor (m_1). These floors can limit performance, but only for a limited amount of classes. For the example classes, the floors applicable are shown in the last column of table 1. The floors are given as:

$$c_1 = \frac{c_0}{2} \quad \text{(Non fused multiply add)}$$

$$m_1 = \frac{d}{P_{uncoalesced}} \quad \text{(Scattered memory accesses)}$$

To obtain the execution time including host-accelerator data transfers, we have to accumulate the presented equations (c_x and m_x) with CPU-GPU data transfer cost (t_0). We assume a copy-in and a copy-out of all the input and output data over a data bus (e.g. PCI Express). The total data transfer time is dependent on the peak practical bandwidth of the bus (B_{bus}) and the amount of data transferred (the class variable d). The equation for t_0 is as follows:

$$t_0 = \frac{d}{B_{bus}} \quad \text{(Host-accelerator data transfer)}$$

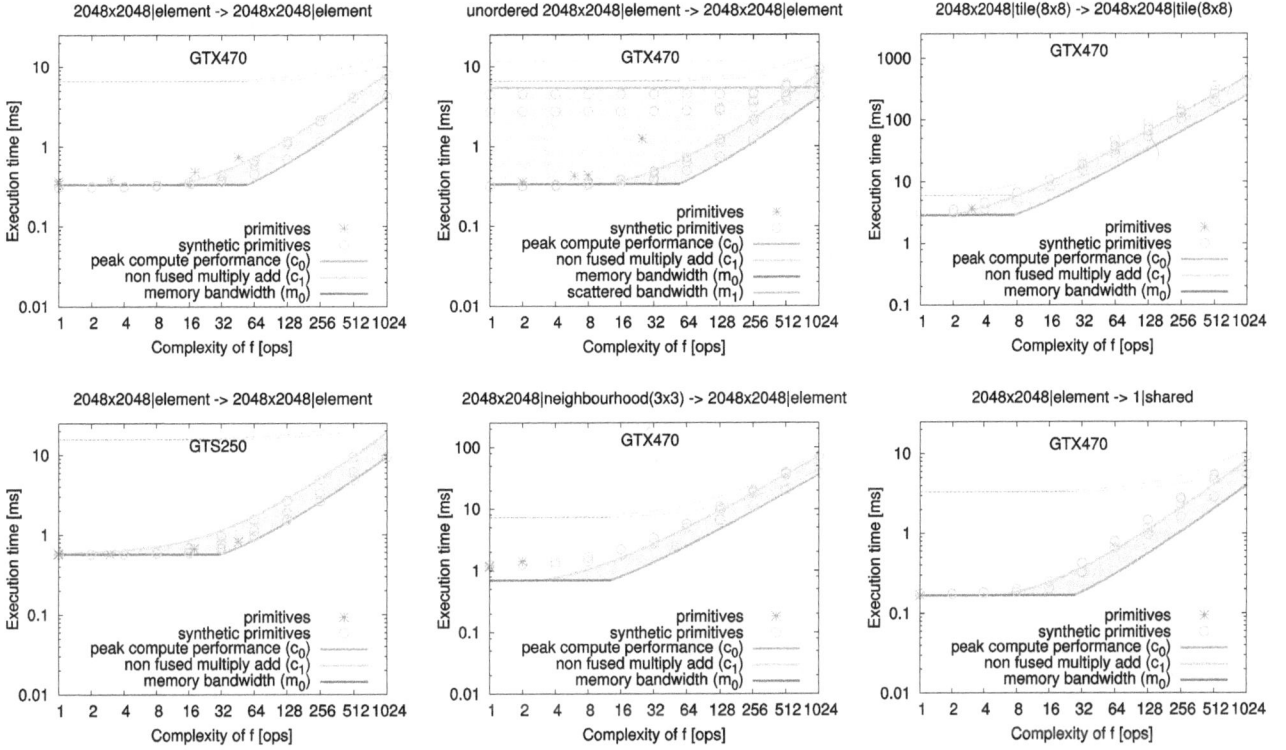

Figure 2: Six examples of the boat hull model applied to GPUs. We show five different classes taken from table 1 for the GTX470 GPU and show one example class for the GTS250 (bottom left). The model is validated against synthetic primitives (orange circles) and real-life examples (red stars). The dashed lines furthermore show the total predicted execution time, including host-accelerator data transfers.

4.3 Validating the boat hull model

To validate the boat hull model, we take primitives from the image processing domain as examples. We target two different GPUs from NVIDIA: a Geforce GTS250 and a GeForce GTX470. The characteristics of these two example GPU models are given in table 2. $P_{compute}$ is obtained from the product specification of the GPUs, while the bandwidth values are obtained using the `bandwidthTest` program supplied by the NVIDIA CUDA SDK [17].

Table 2: Characteristics of two example NVIDIA GPUs, further referred to as GTX470 and GTS250.

	GeForce GTX470	GeForce GTS250
compute capability	sm_20	sm_11
$P_{compute}$	1089 GFLOPS	470 GFLOPS
$P_{coalesced}$	95 GB/s	56 GB/s
$P_{uncoalesced}$	5.9 GB/s	3.5 GB/s
B_{bus}	5.1 GB/s	2.1 GB/s

We show examples of the boat hull model in figure 2 for five different classes[1] taken from table 1. For the class '2048x2048|element → 2048x2048|element', we show a graph for both the GTX470 and the GTS250 GPU. For the other five classes, only the graph for the GTX470 GPU is shown. In figure 2, we show the predicted execution time based on the equations c_0, c_1, m_0 and m_1. To verify correctness of the

model, we add a number of synthetic primitives (orange circles in figure 2) and real-life primitives (red stars in figure 2). The synthetic primitives are artificially constructed and vary in complexity, instruction mix (`add`, `mul`, `fma`) and instruction type (`int`, `float`). For classes with the 'unordered' prefix, they also vary in memory access pattern. The real-life primitives are taken from the image processing domain and contain primitives such as binarization, gamma correction, rotation, xy-mirroring, 2D-DCT, 2D-convolution, adaptive binarization, sum and dilation.

Furthermore, by accumulating c_0, c_1, m_0 and m_1 with the equation for the host-accelerator data transfers (t_0), we achieve a predicted total execution time, including CPU-GPU data transfer. This is given in figure 2 as dashed lines. The colour of the dashed lines is based on the same colour scheme as for the solid lines. Because data transfer is trivial to model and to improve the clarity of the graphs, we show no measurements for the total execution time in figure 2.

We briefly evaluate the results of figure 2 and draw the following conclusions:

- The predicted performance matches the measured performance closely: the measured execution time is either equal or slightly higher compared to the predicted value. The higher execution time can be attributed to the model's simplified view of the architecture.

- The boat hull model's quality is consistent between two different GPU models, even though they have different specifications and architectural properties (e.g.

---

[1]We assume elements to be 32-bit integers in these examples.

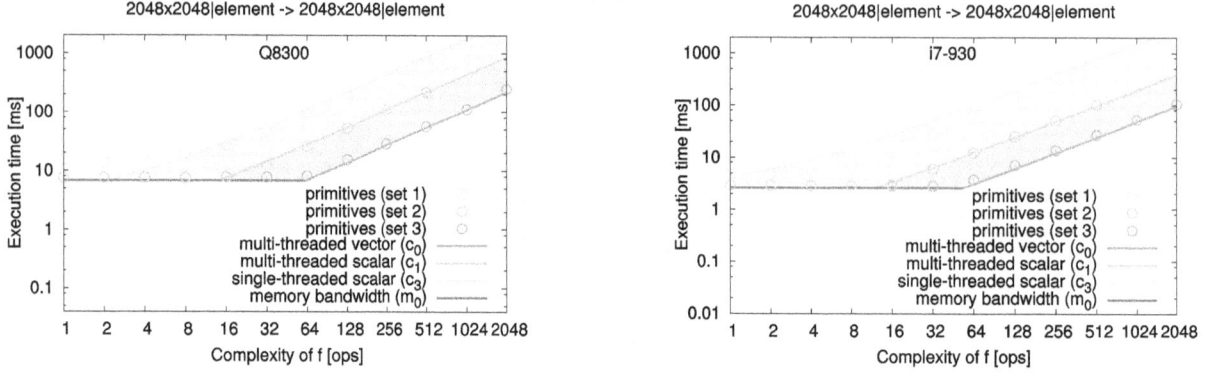

Figure 3: The boat hull model for an example class for both the Q8300 and the i7-930 CPUs. The model is validated against synthetic primitives, shown as circles in the graphs.

the GTX470 includes two levels of caches, which is not present in the GTS250 GPU).

- The additional memory ceiling causes the 'unordered 2048x2048|element → 2048x2048|element' class to give a wide prediction range. The synthetic primitives show that different memory access patterns indeed fit within this range, yielding a better performance when the fraction of coalesced memory accesses is larger.

- A large number of the tested non-synthetic primitives have a low complexity ($f_{complexity} < 10$) making them memory bound rather than compute bound.

4.4 The boat hull model for a multi-core CPU

So far, we have only demonstrated the use of the boat hull model for NVIDIA GPUs. To demonstrate the suitability of the model for a different type of processor, we apply the boat hull model in this section to Intel multi-core CPUs. Similar as for the GPUs, we take two CPU models with different specifications and a different micro-architecture. In this section, we use notations for the theoretical peak ALU performance ($P_{compute}$), the practical peak memory bandwidth (P_{memory}) measured using STREAM [14], the supported number of simultaneous threads ($N_{threads}$) and the width of the vector lane (W_{vector}). The characteristics of the two CPUs are given in table 3.

Table 3: Characteristics of two Intel multi-core CPUs. They are further referred to as Q8300 and i7-930.

	Core 2 Quad Q8300	Core i7-930
micro-architecture	Core	Nehalem
$P_{compute}$	40 GFLOPS	90 GFLOPS
P_{memory}	4.7 GB/s	12.2 GB/s
$N_{threads}$	4 threads	8 threads
W_{vector}	128 bits	128 bits

For the multi-core CPUs we re-use the compute and memory equations as given for the NVIDIA GPUs, but with a slight modification to the memory equation, since memory coalescing is not an issue. We also re-use the class dependent variables w, m, o and c, which have the same meaning as those given for GPUs. The equations are given as follows:

$$c_0 = \frac{w \cdot (f_{complexity} \cdot m + o)}{P_{compute}} \quad \text{(Compute equation)}$$

$$m_0 = \frac{c}{P_{memory}} \quad \text{(Memory equation)}$$

Compute performance on the CPU might be limited by single-threaded execution, scalar execution, or both. We therefore introduce three compute floors. Without using the vector extensions of the architecture, the peak compute performance decreases by the vector lane width (W_{vector}). Furthermore, single-threaded performance causes the peak computer performance to drop by a factor $N_{threads}$. The compute floors are therefore defined as follows:

$$c_1 = \frac{c_0}{W_{vector}} \quad \text{(Multi-threaded scalar)}$$

$$c_2 = \frac{c_0}{N_{threads}} \quad \text{(Single-threaded vector)}$$

$$c_3 = \frac{c_0}{W_{vector} \cdot N_{threads}} \quad \text{(Single-threaded scalar)}$$

We furthermore identify instruction level parallelism (ILP) as another compute floor. To simplify results, we assume in this case that any loops are unrolled and ILP is maximized.

To illustrate the boat hull model for multi-core CPUs, we select the '2048x2048|element → 2048x2048|element' class as an example. We enable all floors for this class and set the class-specific variables as follows:

$$w = 2048 \cdot 2048 \qquad m = 1$$

$$o = 4 \qquad c = d = 2 \cdot 2048 \cdot 2048$$

For the example class, we run three sets of synthetic primitives on both architectures, while varying the complexity of $f()$ in terms of number of operations. Each set enables either: 1) single-threaded scalar execution, 2) multi-threaded scalar execution, or 3), multi threaded vector execution. The boat hull models along with the performance of the synthetic primitives are shown in figure 3 for the Q8300 and the i7-930 processors. We make the following observations with respect to the results:

- For both CPU models, we see a good match between the predicted and measured performance for the compute bound synthetic primitives. The multi-threaded vector operations match the peak compute rate of the architecture, while the performance for multi-threaded scalar operations is a factor 4 lower (assuming 32-bit data elements). Single-threaded operations perform a factor 4 or 8 lower, as predicted by the model.

- The multi-threaded synthetic primitives are able to achieve the predicted memory performance. The prediction is based on the OpenMP version of the benchmark STREAM [14], and does therefore not represent the theoretical peak memory bandwidth. Reasons for not reaching the theoretical peak bandwidth due to the complex memory sub-system of a CPU are discussed in more detail in [21].

4.5 The boat hull model tool

The boat hull model creates a different graph for each processor-class combination. Since classes contain parameters, a tool to automate the creation of such graphs can be very helpful. We present in this section a small tool for this purpose, which is available through our website[2].

Similar to the boat hull model, the tool takes as an input processor parameters and a class description. The processor parameters are as shown in tables 2 and 3. The class description is the full class name, as given in table 1. The class dependent variables w, m, o, c and u and the equations are set by the tool itself. Currently, the tool supports GPUs and CPUs for the 11 classes as shown in table 1.

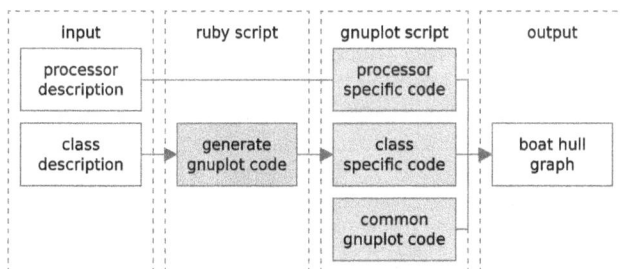

Figure 4: An overview of the tool corresponding to the boat hull model.

We give an overview of the tool in figure 4. Its main component is a script using the graphing utility *gnuplot*, which, after execution, generates a graph as shown in figures 2, 3 and 7. The script consists of three parts:

- A processor specific part, which is based on the processor description given as input to the tool.

- A class specific part, which is generated from a user supplied class description. The generator is written in the Ruby scripting language.

- A common part, which is processor and class independent. It contains the equations and the plot markup settings.

[2]http://parse.ele.tue.nl/

4.6 Evaluating the boat hull model

In this section, we evaluate the boat hull model. Since the model is solely based on class information and the primitive's operational intensity, we cannot expect a performance prediction comparable to detailed architectural models or simulators. With this in mind, we reflect on the boat hull model in this section.

We have seen in this work that the boat hull model's predicted performance is only roughly equivalent to the measured performance. This is due to the fact that many minor limitations are not taken into account. For example, the model does not take load balancing, cache behaviour and register pressure into account. Furthermore, the operator complexity ($f_{complexity}$) will at best yield an estimate due to aspects such as special instructions or compilation optimizations, both of which could alter the prediction. Because of these limitations, we presented the boat hull model as a technique to enable a rough performance prediction which can be used in an early design stage to determine whether or not to select a certain processor and whether or not to develop code for that processor. Once a processor is selected, a more precise performance prediction could be made with a detailed architectural model or simulator if necessary.

Although the presented technique does not rely on the availability of optimized code for a target processor, we do base the values for the class dependent variables w, m, o, c and u on the best available code implementations. The class dependent variables can simply be updated whenever faster code implementations are available. If the programmer eventually decides to develop code for the target architecture, the predicted performance will only be reached if the code is fully optimized for the target architecture.

Because the roofline model is intended to be used to help a programmer improve performance rather than to predict performance, it is of no surprise that the boat hull model gives a much tighter bound on execution time. This is due to the fact that the boat hull model creates multiple instances of the roofline model, each specific to a given class. Since algorithm classes embed information on parallelism as well as on data access dependencies, much more information is available to the boat hull model. This includes for example data re-use information and synchronization requirements.

If we compare the boat hull model to detailed mathematical models and simulators, we find that the boat hull model has the following advantages: 1) it is straightforward to extend to other or future processor architectures, 2) it requires very little architectural information (only four parameters for a GPU or CPU), and 3), most importantly, the boat hull model does not require code implementation nor code optimizations for the target architecture to be available. This allows for rapid performance estimation early in product design trajectories.

5. CASE-STUDY APPLICATION

To illustrate the boat hull model we evaluate a real-life computer vision application targeted at GPU acceleration. This particular application is selected because of its wide variety of (image processing) primitives. In the production process of organic LEDs, the centers of individual LEDs have to be identified under challenging throughput and latency requirements. As explained in [10], this can be achieved using the 3-stage *fast focus on structures* flow.

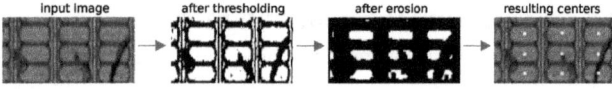

Figure 5: An example of the fast focus on structures application, which finds the centers of 9 LED structures.

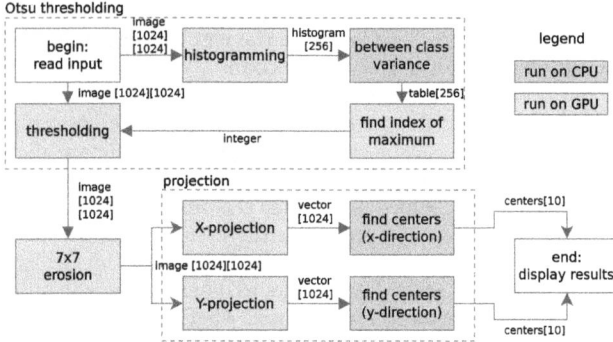

Figure 6: The case-study fast focus on structures flow, in which a 1024x1024 pixel input image is used and 10x10 LED structures are assumed to be present.

An example of the fast focus on structures application is shown in figure 5, in which the 3-stages are applied subsequently: Otsu thresholding, erosion, and projection. A flow chart is given in figure 6, in which the individual image processing primitives are shown. As shown in figure 6, six image processing primitives are targeted for acceleration, in this case using a GPU. More information on the fast focus on structures application is given in [10].

Table 4: Classification of the application's image processing primitives according to the algorithm classification.

primitive	classification
histogram	1024x1024|element $\rightarrow$ 256|shared
maximum	262144|element $\rightarrow$ 1|shared
threshold	1024x1024|element $\rightarrow$ 1024x1024|element
erode 7x7	1024x1024|neighb(7x7) $\rightarrow$ 1024x1024|element
X-projection	1024x1024|tile(1x1024) $\rightarrow$ 1024|element
Y-projection	1024x1024|tile(1024x1) $\rightarrow$ 1024|element

We classify the six primitives according to the algorithm classification presented in [15]. The results[3] are shown in table 4. The application is executed using both of the GPUs introduced in table 2: the GTX470 and the GTS250. For each primitive we generate a graph using the boat hull model tool. As input to the tool we supply the class names as shown in table 4 and the GPU specifications as given in table 2. The resulting graphs are shown in figure 7 for both the GTX470 (top) and the GTS250 (bottom). In these figures, we mark the measured performance with a red star symbol. We make the following observations with respect to the results as shown in figure 7:

[3]The problem size of the primitive maximum is artificially increased from 256 to 262144 elements, because the original problem size is too small to be measured accurately.

- The performance of the primitives histogram, threshold and erode is accurately predicted for both GPUs.

- The maximum primitive shows a higher execution time for both GPUs compared to the predicted time. Even though the problem size has been artificially increased, it is still too small to yield a high occupancy on the GPU and to reach its peak memory bandwidth. Although the prediction is a factor 3 lower compared to the measured performance, it hardly affects the absolute performance of the complete application due to the low execution time.

- Both the X-projection and Y-projection primitives suffer from similar inefficiencies because of their relatively small problem sizes. A wide prediction range is given for primitives such as X-projection, because memory accesses for this class might be uncoalesced.

- The results are consistent over both GPU models, except for the X-projection algorithm. In that case we see that the tighter constraints on memory coalescing for the GTS250 results in a significantly higher execution time. Nevertheless, the measured performance is still within the predicted range for both GPU models.

Furthermore, we evaluate the total execution time of the fast focus on structures application and compare it to the predicted performance. To do so, we assume that fused multiply add instructions do not occur, but make no assumptions on memory access patterns. We show the results in table 5, in which we separately show kernel execution time and CPU-GPU data transfer time.

Table 5: Predicted and measured execution time of the case-study application. The difference is calculated using the average of the predicted execution time.

GTX470	predicted	measured	difference
GPU kernels	1.66-2.32 ms	1.96 ms	2%
data transfers	0.95 ms	1.07 ms	11%
total	2.61-3.27 ms	3.03 ms	3%

GTS250	predicted	measured	difference
GPU kernels	3.21-4.24 ms	3.99 ms	7%
data transfers	1.90 ms	2.13 ms	11%
total	5.11-6.14 ms	6.12 ms	8%

From the results, we conclude that the measured performance of the kernels falls well within the predicted performance range for both GPUs. The range is due to the fact that we assume the fraction of coalesced memory accesses for the X-projection primitive to be unknown. Concerning the CPU-GPU data transfer time, we observe that the predicted values are too optimistic. This is attributed to the fact that transferring smaller amounts of data over the PCI-Express bus yields an increasingly higher overhead.

The roofline model is not designed to predict performance, but can still be used for performance prediction. We therefore compare it briefly with the boat hull model. To do so, we map the 6 primitives of the fast focus on structures application onto the roofline model. We compare the results (figure 1) for the GTX470 architecture with the boat hull model (top half of figure 7). We observe three major

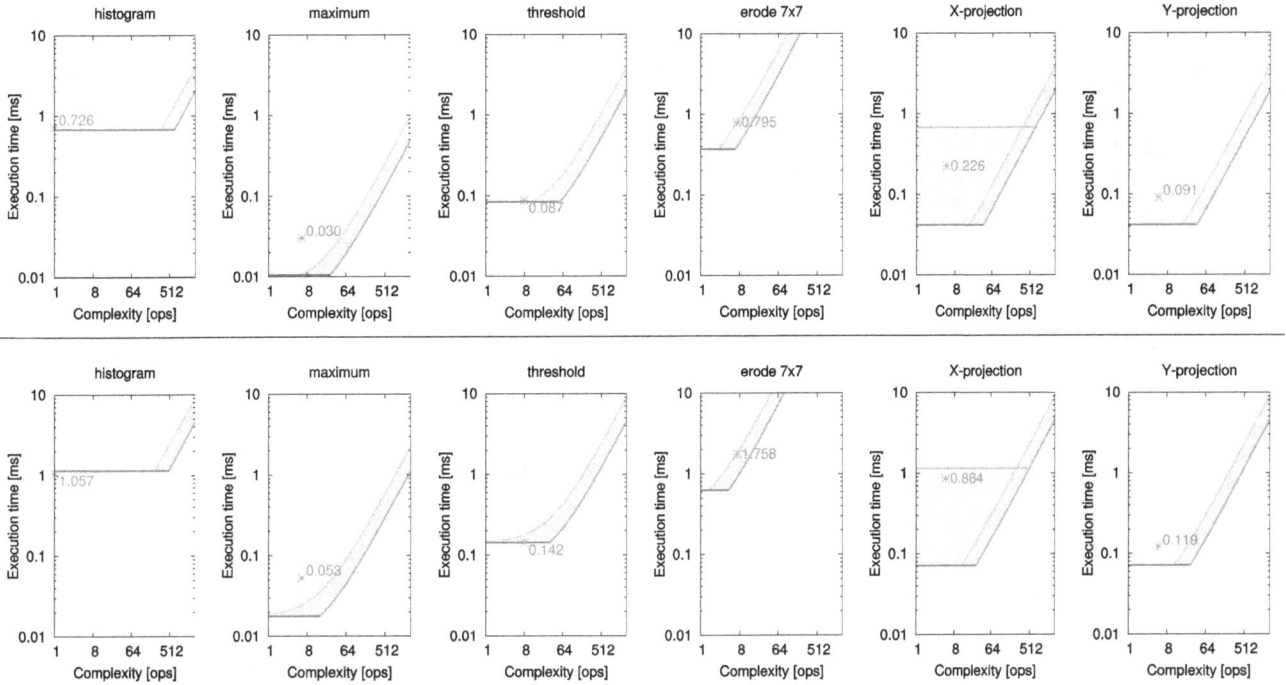

Figure 7: Applying the boat hull model to the fast focus on structures application for the GTX470 (top) and the GTS250 (bottom) GPUs. Red star symbols show the measured performance of a CUDA implementation running on these GPUs, while the curves show the predicted performance. The legend is as shown in figure 2.

differences. Firstly, the roofline model does not show the execution time directly. This can cause a problem when comparing two primitives, as one might have both a higher 'performance' and a larger execution time (e.g. **erode**). Not showing the execution time makes it also less intuitive to accumulate multiple primitives and/or data transfers for a total performance prediction. Secondly, we observe that the boat hull model gives a much tighter prediction. This is due to the creation of class-specific models, as explained in the paper. Lastly, we observe that the roofline model's x-axis requires the amount of loads and stores to off-chip memory, while the boat hull model embeds this information in the algorithm class. Determining which accesses go to off-chip or on-chip memory might not be a trivial task.

6. FUTURE WORK

The applicability of a technique such as the introduced boat hull model depends on the level of automation. In this work, we presented a tool to automatically generate a boat hull model graph. The generation of such a graph depends on the availability of class parameters (as for example given in table 1) and on architectural parameters. Class parameters are given for a number of example classes for GPUs and CPUs. Other, currently not supported classes, will be added in future work. Architectural parameters can be obtained from processor specifications and existing benchmark tools. Nevertheless, the identification of an algorithm class currently remains a manual effort. In separate work, we aim to identify classes automatically under the assumption that a basic C implementation is available.

Currently, the boat hull model predicts performance for a single primitive on a single (multi-threaded) processor. If an application such as fast focus on structures would be executed on a system consisting of multiple processors, kernel execution and data transfer might partly overlap. Future work aims to provide a methodology to support complete homogeneous and heterogeneous multi-processor systems.

We believe that the boat hull model can be a useful tool for system and application designers, provided that the algorithm classification can successfully classify a given application. Therefore, we aim to validate the boat hull model and the algorithm classification against a different domain in future work. For example using the PolyBench benchmark suite [18], which contains various linear algebra kernels and solvers.

Lastly, we work towards integrating the boat hull model as a run-time component into our skeleton-based source-to-source compiler 'Bones' [16]. This enables performance prediction at run-time based on the available hardware, which can be used for task scheduling and mapping onto a suitable processor.

7. CONCLUSION

In this work, we have introduced a method to estimate performance of applications on multi-core and many-core architectures prior to the implementation and optimization of target specific code.

Our new method of performance prediction is based on an existing algorithm classification and a modification to the *roofline model*. We modified the existing roofline model such that it generates multiple rooflines, each specific for a given algorithm class. This new model, the *boat hull model*, gives a prediction of an algorithm's execution time on a given processor based on the properties of the corresponding algorithm class. The boat hull model gives a much tighter bound on performance compared to the roofline model because of the integration of class specific information. In contrast to performance models and architecture simulators, the boat hull model gives a performance prediction prior to the implementation and optimization of target architecture specific code. Moreover, the presented model does not even require code to be available, pseudo-code or a high-level description can be sufficient to predict an application's performance.

In this paper we applied our methodology to different GPUs and CPUs. We evaluated the model for a number of synthetic benchmarks as well as for real-life examples, from which we have shown that the boat hull model is applicable in practice. We furthermore demonstrated the use of the new model for a case-study application. The application's algorithms were classified and their performance predicted using the boat hull model. We implemented a GPU accelerated version of the application and showed that our prediction for the complete application is within 8% of the measured performance.

8. REFERENCES

[1] K. Asanovic, R. Bodik, J. Demmel, T. Keaveny, K. Keutzer, J. Kubiatowicz, N. Morgan, D. Patterson, K. Sen, J. Wawrzynek, D. Wessel, and K. Yelick. A View of the Parallel Computing Landscape. *Communications of the ACM*, 52:56–67, October 2009.

[2] S. S. Baghsorkhi, M. Delahaye, S. J. Patel, W. D. Gropp, and W.-m. W. Hwu. An Adaptive Performance Modeling Tool for GPU Architectures. In *PPoPP '10: 15th Symposium on Principles and Practice of Parallel Programming*. ACM, 2010.

[3] A. Bakhoda, G. Yuan, W. Fung, H. Wong, and T. Aamodt. Analyzing CUDA Workloads using a Detailed GPU Simulator. In *ISPASS '09: International Symposium on Performance Analysis of Systems and Software*. IEEE, 2009.

[4] W. Caarls, P. Jonker, and H. Corporaal. Algorithmic Skeletons for Stream Programming in Embedded Heterogeneous Parallel Image Processing Applications. In *IPDPS '06: 20th International Parallel and Distributed Processing Symposium*. IEEE, 2006.

[5] D. K. G. Campbell. Towards the Classification of Algorithmic Skeletons. Technical Report YCS 276, University of York, 1996.

[6] L. Carrington, M. M. Tikir, C. Olschanowsky, M. Laurenzano, J. Peraza, A. Snavely, and S. Poole. An Idiom-finding Tool for Increasing Productivity of Accelerators. In *ICS '11: International Conference on Supercomputing*. ACM, 2011.

[7] B. Catanzaro, A. Fox, K. Keutzer, D. Patterson, B.-Y. Su, M. Snir, K. Olukotun, P. Hanrahan, and H. Chafi. Ubiquitous Parallel Computing from Berkeley, Illinois, and Stanford. *IEEE Micro*, 30:41–55, March 2010.

[8] M. Cole. *Algorithmic Skeletons: Structured Management of Parallel Computation*. MIT Press, 1991.

[9] S. H. Fuller and L. I. Millett. Computing Performance: Game Over or Next Level? *IEEE Computer*, 44:31–38, January 2011.

[10] Y. He, Z. Ye, D. She, B. Mesman, and H. Corporaal. Feasibility Analysis of Ultra High Frame Rate Visual Servoing on FPGA and SIMD Processor. In *ACIVS '11: Advanced Concepts for Intelligent Vision Systems*. Springer Berlin, 2011.

[11] S. Hong and H. Kim. An Integrated GPU Power and Performance Model. In *ISCA '10: 37th Annual International Symposium on Computer Architecture*. ACM, 2010.

[12] S. W. Keckler, W. J. Dally, B. Khailany, M. Garland, and D. Glasco. GPUs and the Future of Parallel Computing. *IEEE Micro*, 31:7–17, September 2011.

[13] K. Keutzer and T. Mattson. A Design Pattern Language for Engineering (Parallel) Software. In *Intel Technology Journal*, 2010.

[14] J. McCalpin. Memory Bandwidth and Machine Balance in Current High Performance Computers. *IEEE Computer Society Technical Committee on Computer Architecture Newsletter*, pages 19–25, December 1995.

[15] C. Nugteren and H. Corporaal. A Modular and Parameterisable Classification of Algorithms. Technical Report No. ESR-2011-02, Eindhoven University of Technology, 2011.

[16] C. Nugteren and H. Corporaal. Introducing 'Bones': A Parallelizing Source-to-Source Compiler Based on Algorithmic Skeletons. In *GPGPU-5: 5th Workshop on General Purpose Processing on Graphics Processing Units*. ACM, 2012.

[17] NVIDIA. *CUDA C Programming Guide 4.0*, 2011.

[18] L.-N. Pouchet. PolyBench: The Polyhedral Benchmark Suite. http://www.cse.ohio-state.edu/~pouchet/software/polybench/.

[19] J. Sim, A. Dasgupta, H. Kim, and R. Vuduc. A Performance Analysis Framework for Identifying Potential Benefits in GPGPU Applications. In *PPoPP '12: 17th Symposium on Principles and Practice of Parallel Programming*. ACM, 2012.

[20] S. Williams. *Auto-tuning Performance on Multicore Computers*. PhD thesis, University of California, Berkeley, 2008.

[21] S. Williams, A. Waterman, and D. Patterson. Roofline: an Insightful Visual Performance Model for Multicore Architectures. *Communications of the ACM*, 52:65–76, April 2009.

Parameterized Micro-benchmarking: An Auto-tuning Approach for Complex Applications

Wenjing Ma
Pacific Northwest National
Laboratory
wenjing.ma@pnnl.gov

Sriram Krishnamoorthy
Pacific Northwest National
Laboratory
sriram@pnnl.gov

Gagan Agrawal
The Ohio State University
agrawal@cse.ohio-
state.edu

ABSTRACT

Auto-tuning has emerged as an important practical method for creating highly optimized implementations of key computational kernels and applications. However, the growing complexity of architectures and applications is creating new challenges for auto-tuning. Complex applications can involve a prohibitively large search space that precludes empirical auto-tuning. Similarly, architectures are getting more complicated, making it hard to model performance.

In this paper, we focus on the challenge to auto-tuning presented by applications with a large number of kernels and kernel instantiations. While these kernels may share a somewhat similar pattern, they differ considerably in problem sizes and the exact computation performed. We propose and evaluate a new approach to auto-tuning which we refer to as *parameterized micro-benchmarking*. It is an alternative to the two existing classes of approaches to auto-tuning: *analytical model-based* and *empirical search-based*. Particularly, we argue that the former may not be able to capture all the architectural features that impact performance, whereas the latter might be too expensive for an application that has several different kernels. In our approach, different expressions in the application, different possible implementations of each expression, and the key architectural features, are used to derive a simple micro-benchmark and a small parameter space. We have evaluated our approach in the context of GPU implementations of tensor contraction expressions.

Categories and Subject Descriptors

C.4.4 [**Computer Systems Organization**]: Performance of Systems—*Modeling techniques*; C.4.5 [**Computer Systems Organization**]: Performance of Systems—*Performance attributes*

Keywords

auto-tuning, micro-benchmarking, GPU, tensor contraction, cost model

1. INTRODUCTION

Auto-tuning has emerged as a key approach to optimizing important computational kernels [31, 34, 10]. One reason for the success of auto-tuning, over other approaches like code generation driven by modeling [6], is the increasing complexity of architectures. The initial work on auto-tuning was driven by processors in late 90s, which had multiple levels of cache. Even a relatively simple kernel, say matrix-matrix multiplication, had many parameters (such as unrolling factor and tile size for each level of cache hierarchy) that needed to be determined to achieve the best performance. Rather than employing complicated yet inaccurate model-based approaches, an empirical search, with intelligent heuristics to reduce the search space, was proposed as a practical means to optimizing a specific kernel [31].

Performance tuning of many complex real-world applications involves challenges that are not adequately addressed by the current frameworks. As a motivating example, consider NWChem, where the Coupled Cluster theory, a post-Hartree Fock ab initio quantum chemistry method, is used in electronic structure calculations [28]. The dominant computation is in the form of *tensor contractions*. A tensor is a multi-dimensional matrix and a tensor contraction is a generalized matrix multiplication [4]. The interesting challenge that arises with such an application is that a single application involves many different contractions, which differ significantly in the dimensionality of the operands and the nature of the computations. Moreover, in the same context, the same expression may be executed with different data sets, leading to different problem sizes for each task. Therefore, the optimized versions of these expressions can be quite different. Thus, some of the existing auto-tuning approaches, if applied to NWChem, will involve extremly expensive empirical search for each of the contractions. Other methods, which might involve accurate cost models [34], are applicable only if the underlying architecture can be modeled very accurately. Unfortunately, modern multi-core and many-core architectures have features that are not well understood, and one cannot expect performance of a tensor contraction on one of these to be succinctly captured through an accurate and complete cost model.

As another example, we consider signal-processing applications (eg., FFT [30], Walsh-Hadamard transforms [16]). In these cases, a single application can involve a complex set of kernel invocations, which are characterized as recurrence relations. Dynamic programming approaches have been developed to optimize invocations on larger problem sizes in terms of those on smaller problem sizes [23].

Driven by the need for tuning such applications, this paper presents a novel approach to auto-tuning. We used tensor contraction expressions as our focus of the auto-tuning object. The key aspect of our approach is the use of *parameterized micro-benchmarks*. Our approach involves the following features: 1) Based on a broad knowledge of the target architecture and the class of kernels being optimized, we choose the micro-benchmarks and their parameter space, 2) The micro-benchmarks are executed with their chosen parameter space to learn how the architectural features can impact the performance of the target kernels, 3) Based on the performance characteristics learned from micro-benchmarks, the best versions of kernels are chosen and executed.

Our approach has several advantages over the existing methods. First, by using a single micro-benchmark or a small number of micro-benchmarks, we avoid expensive empirical search on each distinct compute-intensive kernel in the application. Second, since the micro-benchmarks and their parameter space are created keeping the target kernels in mind, we focus only on the architectural features that actually impact the performance of the target kernels.

Though our approach is not specific to any particular architecture, the studies performed in this paper target modern GPUs. While GPUs have rapidly gained a very substantial HPC market, significant effort is typically needed to extract performance from a particular application such as NWChem [20] on a modern GPU. Given the challenge of extracting performance from a modern GPU, there has been a lot of interest in auto-tuning for GPUs as well, with extensive studies focusing on kernels like dense matrix multiplication [18], sparse matrix computations [8], and FFTs [12]. However, none of these approaches can be effective on an application like NWChem.

2. AUTO-TUNING FRAMEWORK

This section describes our overall approach for auto-tuning. This framework is designed to be semi-automatic, i.e. to a large extent, it can be supported as part of an automatic code generation and optimization system.

The first step in the process is to focus on architectural features to be modeled. This step cannot currently be automated, and instead, it requires that a general micro-benchmark and a corresponding parameter space be obtained or created, which can model the architectural features of interest. The subsequent steps, however, are automatically performed. A compilation system can analyze the target expressions and their different possible implementations, and obtain a *specialization* of the general micro-benchmark. The specialized micro-benchmark is then executed on the target architecture. Using regression analysis, cost functions are extracted, which can then be applied to choose the appropriate implementation of each target expression.

We next explain the concept of a general micro-benchmark and its specialization through an example. Suppose we are interested in modeling the memory hierarchy of the GPU. One needs to have a micro-benchmark that is aware of the execution model of the GPUs, though it does not need to be specific to a particular GPU. The micro-benchmark we create for this purpose is as follows. Based on how a kernel is executed on a GPU, we consider three types of locality: 1) *temporal locality*, which is the stride between consecutive accesses to an array from a particular thread, 2) *intra-warp spatial locality*, which is the stride between accesses to an array by consecutive threads within a warp, and 3) *inter-warp spatial locality*, which is the stride between accesses to an array by threads of consecutive warps.

Based on this classification, our general micro-benchmark works as follows. In the iteration i, the jth thread in the kth warp reads/writes the element $F_1(i, j, k)$ of the first array, the element $F_2(i, j, k)$ of the second array, and finally, the element $F_n(i, j, k)$ of the nth array. The value n, the corresponding n functions, and whether read or write is performed on each of these, depends upon the target expressions.

In Section 3, we explain the key properties of tensor contractions, and subsequently, explain the specialized micro-benchmarks we extract for modeling memory hierarchy in Section 4. However, just for an illustration, we can analyze target expressions and extract the following information: 1) functions F_i are affine with respect to i, j, and k, 2) we need to focus on two arrays, one of which is being read and another being written, and 3) only certain stride values are of interest, depending upon the specific target expressions being considered. Based on this analysis, the specialized micro-benchmark we extract has the jth thread in the kth warp executing the following code:

```
for(int i=0;i<iters;i++)  {
  tmp += t1[j];
  t2[i*stride_iter+j*stride_x+k*stride_y]=tmp;
}
```

By executing such a specialized micro-benchmark with different values of *stride_iter*, *stride_x*, and *stride_y*, corresponding to the three types of locality explained above, we can learn the impact of these parameters on the performance of the kernel. Subsequently, the resulting cost model can be used to compare the performance of different candidate implementations of each expression.

Overall, our goal is not to develop a complete cost model, since such models tend to be very complex and difficult to apply for a real machine. Instead, our goal is to capture the features we see in tensor contraction expressions and their different implementations, on typical problem sizes, and design micro-benchmarks and identify their parameter space. These, in turn, are used to predict the relative performance of different implementations of the same expression, and choose the best version.

3. BACKGROUND

Throughout this paper, we use our auto-tuning framework to optimize tensor contractions. This section gives background on this class of computations.

While prevalent in many-body formalisms in electronic-structure theory, we focus on tensor contractions that occur in the context of the Coupled Cluster (CC) theory [2], a widely used method for solving the electronic Schrödinger equation, for illustration. The methods such as the CCSD(T) approach [24] enable accurate predictions for the molecular structure, inter-molecular interactions, transition states, and activation barriers. These computations, however, have a high computational complexity ($O(N^7)$), and thus require the use of parallel machines and/or accelerators. The primary data structures in the coupled cluster theory are the *tensors*, which are multi-dimensional matrices. Tensor contractions are products of such multi-dimensional arrays.

Consider the following tensor contraction.

$$R[h1,h2,h3,p1,p2,p3] -= T[p2,h3,p4,h2] * V[h1,p4,p1,p2] \quad (1)$$

The tensor contraction involves computing tensor R from tensors T and V. The index p4 above is common to both input tensors, corresponding to the *common dimension* in matrix-matrix multiplication, and is referred to as the *contracted* or *common* index. Unlike conventional matrix multiplication, several dimensions can be contracted in a binary tensor contraction. In comparison, *uncommon index set* denotes the indices that appear in the output matrices, and one (but not both) of the input tensors.

Coupled Cluster theory consists of a collection of methods, each with increasing accuracy and cost. In addition to the computational complexity, each higher theory consists of a larger number of contractions. In the Coupled Cluster implementation in NWChem, the CCD, CCSD, CCSDT, and CCSDTQ methods consist of 10, 43, 100, and 189 tensor contractions, respectively. These are distinct contractions produced from a chemical formalism that minimizes the total operation count.

The tensors themselves incorporate various forms of sparsity. A tensor contraction is load-balanced at runtime through dynamically distributing the sub-contractions involving dense blocks in both input tensors to produce a contribution to the output tensor. Depending on the sparsity, the dense blocks could vary widely in their sizes. The high-dimensionality of the contractions, together with the sparsity, often results in each individual dimension of a dense block being small (10s of doubles). The contractions vary widely in the FLOP count ($O(N^3)$ to $O(N^7)$ or higher) with tensors consisting of two, four, six, or eight dimensions. This coupled with the potentially arbitrary choice of summation indices can result in tensor contractions with very high reuse (the equivalent of outer-products) or being bandwidth bound (the equivalent of inner-products).

It is clear that optimizing all these variants individually can be prohibitively expensive. In our *parametrized micro-benchmark* based auto-tuning approach, we consider how the expressions could differ from each other, as well as how their different implementations can differ from each other. Based on these differences, the micro-benchmark(s) and their corresponding parameter spaces are chosen.

4. MICRO-BENCHMARKING FOR ANALYZING DEVICE MEMORY ACCESSES

In this section, we describe how we use our parameterized micro-benchmarking approach to develop cost models of memory access performance.

The most studied memory hierarchy optimization on GPUs has been the use of shared memory for frequently accessed data [3, 21, 17]. Other important characteristics associated with the cost of device memory accesses on Fermi and T10 architectures include coalesced accesses and the cache hierarchy. First, *coalesced accesses*, where simultaneously executing threads access consecutive memory locations, help improve performance over the cases where a large stride value is involved. Second, the Fermi series of cards also have a L1 and a L2 cache. The L1 cache is either 16 or 48 KB, depending upon the size of the shared memory that is chosen, whereas L2 cache is 768 KB. It should be noted that some existing frameworks do optimize coalesced accesses [33].

4.1 Memory Hierarchy Related Optimizations

Recall from Section 2 the access strides for a kernel can be classified into three types: stride between consecutive threads within a warp, denoted as $stride\_x$, stride between threads in consecutive warps, denoted as $stride\_y$, and the stride between two iterations of one thread, denoted as $stride\_iter$. In executing tensor contractions on a GPU, it turns out that consecutive threads within a warp and/or threads in consecutive warps access consecutive locations along a certain dimension of the input matrix. To illustrate this, consider the following expression:

$$C[a,b,c,d] = A[b,e,a,f] * B[f,e,d,c]. \quad (2)$$

To facilitate our discussion, we view the threads as forming a two-dimensional ((x,y)) grid, with consecutive x values denoting consecutive threads within a warp, and consecutive y values denoting consecutive warps. With a (x,y) block of threads, two threads with adjacent values along the x dimension will read adjacent elements along the common index of the input A. They will also read adjacent elements along the uncommon index of the input B. When writing to the output, they will access adjacent elements along the x dimension of C, which is calculated by the uncommon index of the input B. Similarly, two threads with adjacent values along the y dimension will access adjacent elements along the uncommon index of A, and adjacent elements along common index of B, and adjacent elements along the y dimension of C, which comes from the uncommon index of A.

The common indices here are $\{e, f\}$, where the uncommon indices are $\{b, a\}$ in A, and $\{d, c\}$ in B. Suppose the index calculation order is determined by the output matrix. The access of uncommon index of A will be in the order of $\{a, b\}$. This implies that the index b is the innermost index, and the $stride\_y$ for A will be T^3, where T is the size of each dimension. On the other hand, if index calculation order is done with the index order of the input tensor A, then the $stride\_y$ for A is T, because now a is the innermost index in the uncommon index set.

Because of the features of the GPU memory hierarchy described above, the choices of index calculation can have a significant impact on the performance. Particularly, we need to choose the index calculation order among uncommon indices, and the index calculation order among common indices. In both cases, we have two options to choose from. Revisiting the example above, if we choose the *output-favored* index order, the index calculation order for C will be $\{a, b, c, d\}$. In contrast, if we choose *input-favored* index order, the index calculation orders will be changed according to their order in the input, leading to $\{b, a, d, c\}$. For the common index, if we choose the index order that favors A, the calculation order of common index will $\{e, f\}$. If we choose the index order that favors B, the order of common index is now reversed.

All these options lead to different strides between threads along x and y dimensions, and iterations. Thus, our goal is to use our parametrized benchmarks to evaluate the performance of different access orders on a given machine, and to choose the best orders.

4.2 Micro-benchmarks and Parameter Space

In Section 2, we outlined how the generic micro-benchmark can be specialized for extracting cost models relevant to tensor contractions. Particularly, by considering two arrays and

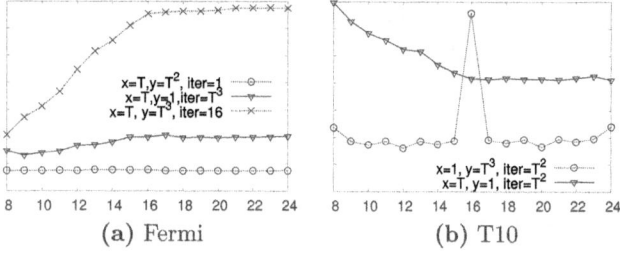

Figure 1: Micro-benchmark performance (major cases) for various access patterns. y-axis is the time in milliseconds, x-axis is the value of parameter T.

three parameters $stride\_x$, $stride\_y$, and $stride\_iter$, we can capture the memory hierarchy features relevant for optimizing tensor contractions. More detailed examination of the optimization issues leads to further narrowing of the parameter space. Particularly, for tensor contractions, the data accesses follow such a pattern: for the same matrix being accessed, the values of $stride\_x$, $stride\_y$, and $stride\_iter$ are either 1 or a power of the dimension size. For example, suppose the dimension size is T, then if $stride\_x$ is 1, $stride\_y$ could be T, T^2, T^3, ... Therefore, our tests are conducted with permutations of these three parameters, assuming that the four candidate values are 1, T, T^2 and T^3.

With larger numbers of dimensions, the number of configurations can be larger, but follows a similar trend. However, to shrink the parameter space, we measured strides only less than or equal to T^3. This is a reasonable simplification, because the cost of accesses with a stride larger than T^3 is usually similar to the cost with a stride equal to T^3. In the expressions we derive, x, y, and $iter$ are used to represent $stride\_x$, $stride\_y$, and $stride\_iter$.

4.3 Analyzing Device Memory Accesses on Fermi

Register tiling has been shown to be beneficial on Fermi GPUs [22], in which each thread calculates the output matrix with a stride of 16 elements. Thus, for the output matrix, $iter$ is almost always 16.

We empirically evaluated the various memory access patterns taking x, y, and $iter$ as input parameters. Simplifying the presentation, we show the performance for the main cases considered in Figure 1(a). Other choices evaluated presented similar trends, and were considered in the full evaluation.

Rather than retain the large number of performance numbers explicitly, we employ a piece-wise fit of linear functions to the data. In the following formula (and the formula in the next subsection), S represents a constant value.

$$cost = \begin{cases} 2S, \; if \; x = 1, \; 4S, \; if \; y = 1, \\ (1.1T - 5)S, \; if \; x = T, y = T^3, iter = 16, T < 16 \\ 13S, \; if \; x = T, \; y = T^3, \; iter = 16, \; T \geq 16; \end{cases}$$

When x is 1, the accesses to the device memory are coalesced, therefore, irrespective of the other parameters, the cost is low. When y is 1, it means consecutive half warps are also accessing the same data, which will enable good cache reuse, therefore the costs are again low. In the other cases, because the accesses are not coalesced, and the cache miss rates are potentially higher, the cost is increased. There-

fore, the last case in the above equation has a fixed cost of $13S$ when the dimension size is ≥ 16. The third case has the same expression pattern as the fourth case, while the dimension size is smaller than 16. In this situation, a smaller dimension size will enable better cache performance, therefore, the cost increases linearly with the dimension size. After the dimension size reaches 16, the miss rate becomes stable, resulting in a constant cost.

4.4 Analyzing Device Memory Access on T10 GPU

The experiments on T10 were done with the same configurations, except that to match the access pattern of the output, $iter$ is always 1 instead of 16. This is because register tiling is not used for tensor contraction implementations on these cards. Similar to the cases on Fermi, we can group the configurations into several categories. A set of them (but not all) are shown in Figure 1(b). The cost expressions derived from them are listed below.

$$cost = \begin{cases} 4S, \; if \; x = 1 \\ (-1.7T + 36)S, \; if \; x = T, y = 1, iter = 1, T < 16 \\ 9S, if \; x = T, y = 1, iter = 1, T \geq 16 \end{cases}$$

Similar to the model derived for Fermi, when x is 1, coalesced accesses enable the lowest possible overhead. In the other configurations, the memory accesses are more expensive. The slope in the upper line of Figure 1(b) is due to the uncoalesced accesses caused by smaller dimension sizes. One important observation is that the cost difference among various cases is smaller for T10 GPUs, and therefore, the performance differences caused by index calculation order may be less significant for most of the expressions. We believe this is due to the absence of L1 and L2 caches on this generation of GPUs.

However, there are still situations in which performance could differ a lot when strides are different. Particularly, we see spikes in the costs. One example is when the dimension size is 16, $x = 1$, $y = T^3$, $iter = T^2$, as shown in Figure 1(b). These spikes are hard to explain from the documented architectural characteristics given by the vendor. We can conjecture that for some combinations of configuration and stride, there are certain conflicts in the memory accesses by adjacent warps, leading to worse performance.

Overall, from the analysis presented in this section, we can see that: 1) parameterized micro-benchmarks can help summarize cost factors which cannot always be explained from the known features of the architectures, and 2) there are significant differences in the behavior of device accesses between two GPU architectures we have considered, leading to the possibility that the best version for a given expression may differ across the two cards. Later, we will evaluate if the models learned from these micro-benchmarks can help choose the optimal implementation of real tensor contractions.

4.5 Generality to a Multi-Core CPU

To show that our approach is not restricted to GPUs, we applied the same micro-benchmark to extract a cost model for a multi-core CPU.

The same micro-benchmark was written in OpenMP. Due to the characteristics of the multi-core CPU, we used two parameters, $stride\_x$ and $stride\_iter$. $stride\_y$ is not required since there is no concept of warp on the multi-core CPU. Using 4 threads on a quad-core Intel E5520 CPU with 64KB L1 cache/core and 256KB L2 cache/core, the following cost model was extracted.

$$cost = \begin{cases} (0.1T + 5.5)S, \ if \ iter = T^3 \\ 5S, otherwise \end{cases}$$

This cost model implies that for execution of these kernels on the multi-core CPU, the important factor is the temporal stride. This is because the kernels can effectively reuse L1 and L2 cache in most cases, and each core has its own L1 and L2 cache, which makes $stride\_x$ irrelevant.

5. MICRO-BENCHMARKS FOR KERNEL CONSOLIDATION

In this section, we apply our parameterized micro-benchmarking approach to learn the benefits from *kernel consolidation* supported in modern GPUs.

Though GPUs initially focused on exploiting data parallelism, recently task parallelism has also been supported through *concurrent kernels*. Different kernel functions can be launched simultaneously, with each kernel performing a distinct task. There are at least two cases where concurrent kernels can help improve performance of an application with several independent computations. First, if the amount of computation in a single kernel is not very high, one could run several such kernels together, and obtain overall higher performance for the entire application. This is because modern GPUs have a high-degree of parallelism, which cannot be adequately used by single kernel with a modest amount of computation. Second, consolidation also provides an easy mechanism to achieve an overlap between data movement and computation. By launching several kernels at the same time, we can have one or more of them performing the computation, while others may be transferring data between device and host at the same time. This can further help reduce the total execution time for these sets of kernels.

Kernel consolidation turns out to be useful for tensor contraction based applications as well. This is because in an application like NWChem, a fixed *tile size* (along each dimension) is used for all tensor contractions, according to the memory limit and the *dominant matrix*. For example, suppose on a system with 1 GB device memory, the *dominant matrix* is 6-dimensional, i.e., it has the size T^6, where T is the tile size along each dimension. With double precision numbers, we can determine that T should be no more than 22, to meet the memory constraints. Consequently, for expressions involving matrices with only a small number of dimensions (for example, two-dimensional or four-dimensional matrices), which tend to be quite common, a GPU's resources are not fully utilized. Fortunately, there exists a significant amount of task parallelism across such computations. In these cases, we can launch the kernels together, or *consolidate* them.

As we stated above, besides using task parallelism, there is another advantage of kernel consolidation–achieving an overlap between data movement and computations. But, it turns out that different methods of consolidation need to be used for exploiting task parallelism and achieving overlap between data movement and computations. We refer to these as *tightly-coupled* and *loosely-coupled* consolidation.

In both consolidation schemes, one task will be executed as one stream on the GPU, in three phases: data copy from host memory to device memory, kernel execution, and data copy from device memory to host memory. In *loosely-coupled consolidation*, asynchronous data copy functions are invoked in a batch, then the N kernels are launched, followed by another batch of asynchronous data copy. In other words, the three phases of execution of a single task or kernel are loosely-coupled. In comparison, with tightly-coupled consolidation, we iterate all the N tasks, and invoke the three phases for each task one by one.

We only consider kernel consolidation on the T20 (Fermi) cards for two reasons. First, the T10 cards cannot actually execute multiple kernels at the same time, i.e., multiple kernels launched at the same time are executed sequentially. Second, unlike Fermi, which has bi-directional data transfer on PCIe that enables overlapping of data transfer in two directions, the T10 cards only have one-directional data transfer on the PCIe bus. Thus, consolidation cannot help achieve better overlapping on the T10 cards.

In auto-tuning for consolidation, we focus on choosing the right method for a given expression, since different tensor contraction expressions get different benefits from the two methods. Deciding whether or not to perform consolidation is not the critical issue, as long as correctness is maintained, and memory constraints are met. This is because our experiments have determined that consolidation does not degrade the performance in any case.

5.1 Micro-benchmarks and Parameter Space Selection

We now describe the rationale underlying the choice of micro-benchmarks and the possible parameters to understand the impact of consolidation on the performance of tensor contractions on the Fermi architecture. We start off by examining the characteristics of the tensor contraction that impact benefits from consolidation.

It turns out that the key factor is the ratio between sizes along the common indices and the sizes along the uncommon indices. Particularly, the product of the sizes along the uncommon index determines the amount of data movement between CPU and GPU, and the size of common index determines the ratio between computation and the data transfer. For example, consider the following two expressions:

$$C[a,b,c,d]=A[a,b,e,f]*B[e,f,d,c] \qquad (3)$$

$$C[a,b,c,d] = A[a,f]*B[b,f,d,c] \qquad (4)$$

Assuming each dimension has the same size, the first expression above has a larger computation to I/O ratio, whereas the total output costs for both the expressions are identical.

The goal in micro-benchmarking is to avoid experimenting with each individual tensor contraction, i.e. those with different number of dimensions and sizes along each dimension. Therefore, we used a GPU implementation of matrix multiplication, closely based on the one available from CUDA SDK[1], with various sizes of input and output matrices.

Specifically, we created test cases as follows. Suppose the matrix multiplication we test is $C \mathrel{+}= A \times B$, where A is a matrix of size $HA \times WA$, and B is a matrix of size $WA \times WB$. Then, the size of C is $HA \times WB$. The absolute and relative costs of computation and data movement can be

---

[1]http://developer.download.nvidia.com/compute/
cuda/sdk/website/samples.html

varied by choosing different values for the dimension sizes. The product of two *uncommon* indices, i.e. $HA \times WB$, determines the amount of data being moved for the array C. This turns out to be the dominant I/O cost, since C needs to be copied both in and out of the GPU memory. Also, most tensor contractions have the pattern that C is at least as large as the maximum of the sizes of A and B. The *common* index WA determines the ratio between the computation and the data movement.

Overall, we chose three sets of cases, which are as follows. **Pattern 1:** The size of the matrix A is small, where matrices B and C have the same size. **Pattern 2:** All three matrices have the same size. **Pattern 3:** A and B have the same size, whereas C is much larger than A and B.

In all the 3 patterns, large problem sizes are considered to effectively capture the behavior of higher-dimensional tensor contractions. As overall problem sizes are scaled, the three cases above capture different scenarios. In the second case, the ratio of computation to data movement also increases with problem size. On the other hand, the first and third cases are dominated by data copy times with the above ratio increasing at a slower rate.

5.2 Experiments with Micro-benchmarks

Figure 2 shows the performance of the two methods of consolidation, compared for the three patterns, with varying problem sizes. We can see that the two consolidation methods can outperform each other for different cases. For patterns 1 and 3, tightly-coupled consolidation has a better performance, whereas loosely-coupled consolidation is better for pattern 2. This is because patterns 1 and 3 are dominated by data copy times. Thus, the main advantage of consolidation for these cases is in achieving an overlap between the computation and data movement, which is accomplished by tightly coupled consolidation. On the other hand, expressions following pattern 2 are more compute-intensive. In such cases, loosely-coupled consolidation will enable better utilization of the computing resources on the GPU. While the relative performance difference from the two methods are quite small in most cases, the overall benefit from consolidation is quite high (up to 1.5 speedup).

Overall, our results from micro-benchmarking show that tensor contractions with a larger common index should use loosely-coupled consolidation, whereas expressions with a smaller common index should use tightly-coupled consolidation. Later, we will apply this observation to tensor contractions with different number of dimensions, and determine if the observations from micro-benchmarks are still applicable.

6. EXPERIMENTAL RESULTS

This section reports on a series of experiments we conducted to evaluate the effectiveness of our parameterized micro-benchmarking approach. Particularly, we conducted experiments with the following three goals: 1) To demonstrate that the cost models about device memory accesses we learned from micro-benchmarks can help us choose the best implementation for real tensor contractions. These experiments were performed on both Fermi and T10 architectures. 2) To demonstrate that observations about the benefit from different consolidation patterns learned from micro-benchmarks match the observations on actual expressions, on the Fermi architecture. 3) To demonstrate that our

approach can obtain a significant performance improvement on an application comprising several tensor contractions.

6.1 Applying the Memory Access Cost Models

The cost models for device memory accesses we learned in Section 4 are used to choose between different index orders for a given tensor contraction. First, given an expression, the potential index orders are determined. In some cases, there is only one choice. For example, there will be only one index order of uncommon index if both input indices and output indices follow the same order. In this situation, we do not have to make any choice. Second, for each index order choice, we determine the three stride values, and the associated cost, by looking at the expression, dimension size, and index calculation order. The choice with the lowest cost is selected.

Evaluation on Fermi As we mentioned before, there are two cases in which we can choose among different index calculation orders. One is selecting the index calculation order for the uncommon index, which could either be in the order of the output matrix, or in the order of the input matrices. The other is selecting the index order for the common indices, where we could use the order from the first or the second input matrix.

Focusing on the first case, we show the effectiveness of our approach with two representative tensor contraction expressions, which are listed below:

$$R2[i,j,k,b,c,a] \mathrel{-}= I1[a,j,i,d]*I2[d,k,b,c]$$
$$R2[b,a,e,l] \mathrel{+}= I1[d,a,m,l]*I2[m,d,e,b]$$

In our experiments, we used block configuration of 16×16, which is the best configuration according to prior work [22]. The size of each dimension, T, is varied between 10 and 20. To use the cost models extracted in Section 4, the strides and number of accesses for each matrix are calculated according to the tile size.

In Expression 1, there are 6 uncommon indices. First, let us consider the case when the index calculation is done in the order of the input. For $I1$, we get the following stride values: $stride\_x$ for $I1$ is 1, because when loading $I1$, adjacent threads load adjacent elements along the common index. $stride\_y$ is T, because the threads with adjacent y values access adjacent elements along the uncommon index. $stride\_iter$ is not important here (set as 1 in the calculations), because there is only one consumed index, implying that each thread will not access the same set of unconsumed indices more than once. For $I2$, the strides are calculated in a similar way, except that the threads with adjacent x index access adjacent elements along the uncommon index, and threads with the adjacent y index access adjacent elements on the common index. For $R2$, since the indices are calculated in the order of the input matrices, $stride\_x$ is T, $stride\_y$ is T^5, and $stride\_iter$ is 16, because of the register tiling in the algorithm we use.

If the index calculation is done favoring the output, then, for $I1$, $stride\_x$ is still 1 and $stride\_y$ is T^3. For $R2$, $stride\_x$ is T, $stride\_y$ is 1, since a is the inner loop index, and $stride\_iter$ is 16. Strides with $I2$ is the same as in the case in which the input order is used.

The predicted memory access times and the actual execution times are listed in Table 1(a). Here, *In* implies that the index order is calculated in the order of the input data,

Tile Size	Pred. In	Pred. Out	Act. In	Act. Out
12	272	144	5.8	1.6
13	304	144	10	2.7
14	336	144	17	4.3
15	368	144	28	6.8
16	432	144	43	10
17	448	160	64	17
18	448	160	91	25
19	448	160	124	36
20	448	160	169	48

(a) Different uncommon index orders - expression 1

Tile Size	Pred. In	Pred. Out	Act. In	Act. Out
12	272	144	5.8	1.6
13	304	144	10	2.7
14	336	144	17	4.3
15	368	144	28	6.8
16	432	144	43	10
17	448	160	64	17
18	448	160	91	25
19	448	160	124	36
20	448	160	169	48

(b) Different uncommon index orders - expression 2

Tile Size	Pred. I2	Pred. I1	Act. I2	Act. I1
12	96	98	0.29	0.33
13	104	114	0.30	0.31
14	112	131	0.49	0.52
15	120	150	0.58	0.62
16	128	169	0.57	0.67
17	136	190	0.75	0.88
18	144	212	1.26	1.49
19	152	235	1.30	1.57
20	160	260	1.60	2.02

(c) Different common index orders

Table 1: Predicted device memory access costs ($\times S$) and actual execution times (ms) on Fermi (Pred. is the prediced time, Act. is the actual time, "I1" means the index is calculated according to order in I1, "In" means index is calculated according to the order of inputs).

Tile Size	Pred. In	Pred. Out	Act. In	Act. Out
12	32	27	0.22	0.21
13	32	27	0.28	0.27
14	31	26	0.36	0.35
15	31	26	0.51	0.48
16	36	25	0.85	0.64
17	40	40	0.94	0.92
18	36	36	1.19	1.12
19	33	33	1.45	1.35
20	30	30	1.66	1.55

(a) Different uncommon index orders

Tile Size	Pred. I2	Pred. I1	Act. I2	Act. I1
12	216	237	0.31	0.32
13	234	249	0.52	0.53
14	252	260	0.73	0.74
15	270	270	1.04	1.04
16	304	278	4.29	1.33
17	306	306	2.42	2.43
18	324	324	3.04	3.05
19	342	342	4.08	4.07
20	360	360	5.35	5.19

(b) Different common index orders

Table 2: Predicted device memory access costs ($\times S$) and actual execution times (ms) on T10 GPU

and *Out* indicates that the order of the output matrix is used. The predicted device memory access cost is a multiplication of S, which is the constant value used in the cost model. The actual time is in milliseconds. Note that our cost model is used for predicting the device memory access costs, not the actual execution times. However, different implementations arising from different index order selection can only vary in the device memory access costs. Thus, while the device memory access costs may not be proportional to the execution times, they can be used to predict which implementation will have a lower execution time. For this expression, it turns out that *Out* is always better, irrespective of the dimension size, and this is predicted by the cost model learned from micro-benchmarks as well.

In the second contraction, the number of accesses are calculated similarly, according to the dimension sizes. The predicted device memory access costs and the actual execution times are shown in Table 1(b). In all cases, the *In* implementation is predicted to have a lower execution time. This matches the actual observation, in all but one case, where the difference between two versions is only 3%. Thus, overall, the results show that our prediction methodology is very accurate, and can lead to optimal or near-optimal code.

Choosing between the input and the output order is not the only choice made for these expressions. Another important consideration is determining the processing order of the common index. We consider the following representative contraction:

R2[b,a,d,i]+= I1[c,a,j,i]*I2[b,d,j,c]

For this expression, the common index can be calculated in the order of I1 or I2, resulting in different access strides.

Using these strides and the cost models extracted earlier, we can predict the device memory access costs. The comparison between the predicted device memory costs and the actual execution times is shown in Table 1(c). We can see that the cost model directs the correct selection of index order for every dimension size.

Evaluation on T10: The same index order selection approach is tested on T10 GPUs, where the extracted cost models are quite different. First, to test uncommon index order selection, we used the following tensor contraction:

R3[j,i,b,a]+=I1[k,i]*I2[b,a,k,j]

The trends observed for this expression were identical to that for the two expressions evaluated on the Fermi GPU. A distinct expression is used to broaden the use cases considered. The calculated costs and actual performance are shown in Table 2(a). The notations used here have the same meaning as in the results reported on the Fermi cards (Table 1). From the table, we can see that for every dimension size, either the cost model directs the right selection, or the model does not show a significant difference in performance of the two versions, and the actual performance between the versions only differs marginally.

Next, to evaluate the effectiveness in predicting the common index order, we consider the following contraction:

R2[b,a,d,i]+=I1[c,a,j,i]*I2[b,d,j,c]

Similar to the evaluation study we performed on Fermi, we have the two index calculation orders here, corresponding to the index orders of tensors $I1$ and $I2$, respectively. Table 2(b) shows the predicted device memory costs, and the actual execution times. In most cases, the predictions with

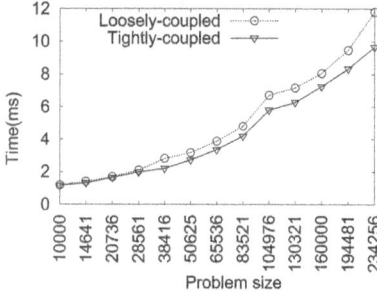
(a) Pattern (1)

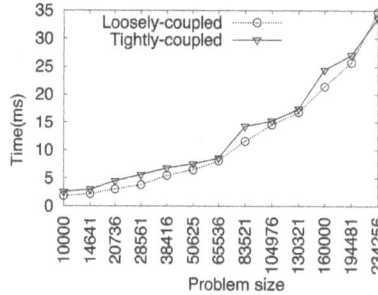
(b) Pattern (2)

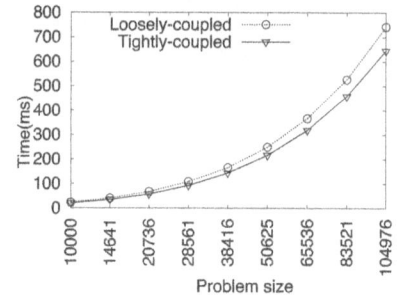
(c) Pattern (3)

Figure 2: Comparison of consolidation micro-benchmark with copy on Fermi. x-axis on all three figures show size of square matrix B (in number of doubles)

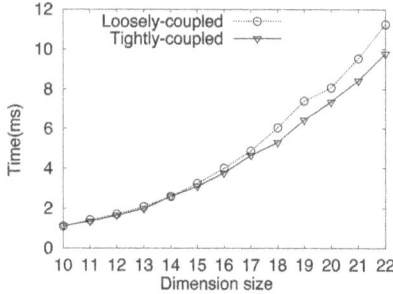
(a) Expression (I)

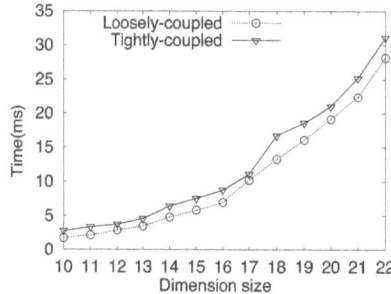
(b) Expression (II)

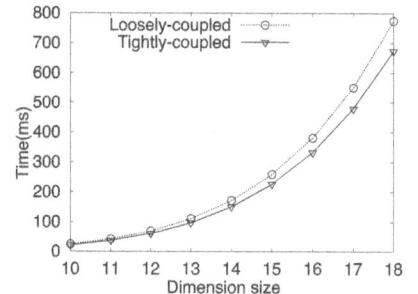
(c) Expression (III)

Figure 3: Comparison of consolidation for expression (i), (ii), (iii) with copy on Fermi

the two versions are the same, and correspondingly, there are no noticeable differences in the observed performance. An exception arises when the dimension size equals 16. We had seen from our micro-benchmarking that the performance degrades sharply in this case, and this is captured through our cost model. The prediction from the cost model indeed matches the performance of the actual expressions. Thus, we can see that our micro-benchmarking based approach can help guide optimizations that would not be possible from completely analytical approaches.

6.2 Evaluation of Kernel Consolidation

We now focus on determining if the observations made from micro-benchmarking in Section 5 are valid in practice for actual tensor contraction expressions. We used the following three tensor contractions:

```
R2[b,a,d,i]+=I1[n,i]*I2[b,a,n,d]
R2[b,a,e,i]+=I1[d,a,n,i]*I2[b,e,n,d]
R3[j,k,l,a,b,c]-=I1[b,a,j,m]*I2[k,l,c,m]
```

While these tensor contractions involve significantly more complex computations than the matrix-multiplication based micro-benchmarks, there is an important correspondence between the above three expressions and the three patterns of micro-benchmarks used in Section 5. Specifically, the first expression above has one large input matrix and one large output matrix, the second expression has three operands with the same size, and the third expression has one small input matrix and a very large output matrix. Note that if we assume that the size of each dimension is the same, these properties are easy to see from the dimensionality of each

operand. In this way, these three expressions correspond to the three patterns of the micro-benchmarks used earlier.

Figure 3 shows the experimental results on each pattern on the Fermi card. The dimension size is varied in these experiments such that the resulting problem sizes correspond to the problem sizes in Figure 2. Now, comparing Figures 2(a) and 3(a), we can see that the micro-benchmark and the real contraction show very similar trends. For all of the problem sizes, tightly-coupled consolidation is better. Larger problem sizes get more benefit from the tightly-coupled consolidation, because of greater benefit from overlapping data movement and computation. Figure 3(b) plots the performance of the second expression. Similar to the previous case, the micro-benchmark (shown in Figure 2(b)) predicts the performance of the real contraction correctly, with loosely-coupled consolidation having better performance. Figure 3(c) shows the performance on the last expression, which is also consistent with our tests using the micro-benchmarks in Figure 2(c). We can see that the trend is similar to what is shown by the micro-benchmark.

6.3 Evaluation on a Collection of Tensor Contractions

To evaluate the overall effectiveness of our auto-tuning framework, we experimented with the following collection of eight tensor contractions:

```
R3[i,e,a,b] += I1[n,a,d,i] * I2[d,e,n,b]
R3[i,e,a,b] += I1[i,n,a,d] * I2[b,e,d,n]
R3[i,d,a,b] += I1[i,n] * I2[d,n,a,b]
R3[a,b,i,m] += I1[i,n] * I2[m,n,a,b]
R3[i,e,a,b] += I1[i,n,a,d] * I2[b,e,d,n]
```

220

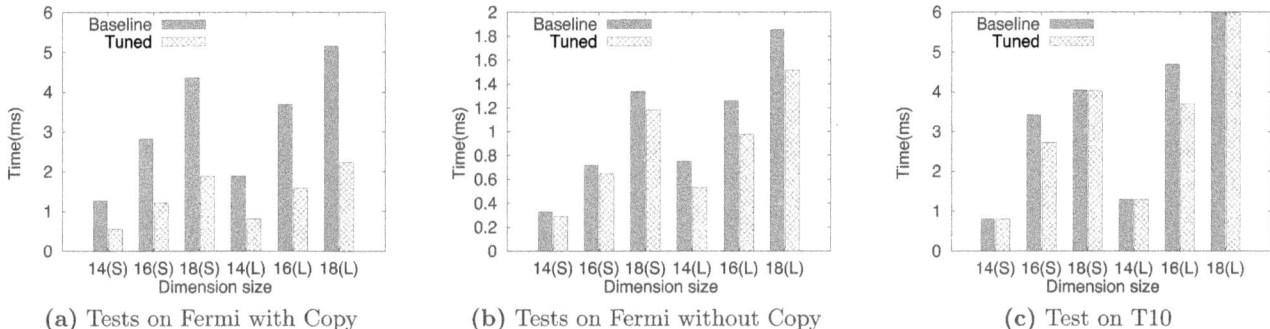

(a) Tests on Fermi with Copy   (b) Tests on Fermi without Copy   (c) Test on T10

Figure 4: Comparison between baseline and auto-tuned versions

```
R3[a,c,b,l,k,j] -= I1[d,j,k,a] * I2[c,b,l,d]
R3[c,b,a,l,j,k] += I1[m,j,a,b] * I2[m,c,l,k]
R3[j,k,l,b,c,a] -= I1[a,b,d,j,k,l] * I2[d,c]
```

We considered two scenarios. First, eight instances of each of the eight contractions, all of which can be executed in any order, were considered. In the second scenario, we increased the total work using 240 instances of the first two contractions and 8 instances of the remaining contractions. These correspond to the work done by a single process in a parallel execution involving block-sparse tensors, under different load-balancing scenarios. In all experiments involving both scenarios, we considered the largest consolidation possible, subject to the GPU memory constraint.

Three sets of experiments were performed using these applications. On the Fermi GPU, we created two versions, one with the output data being copied after execution of each task, and another where it did not need to be copied (since it was assumed that the same data is needed for the next task). The third experiment was performed using the T10 GPU, where we tested the version without data copy.

Before applying auto-tuning, we created a *baseline* version, which itself incorporated several optimizations – register tiling, use of shared memory, etc – but were not tuned for the specific GPU architecture, expression, or problem size. Particularly, in the baseline version, no consolidation is done, uncommon indices are calculated in the order of the output matrix for Fermi, and in the order of input data for T10. We chose uncommon index order in this way because there is more redundant data movement for input data in the algorithm of T10, and output is the dominant factor in terms of execution time on Fermi. Common indices are calculated in an arbitrarily chosen order by the code generator.

From the baseline version, an auto-tuned version was created for each case, using the methods presented in this paper. Figure 4(a) and Figure 4(b) show the performance of the baseline version and the tuned version on Fermi, with and without data copy. For both applications, we selected three dimension sizes: 14, 16, 18. The dimension size denoted with (S) refers to the first application (with smaller number of tasks), while the one denoted with (L) refers to the second application (with larger number of tasks).

On Fermi, with data copy, the auto-tuned version has a speedup of more than 2 over the baseline version. Without data copy, the benefits are lower, but still substantial. When the number of small tasks is increased, the benefit is more obvious. Figure 4(c) shows comparison between the

tuned version and the baseline version without data copy on the T10 GPU, with the same dimension sizes and the same collections of tensor contractions. Since we did not do kernel consolidation for T10, the version with data copy is not tested. We can see that the tuned version is about 27% faster than the baseline version when tile size is 16, and the performance is the same for other tile sizes. This is consistent with the prediction from our cost model, and earlier results with individual tensor contractions.

Overall, we show that our approach can help explore optimizations not immediately obvious to the programmer, and could be dependent on the specific GPU architecture and/or problem size. Moreover, for a complex application involving several different compute-intensive expressions, we are able to effectively apply the cost models learned from simple micro-benchmarks.

7. RELATED WORK

Auto-tuning has been extensively studied over the last decade, based on empirical search [31, 26, 32] and/or analytical models [34, 19]. Belter et al. used auto-tuning to evaluate the profitability of each optimization [5]. Chen et al. select code patterns that benefit certain applications for particular problem sizes by analyzing memory footprint and cache reuse [7].

In recent years, auto-tuning has been applied to GPG-PUs. Early work in this area considered matrix multiplication with the BrookGPU language [15]. Analytical models of applications on GPU were used for evaluating performance [13, 1] and power consumption [14]. Volkov and Demmel conducted a detailed study to investigate memory access patterns on a GPU [29]. Some of the recent auto-tuning efforts have been specific to particular kernels, such as sparse matrix-vector multiplication [8], FFTs [12], stencil computations [10], DGEMM [18], and large tridiagonal systems [11]. Investigation on existing libraries such as BLAS has also been done to enable tuning on GPUs [9]. Yet another recent effort has been specific to OpenCL [25]. Machine learning has also been used for compile-time and runtime optimization [27]. In comparison to all these approaches, we employ a novel approach, where the implications of the architectural features are learned by choosing a micro-benchmark and an associated parameter space.

8. CONCLUSIONS

Driven by the need for optimizing a tensor contraction based application on GPUs, this paper has developed a new approach to auto-tuning, which we refer to as parameterized micro-benchmarking. Simple micro-benchmarks are used to understand the performance factors that are important for the choice of implementation of target kernels. We have applied this approach to optimize for two aspects of two latest series of GPUs, namely, device memory accesses and kernel consolidation. On an application with a collection of tensor contractions, the tuned version obtained a speedup of up to 2, showing that our auto-tuning method is effective.

9. REFERENCES

[1] S. S. Baghsorkhi, M. Delahaye, S. J. Patel, W. D. Gropp, and W.-m. W. Hwu. An adaptive performance modeling tool for GPU architectures. *SIGPLAN Not.*, 45:105–114, January 2010.

[2] R. J. Bartlett and M. Musiał. Coupled-cluster Theory in Quantum Chemistry. *Rev. Mod. Phys.*, Feb 2007.

[3] M. M. Baskaran, U. Bondhugula, S. Krishnamoorthy, J. Ramanujam, A. Rountev, and P. Sadayappan. Automatic data movement and computation mapping for multi-level parallel architectures with explicitly managed memories. In *PPoPP '08*, pages 1–10, 2008.

[4] G. Baumgartner, A. Auer, D. Bernholdt, A. Bibireata, V. Choppella, D. Cociorva, X. Gao, R. Harrison, S. Hirata, S. Krishnamoorthy, et al. Synthesis of high-performance parallel programs for a class of ab initio quantum chemistry models. *Proceedings of the IEEE*, 93(2):276–292, 2005.

[5] G. Belter, E. R. Jessup, I. Karlin, and J. G. Siek. Automating the generation of composed linear algebra kernels. In *SC '09*, pages 59:1–59:12, 2009.

[6] S. Carr, K. S. McKinley, and C.-W. Tseng. Compiler optimizations for improving data locality. In *ASPLOS'94*, pages 252–262, 1994.

[7] C. Chen, C. Jacqueline, and M. Hall. Combining models and guided empirical search to optimize for multiple levels of the memory hierarchy. In *CGO '05*.

[8] J. W. Choi, A. Singh, and R. W. Vuduc. Model-driven autotuning of sparse matrix-vector multiply on gpus. PPoPP '10.

[9] H. Cui, L. Wang, J. Xue, Y. Yang, and X. Feng. Automatic Library Generation for BLAS3 on GPUs. In *IPDPS, 2011*.

[10] K. Datta, M. Murphy, V. Volkov, S. Williams, J. Carter, L. Oliker, D. Patterson, J. Shalf, and K. Yelick. Stencil computation optimization and auto-tuning on state-of-the-art multicore architectures. In *SC '08*, pages 4:1–4:12, 2008.

[11] A. Davidson, Y. Zhang, and J. D. Owens. An auto-tuned method for solving large tridiagonal systems on the GPU. In *Proceedings of the 25th IEEE International Parallel and Distributed Processing Symposium*, may 2011.

[12] Y. Dotsenko, S. S. Baghsorkhi, B. Lloyd, and N. K. Govindaraju. Auto-tuning of Fast Fourier Transform on graphics processors. In *PPoPP '11*, 2011.

[13] S. Hong and H. Kim. An analytical model for a GPU architecture with memory-level and thread-level parallelism awareness. In *ISCA '09*, 2009.

[14] S. Hong and H. Kim. An integrated GPU power and performance model. In *ISCA'10*, pages 280–289, 2010.

[15] C. Jiang and M. Snir. Automatic tuning matrix multiplication performance on graphics hardware. In *PACT'05*, pages 185–196, 2005.

[16] J. Johnson and M. Puschel. In search of the optimal Walsh-Hadamard transform. In *Proceedings of the Acoustics, Speech, and Signal Processing, 2000. Volume 06*, pages 3347–3350.

[17] S. Lee and R. Eigenmann. OpenMPC: Extended OpenMP programming and tuning for GPUs. In *SC'10*, pages 1–11, 2010.

[18] Y. Li, J. Dongarra, and S. Tomov. A Note on Auto-tuning GEMM for GPUs. In *ICCS '09*, pages 884–892, 2009.

[19] W. Ma, S. Krishnamoorthy, and G. Agrawal. Practical loop transformations for tensor contraction expressions on multi-level memory hierarchies. In *CC*, pages 266–285, 2011.

[20] W. Ma, S. Krishnamoorthy, O. Villa, and K. Kowalski. Acceleration of Streamed Tensor Contraction Expressions on GPGPU-based Clusters. In *IEEE International Conference on Cluster Computing*, September 2010.

[21] M. Moazeni, A. Bui, and M. Sarrafzadeh. A memory optimization technique for software-managed scratchpad memory in gpus. In *SASP '09*.

[22] R. Nath, S. Tomov, and J. Dongarra. An improved magma gemm for fermi graphics processing units. *International Journal of High Performance Computing Applications*, 24(4):511–515, 2010.

[23] M. Püschel, J. M. F. Moura, J. Johnson, D. Padua, M. Veloso, B. Singer, J. Xiong, F. Franchetti, A. Gacic, Y. Voronenko, K. Chen, R. W. Johnson, and N. Rizzolo. SPIRAL: Code generation for DSP transforms. *Proceedings of the IEEE, special issue on "Program Generation, Optimization, and Adaptation"*, 93(2):232– 275, 2005.

[24] K. Raghavachari, T. G.W., J. A. Pople, and M. Head-Gordon. A 5th-Order Perturbation Comparison of Electron Correlation Theories. In *Chemical Physics Letters 157(6): 479–483*, 1989.

[25] K. Spafford, J. Meredith, and J. Vetter. Maestro: data orchestration and tuning for opencl devices. In *Proceedings of the 16th international Euro-Par conference on Parallel processing: Part II*, Euro-Par'10, 2010.

[26] A. Tiwari, C. Chen, C. Jacqueline, M. Hall, and J. K. Hollingsworth. A scalable auto-tuning framework for compiler optimization. In *IPDPS*, pages 1–12, 2009.

[27] G. Tournavitis, Z. Wang, B. Franke, and M. F. O'Boyle. Towards a holistic approach to auto-parallelization: integrating profile-driven parallelism detection and machine-learning based mapping. PLDI '09, 2009.

[28] M. Valiev, E. Bylaska, N. Govind, K. Kowalski, T. Straatsma, H. V. Dam, D. Wang, J. Nieplocha, E. Apra, T. Windus, and W. de Jong. NWChem: A comprehensive and scalable open-source solution for large scale molecular simulations. *Computer Physics Communications*, 181(9):1477 – 1489, 2010.

[29] V. Volkov and J. W. Demmel. Benchmarking GPUs to tune dense linear algebra. In *SC '08*, 2008.

[30] Y. Voronenko and M. Püschel. Algebraic signal processing theory: Cooley-Tukey type algorithms for real DFTs. *IEEE Transactions on Signal Processing*, 57(1):205–222, 2009.

[31] C. Whaley, A. Petitet, and J. Dongarra. Automated empirical optimization of software and the ATLAS project. *Parallel Comp.*, 27:2001, 2000.

[32] D. B. Whalley. Tuning high performance kernels through empirical compilation. In *ICPP*, 2005.

[33] Y. Yang, P. Xiang, J. Kong, and H. Zhou. A GPGPU compiler for memory optimization and parallelism management. In *PLDI '10*, pages 86–97, 2010.

[34] K. Yotov, X. Li, G. Ren, M. Garzaran, D. Padua, K. Pingali, and P. Stodghill. Is search really necessary to generate high-performance blas? *Proceedings of the IEEE*, 93(2):358 –386, feb. 2005.

A Flexible OS-based Approach for Characterizing Solid-State Disk Endurance

Gokul B. Kandiraju   Kaoutar El Maghraoui
IBM T.J Watson Research Center, Yorktown Heights, NY 10598
{gokul, kelmaghr}@us.ibm.com

Abstract

The performance and power benefits of Flash memory have paved its adoption in mass storage devices in the form of Solid-State Disks (SSDs). Despite these benefits, Flash memory's limited write endurance remains a big impediment to its wide adoption in the enterprise server market. Existing research efforts have mostly focused on proposing various mechanisms and algorithms to improve SSD's performance and reliability. However, there is still a lack of flexible tools that allow characterizing SSD endurance (i.e., wear-out behavior) and investigating its impact on applications without affecting the lifetime of the real SSD device. To address this issue, *SolidSim*, a kernel-level simulator has been enhanced with capabilities to simulate state-of-the-art wear-leveling, garbage-collection and other advanced internal management techniques of an SSD. These extensions have further increased SolidSim's flexibility to study both SSD performance and endurance characteristics. Our approach allows investigating these characteristics without requiring any changes to applications or gathering any workload traces. The paper presents insights into wear-out behavior including logical, physical and translation characteristics, and correlates them with application behavior and SSD life-times using a set of representative workloads.

Categories and Subject Descriptors

D.4 [**Software**]: Operating Systems—*Storage Management, Performance*

Keywords

SSD, Characterization, Flash, Endurance, Simulation

1. INTRODUCTION

The use of Flash based Solid-state Disks(SSDs) is gaining a lot of momentum on both personal computing [17] and enterprise system [20] fronts. A key determinant to the use of SSDs in either of these environments is its life-time. The life-time of an SSD is dependent on (i) the characteristics of an SSD (which include the technology, internal block

and page sizes, the total size of the SSD and the type of wear-leveling and garbage-collection algorithms) and (ii) the (use-case) workload pattern. Since the characteristics of a given SSD are fixed, the workload pattern determines how long a given SSD will survive for that particular use. It is important for one, in particular the *producer* of the SSD, to understand how the *consumer* would use it so that an SSD can be designed for increased longevity. Designing an SSD for the needs of an Enterprise would require a good understanding of access characteristics of enterprise workloads and *more importantly*, the effect of such a pattern on an SSD. A typical approach by vendors ([20]) has been to estimate the life-time using worst case scenario calculations. While such life-time figures are advertised in the device specification manuals, the effects of enterprise applications on SSDs still remains to be understood. Once an SSD has been shipped, its internal policies (such as wear-leveling, garbage-collection etc.) are fixed and it is very difficult to extract out all the internal behavioral changes. SSDs usually do not expose detailed block-level statistics such as current state of the blocks, erase counts, translation mappings etc. Even if one were to extract all this information, it is very difficult to re-construct the temporal dependencies that led an SSD to that state. Therefore, simulators are a much better choice to investigate the endurance effects of applications on SSDs. While simulators exist for SSDs [21, 15], these are typically user-level simulators driven by traces. Extracting traces for applications is still a cumbersome task, and the traces usually do not reflect a complete picture of the I/O behavior. While some of the behavioral patterns might have been investigated before manufacturing, vendors typically use very detailed simulators with concocted workloads and not realistic applications.

This paper brings out the *wear-out behavior* of an SSD for two representative enterprise applications and some micro-benchmarks by using *SolidSim*, an infrastructure to simulate SSDs. By enhancing the SSD performance simulation methodology validated in [7], and making it flexible for detailed SSD endurance simulation, SolidSim is able to capture effects that a running application would have on real SSDs. The following key aspects make SolidSim a very flexible infrastructure:

- *Easy Setup* : SolidSim can be loaded as a kernel extension on a running OS and configured in minutes. Creating file-systems, paging devices, logical volumes etc. can be done using standard OS commands.

- *Enterprise Applications*: Enterprise applications (including multi-tier) can be run on SolidSim with no changes. There is no need to collect traces.

- *Simulation Methodologies* : SolidSim can be used for performance or endurance investigations. However, this paper is focused on endurance aspects of SSDs.

- *Configuration and Reporting* : SolidSim can be configured using tools that change the internal parameters of the simulator. Tools are also provided to extract plethora of statistics that are collected in the simulator.

Using this infrastructure, we simulate the SSD in a great detail including wear-leveling details, garbage collection, translation and block/page mappings, and capture the effects for enterprise and microbenchmark applications. We observe a few characteristics of the wear-out behavior and correlate them with application access patterns. We also show that looking at the translation mapping in the SSD can give a good hint about the application's access pattern, which can be used to construct techniques to dynamically set SSD parameters for better performance and endurance.

The rest of the paper is organized as follows: Section 2 gives a brief background about the basics of Flash-based SSDs and discusses related work. Section 3 presents the design of the Flash simulator and its internal algorithms. In Section 4, we present the endurance simulation methodology. Experimental results are presented in Section 5. Section 6 presents over-all observations and finally, concluding remarks and future work are discussed in Section 7.

2. BACKGROUND AND RELATED WORK

In this section, we provide a brief background about solid-state disks. We then describe related work and how they compare with our approach.

2.1 Solid-state Disks

SSD devices provide persistent storage through a non-volatile memory technology that is based on NAND Flash memory. A key feature of SSD devices is the lack of any mechanical moving parts compared to a Hard Disk Drive (HDD). SSDs have no seek time, which are inherent in conventional disks. Therefore, they can provide a much faster, and a more uniform random access speed compared to HDD. A typical NAND-Flash package is composed of a number of dies, each containing an even number of planes which itself comprises of several blocks that are typically made up of 64/128 pages. Each page reserves a region to store metadata (error detection and correction checksum). Standard block I/O interfaces are used to connect SSDs to the rest of the computing system.

Due to the absence of mechanical parts in Flash chips, their random read performance is almost as good as the sequential read performance. Reading is done at the granularity of a page. A Program operation is also done at a page granularity. Within the same blocks, page programs are performed sequentially. Erase operations on the other hand can only be done at the block level (typically 64 pages). A block erase sets all the bits in the block to 1. So any time a bit has been set to 0, changing this bit back to 1 requires erasing the entire block that it belongs to. An erase operation is also expensive (typically 1.5 ms to erase a block). Due to this major limitation, the cost of write performance can

vary depending on whether the operation requires an erase operation or not. Another important aspect of Flash SSDs is the wearing behavior. Flash memory has a finite number of erase-write cycles. Most commercially available products guarantee a life-span of about 10^5 write-erase cycles per block. Wear-leveling algorithms are used inside Flash-controllers to spread the erase operations across the Flash device in an attempt to increase its lifespan.

To hide the expensive erase operations and create abstractions for an in-place write, SSDs have an integrated controller that implements address translation, garbage collection and wear-leveling algorithms in a software layer called the Flash translation layer (FTL). The FTL emulates a block device so that unmodified files systems can run on top of the Flash SSD just as they run on top of regular block devices. Several FTL schemes have been implemented such as paged-based, block-based, FAST [16], and DFTL [12].

2.2 Related Work

Numerous research efforts have attempted to understand the behavior of Flash SSDs and improve their overall performance and reliability [6, 4, 8, 9, 12]. Work has also been done to simulate SSD operations. Existing SSD simulators have attempted at simulating some wear-leveling algorithms. Agrawal et al. [4] built a NAND-Flash simulator based on the DiskSim simulation environment [10]. DiskSim is driven by externally-provided I/O request traces or internally-generated synthetic workloads. Agrawal et al's SSD simulator extends DiskSim by adding SSD features and implementing the page-based FTL scheme. CPS-SIM [15] is another Flash SSD simulator that is limited by a single FTL scheme. FlashSim [21] has an object-oriented design and supports simulating multiple FTL schemes using workload traces. All these simulators rely on existing traces, artificial workloads and/or are limited by one FTL scheme. SolidSim does not rely on traces. It is capable of running unmodified workloads as if they were running on a real SSD device. Hence, it is capable of capturing more realistic access patterns that would be difficult to capture through traces. SolidSim also has pluggable components that allows it to simulate various FTL algorithms.

Boboila et al. [5] conduct experiments at the chip-level and show that the endurance observed is far more than what is quoted by manufacturers. Other studies such as [20] estimate the life-time of Flash based on 'heavy-stream' usage. Soundararajan et al. [19] propose using HDD as write cache for SSD to extend the lifetime of the SSD device by reducing the number of writes to SSD. Little work has been done to characterize SSD endurance for enterprise workloads. Mohan et al. [18] build a model for the physical processes that affect endurance based on physical cell stress and recovery process. Their model focuses mainly on the physical characteristics of the SSD device and how they relate to endurance. This paper focuses on studying endurance characteristics at the application-level. SolidSim's unique architecture and features allow easily conducting an in depth characterization of endurance for many applications.

3. OVERVIEW OF SOLIDSIM

Several features render SoliSim a flexible framework for characterizing SSDs, investigating performance impact, and studying various wear-leveling algorithms using realistic workloads. Firstly, *SolidSim* is a dynamically loadable kernel ex-

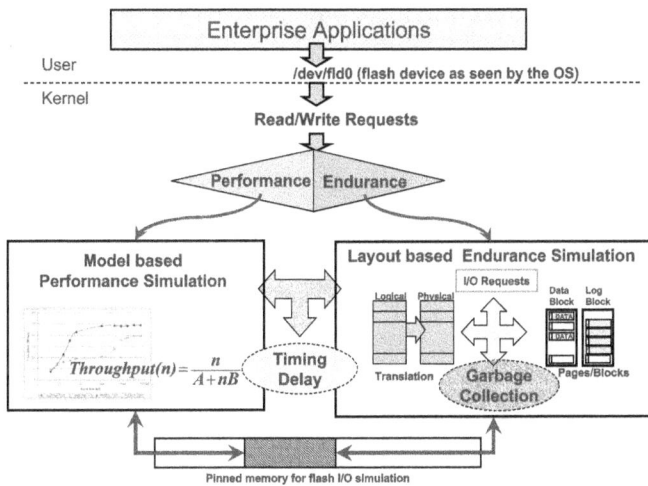

Figure 1: Flexible Architecture of SolidSim

4. ENDURANCE SIMULATION

Figure 2 shows the internal architecture of SolidSim. Every read/write operation arrives as an I/O request and is examined to see if it is a read or a write operation. A delay for that operation is simulated. A dedicated kernel-process handles all these requests (resembling the notion of a Flash controller). In addition, the data transfer part is simulated using a high-performance memcpy operation implemented using firmware calls (*hypervisor* calls). This allows for minimal overhead in copy operations. Delays are simulated using high-resolution nanosecond granularity timer services that are provided by the kernel.

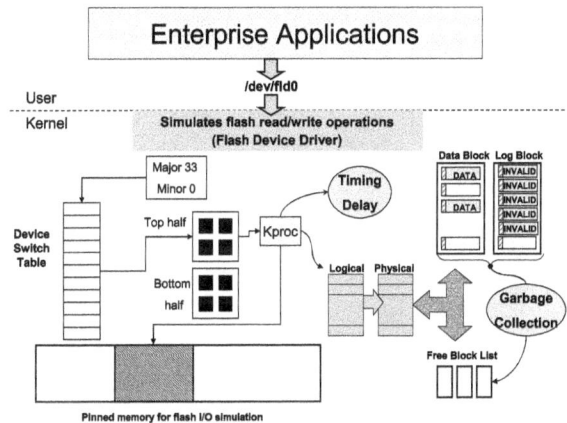

Figure 2: Internal Architecture of the Flash Simulator

SolidSim has been extended with functionality to allow simulating block-level translation and log-block based garbage collection mechanisms. Block-level translation in Flash drives, as opposed to page-level translation, reduces the overhead of resources required to maintain translation information which is crucial for cost and power consumption reasons. But maintaining block-level translation may lead to quicker wear-out of the drive due to a larger number of erases. In order to prevent this, [14] proposed Log-block based FTL that uses a hybrid approach (block-level translation while efficiently handling small size writes using log-blocks) to extend the life-time of Flash memories. In addition, we implement *cyclic wear-leveling* [11] where we re-cycle the erased blocks in a circular manner to maximize the life-time of all the blocks.

In the hybrid FTL scheme implemented as part of Solid-Sim, most of the simulated SSD drive is block-mapped. These blocks are referred to as *data blocks*. A small number of blocks, called *log blocks* are page-mapped. The main purpose of log blocks is to deal with overwrites to the data blocks. Since log blocks usually constitute a small portion of the entire address space, the page mapping table used for them is relatively small. When the first overwrite happens to a page in a data block, a log block is associated with this data block. This is illustrated in Figure 3 in step 3. In this example, *page3* in a new data block is being written to for the first time in step 1. *page5* is then written in step 2. In these cases, since there are no overwrites, writes can directly

tension (kernel module) on the AIX operating system that 'pins' a chunk of memory and simulates it as Flash memory. Once the extension is loaded, the simulated Flash device appears on the system as a disk device. The OS simply knows the kernel extension as a driver for a disk device and passes I/O requests to the kernel extension strategy routine to handle read/write operations, which does data transfers and simulates delays. Logical volumes and paging devices can be configured on top of the simulated device. Hence, many configurations are possible which narrow the gap between the simulator and realistic deployments of SSDs.

Secondly, due to the seamless integration of SolidSim with the OS, any application can run on top of solidSim as if it were running on a real SSD device. The advantage of this feature is that complex application scenarios can be run with SolidSim without any changes. Usually, this is not possible with state of the art simulators, which require capturing traces of workloads and then simulating them offline.

Last but not least, SolidSim provides two different ways of simulating an SSD device (as shown in Figure 1): A model-based performance simulation and a layout-based endurance simulation. The performance model allows simulating an SSD drive without having any knowledge about its internal characteristics such as read/write timings, block/page-level translation, wear-leveling algorithms, etc. The performance model parameters are extracted using a real SSD device and then fed into the simulator. More details about the performance simulation are described in [7]. Model-based performance simulation is especially important when one needs to investigate performance-related issues of using SSD in their enterprise and how they compare with other storage types like HDD. On the other hand, when it is becomes important to investigate the inner details of Flash memory, SolidSim provides another way of simulating various details about wear-leveling, logical-to-physical translation and garbage collection. This Layout-based endurance simulation is the focus of this work. More details about the algorithm implemented are explained in Section 4.

go to the data block. In step 3, the overwritten page in the data block is invalidated and copied to the first page in the corresponding log block. Any subsequent overwrites to this data block are written to the next available pages in the log block as illustrated in steps 4 and 5. When all the pages in the log block are used up, the data block and its log block need to be *merged* into a free (erased) data block (step 6). After merge, the old data block and its log block are erased and recycled to the free pools (FIFO queues) of data and log blocks (as illustrated in step 7). In order to maximize life-time of the blocks, we add the erased log block into the free data block pool and vice versa. This way, the wear-out is distributed evenly in a cyclic manner. Otherwise, the few log blocks would wear out quickly.

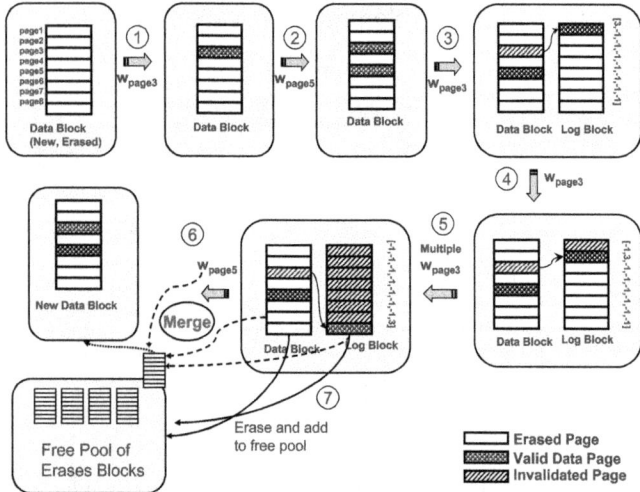

Figure 3: Sample write, erase, and merge operations in the log-block-based wear-leveling algorithm

5. PERFORMANCE EVALUATION

All the experiments were conducted on the IBM AIX v6 Operating System running on POWER6 processor with 4.7 GHz clock speed, 2 physical CPUs, and 2 hardware threads (SMTs) per CPU.

5.1 Benchmarks

We used several applications to capture the variation in characteristics of diverse workloads. For all of the benchmarks described below, we created necessary devices (logical volumes for the file-system benchmarks, paging devices for paging benchmarks and raw volumes for others) on top of the simulator. Our page size is fixed at 4K and we internally have 64 pages per Flash block (i.e., block size is 256K). In all the experiments, we have 64 log blocks and the remaining are data blocks. We briefly describe the benchmarks here:

- *Fileop File-system Benchmark* : *fileop* is a benchmark from the IOzone benchmark package [2]). It creates a set of directories/sub-directories/files hierarchy and tests the performance of the file-system by stressing the system using various operations such as mkdir, rmdir, create, open, read, write, link, unlink, delete, etc. We use the benchmark to create smaller (4KB

Benchmark	Execution Time	Disk Space	Reads	Writes
Sequential	3.5 min	1GB	(no reads)	3.67 M
Random	6.3 min	1GB	3.3 M	3.59 M
fileop4K	7 min	1GB	272 K	3.63 M
fileop1M	5 min	1GB	2.47 M	3.36 M
SPECJbb	20 min	1.5GB	3.76 M	3.79 M
DayTrader	20 min	1.5GB	18.3 M	8.87 M

Table 1: Global Statistics for all the Applications (K=Thousands, M=millions).

size) files as well as larger (1MB size) files. In the first scenario, 256K files/directories are created/deleted in the file system, thus effectively taking up 1GB of disk space (i.e., simulator memory). In the second scenario, 1024 files/dirs are created/deleted, again using about 1GB of the disk space. In the results shown below, we represent these two scenarios by *fileop4K* and *fileop1M* respectively.

- *SPECJbb 2005 benchmark* : SPECJbb [3] is a benchmark from the Standard Performance Evaluation Corporation (SPEC) based on the TPC-C benchmark specifications. It emulates a 3-tier system in a JVM with emphasis on the middle tier. We ran SPECJbb with 1.5GB memory and used the SolidSim as a paging device for it. The benchmark mainly exercised 1GB of the SSD space. SPECJbb was configured and executed with 8 warehouses.

- *Day Trader* : DayTrader [1] is a Websphere benchmark application that emulates an on line stock trading system. The application allows users to perform typical trading operations such as login, viewing portfolios, looking up stock quotes, and buying or selling stock shares. The DayTrader server was hosting an instance of the DB2 database and an instance of the WebSphere Application Server (WAS). The DayTrader client is a Linux Intel Xeon machine running the JIBE (WebSphere Studio Workload Simulator), which simulates a specifiable number of concurrent browser clients. We simulated 500 clients for stressing the DayTrader application running on the DayTrader server. We configured SolidSim as a paging device to the DayTrader. About 1GB of the simulator space was actively exercised.

- *Microbenchmarks* : We also stressed the system with sequential and random microbenchmarks. *Sequential* benchmark repeatedly accesses the entire device in a sequential manner, writing to every page (there are no reads). *Random* benchmark access the device using a uniform random number generator. Each request randomly 'seeks' to an offset in a device and randomly reads or writes.

Table 1 shows statistics for applications at a global level. Our attempt was to run each benchmark for certain amount of time so that the resulting number of writes across the benchmarks roughly remains the same (for ease of analysis and comparison). Table 1 shows that for the benchmarks, we had about 3.3-3.7 million writes, except for *DayTrader* where we could not exercise detailed control due to its complex setup. Number of reads varies with the application and we consistently exercised disk space of about 1-1.5GB for all the benchmarks.

5.2 Logical Level Behavior

We first look at *logical block behavior* of the applications. This represents the behavior of the I/O requests of the application that arrive at the SSD (hence *logical* from an SSD perspective, since this is before the internal translation). Looking at the logical level behavior can give us a picture of how application reads/writes are distributed in the application I/O space. Block level read/write counts can give us an understanding if there are any 'hot' (frequently accessed) blocks. It can also serve as a good reference point to evaluate physical level behavior (for example, the performance of an SSD wear-leveling algorithm can be evaluated by analyzing if the 'hot' blocks at logical-level get evenly distributed to the physical level).

Figure 4 shows logical level behavior of the applications. For each application, we present the read/write counts for each logical block accessed. Each logical block will be associated with log blocks (as described in section 4) on multiple writes. At some point, when the log block is full, the physical block associated with the logical block and the log block are *merged* together into a new physical block, and the logical-to-physical block mapping is updated. Therefore, we also present the *number of merges* that each logical block goes through during the application run. For each application, the range on the x-axis that has been exercised has non-zero y-values.

Figure 4(a) shows that for *Sequential*, every block is written about 1000 times on average and this results in 14-15 merges for each logical block. SolidSim was configured to have 64 pages per block. So, If the pages are written sequentially, then there is a merge roughly every 64 pages (64 writes). On the other hand, from Figure 4(b) for *Random*, while the number of writes are almost the same, the merges are far higher (averaging about 800). This is because the *Random* workload writes all over the logical space quickly consuming all the log blocks and forcing SSD to merge more often. Therefore, the quality of merges is far poorer (looking at the statistics in detail showed that for a large number of cases, only one page of the log-block was actually used or 'dirty' compared to the *Sequential* case where most of the pages of the log blocks were dirty). While *Sequential* and *Random* represent two extreme cases, Figures 4(c) and 4(d) show the logical counts for the *fileop* benchmark. *fileop4K* has about 100 writes per block on average, but the majority of logical blocks cause only about 5-6 merges. The only exception are a set of 10 blocks (around block number 1900, represented by the peak in the graph) that have about 190K writes (causing 3000 merges) each. *fileop1M*, on the other hand, has about 1000 writes per block on average, but causing only 10 merges per block. An observation here is that while the average number of writes for *fileop1M* is at least 10 times that of *fileop4K*, the number of merges only doubles (10 merges for most of the blocks as shown in Figure 4(d)). This is attributed to the fact that *fileop1M* creates and access 1MB files/chunks in a sequential manner. Hence, the log block usage is much more efficient.

Figures 4(e) and 4(f) show the logical counts for the *SPECJbb* and the *DayTrader* benchmarks respectively. Accesses are much more non-deterministic compared to the other benchmarks in these cases. However, general correlation between the number of writes and merges can be seen.

5.3 Physical Level Behavior

This section focuses on the physical level behavior of the applications. Figure 5 shows the statistics gathered at the physical level. The main metrics to observe at this level are the read, write and erase counts. Merges at logical level get translated to erases at physical level. However, a merge combines a data block and a log block into a new data block. Therefore, physically, a merge results in using an already erased block but producing two new erased blocks. Figure 5(a) shows write and erase counts for all the physical blocks for *Sequential*. Most of the blocks have 14 erases and all the blocks wear out *evenly* due to the cyclic wear-leveling explained in Section 4. Figure 5(b) shows similar counts for *Random*. It can be seen that while the number of writes for every physical block is roughly the same (as *Sequential*), the erase counts are very high. This is due to the fact that as *Random* workload writes to different blocks of the device, the system quickly runs out of the log blocks, forcing more merges/erases. In other words, the utilization of a log block is reduced (with only one or two valid data pages) as mentioned in the previous section. The erase counts in Figure 5(b) can also be correlated with logical merge counts shown in Figure 4(b).

For a workload like *Random*, the larger the number of log blocks, the better it is. However, given an SSD of fixed size, increasing the number of log blocks corresponds to a direct reduction of data blocks. On the other hand, for a workload like *Sequential*, a low number of log blocks is acceptable. Therefore, an important observation here is that one needs the right balance between data and the log blocks based on the workload.

Figures 5(c) and 5(d) show physical counts for the *fileop* benchmarks (y-axes are in the log scale). The Figures show that the erase counts for *fileop1M* are lower than those of *fileop4K*. This is again attributed to the sequentiality in access patterns of *fileop1M*. It is also interesting to note that despite the fact that there is cyclic wear-leveling built into the SSD simulator, there is still some unevenness in the way blocks wear-out because of the limited nature of log blocks. When a write arrives for a new data block after all the log blocks are in use, a *forced* merge needs to happen. Therefore using the right number of log blocks is an important parameter to wear-leveling. If there were no cyclic wear-leveling in the system, then the erase counts of the physical blocks would have been much more directly related to the 'logical write behavior', thus causing uneven wear-out and making certain blocks defective before others. Figures 5(e) and 5(f) show physical counts for *SPECJbb* and *DayTrader* benchmarks respectively. The variation in erase counts is very high for these two benchmarks.

5.4 Logical to Physical Translation

Having seen characteristics at Logical and Physical levels individually, we now present Logical to Physical translation characteristics. SSDs typically maintain tree-like structures to maintain Logical to Physical block map [13]. This mapping changes on every write. For the log block scheme, a second write to a page in the data block causes the write to be written to the log block and update the mapping. Further periodic merges cause the map to change again, complicating its evolution. In order to study the characteristics of this map, we initialize the map to a linear map and observe how the map changes due to an application run. Figure 6 shows

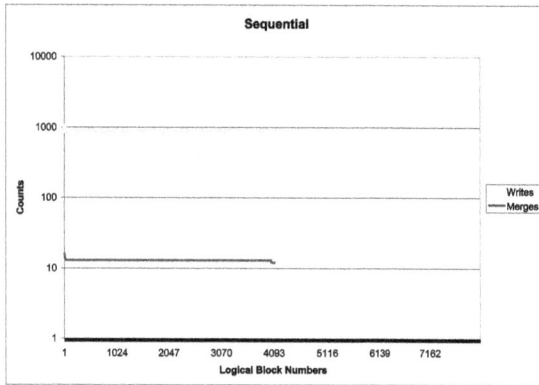

(a)

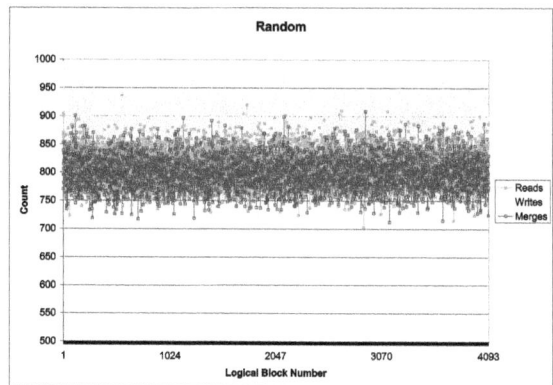

(b)

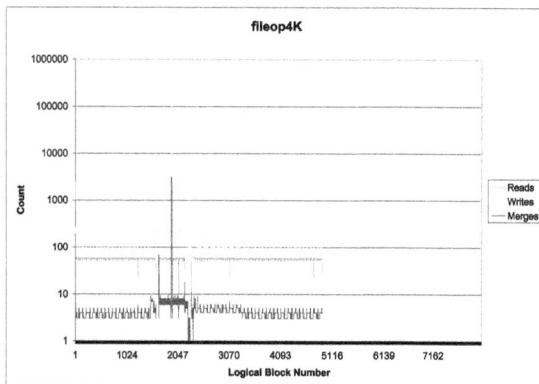

(c)

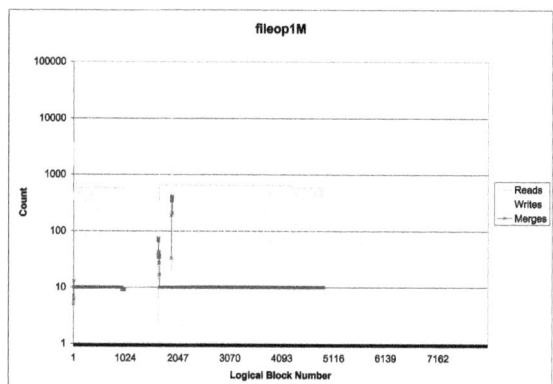

(d)

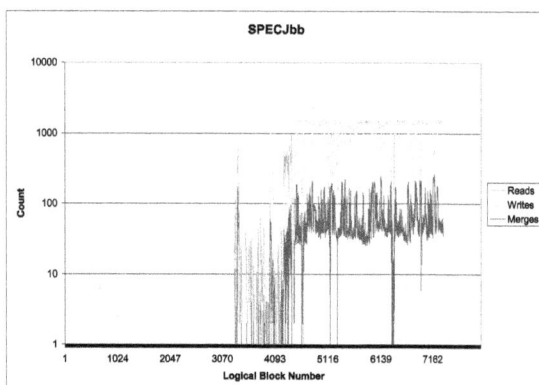

(e)

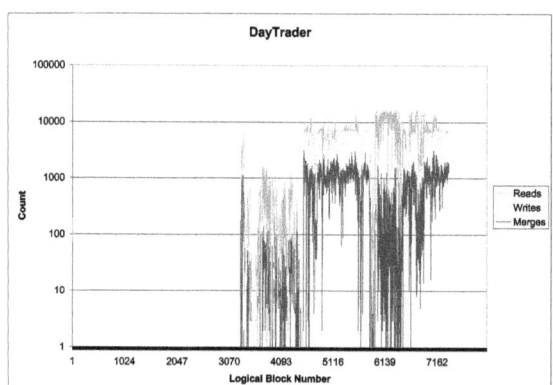

(f)

Figure 4: Logical Block Statistics for all the Applications

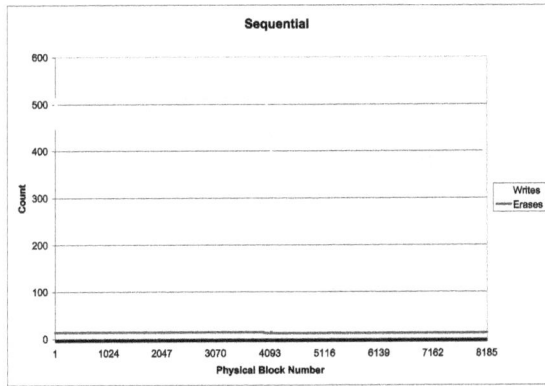

(a)

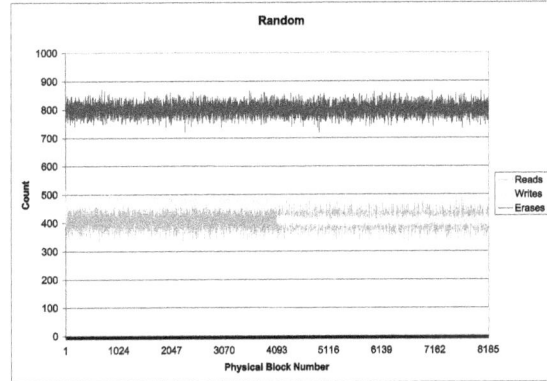

(b)

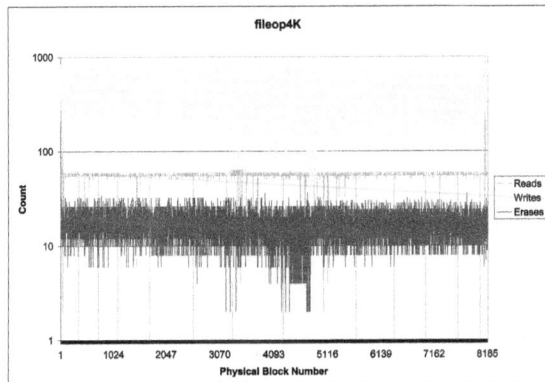

(c)

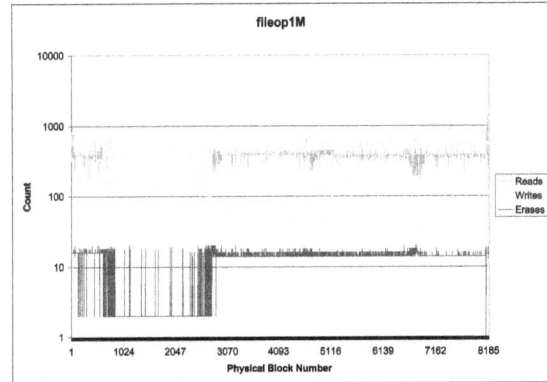

(d)

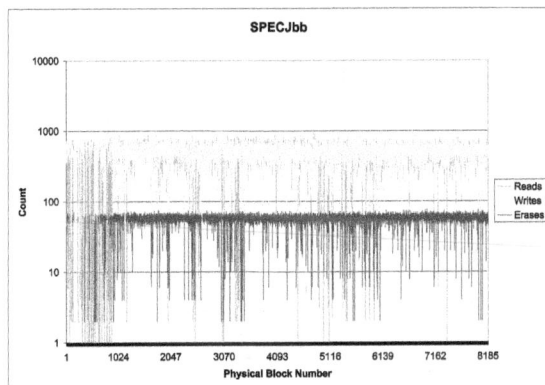

(e)

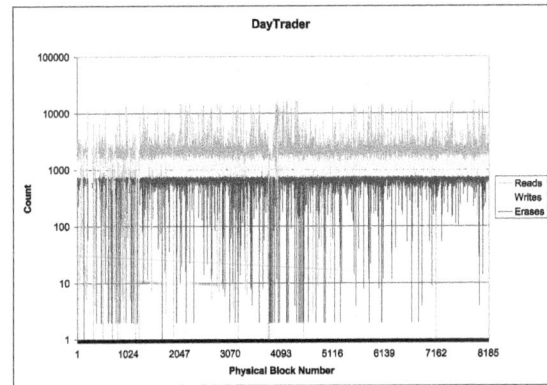

(f)

Figure 5: Physical Block Statistics for all the Applications

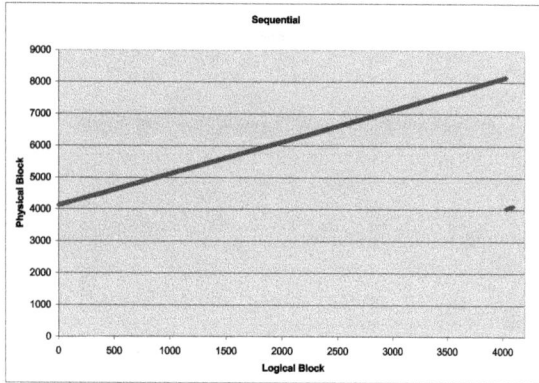

(a)

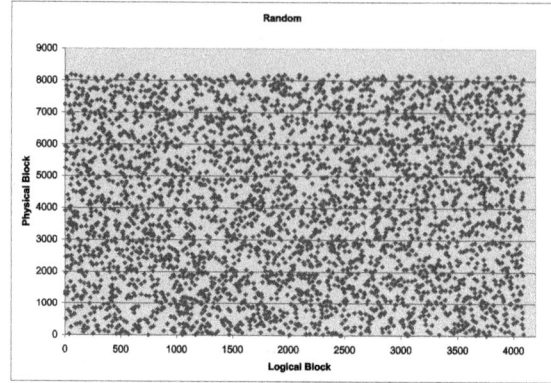

(b)

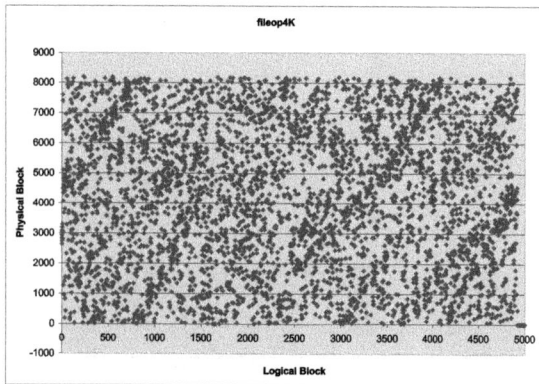

(c)

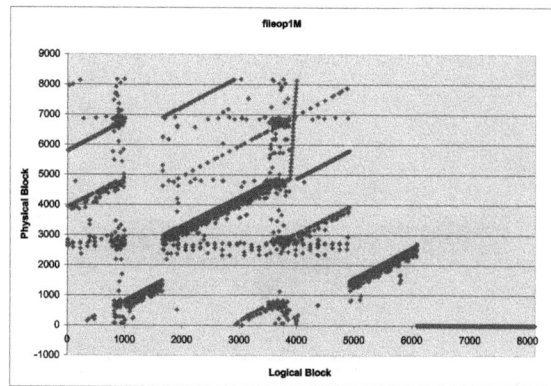

(d)

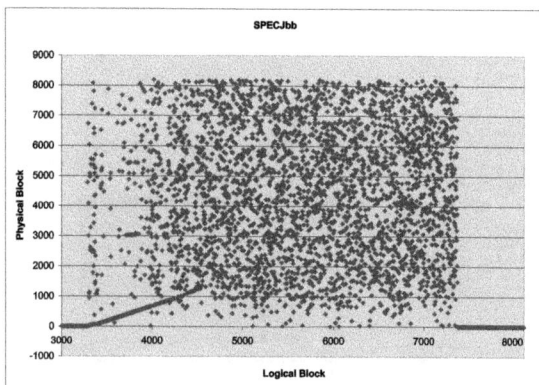

(e)

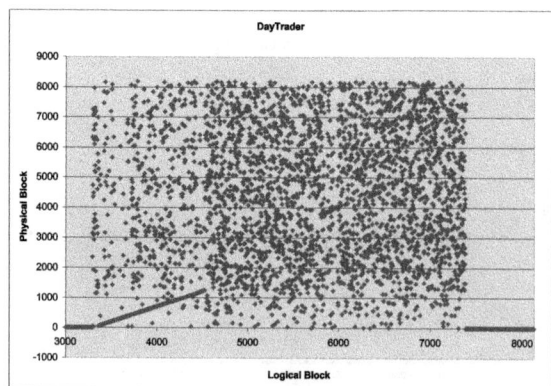

(f)

Figure 6: Logical-to-physical Mappings in the SSD after each Application's Run (map was a simple linear map before the run)

this logical-to-physical mapping for all the applications. For each application, the $x - axis$ represents the logical block number and the $y - axis$ represents the physical block number.

Figure 6(a) shows the resulting map after the execution of *Sequential* workload. The sequential behavior of the application hardly does anything to the linearity of the map. In fact, all that happens is that there is a shift in the map. This is also consistent with the merge/erase counts observed in the previous sections. On the other hand, Figure 6(b) shows the map after the *Random* workload finishes. In this case, random access has distorted the map from linearity. Figures 6(c) and 6(d) show the map for the *fileop* workloads. For *fileop1M*, we observe that the linearity has been preserved much more compared to *fileop4K*. This is attributed to the fact that *fileop1M* uses 1MB blocks causing periodic linear access. Finally, we observe that both the applications *SPECJbb* and *DayTrader* exhibit similar map behavior. Figures 6(e) and 6(f) show that the way the map is 'distorted' is very similar. Both applications cause paging to the simulated SSD device through the Operating System. Hence, OS interference (and characteristic) is causing similar mapping changes in both these applications.

Benchmark	r^2
Initialization	1
Sequential	0.825
Random	0.000469
fileop4K	0.000314
fileop1M	0.0204
SPECJbb	0.1335
DayTrader	0.1323

Table 2: r^2 Values for Linear Regression Fit for the Logical-to-physical Translation Maps after the Application Runs.

We now quantify the linearity change in the logical-to-physical mappings to confirm our observations from the graphs. We do a linear regression fit across the logical-to-physical translation mappings for all the applications. Table 2 shows the r^2 values for all the curves. The higher the r^2 value (i.e., the closer it is to 1), the more linear is the mapping. The *Initialization* row corresponds to the r^2 value before running any benchmark and hence the r^2 value of 1(linear mapping).

As expected, *Sequential* workload has the highest r^2 value. r^2 values for *Random* and *fileop4K* are very close. We observe that the r^2 value of *Random* has a slightly better value than *fileop4K*. This is attributed to the fact that *fileop4K* also handles metadata read/writes which have variable small sizes. This causes more randomness than what is observed in the *Random* workload, which consistently handles $4K$ sized data blocks. This also could be attributed to the randomness behavior of the *Random* workload. However, the two values are very close and both workloads can be considered as having a random behavior. On the other hand, *fileop1M* has higher value due to the linearity of accesses while accessing 1MB files. Although *SPECJbb* and *DayTrader* are different applications, their r^2 values are almost the same. This further corroborates that although applications have different access patterns, their I/O requests exhibit similar behavior due to paging.

5.5 Relative SSD Life-time

In this section, we compare the applications and compute *relative wear-out rate* of the SSDs. The number of erases is used as an important determinant in deriving the relative wear-out ratios. Table 3 shows *normalized* erase counts for 3 million writes in Column 4 and uses that to calculate normalized erases per block (Column 6). Relative wear-out rate is calculated w.r.t *Sequential* workload, assuming that the wear-out rate of *Sequential* is 1.

The way to interpret the last column of Table 3, *relative wear-out*, is that if an application has a relative wear-out of x, then the application would wear-out an SSD block on average x times faster than the *Sequential* workload. For example, if an SSD is used only to run the *Random* workload, it would live on average 63 times shorter compared to an SSD that runs only a *Sequential* workload (since the number in *Random* row is 63). In our experiments, we used a block size of 64 pages and a completely random workload would cause 63 more erases for every one erase of a sequential workload. Similarly, running only *DayTrader* on an SSD would have its life time 17.8 times less than the SSD that would be used to run only *Sequential* on average. However, it should be noted that the purpose of these numbers is to give an idea of *relative wear-out* only. We used in these experiments a disk size of 1GB throughout and run the experiment continuously. In real world, where disk sizes are much larger, we expect a lower value of normalized erases per block.

6. OVERALL OBSERVATIONS

We presented logical, physical and logical-to-physical characteristics for different applications and correlated them with application behavior. We presented write, merge (logical level), erase (physical level) counts, translation mapping details and explained how application behavior might impact SSD life-times. However, we would like to emphasize some important observations:

- Logical-level characteristics translate into very different physical level characteristics. Translation mechanism, wear-leveling methods and the garbage collection scheme play an important role in determining this mapping.

- Blocks may wear-out *slightly unevenly* even in the presence of cyclic wear-leveling. This may occur due to other restrictions imposed by garbage collection or translation mechanism (for example, number of log blocks may be limited, thus forcing a merge)

- In a log block based garbage collection scheme, it is important to maintain the right number of log blocks based on the workload: balancing between more log blocks (to capture application randomness) and more data blocks (to cater to application working set).

- Logical-to-physical mappings' changes can be correlated with application logical reference patterns. Thus, a sequential workload will probably preserve the linearity in the logical-to-physical mappings whereas a random workload will 'distort' it.

- Therefore, Linear regression models, when applied to logical-to-physical mappings can give a good hint of how sequential the workload is and could be used to determine the garbage collection parameters (such as number of log blocks).

Benchmark	Writes	Erases	Normalized Erases (for 3M writes)	Number of Phys. Blocks accessed	Normalized erases per block	Relative Wear-out Rate
Sequential	3.67 M	106420	86992	8192	10.6	1
Random	3.59 M	6.56 M	5.48M	8192	668.2	63
fileop4K	3.63 M	137974	114028	8192	13.9	1.3
fileop1M	3.36 M	94258	84159	8192	10.3	0.97
SPECJbb	3.79 M	417826	330733	8192	40.4	3.8
DayTrader	8.87 M	4.59 M	1.55M	8192	189.5	17.8

Table 3: Relative Life-times for SSDs Relative to Sequential Workload. (in the table, M = million)

We think that the last observation is a particularly important one for the research community. Translation data (which is persistent on the SSD) can be used to derive intelligent metrics to predict application access patterns. By using this data, one can develop schemes for SSD to adapt itself to the application.

7. CONCLUSIONS AND FUTURE WORK

This paper presents a methodology to characterize the wear-out behavior of an SSD for applications through simulation. Two enterprise applications and several micro-benchmarks have been used. The methodology uses SolidSim, an OS kernel level simulator that can simulate sophisticated SSD algorithms. The characterization presented includes analysis at logical and physical levels and correlates observed characteristics with application behavior. Translation patterns and their linearity properties are studied to see how applications change the translation. Relative impact on SSD life-times is presented and key observations from the study are enumerated.

This is still a very fertile area of research. This paper not only brings out all the details of the characterization but also identifies potential ways to further optimize SSDs and improve their performance and endurance. For example, capturing the 'linearity' of logical-to-physical block mapping on an SSD dynamically (or periodically), and using that information to determine (or change) parameters of garbage collection algorithm (such as the number of log blocks), is an interesting idea that is worth exploring. Work is also underway to further study the impact of SSD wear-out on the performance of applications and analyze more enterprise workloads.

8. REFERENCES

[1] Apache DayTrader Benchmark Sample:
http://cwiki.apache.org/GMOxDOC20/daytrader.html.
[2] IOzone Filesystem Benchmark: http://www.iozone.org/.
[3] SPECJbb2005(Java Performance Benchmark),
http://www.spec.org/jbb2005/.
[4] N. Agrawal, V. Prabhakaran, T. Wobber, J. D. Davis, M. Manasse, and R. Panigrahy. Design tradeoffs for SSD Performance. In *ATC'08: USENIX 2008 Annual Technical Conference on Annual Technical Conference*, pages 57–70, Berkeley, CA, USA, 2008. USENIX Association.
[5] S. Boboila and P. Desnoyers. Write endurance in flash drives: measurements and analysis. In *Proceedings of the 8th USENIX conference on File and storage technologies*, FAST'10, pages 9–9, Berkeley, CA, USA, 2010. USENIX Association.
[6] Y.-H. Chang, J.-W. Hsieh, and T.-W. Kuo. Endurance enhancement of Flash-memory Storage Systems: An efficient static wear leveling design. In *DAC '07: Proceedings of the 44th annual Design Automation Conference*, pages 212–217, New York, NY, USA, 2007. ACM.
[7] K. El Maghraoui, G. Kandiraju, J. Jann, and P. Pattnaik. Modeling and simulating flash based solid-state disks for operating systems. In *Proceedings of the first joint*

WOSP/SIPEW international conference on Performance engineering, WOSP/SIPEW '10, pages 15–26, New York, NY, USA, 2010. ACM.
[8] E. Gal and S. Toledo. A Transactional Flash File System for Microcontrollers. In *ATEC '05: Proceedings of the annual conference on USENIX Annual Technical Conference*, Berkeley, CA, USA, 2005. USENIX Association.
[9] E. Gal and S. Toledo. Algorithms and Data Structures for Flash Memories. *ACM Comput. Surv.*, 37(2):138–163, 2005.
[10] G. R. Ganger, B. L. Worthington, and Y. N. Patt. The DiskSim Simulation Environment - Version 2.0 Reference Manual. Technical report, 1999.
[11] S. A. Gorobets, A. D. Bennett, P. J. Smith, A. W. Sinclair, K. M. Conley, and P. D. Royall. Cyclic flash memory wear leveling : SanDisk Corporation. Patent number: 7441067, 2008 (issued).
[12] A. Gupta, Y. Kim, and B. Urgaonkar. DFTL: A Flash Translation Layer employing demand-based selective caching of page-level address mappings. In *ASPLOS '09: Proceeding of the 14th international conference on Architectural support for programming languages and operating systems*, pages 229–240, New York, NY, USA, 2009. ACM.
[13] D. Kang, D. Jung, J.-U. Kang, and J.-S. Kim. μ-tree: an ordered index structure for nand flash memory. In *Proceedings of the 7th ACM & IEEE international conference on Embedded software*, EMSOFT '07, pages 144–153, New York, NY, USA, 2007. ACM.
[14] J. Kim, J. M. Kim, S. H. Noh, S. L. Min, and Y. Cho. A Space Efficient Flash translation layer for CompactFlash systems. *IEEE Transactions on Consumer Electronics*, 48:366–375, 2002.
[15] J. Lee, E. Byun, H. Park, J. Choi, D. Lee, and S. H. Noh. CPS-SIM: Configurable and accurate clock Precision Solid State drive Simulator. In *SAC '09: Proceedings of the 2009 ACM symposium on Applied Computing*, pages 318–325, New York, NY, USA, 2009. ACM.
[16] S.-W. Lee, D.-J. Park, T.-S. Chung, D.-H. Lee, S. Park, and H.-J. Song. A Log buffer-based Flash Translation Layer using fully-associative sector translation. *ACM Trans. Embed. Comput. Syst.*, 6(3):18, 2007.
[17] Lenovo. Lenovo Products, 2009.
http://lenovo.com/us/en/index.html.
[18] V. Mohan, T. Siddiqua, S. Gurumurthi, and M. R. Stan. How I learned to stop worrying and love flash endurance. In *HotStorage'10: Proceedings of the 2nd USENIX conference on Hot topics in storage and file systems*, pages 3–3, Berkeley, CA, USA, 2010. USENIX Association.
[19] G. Soundararajan, V. Prabhakaran, M. Balakrishnan, and T. Wobber. Extending ssd lifetimes with disk-based write caches. In *Proceedings of the 8th USENIX conference on File and storage technologies*, FAST'10, pages 8–8, Berkeley, CA, USA, 2010. USENIX Association.
[20] Texas Memory Systems. An In-depth Look at the RamSan-630 Flash Solid State Disk, 2010. http://www.ramsan.com.
[21] K. Youngjae, T. Brendan, G. Aayush, and U. Bhuvan. FlashSim: A Simulator for NAND Flash-based Solid-State Drives. In *The First International Conference on Advances in System Simulation*, 2009.

An Out-of-Order Vector Processing Mechanism for Multimedia Applications

Ye Gao[†], Ryusuke Egawa[†‡*], Hiroyuki Takizawa[†*], Hiroaki Kobayashi[†‡*]

[†]Graduate School of Information Sciences, Tohoku University, Sendai, 980-8578, Japan.
[‡]Cyberscience Center, Tohoku University, Sendai, 980-8578, Japan. [*]JST CREST.
{gaoye@sc., egawa@, tacky@, koba@}isc.tohoku.ac.jp

ABSTRACT

Next generation multimedia applications (MMAs) will become a heavy workload for general-purpose processors (GPPs). Although the current single instruction multiple data (SIMD) extensions enable to improve the performance of MMAs, their limited parallel-processing capability is a drawback to execute next generation MMAs in the era of data explosion. This paper proposes an out-of-order vector processing mechanism named OVPM, in order to expand the potential of GPPs on next generation media processing. OVPM can more efficiently utilize memory bandwidth and vector function units than a conventional in-order vector processing mechanism (IVPM), especially for the MMAs with short vectors. The results of performance evaluations using kernels of MMAs show that OVPM achieves a higher performance than that with IVPM.

Categories and Subject Descriptors

C.1.2 [**Processor Architectures**]: Multiple Data Stream Architectures(Multiprocessors)—*Single-instruction-stream, multiple-data-stream processors (SIMD)*

General Terms

Design, Performance

Keywords

vector architecture, SIMD extension, multimedia application

1. INTRODUCTION

With the development of computer science and technologies, our society is experiencing a new era of data explosion. In the multimedia domain, the unprecedented amount of data is derived from the ever-growing demands for high quality media processing. The explosion of data leads to high computation requirements. For example, high definition video decoders have 10-100x longer computation times than standard definition video decoders, and a 3-D computer visual algorithm for super resolution images needs 25-200x higher computational cost [4].

A popular approach to high-performance computing of various MMAs is to enhance GPPs with SIMD ISA exten-

sions [1]. A SIMD extension makes one instruction operate on vector data. By utilizing data level parallelism (DLP) of the vector operations, these extensions can improve the performance of many MMAs. However, the existing SIMD extensions have a limitation on the parallel-processing capability on a large amount of data. Even in the latest SIMD extension, AVX, the maximum vector length processed by one instruction is 512 bits [3]. Such a limitation restricts the potential of SIMD extensions on media processing in the era of data explosion. Moreover, due to the lack of mechanism on hiding the memory access latency and pipeline latency of function units, simply increasing the width of SIMD datapath is difficult to increase the sustained performance of next generation MMAs [5]. Therefore, a novel approach for high quality MMAs should be considered to efficiently handle this new era of data.

To address the challenge, this paper proposes an out-of-order vector architectural extension instead of conventional SIMD one. Compared to existing SIMD extensions, the vector architectures employ longer vector registers. Longer registers make one vector instruction process more data than one SIMD instruction does. In addition, vector architectures employ the instruction chaining technology and interleaved memory accesses. These technologies help vector architectures more efficiently use the vector function units (VFUs) and tolerate longer memory access latencies.

2. RELATED WORK

Except ISA extensions, there are other two hardware approaches to high quality media processing: application-specific integrated circuits (ASICs), and accelerators. ASICs [6] are designed for only one or one type of specific MMA. They could achieve high performance with low power consumption for the media processing. However, the lack of high level language programmability and flexibility over a wide range of MMAs is the main downside of the ASICs approach.

Use of accelerators such as GPUs is the second approach to improve the performance of MMAs. They enable to exploit both thread-level parallelism (TLP) and DLP by simultaneously executing multiple threads of vector instructions. Each thread, called a warp, is a basic unit to perform vector processing. However, GPUs fix the length of vector operations in the wrap. When the length of vector data is shorter than that of a warp, the SIMD function units in the GPUs would idle, which leads to the performance loss. In contract, vector architectures have a vector length register that specifies the vector length for the current operation. The flexible vector length make vector architectures more easily accom-

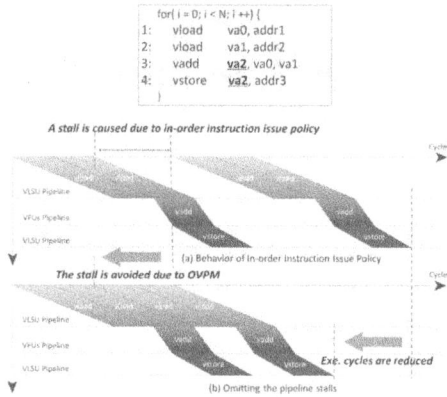

Figure 1: Time-Space Diagram on the Behavior of the in-order instruction issue policy.

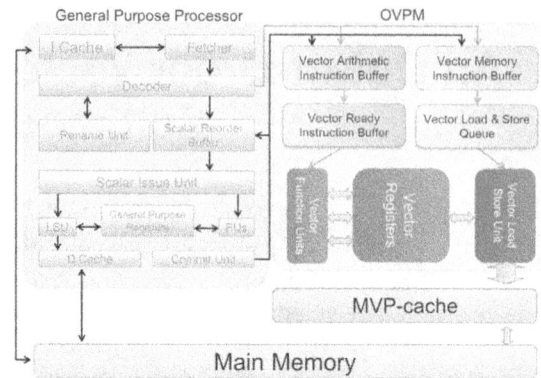

Figure 2: Block Diagram of OVPM

modate programs that naturally have shorter vectors than the maximum size the architecture supports.

Although vector architectures can efficiently take advantage of high DLP in MMAs [2], the conventional vector processors are not efficient for media processing. Conventional vector processors employ IVPM, which easily causes pipeline stalls. The stalls would expose the memory access latency and the latencies of deeply pipelined VFUs. The performance loss due to IVPM becomes even worse when executing MMAs with short vectors, because there are no enough data to fill the deep pipelines and hide the memory access latency. Figure 1(a) presents an example of a simple loop to illustrate the inefficiency of IVPM, and its time-space diagram. Each parallelogram in Figure 1 shows a vector pipeline operation. A vector store instruction is held in the issue stage. It blocks the subsequent instructions, such as the vector load instruction for the second loop, from being issued. The same stall will occur in each iteration, resulting in underutilization of hardware resources in terms of memory bandwidth and VFUs. This underutilization leads to exposure of memory access latency and performance loss.

Under this situation, this paper proposes an out-of-order vector processing mechanism (OVPM) in order to efficiently execute the MMAs with short vectors. As a result, the vector architectural extension is expected to extend the potential of GPPs on efficiently processing a wide range of MMAs.

3. OUT-OF-ORDER VECTOR PROCESSING MECHANISM

In this section, OVPM is proposed to increase the potential of vector architectures on media processing.

Figure 2 illustrates the architecture of OVPM. It consists of three units: renaming unit, reorder unit and commit unit. The renaming unit is used to remove the false data dependencies and check the true data dependence among vector instructions. The commit unit is used to manage the retirement of vector registers in the register alias table. Only after all preceding instructions have been committed, the vector register used in the vector instruction is returned to the free list. In order to decrease the hardware overhead, OVPM uses GPP's rename unit and commit unit to perform the renaming and commit processes.

Regarding the reorder unit, we add two new instruction buffers, a vector arithmetic instruction buffer (VAIB) and

a vector memory instruction buffer (VMIB), in the vector datapath as the reorder buffers. The proposed OVPM adopts a physical register file based approach. Unlike a reservation station based approach, the reorder buffers do not need to hold the values of a vector register. The reorder buffers just contain a few bits to identify instructions and input/output registers without the values of vector registers. Therefore, VAIB and VMIB can be implemented at a low hardware cost. In detail, they store the control information including ID, $opcode$, $output\_dependency$, and $input\_dependency$. ID is used to distinguish the instructions in the buffer. $opcode$ is an operation code from decoder. $output\_dependency$ and $input\_dependency$ are used to control and check the data dependency. The states of $output\_dependency$ and $input\_dependency$ are updated in the writeback stage.

Figure 1(b) shows how OVMP can improve performance by removing the pipeline stalls. The first instruction of the second iteration ($vload$) is decoded and dispatched to VMIB. As long as its operands are ready, it is delivered to the next vector pipeline stage, no matter whether it is the first element in VMIB or not. As a result, the first $vload$ of the second loop can be issued rather than be stalled by the previous instruction that has not been issued yet. Even if MMAs with short vectors are executed, OVPM potentially enables to make their behavior close to the ideal case shown in Figures 1 (b). Consequently, OVPM could potentially improve the performance of both MMAs with long vectors and short vectors by taking advantage of memory bandwidth and VFUs.

4. PERFORMANCE EVALUATION

In this section, to illustrate the potential of OVPM, the computation efficiency of OVPM is compared with that of a conventional vector processor with an in-order instruction issue policy.

4.1 Experimental Setup

We developed a simulator of vector extension with OVPM based on the SimpleScalar toolset to investigate its performance on media workloads. The GPP is modeled as a 4-way superscalar processor, and OVPM employs 8-way parallel pipelined VFUs. The vector instruction set is implemented by manually inserting vector instructions as instruction annotations to the PISA instruction set of SimpleScalar.

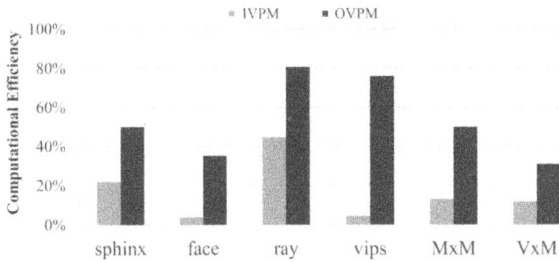

Figure 3: Impact of Different Issue Policies.

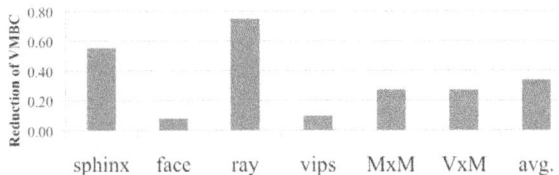

Figure 4: Reduction of Underutilization of Memory Bandwidth

Six multimedia benchmarks are used to evaluate the vector extension. These benchmark programs are selected from the PARSEC benchmark suite. Both of them include emerging MMAs that contain massive DLP.

4.2 Evaluation Results

The computation efficiencies of an IVPM and OVPM are compared in order to demonstrate that OVPM could exploit DLP in MMAs more efficiently. Here, the computational efficiency is defined by the ratio of sustained performance to peak performance. The higher th e computational efficiency means the better use of vector execution units. Specially, computational efficiency at 100 % represents that the MMA always makes the full use of the vector execution units during the execution.

Figure 3 the evaluation results obtained by comparing the maximum performance of IVPM with OVPM when changing the size of vector registers. The sizes of vector registers for IVPM and OVPM are 512 entries and 128 entries, respectively. The computational efficiencies of the proposed architecture are always higher than those of IVPM. The improvement of computation efficiency is derived from the good use of VFUs due to omitting the pipeline stalls. With the help of out-of-order issue policy, even if OVPM employs smaller size of vector registers, it also enables to effectively hide the memory access latency and pipeline latency of VFUs by using small size of vector registers. Specially, the benchmark programs *face* and *vips* show significant performance improvement. These two benchmark programs often need to process short vectors. In the benchmark programs, short vector operations cannot be always overlapped with memory operations. Therefore, they are easier to expose the pipeline stalls, leading to the low computational efficiency. OVPM could efficiently eliminate these stalls, and thereby allows vector extension to achieve a much higher efficiency on processing the short vectors. In spite of the significant performance improvement, their computational efficiencies are still less than 50 %. This is because their vectorization ratios are lower than those of other benchmark programs.

To demonstrate that OVPM can take advantage of mem-

ory bandwidth, vector memory access blank cycles (VM-BCs) are also evaluated. VMBCs represent the utilization of memory bandwidth. For a given program, a VMBC becomes smaller if the period of underutilizing memory bandwidth is shorter. Therefore, a smaller VMBC implies more efficient utilization of memory bandwidth. Figure 4 shows the relative VMBCs of OVPM to IVPM. VMBCs of all the benchmark programs are reduced when employing OVPM, especially for the programs with short vectors such as *face* and *vips*. Compared with Figure 3, VMBCs decrease as the speedup ratio increases. This proves that the main factor of performance improvements by the proposed architecture is efficient use of the memory bandwidth. The VMBCs of benchmarks *face* and *vips* are especially reduced. Consequently, these evaluations clarify that OVPM extends the potential of a vector extension on short vector processing.

5. CONCLUSIONS

Aiming to enhance the potential of GPPs on MMAs, a vector extension with OVPM has been proposed. OVPM overcomes the inefficiencies in executing MMAs by conventional vector architectures, which obey an in-order instruction issue policy. OVPM is implemented by using two instruction buffers. The two instruction buffers ensure that vector instructions can be issued as long as their operands are ready. The evaluation results show that OVPM obtains 3.25x speedup on average. The results indicate that a vector extension with OVPM could efficiently execute MMAs with short vectors as well as those with long vectors.

6. ACKNOWLEDGMENTS

This research was partially supported by Core Research for Evolutional Science and Technology (CREST), Japan Science and Technology Agency (JST).

7. REFERENCES

[1] J.-C. Chiu, Y.-L. Chou, and H.-Y. Tzeng. A Multi-Streaming SIMD Architecture for Multimedia Applications. In *Proceedings of the 6th ACM Conference on Computing frontiers*, CF '09, pages 51–60, 2009.

[2] J. Gebis and D. Patterson. Embracing and Extending 20th-Century Instruction Set Architectures. *IEEE Computer*, 40(4):68–75, April 2007.

[3] Intel. Intel 64 and IA-32 Architectures Optimization Reference Manual. http://software.intel.com/en-us/avx/, 2011.

[4] H. Park, Y. Park, and S. Mahlke. Polymorphic Pipeline Array: A Flexible Multicore Accelerator With Virtualized Execution For Mobile Multimedia Applications. In *Proceedings of the 42nd Annual IEEE/ACM International Symposium on Microarchitecture*, MICRO 42, pages 370–380, 2009.

[5] M. Woh, S. Seo, S. Mahlke, T. Mudge, C. Chakrabarti, and K. Flautner. AnySP: Anytime Anywhere Anyway Signal Processing. *IEEE Micro*, 30:81–91, January 2010.

[6] N. Wu, M. Wen, W. Wu, J. Ren, H. Su, C. Xun, and C. Zhang. Streaming HD H.264 Encoder on Programmable Processors. In *Proceedings of the 17th ACM international conference on Multimedia*, MM '09, pages 371–380, 2009.

Towards Player-Driven Procedural Content Generation

Noor Shaker
Center for Computer Games
Research at the IT University
of Copenhagen
Rued Langaards Vej 7
2300 Copenhagen, Denmark
nosh@itu.dk

Georgios N. Yannakakis
Center for Computer Games
Research at the IT University
of Copenhagen
Rued Langaards Vej 7
2300 Copenhagen, Denmark
yannakakis@itu.dk

Julian Togelius
Center for Computer Games
Research at the IT University
of Copenhagen
Rued Langaards Vej 7
2300 Copenhagen, Denmark
juto@itu.dk

ABSTRACT
Generating immersive game content is one of the ultimate goals for a game designer. This goal can be achieved by realizing the fact that players' perception of the same game differ according to a number of factors including: players' personality, playing styles, expertise and culture background. While one player might find the game immersive, others may quit playing as a result of encountering a seemingly insoluble problem. One promising avenue towards optimizing the gameplay experience for individual game players is to tailor player experience in real-time via automatic game content generation. Specifying the aspects of the game that have the major influence on the gameplay experience, identifying the relationship between these aspect and each individual experience and defining a mechanism for tailoring the game content according to each individual needs are important steps towards player-driven content generation.

Keywords
Player modeling, procedural content generation, game personalization, game adaptation, neuroevolutionary preference learning

Categories and Subject Descriptors
I.2.m [**Artificial Intelligence**]: Miscellaneous

1. INTRODUCTION
As players tend to vary significantly in their preferences, it would be useful to have an algorithm that could observe a human playing a game and accurately judge what the human is experiencing as he/she is playing, as this could allow us to adapt the game to the player, and also help us understand how human affect is expressed in behavior. Our approach towards achieving this goal is first to construct accurate models of the relationship between player experience and game content. This requires the construction of data-driven models based on data collected about the game, the player behavior and correlating this data with data annotated with player experience tags. Our ultimate aim is to tailor player experience in real-time via automatic game content generation based on accurate computational models of in-game player experience.

2. RELATED WORK
The following sections review previous work on topics related to our work.

2.1 Modeling of Player's Emotion
Emotions are critical in game design. Identifying what is "fun" and what makes computer games more engaging have been the focus of many research [3, 7]. Closing the *affective loop* [6] is one of the ultimate aims of the research carried out in the field of affective computing [10]. A few attempts can be found on incorporating players' emotions into the game in a closed-loop manner where player's emotion is actively manipulated to ensure engagement [4]. Existing work [22, 2] demonstrates the power of using affective player models to generate in-game situations of high interest and satisfaction for the players. Most studies in this direction can be classified as qualitative in a sense that they have been based on intuition in combination with some qualitative theories of player experience [3, 7]. On the other hand, the quantitative approaches have received more attention recently. Computational intelligence techniques have been adopted recently to build quantitative models of player experience for platform games [9, 23].

2.2 Experience-Driven Procedural Content Generation
A Research direction that has received increased attention recently is the automatic generation of game content. Procedural Content Generation (PCG) via artificial and computational intelligence methods have been utilized to generate different aspects of content with or without human interference. A recent overview of recently used techniques can be found in [19, 24]. An interesting direction within the automatic content generation is the creation of personalized content [5, 18, 12]. Optimization of game aspects based on empirically derived models has mostly been focused on the impact of non player character NPC behavior and the adjustment of NPC behavioral parameters for maximizing satisfaction in games [1, 8]. Few attempts emerged recently focusing on adapting game content using computational models of player emotion built from the interaction between the player and the game [20, 9]. The literature on personalized and player-adaptive PCG is so far scarce, as it is a new research direction.

3. PLAYER-DRIVEN PROCEDURAL CONTENT GENERATION
Mainly motivated by the current lack of a quantitative entertainment formulation of computer games, the need for a better understanding of the relationship between game content and players' affective state and the increasing interest in personalized and online (during play) automatic adaptation mechanisms, the focus of the work carried out is on constructing an estimator of players' emotional state derived from the in-game interaction, this can serve as a fitness function for game content generation, the content genera-

tion will be done online, serving players new game content based on how they individually have played previously. To achieve these goals a number of fundamental objectives need to be carried out:

1. Constructing an accurate indicator of player experience based on the interaction between the player and the game.

2. Applying an online adaptation to change game content to accommodate specific player experience.

In the work carried out we are trying to give answers to the following sub-goals that the aforementioned research objectives generate:

1. How can we recognize players' affect while playing?

2. What are the features from the game content and players' in-game behavior that help predict players' affect?

3. How to construct models of players' experience that can predict players' emotional state with high accuracy?

4. What is the best representation of players' behavior and game content that can be used to construct the models?

5. How and how often the game should be adapted to enrich particular player experience?

We chose *Super Mario Bros* as the testbed for our research. The remaining sections present our approach to tackle the research questions and explore our view on the future directions.

3.1 Data Collection

In our study we rely on data expressed by players themselves about their playing experience along with features of how they play the game and we construct our models based on these data. The following features have been extracted from data collected from hundreds of players playing Infinite Mario Bros.

- Content features: these are also named *Controllable* as they are used to generate the levels and are varied to make sure several variants of the game are played and compared. These features have been selected with the intent to cover the features that have the most impact on the investigated affective states [14, 15].

- Gameplay Features: All player actions and interactions with game items and their corresponding time-stamps have been recorded with the full trajectory of Mario.

- Reported Player Experience: Player experience is annotated via a 4-alternative forced choice questionnaire. The questionnaire asks the player to report the preferred game for the three user states: engagement, challenge and frustration. The selection of these states is based on earlier game survey studies [9] and our intention to capture both affective and cognitive/behavioral components of gameplay experience [24].

A number of limitations are embedded in the players' self-reporting experience modeling [24]. To overcome these limitations, a set of experiments has been conducted to assess the estimation of players' affect by introducing *expressivity features*; a set of head movement parameters extracted for creating behavioral correlations to game events by analyzing video recording of players.

3.2 Feature Representation

Two types of representations have been used for the recorded content and gameplay features via direct and sequential feature extraction. Direct features provide quantitative measure about game content and playing style such as the number of collected items. Alternatively, sequential features allow including features that are based on ordering in space or time and yields patterns that might be directly linked to player experience. Sequential features have been extracted by applying sequence mining techniques [25, 16] to extract useful patterns from the sequences generated [15, 13].

3.3 Player Experience Modeling

The very first step towards designing accurate, reliable and computationally efficient models of players' experience is to identify relevant features from game content and gameplay that affect player experience. A large set of features have been extracted and not all of these features are necessarily relevant for modeling player experience. Therefore, automatic features selection is used to extract the minimal subset of relevant features for predicting players' affective states with high accuracy. Neuroevolutionary preference learning [21] has been used in order to construct models that approximate the function between the selected subset of gameplay features, controllable features, expressivity features and reported affective preferences. Different experiments with different setups and features has been conducted on different portions of the dataset [14, 15, 13, 11]. Using the proposed approach, we were able to predict engagement with accuracy up to 75.21%. The best constructed model for predicting frustration has an accuracy of 85.88%, while challenge can be best predicted with an accuracy of 91.23% [13].

3.4 Online Game Adaptation

Once a model that capture player experience has been constructed, and as an initiative to close the affective-loop, the content generator needs to search within the resulting search space for content that maximizes particular aspects of player experience. Ideally, the content generator should be able to identify if, how much and how often content should be generated for a particular player [24].

3.4.1 Adaptation Frequency

Successfully defining the smallest possible segment of the level for which the player experience models can still predict reported affect with acceptable accuracy is important since this segment size can then potentially be used to set the frequency of a real-time adaptation mechanism for the purpose of maximizing specific players' affective state. Therefore, the game sessions have been segmented into up to three segments and models have been constructed from the different segments. The results suggested that player reported challenge can be best predicted with longer sessions' size than the ones needed for predicting frustration or engagement [13].

3.4.2 Adapting Game Content

A step toward achieving the online content adaptation was carried out in [14] where the constructed models of players' experience from content and gameplay direct features were used to optimize game levels for particular players. Since content was represented via a small number of dimensions (four controllable features were used in that experiment), exhaustive search was used as the online adaptation mechanism. The space of controllable features has been explored to find the best combination of game features that yields the best performance in predicting the player's reported emotional states. This best combination found was then used to set the value for the four controllable features to generate a new level that is personalized according to the behavior of a specific player [14].

4. CONCLUSION AND FUTURE WORK

The work carried out is primarily based on two research questions: how to accurately model player experience and how to tailor game content generation according to specific player behavior. Super Mario Bros game was used as the testbed. A number of experiments have been conducted to construct player experience models based of different categories of features collected from hundreds of players. Direct and sequential feature representation have been employed and tested for constructing efficient models. The experiments showed that players' reported affect of the three emotional states, engagement, frustration and challenge could be predicted with high accuracies using automatic feature selection and neuroevolutionary preference learning. As for game adaptation, our goal is to give answers to the questions of how, how much and how often game content should be adapted for a particular player. To answer these questions, the smallest possible sessions' size for which the constructed models can still predict the reported affect with high accuracies has been investigated. This size can be potentially used to set the adaptation frequency. A further experiment has been conducted to generate personalized level by exhaustively searching the content space for a combination that maximizes specific player experience. The future directions include constructing a more accurate models based on more controllable features. Grammatical evolution is being adopted to construct playable levels and a study will be conducted to analyze and construct player experience models from these levels. Another direction includes a more in-depth investigation of the adaptation mechanism. Evolutionary algorithms could be used to explore the content space when exhaustive search algorithm could fail due to larger search space. Other approaches could also be investigated to personalize the structure of the player models. For this purpose, the NeuroEvolution Augmenting Topologies (NEAT) [17] could be potentially used. A thorough analysis of the direct and sequential features selected by automatic feature selection is an interesting direction towards constructing data-driven models of game aesthetics that can also be used by designers to construct more engaging, challenging, or frustrating content. The work presented and the approach followed constitute an important step for future work on other game genre. The findings can also be generalized and applied for personalizing other digital media content based on human-computer interactions.

Acknowledgments

The research was supported in part by the Danish Research Agency, Ministry of Science, Technology and Innovation; project *AGameComIn* ; project number: 274-09-0083.

5. REFERENCES

[1] G. Andrade, G. Ramalho, H. Santana, and V. Corruble. Automatic computer game balancing: a reinforcement learning approach. In *Proceedings of the fourth international joint conference on Autonomous agents and multiagent systems*, AAMAS, pages 1111–1112. ACM, 2005.

[2] D. Charles and M. Black. Dynamic player modeling: A framework for player-centered digital games. In *Proc. of the International Conference on Computer Games: Artificial Intelligence, Design and Education*, pages 29–35, 2004.

[3] M. Csikszentmihalyi. *Beyond Boredom and Anxiety: Experiencing Flow in Work and Play*. Jossey-Bass, 25th anniversary edition, 2000.

[4] E. Hudlicka. Affective computing for game design. In *GAMEON-NA'08: Proceedings of the 4th Intl. North American Conference on Intelligent Games and Simulation*, pages 5–12, Montreal, Canada, 2008.

[5] S. Kazmi and I. Palmer. Action recognition for support of adaptive gameplay: A case study of a first person shooter. *International Journal of Computer Games Technology*, 2010:1, 2010.

[6] I. Leite, A. Pereira, S. Mascarenhas, G. Castellano, C. Martinho, R. Prada, and A. Paiva. Closing the loop: from affect recognition to empathic interaction. In *Proceedings of the 3rd international workshop on Affective interaction in natural environments*, AFFINE, pages 43–48. ACM, 2010.

[7] T. Malone. What makes computer games fun? (abstract only). In *Proceedings of the joint conference on Easier and more productive use of computer systems. (Part - II): Human interface and the user interface - Volume 1981*, CHI '81, pages 143–. ACM, 1981.

[8] O. Missura and T. Gartner. Player Modeling for Intelligent Difficulty Adjustment. In *Proceedings of the 12th International Conference on Discovery Science*, DS '09, pages 197–211. Springer-Verlag, 2009.

[9] C. Pedersen, J. Togelius, and G. N. Yannakakis. Modeling player experience for content creation. *IEEE Transactions on Computational Intelligence and AI in Games*, 2(1):54–67, 2010.

[10] R. W. Picard. *Affective Computing*. Cambridge, MA: The MIT Press, 1997.

[11] N. Shaker, S. Asteriadis, G. Yannakakis, and K. Karpouzis. A game-based corpus for analysing the interplay between game context and player experience. *Affective Computing and Intelligent Interaction*, pages 547–556, 2011.

[12] N. Shaker, J. Togelius, G. N. Yannakakis, B. Weber, T. Shimizu, T. Hashiyama, N. Sorenson, P. Pasquier, P. Mawhorter, G. Takahashi, G. Smith, and R. Baumgarten. The 2010 Mario AI championship: Level generation track. *IEEE Transactions on Computational Intelligence and Games*, 2011.

[13] N. Shaker, G. Yannakakis, and J. Togelius. Digging deeper into platform game level design: session size and sequential features. In *Proceedings of the European Conference on Applications of Evolutionary Computation (EvoApplications)*. Springer LNCS, 2012.

[14] N. Shaker, G. N. Yannakakis, and J. Togelius. Towards Automatic Personalized Content Generation for Platform Games. In *Proceedings of the AAAI Conference on Artificial Intelligence and Interactive Digital Entertainment (AIIDE)*. AAAI Press, 2010.

[15] N. Shaker, G. N. Yannakakis, and J. Togelius. Feature Analysis for Modeling Game Content Quality. In *IEEE Transactions on Computational Intelligence and AI in Games (CIG)*, 2011.

[16] R. Srikant and R. Agrawal. Mining sequential patterns: Generalizations and performance improvements. pages 3–17, 1996.

[17] K. Stanley and R. Miikkulainen. Evolving neural networks through augmenting topologies. *Evolutionary computation*, pages 99–127, 2002.

[18] J. Togelius, R. De Nardi, and S. Lucas. Towards automatic personalised content creation for racing games. In *Computational Intelligence and Games, 2007. CIG 2007. IEEE Symposium on*, pages 252–259. IEEE, 2007.

[19] J. Togelius, G. N. Yannakakis, K. O. Stanley, and C. Browne. Search-based procedural content generation. In *Proceedings of EvoApplications*, volume 6024. Springer LNCS, 2010.

[20] G. Yannakakis and J. Hallam. Real-time Game Adaptation for Optimizing Player Satisfaction. *IEEE Transactions on Computational Intelligence and AI in Games*, 1(2):121–133, June 2009.

[21] G. Yannakakis, H. Lund, and J. Hallam. Modeling children's entertainment in the playware playground. In *IEEE Symposium on Computational Intelligence and Games*, pages 134–141. IEEE, 2006.

[22] G. N. Yannakakis, M. Maragoudakis, and J. Hallam. Preference learning for cognitive modeling: a case study on entertainment preferences. *Trans. Sys. Man Cyber. Part A*, 39:1165–1175, November 2009.

[23] G. N. Yannakakis, H. P. Martí£¡nez, and A. Jhala. Towards affective camera control in games. *User Modeling and User-Adapted Interaction*, 20:313–340, 2010. 10.1007/s11257-010-9078-0.

[24] G. N. Yannakakis and J. Togelius. Experience-Driven Procedural Content Generation. *IEEE Transactions on Affective Computing*, 2011.

[25] M. J. Zaki. Spade: An efficient algorithm for mining frequent sequences. *Mach. Learn.*, 42:31–60, January 2001.

An Efficient Vectorization of Linked-Cell Particle Simulations

Wolfgang Eckhardt
Technische Universität München
Fakultät für Informatik
85748 Garching, Germany
eckhardw@in.tum.de

Alexander Heinecke
Technische Universität München
Fakultät für Informatik
85748 Garching, Germany
heinecke@in.tum.de

ABSTRACT

Molecular dynamics simulations for short-range potentials represent an important class of applications in scientific computing. While a lot of work has been spent on the efficient implementation of such simulations on vector machines in general, not much effort has been invested into the efficient implementation for current x86 processor architectures' SIMD extensions such as SSE and AVX.

We describe an implementation of the linked-cell algorithm for the SSE and AVX instruction set, which achieves the theoretical limit for SSE. Moreover, the proposed scheme will allow the efficient usage of future architectures with wider vector units. We implemented the kernel using intrinsics within a small test program and conducted a number of runs for different setups of the Lennard-Jones fluid on an Intel- and AMD-based cluster, respectively.

Categories and Subject Descriptors

G.4 [**MATHEMATICAL SOFTWARE**]: Parallel and vector implementations

General Terms

Algorithms, Performance

Keywords

particle simulation, n-body, linked cell, SIMD, many/multi-core

1. MOTIVATION AND RELATED WORK

During the last decades molecular dynamics simulation (MD) has become an important tool for the simulation and prediction of material properties at the nano-scale.

Although significant progress has been made, for many applications, the number of particles that can be simulated is still quite limited compared to realistic setups due to demands for both memory and computational power. The most time consuming part is the calculation of the inter-atomic forces. Efficient implementation exploiting SIMD parallelism has been a focus of research from the early days on. In this paper, we propose an efficient implementation on current microprocessors using SSE and AVX.

For MD simulation a solid or fluid is modeled as a system of N discrete particles. All molecules i and j interact pairwise through a potential $U(r_{ij})$, where r_{ij} is the distance of the two particles, which results in a force $F_i = \sum_{j \in particles} F_{ij}(r_{ij})$ on each of the particles.

As described by Newton's third law, the mutual force between two particles is equal according to amount: $F_{ij} = -F_{ji}$, a fact our implementations strictly adhere to. The interaction is determined by the Lennard-Jones-12-6 (LJ-12-6) potential [9]:

$$U(r_{ij}) = 4\varepsilon \cdot \left(\left(\frac{\sigma}{r_{ij}} \right)^{12} - \left(\frac{\sigma}{r_{ij}} \right)^6 \right),$$

where ε and σ are material parameters.

The force calculation for one particle involves all others particles, and thus has complexity $O(n^2)$. For short-range potentials like the LJ-12-6, the contributions of distant particles can be neglected. Then only particles within a cutoff radius r_c have to be considered. This can be efficiently implemented with the linked-cell algorithm, where the computational domain is subdivided into cells of length r_c. In order to find the neighbors of a given molecule in 3D, only the cell of the molecule plus the 26 adjacent cells have to be searched, resulting in a linear complexity of the force calculation.

Due to the reduced computational load, usually small cutoff radii in the range of 2.5 to 5.0 σ are chosen. Nevertheless, the effect of the truncation of the potential has to be analyzed and compensated for, and there exist also applications, e.g. the simulation of properties of liquid-vapor interfaces, which require higher values [6].

Apart from the force calculation, the computationally most expensive part is the neighbor search, which may add substantial overhead. Here, an obvious idea is to choose cells of smaller size to approximate the geometry of the sphere more precisely, called generalized linked-cells. For a comparison of different linked-cell variants we refer the reader to [11] and references therein.

The efficient implementation of the linked-cell algorithm for vector architectures has been subject of several publications. Improvements include the combined use of Verlet neighbor lists and linked cells [10] as well as the layered linked-cells [9] which applies vectorization over cells rather than molecules. Different implementations for NEC Vector systems have been evaluated by Benkert [1], concluding that existing algorithms achieve rather unsatisfactory performance and do not really seem to be well-suited for vectorization.

Since the introduction of vector extensions to commodity processors, efforts have been made to efficiently utilize them in the quite complex context of application software. E.g. the MD code Gromacs has been vectorized using SSE [5] and has been ported to other SIMD-type architectures like the cell architecture by Olivier [7].

Work similar to the presented one has recently been done by Peng [8]. However, he focuses on hierarchical parallelization using MPI, Multithreading and SIMD. Both Peng and Olivier vectorize over the three dimensions of coordinates, velocities, forces, etc. in single precision, which reduces the theoretically possible speedup from 4 to 3 by design.

Commonly the linked-cell data-structure is implemented as follows: the molecules are arranged as a list in memory, the cells are stored in an array and hold pointers to the molecules, which belong to each cell. The advantage here is that molecule objects do not have to be moved in memory if they migrate to a different cell. We implemented the generalized linked-cell method and store the molecule objects explicitly in cells, so that a performance degradation due to diffusion as reported by [8] cannot occur.

The code is parallelized based on a spatial domain decomposition with MPI. The sub-domain of each process is surrounded by a layer of ghost cells, which contain particles residing on the neighboring processes, so the particles at the boundaries have to be exchanged at the beginning of each time step. As there exist applications which require double precision [5], we perform our calculations in double precision to be as general as possible.

2. IMPLEMENTATION

As stated, we follow a completely different approach for memory organization and vectorization than discussed in most of the literature. Our application is written in C++ and therefore applies standard object-oriented design principles. Cells are container-classes storing each a private list of particle objects owned by the actual cell. After each timestep, the linked-cell algorithm recalculates the particle cell membership and copy-moves particles, if needed, to neighboring cells. By using such a memory organization, locality, which is rather important due to caching, is implicitly given, as we execute all subroutines on a per-cell basis. Furthermore, this approach allows an easy to read and maintainable code.

Although our implementation offers many advantages, we introduce one major drawback for the vectorization of the subroutines: the particles stored in a list must be regarded as a so-called *array of structures (AoS)* memory layout. Here, data cannot be processed without costly gather and scatter instructions in order to use vectorized routines if several members have to be touched, see [3] for details. Only in simple cases (e.g., updates of one member, etc.) this drawback does not matter as prefetch logic inside the hardware loads only cache-lines containing the data to be modified. In our application this applies to subroutines like thermostats, velocity scaling, or calculation of statistics which are directly executed on the AoS-structure.

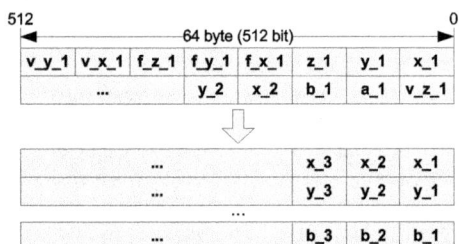

Figure 1: AoS- in comparison to SoA-cache-line-occupancy for sample members of particles: position, forces, velocity, etc.

When implementing the force calculations, here LJ-12-6, the AoS-structure imposes major challenges as depicted in Fig. 1. Its upper part shows elements scattered across several cache-lines. Those have to be accessed multiple times during force calculations. Taking into account that only a small portion of the members is needed for the force calculation, a temporary *structure of arrays (SoA)* can be constructed in order to address cache-line pollution and vectorization opportunities, illustrated in the lower part of Fig. 1.

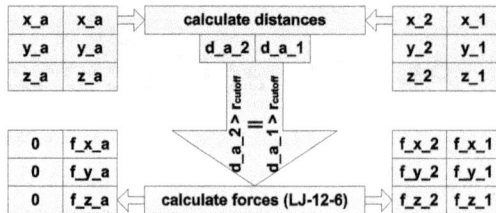

Figure 2: Vectorization of the LJ-12-6 force calculation kernel.

Given a SoA-storage, we are able to vectorize the LJ-12-6 kernel across particle pairs. Please note that this approach scales with the number of particles per cell and does not require zero-padding or is limited to a vector-length of four as methods presented by Peng and Olivier [8, 5]. In our case the only limitations are the number of particles per cell, the size of the cutoff-radius r_{cutoff} and cell-length r_c as these factors influence the vector load.

Figure 2 sketches the applied vectorization of the LJ-12-6 calculations. As we need to deal with double precision floating point numbers we can store a maximum of two elements per SSE register. The calculation is performed on particle pairs, therefore we broadcast-load (duplicating by vector-length) the required data of one particle in the first register (a) and the second register is filled by data of two different particles (1 and 2). With this approach we can theoretically reduce the number of operations by a factor of two. Since we are calculating two interactions within one step, we need to apply some pre- and post-processing, which can be performed by regular logical operations directly in hardware: the SSE/AVX instruction set offers compare, logical and sign-bit operations that can be used to decide if the force calculation should be initiated (at least one particle pair distance is smaller than r_{cutoff}, pre-processing) and if calculated results need to be zeroed by a mask (a particle pair distance is greater than r_{cutoff}). In case of SSE this should already gain a factor of two for small particle numbers. The lower performance bound is the scalar performance as these algorithms will not execute more instructions than necessary in the scalar case. We want to close this section by noting two minor issues (which may change in future): currently the AVX implementation is just an extended version of the SSE implementation. Optimization may be possible by better exploiting the lane-concept, see [4] for details. As we are calculating everything with double precision, we have to use costly square root and division instructions and cannot use reciprocal functions as they are often use in the field of MD, see [5].

3. RUNTIME EXPERIMENTS

We evaluated the performance of the proposed implementation on two different systems at Leibniz Supercomputing Centre in Munich: an SGI ICE cluster; one blade features two Intel Nehalem Xeon processors (Intel Xeon E5540 at 2.53 GHz) and two Infiniband connects. The second system is the so-called MiniMUC-cluster. It is based on two socket AMD Opteron blades (AMD Opteron 6128HE at 2.00 GHz) connected by a fat tree Infiniband network. We simulated a Lennard-Jones fluid with $\rho \approx 0.72$ and different particle counts though different domain sizes. Simulations with 68K, 160k, 551k and 1300k particles where executed for three linked-cell configurations: $[r_c = 1.5, r_{cutoff} = 3.0]$ (≈ 8 particles per cell), $[r_c = 3.0, r_{cutoff} = 3.0]$ (≈ 20 particles per cell) and $[r_c = 5.0, r_{cutoff} = 5.0]$ (≈ 100 particles per cell). Due to space limitations, we only plot results for the 1300k particle run in Fig. 3. Also the mentioned smaller scenarios show a similar scaling behavior.

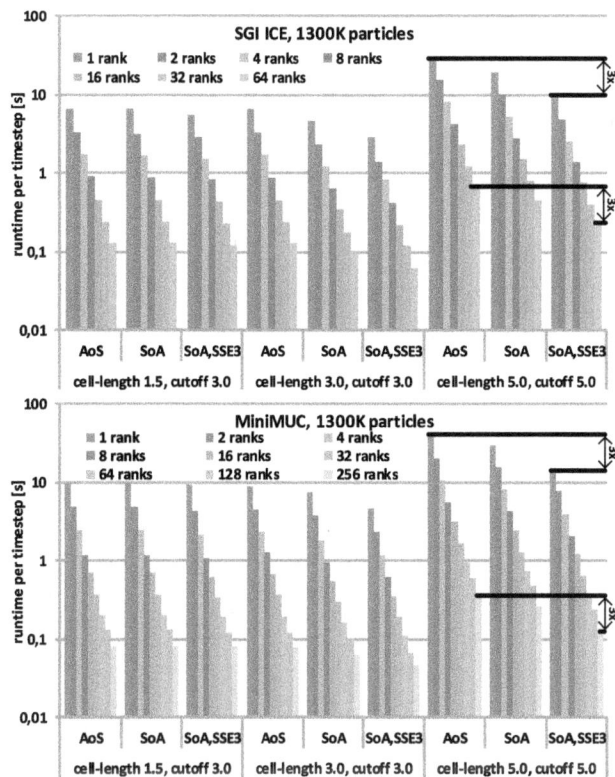

Figure 3: Runtimes in seconds for a scenario with 1300k particles on both clusters, one MPI rank per core.

We executed each linked-cell configuration in three different modes in order to measure the quality of our vectorization approach: with the described AoS memory layout, a SoA memory organization with scalar kernel code and SoA with a vectorized kernel. On both clusters, we were able to obtain nearly identical results. For the first configuration with 8 particles per cell a SoA storage scheme vectorization does not gain a lot, as the calling overhead dominates. But with 20 particles per cell the vectorized version is able double the execution of AoS version. Here, around 20% of this speed-up is delivered by the mandatory SoA structure as depicted in the performance plot. In case of 100 molecules per cell, performance improves even more: the vectorized version yields a factor of 3. Around one third of this factor is due to the SoA memory organization. As these speed-ups hold also for the highly-parallel executions our vectorization is very promising.

We want to close our result discussion by a short outlook on the AVX instruction set. Therefore Tab. 1 gives a comparison of the runtimes on a desktop Sandy Bridge processor (Core i7 2600 @ 3.6 GHz, 4 MPI ranks) of the SSE and AVX implementation. In case of AVX we need more particles per cell to really exploit this new instruction set. This is due to the fact that we just extend our approach to the wider vector units.

linked-cell configuration	#particles	SSE3 [s]	AVX [s]
$r_c = 3.0, r_{cutoff} = 3.0$	20	0.58	0.58
$r_c = 5.0, r_{cutoff} = 5.0$	100	1.63	1.43
$r_c = 7.5, r_{cutoff} = 7.5$	300	5.01	3.97

Table 1: Comparison of SSE3 and AVX implementation.

Therefore it may happen that the number of executed LJ-12-6 kernels does not decrease as often only one vector component forces a LJ-12-6 kernel call with three elements being zero. Such zero-pair elements are just skipped if the SSE version is executed. However, with an AVX vectorization, we are able to increase the accuracy of our simulations, as we compute with bigger cell-lengths and cutoffs.

4. CONCLUSION AND FUTURE WORK

In this paper we proposed a SoA-based on-the-fly vectorization for the linked-cell algorithm. We demonstrated perfect speed-up on SSE capable platforms (our vectorization yields a speed-up of 2), even for only a few particles per cell. Results obtained using AVX are good, especially for bigger cell-length or cutoff-radius. By a better usage of the lane concept of AVX, we are quite confident to be able to further improve performance, even on devices like Intel MIC and GPGPUs.

Besides architectural improvements we are also working on the integration of the vectorized calculation into the simulation program ls1/Mardyn [2], which supports more complex models like molecules with multiple interaction centers of different potential types.

5. REFERENCES

[1] K. Benkert and F. Gähler. *Molecular Dynamics on NEC Vector Systems*, pages 145–152. Springer, 2007.

[2] M. Buchholz, H.-J. Bungartz, and J. Vrabec. Software design for a highly parallel molecular dynamics simulation framework in chemical engineering. *Journal of Computational Science*, 2(2):124–129, May 2011.

[3] C. Gou, G. Kuzmanov, and G. N. Gaydadjiev. SAMS multi-layout memory: providing multiple views of data to boost SIMD performance. In *Proceedings of the 24th ACM International Conference on Supercomputing*, ICS '10, pages 179–188, New York, NY, USA, 2010. ACM.

[4] Intel Corporation. Intel 64 and IA-32 Architectures Software Developer's Manual Combined Volumes: 1, 2A, 2B, 3A and 3B, 2011. Document Number 325462-039US.

[5] E. Lindahl, B. Hess, and D. van der Spoel. Gromacs 3.0: a package for molecular simulation and trajectory analysis. *Journal of Molecular Modeling*, 7:306–317, 2001.

[6] M. Mecke, J. Winkelmann, and J. Fischer. Molecular dynamics simulation of the liquid–vapor interface: The lennard-jones fluid. *The Journal of Chemical Physics*, 107(21):9264–9270, 1997.

[7] S. Olivier, J. Prins, J. Derby, and K. Vu. Porting the gromacs molecular dynamics code to the cell processor. In *Parallel and Distributed Processing Symposium, 2007. IPDPS 2007. IEEE International*, pages 1 –8, march 2007.

[8] L. Peng, M. Kunaseth, H. Dursun, K.-i. Nomura, W. Wang, R. Kalia, A. Nakano, and P. Vashishta. Exploiting hierarchical parallelisms for molecular dynamics simulation on multicore clusters. *The Journal of Supercomputing*, 57:20–33, 2011.

[9] D. C. Rapaport. *The Art of Molecular Dynamics Simulation*. Cambridge University Press, Apr. 2004.

[10] M. Schoen. Structure of a simple molecular dynamics fortran program optimized for cray vector processing computers. *Computer Physics Communications*, 52(2):175 – 185, 1989.

[11] U. Welling and G. Germano. Efficiency of linked cell algorithms. *Computer Physics Communications*, 182(3):611–615, 2011.

Dynamic Percolation: A Case of Study on the Shortcomings of Traditional Optimization in Many-core Architectures

Elkin Garcia
University of Delaware
egarcia@udel.edu

Daniel Orozco
University of Delaware
orozco@udel.edu

Rishi Khan
ET International
rishi@etinternational.com

Ioannis E. Venetis
University of Patras
venetis@ceid.upatras.gr

Kelly Livingston
University of Delaware
kelly@udel.edu

Guang Gao
University of Delaware
ggao@capsl.udel.edu

ABSTRACT

This paper provides a discussion on the shortcomings of traditional static optimization techniques when used in the context of many-core architectures. We argue that these shortcomings are a result of the significantly different environment found in many-cores. We analyze previous attempts at optimization of Dense Matrix Multiplication (DMM) that failed to achieve high performance despite extensive efforts towards optimization.

We have found that percolation (prefetching data) and scheduling play a central role in the performance of applications. To overcome those difficulties, we have (1) fused dynamic scheduling and percolation into a *dynamic percolation* approach and (2) we have added additional percolation operations. Our new techniques enabled us to increase the performance of the application in our study from 44 GFLOPS (out of 80 GFLOPS possible) to 70.0 GFLOPS (operands in SRAM) or 65.6 GFLOPS (operands in DRAM).

Categories and Subject Descriptors

C.4 [**Performance of Systems**]: [Modeling techniques]; D.1.3 [**Programming Techniques**]: Concurrent Programming—*Parallel programming*; G.1.0 [**Numerical Analysis**]: General—*Parallel algorithms*

Keywords

Many-cores, Dynamic Scheduling, Percolation, Cyclops64

1. INTRODUCTION

This paper presents a comprehensive case of study that shows how to obtain high performance in modern many-core processors. This study is important because it addresses situations not previously encountered in multi-core architectures, other shared memory processors or distributed memory systems. Many-cores provide an environment where hardware resources are uncomplicated and abundant. Large numbers of thread units are present, on-chip memory is user-managed, no automatic data cache is present and hardware

support for synchronization is available. The environment is different and requires new optimization paradigms.

Even in the simple case of Dense Matrix Multiplication (DMM) running on IBM's Cyclops-64 processor (C64) [2], extensive efforts toward optimization using a broad range of static optimization strategies such as multiple levels of tiling, instruction scheduling, register allocation, manual instruction selection, optimized synchronization and several other only resulted in disappointing performance of 44.12 GFLOPS [4] (out of 80 GFLOPS possible).

These results ultimately show that peak performance could not be achieved by static techniques alone, even for simple, highly parallel and regular programs such as DMM. Mainly, this happens because it is not possible to statically create a plan that efficiently schedules data prefetching (percolation) and computation at the right times. The reason is that small variations in the execution of tasks voids the possibility of making optimal scheduling decisions a-priory.

To solve the difficulties in percolation and scheduling, we propose to take advantage of the fine-grain synchronization primitives available in many-core architectures. Percolation and dynamic scheduling can be fused together in what we call *dynamic percolation* which dynamically schedules data prefetching at an appropriate time so that (1) data is available when the computation needs it and (2) the percolation operation is done when enough memory bandwidth is available. We apply this technique for the optimization of DMM.

2. BACKGROUND

Cyclops-64: C64 is a homogeneous many-core system on a chip architecture designed by IBM [2]. A C64 chip is an aggregation of 160 simple MIMD Thread Units (TU). It has 80 floating point units (FPU), 5 MB of user-managed on-chip memory (SRAM) with total bandwidth of 320 GB/s and 1 GB of DRAM with a total bandwidth of 16 GB/s. There is no automatic data cache. C64 has a total performance of 80 GFLOPS per chip when running at 500MHz. In addition, C64 incorporates efficient support for hardware barriers and atomic in-memory operations. Each memory controller has an ALU that allows it to execute atomic operations directly inside the memory controller (both SRAM and DRAM), without help from a thread unit.

Tiling: Bandwidth is the bottleneck for most naively-implemented algorithms in C64. On-chip memory is frequently used to perform partial computations (tilings) [1, 4, 8] decreasing the amount of bandwidth required.

Static Scheduling and Data Partitioning: Scheduling is an important optimization for programs once the bottleneck of memory bandwidth has been removed through tiling. Scheduling presents challenges in itself since it requires assignment of work to processors at the appropriate time, taking into account issues such as availability of resources and availability of data. The scheduling problem is complicated by the fact that the tasks scheduled to each processor are not necessarily identical. The problem seems simpler for regular and embarrassingly parallel applications, where the amount of data can be distributed uniformly between TUs, expecting similar execution times.

Two main factors, under the scenario imposed by many-core architectures, decrease the expected performance of this static approach to the point of making it impractical even for regular applications: 1) The imbalance, due to competition for shared resources, produced by shared resources even with tasks that perform similar amounts of work. 2) Partitioning the problem statically (in equal amounts of work per TU) may result in non-optimal tile sizes with poor performance.

Percolation: Uninterrupted computation by the processing units in a many-core chip requires data to be available continuously. Percolation is the process by which data is moved across the levels of memory hierarchy to meet the necessities of locality for computation. Percolation is related to data prefetching in that both achieve the same objective. As opposed to conventional data prefetching, percolation operations are expressed as tasks on their own, with precedence relationships with other computational tasks and with restrictions to available resources such as bandwidth or on-chip memory space.

It is difficult to know *a priori* when percolation should be done. As explained before, not all tiles are of the same size, and not all tiles take the same amount of time, even when they perform similar amounts of computations.

3. DYNAMIC SCHEDULING: SCALABILITY AND PERCOLATION

Our target operation is DMM ($C = A \times B$) for matrices with size $m \times m$. We propose a separation of the problem into two orthogonal subproblems: 1) optimizing DMM in SRAM moving operands between SRAM and Registers and 2) moving data between DRAM and SRAM. To extend the matrices to DRAM we simply partition the matrices A, B and C into $n \times n$ blocks $A_{i,k}$, $B_{k,j}$ and $C_{i,j}$ that fit in SRAM. This is similar to the blocking performed in traditional cache hierarchies, resulting in a trade off between computation and data movement. Each block of C is calculated by

$$C_{i,j} = \sum_{k=0}^{\frac{m}{n}-1} A_{i,k} \cdot B_{k,j} \qquad (1)$$

Considering the limitation of bandwidth in the crossbar and the unpredictable effects of resource sharing, we must devise a schedule that considers both computation and data movement efficiently. DMM with operands on DRAM will require two kind of tasks: Data movement tasks and computation tasks. Our analysis will follow a bottom-up approach:

1. We will analyze how to optimize MM in SRAM. Two

major aspects are studied and solutions are given in each case: A load balanced scheduler with low overhead and an optimized computation task with proper *percolation* of operands between SRAM and Registers.

2. We will analyze the MM in DRAM. The main aspect studied here is a load-balanced scheduler that effectively overlaps data movement and computation tasks using *dynamic percolation*

Dynamic Scheduling for Computation Tasks: Static Scheduling (SS) is suboptimal because it does not consider two main sources of imbalance in a many-core environment: 1) The amount of work is a function of how the block is tiled and what fraction of tiles are not of optimum size. 2) Possible stalls due to arbitration of shared resources.

The unpredictable effects of resource sharing are a formidable challenge for SS. A static block partition exacerbates problems, especially when the number of processors (P) is increased. Despite the simplicity and regular behavior in computation and data access of DMM, static techniques cannot overcome these problems. At that point, Dynamic Scheduling (DS) arises as a feasible solution able to alleviate the overhead and scalability problems of SS.

We propose a work-stealing approach where the computation of optimum size tiles in matrix C are scheduled dynamically using atomic in-memory operations. The advantages of this technique are low overhead and improved load-balance in the presence of stalls.

Percolation in the Computation Tasks: Most of the time is spent computing tiles. Therefore, computation deserves special attention. Previous Instruction Scheduling [4], partially hides the latency incurred while fetching operands from SRAM to registers. The remaining stalls due to latencies in memory movements from SRAM are avoided with a combination of loop unrolling and percolation.

Dynamic Percolation: A DMM algorithm, that has been highly optimized through SRAM percolation, is severely limited in the size of the matrices that can fit in SRAM (i.e. 500×500). We extend DMM into DRAM by blocking at the SRAM level and using our percolated MM algorithm in SRAM. We assume that the target many-core architecture has no hardware mechanisms for block transfers (e.g. caches or DMA engines), forcing us to use TUs for memory movement. The computational TUs must be orchestrated with data movement TUs to enforce data dependencies: work cannot be done before a matrix is loaded and a matrix cannot be unloaded until work using it is completed. Further, TUs performing data movement should help with computation if there is no data to move. The straightforward static scheduling approach using barriers will waste resources while TUs are waiting on barriers. Also, it is inefficient for all TUs to copy data at the same time given the limited DRAM bandwidth. A dynamic scheduling approach replaces the barriers with finer-grained signals while still enforcing data dependencies.

We introduced *Dynamic Percolation*, where data movement tasks and computation tasks were assigned dynamically. Helper Threads (HT) are in charge of the data movement tasks and Computation Threads (CT) are in charge of the computation tasks. Computation and data movement tasks are overlapped by a pipelined schema using a double buffer in SRAM. Moreover, the distribution of computation

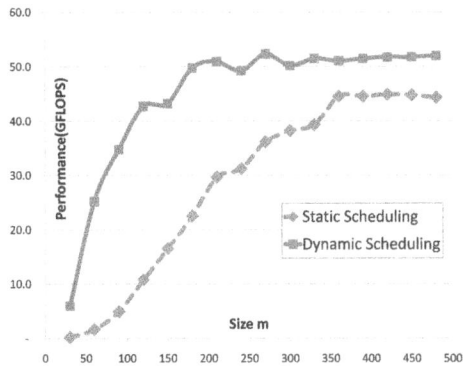

Figure 1: Scalability vs Matrix Size with 156 TUs

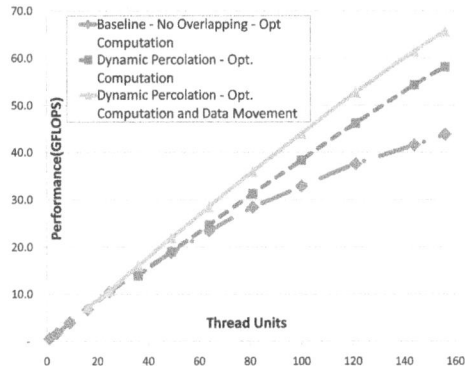

Figure 2: Performance of MM in off-chip DRAM

tasks and data movement tasks will vary in the course of Dynamic Percolation.

The Dynamic Scheduler for each set of tasks is implemented using atomic in-memory additions. The main advantage of this implementation is the low overhead given by the low latency of in-memory operations. They avoid unnecessary roundtrips to memory and they provide the necessary synchronization due to the atomicity supported by the hardware.

There is also a hierarchy of tasks. Tasks related with data movement of the $C_{i,j}$ blocks are at the highest level, data movement of the blocks $A_{i,k}$ and $B_{k,j}$ is next with computation tasks at the lower level.

4. EXPERIMENTAL EVALUATION

This section describes the experimental evaluation based on the analysis done in section 3 using the C64 architecture described in section 2. Our baseline parallel DMM implementation uses Static Scheduling (SS) and the set of optimizations described in [4].

Using the DMM in on-chip SRAM, we compared the scalability of SS and DS with several matrix sizes. Figure 1 shows that SS not only has a lower performance than DS, but also its performance is affected drastically for smaller matrices. This is critical to extend our algorithm to off-chip DRAM because smaller block sizes are required to hide the latency of data movement tasks.

Figure 2 compares three implementations. (1) A fully parallel DMM that uses off-chip DRAM without overlapping computation and data movement. This implementation is based in the already optimized version of DMM that uses on-chip SRAM. (2) A version with the proposed Dynamic Percolation with optimized computation tasks, the optimum number of HTs is 24. (3) A version that uses Dynamic Percolation, optimized computation tasks, and communication that was optimized for the on-chip block sizes and the required transposition of matrix A.

In the best implementation, only 8 HTs were needed, increasing the performance due to the larger number of TUs available for computation, and ultimately achieving 65.63 GFLOPS with matrices of 6336×6336 using 156 TUs: 82.02% of the theoretical peak performance of C64.

5. CONCLUSIONS AND FUTURE WORK

In this paper we have proposed a Dynamic Percolation technique using two types of tasks – computation tasks and data movement tasks. The distribution of computation tasks and data movement tasks will vary in the course of dynamic percolation. Therefore, our method allows runtime redistribution between computational threads and data movement threads to achieve better utilization of thread unit resources. We have shown several advantages of the method proposed over well-known static techniques for many-core architectures in terms of scalability as a function of the matrix size for DMM. Our method also load-balances tasks across the machine because it handles well the unpredictable effects of resource-sharing, drastically improving performance. We report experimental results of our methods on a real C64 chip achieving 70.0 and 65.6 GFLOPS (out of 80 GFLOPS) for DMM with operands in SRAM and DRAM respectively.

Future work will apply this techniques to a broader set of applications, extending the work on Dynamic Scheduling [3], High Throughput Algorithms [5, 6] and Efficient Task Representation [7] for many-cores.

6. REFERENCES

[1] Chen, L., Gao, G.R.: Performance Analysis of Cooley-Tukey FFT Algorithms for a Many-core Architecture. In: HPC 2010 (2010)

[2] Denneau, M., Warren Jr., H.S.: 64-bit Cyclops: Principles of Operation. Tech. rep., IBM Watson Research Center, Yorktown Heights, NY (April 2005)

[3] Garcia, E., Orozco, D., Pavel, R., Gao, G.R.: A discussion in favor of Dynamic Scheduling for regular applications in Many-core Architectures. In: MTAAP'12. IEEE, Shanghai, China (May 2012)

[4] Garcia, E., Venetis, I.E., Khan, R., Gao, G.: Optimized dense matrix multiplication on a many-core architecture. In: Euro-Par'10. Ischia, Italy (2010)

[5] Orozco, D., Garcia, E., Khan, R., Livingston, K., Gao, G.: Toward high-throughput algorithms on many-core architectures. TACO 8(4), 49:1–21 (January 2012)

[6] Orozco, D., Garcia, E., Khan, R., Livingston, K., Gao, G.R.: High throughput queue algorithms. CAPSL Technical Memo 103 (January, 2011)

[7] Orozco, D., Garcia, E., Pavel, R., Gao, G.: TIDeFlow: The Time Iterated Dependency Flow Execution Model. In: DFM 2011. Galveston Island, TX, USA (October 2011)

[8] Orozco, D.A., Gao, G.R.: Mapping the fdtd application to many-core chip architectures. In: ICPP'09. pp. 309–316. IEEE Computer Society, Washington, DC, USA (2009)

CoreSymphony Architecture

Tomoyuki Nagatsuka, Yoshito Sakaguchi, Kenji Kise
Graduate School of Information Science and Engineering
Tokyo Institute of Technology
2-12-1, Ookayama, Meguro-ku, Tokyo, Japan
{nagatsuka, yoshito}@arch.cs.titech.ac.jp, kise@cs.titech.ac.jp

ABSTRACT

We propose *CoreSymphony architecture*, which aims at balancing single-thread performance and multi-thread performance on CMPs. The former version of CoreSymphony had complex branch predictor, re-order buffer, and in-order state management mechanism. In this paper, we solve these problems and evaluate the performance of CoreSymphony.

Categories and Subject Descriptors

C.1.3 [**Processor Architectures**]: Other Architecture Styles—*adaptable architectures*

General Terms

Performance, Design

Keywords

Multi-core Architecture, Reconfigurable Architecture, Single-thread Performance

1. INTRODUCTION

Current chip multiprocessors (CMPs) with between two and eight cores achieve high performance by executing a number of threads in parallel. With the development of semiconductor technology, the number of cores on a chip is expected to increase towards many-core era.

On the multi-core/many-core era, as Amdahl's Law [1] says, the performance improvement of multi-threaded programs on CMPs is restricted by single-threaded region. Unfortunately, some portion of single-threaded region remains on complicated and large programs like SPEC CPU. Therefore, we must improve single-thread performance.

In order to improve the single-thread performance, we proposed *CoreSymphony architecture* [4], which balances single-thread performance and multi-thread performance. CoreSymphony is able to fuse up to four 2-issue cores, and the fused virtual core behaves as a single wide-issue core. The wide-issue core exploits instruction-level parallelism (ILP) and is able to execute the single-thread faster than a baseline core. CoreSymphony splits a single wide-issue virtual core into some narrow issue cores, and executes multi-threaded program effectively. Figure 1 shows a conceptual diagram of CoreSymphony. For simplicity, we show 2-core configuration, where two 2-issue cores are fused into a single 4-issue core.

2. PROBLEMS OF CORESYMPHONY

The first version of CoreSymphony has three major problems.

(1) Complex branch predictor: The Bimode branch predictor is used, and it complicates the instruction fetch mechanism.

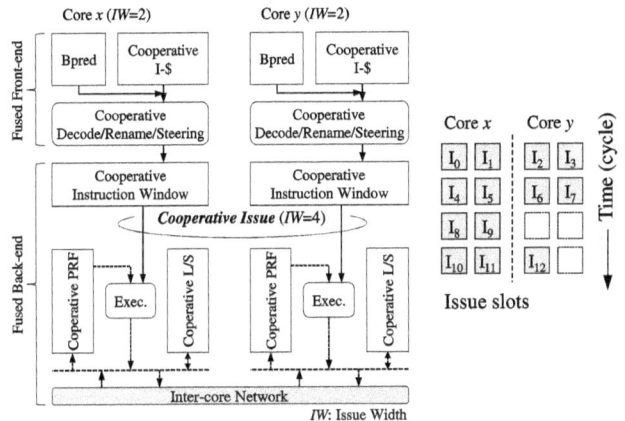

Figure 1: Conceptual diagram of 2-core fusion CoreSymphony.

(2) Complex re-order buffer (ROB): A ROB entry is allocated to each in-flight instruction. On CoreSymphony, the number of in-flight instructions increases by fusion, and it also increases the number of ROB entries. Moreover, the ROB requires many read/write ports, because the issue width is increased by fusion.

(3) Inefficient in-order state[1] management: Although all fused cores need the in-order state to recover from speculation miss, it is unrealistic for all cores to have the complete in-order state redundantly. Its hardware is too complex.

3. PROPOSAL ARCHITECTURE

We show the overall structure of new CoreSymphony in Figure 2. The shaded areas are the modules that are added or modified from a conventional out-of-order core. In this chapter, we discuss the differences from the former version of CoreSymphony.

3.1 Branch Predictor

On CoreSymphony, all fused cores predict a branch outcome using the same branch history. Although this makes it easy to synchronize control flows of fused cores, it doesn't increase the number of predictor entries by fusion.

As a branch predictor, we adopt Tree-Based Multiple Branch Predictor (TMP) [3]. TMP is applied to CoreSymphony easily, because it is a branch predictor suitable for trace cache and *Local Instruction Cache* (Local I-$) [4] is a trace cache.

TMP uses one entry for prediction of one instruction trace. A *Fetch Block* (FB) [4] is an instruction trace on CoreSymphony, and a FB tends to contain more instructions by fusion. This decreases the number of necessary static FBs for program execution by fusion. Therefore, it decreases the number of necessary TMP entries, and improves branch prediction accuracy by fusion.

---

[1]State constructed by last assignment of non-speculative instructions to each logical register.

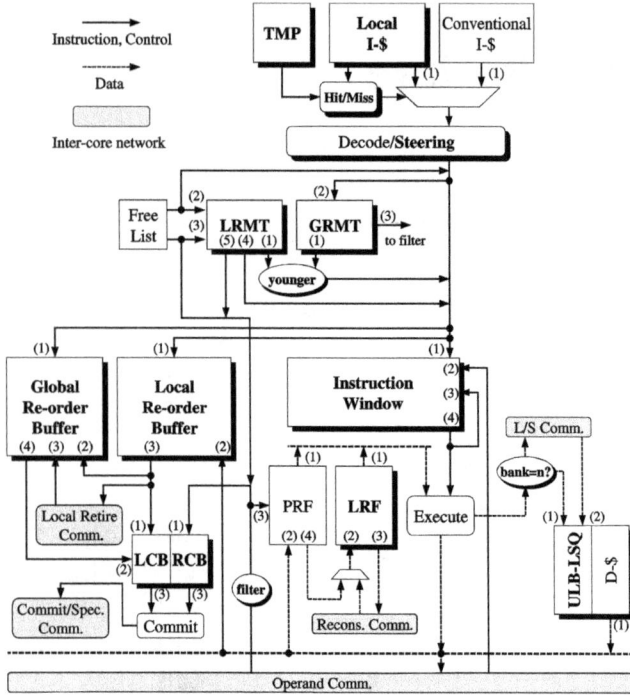

Figure 2: Block diagram of CoreSymphony architecture.

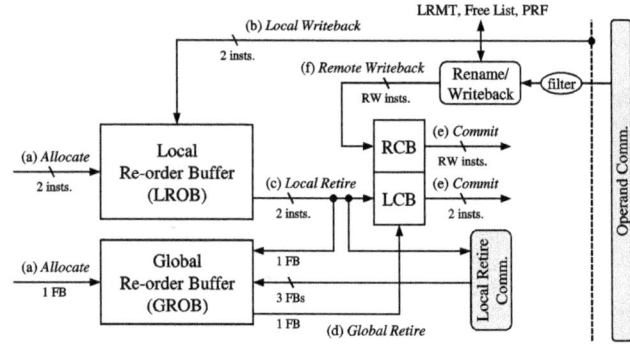

Figure 3: ROB distribution.

3.2 Re-order Buffer Distribution

In order to reduce ROB complexity, we separate ROB into two types of ROBs, *Local ROB* (LROB) and *Global ROB* (GROB). LROB stores only instructions steered to the core itself. Therefore, the size of LROB is equal to the size of 2-way out-of-order core's ROB. We are able to increase the number of effective ROB entries by fusion. However, this makes it difficult to take control precisely, because information, such as speculation misses, is distributed over all fused cores. Therefore, all fused cores need to share necessary information for precise control. Such information is managed in GROB, and the contents of GROBs are the same on all fused cores. A GROB entry is allocated for each dispatched FB. The number of GROB entries is equal to the maximum number of in-flight FBs (e.g. eight entries).

Figure 3 shows the block diagram of distributed ROB. We explain the detailed behavior.

(a) When a FB is dispatched in a core, only instructions steered to the core is allocated to its LROB and one GROB entry is allocated for the FB.

(b) Completions of instructions are notified only in the core where these instructions are steered. LROB is updated in the same manner as a conventional ROB.

(c) We then broadcast compressed information for precise control to all GROBs in all fused cores. The information

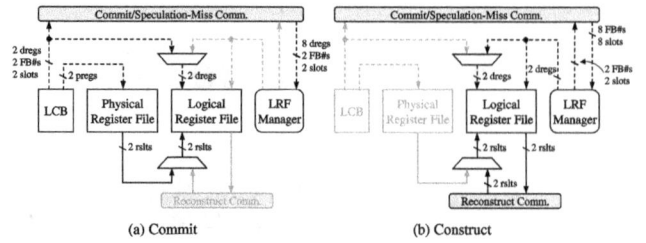

(a) Commit (b) Construct

Figure 4: In-order state distribution.

is FBID[2] of completed instruction, position of completed instruction in FB, result of branch instruction, speculation hit/miss, and so on. We update GROBs in all fused cores using the same information. Therefore, the contents of all GROBs are the same in all fused cores. The instructions that are broadcasted to all GROBs are allocated to *Local Commit Buffer* (LCB).

(d) GROB entry collects information, such as completion flags of instructions in the FB, result of branch instruction in the FB, speculation hit/miss, and so on. After all instructions in the FB are completed, instructions in LCB and RCB (discussed later) are woken up using the information. If speculation miss occurs, precise PC is sent to the front-end. We set ready flags of instructions in precise control flow.

(e) CoreSymphony commits instructions that has ready flag from LCB and RCB.

On CoreSymphony, execution result is broadcasted to all fused cores with inter-core network. If an instruction in a core needs the execution result, a physical register file (PRF) entry is allocated and stores the execution result. This and distributed ROB causes a problem about physical register deallocation.

On a conventional out-of-order processor, on register renaming of an instruction, we read the identifier of the physical register (PRID) where the destination register is already mapped (ppreg) from RMT, and register the PRID that is assigned to the instruction as the destination (preg) into RMT. ppreg is stored to ROB entry that is allocated for the instruction. When the instruction is committed, to deallocate physical register, the ppreg is brought back to free list if the instruction is in precise control flow.

On CoreSymphony, LROB has no entry for instructions that are steered to other cores. When execution result of a remote instruction is written back to PRF, we aren't able to bring back its ppreg to free list. Therefore, CoreSymphony needs special mechanism for bringing back the ppreg to free list.

For physical register deallocation for remote instructions, we use *Remote Commit Buffer* (RCB) in Figure 3. RCB is constructed in a similar way of LCB. An entry is allocated to RCB when a remote instruction writes back the result to PRF, and ppreg is stored to the RCB entry (Figure 3(f)). When the instruction is committed, the ppreg is brought back to free list.

3.3 In-order State Distribution

In order to recover from speculation miss, *Logical Register File* (LRF) is used. LRF keeps the in-order state and supply operands after recovery from speculation miss. LRF has as many entries as logical register file on ISA.

LRF stores execution results of committed instructions. When instructions are committed from LCB, each core reads execution results from PRF and copies these values to LRF. On CoreSymphony, the number of commits per cycle in all fused cores increases by fusion. Therefore, LRF needs many write ports in order to keep the correct in-order state in all fused cores redundantly.

In order to manage the in-order state effectively, we distribute the in-order state in all fused cores. The basic idea of in-order state distribution is as follow: (a) LRF in each core

---

[2]FBID is an identifier that is assigned to each in-flight FB in cyclic manner.

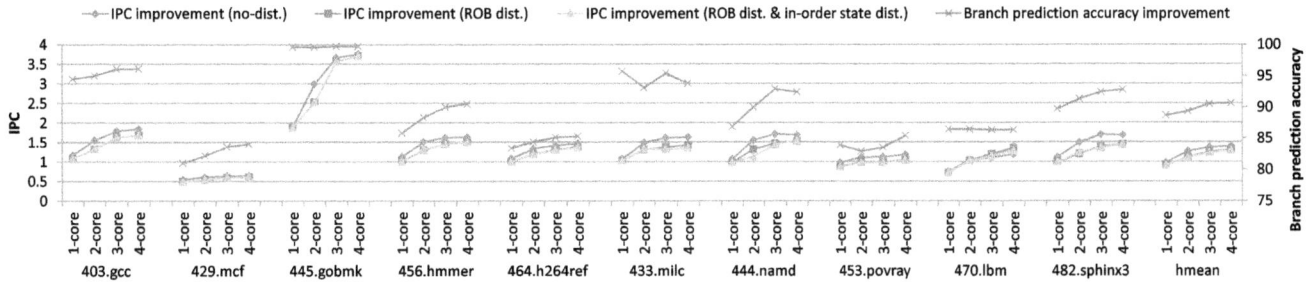

Figure 5: Performance improvement obtained by fusion. IPC improvement (left axis). Branch prediction accuracy improvement (right axis).

has incomplete in-order state constructed by only the instructions executed in the core; and (b) when speculation miss occurs, we construct the complete in-order state with inter-core communication between LRFs.

Figure 4 shows (a) update of in-order state when instructions are committed; and (b) construction of in-order state when speculation miss occurs.

When instructions are committed from LCB, each core reads the results from PRF using `preg`, and copies the results to LRF in the core using the identifier of the destination logical register (`dreg`). At the same time, `dreg` is broadcasted to all fused cores and each core records the `dreg` in *LRF Manager*. Furthermore, `FBID` and the position of the instruction in FB (`slot`) are recorded only to the LRF Manager in the core. By this way, each LRF has incomplete in-order state constructed by only the instructions that is steered to the core.

When recovering from speculation miss, we construct the complete in-order state. The values of logical registers that aren't updated recently[3] in any core are always the same in all fused cores. Therefore, it is sufficient to construct logical registers that are updated recently. The identifiers of the recently updated logical registers are recorded in LRF Manager. Furthermore, it is sufficient to broadcast only the latest values of recently updated instructions. We are able to know which core's LRF entry has the latest value by communicating and comparing `FBID` and `slot` in LRF Manager between cores. The core that has the latest value reads the value from LRF and copies it to all LRFs in all fused cores. Then, the constructed logical register flag is set. This process is done for every logical register.

During construction, we don't issue an instruction whose any source register isn't constructed. The scheduler sees whether the source register of the instruction is already constructed or not, and issues the instruction when its all source registers are ready.

In order to update the in-order state, LRF needs write ports that are the same in number of retirement width of LCB. Moreover, in order to construct the in-order state, LRF needs as many ports as the number of LRF entries that we desire to construct per cycle. Here, we focus on the point that it is only after speculation miss to construct the in-order state. Because the pipeline is flushed after a speculation miss, it takes some time to commit the instructions that is in the correct path. Therefore, even if we use the same ports for both update and construction, it would have a small effect for performance. Thus, we stall the instruction commit during construction of the in-order state, and after the construction, the instruction commit is started.

4. EVALUATION

We used a cycle-accurate software-based simulator, *SimMips* [2], and SPEC2006 benchmarks to evaluate CoreSymphony. We modified SimMips for the simulation of CoreSymphony. Figure 5 shows IPC and branch prediction accuracy obtained by fusion on each benchmark. In the figure, 1, 2, 3, 4-core respectively mean 1-core execution, 2-core fusion, 3-core fusion, and 4-core fusion. `no-dist.`, `ROB dist.`, and `in-order state dist.` respectively mean no-distribution, ROB distribution, and in-order state distribution.

[3]From the latest speculation miss recovery to the present.

The evaluation results show that the IPC of CoreSymphony is improved by fusion. On the harmonic mean (hmean) of all benchmarks, 2, 3, and 4-core fusion achieve 22%, 36%, and 43% higher IPC respectively than 1-core execution.

As discussed in Section 3.1, on almost all benchmarks, branch prediction accuracy is improved by fusion. On hmean of all benchmarks, the branch prediction accuracy on 4-core fusion is 1.9% higher than that on 1-core execution.

Although ROB/in-order state distribution reduce hardware complexity, these degrade the performance. This is because the number of the pipeline stages is increased by ROB distribution, and the issue stage may stall by in-order state distribution. On harmonic mean, compared to IPC of ROB distribution, IPC degradation ratio by in-order state distribution is 0%, 1.0%, 1.6%, and 1.1% on 1, 2, 3, and 4-core respectively. In-order state distribution degrades the performance a little.

On harmonic mean, compared to IPC of no-distribution, IPC degradation ratio by ROB distribution is 8.3%, 12%, 8.8%, and 6.5% on 1, 2, 3, and 4-core respectively. Although the performance degradation by ROB distribution is not negligible, it realizes the ROB's ports reduction and it is necessary for realistic hardware implementation.

5. CONCLUSION

In this paper, we solved three major problems on the former version of CoreSymphony. It had complex branch predictor, ROB, and in-order state management mechanism. We simplified the branch predictor by adopting TMP, and reduce complexity of ROB and in-order state management mechanism by distribution.

Future work is as follows: (1) estimation of the hardware budget; and (2) performance evaluation with dynamic fusion/split mechanism. In order to estimate the hardware budget of CoreSymphony strictly, we describe CoreSymphony with HDL and implement it on FPGAs. Furthermore, there are some overhead when CoreSymphony fuses/splits cores. In order to realize higher performance than heterogeneous multi-core architectures, we develop an effective mechanism that fuses and splits cores during execution.

6. ACKNOWLEDGEMENTS

This work was supported by MEXT KAKENHI 22700046.

7. REFERENCES

[1] M. D. Hill, et al. Amdahl's Law in the Multicore Era. *IEEE Computer*, 41(7):33–38, 2008.

[2] N. Fujieda, et al. A MIPS System Simulator SimMips for Education and Research of Computer Science. In *IPSJ Journal, Vol.50, No.11*, pages 2665–2676, 2009.

[3] R. Rakvic, et al. Completion Time Multiple Branch Prediction for Enhancing Trace Cache Performance. In *Proceedings of the 27th International Symposium on Computer Architecture (ISCA-2000)*, pages 47–58, 2000.

[4] T. Nagatsuka, et al. CoreSymphony: An Efficient Reconfigurable Multi-core Architecture. In *ACM SIGARCH Computer Architecture News, Vol.39, Iss.4*, pages 32–37, 2011.

Instructions Activating Conditions for Hardware-Based Auto-Scheduling

Silvia Lovergine, Fabrizio Ferrandi
Politecnico di Milano - Dipartimento di Elettronica ed Informazione
via Ponzio 34/5, Milan, Italy
{lovergine,ferrandi}@elet.polimi.it

ABSTRACT

Nowadays, implementing hardware accelerators by hand-writing the RTL still leads to better quality of the results with respect to those obtained by automating the design process. Manually developing and maintaining hardware designs, however, is a complex, time-consuming and error prone task, making improvements in the automatic design flow definition a fervent ongoing research topic. The most common approach is based on a statically computed scheduling order. Supports for features such as dynamic scheduling or unbounded latency of operations and functional units have been proposed with some limitations. Instructions auto-scheduling is an alternative to overcome such restrictions, while facing those situations that need or take advantage of run-time adaptive reordering of the instructions. This paper focuses on how to improve the synthesis of hardware cores by increasing automatic parallelism exploitation. The proposed approach computes the set of conditions to be satisfied for each instruction to be executed as soon as possible, allowing run-time auto-scheduling. Representing such conditions as logic functions, the corresponding hardware implementation can be easily automated. Experimental results have shown an encouraging enhancement in terms of performance, with a limited increase of area.

Categories and Subject Descriptors

B.5.2 [**Design Aids**]: Automatic Synthesis

General Terms

Design, Performance

Keywords

Autoscheduling, Automatic Parallelism Exploitation, High-Level Synthesis, Dynamic Scheduling

1. INTRODUCTION

As hardware description languages (HDLs) reside at a low abstraction level, manually implementing efficient hardware designs requires great skills and extensive knowledge about the underlying infrastructure. RTL designs quickly becomes complex, making their creation, testing and integration a time-consuming and error prone process. Automating the design of hardware accelerators can reduce the development time from weeks to minutes.

In this paper we propose an auto-scheduling methodology based on the computation of the Instructions *Activating Conditions (ACs)* and on the integration of their computation into an automatic synthesis flow. Once identified, the ACs are expressed as logic functions, and consequently straightforwardly implemented into hardware.

The remainder of this paper is organized as follows. Section 2 describes some related work about scheduling techniques and about architectural choices that impact on the scheduling task. The proposed methodology for the instructions auto-scheduling, based on the Instructions Activating Conditions, is presented in Section 3. Experimental results are shown in Section 4, while Section 5 concludes outlining possible future directions for the work.

2. RELATED WORK

Instruction scheduling and resource binding represent the main tasks in high-level synthesis, and consequently those impacting more on the quality of the results. These two problems can be modeled together as scheduling under resource constraint. Unfortunately such problem is computationally prohibitive [7]. For this reason these two tasks either are faced separately, or with heuristic approaches.

In this paper we consider the scheduling problem for the high-level synthesis of efficient hardware cores. Over the years, with the increasing interaction of such systems with external modules, such as sensors, memories or IP cores, that are often characterized by unpredictable latencies, standard scheduling techniques have come to significantly restrict the performance. Moreover, traditional approaches cannot deal with process variation, making hardware cores unusable in most cases, such as in critical environments. Other scheduling techniques have been proposed to support for example unbounded modules [14] or speculation [8], but with some limitation on the exploitable parallelism.

Automatically designed hardware accelerators are usually composed of a datapath and a centralized Finite State Machine (FSM) acting as controller. The FSM controller requires to establish at design time the set of instructions that will be executed at each control step. As a consequence, potentially independent code fragments must be sequentialized in presence of unknown information at design time, such as number of loop iterations, outcome of conditional instructions evaluation, value of the incoming arguments of a function or latency of unpredictable components. To increase parallelism exploitation, the FSM can be extended with additional states to support the selection at run-time, i.e. when unknown information will be resolved, of the proper scheduling among a set of scheduling orders, pre-computed at design time. This lead, however, to an increase in area up

to the Cartesian product of the original number of states
[10], often producing unfeasible solutions. With this approach, the more the architecture is flexible, the more its
area grows. In general, the scheduling task can affect the
area of the controller part of the designed architecture, and
the model chosen for the controller can restrict the parallelism exploitable during the scheduling. For this reason,
the scheduling problem is strictly coupled with the problem
of designing a proper architectural model for the controller.
More efficient alternatives to the centralized FSM controller
have been proposed, as for example distributed FSMs [16],
parallel FSMs [13], hierarchical controllers [12] and adaptive
controllers [15]. The auto-scheduling technique proposed in
this paper takes advantages of the capabilities of an adaptive controller, as described in [15], that is able to adjust
its behavior at run time. Since such controller is not FSM-
based, it avoids the limitations, related to the use of FSMs
controllers, about parallelism exploitation.

3. PROPOSED APPROACH

This section introduces our methodology to increase parallelism exploitation in the automatic synthesis of hardware
accelerators. Driven by the idea that supporting instructions
auto-scheduling allows to overcome restrictions due to unknown information at design time, with a limited growing
area, our approach aims to identify the Instructions *Activating Conditions (ACs)* in order to automate their computation, to be integrated into an HLS flow. Due to the
sequential nature of the high level languages, describing the
specification, the first step to identify the ACs consists in the
definition of a proper IR able to expose the inherent parallelism. For this purpose, we have defined a proper Intermediate Representation (IR) extending the Program Dependence
Graph [9] with minimum control flow edges, needed to ensure correct execution. Once defined, such IR is analyzed
to compute the Activating Conditions, according to a set of
formal rules. More in detail, the task for the IR construction
must be added in the front-end. Then, the task of the ACs
computation must be added to those commonly performed
during high-level synthesis, in order to create the support
for the synthesis of an adaptive controller.

The Activating Conditions (ACs) are logic formulas that
indicate which conditions must be satisfied at run-time to
correctly enable the execution of each instruction. Such conditions depend not only on data and control dependencies,
but also on control-flow dependences. Such formulation extends the one proposed in [11] with the addition of control-
flow dependences to increase the amount of exploited parallelism. Notice that this approach can be straightforwardly
extended to support optimizations such as loop pipelining,
and speculation.

*Definition 1. Let V the set of instructions in the specification, and E the set of dependences among them. Given an
instruction $i \in V$, the Activating Condition $AC(i)$ is a logic
function of other instructions and of conditional instructions
evaluation outcomes.*

An AC is composed of three parts. The first one guarantees
that data dependences are satisfied, control dependences are
handled by the second part, while the third one manages the
control flow:

$$AC(i) = AC_{data}(i) \wedge AC_{control}(i) \wedge AC_{control\_flow}(i) \quad (1)$$

where the use of the operator $\wedge$ means that all the three
parts must be satisfied for safely activating the execution of
an instruction.

Table 1: Simulation: Clock Cycles

Benchmark	LIST FSM	AutoSched Adaptive	Gain
adpcm	76113	69571	8.59%
bubble_sort	731	354	51.57%
convolutionSeparable	47187	42840	9.21%
fastWalshTransform	33	11	66.67%
gsm	5804	2984	48.59%
popCnt	397	292	26.45%
wavesched	73	39	46.57%
yuv2rgb	168	139	17.26%

4. EXPERIMENTAL EVALUATION

The proposed methodology has been implemented in C++
and integrated into the PandA framework [5], that uses the
GCC compiler ver. 4.5.2 [1] as front-end. The representation taken as input for the construction of the defined
IR is the *gimple* produced by GCC. The designs produced
by the high-level synthesis have been simulated through
Modelsim ver. 6.6 [4], and then synthesized on FPGA by
means of Xilinx ISE ver. 12.4, targeting a Virtex 5 device
xc5vlx50-3ff1153 [6].

The benchmarks used for the experimental evaluation are:

- *adpcm* and *gsm*, from the CHStone test suite [17]
- *bubble_sort*, *fastWalshTransform*, *popCnt* and *yuv2rgb*,
  from [2]
- *convolutionSeparable*, from [3]
- *wavesched*, from [10]

The proposed methodology for high level synthesis, implementing instructions auto-scheduling and targeting an adaptive controller based architecture, has been compared with
a classical approach, implementing a LIST algorithm for the
scheduling and targeting a centralized FSM controller based
architecture. Table 1 shows the simulation results in terms
of clock cycles. Notice that the gain obtained is strictly
related to the amount of parallelism available in the specification. Data-flow intensive parallelism is well exploited
also by traditional techniques, as shown in the results for
the benchmark yuv2rgb. At the contrary, control-flow intensive specifications, as wavesched, show a significant gain
in performance with the proposed approach. More in detail,
yuv2rgb contains a single loop, while wavesched contains two
parallel loops, where the first one contains an if-then-else
construct. Hence, wavesched is a typical example showing
how the LIST-FSM approach, as other standard approaches,
is limited by the presence of control constructs, especially if
they are nested into each other. In general, the results obtained with standard techniques represent the lower bound
of those obtained with the proposed approach.

Finally, Table 2 shows the results of the RTL synthesis on a
Xilinx Virtex 5 FPGA. Despite the number of Flip-Flops increases, notice that this number is still significantly smaller
than the number of LUTs, that is instead reduced by the
proposed approach for most of the presented benchmarks.
When in an FPGA the number of FFs and LUTs is unbalanced, an increase of the smaller may be hidden by the
bigger, since the resources are allocated by cells. This result is well shown by the numbers of LUT-FF pairs, that
for the proposed approach are reasonably close to those obtained with the LIST-FSM approach. Moreover, the results
in terms of FFs numbers can be explained by the absence, at
the state of the art, in the considered model, of an efficient

Table 2: Synthesis: Area

	LIST-FSM			Autosched-Adaptive			Gain		
Benchmark	FF	LUT	PAIRS	FF	LUT	PAIRS	FF	LUT	PAIRS
adpcm	5122	22900	22900	18586	20225	25055	-262.86%	11.68%	-9.41%
bubble_sort	153	935	937	365	741	910	-138.56%	20.75%	2.88%
convolutionSeparable	1359	4432	4471	3571	3945	5497	-162.77%	10.988%	-22.95%
fastWalshTransform	681	2345	2395	1289	2267	2721	-89.28%	3.33%	-13.61%
gsm	5915	19188	19261	16503	15516	21673	-179.00%	19.14%	-12.52%
popCnt	390	1581	1619	618	1513	1769	-58.46%	4.30%	-9.26%
wavesched	182	474	480	613	572	786	-236.81%	-20.67%	-63.75%
yuv2rgb	428	2047	2056	851	1171	1697	-98.83%	42.79%	17.46%

binding technique that not restricts parallelism exploitation. Thus, a unique binding approach has been considered, with a consequent increase in the number of allocated registers, that further researches in such direction could significantly reduce.

5. CONCLUSION

In this paper a methodology for the instructions auto-scheduling in high-level synthesis (HLS) has been proposed, aiming to provide a support for parallelism exploitation and thus for the design of efficient hardware core. The most common approach in HLS is based on a statically computed scheduling order. Such approach, however cannot deal with unknown information at design-time or with unpredictable components. Instructions auto-scheduling can be a possible alternative to adaptively exploit at run-time the available parallelism. The instructions are able to autonomously establish when the conditions enabling their execution are satisfied, avoiding the above mentioned limitations. The proposed approach for auto-scheduling computes the set of Activating Conditions to be satisfied for each instruction to be executed as soon as possible, on the basis of the analysis of a proper IR. Experimental results have shown an encouraging increase in performance with a limited increase of area. Further works on this direction could formalize the AC computation in presence of optimizations such as loop pipelining or speculation. As above mentioned, the proposed approach can be easily extended to deal with such optimizations, leading to further increase the performance. Moreover, future works on the analysis of parallel execution flows for the improvement of other HLS tasks, such as resource allocation and binding, or chaining of the instructions, could impact on the proposed methodology by reducing the resulting area.

6. REFERENCES

[1] GCC - GNU Compiler Collection. http://gcc.gnu.org.
[2] http://c-to-verilog.com/.
[3] http://developer.nvidia.com/cuda-cc-sdk-code-samples.
[4] Modelsim - Advanced Simulation and Debugging, http://model.com/.
[5] PandA - A Framework for Hardware-Software Co-Design of Embedded Systems. http://panda.dei.polimi.it/.
[6] Xilinx. Synthesis tools for FPGA devices. http://www.xilinx.com.
[7] F. D. Brewer and D. D. Gajski. Knowledge based control in micro-architecture design. In *Proceedings of the 24th ACM/IEEE Design Automation Conference,* DAC '87, pages 203–209, New York, NY, USA, 1987. ACM.
[8] A. Del Barrio, S. Memik, M. Molina, J. Mendias, and R. Hermida. A distributed controller for managing speculative functional units in high level synthesis. *Computer-Aided Design of Integrated Circuits and Systems, IEEE Transactions on,* 30(3):350–363, march 2011.
[9] J. Ferrante, K. J. Ottenstein, and J. D. Warren. The program dependence graph and its use in optimization. *ACM Trans. Program. Lang. Syst.,* 9:319–349, July 1987.
[10] G. Lakshminarayana, K.S. Khouri, and N.K. Jha. Wavesched: a novel scheduling technique for control-flow intensive designs. *IEEE Trans. on CAD,* 18(5):505–523, May 1999.
[11] M. Girkar and C. D. Polychronopoulos. Automatic extraction of functional parallelism from ordinary programs. *IEEE Trans. Parallel Distrib. Syst.,* 3:166–178, March 1992.
[12] João M. Fernandes, M. Adamski, and A.J. Proença. "VHDL generation from hierarchical petri net specifications of parallel controllers". *Proc. of IEEE Computer and Digital Techniques,* 1997.
[13] Krzysztof Biliński, E.L. Dagless, J.M. Saul, and M. Adamski. "Parallel controller synthesis from a Petri net specification". *Proc. of European Design Automation Conference,* 1994.
[14] D. Ku and G. De Micheli. Relative scheduling under timing constraints: algorithms for high-level synthesis of digital circuits. *Computer-Aided Design of Integrated Circuits and Systems, IEEE Transactions on,* 11(6):696–718, jun 1992.
[15] Pilato, C., Castellana, V.G., Lovergine, S., and Ferrandi, F. A Runtime Adaptive Controller for Supporting Hardware Components with Variable Latency. *NASA/ESA Conference on Adaptive Hardware and Systems (AHS '11),* June 2011.
[16] S.Devadas and R. Newton. "Decomposition and Factorization of Sequential Finite State Machines". *IEEE Trans. on CAD,* 8:1206–1217, 1988.
[17] H. T. S. H. Y. Hara and H. Takada. Proposal and quantitative analysis of the chstone benchmark program suite for practical c-based high-level synthesis. pages 242–254, 2009.

Selective Search of Inlining Vectors for Program Optimization

Rosario Cammarota
Alex Nicolau, Alex Veidenbaum
Dept. of Computer Science
University of California Irvine
Irvine, CA

Arun Kejariwal, Debora Donato

Yahoo! Inc.
Sunnyvale, CA

ABSTRACT

We propose a novel technique to select the inlining options of a compiler - referred to as an *inlining vector*, for program optimization. The proposed technique trains a machine learning algorithm to model the relation between *inlining vectors* and performance (*completion time*). The training set is composed of sample runs of the programs to optimize - that are compiled with a limited number of inlining vectors. Subject to a given compiler, the model evaluates the benefit of inlining combined with other compiler heuristics. The model is subsequently used to select the inlining vector which minimizes the predicted completion time of a program with respect to a given level of optimization.

We present a case study based on the compiler GNU GCC. We used our technique to improve performance of 403.gcc from SPEC CPU2006 - a program which is notoriously hard to optimize - with respect to the optimization level -O3 as the *baseline*. On the state-of-the-art Intel Xeon Westmere architecture, 403.gcc compiled using the inlining vectors selected by our technique outperforms the baseline by up to 9%.

Categories and Subject Descriptors

C.4 [**Performance of systems**]: [Modeling techniques]; D.3.4 [**Processors**]: [Compilers]; D.4.8 [**Software Engineering**]: [Modeling and prediction, Stochastic analysis]

General Terms

Measurements, Performance

Keywords

Performance modeling, Hardware counters, Random Forest, Cross-validation

1. INTRODUCTION

The widespread use of software engineering methodologies often leads to complex program structures that are composed of a multitude of functions and source files. The presence of these files and functions unfortunately limits the scope of global optimizations and their forced separate compilation reduces the performance in complex and unpredictable ways. As a result, when relying on current compiler technologies and rigid compiler heuristic constraints, programs achieve in practice only a portion of the performance that they could in principle achieve on a given architecture.

Function inlining provides a simple - in principle - way of overcoming these barriers to program optimization and prior studies acknowledge the potential that function inlining offers at compile time to other optimizations, parallelization and vectorization [1, 2]. The importance of function inlining is also evidenced by the fact it is used in all optimizing compilers - e.g., the GNU GCC [3], Intel ICC [4], IBM XLC [5]- as a first pass of their aggressive optimization levels such as −O3.

Despite its importance, most of the effort of prior work was devoted on improving the accuracy of inlining decisions [6, 7, 8, 9, 10] for hot and/or frequently used functions/methods and/or within the same program module, i.e., in the absence of separate compilation.

In this paper we develop a novel technique for function inlining, given a compiler and its parameterized heuristic for optimizing programs exhibiting complex structures. Our technique accounts for compilation and run-time properties of a program and leverages them by training a machine learning model. Our machine learning based model is parameterized with the inlining vector and is subsequently used to select inlining constraints - referred to as an *inlining vector*, which minimizes completion time of this program.

We illustrate the efficacy of our technique in a case study using GNU GCC v4.5. This case study is focused on the optimization of the program 403.gcc from SPEC CPU2006 [11] for a number of input files. The baseline is set to the optimization level -O3. The binary generated using our technique outperforms both the the baseline and the best performance observed during the training phase. For several input files, performance improvements on the state-of-the-art Intel Xeon Westmere architecture range from 2% to 9%.

The rest of the paper is organized as follows: Section 2 provides the background and the motivation aiming our work; Section 3 describes in detail the steps of our technique; Section 4 reports a case study and discusses the findings to it related.

2. BACKGROUND

The selection of inlining constraints for a given program is non-trivial. Not only is the performance of a program for given inlining vector unpredictable - because of the interaction with other compiler heuristics geared toward a given architecture - but also the large number of inlining vectors makes the exploration process intractable. Furthermore, obvious solutions to the problem, such as indiscriminate inlining, either are likely to provide performance degradation or involve compiler/run-time malfunctioning due to code explosion. Such an intractability represents a severe limitation which makes the direct application of specialized search techniques [9, 10] impractical in industry settings when optimizing complex C and C++ programs - the search would involve a (large) number of recompilations and runs ($> 10^{17}$).

The proposed technique differs from prior work utilizing machine learning algorithms to predict near-optimal on-off compiler settings [12, 13, 14, 15] in the following aspects: (a) Our technique focuses on non on-off compiler settings; (b) It leaves the selection of the model unspecified until the training set is available and explicitly selects the model using a rigorous and quantitative procedure based on k-fold cross-validation; (c) The training set contains both examples under-performing and outperforming the baseline in order to enforce the prediction accuracy of the model.

3. TECHNIQUE

Our technique is composed of the four passes described below.

3.1 Building the training set

This pass involves a large number of compilations - one compilation for one inlining vector - followed by a limited number of sample runs. [1] An analysis of binary sizes and layouts is employed to identify binary files with distinct sizes and/or program layouts.

Let F be the total number of inlining vectors generating valid binary files. Let $M << F$ be the number of compilations performed - for example M inlining vectors can be obtained by sampling uniformly each dimension of the inlining vector in F. Compiling a program using different inlining vectors does not guarantee that the corresponding binary files are distinct. Furthermore, among distinct binary files many of them can have the same size - referred to as *aliases*. Therefore, among the M binary files, U ($\leq M$), binary files that are distinct files and not aliases are separated from the set of binary files previously compiled. Despite the fact that these are distinct binary files, aliases achieve nearly equal performance subject to a given input. Thereby, our technique excludes aliases and runs only U unique binary files to populate the training set. Indeed, U binary files are executed and their execution is monitored to collect: (a) The completion time; (b) A set of hardware performance counters - to describe the behavior of a program on a given architecture, subject to its compilation with an inlining vector. The runs above populate the *training set* (T). Each entry of the training set is composed of an inlining vector (iv), a vector of hardware performance counters (cnt) and associate completion time (p) to these two vectors.

3.2 Building the hypothesis

This pass uses supervised learning in the form of regression algorithms to learn a regression model (*hypothesis*) from T. The role of the hypothesis is to approximate the relation between the vector of counters - representing the behavior of an application on a given architecture - and performance, parameterized to the inlining vector.

---

[1]Note that, no matter how large is the number of compilations, these can be performed in parallel to velocize the process.

Processor	Intel X5680 (westmere) @ 3.33GHz
L1 I/D cache [KB]	32
L2 cache	256KB
LLC	12MB
Main memory [GB]	24
Compilers, options	GNU GCCv4.5, -m64 -O3
Operating system	Linux Red Hat AS 4 update 7

Table 1: System configuration

This pass involves the training of multiple regression algorithms using the sample runs above and compares the corresponding models (*hypotheses*). Each hypothesis is subsequently validated using 10-fold cross-validation: mean absolute error and coefficient of correlation are computed for each model - refer to Appendix A. The hypothesis exhibiting the lowest mean absolute error and the highest positive coefficient of correlation is selected. [2]

3.3 Selection of an inlining vector

The third pass of our technique operates as follows: given a program and its binary file corresponding to the baseline and characterized by a vector of hardware performance counters, the hypothesis is used to search and select an inlining vector - iv^* - able to minimize predicted completion time and/or outperform the baseline. This inlining vector is subsequently used to recompile the program. While the training is done using U inlining vectors, the search is performed on the set F.

3.4 Evaluation

The efficacy of the predicted inlining vector is verified by recompiling the program using the inlining vector and measuring its performance on an average of 20 runs. T-test [16] is applied to decide about the equality of the average execution times of the baseline and the predicted inlining vector.

4. CASE STUDY

Using GNU GCC v4.5, we present a case study, which is focused on the optimization of the program 403.gcc from SPEC CPU2006 [11]. The baseline is set to the optimization level -O3. 403.gcc is notoriously hard to optimize because it exhibits (a) a flat function calls profile; (b) it spends approximately half of its execution cycles in external libraries; (c) it has a very complex program structure - its call-graph is composed of 2,072 nodes, 7,868 edges and 216,947,768 function calls. We attempted 30,000 compilations corresponding to the number of inlining vectors in the ranges mentioned in Table 2. Not all the compilation were successful, however, compared to the number of compilations, 403.gcc exhibits a small number of unique binary files - see Table 3 - that are used to build the training set. We consider a vector of performance hardware counters composed of cycles per instructions, the percentage of branch retired and the count of cache misses per kilo instruction at the second and the last level of cache. Our technique selects *M5P* [17], a form of random forest for regression, as the most suitable regression algorithm to model our experimental runs. Indeed, on the training set M5P exhibits a mean absolute error $\mu_{M5P}^{\alpha} = 0.89[s]$ - which accounts for a prediction error of less than 1% compared with the average execution time of 403.gcc on the set of reference input - and coefficient of correlation $\mu_{M5P}^{\rho} = 0.99$.

---

[2]The maximum acceptable mean absolute error is a parameter of our technique and can be set according the to average execution time of the program to optimize.

Constraint	Ranges
inline_call_cost	{10}
max_inline_insns_auto	[10-170]
large_function_insns	[2100-3100]
large_function_growth	[20-100]
large_unit_insns	[6,000-16,000]
inline_unit_growth	[30-300]
inline_recursive_depth	[4-8]

Table 2: GCCv4.5 - Inlining constraints

	Unique	Alias	Clone
403.gcc	1,000	20,000	7,000

Table 3: 403.gcc - Alias and clone analysis

Baseline	Default iv
$-O3$	$< 10, 120, 2000, 300, 10000, 150, 8 >$

(program, input)	iv^*
(403.gcc,I1)	$< 10, 126, 2415, 297, 6000, 135, 8 >$
(403.gcc,I2)	$< 10, 165, 2405, 296, 6000, 66, 8 >$
(403.gcc,I3)	$< 10, 127, 2524, 46, 6000, 103, 8 >$
(403.gcc,I4)	$< 10, 167, 2697, 207, 6000, 105, 8 >$
(403.gcc,I5)	$< 10, 167, 2693, 33, 6000, 95, 8 >$
(403.gcc,I6)	$< 10, 168, 2684, 183, 6000, 145, 8 >$
(403.gcc,I7)	$< 10, 152, 2373, 298, 6000, 106, 8 >$
(403.gcc,I8)	$< 10, 150, 2637, 127, 6000, 149, 8 >$
(403.gcc,I9)	$< 10, 138, 2691, 299, 6000, 44, 8 >$

Table 4: Optimal iv^*

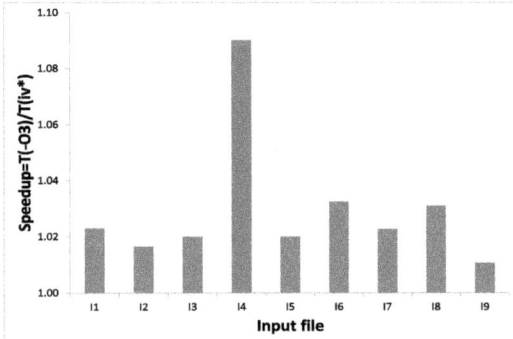

Figure 1: 403.gcc - Performance improvements

We used our technique to predict one iv^* for each of the reference input files of 403.gcc within SPEC CPU2006 - see Table 4. The binary obtained using such inlining vectors outperform both the baseline and the best performance observed during the training phase. Specifically, we achieved speedups of the range 2% to 9% on the state-of-the-art Intel Xeon Westmere (X5680), see Figure 1.

Acknowledgments

This work was supported in part by the National Science Foundation under grant NSF CCF-0811882 and Yahoo! Inc.

5. REFERENCES

[1] J. E. Ball. Predicting the effects of optimization on a procedure body. In *Proceedings of the 1979 SIGPLAN symposium on Compiler construction*, pages 214–220, 1979.

[2] R. Allen and S. Johnson. Compiling c for vectorization, parallelization, and inline expansion. In *Proceedings of the ACM SIGPLAN 1988 conference on Programming Language design and Implementation*, pages 241–249, 1988.

[3] GCC, the GNU Compiler Collection. http://gcc.gnu.org/.

[4] Intel Compilers. http://software.intel.com/en-us/articles/intel-compilers/.

[5] IBM XL C and C++ compilers. http://www-01.ibm.com/software/awdtools/xlcpp/.

[6] R. W. Scheifler. An analysis of inline substitution for a structured programming language. *Commun. ACM*, 20, September 1977.

[7] J. Dean and C. Chambers. Training compilers for better inlining decisions. Technical Report 93-05-05, University of Washington, May 1993.

[8] K. Hazelwood and D. Grove. Adaptive online context-sensitive inlining. In *Proceedings of the international symposium on Code generation and optimization: feedback-directed and runtime optimization*, pages 253–264, 2003.

[9] J. Cavazos and M. F. P. O'Boyle. Automatic tuning of inlining heuristics. In *Proceedings of the 2005 ACM/IEEE conference on Supercomputing*, 2005.

[10] K. D. Cooper, T. J. Harvey, and T. Waterman. An adaptive strategy for inline substitution. In *Proceedings of the Joint European Conferences on Theory and Practice of Software 17th international conference on Compiler construction*, pages 69–84, 2008.

[11] J. L. Henning. Spec cpu2006 benchmark descriptions. *SIGARCH Computer Architecture News*, 34(4):1–17, 2006.

[12] A. Monsifrot, F. Bodin, and R. Quiniou. A machine learning approach to automatic production of compiler heuristics. In *Proceedings of the 10th International Conference Artificial Intelligence: Methodology, Systems, and Applications*, pages 41–50, 2002.

[13] M. Stephenson and S. P. Amarasinghe. Predicting unroll factors using supervised classification. In *3nd IEEE / ACM International Symposium on Code Generation and Optimization*, pages 123–134, 2005.

[14] J. Cavazos, G. Fursin, F. Agakov, E. Bonilla, M. F. P. O'Boyle, and O. Temam. Rapidly selecting good compiler optimizations using performance counters. In *Proceedings of the International Symposium on Code Generation and Optimization*, pages 185–197, 2007.

[15] C. Dubach, T. M. Jones, E. V. Bonilla, G. Fursin, and M. F. P. O'Boyle. Portable compiler optimisation across embedded programs and microarchitectures using machine learning. In *Proceedings of the 42nd Annual IEEE/ACM International Symposium on Microarchitecture*, pages 78–88, 2009.

[16] W. S. Gosset. The probable error of a mean. *Biometrika*, 6(1):1–25, March 1908.

[17] J. R. Quinlan. Learning with continuous classes. In *Australian Joint Conference on Artificial Intelligence*, 1992.

APPENDIX
A. METRICS FOR MODEL COMPARISON

Let $\mathcal{A}$ be a machine learning algorithm which is trained on a set composed of $M = 1000$ entries of the type *(features,outcome)*. Let $\hat{h}_{\mathcal{A}}$ be the corresponding hypothesis. We validate $\hat{h}_{\mathcal{A}}$ using 10-fold cross-validation as follows: the training set is partitioned in 10 folds. Each fold contains 100 entries. For each $j = 1, \cdots, 10$, the fold j is taken out of the set. Subsequently, the hypothesis $\hat{h}_{\mathcal{A},j}$ is used to predict the outcomes for the unseen features in the fold j: $\hat{\mathbf{p}}_j = (\hat{p}_{j,1}; \cdots; \hat{p}_{j,100})$. The true outcomes in the fold j - $\mathbf{p}_j$ - and those predicted by $\hat{h}_{\mathcal{A},j}$ - $\hat{\mathbf{p}}_j$ - are compared. The metrics adopted in this paper for such a comparison are the absolute error

$$\alpha_j = \frac{|p_{j,1} - \hat{p}_{j,1}| + \cdots + |p_{j,100} - \hat{p}_{j,100}|}{100}$$

and the coefficient of correlation

$$\rho_j = \frac{\sum_{s=1}^{100} (p_{j,s} - \mu_j)(\hat{p}_{j,s} - \hat{\mu}_j)}{\sqrt{\sum_{s=1}^{100} (p_{j,s} - \mu_j)^2 \times \sum_{s=1}^{100} (\hat{p}_{j,s} - \hat{\mu}_j)^2}}$$

where $\mu_j = \frac{\sum_{s=1}^{100} p_{j,s}}{100}$ and $\hat{\mu}_j = \frac{\sum_{s=1}^{100} \hat{p}_{j,s}}{100}$. Hence, the mean absolute error and the coefficient of correlation of $\mathcal{A}$ are defined as

$$\mu_{\mathcal{A}}^{\alpha} = \frac{\sum_{j=1}^{10} \alpha_j}{10} \ and \ \mu_{\mathcal{A}}^{\rho} = \frac{\sum_{j=1}^{10} \rho_j}{10}$$

D^{3}AS Project: a Different Approach to the Manycore Challenges

Lorenzo Verdoscia
Institute for High Performance Computing and
Networking (ICAR) - CNR
Via Castellino, 111
80131 Napoli, Italy
lorenzo.verdoscia@na.icar.cnr.it

Roberto Vaccaro
Institute for High Performance Computing and
Networking (ICAR) - CNR
Via Castellino, 111
80131 Napoli, Italy
roberto.vaccaro@na.icar.cnr.it

ABSTRACT

The number of cores integrated onto a single die is expected to climb steadily in the foreseeable future. The main aim of Demand Data Driven Architecture System (D^{3}AS) project is an attempt to provide a new programming model and architecture to allow efficient programming of highly parallel systems based on thousands of simple, thin cores. After a detailed description of the proposed prototype, some experimental results, obtained by a demonstrator, are discussed. Results show that the D^{3}AS approach is feasible and promising.

Categories and Subject Descriptors

C.0 [**System Specification Methodology**]: Other Architecture Styles—*Data-flow architectures*; D.1 [**Programming Techniques**]: Functional Programming

General Terms

Design, Languages, Algorithms

Keywords

Functional languages, data-flow program graphs, many-cores

1. INTRODUCTION

It is widely agreed that many-core microprocessor architectures represent the natural evolution of multi-core. So, if multi-core processing is now mainstream, the future will be massively parallel computing performed on many-core processors [2]. On the other hand, if many-core is destined to be the way forward, one of the main issues is the type of hardware building blocks (cores, networks on chip, etc.) should be used for many-core systems. Thin and simple cores are the most efficient solution, providing the best tradeoff between energy consumption, performance, and manufacturability. High performance applications have to be implemented on processors constituted by a thousand fine-grained cores running at 200 MHz, rather than on a traditional processor running at 20 GHz. The challenge is how to program such systems with an acceptable productivity exploiting such spatial parallelism. In order to give right

answer to these challenges, we need a critical reexamination of our "consolidated wisdoms" in terms of programming style and execution model, trying to look beyond them. The proposed D^{3}AS architecture is based on a serious reconsideration of the functional and dataflow paradigms as programming style and execution model respectively.

2. OUR APPROACH TO THE MANY CORE CHALLENGES

The D^{3}AS project is an attempt to apply a true hardware/software (H/S) co-design approach that can support a variety of H/S research projects. The project's target is to investigate a computing system capable of exploiting the coarse-grained functional parallelism as well as the fine-grained instruction level parallelism. That through the direct hardware execution of static dataflow program graphs created by a functional programming language. The language is both the high and low level programming language for the entire system. D^{3}AS computing system is based on the integration of two *naturally* parallel organizations for computation, the data-driven and demand-driven models.

2.1 The hHLDS model

As far as the data-driven architecture model is concerned, our approach is based hHLDS model [8]. Static dataflow graphs form a very natural model of asynchronous computation in system based on many-core chips where each chip is constituted by thousands of simple, thin, and identical Functional Units (FU), each including the firing circuitry . The hHLDS model, with homogeneous I/O condition actors, is well tailored to directly map dataflow program graphs (DPG)s onto hardware. Homogeneous I/O conditions mean that any actor has two input and one output arcs and only consumes and produces data-tokens. No control arcs, entering or living control links, with tokens of the Boolean type, are provided for.
Despite the model simplicity, with these actors it is possible to generate determinate graphs, including iterative and conditional constructs, where: (1) no feedback interpretation is needed to correctly execute a dataflow program graph. This means that no check needs to verify whether the output token of an actor has been consumed, thus only one-way token flow is present; (2) no extra synchronization mechanism is required to control the token flow, thus the model is completely asynchronous.
To make in hardware the token flow control mechanism as

simple as possible without losing the token-level functionality[1], we augment the token of the model with the concept of *validity*. Validity denotes whether a data inside the processor is ready to be processed or not. Thus, a data-token is constituted by two parts: *value* and *validity*. Validity is coded only by one bit. Token validity, besides supplying a very simple control for the data flow, reduces the design complexity of the dataflow processor architecture by eliminating the data/acknowledgement mechanism between actors present in the classical static dataflow model [6, 4]. In the *h*HLDS model, an actor executes an operation when its two input tokens are ready. Therefore, with this extension, if two valid tokens are ready on the input links of an actor, they fire it. Thus, the new token produced will substitute the previous one even though it has not been yet consumed. Since we do not need any other control besides the token validity, we reduce the communication overhead and eliminate the two opposite flows, data and signal, for the same computation.

Lastly, it is important to underline that in classical dataflow model the arcs receiving data from a single actor and transmitting values to one or more actors, are considered as generic channels of communication, while in *h*HLDS model the arcs represent real hardwired connections between actors.

2.2 The programming language

As far as the demand-driven architecture model is concerned, our approach is based on the choice of functional style as programming model. The D^{3}AS is a demand-data driven machine in the sense that the DPG construction is created in demand mode, while its execution happens in data mode. For D^{3}AS, our approach to the programming language choice has been *language first* oriented, that is, first we decide which will be our system programming language, then we design the machine, true co-design approach.

The D^{3}AS programming language is CHIARA [5], a dialect of Backus' FP language [1]. CHIARA's peculiarity is that it defines a set of elementary operators, directly executable in hardware. That set constitutes the *functionally complete* set of the language, i.e. the set able to generate any other more complex function applying the metacomposition rule. Viceversa, any CHIARA function is reduced by the compiler to a combination of elementary operators. Therefore, if on the one hand this set constitutes the low level programming language for the processor, on the other hand CHIARA is also the D^{3}AS high level programming language. In this way, DPGs produced by compiling a program written in this language can be then directly mapped and executed onto the hardware.

As CHIARA programs are variable free, we can both easily recognize, in the code, the functions that only route data to the places where they are consumed and distinguish such code from that actually performing computations. In a framework where operations and data are distributed over several nodes for the execution of a DPG, this point is very important. In fact, we have the possibility to devise an initial data distribution over the many core processors of D^{3}AS. After that, we have to follow the well defined instructions

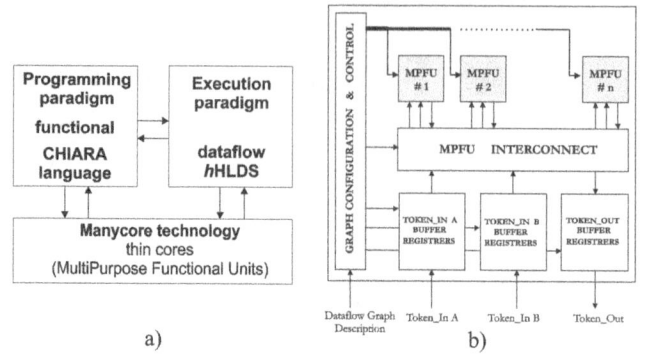

Figure 1: D^{3}AS a) Process design, b) MDP Endo-architecture.

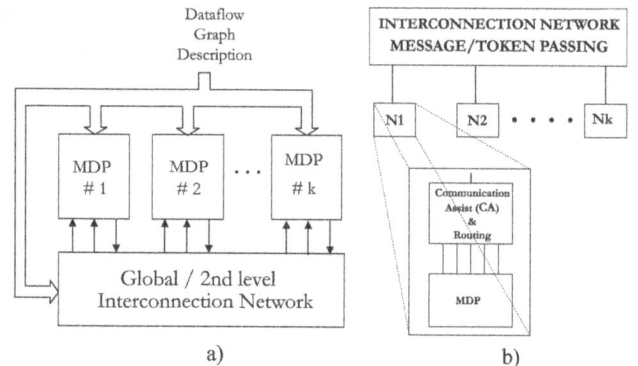

Figure 2: MHS Endo-architecture based on the a) pure dataflow and b) CDP model.

present in the program code to execute the routing of the data in such a way that they reach the destinations where they have to be consumed.

3. D^{3}AS GENERAL ARCHITECTURE

In order to directly map and execute in hardware DPGs created with the *h*HLDS in conjunction with CHIARA, what we need is a Manycore based Hardware System (MHS). MHS, according to the model, executes graphs in completely asynchronous manner. Its co-design process is schematized in Figure 1.a. The MHS/D^{3}AS fundamental building block is a many-core chip named Many-core Dataflow Processor (MDP) and is based on n FUs. The MDP Endo-architecture is shown in Figure 1.b. When in a DPG the actor number is greater than n, first the graph is partitioned in fitting subgraphs and then the MHS is configured, interconnecting the appropriate number of MDP as shown in Figure 2.a.

To preserve the globally pure dataflow model, also the 2nd level interconnection network is a non-blocking cross-bar switch. Such interconnect can be implemented, for example, via a Field Programmable Interconnection Chip. Obviously, growing the number of the MDP constituting the MHS, different cheaper network solutions (dynamic, static, etc.) can be adopted. In this case, the interconnections that implement the DPG edges among the DPG parts (subgraphs), mapped on different MDPs, are made virtual by messages routed through the adopted network. In this case the execu-

---

[1] Token level functionality means that an actor with the same tokens on its incoming arcs will always produce the same token on its outgoing arc, independently from the arrival times of the incoming token and the computation state.

tion model becomes an hybrid model we call *Communicating Dataflow Processes* (CDP). Subgraphs belonging to different MDPs exchange data tokens through messages. The Endo-architecture of a system based on this execution model is shown in Figure 2.b.

3.1 The demonstrator

To verify the correctness and validity of the basic design choices, we have developed a demonstrator for D^3AS, an FPGA based system. In this demonstrator, the Global/2nd level Interconnection Network is constituted by a WK-recursive [3] ($N_d = 4, L = 1$); so, the execution model is a hybrid CDP. In the D^3AS demonstrator a node is constituted by a Smart Router Subsystem and a Platform-Processor Subsystem [7].

4. PERFORMANCE

To evaluate the D^3AS effectiveness, we have utilized its demonstrator to solve the linear equation system

$$Ax = B \qquad (1)$$

with the Jacobi and Gauss-Seidel iterative algorithms. They calculate an approximation of the exact solution:

$$x_i = \frac{1}{a_{ii}} \sum_{i \neq j} a_{ij} x_j - b_i \quad i = 1...n. \qquad (2)$$

To execute the two algorithms, we tailored the corresponding DPG description tables according to the resources of the demonstrator. In this way, we have obtained the configuration files for different values of n. The execution time for one iteration is given by:

$$T_{iter} = (T_{com} + T_{cal}) \qquad (3)$$

where T_{iter} can be evaluated as a function of n. In fact:

$$T_{com} = t_{CT} + t_{TT} = (n_{FU} * n_{b_{FU}} + n_t * n_{bt}) * t_b * n_s \qquad (4)$$

$$T_{cal} = t_{FU} * n_o * n_s \qquad (5)$$

where t_{CT} is the configuration transfer time, t_{TT} the token transfer time, t_{FU} the FU execution time, t_b the transfer time for a single byte, n_o the number of sequential elementary operations to upgrade an x_i value, n_s the number of steps to upgrade all the x_i values, n_{FU} the number of clusters to be configured, $n_{b_{FU}}$ the number of bytes to configure a cluster, n_t the number of tokens transferred in a cycle, and n_{bt} the number of bytes per token. $t_{FU}, n_{b_{FU}}, t_b$, and n_{bt} depend on technology and architecture. The total execution time in the computational engine is given by:

$$T_{tot} = n_i * T_{iter} \qquad (6)$$

where n_i (number of iterations) depends on the initial value set goodness. The other parameters can be known for each n by the size of the graph description tables and the longest path in the DFG. For instance, it results $n_s = 1$ for the Jacobi method if $n \leq 20$, whereas for the Gauss-Seidel method $n_s = n$, and $n_o = 6 + \lceil \log_2 n \rceil$. In a sequential environment, the time T_s needed to execute an iteration is given by:

$$T_s = k_1 * n^2 + k_2 * n \qquad (7)$$

where k_1 and k_2 depend on the environment and can not be exactly evaluated a priori. However, with a processor power equal to 1.4 Gflops, the minimum values for k_1 and k_2 can be set at 20 nsec.

Table 1: Time evaluation expressed in μsec

		Gauss-Seidel		Jacobi	
n	T_s	T_{com}	T_{cal}	T_{com}	T_{cal}
64	83.2	68.38	22.75	22.16	3.20
256	1315.8	547.14	238.23	170.56	65.20
1024	20992.0	7494.25	1436.61	1243.70	612.38

Table 2: Performance

	Gauss-Seidel		Jacobi	
n	CP	Sp	CP	Sp
64	3.01	0.91	6.92	3.28
256	2.30	1.68	2.62	5.58
1024	5.22	2.35	2.03	11.31

With $t_{FU} = 30$ nsec, $t_b = 5$ nsec, and $n_{bt} = 4$, Table 1 shows the values of T_{com} and T_{cal} for several values of n. Due to fine grain dataflow operations and no scheduling optimization, most of the time is spent in communication. Some performance indices defined to compare the two methods and evaluate the proposed architecture are shown in Table 2. In particular, CP is the communication penalty defined as the ratio between Equation 4 and 5 and speedup Sp is the ratio between the Equation 7 and 3.

5. CONCLUDING REMARKS

In this paper we describe the D^3AS architecture with its MDP basic building block. After a description of hHLDS model and CHIARA programming language, some promising results, obtained with a demonstrator, are presented.

6. REFERENCES

[1] J.W. Backus. Can programming be liberated from von Neumann style? a functional style and its algebra of programs. *CACM*, 21:613–641, August 1978.

[2] S. Borkar. Thousand Core Chips-A Technology Perspective. In *44th Design Automation Conference*, pages 746–749, San Diego, Ca, USA, June 2007. ACM.

[3] G.H. Chen and D.R. Du. Topological properties, communication, and computing on WK-recursive networks. *Networks*, 24:303–317, 1994.

[4] J.B. Dennis. Dataflow computation, control flow and data flow: Concepts of distributed programming. *NATO ASI Series F: Computer and system sciences*, vol.14, 1985.

[5] L. Verdoscia et al. CODACS prototype: CHIARA language and its compiler. In *First Int. Workshop on Embedded Computing*, Hachioji, Tokyo, Japan, March 23–26, 2004. IEEE Computer Society Press.

[6] G.R. Gao. *A Code Mapping Scheme for Dataflow Software Pipelining*. Kluwer Academic Publishers, 1991.

[7] L. Verdoscia. CODACS Prototype: a Platform-Processor for CHIARA Programs. In *19th IEEE IPDPS-PDSEC05*, Denver, Colorado, USA, April 4–8, 2005. IEEE Computer Society Press.

[8] L. Verdoscia and R. Vaccaro. A high-level dataflow system. *Computing*, 60(4):285–305, 1998.

A Capacity-Efficient Insertion Policy
for Dynamic Cache Resizing Mechanisms

Masayuki Sato[†], Yusuke Tobo[†], Ryusuke Egawa[†‡*], Hiroyuki Takizawa[†*], Hiroaki Kobayashi[†‡*]

[†]Graduate School of Information Sciences, Tohoku University, Sendai, 980-8578, Japan.
[‡]Cyberscience Center, Tohoku University, Sendai, 980-8578, Japan. [*]JST CREST.
{masayuki@sc., tobo@sc., egawa@, tacky@, koba@}isc.tohoku.ac.jp

ABSTRACT

Dynamic cache resizing mechanisms have been proposed to achieve both high performance and low energy consumption. The basic idea behind such mechanisms is to divide a cache into some parts, and manage them independently to resize the cache for resource allocation and energy saving. However, dynamic cache resizing mechanisms waste their resource to store a lot of dead-on-fill blocks, which are not reused after being stored in the cache. To reduce the number of dead-on-fill blocks in the cache and thus improve energy efficiency of dynamic cache resizing mechanisms, this paper proposes a dynamic LRU-K insertion policy. The policy stores a new coming block as the K-th least-recently-used one and adjusts K dynamically according to the application to be executed. Therefore, the policy can balance between early eviction of dead-on-fill blocks and retainment of reusable blocks.

Categories and Subject Descriptors

B.3.2 [**Memory Structures**]: Design Styles—*Associative memories, Cache memories*; C.1.2 [**Processor Architectures**]: Multiple Data Stream Architectures (Multiprocessors)

General Terms

Algorithms, Design, Performance

Keywords

Dynamic Cache Resizing, Cache Replacement Policy, Energy Efficiency

1. INTRODUCTION

In modern microprocessors, cache memories have significant impacts upon energy consumption and performance. Since cache memories occupy a large portion of the area of microprocessors, their static energy is not ignorable. Moreover, in recent years, chip multiprocessors (CMPs) have become common forms of microprocessors. In a CMP, multiple cores share a cache on a chip to make good use of the cache capacity. However, such cache sharing often causes inter-thread cache conflicts, and thus increases the cache

misses of mutually executed threads sharing the cache. Under this situation, dynamic cache resizing is one of the main research topics in cache management. The objectives of dynamic cache resizing mechanisms are mainly energy saving and cache partitioning on CMPs. As one of dynamic cache resizing mechanisms, this paper focuses on the power-aware dynamic cache partitioning mechanism [6]. In this mechanism, ways of a set-associative cache are individually managed for both improving performance and saving energy. Some ways are activated and allocated to running threads, and the others are deactivated for energy saving.

One important technical issue of dynamic cache resizing mechanisms is the existence of *dead-on-fill blocks* [1]. In recent years, various applications have become more complex, and their data sets become larger. As a result, some applications use most data blocks only once, or take a long time to reuse the blocks. If such blocks are once inserted in the cache, they are evicted from the cache without being reused. Furthermore, the number of dead-on-fill blocks tends to become very large in dynamic cache resizing mechanisms because they rely on the LRU replacement policy and are mainly applied to last-level caches. Therefore, dynamic cache resizing mechanisms waste their resource to store a lot of dead-on-fill blocks, even though they do not contribute to performance improvement but consume energy.

This paper proposes a dynamic LRU-K insertion policy to reduce the number of dead-on-fill blocks. The proposed policy inserts a new block into the K-th LRU position that is the K-th lowest resident priority position in an n-way set associative cache ($1 \le k \le n$). Furthermore, the policy determines K flexibly during execution. As a result, the policy can evict dead-on-fill blocks earlier than the LRU replacement policy while keeping reusable blocks. If the number of dead-on-fill blocks in the cache is reduced, dynamic cache resizing mechanisms can deactivate the ways, which would store dead-on-fill blocks if the LRU replacement policy is used. Therefore, the proposed policy allows dynamic cache resizing mechanisms to carry out capacity-efficient resizing.

2. RELATED WORK

Data management policies are important for improving the cache efficiency. The main idea of this paper is to change the *insertion position* of a newly coming block. There are some papers related to this idea. The Segmented LRU (SLRU) replacement policy [4] was originally proposed for cache management of a disk system. Its basic concept is the same as the proposal in this paper. However, dynamic adjustment of the insertion position was not discussed well.

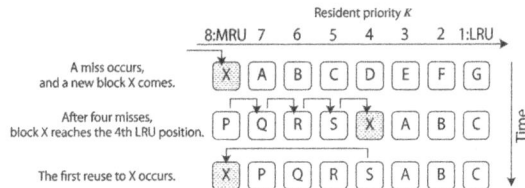

Figure 1: First reuse to a newly inserted block X and its resident priority change in the cache.

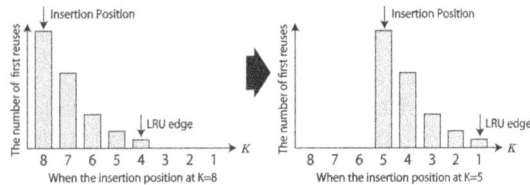

Figure 2: Profiling results of the number of first reuses to the newly inserted blocks in each priority position.

Qureshi et al. proposed the adaptive insertion policy [7] and Jaleel et al. proposed its enhanced version [2], in which the insertion position is switched either the MRU position or the LRU position. However, their policies do not insert blocks into the other positions. Khan et al. [5] presented an insertion position selection mechanism. The number of candidates is still limited because of the verification overhead of decision tree analysis. These limits of the insertion position deprive chances to further improve energy efficiency of dynamic cache resizing mechanisms.

There are some insertion policies based on other replacement policies. PIPP [8] is based on the Least Frequently Used replacement policy, and DRRIP [3] was based on the Not Recently Used replacement policy. However, these other replacement policies are beyond the scope of this paper. This paper focuses on the LRU replacement policy, which is the representative one that exploits the temporal locality of reference and is effective for almost all benchmarks except ones causing dead-on-fill blocks.

3. DYNAMIC LRU-K INSERTION POLICY

3.1 Principle of Optimal Insertion Position

In dynamic cache resizing mechanisms, the resized cache capacity should be as small as possible unless reusable blocks are evicted. Hence, the policy has to decide the optimal insertion position under this condition.

Figure 1 illustrates how the resident priority of a new cache block X changes in a set of an 8-way set-associative cache with the LRU replacement policy. First, X is inserted at the MRU ($K = 8$) position. After four misses occur, X is placed at the fourth LRU position. Then, when the first reuse of X occurs, the block is again moved to the MRU position. Focusing on this block, the optimal insertion position is the fifth LRU position. Even if X is inserted at the fifth LRU position, the first reuse of X occurs before X is evicted.

The position where X is reused for the first time is called the first reuse position of X. Figure 2 shows an example of

histograms of first reuse positions. The vertical axis means the frequency of first reuses at each LRU position. The left-side histogram is a typical one in the case where a new cache block is always inserted at the MRU position. This histogram indicates that first reuses do not occur at the third, second, and first LRU positions. Therefore, a cache block that reaches the third LRU position without being reused should be evicted. In this situation, the insertion position of a new cache block should be changed to the fifth position as shown in the right-side histogram. As a result, dead-on-fill blocks are evicted earlier without evicting reusable blocks. It should be noted that the total number of first reuses in the left-side histogram is the same as that in the right-side one. This means that the newly coming reusable blocks are not evicted before being reused, even after the change of the insertion position.

3.2 An Adjusting Mechanism of Insertion Position

A key to achieve automatic adjustment of the insertion position is to find the position of the right-most edge (the LRU edge) of the histogram of first reuse positions. At lower LRU positions after this edge position, there is no more first reuse in the histogram. As the insertion position moves to the lower LRU position, the LRU edge of the histogram also becomes closer to the LRU position. When the LRU edge reaches the LRU position, the insertion position becomes the lowest under the condition of not reducing first reuses. Hence, the adjusting mechanism may check the existence of the first reuses of blocks at the LRU position because the histogram typically decreases with K due to the temporal locality of reference.

In addition, phase changes in executing an application affect cache block reusability. This means that the shape of the histogram changes during the execution. Hence, the insertion position K should be changed at a fixed interval according to the algorithm described below.

$$K := \begin{cases} K + 1 & (\text{if } C_{f,LRU} \geq A) \\ K - 1 & (\text{if } C_{f,LRU} < A), \end{cases} \quad (1)$$

where,

$$K = (\text{the insertion position}),$$
$$C_{f,LRU} = (\text{the number of first reuses at the LRU position}),$$
$$A = (\text{the threshold for judgement of first reuses}).$$

According to Equation (1), the insertion position is shifted to the right by reducing K if the number of first reuses at the LRU position is small. On the other hand, the insertion position is moved to the left if the number of first reuses at the LRU position is large. As a result, the insertion position is adjusted to be the lowest under the condition of not causing significant performance degradation. Accordingly, it is expected that the dynamic cache resizing mechanism can activate only the minimum number of ways to keep the performance.

4. EVALUATIONS

We have developed a simulator based on the M5 simulator system and CACTI 6.5. In this evaluation, the power-aware dynamic cache partitioning mechanism [6] is applied

266

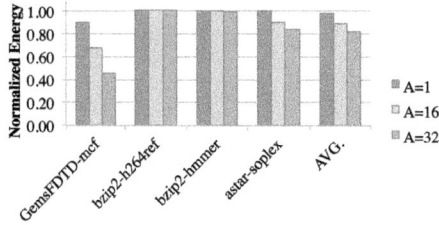

Figure 3: Energy consumption of the L3 cache on the 2-core CMP.

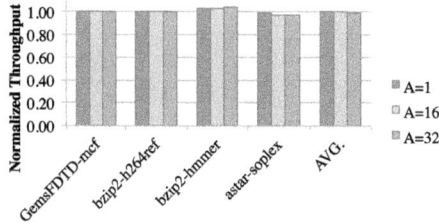

Figure 4: Performance on the 2-core CMP.

to the last-level shared L3 cache of a 2-core CMP with private L1 and L2 caches. The simulation is performed by the 2-thread workloads, each of which consists of two benchmarks. Benchmark programs examined on the simulator are selected from the SPEC CPU2006 benchmark suite. Each simulation is done by executing first 2 billion cycles of the simulated CMP. We have carried out experiments with 66 ($= {}_{12}C_2$) workloads, however, the results of overall average and some representative workloads are shown in this paper.

Figure 3 shows the energy consumption of the power-aware dynamic cache partitioning with the proposed policy. In the figure, the vertical axis indicates the energy consumption, which is normalized by that of the power-aware dynamic cache partitioning mechanism with the LRU replacement policy. The three bars of each workload indicate the results with $A = 1, 16$, and 32, respectively. The results with $A = 1$ indicate the normalized energy consumptions achieved when eviction of reusable blocks is avoided as much as possible. The results with $A = 16$ or 32 show the normalized energy consumptions when the eviction of some reusable blocks is allowed, and the reusability becomes the higher. The energy consumption dramatically decreases with `GemsFDTD-mcf` about 55% ($A = 32$). These benchmarks include a lot of dead-on-fill blocks, and the time between insertions and first reuses to reusable blocks are very short. As a result, the proposed policy can effectively reduce the number of dead-on-fill blocks. The maximum energy consumption is observed with `bzip2-h264ref`, however, the increase in energy is quite small about 2% with $A = 32$.

Figure 4 shows throughput, which is normalized by those of the power-aware dynamic cache partitioning mechanism with the LRU replacement policy. The proposed policy can improve throughput with `bzip2-hmmer` about 4%. These benchmarks originally require a lot of reusable blocks to be retained in the cache to improve the performance. The proposed policy can retain them for a longer time than the LRU replacement policy by reducing dead-on-fill blocks preferen-

tially. Hence, the proposed policy can improve their performances. Moreover, this figure indicates that the significant performance degradations do not occur in any workloads. The maximum performance degradation is observed with `astar-soplex` because some reusable blocks are early evicted by the proposed policy. However, the degradation is quite small about 3% ($A = 32$).

The average results of Figures 3 and 4 also indicate that the proposed policy can improve the energy efficiency of the power-aware dynamic cache partitioning mechanism. The proposed policy can reduce energy about 3%, 11%, and 19% when $A = 1, 16$, and 32 respectively, without significant performance degradation.

5. CONCLUSIONS

Dynamic cache resizing mechanisms are promising approaches toward performance improvement and energy reduction. However, dead-on-fill blocks spoil the advantages of the mechanism. To reduce dead-on-fill blocks in the cache, this paper has proposed the dynamic LRU-K insertion policy. This policy evicts dead-on-fill blocks earlier than the LRU replacement policy by inserting new blocks into the K-th LRU position. Furthermore, the policy dynamically adjusts K according to the executed application. Evaluation results show that the proposed policy can save energy consumption without significant performance degradation.

In future work, dead blocks will also be considered as well as dead-on-fill blocks. Dead blocks are blocks that are no longer reused after their final accesses. They do not contribute to performance, and hence the reduction of them will also be effective for dynamic cache resizing mechanisms.

6. ACKNOWLEDGMENTS

This research was partially supported by Core Research for Evolutional Science and Technology (CREST), Japan Science and Technology Agency (JST).

7. REFERENCES

[1] M. Chaudhuri. Pseudo-LIFO: The Foundation of a New Family of Replacement Policies for Last-level Caches. In *Proc. of MICRO*, pages 401–412, 2009.

[2] A. Jaleel, et al. Adaptive Insertion Policies for Managing Shared Caches. In *Proc. of PACT*, pages 208–219, 2008.

[3] A. Jaleel, et al. High Performance Cache Replacement Using Re-Reference Interval Prediction (RRIP). In *Proc. of ISCA*, pages 60–71, 2010.

[4] R. Karedla, et al. Caching Strategies to Improve Disk System Performance. *Computer*, 27(3):38–46, 1994.

[5] S. Khan, et al. Insertion Policy Selection using Decision Tree Analysis. In *Proc. of ICCD*, pages 106–111, 2010.

[6] I. Kotera, et al. Power-Aware Dynamic Cache Partitioning for CMPs. *Transaction on HiPEAC*, 3(2):149–167, 2008.

[7] M. K. Qureshi, et al. Adaptive Insertion Policies for High Performance Caching. In *Proc. of ISCA*, pages 381–391, 2007.

[8] Y. Xie, et al. PIPP: Promotion/Insertion Pseudo-Partitioning of Multi-Core Shared Caches. *ACM SIGARCH Computer Architecture News*, 37(12):174–183, 2009.

Accelerated High-Performance Computing Through Efficient Multi-Process GPU Resource Sharing

Teng Li
ECE Department
The George Washington
University
tengli@gwu.edu

Vikram K. Narayana
ECE Department
The George Washington
University
vikram@gwu.edu

Tarek El-Ghazawi
ECE Department
The George Washington
University
tarek@gwu.edu

ABSTRACT

The HPC field is witnessing a widespread adoption of GPUs as accelerators for traditional homogeneous HPC systems. One of the prevalent parallel programming models is the SPMD paradigm, which has been adapted for GPU-based parallel processing. Since each process executes the same program under SPMD, every process mapped to a CPU core also needs the GPU availability. Therefore SPMD demands a symmetric CPU/GPU distribution. However, since modern HPC systems feature a large number of CPU cores that outnumber the number of GPUs, computing resources are generally underutilized with SPMD. Our previous efforts have focused on GPU virtualization that enables efficient sharing of GPU among multiple CPU processes. Nevertheless, a formal method to evaluate and choose the appropriate GPU sharing approach is still lacking. In this paper, based on SPMD GPU kernel profiles, we propose different multi-process GPU sharing scenarios under virtualization. We introduce an analytical model that captures these sharing scenarios and provides a theoretical performance gain estimation. Benchmarks validate our analyses and achievable performance gains. While our analytical study provides a suitable theoretical foundation for GPU sharing, the experimental results demonstrate that GPU virtualization affords significant performance improvements over the non-virtualized solutions for all proposed sharing scenarios.

Categories and Subject Descriptors

C.4 [**PERFORMANCE OF SYSTEMS**]: Modeling techniques; C.1.3 [**PROCESSOR ARCHITECTURES**]: Other Architecture Styles—*Heterogeneous (hybrid) systems*

General Terms

Design, Performance, Measurement, Verification

Keywords

GPU, Resource Sharing, Virtualization, HPC, SPMD

1. INTRODUCTION

Recent years have seen the proliferation of GPUs as application accelerators in HPC systems. Contemporary examples include the latest Cray XK6 [5], SGI Altix UV [10]

and the Tianhe-1A supercomputer [1]. To program current GPU-based heterogeneous HPC systems, Single-Program Multiple-Data (SPMD) [6] is still the most common parallel programming model, under which all processors execute the same program. However, it can be challenging to execute programs under SPMD for GPU-based HPC systems, primarily due to the asymmetrical CPU/GPU distribution and thus leading to system resource (CPUs) underutilization. While SPMD requires a 1 to 1 CPU/GPU ratio, with the fast advancement of multi/many core technologies, the increasing CPU/GPU ratio is making the resource underutilization a more severe problem. In this paper, we propose to share the GPU resource among multiple processors under multiple sharing scenarios. The proposed sharing scenarios are primarily based on our GPU virtualization approach [7], which provides a virtual 1 to 1 CPU/GPU ratio and efficient GPU sharing among multiple processes. It allows GPU kernels from multiple processes to achieve concurrent execution as well as overlapped execution and GPU I/O. Meanwhile, the profiles of the GPU applications primarily determine the actual resource sharing scenario. Thus, varied sharing efficiency can be achieved under different sharing scenarios. Depending upon the GPU kernel profile and the number of SPMD processes, we propose that multiple identical GPU kernels from the SPMD program can share the GPU under four sharing scenarios, which are analyzed using our proposed analytical model. We conduct further benchmarks as verifications of the proposed sharing scenario modeling analysis as well as experimental studies on comparing GPU sharing efficiencies under the virtualization.

2. GPU SHARING SCENARIOS

Modern GPUs are composed of many Streaming Multiprocessors (SMs) which execute thread blocks. With the virtualization approach, multiple kernels are simultaneously launched from a single daemon process (virtualization layer which intercepts requests from all CPU processes) through CUDA streams. Based on how GPU thread blocks (from all kernels) occupy the SMs, we expect four GPU sharing scenarios: *Exclusive Space Sharing, Non-exclusive Space Sharing, Space/Time Sharing, Time Sharing*. We define necessary parameters for further analysis as shown in Table 1. We assume that the GPU assigns all blocks to free SMs until every SM is occupied, before assigning additional blocks to an SM. Therefore, if the total number of blocks from all SPMD kernels does not exceed (N_{SM}), kernels will execute on independent SMs, resulting in a space-sharing scenario.

When kernels from all processes can co-exist on the GPU

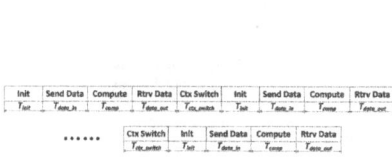

Figure 1: Native GPU Sharing

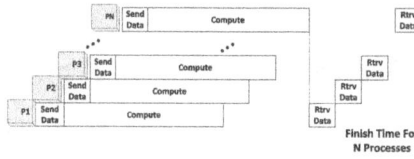

Figure 2: Model for Ex Space Sharing

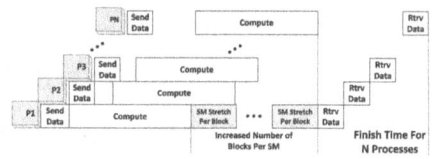

Figure 3: Model for Non-ex Space Sharing

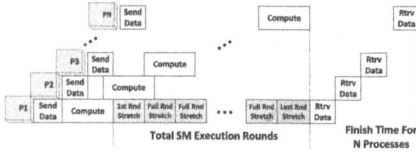

Figure 4: Model for Space/Time Sharing

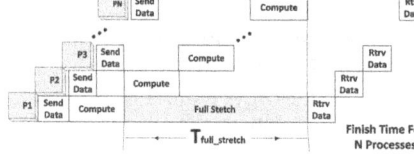

Figure 5: Model for Time Sharing

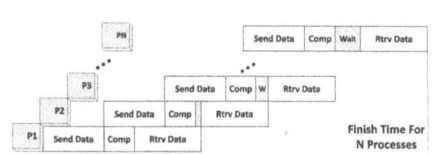

Figure 6: Model for I/O-I applications

Table 1: Parameters Defined For GPU Sharing Scenarios

N_{SM}	The # of SMs in the GPU
$N_{max\_blks\_per\_SM}$	The max possible # of blocks per SM
$N_{blks\_per\_knl}$	The # of blocks per SPMD kernel
$N_{process}$	The # of SPMD processes sharing GPU

and be processed by different SMs simultaneously, we have *Exclusive Space Sharing*, occurring under condition (1).

$$N_{blks\_per\_knl} \times N_{process} \leq N_{SM} \qquad (1)$$

If each GPU kernel requires many blocks and consequently does not satisfy condition (1), more than one block (from different kernels) will be assigned to an SM, when an SM can execute multiple blocks simultaneously. The scenario qualifies as space-sharing. Nevertheless, each SM is not exclusively used by one kernel; we therefore term this case as *Non-exclusive Space Sharing*, under condition (2) and (3).

$$N_{max\_blks\_per\_SM} > 1 \qquad (2)$$

$$N_{SM} < N_{blks\_per\_knl} \, N_{process} \leq N_{max\_blks\_per\_SM} \, N_{SM} \qquad (3)$$

If the total number of blocks is so large that it exceeds the RHS of (3), the available SMs will have to be time-shared through multiple rounds of SM executions. Within a round, there is space-sharing, and across multiple rounds, time sharing occurs. Thus we define this scenario as the *Space/Time Sharing* under condition (4) and (5). Note that the space-sharing that is exhibited within an execution round may be exclusive or non-exclusive.

$$N_{blks\_per\_knl} \, N_{process} > N_{max\_blks\_per\_SM} \, N_{SM} \qquad (4)$$

$$N_{blks\_per\_knl} < N_{max\_blks\_per\_SM} \, N_{SM} \qquad (5)$$

Time Sharing Scenario happens when (a) multiple rounds are required as exemplified by (4) and (b) $N_{blks\_per\_knl}$ is large enough to occupy at least one round as shown in (6).

$$N_{blks\_per\_knl} \geq N_{max\_blks\_per\_SM} \, N_{SM} \qquad (6)$$

3. GPU SHARING ANALYTICAL MODEL

Our previous scenario analysis only considers the execution phases of the kernels. Accurate performance estimates can not be achieved unless the GPU I/O is taken into account. Here we model the kernel execution from one process to consist of four stages: T_{init}, T_{data_in}, T_{comp} and T_{data_out}, as explained in Table 2 along with necessary analytical parameters. Figure 1 models the native process-level GPU sharing (without virtualization), under which all SPMD processes share the GPU sequentially with context-switch overhead (one context per process). The native sharing model is used as our performance baseline for comparison.

Table 2: Parameters Defined For Analytical Modeling

T_{init}	Time overhead for the GPU to be initialized
T_{data_in}	Time to transfer input data to the GPU mem
T_{data_out}	Time to transfer result data to the main mem
T_{comp}	Time for the GPU kernel computation
T_{ctx_switch}	Context-switch overhead between processes
T_{SM_str}	SM time stretch of adding a block per SM
R_{SM}	Total number of SM execution rounds
$T_{full\_rnd\_str}$	Time stretch of one full SM execution round
$T_{fs\_rnd\_str}$	Time stretch to add the 1st SM round to full
$T_{ls\_rnd\_str}$	Time stretch of the last SM execution round
T_{full_str}	Full "comp" time stretch under time sharing

Different from the native sharing, GPU virtualization achieves inter-process parallelisms using CUDA streams with two programming styles [9] targeting: (a) kernel concurrency (concurrency between T_{data_in} and T_{comp}; T_{comp} and T_{comp}) (b) I/O concurrency (concurrency between T_{data_in} and T_{comp}; T_{data_in} and T_{data_out}). Our proposed model is to estimate the total execution time based on interprocess concurrency behaviors while considering two types of applications: Compute-Intensive(C-I) and I/O-Intensive (I/O-I). For C-I applications, I/O time is relatively small such that T_{comp} always overlaps by using programming style (a), and thus varied sharing scenarios can be achieved.

Under *Exclusive Space Sharing*, T_{comp} achieves complete concurrency since all kernel blocks are executed on different SMs. T_{data_in} can also be overlapped with T_{comp}. However, the T_{data_out} stages have to wait till all T_{comp} stages finish due to programming style (a), as shown in Figure 2.

For *Non-exclusive Space Sharing*, blocks from all kernels reside in all SMs simultaneously within one SM execution round. However, scheduling more blocks on SMs stretches the execution time of each SM. Thus we model the term "SM time stretch" (T_{SM_str}) to denote the increased execution time when the number of blocks per SM increases by 1. As shown in Figure 3, the total time stretch of T_{comp}, is the product of T_{SM_str} and the increased number of blocks per SM with the added ($N_{process}$-1) SPMD kernels.

Under *Space/Time Sharing*, while using the same T_{SM_str} for each of the single SM execution rounds, we further model time stretches of different rounds to be added to T_{comp} of the 1st kernel, shown in Figure 4. The added components consist of $T_{fs\_round\_str}$; $T_{full\_rnd\_str}$; $T_{ls\_rnd\_str}$. R_{SM} is computed by dividing the total number of blocks from all kernels by the maximum SM capacity in each SM execution round.

Time Sharing(C-I) happens when a single kernel is large enough to occupy one or more SM rounds, which makes all SPMD kernels sequential, as shown in Figure 5. Here we further define T_{full_str}, which is $\approx (N_{process}$-1)T_{comp}.

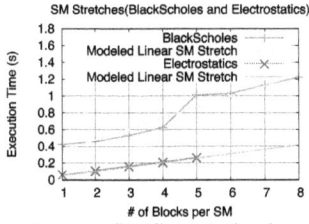

Figure 7: SM Stretch Analysis   *Figure 8*: Modeled Speedups(1)   *Figure 9*: Modeled Speedups(2)   *Figure 10*: Actual Speedups

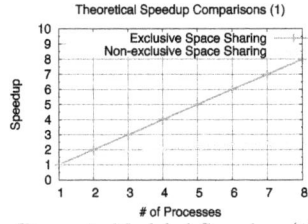

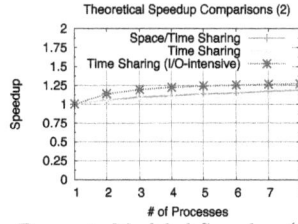

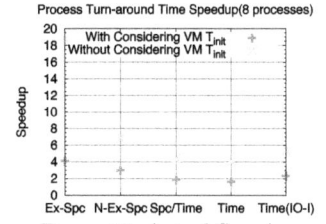

I/O-I applications always time-share the GPU since T_{comp} stages cannot overlap due to the dominating I/O time. Our virtualization layer thus uses programming style (b), which is captured in Figure 6 - both T_{data_in} and T_{data_out} can be inter-overlapped as well as overlapped with T_{comp}, while T_{data_out} can only be sequential.

4. RESULTS AND CONCLUSIONS

We conduct several benchmarks to verify the proposed analytical model and demonstrate the GPU sharing efficiencies under varied scenarios. The experiments are conducted by using our GPU virtualization implementation on NVIDIA Tesla C2070 GPU (14 SMs) under CUDA 4.0. Five benchmarks are utilized and profiled to represent a different sharing scenario. We emulate SPMD execution by launching the same benchmark on multiple processes simultaneously in our virtualization infrastructure. The resulting GPU time, which is the duration spent by each process on GPU tasks, is compared with the model prediction. The model parameters are derived using profiling results for each sharing scenario. With each process affinity assigned to a unique CPU core, we vary the number of processes from 1 to 8 (8 cores). We then compare the model deviations from the experimental results, as shown in Table 3 (averaged from 1 to 8 processes). We utilize NPB [3] EP GPU kernel (1 block) [8] merely to verify *Exclusive Space Sharing*. For *Non-exclusive Space* and *Space/Time Sharing Scenarios*, we respectively utilize BlackScholes (BS) [4], a European option pricing benchmark and the fast molecular electrostatics algorithm (ES) (molecular visualization program VMD [2]). Two micro benchmarks are conducted to analyze the T_{SM_str}, for both BS and ES. As shown in Figure 7, the execution time of BS and ES are plotted for each number of blocks per SM (1 to 8 for BS and 1 to 5 for ES). Since we previously modeled T_{SM_str} as an average factor, we therefore linearly fit both BS and ES as shown in Figure 7; derive the average T_{SM_str} for both and thus get the model time of BS. SM execution rounds (R_{SM}) and corresponding $T_{full\_rnd\_str}$, $T_{fs\_rnd\_str}$ and $T_{ls\_rnd\_str}$ are also derived accordingly to get the model time of ES. We further use our NPB MG kernel (Class W with 4K block size) [8] to verify the *Time Sharing Scenario*. For I/O-I applications (Time Sharing), we use a simple Vector Multiplication benchmark. Table 3 summarizes the average model deviations from the experimental results and demonstrate good model accuracy for all scenarios. Note that the relatively higher deviation from BS(Non-exclusive Space) is due to inaccuracies from linearly modeling T_{SM_str}.

To evaluate the GPU sharing efficiency, we analyze the speedups over the native sharing approach by using both the verified model and experimental results. Figure 8 and 9 demonstrate the speedups by using the model results of the five benchmarks. Since we use $T_{init}=0$ for native sharing in our analysis, the model results provide the speedup lower

Table 3: Average Model Deviations for All Described Scenarios

Ex Space	Non-ex Space	Space/Time	Time	I/O-I
0.42%	14.29%	1.92%	4.10%	4.76%

bounds. We obtained experimental speedups using the five benchmarks by measuring the process turn-around time (the time for all processes to finish after simultaneous launch) under virtualization and comparing it with the turn-around time under native sharing. 8 processes were launched and speedups are shown in Figure 10. Our virtualization incurs a one-time T_{init} (single process) that can be hidden, while the native sharing always suffers multiple T_{init}. We evaluate both speedups with and without the T_{init}. The results demonstrate a *minimum* 1.64/4.03 times speedup and up to 4.1/18.7 times speedup (with/without T_{init}). It also demonstrates that the performance gain potential for each scenario shown in Figure 8 and 9 matches the experimental speedups.

To summarize, in this paper, we proposed four possible GPU sharing scenarios with our GPU virtualization approach. Both theoretical performance modeling and experiments were conducted for each sharing scenario. Our results demonstrated that the theoretical analysis was fairly accurate and also proved that efficient GPU sharing can be achieved by using our virtualization approach.

Acknowledgement

This work was supported by the I/UCRC Program of the National Science Foundation under Grant No. IIP-0706352.

5. REFERENCES

[1] *Tianhe-I, http://en.wikipedia.org/wiki/Tianhe-I.*

[2] *Visual Molecular Dynamics Program, http://www.ks.uiuc.edu/Research/vmd/.*

[3] D. Bailey, E. Barszcz, J. Barton, D. Browning, R. Carter, L. Dagum, R. Fatoohi, P. Frederickson, T. Lasinski, R. Schreiber, et al. The NAS parallel benchmarks. *International Journal of High Performance Computing Applications*, 5(3):63, 1991.

[4] F. Black and M. Scholes. The pricing of options and corporate liabilities. *The journal of political economy*, pages 637–654, 1973.

[5] Cray Inc. *Cray XK6 Brochure*. Available online on http://www.cray.com/Assets/PDF/products/xk/CrayXK6Brochure.pdf.

[6] F. Darema. The SPMD model: Past, present and future. *Recent Advances in Parallel Virtual Machine and Message Passing Interface*, pages 1–1, 2001.

[7] T. Li, V. K. Narayana, E. El-Araby, and T. El-Ghazawi. GPU resource sharing and virtualization on high performance computing systems. In *Proceedings of the 40th International Conference on Parallel Processing*. IEEE, Sep 2011.

[8] M. Malik, T. Li, U. Sharif, R. Shahid, T. El-Ghazawi, and G. Newby. Productivity of GPUs under different programming paradigms. *Concurrency and Computation: Practice and Experience*, 24(2):179–191, 2012.

[9] NVIDIA Corp. *NVIDIA CUDA C-Programming Guide V4.0*, May 2011.

[10] SGI Corp. *SGI GPU Compute Solutions*. Available online on http://www.sgi.com/pdfs/4235.pdf.

Improving the Performance of k-means Clustering Through Computation Skipping and Data Locality Optimizations

Orhan Kislal
The Pennsylvania State
University
University Park, PA 16802
omk103@cse.psu.edu

Piotr Berman
The Pennsylvania State
University
University Park, PA 16802
berman@cse.psu.edu

Mahmut Kandemir
The Pennsylvania State
University
University Park, PA 16802
kandemir@cse.psu.edu

ABSTRACT

We present three different optimization techniques for k-means clustering algorithm to improve the running time without decreasing the accuracy of the cluster centers significantly. Our first optimization restructures loops to improve cache behavior when executing on multicore architectures. The remaining two optimizations skip select points to reduce execution latency. Our sensitivity analysis suggests that the performance can be enhanced through a good understanding of the data and careful configuration of the parameters.

Categories and Subject Descriptors

I.5.3 [**Computing Methodologies**]: Pattern Recognition—*lustering*

Keywords

Clustering, k-means algorithm, Data mining

1. INTRODUCTION

k-means clustering is a widely used and well studied geometric clustering method [3]. Its simple nature and good runtime performance keep k-means clustering popular in a number of different disciplines. Although the basic problem is defined for a fixed number of centers (*le el*); it is usually applied on a range of levels to find an optimal pair (k, total distance).

As the multicore architectures with multiple levels of caches emerge as mainstream computer architectures, algorithms that can exploit these features can provide significant reductions in execution times. However, the reuse distance, the amount of data accessed between two accesses to the same point, of Lloyd's algorithm is too large to exploit caches of multicores without special optimizations.

It is also important to note that k-means clustering does not guarantee an optimal cluster set. This creates an interesting *tradeoff* between speed and accuracy. In particular, applications that execute the algorithm several times for better clusters might benefit from a modified k-means with better speed but slightly worse accuracy.

This paper proposes three different optimizations on parallel k-means algorithm. Our first optimization reorders loop structures of the algorithm to maximize its on-chip cache

performance, while the other two employ different heuristics to skip some of the points at certain iterations of the algorithm. Our goal with these heuristics is to reduce parallel execution time of the algorithm without much distortion of its accuracy.

2. OUR PROPOSED ALGORITHMS

2.1 Reordering Algorithm

The nature of k-means does not allow reusing the data points unless the whole dataset fits in the cache. This is because the same point is reused only across different iterations. However, we also note that computations on different levels are independent of each other. Our proposed strategy exploits this observation by *reordering co putations* to improve cache performance.

The basic principle behind the Reordering algorithm is simple: If a data point is brought to the cache, use it as much as possible. Specifically, after the basic algorithm brings a data point into cache, it calculates the distances for every center and then moves to the next point. In comparison, after our Reordering algorithm brings a data point into the cache, it calculates the distances for every center *or e ery le el* and then moves to the next one. Convergence is still computed per level basis; if a level finishes its computation, it is deemed as inactive and the algorithm continues to run for the remaining levels.

2.2 2 Bin Algorithm

In an iteration of Lloyd's algorithm, the most time consuming task is computing, for each point, the distances to every center. However, we observed that the number of points changing the membership is quite small after the first few iterations. This suggests that we can save work by skipping, with a certain frequency, points that are unlikely to change their membership. We will employ two types of points; mobile and slow, and two types of iterations; complete and skipping. Of course, with a bad choice of slow points (the points that will change their membership in basic algorithm), we may increase the number of iterations needed to converge, and thus make the algorithm slower. We tested the 2 Bin algorithm with the following criterion: *a point is considered to e slo i it changed its e ership.*

The implementation of our proposed 2 Bin strategy is fairly straightforward. For each and every point, we track the center change information. At the beginning of every iteration, we check if that point has changed its membership, and if so, skip according to the frequency. We update the

Table 1: L2 hit rates for proposed algorithms. Re + 2 Bin and Re + LC denote the combined schemes. Higher hit rate means better performance.

Dataset	Base	Reorder	2 Bin	Last Change	Re + 2 Bin	Re + LC
Small	81.49%	98.60%	82.14%	83.43%	95.12%	98.14%
Medium	80.17%	99.02%	85.06%	81.24%	98.95%	98.95%
Large	80.42%	99.68%	81.44%	81.06%	99.60%	99.65%
Wide	97.24%	96.03%	97.31%	95.93%	97.04%	96.73%

bin information after a membership change, as well as the delta (our convergence metric).

2.3 Last Change Algorithm

We observed that, nearly 35% of the points *ne er* change their assigned centers after the initial step. We refer to these points as *true sta le points*. Just like the 2 Bin Algorithm, the Last Change algorithm predicts which points will not change their membership and skips them in select intervals. In contrast, reasons why to select a point to be skipped are quite different in these two algorithms. Specifically, Last Change skips points if they do not change their memberships assuming that trend will continue, while 2 Bin skips points if they do change their membership assuming they will not change again. Keeping the accuracy loss at minimal requires a heuristic to distinguish true stable points from temporary ones. To address this, we define a concept called the *change-li it*. Change-limit indicates the starting iteration of our heuristic. Before the change-limit is reached, the membership changes for every point are recorded to use afterwards. Afterwards, the points with no membership change are skipped according to the skipping frequency.

2.4 Exploring Combinations

The aforementioned techniques are expected to work well by themselves but they could also be combined. The conflicting nature of the 2 Bin and Last Change algorithms makes this combination troublesome. Combining a skipping heuristic with reordering will work correctly but not optimally. Accessing a particular point in one level and skipping it at the next level will not take advantage of the data that is already in the cache. On the other hand, accessing that point might increase the accuracy. Based on this insight, we can modify our heuristics for skipping: Skip a point if the conditions for skipping are met in *e ery* active level.

3. EXPERIMENTAL RESULTS

We used physical and simulated systems to evaluate our proposed algorithms. Physical system has four cores, 32 KB private L1 cache and 256 KB private L2 cache. Simulated system (created in SIMICS [5]) has four cores, 16 KB L1 cache and 1 MB shared L2 cache. Our baseline algorithm is the *k*-means clustering implementation from the NU-MineBench suite [4] and the parallelization in our proposed algorithms is handled by OpenMP constructs as in the original NU-MineBench code. All reported execution time results are in *seconds*.

The small dataset [1] is a set of edge vectors (with 18 coordinates) from 17,695 pictures. The medium dataset is a gene expression dataset obtained on Affymetrix HT HG133t platform for 18 cell samples, thus having 54,143 vectors with

Table 2: Execution time analysis of skipping algorithms.

Dataset	Base	2 Bin	Last Change
Small	0.55	0.44	0.40
Medium	2.98	1.82	2.91
Large	6.83	4.16	6.31
Wide	9.51	8.50	7.53

18 coordinates. The large dataset is the KDD Cup 1998 data. It has 56 coordinates and 95413 vectors. The wide dataset is from Bag of Words dataset of UC Irvine Data Repository [2]. This dataset has 3430 vectors with 6906 coordinates. We used a range of k values (4 to 13) for all four datasets. In our skipping algorithms, the default skipping frequency is set to 1:2 for small, medium and large datasets and 3:4 for wide dataset. Change-limit (in the Last Change algorithm) is 10 for small and wide datasets and 20 for other datasets.

3.1 L2 Hit Rates

The Reordering algorithm improves the cache hit rates, except the wide dataset (Table 1). The hit rates achieved by combinations (Re + 2 Bin and Re + LC) also meet the expectations; i.e. within 95% - 99% range but also less than the Reordering scheme. The slight decreases in the cache performances of the 2 Bin and Last Change schemes are not very surprising. It should be noted that all of the datasets we experiment with are larger than the total L2 cache.

3.2 Execution Times

Table 2 shows running time improvements. It is important to note that 2 Bin is significantly more successful for larger datasets. Increasing the number of points generally increases the required number of iterations to converge, which leads to more point skipping for 2 Bin, as size of the second bin always increases. In comparison, Last Change algorithm works even better than 2 Bin for the small and wide datasets. Last Change fills the second bin at the limit iteration and reduces its size through the process; a large dataset will have a smaller ratio of true stable points and reduce the effectiveness.

Since our physical architecture does not have a shared L2 cache, we computed the execution time of the Reordering algorithm using the Simics environment, and found that under L1, L2 and memory latency values of 2, 8 and 200 cycles, our approach improves upon the base algorithm by 21,8% (resp. 22.9%, 23.8%) for the small (resp. medium, large) dataset.

Table 3: Average percentage increase in sum of point-to-center distances against base algorithm.

Dataset	2 Bin	LC	Re + 2 Bin	Re + LC
Small	0.0320%	0.0046%	0.0039%	0.0001%
Medium	1.8323%	0.0069%	0.8504%	0.0001%
Large	0.1731%	0.0003%	0.0005%	0.0001%
Wide	0.0918%	0.0058%	0.0023%	0.0001%

Table 4: L2 hit rate analysis for the Reordering algorithm with various cache sizes.

Dataset	Algorithm	512KB	1MB	2MB
Small	Base	82.67%	81.49%	98.72%
	Reordering	98.04%	98.60%	98.73%
Medium	Base	78.85%	80.17%	83.26%
	Reordering	98.85%	99.02%	98.95%
Large	Base	79.61%	80.42%	81.10%
	Reordering	99.48%	99.68%	99.74%
Wide	Base	97.12%	97.24%	98.05%
	Reordering	95.68%	96.03%	96.27%

3.3 Accuracy Analysis

None of the skipping heuristics proposed in this paper can detect points to skip with 100% accuracy; consequently, some points that should change their membership might be skipped. Therefore, the final centers can be different than what Lloyd's algorithm finds. Our metric of comparison is the sum of the square of Euclidian distances for every point to its assigned center (Table 3). It is important to note that, even though the accuracy losses for 2 Bin seems to be higher than others, they are still low enough for most practical purposes (the worst observed accuracy loss is less than 4%). However, Last Change proves to be a better solution if extremely high precision is needed. The accuracy losses incurred by the combined techniques are much lower as skipping limitations are more strict in these cases.

3.4 Sensitivity Experiments

The architecture-centric nature of Reordering algorithm requires further experiments with different multicore configurations to fully understand its behavior. We repeat our tests with two different shared cache sizes, namely, 512 KB and 2 MB (Table 4). It is important to note that 2 MB configuration can fit the whole small dataset into the cache. 512 KB hit rates are lower than 1 MB hit rates especially for base algorithm, which shows that it is more sensitive to the cache size. The Reordering algorithm provides relatively stable L2 hit rates for different datasets and configurations.

The skipping factor is an important parameter for 2 Bin heuristic. We experimented with 1:2, 1:4 and 3:4 frequencies to observe the sensitivity of performance (Table 5). Furthermore, 2 Bin heuristic might be too simplistic for some datasets and the technique is suitable for expansion. One can accommodate additional bins for different number of center changes. We implemented a 3 Bin technique with skipping frequencies 1:2 and 3:4. As expected, skipping more

Table 5: Execution time analysis for 2 Bin modifications. x:y indicates that first x iterations are skipped in every y iterations.

Dataset	2 Bin			3 Bin
	1:2	1:4	3:4	1:2 , 3:4
Small	0.44	0.47	0.32	0.30
Medium	1.82	1.85	1.35	1.11
Large	4.16	4.30	3.17	3.32
Wide	11.27	10.27	8.50	8.41

Table 6: Execution time analysis for the Last Change algorithm.

Dataset	Freq. , Limit	Frequency		Limit	
	1:2 , Normal	1:4	3:4	Low	High
Small	0.40	0.48	0.44	0.43	0.42
Medium	2.91	2.97	2.89	3.05	2.90
Large	6.31	6.54	5.04	6.25	6.64
Wide	7.39	8.26	7.53	5.48	9.51

points results in a faster algorithm. 3 Bin performs better than all of 2 Bin configurations as it makes better skipping decisions with additional information.

The performance of the Last Change scheme is affected by skipping factor, like 2 Bin (Table 6). Another parameter to study is the limit to start skipping points. We defined low, normal and high limits for each data set (5, 10, 20 for small and wide, 10, 20, 40 for others). The low limit for the medium dataset skips enough non-stable points to decrease convergence rate and ergo the performance, while the same low limit improves the performance for the wide dataset significantly which supplements our idea of the effect of the dataset structure.

4. CONCLUDING REMARKS

We have presented three different optimizations on k-means algorithm. Further, we explored combinations and variations of these algorithms. The proposed algorithms differ from previous works in optimizing the cache performance and/or reducing the computation by skipping points. They are implemented and tested on multicore architectures for their performances against parallel Lloyd's algorithm. Our experiments showed promising results with different datasets and architectures.

5. REFERENCES

[1] Corel Corporation. http://www.corel.com/.
[2] A. Frank and A. Asuncion. UCI machine learning repository, 2010.
[3] S. P. Lloyd. Least squares quantization in pcm. *ransactions on n or ation heory*, 28(2):129–136, 1982.
[4] NU-MineBench. http://cucis.ece.northwestern.edu/ projects/DMS/MineBench.html.
[5] Wind River Simics. http://www.virtutech.com/.

Learning, Evolution and Adaptation in Racing Games

Daniele Loiacono
Politecnico di Milano
P.zza Leonardo da Vinci, 32
I-20133, Milano, Italy
loiacono@elet.polimi.it

ABSTRACT

Modern racing games offer a realistic driving experience and a vivid game environment. Accordingly, developing this type of games involves several challenges and requires a large amount of game contents. Computational intelligence represents a promising technology to deal effectively with such challenges and, at the same time, to reduce the cost of the development process. In this paper, we provide an overview of the most relevant applications of computational intelligence methods in the domain of racing games. In particular, we show that computational intelligence can be successfully applied (i) to develop highly competitive non-player characters, (ii) to design advanced racing behaviors such as overtaking maneuvers, and (iii) to automatically generate tracks and racing scenarios.

Categories and Subject Descriptors

I.2.1 [**Artificial Intelligence**]: Applications and Expert Systems—*Games*; K.8 [**Personal Computing**]: Games

General Terms

Algorithms, Design

Keywords

Racing Games, TORCS, Simulated Car Racing, Computational Intelligence

1. INTRODUCTION

Nowadays, racing games are one of the most popular game genre as they can provide a realistic driving experience in a vivid scenario. Accordingly, racing games are getting more sophisticated and expensive to develop. In fact, non-player characters have to deal with increasingly accurate physics engines and with a large variety of complex racing situations. In addition, racing games usually involves a huge amount of game contents (e.g., car models, tracks, racing scenarios,

etc.) requiring an extremely expensive design process. Computational intelligence represents a promising technology to deal with such development challenges and to reduce the design costs. Recently, several works in the literature proved that computational intelligence methods are well suited both to improve the development of non-player characters and to design effectively innovative game contents. At the same time, racing games represent an ideal testbed to compare different computational intelligence approaches on challenging problems as proved by the large number of scientific competitions organized on this topic in the recent years.

A comprehensive survey of the computational intelligence applications to racing games is out of the scope of this paper (we refer the interested readers to [42] for a survey of the field). In contrast, our aim is to provide an overall picture of the most interesting problems in the domain of racing games and to suggest possible research directions for future works in this area.

This paper is organized as follows. In Section 2 we provide an overview of the most popular racing simulators and research platforms used so far in the literature. In Section 3 we discuss the development of competitive non-player characters with evolutionary computation approaches while, in Section 4, we focus on the design of advanced racing behaviors such as overtaking. Finally, in Section 5 we deal with the automatic generation of tracks with evolutionary algorithms.

2. RACING SIMULATORS AND RESEARCH PLATFORMS

In this section we provide a brief overview of the most popular racing simulators and platforms used so far in the literature.

2.1 Evolutionary Car Racing

Evolutionary Car Racing is a 2D racing environment developed in Java by Togelius et al. [39]; it features a rather simple car dynamics inspired to the behaviors of real R/C racing car models; its racing environment (see Figure 1a) consists of walls, which delimit the track, and of a sequence of waypoints, which define the path the car must follow to complete a lap on the track. In order to compute their actions, controllers are provided with several sensory information such as the position with respect to the next waypoint, a rangefinder to perceive walls along some given directions (Figure 1b), the current speed, etc. Evolutionary Car Racing was designed to study the application of evolutionary computation for developing a controller in a simple racing

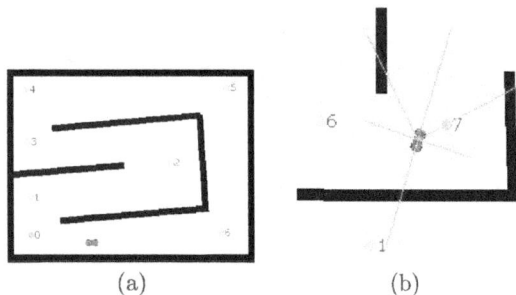

Figure 1: Screenshots of Evolutionary Car Racing: (a) an example of track and (b) details of the sensory information provided to the controllers.

Figure 2: A screenshot from TORCS.

game; despite being a very simple environment, it allows to study effectively several relevant topics ranging from the optimization of sensors configuration to the comparison among different approaches [39, 41, 38, 36, 2, 28].

2.2 The Open Racing Car Simulator

The Open Racing Car Simulator (TORCS) [17] is a state-of-the-art open source car racing simulator. It falls somewhere between being an advanced simulator, like recent commercial car racing games, and a fully customizable environment, like the ones typically used by researchers in computational intelligence for benchmarking purposes. It features a rather sophisticated physics engine, which takes into account many aspects of the racing car (e.g. collisions, traction, aerodynamics, fuel consumption, etc.); it provides a rather sophisticated 3D graphics engine for the visualization (Figure 2); finally, it also provides a lot of game content (i.e., several tracks, car models and controllers, etc.), resulting in a countless number of possible game situations. On the other hand, TORCS has been specifically devised to allow the users to develop their own car controllers, their own bots, as separate C++ modules, which can be easily compiled and added to the game. At each control step (game tick), a bot can access the current game state, which includes information about the car and the track as well as the other cars on the track; a bot can control the car using the gas/brake pedals, the gear stick, and steering wheel. The game distribution includes many programmed bots, which can be easily customized or extended to build new bots. TORCS users developed several bots, which often compete in international competitions such as the driver championship[1] or those organized by the TORCS racing board[2].

In the recent years, TORCS has quickly become the de-facto standard in the computational intelligence research being used in a large amount of works [1, 5, 6, 7, 10, 9, 8, 12, 16, 20, 23, 25, 30, 31, 29, 32, 33, 34, 35, 45, 49, 50].

2.3 Simulated Car Racing

Racing games are an ideal testbed for organizing scientific competitions as they allow researchers to compare different techniques in a challenging problem domain. In the recent years, several of these competitions have been organized at major scientific conferences. The first *simulated*

car racing competition was organized by Togelius during the 2007 IEEE Congress on Evolutionary Computation and was based on the Evolutionary Car Racing environment described in Section 2.1. The same competition was later organized also as part of the 2007 IEEE Conference on Computational Intelligence and Games. In this competition, two controllers compete against each other in a square racing environment to reach randomly generated waypoints; each controller knows the position of the opponent, the position of the current waypoint and the position of the next waypoint to reach after the current one. Accordingly, submitted entries require also some planning capabilities to decide which waypoint they should target. A report about these competitions, with a description of the rules, of the submitted entries, and of the results, was published in [40]. Since 2008, the simulated car racing competition was organized by Loiacono et al. [27] using a TORCS-based racing environment. From 2009, this competition evolved in the *Simulated Car Racing Championship*, an event joining every year three scientific competitions (dubbed *legs*) organized at major conferences in the field of Computational Intelligence. The racing environment is based on TORCS but involves three major changes. First, it is organized as a client-server application: the bots run as external processes connected to the race server through UDP connections (see Figure 3). Second, it adds real-time: every game tick (which roughly corresponds to 20ms of simulated time), the server sends the current sensory inputs to each bot and waits for 10ms (of real time) to receive an action from the bot. If no action arrives, the simulation continues and the last performed action is used. Finally, the competition software provides an abstraction of the actual TORCS racing environment, that is, it provides a sensors and actuators model, which (i) gives complete freedom of choice regarding the programming language used for bots; (ii) restricts the access to the information provided by the organizers of the competition; (iii) allows to make the problem more challenging by applying an artificial noise to the sensors model.

The Simulated Car Racing Championship involves every year different tracks, that are not known in advance by the competitors. For each track, the competition consists of three stages: (i) the warm-up, where each controller races alone and can collect useful information about the track; (ii) the qualifying, where each controller races alone as fast as

---

[1] http://speedy.chonchon.free.fr/tdc/
[2] http://www.berniw.org/trb/

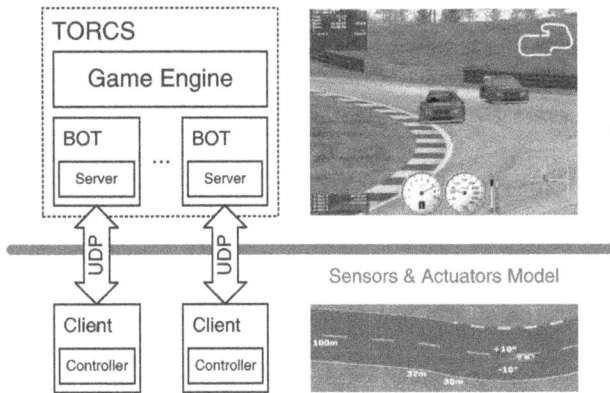

Figure 3: The architecture of the API developed for the Simulated Car Racing Championship.

Figure 4: A screenshot from VDrift.

possible on the track; (iii) the race, where the best eight controllers according to the qualifying stage race together. During these years, the Simulated Car Racing competition, had a great success receiving many submissions with a good variety of approaches (e.g., fuzzy logic, neuroevolution, potential fields, genetic algorithms, etc). Several submissions to the competition, resulted into one or more scientific publications [35, 6, 33]. Part of the results and more details about these competitions can be found in [26, 22, 24].

2.4 Other Platforms

A few more relevant open source racing simulators are *RARS*[3], *Speed Dreams*[4], and *VDrift*[5]. RARS (Robot Auto Racing Simulator) is an old project designed to easily allow users to program their own AI drivers. RARS has been now discontinued but it was used as a starting point for the TORCS project. Speed Dreams is a fork of TORCS which aims at implementing innovative features as well as constantly improving visual and physics realism. The main idea behind this fork, is to implement a faster release process (e.g., 1 or 2 releases per year) than the one implemented for TORCS, thanks to a more active community of users. VDrift is one of the best open-source car racing game. It features a high quality 3D visualization (see Figure 4) and an arcade-like playability. Concerning the physics, it exploits Bullet[6], a popular open source physics engine.

Beyond the open source racing platforms covered so far, it is finally worth to name at least two commercial platforms: Trackmania by Nadeo[7] and rFactor by Image Space Inc.[8]. In fact, although they don't provide any access to the game sources, they are two of the most important commercial products that can be rather easily extended with user-created contents.

3. NON-PLAYER CHARACTERS

A racing game involves several problems but the most im-

portant one is controlling effectively the car in the racing environment. In fact, non-player characters are generally required to race as fast as possible along the track without loosing the control of the car and without suffering any damage. In this section we provide an overview of the most significant applications of computational intelligence to this problem.

3.1 Optimizing the racing lines

In racing games, non-player characters typically consist of a controller designed to follow a target racing line [21]. The optimal racing line, i.e., the line that a driver should follow to achieve the best lap-time possible on given track with a given car, depends on several factors [15, 4] including the track shape, the car aerodynamics, the grip, etc. In commercial games, the target racing lines are usually drawn by domain experts [21] and then tested and tuned by game developers through actual game-play. Unfortunately, this a rather time-consuming process especially for games that include a large number of tracks and of car models. While the problem of computing the optimal racing line is well studied in the real car racing domain [15, 4], so far, only few works focused on the problem of optimizing the racing lines to speedup the development of non-player characters in racing games. In [14] Coloum introduced *K1999*, a heuristic to automatically design an optimal racing line on a given track. The same approach was later followed for developing some of the non-player characters available for TORCS, like *Simplix* [3] that is perhaps the best performing one. In [12], Cardamone et al. presented a preliminary work toward the development of a tool for the automatic design, tune and test of the best racing line for a given track and car model. Following the same principles introduced in [4], they modeled the problem of finding the best racing line as an optimization problem to compute the optimal trade-off between two conflicting objectives: (i) driving fast, i.e., following the fastest racing line and (ii) following the shortest path. Thus, they applied genetic algorithms for search this optimal trade-off as follows. Tracks are decomposed into several sections; for each section, the target racing line is defined as a convex combination between the fastest line and the shortest path; therefore, genetic algorithms are exploited to find the optimal convex combinations in each section of the track. The racing lines discovered with this approach led to improve the

[3]http://rars.sourceforge.net/
[4]http://www.speed-dreams.org/
[5]http://vdrift.net/
[6]http://bulletphysics.org/
[7]http:// www.trackmania.com
[8]http://www.rfactor.net

performances of the existing non-player characters in most of the tracks tested.

3.2 Optimizing the car parameters

Developing a racing controller generally requires also to tune several parameters involving the aerodynamics and the mechanics of the car. In this problem evolutionary computation might be successfully exploited to search for an optimal parameters setting. In [48] Wloch et al. applied a standard genetic algorithm to optimize the setup of a F1 car in the commercial game *Formula One Challenge* by Activision. More recently, Cardamone et al. [10] applied a cooperative evolution approach to optimize the car parameters of a racing controller for TORCS. In particular, Cardamone et al. applied a coevolutionary approach introduced in [18] to optimize a subset of the car parameters modeled in TORCS involving wings, suspensions, wheels, brakes, etc. The resulting optimized controller was then submitted to the 2009 TORCS Endurance World Championship, an international competition organized by community of TORCS users. The results showed that coevolution could effectively optimize the car parameters leading to competitive performances (the submitted racing controller placed 4th in the final standings among 12 participants). Finally, in [6, 5] Butz et al. applied evolutionary strategies to optimize the parameters of an heuristic controller; the results reported in their work suggest that evolutionary computation can be effectively applied to improve significantly the performance of a controller that involves several parameters.

3.3 Other Approaches

As discussed in the previous sections, in racing games the most common approach to develop a non-player characters typically involves a controller that follows a given racing line. However, several works in the literature investigated different approaches to this problem such as evolved neural controllers [8, 13], fuzzy systems [24, 33], learning by imitation [9, 29, 30], track modeling [34, 35], and genetic programming [16]. Although the non-player characters developed with these approaches are generally outperformed by *standard* ones, many of these research directions provided very promising results and are worth to be further investigated. As an example, supervised learning techniques has been applied [29, 30] to train a human-like non-player characters from data of real players. A similar approach was also used in *Colin McRae Rally 2.0* (by Codemasters) where a feedforward multilayer neural network has been trained to follow the target racing line from the game data of an expert player [19].

4. ADVANCED RACING BEHAVIORS

Racing fast along the track is very important but it is not the only skill of a non-player character in a racing game. In fact, racing games involve several challenges for non-player characters such as avoiding collisions, overtaking opponents, recovery the car from a crash, choosing a pit-stop strategy, etc. Dealing successfully with these challenges is essential for developing an effective non-player character.

Developing non-player characters with such a sophisticated variety of behaviors generally requires a modular approach: the whole non-player character can be decomposed in several *behaviors*; each *behavior* is devised to deal with a specific problem or situation; all the *behaviors* are thus com-

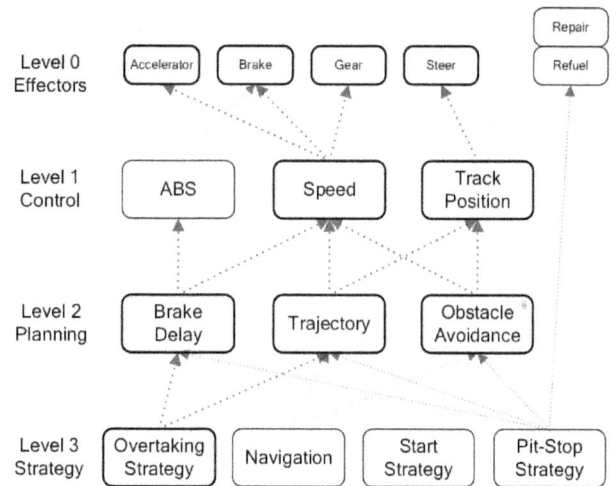

Figure 5: An example of modular decomposition of the most important behaviors in a racing game [25].

bined together to define the final response of the non-player character to every situation. Figure 5 shows an example of such a modular architecture proposed by Loiacono et al. in [25]; it involves four abstraction layers that identify (i) high-level behaviors which operate at a strategic level, (ii) behaviors which represent macro-actions needed for planning, (iii) tasks which implement middle-level control (e.g., ABS), and (iv) elementary actions on the actuators.

In this scenario, computational intelligence techniques might be effectively applied to either develop specific behaviors or to decide how they should be combined together, as suggested by the two case studies presented in this section.

4.1 Overtaking Behaviors

Overtaking is at the same time one of the most important and one of the most challenging racing behaviors. As suggested by Figure 5 it might be further decomposed in specialized behaviors for specific overtaking situations. In particular, Loiacono et al. [25] focused on the following overtaking behaviors: (i) the overtaking of a fast opponent either on a straight stretch or on a large bend; (ii) the overtaking on a tight bend which typically requires a rather advanced brake policy. Instead of programming such behaviors, Loiacono et al. applied Q-Learning [47], a very simple reinforcement learning algorithm, to learn them in TORCS. Their results suggested that, through a suitable task decomposition, even a rather simple learning algorithm like Q-Learning can effectively learn sophisticated behaviors and outperform programmed non-player characters. In addition, the proposed approach was successfully applied to learn the target behaviors in different conditions (e.g., using a different car aerodynamics model), without requiring any ad-hoc adjustments.

4.2 Blocking Behaviors

Blocking is a rather typical maneuver in racing games that is frequently employed both by human players and non-player characters. The term identifies all those strategies that a driver can use to prevent, disturb or possibly block an overtaking action by an incoming car. Onieva et al. [32],

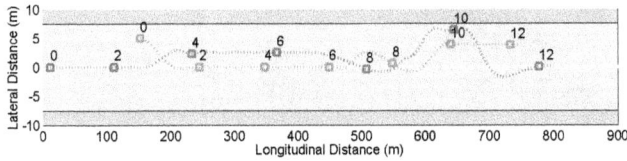

Figure 6: An example of the overtaking behavior developed by Onieva et al. in [32]. Red line represents the path followed by an opponent implementing a reactive blocking strategy, while blue line is the path followed by the fuzzy-based non-player characters developed by Onieva et al. Square dots are the positions of the two controllers at given time steps specified by the small label over the dots.

showed that even the most competitive drivers available for TORCS are not able to deal effectively with opponents implementing rather simple blocking strategies. Accordingly, they designed a set of fuzzy rules to develop an overtaking behavior capable of dealing with challenging opponents that implement blocking strategies of increasing difficulty. Figure 6 shows an example of the resulting overtaking behavior developed by Onieva et al. in [32]. The example shows how the non-player characters is capable of trying a fake overtake on the left side of the opponent (at time step 10 in Figure 6) and then completing the overtake on the right side. Noticeably, such a rather sophisticated behavior was achieved with a quite simple set of fuzzy rules, while is much more difficult to achieve with a programmed heuristic [32].

5. PROCEDURAL CONTENT GENERATION OF TRACKS

Providing a rich set of contents such as car models, tracks and scenarios, plays a key role for the commercial success of many racing titles (see for instance, Trackmania by Nadeo[9], rFactor by Image Space Inc.[10], and Gran Turismo series by Polyphony[11]). Unfortunately, providing such a large amount of game contents is an extremely time consuming process and it is perhaps one the most expensive task in the development of a commercial game nowadays.

Accordingly, several researchers have recently investigated the application of evolutionary methods for the automatic discovery of innovative and interesting game content. In this area, called Search-Based Procedural Content Generation (SB-PCG) [44], the quality assessment of the evolved content is probably the most critical issue. So far, three major approaches have been proposed in the literature [37, 46, 11]: (i) *theory-driven approaches*, that rely on design principles and ad-hoc heuristics to measure the quality of game content; (ii) *data-driven approaches*, that exploit a large amount of game data to predict the quality of unseen contents; (iii) *interactive approaches*, that involve the direct feedback of the players community to evaluate the game contents discovered.

In the remainder of this section we will focus on Search-Based Procedural Content Generation applied to generation of tracks in racing games.

[9]http://www.trackmania.com
[10]http://www.rfactor.net
[11]http://www.gran-turismo.com/

5.1 Theory and Data Driven Track Generation

In their early works, Togelius et al. [37, 43] combined a data-driven procedural content generation approach with an evolutionary algorithm to evolve racing tracks that would fit a target player profile. As a first step, they profiled a human player on a test track by recording game data such as the number of waypoints reached in a fixed amount of time, the driving speed, the driving path, etc. Then, they applied an evolutionary computation to evolve a controller that match the player's driving profile. Finally, the same controller was used to evolve tracks which would provide the right amount of challenge to the profiled human player.

More recently, Loiacono et al.[23] proposed a *theory-driven* procedural content generation approach to evolve tracks for TORCS. While Togelius et al. [43, 37] focused on evolving personalized tracks for a target player, Loiacono et al. [23] focused on evolving of tracks that provide a *large degree of diversity* and an adequate amount of challenge. For this purpose, they defined the *curvature profile* of a track, as the distribution of curvature values of all the track segments, and the *speed profile* of a track, as the distribution of the speed values that a competitive driver achieves along the track. Thus, they applied both single-objective and multi-objective genetic algorithms to evolve tracks that maximize the *entropy* of these profiles. Finally, they performed a preliminary validation with human subjects on the evolved tracks and the results suggest that there is a statistically significant correlation between the metrics proposed (i.e., the entropy of curvature and speed profiles) and the preferences expressed by the human players. As a proof of concept, some of the tracks evolved (see Figure 7) were also used to run the 2010 Simulated Car Racing Championship described in Section 2.3).

5.2 Interactive Track Generation

The main underlying idea of *interactive* procedural content generation approaches is the direct evaluation by the users of the game contents. For this purpose, Cardamone et al. [11] developed a framework which enables the interactive evolution of racing tracks both by single users, working alone on their own population, and by a community of users sharing (a typically much larger) population. The framework employs (i) a web frontend to provide discovered contents and to allow the interaction with the users; (ii) an evolutionary backend to discover new game content and to perform all the evolutionary tasks (i.e., selection, recombination and mutation). As a proof of concept, the authors deployed online the *Interactive Track Generator*[12], a working version of their framework that allows the collaborative evolution of tracks for TORCS and Speed Dreams (see Section 2.2) and Section 2.4). Figure 8 shows a screenshot of the user interface of the *Interactive Track Generator* with a preview of some of the best tracks evolved so far. The web frontend allow to the users to see the tracks generated so far, to provide a feedback on them and to download the tracks they would like to race on.

6. CONCLUSIONS

In this paper we discussed some among the most challenging problems in the domain of racing games from a computa-

[12]http://trackgen.pierlucanlanzi.net/besttracks.php

(a)

(b)

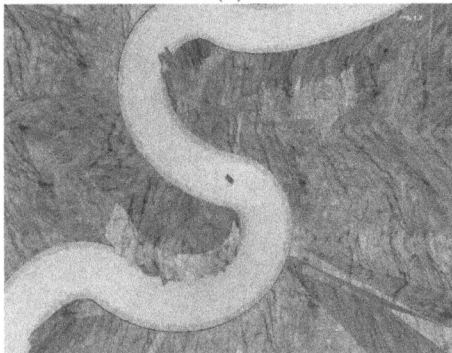

(c)

Figure 7: The track Rocky **used in the third leg of the 2010 Simulated Car Racing Championship held at CIG-2010, Copenhagen, Denmark: (a) the shape of the track, (b) and (c) screenshots of the track in the game.**

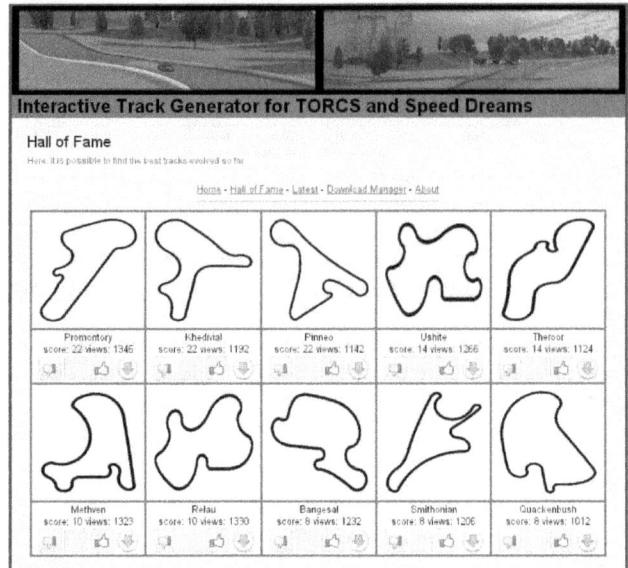

Figure 8: A screenshot of the *Interactive Track Generator.*

tional intelligence perspective. We also provided a showcase of the most successful applications of computational intelligence methods in this area. First of all, we focused on the development of non-player characters where evolutionary algorithms have been applied to improve both the racing line and the car parameters. Then, we investigated the application of reinforcement learning and fuzzy logic to the design of sophisticated racing behaviors. Finally, we provided an overview of the procedural content generation approaches applied to the automatic discovery of new tracks. The contributions briefly summarized in this paper suggest that, although some research directions still requires future investigations, computational intelligence might be a promising technology for developing racing games.

7. REFERENCES

[1] A. A. Abdullahi and S. M. Lucas. Temporal difference learning with interpolated n-tuples: Initial results from a simulated car racing environment. In *Proc. IEEE Conf. Computational Intelligence and Games (CIG)*, pages 321–328, 2011.

[2] A. Agapitos, J. Togelius, S. M. Lucas, J. Schmidhuber, and A. K. 0002. Generating diverse opponents with multiobjective evolution. *CIG*, pages 135–142, 2008.

[3] W.-D. Beelitz. The SIMPLy mIXed best practice TORCS robot. http://www.wdbee.gotdns.org:8086/SIMPLIX/SimplixDefault.aspx.

[4] F. Braghin, F. Cheli, S. Melzi, and E. Sabbioni. Race driver model. *Comput. Struct.*, 86(13-14):1503–1516, 2008.

[5] M. V. Butz, M. J. Linhardt, and T. D. Lonneker. Effective racing on partially observable tracks: Indirectly coupling anticipatory egocentric sensors with motor commands. *IEEE Transactions on Computational Intelligence and AI in Games*, 3(1):31–42, 2011.

[6] M. V. Butz and T. D. Lonneker. Optimized

sensory-motor couplings plus strategy extensions for the torcs car racing challenge. In *Computational Intelligence and Games, 2009. CIG 2009. IEEE Symposium on*, pages 317–324, Sept. 2009.

[7] L. Cardamone, A. Caiazzo, D. Loiacono, and P. L. Lanzi. Transfer of driving behaviors across different racing games. In *Proc. IEEE Conf. Computational Intelligence and Games (CIG)*, pages 227–234, 2011.

[8] L. Cardamone, D. Loiacono, and P. Lanzi. On-line neuroevolution applied to the open racing car simulator. In *Evolutionary Computation, 2009. CEC '09. IEEE Congress on*, pages 2622–2629, May 2009.

[9] L. Cardamone, D. Loiacono, and P. L. Lanzi. Learning drivers for torcs through imitation using supervised methods. In *Proc. IEEE Symp. Computational Intelligence and Games CIG 2009*, pages 148–155, 2009.

[10] L. Cardamone, D. Loiacono, and P. L. Lanzi. Applying cooperative coevolution to compete in the 2009 torcs endurance world championship. In *Evolutionary Computation (CEC), 2010 IEEE Congress on*, pages 1 –8, jul. 2010.

[11] L. Cardamone, D. Loiacono, and P. L. Lanzi. Interactive evolution for the procedural generation of tracks in a high-end racing game. In *Proceedings of the 13th annual conference on Genetic and evolutionary computation*, GECCO '11, pages 395–402, New York, NY, USA, 2011. ACM.

[12] L. Cardamone, D. Loiacono, P. L. Lanzi, and A. P. Bardelli. Searching for the optimal racing line using genetic algorithms. In *Proc. IEEE Symp. Computational Intelligence and Games (CIG)*, pages 388–394, 2010.

[13] L. Cardamone, Loiacono, Daniele, and P. L. Lanzi. Evolving competitive car controllers for racing games with neuroevolution. *GECCO*, pages 1179–1186, 2009.

[14] R. Coulom. *Reinforcement Learning Using Neural Networks, with Applications to Motor Control*. PhD thesis, Institut National Polytechnique de Grenoble, 2002.

[15] R. S. D. Casanova. *On minimum time vehicle manoeuvring: the theoretical optimal time*. PhD thesis, Cranfield University, 2000.

[16] M. Ebner and T. Tiede. Evolving driving controllers using genetic programming. In *Computational Intelligence and Games, 2009. CIG 2009. IEEE Symposium on*, pages 279–286, Sept. 2009.

[17] E. Espié, C. Guionneau, B. Wymann, C. Dimitrakakis, R. Coulom, and A. Sumner. TORCS, the open racing car simulator. http://www.torcs.org, 2005.

[18] F. Gomez, J. Schmidhuber, and R. Miikkulainen. Accelerated neural evolution through cooperatively coevolved synapses. *Journal of Machine Learning Research*, pages 937–965, 2008.

[19] J. Hannan. Interview to jeff hannan, 2001. http://www.generation5.org/content/2001/hannan.asp.

[20] M. Kemmerling and M. Preuss. Automatic adaptation to generated content via car setup optimization in torcs. In *Proc. IEEE Symp. Computational Intelligence and Games (CIG)*, pages 131–138, 2010.

[21] S. Lecchi. Artificial intelligence in racing games. In *CIG'09: Proceedings of the 5th international conference on Computational Intelligence and Games*, pages 1–1, Piscataway, NJ, USA, 2009. IEEE Press.

[22] D. Loiacono, L. Cardamone, and P. L. Lanzi. Simulated car racing championship 2009: Competition software manual. Technical report, Dipartimento di Elettronica e Informazione, Politecnico di Milano, 2009.

[23] D. Loiacono, L. Cardamone, and P. L. Lanzi. Automatic track generation for high-end racing games using evolutionary computation. *Computational Intelligence and AI in Games, IEEE Transactions on*, 3(3):245 –259, sept. 2011.

[24] D. Loiacono, P. Lanzi, J. Togelius, E. Onieva, D. Pelta, M. Butz, T. Lonneker, L. Cardamone, D. Perez, Y. Saez, M. Preuss, and J. Quadflieg. The 2009 simulated car racing championship. *Computational Intelligence and AI in Games, IEEE Transactions on*, 2(2):131 –147, jun. 2010.

[25] D. Loiacono, A. Prete, P. L. Lanzi, and L. Cardamone. Learning to overtake in torcs using simple reinforcement learning. In *Proc. IEEE Congress Evolutionary Computation (CEC)*, pages 1–8, 2010.

[26] D. Loiacono, J. Togelius, P. L. Lanzi, L. Kinnaird-Heether, S. M. Lucas, M. Simmerson, D. Perez, R. G. Reynolds, and Y. Saez. The wcci 2008 simulated car racing competition. In *Proc. IEEE Symp. On Computational Intelligence and Games CIG '08*, pages 119–126, 2008.

[27] Loiacono, Daniele and J. Togelius. Competitions @ WCCI-2008: simulated car racing competition. *SIGEVOlution*, 2(4), Dec. 2007.

[28] H. Marques, J. Togelius, M. Kogutowska, O. Holland, and S. Lucas. Sensorless but not Senseless: Prediction in Evolutionary Car Racing. *Artificial Life, 2007. ALIFE '07. IEEE Symposium on*, pages 370–377, 2007.

[29] J. Munoz, G. Gutierrez, and A. Sanchis. Controller for torcs created by imitation. In *Computational Intelligence and Games, 2009. CIG 2009. IEEE Symposium on*, pages 271–278, Sept. 2009.

[30] J. Munoz, G. Gutierrez, and A. Sanchis. A human-like torcs controller for the simulated car racing championship. In *Proc. IEEE Symp. Computational Intelligence and Games (CIG)*, pages 473–480, 2010.

[31] J. Munoz, G. Gutierrez, and A. Sanchis. Multi-objective evolution for car setup optimization. In *Proc. UK Workshop Computational Intelligence (UKCI)*, pages 1–5, 2010.

[32] E. Onieva, L. Cardamone, D. Loiacono, and P. L. Lanzi. Overtaking opponents with blocking strategies using fuzzy logic. In *Proc. IEEE Symp. Computational Intelligence and Games (CIG)*, pages 123–130, 2010.

[33] E. Onieva, D. A. Pelta, J. Alonso, V. Milanes, and J. Perez. A modular parametric architecture for the torcs racing engine. In *Computational Intelligence and Games, 2009. CIG 2009. IEEE Symposium on*, pages 256–262, Sept. 2009.

[34] M. Preuss, J. Quadflieg, and G. Rudolph. Torcs sensor noise removal and multi-objective track selection for driving style adaptation. In *Proc. IEEE Conf. Computational Intelligence and Games (CIG)*, pages 337–344, 2011.

[35] J. Quadflieg, M. Preuss, O. Kramer, and G. Rudolph. Learning the track and planning ahead in a car racing controller. In *Computational Intelligence and Games (CIG), 2010 IEEE Symposium on*, pages 395 –402, aug. 2010.

[36] J. Togelius, P. Burrow, and S. M. Lucas. Multi-population competitive co-evolution of car racing controllers. *IEEE Congress on Evolutionary Computation*, pages 4043–4050, 2007.

[37] J. Togelius, R. De Nardi, and S. Lucas. Towards automatic personalised content creation for racing games. In *Proc. IEEE Symposium on Computational Intelligence and Games CIG 2007*, pages 252–259, 2007.

[38] J. Togelius and S. Lucas. Evolving controllers for simulated car racing. *Evolutionary Computation, 2005. The 2005 IEEE Congress on*, 2:1906–1913, 2005.

[39] J. Togelius and S. Lucas. Evolving robust and specialized car racing skills. *Evolutionary Computation, 2006. CEC 2006. IEEE Congress on*, pages 1187–1194, 2006.

[40] J. Togelius, S. Lucas, H. D. Thang, J. M. Garibaldi, T. Nakashima, C. H. Tan, I. Elhanany, S. Berant, P. Hingston, R. M. MacCallum, T. Haferlach, A. Gowrisankar, and P. Burrow. The 2007 IEEE CEC simulated car racing competition. *Genetic Programming and Evolvable Machines*, 9(4):295–329, July 2008.

[41] J. Togelius and S. M. Lucas. Arms Races and Car Races. *PPSN*, pages 613–622, 2006.

[42] J. Togelius, S. M. Lucas, and R. De Nardi. Computational Intelligence in Racing Games. *Advanced Intelligent Paradigms in Computer Games*, pages 39–69, 2007.

[43] J. Togelius, R. D. Nardi, and S. M. Lucas. Making racing fun through player modeling and track evolution. In *Proceedings of the SAB Workshop on Adaptive Approaches to Optimizing Player Satisfaction*, 2006.

[44] J. Togelius, G. N. Yannakakis, K. O. Stanley, and C. Browne. Search-based procedural content generation. In C. D. Chio, S. Cagnoni, C. Cotta, M. Ebner, A. Ekárt, A. Esparcia-Alcázar, C. K. Goh, J. J. M. Guervós, F. Neri, M. Preuss, J. Togelius, and G. N. Yannakakis, editors, *EvoApplications (1)*, volume 6024 of *Lecture Notes in Computer Science*, pages 141–150. Springer, 2010.

[45] S. Tognetti, M. Garbarino, A. Bonarini, and M. Matteucci. Modeling enjoyment preference from physiological responses in a car racing game. In *Proc IEEE Symp. Computational Intelligence and Games (CIG)*, pages 321–328, 2010.

[46] N. van Hoorn, J. Togelius, D. Wierstra, and J. Schmidhuber. Robust player imitation using multiobjective evolution. In *Proceedings of the IEEE Congress on Evolutionary Computation*, pages 652–659, Trondheim, Norway, 18-21 May 2009.

[47] C. Watkins. *Learning from delayed reward*. PhD thesis, 1989.

[48] K. Wloch and P. J. Bentley. Optimising the performance of a formula one car using a genetic algorithm. In *Proceedings of Eighth International Conference on Parallel Problem Solving From Nature*, pages 702–711, 2004.

[49] E. Yee and J. Teo. Evolutionary spiking neural networks as racing car controllers. In *Proc. 11th Int Hybrid Intelligent Systems (HIS) Conf*, pages 411–416, 2011.

[50] Y. Yu, Z. Li, L. Shi, E. Y.-C. Chen, and H. Xu. Cross-layer optimization for state update in mobile gaming. 10(5):701–710, 2008.

Game AI Revisited

Georgios N. Yannakakis
Center for Computer Games Research
IT University of Copenhagen
Rued Langgaards Vej 7
Copenhagen, Denmark
yannakakis@itu.dk

ABSTRACT

More than a decade after the early research efforts on the use of artificial intelligence (AI) in computer games and the establishment of a new AI domain the term "game AI" needs to be redefined. Traditionally, the tasks associated with game AI revolved around non player character (NPC) behavior at different levels of control, varying from navigation and pathfinding to decision making. Commercial-standard games developed over the last 15 years and current game productions, however, suggest that the traditional challenges of game AI have been well addressed via the use of sophisticated AI approaches, not necessarily following or inspired by advances in academic practices. The marginal penetration of traditional academic game AI methods in industrial productions has been mainly due to the lack of constructive communication between academia and industry in the early days of academic game AI, and the inability of academic game AI to propose methods that would significantly advance existing development processes or provide scalable solutions to real world problems. Recently, however, there has been a shift of research focus as the current plethora of AI uses in games is breaking the non-player character AI tradition. A number of those alternative AI uses have already shown a significant potential for the design of better games.

This paper presents four key game AI research areas that are currently reshaping the research roadmap in the game AI field and evidently put the game AI term under a new perspective. These game AI flagship research areas include the computational modeling of player experience, the procedural generation of content, the mining of player data on massive-scale and the alternative AI research foci for enhancing NPC capabilities.

Categories and Subject Descriptors

I.2.1 [**Artificial Intelligence**]: Applications and Expert Systems—*Games*; H.1.2 [**Models and Principles**]: User — Machine Systems—*Human factors*

Keywords

Game artificial intelligence, player experience modeling, procedural content generation, game data mining, game AI flagships

1. INTRODUCTION

Almost 30 years after the first reported video game conference at Harvard [33] and 12 years after Laird's and van Lent's seminal article [26] that, in part, established the foundations of game artificial intelligence (AI) and inspired early work in the field [34, 22, 25, 14, 3, 30, 58] the game AI term needs to be revisited and restructured.

Since those first days of academic game AI the term was mainly linked to non player character (NPC) behavior (i.e. NPC AI) and pathfinding [8] as most of the early work in that field was conducted by researchers with AI, optimization and control background and research experience in adaptive behavior, robotics and multi-agent systems[1]. AI academics used the best of their computational intelligence and AI tools to enhance NPC behavior in generally simple, research-focused, non-scalable projects of low commercial value and perspective. In almost every occasion the two (academic and industrial game AI), rather immature, communities would meet they would conclude about the gap existent between them and the need of bridging it for their mutual benefit [8]. The key message of academic AI has been that industry does not attempt to use sophisticated AI techniques with high potential (e.g. neural networks) in their games. On the other end, the central complaint of industrial game AI has been the lack of domain-knowledge and practical wisdom when it comes to realistic problems and challenges faced during game production.

While the vast majority of AI academics (including the author) would claim that games are fully scripted and still use 30-year old AI technology — such as A* and finite state machines — the game industry had been making small, yet important, steps towards integrating nouvelle (or modern) AI [8] in their games [55] during the early days of game AI. A non-inclusive list of games that advanced the game AI state-of-practice in industry [42] includes the advanced sensory system of guards in *Thief* (EIDOS, 1989); the advanced opponent tactics in *Half-Life* (Valve, 1998); the fusion of ma-

---

[1]Note that this paper deliberately excludes research in board game AI as — in contrast to the breadth and multifaced nature of AI research challenges met in game development — advances in that field can only be algorithmic with respect to a particular aim (i.e. learn to play a board game) in constrained board game spaces.

chine learning techniques such as perceptrons, decision trees and reinforcement learning coupled with the belief-desire-intention cognitive model in *Black and White* (EA, 2000); the dynamic difficulty adjustment (DDA) features in the *Halo* series (MS Game Studios); the imitation learning *Drivatar* system of *Forza Motorsport* (MS Game Studios, 2005); the AI director of *Left 4 Dead* (Valve, 2008)[2] and the neuroevolutionary training of platoons in *Supreme Commander 2* (Square Enix, 2010).

The key criterion that distinguishes a successful AI in commercial-standard games had always been the level of integration and interweaving of AI in the design of the game [42]. While an unsuccessful coupling of game design and AI may lead to unjustifiable NPC behaviors, break the suspension of disbelief and immediately reduce player incorporation [6], the successful integration of AI in the design process in games such as *Façade* [31] or *Kinectimals* (MS Game Studios, 2010) may absorb potential "catastrophic" failures or limitations of the AI.

The level of AI sophistication in recent games such as *Left 4 Dead* (Valve, 2008) and *The Elder Scrolls V: Skyrim* (Bethesda Softworks, 2011) suggests that advances in NPC AI have converged to highly satisfactory solutions for most NPC control challenges faced during game production. Moreover, a number of game developers (and some game AI academics) have already taken sides arguing that NPC AI is almost solved [7, 35] for most production tasks while some claim that game AI research and development should focus on non-traditional uses of AI [35, 45]. Such indications suggest that further marginal enhancements of NPC AI may require significant effort and cost.

Due to the rise of robust and effective industrial game AI solutions, more frequent and constructive communication with the industry, the convergence to satisfying NPC performances, the support of the multidisciplinary nature of game AI and a more pragmatic and holistic view of the game AI problem, recent years have seen a shift of academic interests with respect to game AI. We have reached an era where the catholic focus of the application of AI in the domain of games is not on agents and NPC behaviors. The focus has, instead, started to shift towards interweaving game design and game technology by viewing the role of AI holistically: AI can help us to make better games but that does not *necessarily* imply better, more human-like or believable NPCs.

There are a number of key research areas, which I name *game AI flagships*, that have recently provided innovative, yet commercially-plausible solutions for a number of game development challenges. Those areas of common (academic and industrial) interest appear to both synthesize the framework of current and future academic research and already influence high-end commercial game technology. It is expected that a focus on these game AI areas (beyond NPC control) will most likely yield a larger impact on the making of better games via the use of AI. Player Experience Modeling (PEM), Procedural Content Generation (PCG), Large-Scale Game Data Mining and new perspectives in NPC AI are the four main game AI flagships considered in this paper. The list provided in this paper is, by no means, inclusive of all high-end potential game AI areas but it is representa-tive of spotlight current research efforts and development advances.

2. THE FLAGSHIPS OF GAME AI

In this section the emerging, non-traditional, flagship research areas of game AI are presented, corresponding successful examples are provided for each flagship, and arguments are listed for their inclusion as key game AI research and development areas.

2.1 Player Experience Modeling

Recent years have seen both a boost in the size of the gaming population and a demographic diversification of computer game players [23]. This, in turn, means that skills, preferences and experience differ widely among players of the same game. Therefore, the need for tailoring games to individual playing experiences is growing and the tasks of user modeling and experience-based adaptation within games become increasingly important and challenging. Game engines that are able to recognize and model the playing style and detect the current emotional and cognitive state of the user will be necessary milestones towards the personalization of the playing experience.

Player experience modeling (PEM) is the study and use of AI techniques for the construction of computational models of experience of players. PEM places an AI umbrella to the multidisciplinary intersection of the fields of user (player) modeling, affective computing, experimental psychology and human-computer interaction. Player experience, player satisfaction and their modeling have recently seen a growing number of dedicated workshops, special sessions and invited talks in top academic venues including the IEEE Conference on Computational Intelligence and Games (IEEE-CIG)[3], the Foundations of Digital Games (FDG)[4] and the Artificial Intelligence and Interactive Digital Entertainment (AIIDE) conference[5] and special issues to journals such as the IEEE Transactions of Computational Intelligence and AI in Games and IEEE Transactions on Affective Computing. In addition, top game developers (such as Valve) have recently started to experiment with multiple modalities of user input (e.g. physiology) for the personalization of experience in popular games such as *Left 4 Dead* (Valve, 2008) [1].

2.1.1 General PEM Principles

A model of player experience predicts some aspect of the experience of a player in general, a type of player, or a particular player would have in some game situation. There are many ways this can be achieved, with approaches to PEM varying both regarding the inputs (from what the experience is predicted, e.g. physiology, level design parameters, playing style or game speed), outputs (what sort of experience is predicted, e.g. fun, frustration, attention or immersion) and the modeling methodology.

Computational models of player experience can be built on different types of data collected from the players which in turn define different approaches to player experience modeling (PEM). We can identify three main classes of approaches for modeling player experience in games which rely on (1) data expressed by players (*subjective* PEM); (2) player data

---

[2]The success of the AI director and its positive impact to player experience has influenced game AI architectures in a number of other game productions including *Resistance 3* (Insomniac Games, 2011).

[3]www.ieee-cig.org/
[4]www.foundationsofdigitalgames.org/
[5]http://www.aiide.org/

obtained from alternative modalities of player response (*objective* PEM); and (3) contextual and behavioral data obtained through the interaction between the player and the game (*gameplay-based* PEM). Data from multiple modalities and types can be fused to better predict annotated player experience states.

If data recorded includes a scalar representation of experience, or classes and annotated labels of user (cognitive and affective) states any of a large number of machine learning (regression and classification) algorithms can be used to build models of experience. Available methods include neural networks, Bayesian networks, decision trees, support vector machines and standard linear regression. On the other hand, if experience is annotated in a ranking format (e.g. game version X is more frustrating than game version Y) standard supervised learning techniques are inapplicable, as the problem becomes one of *preference learning* [15, 57]. In particular, neuro-evolutionary preference learning has proven suitable for this task; in this method, the weights of neural networks are evolved to minimize the error between reported and predicted preferences [63, 57].

The following subsections provide further details about each of the three PEM approaches and corresponding successful examples of each approach. The section ends with a discussion on the potential of personalization of both the experience and the player experience model.

2.1.2 Subjective PEM

The most direct way to develop a model of experience is to ask the players themselves about their playing experience and build a model based on such data. Subjective PEM considers first person reports (self-reports). Reports expressed indirectly by experts or external observers can potentially provide reliable player experience annotations; however, third-person assessment is not covered in this paper. Subjective player experience modeling can be based on either players' *free-response* during play or on *forced* data retrieved through questionnaires. Forced self-reports can be further classified as *ratings*, in which the players are asked to answer questionnaire items given in a Likert scale or *rankings*, in which players are asked to compare their player experience in two or more sessions of the game [60, 57, 51]. A recent study has exposed the limitations of rating approaches over ranking questionnaire schemes (e.g. pairwise preference) including increased order of play and inconsistency effects [56].

While self-reports have inherent limitations including user self-deception, memory-dependencies and ordering effects numerous studies have shown that ranked self-reporting can successfully guide machine learning algorithms to capture aspects of player experience in prey/predator [59], physical interactive [61], platform [41, 40] and racing [51] games.

2.1.3 Objective PEM

Player experience can be linked to a stream of emotions, which may be active simultaneously, usually triggered by events occurring during gameplay. Games can elicit player emotional responses which in turn may affect changes in the player's physiology [64, 51], reflect on the player's facial expression [39, 24], posture and speech, and alter the player's attention and focus level [2]. Monitoring such bodily alterations may assist in recognizing and synthesizing the emotional responses of the player. The *objective* approach to player experience modeling incorporates access to multiple modalities of player input for the purpose of modeling the affective state of the player during play.

Models built via the objective PEM approach may be very accurate representations of player experience since player experience is approached in a holistic manner via the use of multiple input modalities. The key limitations of the objective PEM approach include its high intrusiveness and questionable feasibility. Most modalities are still nowadays not technically plausible within commercial computer games. For instance, existing hardware for physiology requires the placement of body parts (e.g. head, chest or fingertips) to the sensors making physiological signals such as EEG, respiration, blood volume pulse and skin conductance rather impractical and highly intrusive for most games. However, recent advances on biofeedback sensor technology have resulted in low-cost, unobtrusive biofeedback devices (bracelet sensors) appropriate for gaming applications[6].

Pupillometry and gaze tracking are very sensitive to distance from screen and variations in light and screen luminance, which makes them rather impractical for use in a game application. Modalities such as facial expression and speech could be technically plausible in games even though the majority of the vision-based affect-detection systems currently available cannot operate in real-time [67]. At the positive end of the spectrum, Microsoft's XBox 360 Kinect[7] sensor device is pointing towards more natural game interaction and showcases a promising future of objective PEM.

2.1.4 Gameplay-based PEM

The main assumption that drives *gameplay-based* PEM is that player actions and real-time preferences are linked to player experience since games may affect the player's cognitive processing patterns and cognitive focus. On the same basis, cognitive processes may influence emotions as one may infer the player's emotional state by analyzing patterns of the interaction and associating user emotions with context variables. Any element derived from the interaction between the player and the game forms the basis for gameplay-based PEM. This includes parameters from the player's behavior derived from responses to system elements.

The inputs to a gameplay-based player experience model are statistical spatio-temporal features of game interaction. Those features are usually mapped to levels of cognitive states such as attention, challenge and engagement [11]. General measures such as performance and time spent on a task have been used in the literature, but also game-specific measures such as the weapons selected in a shooter game [18]. Moreover, several dissimilar difficulty and challenge measures (see [21, 37, 52] among many) have been proposed for different game genres. In all of these studies, difficulty adjustment is performed, based on a player experience model that implies a direct link between challenge and player satisfaction. Sometimes a player model [62, 20, 10] is embedded in the process of PEM. Data mining attempts to predict player actions and intentions as well as to identify different playing patterns within a game [12, 53] can also be viewed as gameplay-based PEM. Game data mining is covered in Section 2.3 in further detail as it is considered a game AI flagship on its own.

---

[6]http://www.emoticalab.com/
[7]http://www.xbox.com/kinect/

Gameplay-based PEM is arguably the most computationally efficient and least intrusive PEM approach but it usually results in a low-resolution model of playing experience.

2.1.5 Personalizing PEM

AI methodology can be used not only to construct a computational model of player experience but to also tailor the player experience model itself to the player's individual preferences during the interaction. An example of this promising direction within PEM research is the work of Liapis et al. [28] where computational models of player aesthetics are tailored to the player's selections and are further used for the design of personalized spaceships with respect to player aesthetics (see Fig. 2).

2.2 Procedural Content Generation

Procedural content generation (PCG) can be viewed as the study and development of algorithms that generate content automatically. *Game content* refers to all adjustable game elements that may affect player experience (excluding NPC behavior) which may include elements such as terrains, maps, levels, stories, quests, rulesets, camera profiles and music. There are several benefits obtained from the automatic creation of content in games [50]: first, PCG can alleviate the enormous effort and cost of content creation and make it easier to tailor content to the player; second, content can automatically adapt the game to the needs and preferences of individual players and yield maximal game replayability; third, PCG can challenge human creativity and generate solutions beyond the designer's imagination in a stand-alone or mixed-initiative design [44, 4] fashion.

Even though PCG techniques have been incorporated in games since *Rogue* (1980) it is only very recently that an academic community is devoted to the study of PCG signaling the shift of interest towards this use of AI in games. That trend is reflected by an IEEE CIS Task Force[8] and a wiki[9] on the topic, a series of dedicated workshops at the FDG conference, an international PCG competition[10] and a special issue on PCG at the IEEE Transactions of Computational Intelligence and AI in Games. The use of PCG for the design of better games has reached a peak of interest in commercial game development which is showcased by successful (almost entirely procedurally generated) games such as *Minecraft* (Mojang, 2011) and *Love* (Eskil Steenberg, 2010) and the broad coverage of PCG topics in relevant conferences (such as the Paris Game AI conference series).

Research efforts that couple the PEM and the PCG flagships has resulted to research projects of high commercial potential under the *experience-driven procedural content generation* (EDPCG) framework [65]. According to the EDPCG framework, content is viewed as a building block of player experience which can be adjusted to optimize the experience of the player (predicted via player experience models). Examples of EDPCG work include the adaptive content creation framework of Shaker et al. [43] where personalized Super Mario Levels are generated for maximizing models of player experience states, such as *fun*, which are built via crowdsourced *fun* reports about mini Super Mario Bros levels (see Fig. 1 for two example levels).

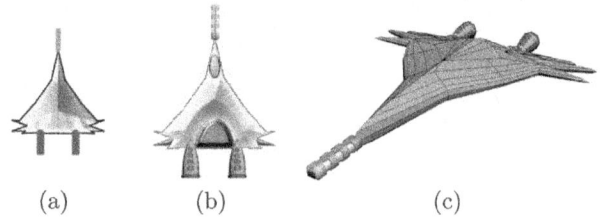

(a)   (b)   (c)

Figure 2: Example spaceship (rendered with three different methods) generated via an EDPCG algorithm. The algorithm both tailors computational user aesthetics models and generates personalized spaceships based on those tailored models.

In addition to Super Mario Bros levels, racing tracks [47], strategy maps [48], game rule sets [5], buildings [29] and weapons [17] (among other types of content) have been generated based on models of player experience. The work of Liapis et al. [27, 28] is indicative of the power of EDPCG for game design as personalized spaceships can rapidly be generated based on player aesthetics models via interactive evolution. Both the models of user aesthetics and the aesthetic attributes of the spaceships are adapted to the preferences of the user/designer yielding personalized spaceship designs such as those presented in Fig. 2.

2.3 Massive-Scale Game Data Mining

Game data mining may be loosely defined as the use of AI (data mining algorithms) for addressing questions such as: *how do people play a game?*; *is the game played as intended?*; *why do people stop playing a game?*; *why do we play a game this way?*; *can we predict what a player will do?*; *does the game offer the right experience?*; *what is the personality of a player?*. All these are critical questions that are tied to user-oriented testing procedures used in the game industry. In iterative-phased game development, representative samples of the target audience as well as internal professional testers spend time and put effort on testing the games and evaluating the quality of the gaming experience.

During the last five years — as an alternative to traditional testing — key game developers (including Zynga, Blizzard, Bioware, Square Enix Europe and EA Games) have been collecting and analyzing detailed and massive-scale player behavioral and contextual data (i.e. game metrics) via specialized monitoring software. As argued by big data analysts we have now reached a point were existing data mining algorithms cannot follow the growth of data availability and the massive size of datasets available and, thereby, cannot fully support the analysis of such data. This poses new exciting challenges and avenues of research for AI in games since the use of AI for inferring playing patterns from data can provide a quantitative approach to and supplement of traditional qualitative approaches of user and playability testing [13].

Even though directly linked to context-based PEM (see Section 2.1), the mining of gameplay data deserves its own game AI flagship as game metrics and game metric analysis is currently a spotlight research and development area within the games industry supported by a growing number of game data analytics companies. Game data mining has seen extensive coverage in game developer meetings such as

---

[8]http://game.itu.dk/pcg/
[9]http://pcg.wikidot.com
[10]http://www.marioai.org

(a) Human

(b) World-Champion AI

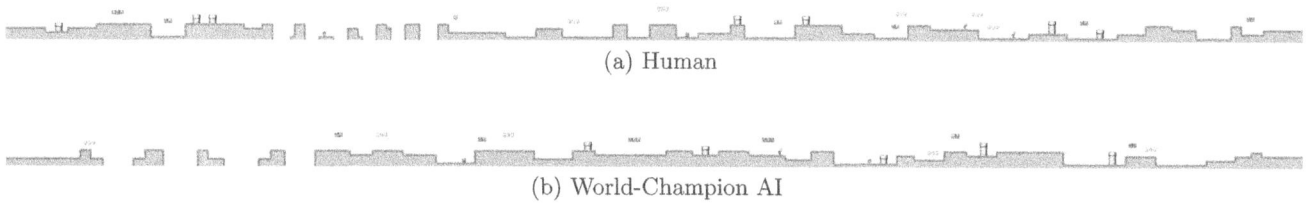

Figure 1: Example levels generated for two different Super Mario players. The levels generated maximize the modeled *fun* value for each player. The level on top depicts the level generated for a human player while the level below is the level generated for the world champion agent of the Mario AI competition.

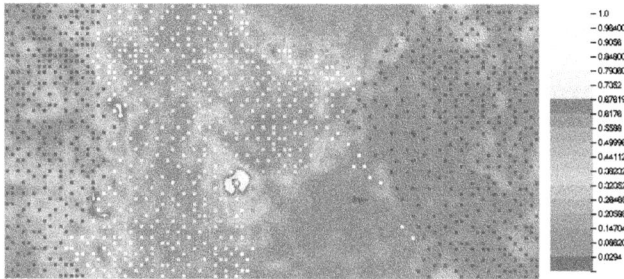

Figure 3: U-matrix visualization of a self-organizing map depicting the 4 player clusters identified in a population of 1365 Tomb Raider: Underworld players (shown as small colored squares). Different square colors depict different player clusters. Valleys represent clusters whereas mountains represent cluster borders.

the game AI summit at GDC[11] and the Paris Game AI Conference[12] as well as dedicated panels, tutorials and special sessions in top game AI academic conferences such as IEEE-CIG and AIIDE.

Among the relatively few studies in the young field of game data mining [13], Yee has analyzed the relationship between player motivations, demographic variables and in-game behaviors of 3000 MMORPG players [66]. Drachen et al. [12] have identified four potential player types in *Tomb Raider: Underworld* using self-organization (see Fig. 3) in direct collaboration with the developer of the game (i.e. Crystal Dynamics). Thurau et al. [46] have applied non-negative-matrix factorization to mine 1.6 million images on World of Warcraft guilds while Mateas and Weber [54] have mined game metrical data for the prediction of player strategies in StarCraft. In addition to empirical player data, alternative analytical apporaches have been proposed for evaluating games and their playability [36].

2.4 NPC AI: Different Perspectives

As AI has already provided satisfactory solutions to most NPC tasks (including navigation and lower levels of NPC control) the focus of research on NPC AI may shift towards under-researched, yet very promising, directions that will enhance NPC capabilities. A different perspective to NPC AI is to view NPC control as a mapping of the NPC's context (environment) and attempt to alter the latter to observe

changes in the perception of the first. So far, the question of whether empirical research efforts should be put more on the agent or its environment (or both) in order for the agent to appear more believable, human-like, or intelligent remains largely unanswered. The ability of the environment — instead of, or in addition to NPC attributes — to absorb non-believable agent behaviors can define new variables for optimization. This raises new research questions such as *how can the design of a game be altered to allow for maximal absorption of AI weaknesses with minimal effort* and *how can constructive or search-based* [50] *content creation processes be coupled with NPC AI control for achieving such a goal.* The issue of assessing NPC believability through contextual content creation and adaptation has already been addressed by a recent study on the believability of Super Mario Bros players [49]. In addition, game Turing test competitions such as those in Super Mario Bros[13] and in *Unreal Tournament* (Epic Games, 1999) [19] define attempts on further exploring the unknown mapping between NPC agent behavior, game context and NPC believability.

Beyond standard single NPC control, a promising trend on NPC AI research — which already has an impact on recent game productions — appears to be the generation and detection of patterns of complex social behavior and interaction among NPCs and humans [68, 38] with a focus on cognitive/affective agent architectures for social games such as the *Prom Week* game [32]. In addition, data-driven modeling of groups of NPCs and players via group structure identification [16] can offer a complementary perspective towards well-grounded human behavior models [9] that can guide personalization in social games.

3. CONCLUSIONS

More than ten years after the establishment of the game AI field the term needs to be revisited and enhanced with non-traditional research and development areas beyond NPC control. The plethora of ways AI is currently used in games, beyond traditional areas such as NPC AI, showcases the potential and impact of a broader conception of the research field, and can enlarge the boundaries of design within these creative industries.

This paper listed a number of flagship areas that are currently at the spotlight of game AI state-of-the-art research and commercial-standard development. Methods for modeling player experience, algorithms and processes for generating content of high value automatically, approaches for mining massive-scale data of players and alternate perspec-

---

[11]http://www.gdconf.com/
[12]http://gameaiconf.com/

[13]http://www.marioai.org/turing-test-track

tives on NPC AI research define the framework of the four key game AI areas presented.

The list of flagships is not inclusive of all potential core uses of AI in the years to follow. In addition to the game AI flagships discussed in this paper the current trends of pervasiveness, embedded systems and natural interaction in design have already seen their integration in gaming contexts (e.g. the Primesense camera-based sensor). Thus, natural and multimodal interaction for player behavioral and movement pattern analysis arguably define core AI domains in the near future at the crossroad of the game data mining and the player experience modeling flagships. Finally, at the crossroads of procedural content generation and player experience modeling, substantial effort is expected on the development of sophisticated AI techniques for meaningful story generation and the design of personalized authoring tools.

4. ACKNOWLEDGMENTS

The research was supported, in part, by the FP7 ICT project SIREN (project no: 258453) and by the Danish Research Agency, Ministry of Science, Technology and Innovation project AGameComIn; project number: 274-09-0083. Thanks to Mark J. Nelson and Julian Togelius for comments and pointers.

5. REFERENCES

[1] M. Ambinder. Biofeedback in Gameplay: How Valve Measures Physiology to Enhance Gaming Experience. In *Game Developers Conference*, 2011.

[2] S. Asteriadis, K. Karpouzis, and S. D. Kollias. A neuro-fuzzy approach to user attention recognition. In *Proceedings of ICANN*, pages 927–936. Springer, 2008.

[3] C. Bauckhage, C. Thurau, and G. Sagerer. Learning human-like opponent behavior for interactive computer games. *Pattern Recognition, Lecture Notes in Computer Science 2781*, pages 148–155, 2003.

[4] R. Bidarra, K. de Kraker, R. Smelik, and T. Tutenel. Integrating semantics and procedural generation: key enabling factors for declarative modeling of virtual worlds. In *Proceedings of the FOCUS K3D Conference on Semantic 3D Media and Content, France (February 2010)*, 2010.

[5] C. Browne. *Automatic generation and evaluation of recombination games*. PhD thesis, Queensland University of Technology, 2008.

[6] G. Calleja. *In-Game: From Immersion to Incorporation*. The MIT Press, 2011.

[7] A. Champandard. Tutorial presentation. In *IEEE Conference on Computational Intelligence and Games*, 2012.

[8] A. J. Champandard. *AI Game Development*. New Riders Publishing, 2004.

[9] Y. Chang, T. Levinboim, V. Rajan, and R. Maheswaran. Learning and Evaluating Human-Like NPC Behaviors in Dynamic Games. In *Artificial Intelligence and Interactive Digital Entertainment (AIIDE)*, 2011.

[10] D. Charles and M. Black. Dynamic player modelling: A framework for player-centric digital games. In *Proceedings of the International Conference on*

[11] C. Conati. Probabilistic Assessment of User's Emotions in Educational Games. *Journal of Applied Artificial Intelligence, special issue on "Merging Cognition and Affect in HCI"*, 16:555–575, 2002.

[12] A. Drachen, A. Canossa, and G. N. Yannakakis. Player Modeling using Self-Organization in Tomb Raider: Underworld. In *Proceedings of the IEEE Symposium on Computational Intelligence and Games*, pages 1–8, Milan, Italy, September 2009. IEEE.

[13] A. Drachen, C. Thurau, J. Togelius, and G. N. Yannakakis. *Game Telemetry and Metrics*, chapter Large-scale Data Mining in Games. Springer-Verlag, 2012.

[14] M. Freed, T. Bear, H. Goldman, G. Hyatt, P. Reber, A. Sylvan, and J. Tauber. Towards more human-like computer opponents. In *Working Notes of the AAAI Spring Symposium on Artificial Intelligence and Interactive Entertainment*, pages 22–26, 2000.

[15] J. Fürnkranz and E. Hüllermeier. Preference learning. *Künstliche Intelligenz*, 19(1):60–61, 2005.

[16] C. Grappiolo, Y. G. Cheong, R. Khaled, and G. N. Yannakakis. Modelling Global Pattern Formations for Collaborative Learning Environments. In *Proceedings of the 12th IEEE International Conference on Advanced Learning Technologies*.

[17] E. Hastings, R. Guha, and K. Stanley. Automatic content generation in the galactic arms race video game. *Computational Intelligence and AI in Games, IEEE Transactions on*, 1(4):245–263, 2009.

[18] E. Hastings, R. Guha, and K. O. Stanley. Evolving content in the galactic arms race video game. In *Proceedings of the IEEE Symposium on Computational Intelligence and Games*, pages 241–248, 2009.

[19] P. Hingston. A Turing Test for Computer Game Bots. *IEEE Transactions on Computational Intelligence and AI in Games*, 1, 2009.

[20] R. Houlette. *Player Modeling for Adaptive Games. AI Game Programming Wisdom II*, pages 557–566. Charles River Media, Inc, 2004.

[21] H. Iida, N. Takeshita, and J. Yoshimura. A metric for entertainment of boardgames: its implication for evolution of chess variants. In R. Nakatsu and J. Hoshino, editors, *IWEC2002 Proceedings*, pages 65–72. Kluwer, 2003.

[22] D. Isla and B. Blumberg. New challenges for character-based AI for games. In *Proccedings of the AAAI Spring Symposium on AI and Interactive Entertainment*, pages 41–45. AAAI Press, 2002.

[23] J. Juul. *A Casual Revolution: Reinventing Video Games and Their Players*. MIT Press, 2009.

[24] L. Kessous, G. Castellano, and G. Caridakis. Multimodal emotion recognition in speech-based interaction using facial expression, body gesture and acoustic analysis. *Journal on Multimodal User Interfaces*, 3:33–48, 2010.

[25] J. E. Laird. Research in human-level AI using computer games. *Communications of the ACM*, 3(8):32–35, 2002.

[26] J. E. Laird and M. van Lent. Human-level AI's killer

Computer Games: Artificial Intelligence, Design and Education, pages 29–35, 2004.

application: Interactive computer games. In *Proceedings of the Seventh National Conference on Artificial Intelligence (AAAI)*, pages 1171–1178, 2000.

[27] A. Liapis, G. N. Yannakakis, and J. Togelius. Optimizing Visual Properties of Game Content Through Neuroevolution. In *Artificial Intelligence for Interactive Digital Entertainment Conference*, 2011.

[28] A. Liapis, G. N. Yannakakis, and J. Togelius. Adapting Models of Visual Aesthetics for Personalized Content Creation. *IEEE Transactions on Computational Intelligence and AI in Games, Special Issue on Computational Aesthetics in Games*, 2012. (to appear).

[29] A. Martin, A. Lim, S. Colton, and C. Browne. Evolving 3D buildings for the prototype video game subversion. *Applications of Evolutionary Computation*, pages 111–120, 2010.

[30] M. Mateas. Expressive ai: Games and artificial intelligence. In *Level Up: Digital Games Research Conference*.

[31] M. Mateas and A. Stern. Façade: An experiment in building a fully-realized interactive drama. In *Game Developers Conference Game Design track*, volume 2, 2003.

[32] J. McCoy, M. Treanor, B. Samuel, A. Reed, M. Mateas, and N. Wardrip-Fruin. Prom Week. In *Foundations of Digital Games*, 2012.

[33] E. Mitchell. Video games visit harvard yard. *Antic*, 2:24, 1983.

[34] A. Nareyek. Intelligent agents for computer games. In T. Marsland and I. Frank, editors, *Computers and Games, Second International Conference, CG 2002*, pages 414–422, 2002.

[35] A. Nareyek. Game AI is dead. Long live game AI! *IEEE Intelligent Systems*, 22(1):9–11, 2007.

[36] M. J. Nelson. Game metrics without players: Strategies for understanding game artifacts. In *Proceedings of the 2011 AIIDE Workshop on Artificial Intelligence in the Game Design Process*, pages 14–18, 2011.

[37] J. K. Olesen, G. N. Yannakakis, and J. Hallam. Real-time challenge balance in an RTS game using rtNEAT. In *Proceedings of the IEEE Symposium on Computational Intelligence and Games*, pages 87–94, Perth, Australia, December 2008. IEEE.

[38] J. Orkin, T. Smith, and D. Roy. Behavior compilation for ai in games. In *Proceedings of the Sixth Artificial Intelligence and Interactive Digital Entertainment Conference (AIIDE)*, pages 162–167, 2010.

[39] M. Pantic and G. Caridakis. *Emotion-Oriented Systems: The Humaine Handbook*, chapter Image and Video Processing for Affective Applications, pages 101–117. Springer-Verlag Berlin Heidelberg, 2011.

[40] C. Pedersen, J. Togelius, and G. N. Yannakakis. Modeling Player Experience in Super Mario Bros. In *Proceedings of the IEEE Symposium on Computational Intelligence and Games*, pages 132–139, Milan, Italy, September 2009. IEEE.

[41] C. Pedersen, J. Togelius, and G. N. Yannakakis. Modeling Player Experience for Content Creation. *IEEE Transactions on Computational Intelligence and AI in Games*, 2(1):54–67, 2010.

[42] S. Rabin. *AI Game Programming Wisdom*. Charles River Media, Inc, 2002.

[43] N. Shaker, G. Yannakakis, and J. Togelius. Towards automatic personalized content generation for platform games. In *Proceedings of the AAAI Conference on Artificial Intelligence and Interactive Digital Entertainment (AIIDE). AAAI Press*, 2010.

[44] G. Smith, J. Whitehead, and M. Mateas. Tanagra: Reactive Planning and Constraint Solving for Mixed-Initiative Level Design. *Computational Intelligence and AI in Games, IEEE Transactions on*, (99):1–1, 2011.

[45] B. Sunshine-Hill, M. Robbins, and C. Jurney. Off the Beaten Path: Non-Traditional Uses of AI. In *Game Developers Conference, AI Summit*, 2012.

[46] C. Thurau, K. Kersting, and C. Bauckhage. Convex non-negative matrix factorization in the wild. In *Proceedings of the 9th IEEE International Conference on Data Mining (ICDMâĂŞ09)*, Miami, FL, USA, December 2009.

[47] J. Togelius, R. De Nardi, and S. Lucas. Towards automatic personalised content creation for racing games. In *Computational Intelligence and Games, 2007. CIG 2007. IEEE Symposium on*, pages 252–259. IEEE, 2007.

[48] J. Togelius, M. Preuss, N. Beume, S. Wessing, J. Hagelback, and G. Yannakakis. Multiobjective exploration of the starcraft map space. In *Computational Intelligence and Games (CIG), 2010 IEEE Symposium on*, pages 265–272. IEEE, 2010.

[49] J. Togelius, G. Yannakakis, S. Karakovskiy, and N. Shaker. *Believability in Computer Games*, chapter Assessing Believability. Springer-Verlag, 2012.

[50] J. Togelius, G. Yannakakis, K. Stanley, and C. Browne. Search-based Procedural Content Generation: A Taxonomy and Survey. *Computational Intelligence and AI in Games, IEEE Transactions on*, (99):1–1, 2011.

[51] S. Tognetti, M. Garbarino, A. Bonarini, and M. Matteucci. Modeling enjoyment preference from physiological responses in a car racing game. In *Proceedings of the IEEE Conference on Computational Intelligence and Games*, pages 321–328, Copenhagen, Denmark, 18–21 August 2010.

[52] G. van Lankveld, P. Spronck, and M. Rauterberg. Difficulty Scaling through Incongruity. In *Proceedings of the 4th International Artificial Intelligence and Interactive Digital Entertainment Conference*, pages 228–229. AAAI Press, 2008.

[53] B. Weber and M. Mateas. A Data Mining Approach to Strategy Prediction. In *IEEE Symposium on Computational Intelligence in Games (CIG 2009)*, pages 140–147, Milan, Italy, September 2009.

[54] B. Weber and M. Mateas. A Data Mining Approach to Strategy Prediction. In *Proceedings of the IEEE Symposium on Computational Intelligence in Games*, pages 140–147, Milan, Italy, September 2009. IEEE.

[55] S. Woodcock. Game AI: The State of the Industry 2000-2001: It's not Just Art, It's Engineering. August 2001.

[56] G. Yannakakis and J. Hallam. Rating vs. Preference: a comparative study of self-reporting. *Affective*

Computing and Intelligent Interaction, pages 437–446, 2011.

[57] G. N. Yannakakis. Preference Learning for Affective Modeling. In *Proceedings of the Int. Conf. on Affective Computing and Intelligent Interaction*, pages 126–131, Amsterdam, The Netherlands, September 2009. IEEE.

[58] G. N. Yannakakis and J. Hallam. Evolving Opponents for Interesting Interactive Computer Games. In S. Schaal, A. Ijspeert, A. Billard, S. Vijayakumar, J. Hallam, and J.-A. Meyer, editors, *From Animals to Animats 8: Proceedings of the 8th International Conference on Simulation of Adaptive Behavior (SAB-04)*, pages 499–508, Santa Monica, LA, CA, July 2004. The MIT Press.

[59] G. N. Yannakakis and J. Hallam. Towards Capturing and Enhancing Entertainment in Computer Games. In *Proceedings of the 4th Hellenic Conference on Artificial Intelligence, Lecture Notes in Artificial Intelligence*, volume 3955, pages 432–442, Heraklion, Greece, May 2006. Springer-Verlag.

[60] G. N. Yannakakis and J. Hallam. Towards Optimizing Entertainment in Computer Games. *Applied Artificial Intelligence*, 21:933–971, 2007.

[61] G. N. Yannakakis and J. Hallam. Real-time Game Adaptation for Optimizing Player Satisfaction. *IEEE Transactions on Computational Intelligence and AI in Games*, 1(2):121–133, June 2009.

[62] G. N. Yannakakis and M. Maragoudakis. Player modeling impact on player's entertainment in computer games. In *Proceedings of the 10th International Conference on User Modeling; Lecture Notes in Computer Science*, volume 3538, pages 74–78, Edinburgh, 24–30 July 2005. Springer-Verlag.

[63] G. N. Yannakakis, M. Maragoudakis, and J. Hallam. Preference Learning for Cognitive Modeling: A Case Study on Entertainment Preferences. *IEEE Systems, Man and Cybernetics; Part A: Systems and Humans*, 39(6):1165–1175, November 2009.

[64] G. N. Yannakakis, H. P. Martínez, and A. Jhala. Towards Affective Camera Control in Games. *User Modeling and User-Adapted Interaction*, 20(4):313–340, 2010.

[65] G. N. Yannakakis and J. Togelius. Experience-Driven Procedural Content Generation. *IEEE Transactions on Affective Computing*, 2:147–161, 2011.

[66] N. Yee. Motivations for play in online games. *CyberPsychology & Behavior*, 9(6):772–775, 2006.

[67] Z. Zeng, M. Pantic, G. Roisman, and T. Huang. A survey of affect recognition methods: Audio, visual, and spontaneous expressions. *IEEE Trans. Pattern Analysis and Machine Intelligence*, 31(1):39–58, 2009.

[68] R. Zubek and M. Lewis. Managing the Masses: Crafting AI for Online Games. In *Game Developers Conference, AI Summit*, 2012.

Towards More Intelligent Adaptive Video Game Agents:
A Computational Intelligence Perspective

Simon M. Lucas
University of Essex
Wivenhoe Park
Colchester CO4 3SQ
00 44 1206 872048

sml@essex.ac.uk

Philipp Rohlfshagen
University of Essex
Wivenhoe Park
Colchester CO4 3SQ
00 44 1206 874444

prohlf@essex.ac.uk

Diego Perez
University of Essex
Wivenhoe Park
Colchester CO4 3SQ
00 44 1206 874444

dperez@essex.ac.uk

ABSTRACT

This paper provides a computational intelligence perspective on the design of intelligent video game agents. The paper explains why this is an interesting area to research, and outlines the most promising approaches to date, including evolution, temporal difference learning and Monte Carlo Tree Search. Strengths and weaknesses of each approach are identified, and some research directions are outlined that may soon lead to significantly improved video game agents with lower development costs.

Categories and Subject Descriptors

A.1.2 [Artificial Intelligence]: *Applications and expert systems – games.* G.3 [Probability and Statistics]: *Probabilistic algorithms, including Monte Carlo.* I.2.6 [Learning]: *Connectionism and neural nets, Parameter learning.*

General Terms

Algorithms, Performance, Design, Experimentation.

Keywords

Games, Artificial Intelligence, Computational Intelligence, Monte Carlo Tree Search, Evolutionary Algorithms, Temporal Difference Learning.

1. INTRODUCTION

This paper describes a promising approach towards building intelligent adaptive video game agents. The aim is to design an architecture that can be used to provide a variety of intelligent capabilities across a range of games, with a minimum of human design input required for achieving acceptable performance on each individual game. The computational intelligence (CI) approach involves a minimum of game-specific programming. Instead, the main idea behind CI methods is that the intelligence emerges from the statistics of many simple low-level interactions, whether these be activations in a neural network, hypothetical actions explored in Monte Carlo Tree Search, or parameters adjusted to optimize a reward signal while performing Temporal Difference Learning.

To give a human-oriented perspective on the type of intelligence we are aiming for, imagine the task of learning to play a video game to a reasonable standard without any prior knowledge of the game and without explicitly knowing the rules. This is the task typically faced by human players of video games, exemplified by the classic arcade games of the 1980's. With this long-term aim in mind, we also have a significantly simpler version of the problem where the agent has access to the complete game state and the forward model, and hence is able to construct and search game trees using the forward model. This is something that a human player does not have access to, but can be used to significantly simplify the problem of generating intelligent adaptive game agents. Part of being an expert human player may involve constructing an approximate forward model, but this in itself is a major challenge.

There are a number of good reasons for investigating more adaptive game agent AI, including the following:

- Self-learning or adaptive agents are one of the long-term grand challenges of AI, and games provide an excellent test bed on which to evaluate such agents. In addition to providing challenges of wide-ranging complexity, games also enable humans to interact with AI agents in many of these scenarios.

- Incorporating intelligent agents into games could provide players with a more immersive experience, with the spine-tingling feeling of competing against intelligent beings, whether they display human-like intelligence or some strange alien type of intelligence; the commercial opportunities are immense.

- Provision of reasonable-performance intelligent agents with no (or minimal) programming effort is useful in the design, evaluation and testing of procedurally generated game content, such as game-levels, weapons and vehicles.

Regarding the latter point, a recent review of procedural content generation for games can be found in [1]. The idea of using the ability of agents to learn to play a game was explored by Togelius and Schmidhuber [19]. More recently, Tozour[1] has been evolving scripted agents to aid in the design process of a robot tower defence game. Clearly, there is much potential for using automatically designed agents in this way, and as the agents become smarter so the potential for exploitation will increase.

---

[1] http://aigamedev.com/open/interview/evolution-in-cityconquest/

Given that this is a useful and interesting endeavor, the question arises of the best way to create such adaptive agents. Although no one has yet done this, many of the enabling technologies are becoming increasingly mature. This paper presents a perspective on which are the essential and desirable techniques, and how they can be used in conjunction with each other.

2. TECHNIQUES

This section describes the main computational intelligence techniques which have an important role to play in the construction of adaptive game agents, together with discussion of their strengths and weaknesses.

2.1 Evolutionary Algorithms

Evolutionary algorithms (EA) are one of the most popular approaches for adapting an agent to perform well on a problem, and they are one of the easiest to deploy. Unfortunately, it is also very easy to get poor or mediocre results with an EA, and a great deal depends on the choice of representation, and other details. The process is as follows:

1. Design a representation.
2. Design a fitness function.
3. Choose an evolutionary algorithm.
4. Run the algorithm and save a selection of the best or most interesting evolved agents.

Although this can indeed be very simple, there is ample opportunity for expertise and innovation in the above steps, especially in steps 1 and 2. For step 3, Covariance Matrix Adaptation Evolutionary Strategy (CMA-ES) [8] is a good default choice if the adaptive elements of the agent can be coded as a vector of real numbers, which is the case when evolving game agents based on neural networks and many other agent architectures where some real-valued parameters control aspects of an agent's behavior.

Note that the above process focuses on using an EA rather than on designing one, which is why there is no mention of the variation operators (e.g. mutation and crossover). When using an algorithm such as CMA-ES, those details are the responsibility of the algorithm.

There is a good deal of skill in designing an appropriate representation, and one should be aware of the limitations of EAs and what can realistically be achieved within a given number of fitness evaluations. One of the simplest problems for an EA is the standard one-max problem: the aim is to evolve a bit string of length B consisting entirely of ones, where the fitness is given as the number of ones in the string. EAs solve this problem for a bit string of length B in an expected $B\ log\_2(B)$ number of fitness evaluations, learning B bits of information in the process. When co-evolving agents, however, it is common to evaluate a population of N players by playing a full round-robin league of (approximately) N-squared games. If single parent selection is used, the identity of the winning player can be coded in $log\_2(N)$ bits, which places an upper bound on the information gained from that number of games. In practice it is hard to get close to this upper bound [11] even for simple games. Furthermore, evolution is sensitive to the representation used. For example, [10] found evolution to perform relatively well when evolving multi-layer perceptrons, but extremely poorly when evolving interpolated table functions, due to epistasis in the representation.

General discussion of using evolutionary algorithms in conjunction with games can be found in [13],[12].

2.1.1 Evolution versus Coevolution

For single-player games evolution can be used directly to evolve agents, using the game score as a fitness function. By single-player games we include games that involve any number of non-adaptive or generally "not very smart" opponents, such as the enemies in Super Mario or the ghosts in the original version of Ms Pac-Man. In the latter case the ghosts do chase the player while exhibiting some non-determinism (so learning a fixed route for example is ineffective), but some reasonably effective strategies can be learned without even using game-tree search.

However, for evenly balanced two-player games, including classic board games, coevolution offers a more interesting approach than straight evolution if the aim is to generate strong players without using an existing strong player to compete against. Coevolution has the potential to create strong players where none previously existed, whereas using evolution to evolve strong players would require an existing strong player to play against. If evolution is used to evolve agents against a weak player then the evolutionary process will just do enough to beat the weak player convincingly and then have no incentive to progress any further.

Coevolution solves this problem by using a relative fitness function: fitness is estimated by the playing performance of each player against other players in the current population, and perhaps also against players in a dynamically created "hall of fame" archive created from the best players found during an evolutionary run. In principle coevolution could produce a long-running arms race culminating in players that eventually solve the game at hand. However, there are several reasons why this rarely happens in practice, including:

- Limitations imposed by the chosen representation. For example, if a value function is being evolved as a weighted combination of some simple game features, then there is a limit to how smart this could ever be.

- Intransitivities in the population of game players. This leads to problems in measuring the fitness of an individual agent. An agent may appear very strong with respect to the current population, but actually be the weakest member of the current population when in competition with a different set of players. This problem can only occur when the players of a game exhibit intransitivities. The extent to which intransitivities exist depends not only on the nature of the game, but also on the nature of the players.

- Insufficient number of games to effectively train parameters. This arises when the parameter space is large e.g. an N-Tuple network for playing Othello may have thousands or tens of thousands of weights. To learn good values of these weights could require millions of fitness evaluations, and an even larger number of games played.

- Noisy or inaccurate fitness evaluations caused by games with random elements, or even in games of perfect information where games may be played from many different states in order to gain a more accurate picture of the relative merits of each player.

- The search space induced by the chosen representation may be difficult to search, containing many local optima or neutral plateaus.

Note that only the problem of intransitivities between the agents is unique to co-evolution; the other problems pose an equal threat to non-co-evolutionary EAs.

Interestingly, it is possible to design experiments to test which of these problems is most serious for a given combination of game and player architecture. For example, if intransitivities are suspected as being the main problem in co-evolving a game agent, then the same experimental setup can be used with the exception of replacing the relative (co-evolutionary) fitness measure with one based on playing against a controlled strength agent: a strong agent that is artificially weakened using forced random moves to always match the level of the evolving agents, such that the evolving agents win 50% of games on average. This removes any problems caused by intransitivities; if evolution still fails, then one of the other problems listed above could be to blame.

2.2 Reinforcement Learning (RL)

Although technically EAs could be placed within a broad RL umbrella in the sense that they aim to improve over time with respect to some reward function, in practice there are clear differences in how each approach is normally applied. Classic EAs operate at the population level, and measure "bottom-line" fitness i.e. how well an agent performs on a complete task or set of tasks. Conversely, classic RL algorithms such as Temporal Difference Learning (TDL) operate at the level of an individual: an individual modifies its behavior during its lifetime to improve its expected reward, which may be given at the end of each task or during a task. Temporal difference learning works outstandingly well on small toy problems where the game states can be exactly enumerated in a table. In such cases learning then corresponds to estimating the value of each table entry. For most games of interest the state space is either discrete and large, or continuous, and this direct tabular representation cannot be applied. In such cases some form of function approximation must be used, and this can be fraught with difficulty. Choosing the correct form of function approximator is of critical importance and can mean the difference between success and failure.

TDL is also sensitive to parameter choices such as the learning rate. Recent approaches such as Least Squares TD (LSTD) work in batch mode and choose a locally optimal step size for each parameter updated, in the sense of minimizing the mean square error (MSE). Interestingly, recent results [Thomas Runarsson, personal communication] indicate that the common practice of using TDL to minimize the MSE may be far from optimal for game playing. When playing a game, what matters is the action selected at each stage. The actual state value or state-action value estimates are not what really matters: they only matter as a means to select the correct action. For this reason there has been interest in applying preference learning to this problem instead. In preference learning, the aim is to learn the correct decisions directly rather than estimate the expected rewards for each action.

2.3 Monte Carlo Tree Search (MCTS)

Computer chess players have played at super-human levels for over a decade, and during that time Go has been one of the main challenges for reaching or surpassing expert human performance. For many years progress on Computer Go had been rather slow, and reaching expert levels of human play seemed many decades away. MCTS changed all that, causing a radical improvement in performance. The best MCTS-based players are now on a par with the best human players for the smaller 9 x 9 version of the game, and are making good progress on the full size 19 x 19 game. This has naturally sparked a great deal of interest in researching other games that MCTS might be good for, and already it has achieved dominance on connection games such as Hex and Y [1]. For a comprehensive survey see [3]. MCTS is also the leading approach to general game playing.

MCTS builds a game tree selectively by performing random simulations (also known as roll-outs) from a game state to predict the value of being in that state. This is depicted in Figure 1 (from [2]). The tree is grown selectively. A node in the tree is selected for expansion using a tree policy to navigate down the tree (shown as the bold line on the left tree). The Upper Confidence Bounds for Trees (UCT) formula [9] is often used to guide child selection while navigating the tree. UCT aims to optimally balance the opposing needs of exploration versus exploitation, though it is usually used in conjunction with some heuristics to achieve better performance.

A random simulation (also known as roll-out or play-out) is then made from the selected leaf node of the tree. The roll-out normally continues to the end of the game, at which point the exact value is known. This value is then propagated up the tree, and a new leaf node is added where the roll-out was made, as shown on the right tree in the figure. The roll-out may be made by choosing uniform random moves, or may be biased towards more favorable moves.

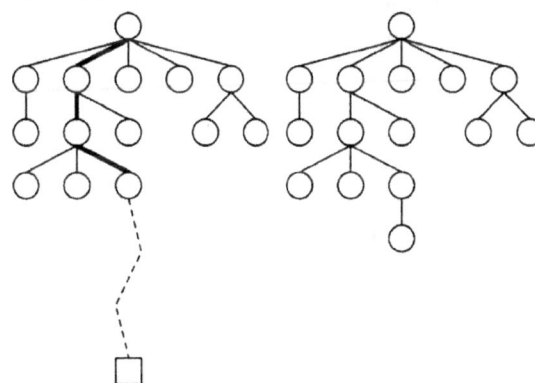

Figure 1: Illustration of how MCTS operates (from [2]).

MCTS has many attractive properties, such as being an anytime algorithm where playing performance typically increases (in some cases logarithmically e.g. [5]) with the number of roll-outs that can be performed given the available time. Perhaps more importantly, MCTS can be used in the absence of any good heuristic evaluation function. The fact that MCTS works at all is at least a little surprising: good players do not play randomly, so why should random simulations which sample only a tiny fraction of the search space provide any clue as to which move is good? Nonetheless, there is clearly important information in the roll-out statistics; at least enough to outperform non MCTS approaches. Furthermore, the tree grows with each roll-out, and increasingly represents more meaningful information. On tasks as difficult as playing Go, it is not that MCTS plays anywhere close to optimal, it is more the case that the problem is hard for any type of agent, and MCTS performs well compared to the competition (though not as well as expert humans yet on the full-size game).

Of more interest to the current paper is whether MCTS can be used to endow video game agents with more intelligence. Many researchers and games industry insiders have questioned the value of this, imagining that an intelligent opponent would be boring to play against because it would simply thrash the human player every time. This is not so, however, for at least three reasons. One is that the intelligent opponent might have a different objective other than winning; for example, it might be aiming to maximize the human player's fun, much as a parent aims to do when playing a game with their child. Secondly, the game can be re-balanced in other ways: it might be fun to play against super-intelligent opponents that are limited in their physical strength, mobility, firepower, health or armor. Thirdly, the aim may be to create an intelligent agent that is not competing against the player, but acts as a partner or an assistant. The illusion of intelligence in this type of agent is crucial, and can be more important than the intelligence of the enemies. For instance, in first person shooter games, a companion may be a partner of the player during the whole game, while typical enemies appear on screen for only 5 seconds on average.[2]

There are some challenges to be overcome in using MCTS to boost the intelligence of video game agents, including making enough roll-outs in the severely limited time available to compute each action, and coping with the long roll-out depth needed to make progress in the game. Depending on the type of game, the game state for a video game may be significantly more complex than for a classic board game, involving many continuous variables describing the position and velocity of each agent. To ameliorate this it may be possible to use a simplified model of the game, or to represent the game state efficiently. For example, when using MCTS to control a Pac-Man agent, the game state can be represented compactly using bit-sets to model the state of each pill (which can change from *available* to *eaten*), and then maintaining a separate data structure of pill positions, which for a given map never changes. In this way it is possible to perform hundreds of roll-outs for each game tick. Further improvements can be made by keeping part of the tree from one game tick to the next (the branch that corresponds to the selected action may be kept). In this way actions may be selected on the basis of tens of thousands of roll-outs even though only a few hundred are made per game tick.

When applying MCTS to video games a significant problem is to decide the value that should be fed back at the end of a roll-out. For games such as Go this is not a problem: each roll-out ends in a terminal state of the game at which time the value is known exactly: either 1 or 0 (either a win or a loss for the current player). The value at each tree node then approximates the probability of winning from that node. In the case of video games, the situation is less clear. Due to the nature of the game, most roll-outs will not end in a terminal state, and some heuristic value must be constructed to estimate the value of a state. Finding a good heuristic is a significant problem, and for this EAs or TDL can be used; so far TDL has been used, but EAs would seem to offer an interesting alternative. Interestingly, there are three distinct ways in which heuristics can be applied within MCTS. They can be used to inform the tree-policy, and/or to bias the roll-outs, or to (as already mentioned) provide a heuristic value at the end of a roll-out (for the frequent cases where the true value is not obvious). Even in arcade games such as Pac-Man, where the

score is updated every time a pill, edible ghost, or fruit is eaten, heuristics play an important part in evaluating game states, since many states with identical scores will have very different true values for the Pac-Man agent.

Without a good heuristic MCTS may fail if applied naively, largely because the vast majority of roll-outs do not do anything of interest. If at each game tick a video game character performs an action selected uniformly at random from the set of available actions, then most roll-outs will not do anything interesting at all, but just dither and not move much. There are a number of ways of overcoming this problem, including choosing a higher-level action space (i.e. a space of macro-actions where each high-level action then has to be translated to a sequence of lower-level actions). Another simpler way is to bias the roll-outs to increase the likelihood that the previous action is repeated.

3. Evaluation and Competitions

One of the most important driving forces behind progress in this area has been regular and rigorous evaluation. For many games there are regular competitions. These provide an ideal means by which to test any number of approaches, and to tune each approach to see which works best in practice. While rigorous evaluation has been the feature of many research communities, this has been embraced with particular enthusiasm in games.

Evaluation in pattern recognition and machine learning normally involves measuring performance on some pattern classification or prediction problem, where the correct answers are already known. In contrast to this, intelligent game-playing agents need to work out for themselves what actions to take in novel situations where no supervised training data exists. Furthermore, game playing algorithms usually compete under strict time limits, so an appropriate balance must be found between optimality and timeliness. Games naturally promote techniques which work well in practice. The remainder of this section discusses two game competitions that are of particular relevance to this paper. The first example, general game playing, is another area where MCTS has proven to be very successful, and the general aspects of this have some relevance to developing general purpose video game agents. The second example, the physical travelling salesman problem is a simple video game being run as an open competition where naïve MCTS only achieves limited success, but more sophisticated MCTS approaches are already showing great promise.

3.1 General Game Playing (GGP)

In focusing on a single game there is a danger that the results will be of limited interest to the goal of developing a general purpose AI agent. This danger may sometimes be overstated, since the AI community has learnt a great deal over the years with results from specific games often having a more general impact. However, the fact remains that achieving high performance on a particular game can involve an enormous amount of game-specific hand tuning. Hence GGP [7] was developed as a way to make games a true challenge for machine learning. GGP games operate in two phases. In the first phase the game rules (specified in a type of first-order logic) are given to each player in order that it can analyse the rules, potentially do some learning about the game, set up any data structures etc. In the second phase play commences and continues until the end of the game. MCTS now seems to be the dominant algorithm in GGP, with the AAAI 2007 and 2008 competitions being won by CadiaPlayer [6], an MCTS-based player, and the 2009 competition being won by Ary [14], another

---

[2] Mikael Hedberg, AI Game Dev Conference 2010, discussing the AI of Battlefield: Bad Company 2, for details see: http://aigamedev.com/open/coverage/paris10-report/#session10.

agent with a significant MCTS component. GGP as it stands offers a fascinating challenge, but its use of a logic-based game description language naturally tailors it toward certain types of game (essentially mind-games), and means it is not appropriate for video or physics-based games. Developing a type of GGP system for this type of game is an interesting possibility, and it remains to be seen which type of algorithm would perform best on this type of problem.

3.2 Physical Travelling Salesman Problem

This competition [15],[16] combines aspects of the classic Travelling Salesmen Problem (TSP) with aspects of vehicle driving (physics) – hence the Physical Travelling Salesman Problem (PTSP). The aim is simply to visit all cities in the minimum time, but the salesman is now driving a physical object and has momentum and steering to take care of: in most cases the optimal TSP city order is very different to the optimal PTSP city order. Figure 2 shows a sample map from the current IEEE World Congress on Computational Intelligence Competition [15].

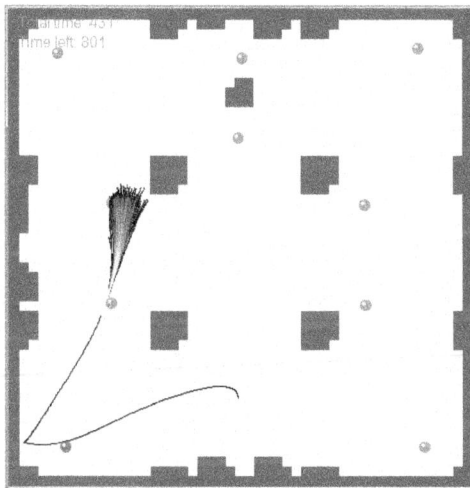

Figure 2: A sample map from a currently running Physical Travelling Salesman Problem (PTSP) Competition.

Applying MCTS to a simple 2D navigation game such as the PTSP provides an ideal way to study its weaknesses. Since the roll-outs can be overlaid on top of the map, it is easy to see how far MCTS is exploring ahead, and whether it is able to incorporate long-term planning considerations into its solutions, or whether it is acting in a greedy manner. If MCTS is applied in its most basic form to this problem, then it tends to do the latter, as also shown in Figure 2. In the standard PTSP configuration, actions are very low level, and specify a force vector to be applied for the next time instant. A good solution for the map in Figure 2 would involve more than 1,000 such actions. Interestingly, if MCTS is used with a higher-level action space [Whitehouse and Powley, personal communication] then this problem is alleviated, and good performance can be obtained. Such an approach is currently leading the rankings on the Human versus Bot version of the PTSP (http://ptsp-game.net/). This is of particular interest here, since it is a type of innovation (i.e. using macro-actions rather than actions from the original more fine-grained set) that could potentially be created through evolutionary adaptation, but not through temporal difference learning. Another way to achieve long-term planning in the PTSP is to explicitly solve the problem in two steps, where one step optimizes the order of cities to visit

and then second step works tries to find the best action sequence to drive that route.

Given that the PTSP is a one-player game (at least in its current form) it would also be interesting to investigate the use of MCTS algorithms that have already been shown to work well on one-player games, such as nested MCTS and Monte-Carlo Beam Search [4].

4. Proposed Approach

Based on the above discussion, the architecture shown in Figure 3 is proposed for a general purpose intelligent game agent generation system. The system involves a population of MCTS game agents which evolves over time. Evolution offers a very flexible way to do this and can easily incorporate major architectural changes. Changes could include the nature of the function approximators used in the agent, such as multi-layer perceptrons or interpolated table functions. Reinforcement learning algorithms such as TDL are unable to do this: they are restricted to adapting a fixed-size parameter vector. Each agent is controlled by a number of parameters, including things such as roll-out depth, the value of the UCT exploration constant, plus many other variables controlling the behavior of the MCTS algorithm. These can be adapted using evolution.

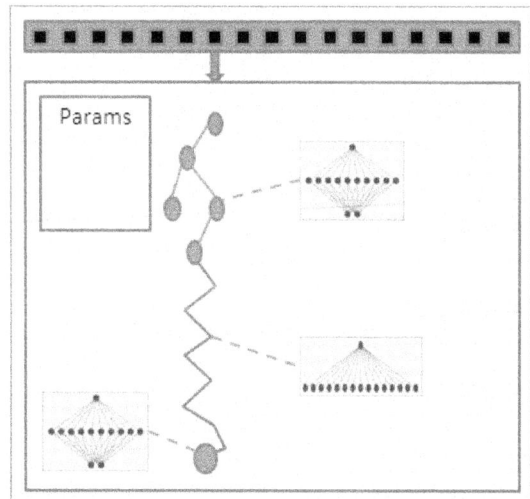

Figure 3: Proposed adaptive MCTS agent architecture. The system evolves a population of MCTS players: major structural changes occur at the evolutionary level. Each player also has many parameters that are adapted during game play. Function approximators help control tree policy, roll-out policy, and heuristic values given to terminal nodes of roll-out which are not terminal game states.

For MCTS to be effective, heuristic value functions (expressed in some form of function approximator, which in the simple case could be a weighted sum of features) are often very important. For video game agents these can be applied in three ways: in the tree policy to help select which node to expand, in the roll-out policy to bias the roll-out to more interesting states, and in the case that a roll-out does not reach a terminal node of the game, to place a heuristic value on that state.

How best to update these is an interesting problem. Silver et al [18] incorporate TDL within MCTS to good effect. Robles et al [17] also found TDL could improve performance by updating a heuristic function both for the tree-policy and for guiding the roll-outs. However, given what was mentioned earlier about the value of preference learning and focusing on actions made rather than mean-square error, alternative approaches are also of great interest. One such approach would be to use an evolutionary algorithm to update the heuristic functions during the execution of the MCTS algorithm. For example, roll-out bias heuristics could be evaluated on the quality of end state that they tend to reach. In this way each roll-out informs the fitness function, and extremely rapid evolution may be possible. Other types of adaptation that TDL is ill-suited to deal with and are best tackled using evolutionary approaches include adapting the temporal resolution of actions (e.g. repeating each movement action N times).

5. Conclusions

This paper discussed the motivation behind developing more intelligent and adaptive video game agents, and described the main research areas needed for this, namely evolution, reinforcement learning and Monte Carlo Tree Search. Some of the strengths and weaknesses of each approach were identified, and placed in the context of some recent game-based competitions. A game agent architecture was proposed, incorporating elements of evolutionary design, temporal difference learning, and Monte Carlo Tree Search. The complete architecture is still a work in progress, but many of the components have been rigorously and independently shown to work in many different games and other domains. The next step is to integrate these into an effective system, able to control agents in a variety of video games with a minimum of programming effort. Although the big-budget game studios have been reluctant to use many statistical AI methods such as evolutionary algorithms and neural networks, there is a burgeoning market for mobile and casual games, and this offers an ideal testing ground for releasing these agents into the wild.

6. ACKNOWLEDGMENTS

Thanks go to members of the Game Intelligence Group at the University of Essex for extensive discussions of many of the ideas in this paper. This work was funded by EPSRC Grant EP/H048588/1: UCT for Games and Beyond.

7. REFERENCES

[1] Arneson, B., Hayward, R.B. and Henderson, P., 2010, Monte Carlo Tree Search in Hex, *IEEE Transactions on Computational Intelligence and AI in Games*, vol.2, no. 4, pp.251-258.

[2] H. Baier and P. D. Drake, 2010, The power of forgetting: Improving the last good reply policy in Monte Carlo Go, *IEEE Transactions on Computational Intelligence and AI in Games*, vol. 2, no. 4, pp. 303–309.

[3] Browne, C., Powley, E., Whitehouse, D., Lucas, S., Cowling, P., Rohlfshagen, P., Tavener, S., Perez, D., Samothrakis, S., Colton, S., 2012, A Survey of Monte Carlo Tree Search Methods, *IEEE Transactions on Computational Intelligence and AI in Games*, vol. 4, no. 1, pp.1–43.

[4] Cazenave, T., 2012, Monte Carlo Beam Search, *IEEE Transactions on Computational Intelligence and AI in Games*, vol.4, no. 1, pp.68-72.

[5] Enzenberger, M., Müller, M., Arneson, B., Segal, R., 2010, Fuego—An Open-Source Framework for Board Games and Go Engine Based on Monte Carlo Tree Search, *IEEE Transactions on Computational Intelligence and AI in Games*, vol.2, no.4, pp.259-270.

[6] Y. Bjornsson and H. Finnsson, 2009, Cadiaplayer: A simulation-based general game player, *IEEE Transactions on Computational Intelligence and AI in Games*, vol. 1, no. 1, pp. 4 –15.

[7] M. R. Genesereth, N. Love, and B. Pell, 2005, General game playing: Overview of the AAAI competition, *AI Magazine*, no. 2, pp. 62 - 72.

[8] N. Hansen, S. Mueller, and P. Koumoutsakos, 2003, Reducing the time complexity of the derandomized evolution strategy with covariance matrix adaptation (CMA-ES), *Evolutionary Computation*, vol. 11, pp. 1-18.

[9] L. Kocsis and C. Szepesvári, 2006, Bandit based Monte-Carlo planning, in *Proceedings of European Conference on Machine Learning*, Berlin, Germany, pp. 282–293.

[10] Lucas, S.M., 2010, Estimating Learning Rates in Evolution and TDL: Results on a Simple Grid-World Problem, *IEEE Conference on Computational Intelligence and Games*, pp. 372-379.

[11] Lucas, S.M., 2008, Investigating Learning Rates for Evolution and Temporal Difference Learning, *IEEE Symposium on Computational Intelligence and Games*.

[12] Lucas, S.M., 2008, Computational Intelligence and Games: Challenges and Opportunities, *International Journal of Automation and Computing*, vol. 5, pages: 45 – 57.

[13] Lucas, S.M. and Kendall, G., 2006, Evolutionary Computation and Games, *IEEE Computational Intelligence Magazine*, vol. 1, pages: 10 – 18.

[14] Méhat, J. and Cazenave, T., 2010, Combining UCT and Nested Monte-Carlo Search for Single-Player General Game Playing, *IEEE Transactions on Computational Intelligence and AI in Games* vol. 2, pp. 271-277.

[15] Perez, D., Rohlfshagen, R. and Lucas, S.M., 2012, The Physical Travelling Salesman Problem: WCCI 2012 Competition, *IEEE Congress on Evolutionary Computation*, to appear.

[16] Perez, D., Rohlfshagen, R. and Lucas, S.M., 2012, Monte-Carlo Tree Search for the Physical Travelling Salesman Problem, *Proceedings of EvoGames*, to appear.

[17] Robles, D, Rohlfshagen, P and Lucas, S.M., 2011, Learning Non-Random Moves for Playing Othello: Improving Monte Carlo Tree Search, *IEEE Conference on Computational Intelligence and Games*, pp. 305 – 312.

[18] Silver, D, Sutton, R.S. and Müller, M., 2008, Sample-based learning and search with permanent and transient memories, in *Proceedings of 25th Annual International Conference on Machine Learning*, Helsinki, Finland, pp. 968–975.

[19] Togelius, J. and Schmidhuber, J., 2008, An Experiment in Automatic Game Design. *Proceedings of the IEEE Symposium on Computational Intelligence and Games (CIG)*, 111-118.

[20] Togelius, J., Yannakakis, G.N., Stanley, K.O. and Browne, C., 2011, Search-Based Procedural Content Generation: A Taxonomy and Survey, *IEEE Transactions on Computational Intelligence and AI in Games*, vol.3, no.3, pp.172-186.

Invited Talk
How AI Can Change the Way We Play Games

Kenneth O. Stanley
Evolutionary Complexity Research Group
Department of EECS
University of Central Florida
Orlando, FL USA

kstanley@eecs.ucf.edu

ABSTRACT

While artificial intelligence (AI) in games is often associated with enhancing the behavior of non-player characters, at its cutting edge AI offers the potential for entirely new kinds of gaming experiences. In this talk I will focus on this frontier of AI in games through three examples of games from my research that are not only enhanced by AI, but would not even be possible without the unique AI techniques behind them. In these experimental games, called NERO, Galactic Arms Race, and Petalz, players become teachers, AI creates its own content, and unique creations are explicitly bred and traded by the players themselves. The discussion will focus on the inspiration for the technologies behind these games (including some related applications) and the long-term implications of unique and creative AI algorithms for gaming.

Categories and Subject Descriptors

K.8.0. [**Personal Computing**]: General – *Games*. I.2.6. [**Artificial Intelligence**]: Learning.

General Terms

Algorithms, Design, Human Factors.

Keywords

Video games, artificial intelligence, machine learning, procedural content generation, neural networks, evolutionary computation, neuroevolution

Invited Talk

CRESTA: A Software Focussed Approach to Exascale Co-design

Mark Parsons
EPCC Executive Director
EPCC, The University of Edinburgh
Edinburgh, UK
m.parsons@epcc.ed.ac.uk

Abstract

The CRESTA project is one of three complementary exascale software projects funded by the European Commission. The three-year project is employing a novel approach to exascale system co-design which focuses on the use of a small, representative set of applications to inform and guide software and systemware developments. This methodology is designed to identify where problem areas exist in applications and to use that knowledge to consider different solutions to those problems which inform software and hardware advances. CRESTA uses a methodology of either incremental or disruptive advances to move towards solutions across the whole of the exascale software stack.

Categories & Subject Descriptors: D.1.0 [**Programming Techniques**]: General

General Terms: Design

TERAFLUX: Exploiting Dataflow Parallelism in Teradevices

Roberto Giorgi
Universita' degli Studi di Siena
Via Roma 56, Siena, Italy
http://www.dii.unisi.it/~giorgi

ABSTRACT

The TERAFLUX project is a Future and Emerging Technologies (FET) Large-Scale Project funded by the European Union. TERAFLUX is at the forefront of major research challenges such as programmability, manageable architecture design, reliability of many-core or 1000+ core chips. In the near future, new computing systems will consist of a huge number of transistors - probably 1 Tera or 1000 billions by 2020: we name such systems as "Teradevices". In this project, the aim is to solve the three challenges at once by using the dataflow principles wherever they are applicable or make sense in the general economy of the system. An Instruction Set Extension (ISE) for the x86-64 is illustrated. This ISE supports the dataflow execution of threads.

Categories and Subject Descriptors

C.1.4 [**Processor Architectures**]: Parallel Architectures---Teradevices; C.1.3 [**Other Architecture Style**]: Dataflow; D.1.3 [**Programming Techniques**]: Concurrent Programming; B.8.0 [**Performance and Reliability**]: General; D.3.4 [**Processors**]: Compilers.

Keywords: Teradevices

1. INTRODUCTION

Most recent updates in the worldwide scenario include the availability of a new type of transistor (3D transistor), which marks the biggest change in the semiconductor industry since 1948 with the introduction of the transistor itself. New materials like Graphene may allow even greater power saving. The technology-node scaling has reached 22nm, with 14nm silicon foundries to be operative by 2013, and it seems the pace will continue at least until 8nm. The 3D layering gives new lymph to the Moore's law too. In this scenario, and in perspective beyond the year 2020, the TERAFLUX project]2] brings together 10 industrial and academic partners to give their best contribution in order to find a common ground to solve at once all the above three challenges. The research in this project is inspired by the Dataflow principle. As recalled by Jack Dennis [1], dataflow is "a Scheme of Computation in which an activity is initiated by presence of the data it needs to perform its function". We believe that, if properly exploited, dataflow can enable parallelism which is orders of magnitude greater than what is achievable by control-flow dominated execution models. To investigate our concepts, we are studying dataflow principles at any level of a complete transformation hierarchy, starting from general and complex applications able to load properly a Teradevice through programming models, compilation tools, reliability techniques and architecture.

One key point it is also the evaluation of this system: our choice has been to rely on an existing simulation infrastructure (HPLabs COTSon) that immediately enabled us to start from a nowadays Teradevice (i.e., a 1000+ cluster of nodes, where each node consists of tens of cores) and progressively evolve such system into a more ambitious system where we can gradually remove major bottlenecks. While relying on solid and well-known reference points such as the x86-64 ISA, GCC tools, StarSs programming model and applications, we wish to demonstrate the validity of our research in such common evaluation infrastructure.

Below, we focus on some part of dataflow execution model as proposed by the partner University of Siena with the author's guidance.

2. THE DATAFLOW THREADS

The TERAFLUX system is not forced to follow entirely the dataflow paradigm: in fact, we distinguish among legacy and system-threads (L-, S-threads) and dataflow threads (DF-threads): this will allow for a progressive migration of programs to the new "dataflow paradigm", while accelerating the available DF-threads on the more dataflow-friendly cores [4]. One other important choice is the exploration of synchronization mechanisms such as transactional memory, and the repetition of a thread on a different core by using the dataflow principles [5] in cases when the cores are detected as failing. We can currently afford to run with an acceptable slowdown and accuracy, parallel, scalable, full-system (with unmodified Linux) simulations of 1000+ x86-64 cores [6] while experimenting with very ambitious changes in the execution model implying a major effort to support the execution model based on dataflow threads [3], especially from the compiler point of view.

Moreover, in recent experiments we were able to boot a kind of "datacenter-in-a-box", thanks to a simulation host HP DL-585-G7 with 64 AMD cores and 1 TB of shared memory. The simulation environment has been able to boot about 7000 guest cores, thanks to the off-the-shelf capabilities of COTSon.

3. THE T-STAR ISA EXTENSION

In order to support the execution of DF-Threads, we designed a minimalistic extension of the x86-64 ISA, that we call T-Star (or T-*) [3] shown in Table 1. The key-points of this ISE are: i) it enables an asynchronous execution of threads, that will execute not under the control-flow of the program but under the data-flow of it; ii) the execution of a DF-thread is decided by an core-external component that we call DTS (or Distributed Thread Scheduler) [3]; iii) the types of memory that are used are distinguished in 4 main types (1-to-1 communication or Thread Local Storage, N-to-1 or Frame Memory, 1-to-N or Owner Writable Memory, and N-to-N or Transactional Memory. More details are available in the public deliverables of the project (see http://teraflux.eu)

Table 1: T* Instruction Set Extension (ISE) for the x86-64 ISA

Synopsis	**TSCHEDULE *RS1, RS2, RD***	**TSCHEDULE(*<IP>, <SC>, &<frame_pointer>*)**
Description	This instruction allocates the resources (a DF-frame of size **RS2** words and a corresponding entry in the Distributed Thread Scheduler – or DTS) for a new DF-thread and returns its Frame Pointer (FP) in **RD**. **RS1** specifies the Instruction Pointer (IP) of the first instruction of the code of this DF-thread and **RS2** specifies the Synchronization Count (SC).	
Notes	The allocated DF-thread is not executed until its SC reaches 0. The TSCHEDULE can be conditional or non-conditional based on the value stored in the zero flag. If the zero flag is set to 1 then the TSCHEDULE will take effect, otherwise it is ignored.	
Synopsis	**TDESTROY**	**TDESTROY**
Description	The thread that invokes TDESTROY finishes and its DF-frame is freed, (the corresponding entry in the Distributed Thread Scheduler is also freed).	
Synopsis	**TWRITE *RS, RD, offset***	***(<frame_pointer> + <offset>) = (<source_register>)**
Description	The data in **RS** is stored into the DF-frame pointed to by **RD** at the specified offset.	
Notes	*Side Effect*: The Distributed Thread Scheduler decrements the SC of the corresponding DF-thread entry (located through the FP): $SC_{FP} = SC_{FP}-1$	
Synopsis	**TREAD *offset, RD***	**(<destination_register>) = *(<self_frame_pointer> + <offset>)**
Description	Loads the data indexed by 'offset' from the self (current thread) DF-frame into **RD**.	
Notes	*Assumption*: the DTS has to load into the register implicitly used by TREAD the value <self_frame_pointer>. In a x86-64 implementation, we can reserve RAX for this purpose.	
Synopsis	**TALLOC RS1, RS2, RD**	**<pointer> = TALLOC (<size>, <type>)**
Description	Allocates a block of memory of **RS1** words. The pointer to it is stored in **RD**. **RS2** specifies the special purpose memory type.	
Notes	The Distributed Thread Scheduler tracks the memory allocated. An implementation can code <type> in the 2 LSBs of <size>	
Synopsis	**TFREE *RS***	**TFREE(<pointer>)**
Description	Frees memory pointed to by **RS**.	
Notes	The Distributed Thread Scheduler tracks the memory deallocated.	

4. ACKNOWLEDGMENTS

This work was partly funded by the European FP7 projects TERAFLUX id. 249013 http://www.teraflux.eu.

5. REFERENCES

[1] J. Dennis, "The Data Flow Concept Past, Present and Future", DFM-2011: Data-Flow Execution Models for Extreme Scale Computing, Oct. 2011

[2] R. Giorgi, "TERAFLUX: Ideas for the Future Many-Cores", ODES: Workshop on Optimizations for DSP and Embedded Systems, Apr. 2011, pp. 38-38.

[3] A. Portero Z. Yu, R. Giorgi, "T-Star (T*): An x86-64 ISA Extension to support thread execution on many cores", HiPEAC ACACES-2011, ISBN:978 90 382 17987, Fiuggi, Italy July 2011, pp. 277-280.

[4] Z. Yu, A. Righi, R. Giorgi, "A Case Study on the Design Trade-off of a Thread Level Data Flow based Many-core Architecture", Future Computing, ISBN:978-1-61208-154-0, Rome, Italy, Sept. 2011, pp. 100-106, Best paper award.

[5] S. Weis, A.Garbade, J. Wolf, B. Fechner, A. Mendelson R. Giorgi, T. Ungerer, "A Fault Detection and Recovery Architecture for a Teradevice Dataflow System", DFM-2011: Data-Flow Execution Models for Extreme Scale Computing, Oct. 2011, pp. 39-45.

[6] A. Portero, A. Scionti, Z. Yu, P. Faraboschi, C. Concatto, L. Carro, A. Garbade, S. Weis, T. Ungerer, R. Giorgi, "Simulating the Future kilo-x86-64 core Processors and their Infrastructure", 45th Annual Simulation Symp. (ANSS12), Orlando, FL, Mar 2012.

DEEP: An Exascale Prototype Architecture Based on a Flexible Configuration

Arndt Bode

Lehrstuhl für Rechnertechnik und Rechnerorganisation at Technische Universität München
Leibniz Supercomputing Centre of the Bavarian Academy of Sciences
München, DE
bode@in.tum.de

Abstract

DEEP is a multipartner international cooperation project supported by the EU FP7 that introduces a flexible global system architecture using general purpose and manycore processor architectures (based on Intel MIC: many integrated core architecture). With XTOLL, DEEP uses a very powerful interconnection structure, which allows for the arrangement of different application oriented ratios between general purpose processor and accelerator. The project includes research and development on program technologies, tools, applications, and looks at energy efficient computing methodologies.

Categories & Subject Descriptors: C.5.1 [**Large and Medium ("Mainframe") Computers**]: Super (very large) computers

General Terms: Design

Mont-Blanc: Towards Energy-efficient HPC Systems

Nikola Puzovic
Barcelona Supercomputing Center
Barcelona, Spain
nikola.puzovic@bsc.es

Abstract

This talk will present the Mont-Blanc project, an European initiative to build exascale systems using energy-efficient parts coming from the embedded market. The energy consumption of current general purpose and high-performance chips would require an unaffordable total power budget for an exascale system to be build using these parts.

The Mont-Blanc project aims to lower the total power of exascale systems by using parts from the embedded market which have a much higher FLOPS/Watt ration than traditional general purpose processor, at the cost of a lower peak performance per chip. Hence, exascale systems built using embedded parts would require a very high number of processors. In this context, overlapping communications and computations is key for applications to reach the system peak performance. This would require highly tuned application code which most users would not be able to afford. The Mont-Blanc project heavily relies on the OmpSs programming model. OmpSs provide a simple parallel programming interface that most users can easily use, and an advanced runtime system that automatically overlaps computation and communication. Furthermore, the OmpSs runtime system is also able to dynamically adapt the load of each node to accomplish the overall system load balance.

Categories & Subject Descriptors: C. Computer Systems Organization; C.5 COMPUTER SYSTEM IMPLEMENTATION; C.5.1 Large and Medium ("Mainframe") Computers; Subjects: Super (very large) computers

General Terms: Performance, Design

Bio

The speaker is a senior researcher at Barcelona Supercomputing Center. He received his PhD degree in Computer Engineering from the University of Siena, Italy. His primary research interests are in the area of energy efficient high performance computing and in parallel programming models.

Author Index